# DATE DUE

| | | | |
|---|---|---|---|
| NO 16 '98 | | | |
| DE 7 98 | | | |
| JE 15 '01 | | | |
| MY 25 02 | | | |
| | | | |
| | | | |
| | | | |
| | | | |
| | | | |
| | | | |
| | | | |
| | | | |
| | | | |
| | | | |

DEMCO 38-296

PRESIDENT LINCOLN AND HIS PRIVATE SECRETARIES,
JOHN G. NICOLAY AND JOHN HAY

# Abraham Lincoln
# Deals with Foreign Affairs

A DIPLOMAT IN CARPET SLIPPERS

## Jay Monaghan

Introduction to the Bison Books edition by
Howard Jones

University of Nebraska Press
Lincoln and London

.ca

m requirements of American
—Permanence of Paper for
34.

.git below:

10    9    8    7    6    5    4    3    2    1

Library of Congress Cataloging-in-Publication Data
Monaghan, Jay, 1891–
[Diplomat in carpet slippers]
Abraham Lincoln deals with foreign affairs: a diplomat in carpet slippers /
Jay Monaghan.—Bison Books ed. / introduction by Howard Jones.
p.  cm.
Originally published: Indianapolis: Bobbs-Merrill Co., 1945 (edition
published as "Diplomat in carpet slippers: Abraham Lincoln deals with
foreign affairs")
Includes bibliographical references and index.
ISBN 0-8032-8231-1 (pbk.: alk. paper)
1. United States—Foreign relations—1861–1865.  2. Lincoln, Abraham,
1809–1865—Contributions in foreign relations.  I. Title.
E469.M75  1997
973.7822—dc21
96-49210  CIP

*For* MILDRED

# INTRODUCTION

## Howard Jones

Anyone interested in the diplomacy of the Civil War must start with this classic work by Jay Monaghan. Elegantly written, engaging in style, and persuasive in argument, it is the result of research primarily in American source materials and, for that reason, provides the American (or, more accurately, the Union) perspective on key foreign policy events during the war. This study, like the more than two dozen other books Monaghan has written or edited on the Civil War and American West, is well researched and innovative in approach.[1] Monaghan graduated from Swarthmore College in 1913 and later received a graduate degree from the University of Pennsylvania. A strong believer in visiting the areas about which he wrote, he emerged as a pioneer of oral history by interviewing Indians for the Colorado Historical Society. His rich and diverse background includes time as professional researcher in Kansas and Nebraska and historian for the Illinois State Historical Society before becoming special consultant for the Wyles Collection of Lincolniana at the University of California at Santa Barbara.

In this distinguished work, Monaghan portrays President Abraham Lincoln as the chief formulator of the Union's foreign policy, thereby providing a valuable reminder to those writers who have virtually ignored the president's contributions to international affairs and who continue to relegate foreign affairs to a status well below that of battles, leaders, and nearly every other feature of this tumultuous period.

Monaghan undermines the arguments of historians who have reduced Lincoln to a virtual stepchild of his arrogant and self-righteous secretary of state, William H. Seward. The president, admittedly inexperienced and lacking either formal training or firsthand knowledge in matters of foreign policy, allegedly deferred to Seward's lead in one crisis after another. Monaghan shows this traditional story to be erroneous, although he goes too far in highlighting Lincoln's role. Recent research shows that Seward emerged as an outstanding secretary of state, safeguarding the national interest from its most dangerous external threat—an intervention by either England or France (or both) that could have helped only the South.[2] But Lincoln deserves praise, too, for working closely with Seward in devising an effective foreign policy. Monaghan's splendidly written account contains numerous human interest stories and wonderfully descriptive passages that make history engrossing and, yes, even entertaining.

Monaghan's finely crafted narrative colorfully and, at times, humorously depicts the human characteristics of the major players in the Civil War. Of Secretary of the Navy Gideon Welles, Monaghan writes: "Hiding always in public behind a wig and beard, he wielded a dangerous pen in the privacy of his own room, stamping up and down the pages of his diary with a rhetorical cutlass in each hand" (14). Thurlow Weed, a prototypical political boss who preferred to remain out of the public limelight, was, "like Lincoln, . . . over six feet tall and the earth would have trembled beneath his stride had Weed been that kind of boss. Instead, he always walked on cat's feet, stalking power and seeking no office for himself. Unscrupulous, according to his enemies, Weed never bared his claws in the light of day" (18). Monaghan intended this work for the intelligent lay reader, not for the small circle of academicians who write solely for each other. Yet his study constitutes a magnificent blend of scholarly respectability and general appeal. Those who want history in the grand old manner of artistic narrative combined with incisive analysis will feel that they experienced a piece of the times, which is the best praise any work can receive.

So often the choice of advisers is as much a mark of effective leadership as are the leader's actions or policies. Seward's appointment as secretary of state exemplified Lincoln's determination to garner candid advice by surrounding himself with political enemies rather than sycophants. "They will eat you up," one warned him about the intense animosity felt by cabinet members toward both him and each other. "They will eat each other up," Lincoln sagely replied (14). No one despised Lincoln more than did Seward at the outset of the administration. The secretary believed that the Lincoln contingent at the Republican convention in Chicago had stolen the nomination from him and thrust a man in the presidency who was nothing more than an ape in human clothing. Only the needs of the country, Seward immodestly wrote his wife, could persuade him to head the state department and thus fill the vacuum in executive leadership left by the crude lawyer and rail splitter who had tumbled into office from the Illinois prairie. But just four months into the new administration, the embittered secretary had developed so much respect for his superior that he told his friend and Union minister in London, Charles Francis Adams, that the president's "most valuable mental attribute" was "a curious vein of sentiment running through his thought" (63). And in June Seward wrote his wife: "There is but one vote in the cabinet and that is cast by the President. . . . The President is the best of us all" (63).

Lincoln was a consummate diplomatist who recognized the importance of patience and calm in molding policy and who also understood the role of diplomacy within the broad picture of the war. Midway into this national cataclysm, one of his personal secretaries, John Hay, acknowledged Lincoln's integral involvement in every aspect of the war. The president, Hay wrote, was "managing this war, the draft, foreign relations, and planning a reconstruction of the Union, all at once. . . . There is no man in the country, so wise, so gentle and so firm. I believe the hand of God placed him where he is" (322).

Lincoln often exasperated his advisers by telling homespun stories in the midst of crisis, but his purpose was to put events in perspective by allowing time for emotions to ease and reason to rule. He grasped the impact of public pressure on policymakers, and he knew his history. In the *Trent* crisis, the president knew he could not release the captives, James Mason and John Slidell, until the American people had felt their honor restored at the expense of both the British and the Confederates. The Crimean War and imperial rivalries, Lincoln also realized, had alienated Russia from England and France and therefore provided the Union with a friend in the Civil War. Further, he feared that his nation's longtime British and French rivals would seize any opportunity to promote their own interests. A diplomat by nature and temperament, Lincoln understood the importance of gathering all available information, of listening to (but not necessarily following) advisers, of avoiding rash decisions, and of having the courage to adopt an unpopular action because it simply was the right thing to do. Most important, he kept the administration's focus on the national interest while covering foreign policy with a veneer of idealism and morality.

Lincoln regarded diplomacy as one of several vital aspects of the Union's effort to win the war. As important as battles and leaders was the necessity of keeping England and France out of the war—particularly in the first eighteen months of the conflict when the verdict hung in the balance and the two European nations seriously considered some form of intervention based on allegedly altruistic reasons. British and French intervention on behalf of the South would have assured its independence. Their declarations of neutrality had already elevated the Confederacy to belligerent status and seemingly put it on the road to diplomatic recognition as a nation. Indeed, a mere mediation would have constituted a further admission to the South's legitimacy, which to the

North came dangerously close to recognition. If the Confederacy won international stature as a separate nation, it could negotiate treaties of both a commercial and military nature. The outcome would confirm secession and shatter the North's argument for a permanent Union. It seems probable that Lincoln purposely conveyed an image of wisdom and serenity while quietly exploiting Seward's heated warnings of war with any nation that dared intervene in the American conflict. As commander in chief, Lincoln grasped the importance of diplomacy as one of his many weapons of war. Monaghan's superb study affirms the president's broad understanding of wartime leadership.

Monaghan was well ahead of his times in showing the intricate relationship between domestic and foreign policy. A European alliance with the Confederacy, Lincoln believed, would guarantee the South's success. Did not a large number of British observers believe the South's cause justified—that the North had become oppressive and that nine million Southern Americans had joined their predecessors from the American Revolution in claiming a natural right to establish an independent nation based on the principle of self-government? Lincoln, however, considered the Union unbreakable and warned of the inherent danger posed to a democracy by a minority willing to fight for its demands. Such a cataclysmic event, he declared, raised the question of

> whether a constitutional republic or democracy—a government of the people by the same people—can or cannot maintain its territorial integrity against its own domestic foes. It presents the question whether discontented individuals, too few in numbers to control administration according to organic law in any case, can always, upon the pretenses made in this case, or on any other pretenses, or arbitrarily without any pretense, break up their government, and thus practically put an end to free government upon the earth. It forces us to ask: "Is there, in all republics, this inherent and fatal weakness?" (124)

During the early stages of the war, Lincoln knew, any form of foreign involvement on behalf of the Confederacy would assure the Union's dissolution.

Monaghan shows that Lincoln personified a balanced combination of idealist and realist who recognized the preeminence of slavery in the war but exercised great caution in making it the central issue. Lincoln regarded slavery as the root of the Civil War. "If slavery is not wrong," he declared, "nothing is wrong" (19). By the summer of 1862 the abolition of slavery had become a military weapon, and by the time of the Gettysburg Address in late 1863 it had become an objective inseparable from Union in defining the real meaning of the war. Shortly after Lincoln signed the Emancipation Proclamation, he made the agonizing observation: "It is a momentous thing to be the instrument under Providence for the liberation of a race" (273). In accepting that heavy burden, he demonstrated an awareness of the principle that in war a profound sense of purpose must drive both warriors and diplomats to accomplish the seemingly impossible. Yet his political sense led him to recognize the danger in prematurely pronouncing the war as antislavery in purpose: such policy would push the border slave states into secession, antagonize believed Unionists in the South, and alienate those many Northerners who refused to fight for black people.

Only gradually did Lincoln shift the direction of the war to an antislavery crusade. In the early part of the war, he appointed abolitionists to foreign posts and, in so doing, rid the United States of people he regarded as troublemakers while demonstrating to Europeans that his administration opposed slavery. He also extended recognition to black regimes in Haiti and Liberia and approved a treaty with England that authorized a longtime opposed mutual search policy considered essential to ending the African slave trade. As the war drummed on and antislavery became both its overriding theme and a crucial component in warding off foreign intervention, these subtle measures emerged as major steps in a strategy that exemplified the president's sound leadership.

Monaghan's writing is clearly anti-Southern in approach. A large part of the British view of the Civil War derived from the writings of *London Times* correspondent William H. Russell, whose firsthand observations in America emphasized that, in Monaghan's words, "the crusade against slavery was only one phase of a crusade against social backwater" (85). The way of life so fervently heralded by the South did not seem worth saving. In the *Times* on 30 May 1861, Russell questioned the Southerners' claim that slavery had civilized the black African savage. American slaves lived in a state of abject poverty that suggested no social advances over that of African villagers. The slave markets, in particular, demonstrated the horrible backwardness of the antebellum South.

Isolation from the outside world, Monaghan asserts, had caused the South to cultivate an intensely negative view toward everything progressive. Violence became the order of the day, as illustrated in the Confederate capital in Montgomery, Alabama, where, Russell declared, the hotel was "full of Confederate congressmen, politicians, colonels, and place-men," all armed with a "bowie-knife, or a six-shooter, or Derringer" (89). Slavery had reduced Southern whites to a status below that of other Anglo-Saxons. "To the correspondent," Monaghan pungently notes, "these people had learned nothing and forgotten nothing for two hundred years" (87). The South that British contemporaries learned about from Russell's news stories constituted, Monaghan wrote in obvious agreement, a "rude people" whose society had "gone to seed" and was "reactionary, closed mentally to new ideas, respecting only property and violence" (90). Despite the vulgarity of Northern democracy and its constant threat to property owners, the conservative society that Russell found in the South proved even more distasteful because it valued property above human rights.

Not every interpretation by Monaghan is above question. In the case of William E. Gladstone's famous speech at Newcastle in October 1862, Monaghan upholds the traditional view that the chancellor of the exchequer was so pro-South that he extolled the certainty of Confederate victory and thereby signaled imminent British recognition of Southern independence. "Jefferson Davis and other leaders of the South have made an army," Gladstone proclaimed; "they are making, it appears, a navy; and they have made what is more than either, they have made a nation" (255). In actuality, Gladstone left the erroneous impression of being pro-Confederate and had only meant to underline the South's independence as a *fait accompli* that the North must accept. And yet, as a seasoned politician, he should have grasped the inadvisability of making such an impolitic declaration. Regardless of Gladstone's real intentions, his speech provided a great boost to southern morale and hence infuriated the Union. In perspective, however, the furor caused by this episode forced the Palmerston ministry to confront the question of intervention in the American war. No longer could government leaders drift in neutrality, hoping that the war would end before they had to make a decision about intervention. The Newcastle speech brought focus to the greatest issue facing the British government since the outbreak of the American war: whether to intervene and perhaps extend diplomatic recognition to the Confederacy.

Monaghan's interpretation of the British reaction to the Emancipation Proclamation is likewise traditional and in need of revision. According to Monaghan, Europe's initial reaction to Lincoln's Emancipation Proclamation was "almost nil" (254). But when Confederate president Jefferson Davis responded with a threat to execute all white officers caught in command of black troops and a convention of Southern Episcopalians declared slavery a positive good, Englishmen finally realized that "the vaunted civilization of the South" rested on a foundation of barbarism (255). Actually, the British at first responded in a mixed fashion that soon grew into righteous indignation. Workers rejoiced at the proclamation while numerous other British observers feared an outbreak of chaos too often generated by democracy. Many believed that Lincoln intentionally sought to inspire a wave of slave revolts aimed at bringing down the South from within. Monaghan does not capture the bitterness of those Britons, both inside and outside government, who regarded the proclamation as a belated piece of hypocrisy resorted to by a desperate Union government frantically attempting to salvage victory in a war that belonged to the Confederacy. Such effort, they charged, guaranteed a racial conflict that would drag in other nations. Indeed, for some time after Lincoln issued his preliminary emancipation proclamation in September 1862, until it took effect on 1 January 1863, many British contemporaries irately spoke of intervening to stop the war—ironically threatening to undermine one of the president's major reasons for taking such a momentous step.

Nor (and understandably, without the use of British sources) does Monaghan highlight the important role played by Secretary for War George Cornwall Lewis in undercutting the quiet but ever-growing interventionist efforts of Lord John Russell. So well did the British foreign secretary conceal his feelings that Adams in London never came to this realization. The Union minister considered Lord Palmerston the culprit in any British interventionist action, and believed that only Russell's rigid adherence to neutrality had blocked a direct involvement. But Adams's son learned long after the war (the elder had died) that the opposite was true. Russell had pursued an interventionist course out of a mixture of humanitarian and realistic considerations. The war, he passionately argued, had taken such an atrocious turn at the battles of Shiloh and Antietam that civilized nations bore the humanitarian duty of bringing it to a close. Further, Lincoln's willingness to instigate slave uprisings guaranteed a racial war that, in turn, assured the involvement of other nations. Finally, steadily diminishing cotton supplies would drive British textile workers into the ranks of the unemployed, leading to domestic violence and resulting pressure on the Palmerston ministry to challenge the Union blockade and forcefully reopen the cotton flow. Defensible reasons for intervention, Lewis admitted in a lengthy memorandum circulated to all cabinet members before a stormy two-day meeting in November 1862; but any form of British involvement in the American conflict, he solemnly warned, ensured a war with the Union that would prove catastrophic for both Atlantic nations while, as a matter of course, putting the ministry in the untenable position of assuring Southern independence. Palmerston agreed with Lewis that the American war must render its own verdict.

Monaghan shows that one of the most dangerous ingredients in this tense international atmosphere was Napoleon III of France. The emperor was strongly pro-South because of his country's need for cotton and his own desire to exploit the weakness of the United States in an effort to fulfill his namesake's dream of reestablishing a French empire in the New World. Seemingly fearless and certainly adventurous, Napoleon became a leading proponent of intervention in the fall of 1862 and again in early 1863. The emperor had favored a multipower mediation in October 1862 because the slowdown in the textile industry had devastated three hundred thousand French people. By November, Napoleon was prepared to use force—even if he had to act alone, according to some accounts. "If the Emperor cannot get us cotton," the popular warning went out in France, "we must get some one else who can" (260). The chief restraint on Napoleon, as Monaghan demonstrates and Lincoln knew, was England. The emperor refused to move unless Palmerston took the lead—which meant that Lincoln's success in dissuading the British from intervening automatically meant that the French would stay out of the war as well.

Historians bear the sacred responsibility of recording events accurately and in a manner that appeals to both the specialist and general reader. The record is clear: no European power intervened in the war and the Union went on to victory in 1865. How tempting it is to ponder the outcome of a foreign intervention that, whether or not formally on the side of the South, would have dealt a devastating blow to the Union. Would the South have won independence and left in the war's wake two American republics, one slave and one free? Whatever the response to such an unsettling question, one observation is certain: Lincoln's carpet-slippered brand of diplomacy played an integral role in preventing a foreign involvement that would have altered the course of Anglo-American relations and the history of Atlantic events in general. Speculation perhaps, but extrapolated from the careful writing, solid evidence, and sound reasoning found in this book. The noted historian of the American West, Ray Allen Billington, himself called Monaghan "a first-rate historian."[3] This admirable study justifies such high praise.

## Notes

1. Among Monaghan's authored works, see *The Great Rascal: The Life and Adventures of Ned Buntline* (Boston: Little, Brown, 1951); *Civil War on the Western Border, 1854–1865* (Boston: Little, Brown, 1955); *The Man Who Elected Lincoln* (Indianapolis: Bobbs-Merrill, 1956); *Swamp Fox of the Confederacy: The Life and Military Services of M. Jeff Thompson* (Tuscaloosa AL: Confederate Publishing Company, 1956); *Australians and the Gold Rush: California and Down Under, 1849–1854* (Berkeley: University of California Press, 1966); *Custer: The Life of General George Armstrong Custer* (Lincoln: University of Nebraska Press, 1971); *Chile, Peru, and the California Gold Rush of 1849* (Berkeley: University of California Press, 1973); and *Schoolboy, Cowboy, Mexican Spy* (Berkeley: University of California Press, 1977). Especially noteworthy among Monaghan's edited works are: *Lincoln Bibliography, 1839–1939*, 2 vols. (Springfield: Illinois State Historical Library, 1943–45), and *The Book of the American West* (New York: Messner, 1963).

2. For recent studies that highlight Seward's diplomacy, see Norman B. Ferris, *Desperate Diplomacy: William H. Seward's Foreign Policy, 1861* (Knoxville: University of Tennessee Press, 1977), and Howard Jones, *Union in Peril: The Crisis over British Intervention in the Civil War* (Chapel Hill: University of North Carolina Press, 1992; reprint, Lincoln: University of Nebraska Press, 1997).

3. Ray Allen Billington, foreword to Monaghan, *Schoolboy, Cowboy, Mexican Spy*, ix.

# TABLE OF CONTENTS

# LIST OF ILLUSTRATIONS

# Diplomat in Carpet Slippers

# I. *Questions that would Unavoidably Come in Due Time*

IT WAS after midnight when the news came. Abraham Lincoln got up from a crowded table in Watson's oyster saloon and started home.[1] "His long arms and giant hands swung down by his side. He walked with even tread, the inner sides of his feet being parallel. He put the whole foot flat down on the ground at once, not landing on the heel; he likewise lifted his foot all at once, not rising from the toe." Thus did William Herndon, Lincoln's law partner, describe the peculiar stride of the man who had just been notified of his election as President of the United States. "The first impression of a stranger, or a man who did not observe closely, was that his walk implied shrewdness and cunning—that he was a tricky man; but, in reality, it was the walk of caution and firmness."[2]

Few people doubted Lincoln's ability as a prairie politician. Civil war loomed and a homely man from the clods and the cornlands had a better chance of uniting the agricultural areas of the North than a sleek and polished man of the cities. But the war, if it came, would be settled partly in Europe, and what chance had this lanky lawyer against trained diplomats?

Abraham Lincoln had never been abroad. American representatives in all the capitals of the Continent, the ministers and diplomats, held their appointments from the party that opposed him, the party that upheld slavery and that would rejoice to see Lincoln fail. Lincoln's task, as he himself said, was "greater than that which rested upon Washington."[3]

When Lincoln arrived at his two-story frame house at Eighth and Jackson streets, he did not retire. A party of townspeople outside blew whistles and horns until they were invited in for refreshments. Early in the morning Lincoln lighted his bedroom candle and climbed the steep narrow stairs. Later he told a friend that he did not sleep until he had constructed the framework of his entire cabinet, selecting in his mind the men who were to be his lieutenants.[4] It was an odd choice—perhaps the strangest cabinet ever formed, yet one of the most able. None of the men Lincoln decided to appoint had any experience or training for the posts he scheduled them to fill and every appointee cordially disliked every other member of the council. Five of them were Lincoln's political rivals. "They will eat you up," he was warned. Lincoln replied, "They will eat each other up."

Foreign affairs Lincoln planned to delegate to William H. Seward, as Secretary of State. The United States Navy, whose ships would deal with all foreign vessels in American waters, Lincoln proposed to turn over to Seward's enemy, Gideon Welles. In politics Seward had been an old Whig. Welles had been a Democrat. Seward was the strongest man politically in the Republican party, Lincoln's chief rival for the Presidency. He was a small man, smooth-shaven, with shaggy eyebrows, beaked nose. His head resembled a wise macaw's.[5] Seward talked raucously and too much. Welles, his counterpoise, was silent in a crowd, a bashful man who buttonholed auditors singly before and after conferences. Hiding always in public behind a wig and beard, he wielded a dangerous pen in the privacy of his own room, stamping up and down the pages of his diary with a rhetorical cutlass in each hand. The combination of Seward and Welles was considered ill-advised by many statesmen. Lincoln's critics had yet to learn that the Rail Splitter thought and acted in the same way that he walked.

On the day following the election, Springfield, a town of 9,000 inhabitants, capital of rural Illinois, prepared to accommodate the promised influx of visitors sure to gather like flies around the President-elect. The little city was accustomed to periodic immigrations of state legislators but not to such a crowd. Hotels were taxed to the utmost. In many of them guests slept three or more in a room, sometimes doubling up in bed, the true Western fashion Lincoln had known for many happy years while riding circuit. Affluent visitors came by train in newfangled contraptions rigged with permanent horizontal shelves for beds.[6] These "sleeping cars" were sidetracked and their occupants, after concluding the day's business uptown, retired at night in the railroad yards.

Lincoln's "audiences" with his people were in marked contrast with the procedure he and his ministers would have to adopt when dealing with foreign powers. For several hours each day Lincoln received visitors in a room in the Statehouse, letting them crowd around his desk or sprawl upon the chairs and a sofa provided for the purpose. Lincoln himself reclined at ease in his own chair, sometimes putting his feet on the table, gossiping and spinning yarns with friends and strangers, farmers, mechanics, office seekers who wanted to tell him how to run the government. This casual hospitality served Lincoln well. In public gatherings office seekers were not so insistent. When privacy was necessary Lincoln slipped away to an inner office at the *Illinois State Journal* or to the St. Nicholas Hotel where his bust was being modeled by a Cincinnati sculptor, T. D. Jones—a name Lincoln whimsically complained he could not remember.[7] The sculptor applied for a consulate in Italy two years later but Lincoln's memory had not improved.[8]

Shortly after the election Donn Piatt and his wife came to town. A wealthy Ohio politician, he had been stumping southern Illinois for Lincoln. The President-elect invited the Piatts to dinner with Mrs. Lincoln and his own two little boys. Piatt remembered the meal as "an old-fashioned mess of indigestion, composed mainly of cake, pies and chickens, the last evidently killed in the morning, to be eaten, as best they might, that evening."[9] After dinner Lincoln's boys climbed over the scaffolding of their father's gaunt frame, making it difficult for him to talk to his exquisite guest. Donn Piatt pretended not to notice the interruptions, and laughed politely at Lincoln's sallies. Furtively he measured the new chief of the nation. The man was a skeptic but not a cynic, Piatt mused, a rude figure to be dealing with European diplomats. Mrs. Lincoln, too, seemed to lack the quality necessary for a woman in her new position. When Seward was mentioned as the future incumbent for the State Department she blurted out, "The country will find how we regard that abolition sneak." Lincoln made no remonstrance and only pushed the remark aside as he did the hand of one of his little boys when it invaded his capacious mouth.[10]

On November 21, Lincoln and his wife took the train to Chicago in company with Senator Trumbull, Donn Piatt and their wives. Enough snow had fallen and mixed with the russet grass to give the Grand Prairie a strange illumination. Steam from the locomotive frosted the windows with fantastic designs. At wayside towns the train stopped to take wood and water. New passengers entered the car with gusts of icy air. Railroad travel to Chicago was a novelty not ten years old, and Lincoln had known these towns and the people in them since stagecoach days. The main topic on everyone's lips was the possibility of war. Lincoln was affable, with a nod or a story for all. Donn Piatt heard him say that he did not believe war was inevitable. "They won't give up the offices." Lincoln paused a moment and then explained, "Were it believed that vacant places could be had at the North Pole, the road there would be lined with dead Virginians."[11]

Finally the train trundled into Chicago, a real city with a population of over a hundred thousand, half of them immigrants from the countries with which Lincoln would soon have to deal. The city was noisy with steamship docks, railroad yards, horse-drawn drays, boys hawking half a dozen newspapers. The *Tribune,* published by Joseph Medill and John Locke Scripps, had campaigned diligently for Lincoln's election. Scripps had written a campaign biography of the President-elect. Another Republican paper in Chicago, the *Journal,* less successful financially, was equally loyal. Its owner, Charles Wilson, was one of the noisy boys who had helped carry the crowd for the Rail Splitter's nomination. Lincoln might have to find a job for him. Diplomatic posts were an obvious solution for political obligations. Lincoln had a blankbook in which all foreign consulates and legations were noted and against this list he penciled the names of deserving friends. His sophisticated advisers were shocked. Such ill-educated riffraff would ruin his foreign relations.

Beside the name of Charlie Wilson, Lincoln wrote the name of Theodore Canisius, his secret partner in a political venture during the late presidential campaign. Lincoln had purchased a case of German script type,[12] Canisius agreeing to issue a newspaper urging his countrymen to vote patriotically. The paper had failed financially and now Canisius might have to be awarded some consular post—another shock to observing statesmen who did not notice that Lincoln made no offers, no rash promises, moving forward always with caution, slowly as he walked.

When he returned to Springfield, the President-elect found great piles of mail awaiting him. Daily the hired man brought market-basket loads of trivial correspondence, some of which must be answered. At first Lincoln was amused by "bad grammar and worse penmanship, stylistic originality, frankness of thought and pertinence of expression,"[13] but even his keen sense of the ludicrous soon became blunted by repetition. From his own desk more important missives were sent out. Letters to the leaders of his party requested them to come to Springfield, not in a body that might unite against him, but singly, one by one—a technique that might work also with foreign powers. Ostensibly Lincoln wished to discuss political policies and appointments, upon which he had already secretly made up his mind. From New York came Horace Greeley to speak for the radical wing of the party. His pink and white complexion fringed with flaxen hair and beard, his blue eyes and a certain rural freshness gave him the air of a successful dairyman[14] or Mennonite preacher. Every week a million farmers read his *Tribune* and pondered over diatribes against a social system which permitted slavery. Lincoln knew that Greeley's readers, together with the immigrant Germans, were the warp and woof that had elected him. In Greeley's room at the hotel Lincoln learned that the great editor wanted John C. Frémont, the Western Pathfinder and presidential candidate four years before, appointed minister to France.[15] Lincoln was affable and noncommittal.

From Missouri, heart of the German-American population, came Edward Bates, Republican leader of the state. He called at Lincoln's office before the President-elect had come down to work. Lincoln's secretary, John G. Nicolay, twenty-eight-year-old Bavarian alien, ex-editor of a country newspaper, tried to entertain the great little man. Nicolay had heard so much about Bates that the real man disappointed him. The old fellow looked dingy gray and acted too polite. Suddenly Nicolay's eyes snapped with pleasure. Bates, he discovered, had a faculty for sharp expression and an aggressiveness that belied his unctuous manners. The Missourian was a determined antisecessionist. The Union, he said impressively, could not be saved with talk—force might be necessary. If so, he always made it a rule *"never to fire blank cartridges."*[16] Nicolay gave Bates the morning paper and went out to hunt Lincoln. In a few minutes the two men entered the office. Lincoln and Bates sat down. The President-elect was gracious, said he was sorry that he could not appoint the Missourian Secretary of State. That position had been offered to Seward. Perhaps the New Yorker would not accept. In any event Bates would not be forgotten.[17]

From Pennsylvania came Simon Cameron, iron magnate accused of playing politics for personal advantage, who in the nominating convention the previous summer had sidetracked the Seward-Weed machine, swung the Pennsylvania delegation to Lincoln and thus assured his nomination. Henry Villard reported to the *New York Herald* that Cameron went away empty-handed, having hoped to become Secretary of the Treasury—a lucrative trough for one of Cameron's reputation. Villard was wrong.[18] Lincoln as usual kept his own counsel. The week before Christmas Lincoln's greatest rival, Thurlow Weed, boss politician of New York state and owner of the *Albany Journal,* pussyfooted into Springfield.

No man in the party controlled more votes at home and at the same time knew more about European politics than Thurlow Weed. With his daughter he had crossed the ocean six times,[19] had been entertained at the American embassies, had met the leading statesmen in both England and France, knew their problems, faiths and foibles. Lincoln realized that this interview was important for his foreign affairs.

Thurlow Weed, like Lincoln, was over six feet tall and the earth would have trembled beneath his stride had Weed been that kind of boss. Instead, he always walked on cat's feet, stalking power and seeking no office for himself. Unscrupulous, according to his enemies, Weed never bared his claws in the light of day. To defeat a party colleague, the great Henry Clay, Weed had once flooded New York with alleged letters from county leaders. Each said in substance, "For God's sake, work for Clay over there; he's sunk here."

Weed's smooth-shaven face had the unperturbed serenity of a Quaker patriarch. His long nose resembled a plowshare[20] and careful observers noted that his left eyebrow curled upward at the extremity. Thus one side of his face was pious, the other resembled Mephistopheles.[21] Calm, even-tempered, always unruffled, Weed had backed Seward for the Presidency against Lincoln and had lost. It was said that the stone lions on Seward's gateposts in

Auburn wept salt tears when the news came. Weed did not flinch. His poker face remained as unmoved as by a hand at cards.

In graciousness and an ability to hold his tongue Weed was Lincoln's match, and the two men looked into each other's eyes, measuring each other's strength. Weed was the older and more experienced in large affairs. His mind was strong and perfectly balanced. Weed had started life as a journeyman printer like Benjamin Franklin. Part of the time he set type with a young man named Harper who dreamed of becoming a great publisher.[22] But while Harper's aspirations were literary, Weed's were political. After a time he organized his own paper in upstate New York. A Whig in politics, his *Albany Journal* made it a practice to laud all ambitious young politicians regardless of party. This increased circulation, and it also gave Weed a remarkable number of supporters for nonpartisan bills.[23]

All one day Weed and Lincoln, both strong self-made men, sat quietly together on the horsehair furniture in Lincoln's little parlor where an ornate stove roared cheerily. Occasionally they walked together downtown to the hotels and the Statehouse. The future life of the nation might depend upon this conference. The policy these two leaders determined upon might make or avert a civil war. Lincoln had been elected by a wave of humanitarian emotionalism on a platform opposed to extending the institution of slavery. On this issue the South was seceding from the Union. Weed wanted to alter the party's position, mollify the slaveholders. Lincoln had said, "If slavery is not wrong, nothing is wrong."[24] On this point he would not concede one jot or tittle, and so Weed lost the first round with the champion. The second round decided the personnel of the new cabinet. Weed would have gladly named them all, but Lincoln did the talking and tallied possible nominees, mentioning only one Weed man, William H. Seward for Secretary of State. To make the blow less hard, Lincoln explained that he wished to fill his cabinet with men from all the border states as a buffer against the South—Free-Soil men, regardless of party, from Maryland, Pennsylvania, Ohio, Indiana, and Missouri. The New England abolitionists he would represent with Gideon Welles, journalist from Connecticut, as Secretary of the Navy.

As Lincoln talked, Weed became dangerously polite. "Four of

your appointees are Democrats," observed the man who had come to Springfield to run the administration from the inside, "and only three are Whigs. Who, may I ask, won this election?"

At times Lincoln's eyes flashed beneath those shaggy brows that jutted from his forehead like scrub pine from a hill. "The fourth Whig in the cabinet," he replied, "will be the President, thus assuring a tie."[25]

The battle had thus been settled in the second round but Weed struggled on. He changed tactics, attempting to show on political grounds how each of Lincoln's proposed appointments was not wise. Montgomery Blair, as Postmaster General, was particularly distasteful. Weed mentioned every conceivable objection except that the Blair family was the traditional enemy of the Weed machine. In like manner Salmon P. Chase of Ohio, slated for the secretaryship of the Treasury, was disparaged and maligned on all counts except that he was Seward's worst enemy. Cameron, the Pennsylvania spoilsman, Weed admitted to be sound on the party but, etc., etc.— allusive objections with no mention that Cameron had double-crossed him at the Chicago convention. As for Welles, the New England Democrat—Weed raised his eyebrows—Welles was not even a border-state man. Weed doubted if Welles, as a seaman, knew a sloop from a yawl—if he had ever in his white-bearded life been on salt water. Calmly and in his sweet sarcastic way, Weed suggested that Lincoln, as he traveled east to assume office, should stop at the harbors of New York, Philadelphia or Baltimore and select an attractive ship's figurehead which would make a more ornamental Secretary for the Navy Department than bewigged Welles.[26]

In spite of the glowing heat from the little ornate stove in Lincoln's parlor the coolness increased between the two great men. But Weed had been in politics too long to give up hope. After all, with his man Seward as Secretary of State, foreign affairs seemed free from danger. Lincoln, with coat off, vest unbuttoned, run-over carpet slippers on his feet, stretched his long legs before the stove. He watched Boss Weed. The New Yorker's power and ability must be bent to his own advantage.

Lincoln's problem was to hold Weed in the administration without giving him the whip hand. The field of foreign affairs might "cut the Gordian knot," as Lincoln liked to say. The two great men discussed this field and became less constrained. Lincoln admitted his own ignorance, offered Weed any diplomatic post he might desire. Weed demurred. He was too keen to be killed with kindness, too shrewd to be kicked upstairs. Always he worked as a lone wolf in sheep's clothing. Lincoln did not urge him further. If Weed would not accept a post for himself he might yet serve the country well as undercover man with Secretary Seward, a team equal to most situations.

For the first time since Lincoln had been elected President he had a chance to talk with a statesman who knew European problems intimately. Weed could tell Lincoln that England was strongly opposed to the institution of slavery, that the author of *Uncle Tom's Cabin* had received an enthusiastic reception from the upper classes in England. The Queen herself had not deemed it becoming to receive Mrs. Stowe openly, since her book was banned by the ruling party in America—the Democrats—but she had arranged an accidental meeting.[27] Abolition of slavery was a principle dear to all Englishmen, but democracy, especially American democracy, was a thing many Britishers feared. The previous generation of Englishmen had experimented with democracy and found it dangerous to property rights. Democracy, many believed, inevitably led to dictatorship. Such a usurper ruled in France. Louis Napoleon, after a lifetime of association with radical socialists, had been elected President of France and forthwith declared himself Emperor.

Weed could explain, too, that France traditionally opposed Great Britain. But Napoleon, shrewd schemer, might propose an alliance with England to ignore the Monroe Doctrine that the Western Hemisphere belonged only to Americans. European countries had maintained colonies in the New World before the United States was born. France and England together were strong enough to dictate to the United States. Moreover, England, as mistress of the seas, was alarmed at the miraculous growth of the United States merchant marine, jealous of the clipper ships which could outsail the best designs in British yards. Weed was sure that Great Britain seriously considered making an agreement with France to rule the world.

Sitting in the Lincoln parlor, Weed may have explained too that England had already taken the first steps toward this alliance. A reciprocity treaty had been signed. Also England and France had been allied in the recent Crimean War against Russia. England feared the Russians above all foreign powers. Thus the Czar might be a useful ally for America. Weed knew that the Russian minister at Washington had hinted that his country stood ready to co-operate with the North in case of trouble with the western European powers.

European armor was weak in one other spot. The common people were restless—dissatisfied. Russia, then, and the common people, were the two strings on which American diplomats must play. Lincoln in all the years of his Presidency never forgot the lesson.

Weed also had reason to suspect that the South was already opening negotiations with Great Britain to return to her allegiance —asking for a king.[28] The aristocratic South was appealing to the aristocrats of Europe for self-preservation. Even the Douglas Democrats, the moderate wing of the party, had catered to the aristocratic ideal.[29] Newspapers reported that the Secessionists were negotiating as well with imperial France.[30] The American experiment with democracy faced its first great crisis. Karl Marx saw this in Germany and he reminded his readers that the impending civil war had all the essential characteristics of a class struggle.

In England the class theme was further publicized by an eccentric American, George Francis Train, who amused large audiences of the underprivileged with his wit and audacity. A member of a prominent shipping family, he had traveled in his youth throughout the British Empire, but the slow grind of commercial competition did not amuse George Francis Train. Once he got a taste of applause on the rostrum he could live on nothing else. The sustained machinations of successful politicians also bored a man with Train's forensic talents. All he wanted to do was talk, toss wit recklessly, and make astonishing statements which he was generally able to prove. Train had two hobbies. One was democracy and the other was the publication of his own addresses. England, with a long tradition of free speech and press, could not deny him ear, but the ruling classes who were opposed to even parliamentary reform feared him as a ghost from red America. Train had been a militant preacher for such shocking democratic innovations as cheap newspapers, penny postage and street railways. "An erratic chap, rather," Britishers would say, fixing their monocles on him when he passed. Arrested once for printing obscene language, Train produced worse words from the Holy Bible. The judge dismissed the case and pronounced him insane.

To an audience near Liverpool, where Train boasted that he had built the first street railway in the British Isles, he shouted, and then printed for distribution:

"I believe in the aristocracy of a good nature . . . the aristocracy of a good hearty laugh, and would advocate that aristocracy in Parliamentary Reform that would remove all taxes on the mind. (applause) I would say to the statesmen . . . remove the tax on knowledge, but tax bachelors, tax widows, tax young men parting their hair in the middle, tax crinoline, and, above all, tax grumbling, but remove the tax on paper! (Laughter and applause) . . . Why pay out of your pocket £2,000,000 for education, and then force half of it back again in taxing the chief agent of education—paper!"[31]

Lincoln knew that American hustings were full of demagogues of this stripe. Perhaps he could use Train sometime. The name was worth remembering. Weed knew, too, that the English Parliament contained a few liberals, idealists worshiped by many of the lower classes. These theorists were a minority, to be sure, but through them the great mass of disfranchised Englishmen might speak. Such men were John Bright and Richard Cobden, who had found wealth in industry and believed it good just as did Vanderbilt and McCormick and others in America. Lincoln, too, believed in labor and capital—laborers who could become capitalists, not laborers fixed in status like slaves. John Bright's political philosophy appealed to 'Abraham Lincoln.

Weed could tell Lincoln of still another source from which he might learn the extent of the European laborers' sympathy with American democracy. An English threepenny newspaper, *Once a Week*, had recently printed an editorial slightly satirical to all things foreign, but showing plainly enough that the common people were friendly to a rail-splitter President-to-be. The British editor had disclosed that his knowledge of American history was weak but that his principles were strong when he wrote, "Abraham Lincoln recently defeated Frederick Douglass for the Presidency." The correspondent meant Stephen A. Douglas, not Frederick, the Negro abolitionist orator. The news article contained other quaint observations. Lincoln, it continued, "wears habitually what we consider evening dress," but as a youth he

"toiled as a farm-labourer, mule-driver, sheep-feeder, deer-killer, and wood-cutter, and lastly as boatman on the waters of the Wabash and the Mississippi. . . . About 1830, Abe . . . went off . . . as volunteer in the New Salem Company, bound for the war in Florida, against either Black Hawk, Billy Bowlegs, or some other desperate Indian chief. . . . When the war was over, Abe returned . . . and sat sturdily in the local parliament for four sessions."[32]

Not very accurate, but Weed and Lincoln both knew that some of the recent campaign biographies were almost as bad.

At the end of the serious consultation in Lincoln's parlor and in his room at the Statehouse, Weed decided that he must go—badly battered but not defeated. He had lost both rounds, on policy and on appointments, with the President-elect. The foreign field alone was open to him and Lincoln frankly admitted that he knew little about it. Weed with his flair for maneuver could bide his time. At present he would go home. Proper farewells in society were lengthy. One must take one's high hat and bow with the formal phraseology which passed for good manners. Weed later remembered that he concluded his farewell with: "I entertain too high a sense of the honor which the confidence of distinguished statesmen in high public position confers, to annoy them or stultify myself by thrusting before them unseasonably mere questions of office,—questions that would unavoidably come in due time to engross their thoughts and perplex their judgment."[33]

After Weed was gone from Springfield, the President-elect settled back into routine political activities, meeting inconsequential people and some not so inconsequential. Hiding away at times, Lincoln worked on his inaugural address and some fifteen other addresses to be delivered on the way to Washington. After Christmas, Mrs. Lincoln went to New York to purchase clothes to wear

in the White House. Lincoln, at home, "batched" in his disorderly
way. People speculated on what Mrs. Lincoln would say when she
saw the house on her return.[34] True to his understanding with
Weed, and already long determined in his own mind, Lincoln sent
Seward formal notification of his nomination as Secretary of State.
The tardiness, however, hurt Seward's feelings and he went to see
Charles Francis Adams, the great Whig leader now turned Repub-
lican.

Adams' sons believed that their own father deserved a place
in the cabinet[35] and that he would eventually be President. They
were incredulous when he introduced a little, insignificant man in
mussed clothes as the future Secretary of State. Seward was offered a cold chair in the formal parlor. Adams gave him a cigar.
Seward puffed and pouted. He wanted to be coaxed and petted.
Adams talked quietly, weighing each word, his face framed in
whiskers as the sun is framed in rays. Seward's petulance boiled
over and then cooled. Soon the simmering New York politician
began to crack jokes and make plans for the future. He decided to
accept the position and went away champing the second of
Adams' cigars and carrying a third in his pocket.[36] As Secretary
of State, with the backing of Weed and Adams, Seward could still
save the administration from Lincoln's incompetence.

Back in Springfield, domestic problems crowded foreign relations
from the mind of the President-elect. January was stormy on the
prairies. Mrs. Lincoln was overdue from her eastern trip, and the
time for Lincoln's departure to Washington drew near. Day after
day he walked down to the station, tall and shambling, making flat-
footed tracks in the snow, standing on the platform like an old
molting crane, watching travelers alight from the cars, looking
for Mrs. Lincoln's pert figure among the hooped and poplin-dressed
passengers. At last she came, with Robert, the Harvard student,
sleek and apple-cheeked, more his mother's than his father's son.
Two days later Lincoln departed on a trip of his own, over to Coles
County to visit his aged stepmother, who had done her best for
him in the log-cabin days.[37] Neighbors came to her little frame
house, hitched their teams along the fence, knocked at the door,
crowded in, shook hands, told stories of the early days. One
farmer showed Lincoln some sulphur matches and how to strike

them. The President-elect was interested and said, "What a blessing to the common people."[38]

On his return to Springfield, Lincoln prepared for Washington. Gifts came by every train. Mrs. Lincoln received "a highly ornamented sewing machine."[39] A new suit of clothes for the President's inauguration was so finely tailored that it was exhibited publicly. A new stovepipe hat Lincoln tried on before a mirror, remarking, "Well, Mother, there is one thing we are going to get out of this mess. We are going to get some new clothes." A hundred-dollar cane was presented to Lincoln by a grasshopper-legged individual in a bottle-green coat, who had come from the gold coast of California for the event.[40] An Ohio colleague, Addison P. Russell, as full of jokes as Lincoln himself, sent the President-elect a pig's tail which emitted a shrill noise when blown. Lincoln's long bony fingers unfolded the note accompanying it and he read: "No whistle can be made out of a pig's tail."[41] Lincoln understood, and amused newspapermen and other visitors by playing with it for an hour. Russell was a young journalist and an admirer of another Ohio joker, Senator Tom Corwin, who, it was said, might have been elected President himself had it not been for his sense of humor. Corwin had stumped actively for Lincoln in the campaign.[42] A laughing Free-Soiler, he called Charles Francis Adams "the Archbishop of antislavery."[43] In Congress, years before, Lincoln had heard Corwin oppose the Mexican War. Now he could pay a political debt by sending Corwin as minister to Mexico, the sunny civilization which seldom let politics or revolutions interfere with entertainment. The "Archbishop of antislavery" might have to have a diplomatic post also, but that would unavoidably come in due time.

In February a spring thaw turned the prairies into quagmires; barnyards became putrid ponds. Wagons on the way to town sank hub-deep in mud black as ink. Horsemen floundered in the main streets of Springfield. February 11, the day before Lincoln's birthday, was scheduled for the departure. His itinerary was in charge of Norman B. Judd, a stubby, silken-haired[44] Chicago lawyer, wealthy organizer of the Rock Island Railway. Lincoln had been an attorney for the road. Judd was capable, unimaginative. He carried in his head endless business details. He had made a successful chairman of the Republican State Central Committee and helped manage Lincoln's campaign. Lincoln had considered him for his cabinet, but Mrs. Lincoln did not like him[45] and had threatened "to raise the roof." Lincoln decided to offer him the ministerial post in Prussia, an honorary but unimportant position in the buffer state between threatening France and friendly Russia. Judd accepted. To assist him with the language Lincoln appointed Herrmann Kreismann as Secretary of Legation in Berlin. Kreismann, another Chicago politician and one-time city clerk,[46] claimed to have swung Chicago's foreign vote to Lincoln.

The presidential party included Ward Hill Lamon, a big, bluff lawyer who had been Lincoln's Danville partner in the circuit-riding days and now acted as his bodyguard; and Orville H. Browning, veteran statesman and polished gentleman who could never be reconciled to uncouth Lincoln's exalted station and watched him constantly for gauche mannerisms which he jotted down in a diary. Parades en route were to be in charge of Elmer E. Ellsworth, a young colonel of Zouaves who had been reading law in Lincoln's office. John G. Nicolay and John Hay, a bright young man just back from college, acted as private secretaries. Military dignity was given the little party by Major David Hunter, Captain George Hazzard, Captain John Pope and Colonel E. V. Sumner, the last fresh from fighting Indians and bushwhackers on the Kansas plains, his face wind-burned, his eyes crowfooted from looking long distances. The "Bull of the Woods" he was affectionately called by his men, who remembered that the colonel always took out his false teeth and put them in his pocket before leading a charge.

The day of departure dawned gloomily. Fog hung over the prairie town. The sun shone wanly, like a metal disk seen through gray crepe. At the railway station a thousand townsmen congregated for a farewell reception in the public waiting room. When the presidential suite assembled, Lincoln was not among them. The reception committee worried. Herrmann Kreismann, running errands for Judd as he would continue to do in Berlin, went in haste to the Chenery House where the Lincolns had moved after renting their residence. Going at once to Lincoln's room, Kreismann stopped. The door was closed and he could hear no sound. He knocked. "Come in," was the prompt reply. Kreismann opened the door. Lincoln was seated in a chair, his head bowed. On the floor, quite beside herself, lay Mrs. Lincoln.

"Kreismann," Lincoln said with a look of utmost misery, "she will not let me go until I promise her an office for one of her friends."[47]

Lincoln left without his wife. He walked into the dreary weather with his peculiar, dejected, flat-footed step, "weariness, and pain, all up and down his person."[48] At the station he shook hands perfunctorily and then mounted the rear platform of his special car. Removing his high hat in a drizzling rain, he looked out across the wet umbrellas and addressed the people of the town into which he had come, plodding through the deep mud of another spring, a ragged and unknown stripling of twenty-two. Now he was leaving to become President of the United States. He began:

"My Friends: No one, not in my situation, can appreciate my feeling of sadness at this parting. To this place, and the kindness of these people, I owe everything."

Tears filled his eyes. Out on the edge of the crowd a carriage stopped. Mrs. Lincoln got out. A bystander handed her an umbrella.

"Here I have lived a quarter of a century, and have passed from a young to an old man. Here my children have been born, and one is buried. I now leave, not knowing when or whether ever I may return. . . ."

Rain dripped from the eaves of the railway station.

"Trusting in Him who can go with me, and remain with you, and be everywhere for good, let us confidently hope that all will yet be well. To His care commending you, as I hope in your prayers you will commend me, I bid you an affectionate farewell."[49]

Wearily Lincoln turned from the wet faces of his neighbors and passed into the car. The train started. In deep dejection he sought solace in his private compartment. Robert Lincoln was gay and happy in the "saloon car."

This simple language from Lincoln's heart was his formal introduction to the people of Europe. The words were admirably suited
for foreign languages. A French translation from the island of
Guernsey preserved the rhythm of the original so artistically that
people said the work had been done by Victor Hugo.[50] The great
novelist was eager to stab the Emperor. He had competed with
Louis Napoleon for the presidency of France and lost. At the time
of the *coup d'état* Hugo made a scene in an omnibus. From a four-
wheeler he harangued the troops in the Place de la Bastille without
effect. Disguised as a workman he escaped arrest for treason. On
Guernsey, under the protection of the British flag and in sight of
the French coast on a clear day, he lived in exile. Lincoln might
help him win France back for the liberals.

The role of international liberal, champion of freedom everywhere, did not appear to be in Lincoln's mind when his train entered Indianapolis. Acres of people greeted him with cheers. Mrs.
Lincoln and the two little boys joined his party, having come on a
later train. During the round of ovations Lincoln entrusted a small
satchel containing his inaugural address to his son Robert[51] who
promptly handed it to a waiter who in his turn mislaid it. Lincoln
lost his temper. The boy had failed in his responsibility. The grip
was found at last in a room full of baggage. Lincoln said that he
would not trust it out of his hands again.

In Cincinnati the streets were gay with bunting in Lincoln's
honor. At Columbus, at Pittsburgh, at Cleveland, at Buffalo, Lincoln passed through lanes of cheering people, from ovation to ovation. In one town his carriage was pulled by six milk-white horses,
in another by eight blacks with red plumes in their bridles and flags
in their harness. Lincoln's spirits had thoroughly revived. A
newspaper correspondent reported that he shouted to some workmen on a railroad trestle, "Do you want any rails split?" When
dignitaries approached for an interview Lincoln's little boys amused
themselves by stepping up to the strangers, asking, "Do you want
to see Old Abe?" Then they pointed out some tall man who was
not Old Abe and slipped away to watch from their elders' coattails.[52] At Albany, Weed's and Seward's bailiwick, the presidential
party, escorted by horsemen, police and troops of soldiers, drove
from the station to the Capitol grounds, past a local theater where

*The Apostate* was being played by a young, dark-eyed tragedian, John Wilkes Booth.[53]

Entraining once more, the party steamed down the Hudson past the Catskills, purple as thunderclouds in the western sky—the most imposing mountains Lincoln had ever seen—past the broad Esopus Valley, Poughkeepsie, the Palisades, across Spuyten Duyvil, arriving at last in the Thirtieth Street Station in New York. Reporters who met the train were amused by a little domestic scene between Mr. and Mrs. Lincoln.

"She took a brush and comb from her reticule, smoothed his hair, arranged his cravat, brushed some of the dust from his coat, and then stood looking at him with evident admiration. 'Am I all right now, mother?' asked the President. Mrs. Lincoln's reply was a hearty kiss. Some of the spectators . . . rushed from the car, unable to restrain their laughter."[54]

Mayor Fernando Wood, handsome, smooth-shaven, dressed in a double-breasted frock coat and black stock, received Lincoln publicly but his welcome was almost insolent. The city was the banking metropolis for the South, "her conscience choked with cotton, her mouth kankered with gold,"[55] as a Northern idealist noted. New York was very important to Lincoln's foreign relations. The city received news from Europe before it reached the State Department in Washington. A few years previously, newspaper employees met incoming ships off Sandy Hook in order to send dispatches to the city by semaphore or carrier pigeon. Since the telegraph had been extended to Halifax, where Cunard steamers touched, news reached New York two days ahead of the steamers. Politically, New York was a Democratic stronghold. Some of its citizens planned to secede along with the South, as a Free City. The president of the Bank of the Republic, Gazaway Bugg Lamar, was plotting to send shipments of guns to the Confederacy. Lincoln heard much of that name in the months ahead. Lamar's cousin, Lucius Quintus Cincinnatus, was later appointed Confederate minister to Russia—the nation whose friendship Lincoln must cultivate. One powerful newspaper in New York, the *Herald,* opposed the coming administration. Its editor, James Gordon Bennett, a Britisher in both blood and sympathy, was in a position to interpret all Lincoln's foreign problems and disseminate his conclusions to foreign-born Americans.

Fernando Wood, Gazaway Bugg Lamar and James Gordon Bennett were not the only New Yorkers of power who were scheming to thwart Lincoln. The operator of a mail steamer between Manhattan and New Orleans, James Dunwody Bulloch, became even more prominent in rebellious circles. As future head of the South's secret service in Europe he was to cause Lincoln endless foreign pains. Bulloch, like many other Southern sympathizers, was a man of means. His sister married into the Roosevelt family of New York City. She named her little son Theodore.

In New York a Verdi opera was being sung. Lincoln attended and shocked the city's elite by wearing black gloves.[56] "Just as we said," they sniffed. "What more could be expected of a red republican?" "Black republican" was the term used by rural aristocrats to designate the party which they feared would take their servants. In Europe, and to a lesser degree in New York, capitalists who feared that Lincoln would take their dollars called him "red"—a nice color distinction. At the Astor House a reception was held for Mrs. Lincoln by the commonalty, wives of politicians, who donned crinoline and chatted elegantly. Newspapers reported that Mrs. August Belmont had been present. She denied it. Mrs. Belmont was the daughter of Commodore Perry, famous for opening isolationist Japan to world trade. Her two uncles were high in the established regime which Lincoln's party had upset. One was captain of a man-of-war. The other, John Slidell, was political boss of Louisiana, master of a planter's mansion. As future commissioner to France his name would be as well known as Lincoln's in all Europe. Such a great family had assured social position to August Belmont, wealthy New York agent for the international bankers, the Rothschilds. Lincoln knew that August Belmont's influence on international problems of finance might be profound.

The potential problems of foreign policy were endless in New York. Across the Hudson in Jersey City, Lincoln and his suite felt more at home. An enthusiastic delegation greeted them, with ex-Senator William L. Dayton, Attorney General of New Jersey, grasping the President-elect's extended hand. Lincoln, tall and sallow, bowed over the ruddy, apoplectic face and satin-upholstered bay window on the man who had once defeated him for the vice-presidential nomination and whom in turn Lincoln had defeated for the presidential nomination.

After an exchange of public addresses Lincoln's train moved across New Jersey toward Dayton's home in Trenton, near where Washington had crossed the Delaware. The flat countryside where Continental soldiers had fought Hessians passed in an endless panorama before the car windows while Lincoln discussed the state of the nation. Dayton, fat and short of breath, could tell Lincoln all about the treachery to be expected from New York City. He had grown up next door to it. Lincoln appreciated Dayton's ability and political importance, his social graces and air of bonhomie. He decided to make him minister to France, but did not mention it at this time.

At four o'clock in the afternoon the presidential party arrived at the City of Brotherly Love.[57] Philadelphia in 1861 was a clean, quiet city with shaded streets named for the trees—Chestnut, Walnut, Spruce and Pine. Quakers in brown knee breeches and broad hats walked the brick sidewalks, but they were no longer numerous.[58] Quaker ladies in dove-gray shawls and bonnets were more common. The City Fathers had not encouraged dirty, noisy locomotives in town. A few railroads had forced their terminals east of the Schuylkill, but the Pennsylvania Railroad still stopped at West Philadelphia, where horses and mules, hitched in tandems of eight and ten, hauled the cars singly across the river.[59] At the Kensington station Lincoln and his party were escorted to carriages and driven to the Continental Hotel, Lincoln bowing to the multitude.

That night in the hotel, while shaking hands with a line of admirers, Lincoln felt his shoulder tapped. It was Nicolay, urging him to come at once to a private conference in Judd's room. A plot had been discovered to assassinate him when his train passed through Baltimore. Lincoln's friends insisted that he change his schedule and thwart the conspirators by going to Washington at once. Lincoln deliberated. Then he said, "I do not feel that I can go to Washington tonight. Tomorrow morning I have promised to raise the flag over Independence Hall, and after that to visit the legislature at Harrisburg. Whatever the cost, these two promises

I must fulfill. Thereafter I shall be ready to consider any plan you may adopt."

The next day, February 22, Lincoln was up at six in the morning. The pink of dawn glowed on the colonial brickwork of old Independence Hall, as the President-elect hoisted the American flag above the colonial eaves.[60] The flagstaff was tall, and when the flag was halfway up he stopped and took off his coat, then finished the task.[61] Inside the venerable building Lincoln spoke to the multitude where the Fathers had signed the Declaration of Independence. Lincoln said he had often pondered over the "dangers" incurred by the men who had assembled there, and he had inquired what principle had kept them so long together. He might have been talking straight to the masses of Europe with whom he was preparing to deal, when he said that hope of liberty "to all the world, for all future time," was the sentiment guiding them. Then, addressing the slaveholding South, he concluded:

"It was that which gave promise that in due time the weights would be lifted from the shoulders of all men, and that all should have an equal chance. This is the sentiment embodied in the Declaration of Independence. . . . But if this country cannot be saved without giving up that principle, I was about to say I would rather be assassinated on this spot than surrender it."[62]

The party drove uptown and embarked for Harrisburg. Lincoln's friends who knew of the assassination plot watched his train with misgivings as it rattled away down the main line of the Pennsylvania Railroad. The President-elect was scheduled to speak three times in Harrisburg, and also to attend a political banquet at the Jones House with Governor Curtin, reputed the handsomest man in Pennsylvania, suave, gracious, well groomed, the beau ideal of statesmen. The gala day passed smoothly until shortly after dark. Then the telegraph wires connecting Harrisburg with Philadelphia and Baltimore were mysteriously cut.[63] Out in the Pennsylvania capital Lincoln had disappeared. Next morning passengers on the New York-Washington train were amazed to see the President-elect towering above them as they filed down the sleeping-car aisle to get off the train at the nation's capital.

Lincoln's future minister to Prussia, Norman Judd, had spirited the President-elect back to West Philadelphia on a special train. In disguise Lincoln had jolted along cobblestoned Market Street in a cab with a detective named Allan Pinkerton and his own body-guard, Ward Hill Lamon.[64] Shortly before midnight Lincoln boarded the Washington sleeping car as it lay in the P. W. & B. station.[65] Mrs. Lincoln, the children and the Army escort arrived in Washington on the presidential special late in the afternoon. Judd came through on the regular passenger train. Having cheated the military out of a triumphal entry, the embryo diplomat did not choose to ride farther with the Bull of the Woods.

# II. *Men Bred in Courts Accustomed to the World*

SHORTLY after noon on March 4, 1861, James Buchanan drove up to Willard's Hotel and walked into the doorway. In a few minutes he reappeared arm in arm with Abraham Lincoln. The two men got into a barouche and drove down Pennsylvania Avenue, a quaint street lined with ailanthus trees in whitewashed sentry boxes.[1] The horses' hoofs and the wheels of the carriage rattled on the round cobblestones. Behind the President and President-elect followed carriages laden with jurists, clergy, members of Congress, governors of states, foreign ministers and their staffs, detachments of the Army and Navy. The carriages of the diplomats carried many men with strange faces under high silk hats—faces that Lincoln would have to learn, faces of friends and of enemies who posed as friends. There was Lord Lyons, representing Great Britain, with a ruddy, hearty, English-squire face fringed with whiskers on the jowls, a face as punctilious as only a bachelor's and a Britisher's may be. His country's traditional enemy, Russia, was represented by a jovial gambler, Baron Edward de Stoeckl. The face of Don Gabriel Garcia y Tassara was morose as a Spanish bull. Another face, pale, intellectual, unhappy, masked Henri Mercier, minister resident from France, famous for his dinners. A good-humored face belonged to De Lisboa from Portugal. Prussian von Gerolt's face appeared kind and timid. Rudolph Schleiden from Bremen appeared rugged and well fed. Abraham Lincoln in time would know them all—Barreda, courtly and elegant; Blondeel, crafty; eccentric Georgi, the invalid; Edward, Count Piper, grotesquely cherubic.[2]

The long procession drove slowly toward the unfinished dome of the Capitol. Washington, after sixty years, was notably unkempt. A city of fine residences and unfinished Greek temples, it was interspersed with shanties and mean shops.[3] Here and there groups of office seekers cheered the incoming President but most of the people sympathized with the South and scowled at the procession. Soldiers marched along the streets flanking Pennsylvania Avenue on both sides, ready to cut in at all cross streets and stop any violent demonstration. Lincoln's carriage was surrounded closely by a blue-coated cavalry guard. On the seat opposite him sat Senator Edward Baker[4]—an early-day Illinois friend. Lincoln had named one of his sons for him. The two men used to ride circuit together. Baker went out West where opportunities were good in politics. Oregon sent him to Washington as Senator. Now he was slated to introduce the President before his inaugural address. Lincoln carried the precious manuscript inside a pocket in his finely tailored coat. All the diplomats and their staffs anxiously awaited the contents of that paper. A civil war would arouse many echoes. For almost a year American affairs had assumed a prominent place in European newspapers. M. Mercier was palely thoughtful, Lord Lyons apprehensive. Coldly judicious and self-contained, the Britisher said:

"Mr. Lincoln has not hitherto given proof of his possessing any natural talents to compensate for his ignorance of everything but Illinois village politics. He seems to be well meaning and conscientious, in the measure of his understanding, but not much more."[5]

Lord Lyons had studied the inaugural address of the newly elected Confederate President, Jefferson Davis, and he knew that the Southern government was getting under way ahead of the Lincoln administration. Davis' inaugural had been a disappointment. The diplomats, as they rattled down Pennsylvania Avenue, might have complained that the Confederate President lacked logic when he stated that Southerners were asserting their constitutional rights and admitted later that they were rebels—an inconsistency that would trouble Davis again and again. This afternoon the diplomats would hear Lincoln's answer and report it to their countries. The diplomats represented monarchies and they knew that the South claimed to be aristocratic.[6] Lord Lyons had read with interest that President Davis, on the way to his inaugural, had spoken at Stevenson, Alabama, saying:

"England will recognize us, and a glorious future is before us. The grass will grow in Northern cities, where the pavements have

been worn off by the tread of commerce. We will carry war where
it is easy to advance—where food for the sword and torch await our
armies in the densely populated cities."[7]

Lord Lyons had read, too, that the Confederate Secretary of
State, Robert Toombs, prophesied that he would call the roll of his
slaves on Bunker Hill.[8] The Englishman knew that Lincoln, on
his way to Washington, had maintained in public that "there was
nothing going wrong." In the *New York Herald* Lyons read that
Lincoln showed "no capacity to grapple manfully with the dangers
of this crisis."

The procession reached the end of Pennsylvania Avenue. Piles
of rock, cables and workmen's tools littered the Capitol grounds.
United States troops stood deployed for action. M. Mercier looked
at the artillery, parked advantageously to rake the avenues. This
precaution resembled those taken to safeguard a change of administration in revolutionary France.

Thurlow Weed, in his usual role of undercover man, prowled on
the outskirts of the procession.[9] America's venerable Lieutenant
General Winfield Scott, hero of the Mexican and British wars,
stood grim and crippled, his elbow on a cannon. Dressed in full
regimentals and gilt epaulets, the chief of the United States Army
was prevented by gout from standing on both feet. The old man
was unable to move from place to place without his buggy, held by
a soldier near by.

Outside the east portico of the Capitol a platform had been
erected for the inauguration. Two sharpshooters crouched behind
windows overlooking the crowd. Dignitaries took their places—
justices of the Supreme Court in black robes, senators in high hats,
representatives, Mrs. Lincoln and the children. Chief Justice
Taney, like an old monk in black, waited to administer the oath to
the ninth President he had sworn in.[10] Taney had been appointed
by Andrew Jackson as a radical to a conservative court and he had
seen the country move away from him on its democratic course
until he now stood as a symbol of conservatism. Lincoln had been
elected by a party bent on reversing his decisions.

Senator Baker arose and introduced the new President. A few
hands clapped dutifully. The diplomats would have to inform their
governments that the applause was not enthusiastic. Lincoln, a

tall, dark figure with white shirt bulging at the breast, stood awkwardly at the edge of the platform. His new, gold-headed, hundred-dollar cane embarrassed him. He finally pushed it into a corner of the railing. Then he removed his hat. Solemnly Lincoln took out his glasses, adjusted them to his angular nose, unfolded his manuscript and began to read. The diplomats and secretaries of legation listened attentively. They noted that the President was moderate, that he talked to America, to the South, and not to Europe. Lincoln did not mention foreign relations, or the abolition of slavery, which would have gained him sympathy abroad. His words were confined to his position as the constitutionally elected president of a democracy—a form of government not popular in the legations. He defined the principles of a democratic government, the constitutional guarantees of minorities, the violations of democratic principles which he would oppose, even with war. His position was clearly stated. The long silence he had maintained since the day of his election was over. Ministers, secretaries of legations and clerks went to their offices after the inauguration. They remembered that Lincoln had been emotionally national, that he had finished with:

"I am loath to close. We are not enemies, but friends. We must not be enemies. Though passion may have strained, it must not break our bonds of affection. The mystic chords of memory, stretching from every battle-field and patriot grave to every living heart and hearth-stone all over this broad land, will yet swell the chorus of the Union when again touched, as surely they will be, by the better angels of our nature."[11]

The inaugural was too superb for a small-town lawyer. English readers were informed that it was "generally attributed to Mr. Seward."[12]

In the afternoon the President moved into the White House. The first floor was open to the public like the lobby of a hotel. On the second floor Lincoln set the east wing aside for his offices, work and sleeping rooms for Nicolay and Hay. The west wing he reserved for Mrs. Lincoln and the family. Lincoln chose a small room at the head of the stairs for cabinet meetings. It contained a sofa, chairs and a baize-covered table.[13] His own office was near by. A massive walnut table served him for a desk. On the wall above a marble fireplace hung a cracked portrait of Andrew Jackson, the doughty Southerner[14] who had said: "Our Federal Union: it must be preserved!"

The Lincoln boys, Willie and Tad, explored the mansion from the basement kitchen to the attic. Mrs. Lincoln planned to change the furniture. Senator Charles Sumner, chairman of the Foreign Relations Committee, called. Sumner and Seward were rivals in the party. Lincoln looked at the Senator's six-foot physique and asked to measure heights with him, back to back. Sumner sniffed, then did so. The yokel from the West was odd indeed. What would the foreign diplomats think?

Lincoln, in his turn, was amused by the pompous New Englander. He told a friend later, "I have never had much to do with bishops down where we live; but, do you know, Sumner is just my idea of a bishop."[15]

On March 6, Lincoln called the first cabinet meeting. The notable enemies assembled. Each watched the others with dignified distrust. Chase stood by the table. His height gave prestige to his words. Seward sat down so that his shortness might not detract from his. Bewigged Welles peered through small spectacles over the ambush of his great beard, suspicious of colleagues who had called him the landlubber seaman. Next to him sat gray-headed Cameron, Secretary of War, quick at business deals, frail in build, with deep-set eyes and cold, thin lips accustomed to discussing money—a spoilsman to his enemies. In a straight-backed chair Secretary of the Interior Caleb Smith sat erect, bright-eyed, efficient, too conservative[16] to be interesting—a placeman to his associates. Behind him stood Postmaster General Montgomery Blair, tall and lean, a hard, practical politician with small ratlike eyes deeply set, slow to talk, nibbling at ideas, and slow to be convinced.[17] Opposed to abolition, he had won national renown arguing in the Supreme Court against the reactionary Taney decision that extended slavery throughout the Union. Blair called Chase "a liar" behind his back.[18] Chase devoted his time to thwarting Seward's influence. Seward grumbled to himself about sitting in the same cabinet with his enemy Chase. Lincoln leaned back in his armchair to survey his official family. He had had no experience in administration. Seward and Chase had both been governors of states. Both expected to run the government and Lincoln knew it.[19] The discussion was desultory and without order, the President a patient listener and learner.[20] Efficient Attorney General Bates fidgeted. Could not the President state his questions and require opinions seriatim?[21]

Foreign relations were considered. The lifeblood of the Confederacy was foreign trade. If this could be cut off, the South would perish. The rebellion could be snuffed out without firing a shot. Southern cotton was the mainstay of both British and French spinning mills. British shipowners profited by the haulage. Interruption of this trade would cause financial distress and unemployment. Lincoln listened. As a practical politician he knew that shipping interests, millowners and factory workers would not side with the North against the South on the constitutional issue of State rights. England's foreign policy for a generation, in Greece, Poland, Italy, Hungary and in Latin America, had favored minorities fighting for their independence. In theory the South's right of rebellion and secession was considered identical with the action taken by the thirteen colonies in their Revolution eighty-five years before.[22] After all, if 9,000,000 Southern Americans chose to set up an independent state, why should the Federal government not let them do so?[23] Britain had just released Canada, the Transvaal and the Orange Free State. The United States should be willing to do as much.

Listening to his cabinet's random conversation, Lincoln heard how an alliance of the European powers with the South would assure Confederate success. Even without this aid the Southerners' chance of victory was reasonably good. The difference in man power, North and South, was only two to one, and military experts maintained that three or four to one was necessary to invade a hostile country as Lincoln would be obliged to do if he re-established the authority of the Federal government. A victory then, doubtful at best, would be impossible if foreign powers took a hand. The job of keeping Europe from joining with the Confederacy fell naturally on the State Department—Seward and Weed.

After the cabinet left, Lincoln heard Washington gossip. Seward was reputed to be a quarrelsome man. The British Foreign Secretary, Lord John Russell, hoped sincerely that the cackling little rooster would be kept out of foreign affairs. For three months Seward had shouted for a foreign war to reunite the republic while Lincoln, out in Springfield, had remained discreetly silent— "nothing going wrong." Now the country lawyer had appointed Seward to the highest post in his cabinet. A dangerous place for him to be. Who in the name of Heaven would be appointed to the lesser posts in this diplomatic madhouse?

Three nations were vital to American diplomatic success— France, England and Mexico. The first two were the most powerful countries in Europe as well as the chief consumers of Southern cotton. Mexico was the doorway through which supplies could be shipped endlessly to the Confederacy in case of a blockade. Moreover, Mexico was not friendly to the United States. Aggressive Americans had provoked a war and taken a third of her territory. Since that time Mexican rulers had looked to Europe for an alliance to protect her from the Colossus of the North. Lincoln would have to use great care in dealing with this suspicious neighbor. His serious diplomatic problems ended here. If he made successful appointments to England, France and Mexico, his other diplomatic posts might be filled with deserving party men. Lincoln had no trouble getting the Senate to approve the appointment of Tom Corwin to Mexico but the French and English posts opened the whole problem of policy and patronage. Lincoln suggested William L. Dayton and Pathfinder Frémont to Seward. "What think you?"[24] Both men had been Republican presidential aspirants and the party owed them this honor although neither had any previous diplomatic experience. Seward said his personal friend Charles Francis Adams should be sent to England. The 'Adams family were by tradition the best-qualified diplomats in America. Unquestionably dignified and aristocratic, no better man could be found than Charles Francis 'Adams to oppose the best talent Jefferson Davis might appoint to represent his civilization in the English court. Such a man would go a long way toward checking the British nobility's belief that the South must win because its citizens were rural and military, used to firearms and the open fields, self-sustaining and accustomed to command.

Lincoln hesitated. He was in a predicament. He did not refuse the appointment but he did not act. Torn between political expedience at home and diplomatic expedience abroad, he did nothing. Charles Francis Adams, waiting at the capital, became discouraged and went home to Boston.[25] Then news arrived in Washington that the South had dispatched three envoys to Europe—William L. Yancey, A. Dudley Mann and Pierre 'A'. Rost. While they were on the water Lord Lyons threatened possible recognition of the Confederacy if British trade were molested.[26]

Lincoln and Seward could wait no longer. Both men met the problem characteristically. Seward stormed and blustered. Talking without restraint,[27] he spread the eagle, and hinted at war with England if the Confederacy were recognized. To the Democratic minister, George M. Dallas, in London waiting for his recall, Seward sent a dispatch urging him to see that the Southern commissioners be not received—a futile gesture. "Dough-face" Dallas, a Northern man with Southern principles, out of touch with the extent to which the rebellion had progressed, suspected a political plot to ruin him in America. Lincoln, in the meantime, said nothing, remained in the background and solved his problem by appointing Adams minister to England, and Dayton as minister to France.[28] Frémont was commissioned a major general in the Army.

Lord John Russell in England was immediately informed of all that was happening. Seward's belligerent bluffing—if it was bluffing—disconcerted him. A war, as Seward foresaw, might upset the precarious balance in Europe. On the other hand, Lord John, like many other Britishers, was confident that the South, with its many advantages, would win the war. In any case England must live with the survivors. To the British minister in Washington, Lord Lyons, he wrote: "Mr. Seward must not be allowed to get us into a quarrel. I shall see the Southerners when they come, but not officially, and keep them at a proper distance."[29]

Three days after the Southern commissioners had left for Europe, Charles Francis Adams received word of his appointment. His son wrote:

"It fell on our breakfast-table like a veritable bomb-shell, scattering confusion and dismay. It had been much discussed in Washington, but Seward had encountered so much difficulty, and the President had seemed so intent on the nomination of Dayton, that the news finally came on us like a thunderbolt. My mother at once fell into tears and deep agitation; foreseeing all sorts of evil consequences, and absolutely refusing to be comforted. . . . [She] took a constitutional and sincere pleasure in the forecast of evil. She delighted in the dark side of anticipation; she did not really think so; but liked to think, and say, she thought so. She indulged in the luxury of woe! . . . It seemed to give her quite a new view of the matter, when presently every one she met, instead of avoiding a painful subject or commiserating her, offered her congratulations."[30]

With the delegates picked for the battle royal of diplomats on the Continent, Lord Lyons wrote a dispatch to Lord John Russell appraising the men he might expect from the North and the South:

"Mr. Adams is son of John Quincy Adams, the fifth P. [*sixth*] of the U. S., and grandson of John Adams, the second P. The grandfather was the first Am. minister in England. The father was one of the Plenipotentiaries who signed in London the convention of the 3rd July, 1815. Mr. Adams as a member of the H. of R. for one of the districts of Mass., acted with the less violent section of the 'Republican' Party. During the last session of Congress he made a very remarkable speech on the state of the Union, denying the reasonableness of the complaints of the Southern States, but stating his desire that every concession not inconsistent with honour and principle should be made to them. He is considered to be a man of great independence of character, and has the reputation of being very tenacious of his own opinions. In manner he is quiet and unassuming. He is a man of good fortune. Mrs. Adams comes of a considerable family in Mass., of the name of Brooks. The late wife of Mr. Edward Everett, who, as your L. is aware, has held the offices of Minister in London and Secretary of State, was her sister."[31]

The British consul, Robert Bunch, at Charleston, South Carolina, also sent in his appraisal of the Southern commissioners to the Foreign Office. William L. Yancey he described as an able lawyer, a stirring orator and a recognized leader of the secession movement, extremely proslavery in his views, one who favored a renewal of the slave trade, a "manifest destiny" man—in short, a territorial expansionist.[32] Bunch might have added that Yancey was a fire-eating politician who in a street brawl had killed his wife's uncle.[33] Consul Bunch described the proud and educated Virginian, A. Dudley Mann, the only one of the commissioners with diplomatic experience, as the son of a "bankrupt grocer." Bunch said that Mann's personal character was "not good." Of the third commissioner, Pierre A. Rost, Bunch professed no knowledge.

Information for the British Foreign Secretary concerning Commissioner Rost did not much matter, as he was bound for France, the country of his birth. He had left Europe as a child. When he returned as a representative of the South, his first diplomatic *faux pas* was to pose as a Frenchman. His broken French caused much ridicule. "Has the South no sons capable of representing your country?" asked the Marquis de Lapressange.[34] Bunch concluded his dispatch to Russell with a description of the extreme confidence of the South in the importance of cotton—the assurance that the economic interests of England would make a recognition of the Confederacy imperative.[35]

Lincoln, with his key posts filled, turned his attention to other available persons. To Belgium he sent Henry S. Sanford, a veteran diplomatist. Dayton, able as he was, would have to learn the official technique of his post. Sanford at Brussels would be near enough to be called upon in an emergency. He had spent much of his life in the diplomatic corps, having served as acting secretary of legation in St. Petersburg, in Frankfort and in Paris. A Connecticut man of independent means, he was also put in charge of the Northern secret service in Europe.

To Madrid, one of the lesser posts, Lincoln planned to send Cassius Marcellus Clay of Kentucky, a Southern fire-eater, a spellbinding orator with a ready pistol in the pocket of his frock coat. In personality and character Clay resembled the type of men Jefferson Davis selected for his diplomatic missions much more closely than he did such sobersided personalities as Charles Francis Adams and William L. Dayton. Clay had been reared in the rural South and his only variation from type was his dislike of slavery. He would shoot and cut and burn to destroy it as readily as his brother planter politicians would to perpetuate the peculiar institution.

Clay was a friend of Lincoln's wife's family, the Todds, in Kentucky. He had been actively engaged in politics—and politics could be active in Kentucky. Once at a rally his opponents imported Sam M. Brown, a fighting man from New Orleans, "hero of forty fights and never lost a battle." Clay attended the meeting, heckled the hero. Brown felled him with a club. Clay got up with his bowie knife in hand. Brown leveled a pistol at Clay's breast but he came on. When the two men were almost within arm's reach Brown fired straight at Clay's heart, but Clay was on him with slash and thrust, cutting off an ear, skewering out an eye, laying open his skull to the brain. The "proud hero of forty fights" was thrown over a wall and rolled ingloriously down the bluff into the waters of Russell's cave.[36] Brown's ball had struck the scabbard of Clay's knife which hung around his neck. Without doubt Clay could show the Spaniards a thing or two.

In 1854, when abolition became a national issue, Clay had traveled to Springfield, Illinois, to speak at a Republican meeting. But Clay was considered so radical—his abolitionism so destructive to property rights—that the authorities did not allow him to speak in the Statehouse. The meeting was held in a field near by. Lincoln attended. He too was accused of being an abolitionist but he had never recommended any action half so radical as this Southerner demanded. Lincoln lay on the ground during the speech, whittling, thinking, watching the reaction of the audience.[37] Four years later, when Lincoln was nominated for the Presidency in Chicago, Clay was also nominated on the first ballot by Kentucky emancipationists. Like Cameron, Dayton and Bates, he had swung his following to the Rail Splitter to defeat Seward. Now Clay expected reward. Lincoln was particularly anxious to favor all border-state men. The ministerial assignment to Spain, on a par with Prussia, Italy or Austria, was a position in which Clay might enjoy himself and do little harm. Before Clay was consulted the Bluegrass Republican read in the papers that he was scheduled for Madrid. The Kentuckian was furious. He summoned his fighting henchmen and boarded the train for Washington. Clay and his resolute-looking devils marched to the White House and demanded an audience.

"Send them in," Lincoln told his doorkeeper. The jut-jawed,

snappy-eyed Kentuckians stood silently around the room, intense, earnest, vital as charged batteries. Cassius Clay stepped forward, an elegant Southern gentleman in blue dress suit, brass buttons, white vest and choker. Tall as Lincoln, he looked the President straight in the face and folded his arms.[38] Lincoln would not have been where he was had it not been for Clay's influence and votes. Clay did not intend to be shunted into Spain. He wanted a place in the cabinet or at least the ministerial post in England or France. Lincoln replied that these positions were filled. Clay stalked out, his gang at his heels. Lincoln could not afford to lose the support of these antislavery border men. He sent a messenger to his old friend, Senator Baker.

Clay in the meantime dined with Sanford, the Belgian minister, and other Republicans. Before long a note was passed to him. Clay read it, and excused himself. Senator Baker wished to see him at the Capitol.

Clay had known Baker in the Mexican War. The two veterans sat down together. Baker owed his position as Senator to his ability to talk convincingly to Western pioneers. Now he sympathized with Clay, deplored the injustice done him, suggested that a post in Russia was still available. Then, appealing to Clay's chivalry, he said, "You have made great sacrifices, but does not patriotism require still more?" Clay agreed to serve. "Get your hat," Baker shouted, jumping to his feet, and the two men hurried off to the White House. Clay remembered later, with a killer's naïveté, that Lincoln was alone "and evidently awaiting us . . . quite sad and thoughtful . . . his head bent down in silence." Clay should have known that Lincoln also bent down his head when suppressing mirth. Baker did not keep him in suspense. "Mr. Lincoln," he said without taking a seat, "our friend Clay will accept the Russian mission."

"Clay, you have relieved me from a great embarrassment," Lincoln said, shaking his hand. A broad smile illuminated the President's face.[39]

On March 30 it was announced that Spain had violated the Monroe Doctrine and reannexed Santo Domingo,[40] raising its red and yellow flag over the island with prayer and cannon. For the first time in American history the tables were turned. Three generations of Americans had expanded from the Appalachians to the Pacific, acquiring territory after territory claimed by European powers, profiting continually from European wars and jealousies. The game of power politics was now to be played the other way. With America at war, Europe intended to do what America had always done. She would profit by American turmoil. Spain had taken the first step. Overnight Madrid became next in importance to Mexico, and Baker had talked Cassius M. Clay into talking himself out of the important post and into a recognized sinecure. Lincoln had good cause to smile.

On the day before Lincoln received word of Clay's acceptance of the change of his appointment, he met one of the most important unofficial ambassadors America received during the war. The growth of democracy would make popular opinion play a major role in international relations, and William H. Russell, correspondent of the London *Times,* could have more influence on European thought than either Lord Lyons or Henri Mercier. The *Times* was the organ of satisfied, well-to-do Englishmen. Its policy also affected government opinion. British statesmen admitted that it was difficult to appoint any man the *Times* disapproved; that it was hardly possible to pass a law the *Times* did not sanction. When the *Times* pointed out a man as deserving favor he rose rapidly.[41] So when the *Times* sent their Crimean War correspondent to report the 'American conflict he was recognized as one of the powerful European influences at Washington. In appearance Russell was a picture of the British gentry of his time, a thick-set man, beefy, bull-headed, sluggish-eyed, throaty as an old terrapin, brave as a Victorian imperialist, and absolutely without what Americans regarded as a sense of humor. He believed and wrote that the American Civil War was a struggle between a conservative middle class and red republicans. He attributed the United States' dilemma to the lowering of the suffrage, the very thing most feared in England by the upper classes. From New York he wrote for publication:

"I met several gentlemen, one of whom said, 'the majority of the people of New York, and all the respectable people, were disgusted at the election of such a fellow as Lincoln to be President, and would back the Southern States, if it came to a split.' "[42]

Russell reported that Americans disliked Great Britain. He believed this due to the great number of Irish immigrants.[43] The correspondent also described one of those democratic abominations, a "street-railway-car,"[44] the pride and product of wild-eyed Mr. Train, whose influence over the common people seemed dangerous. Russell did not prophesy a disastrous civil war. On March 19 he wrote:

"New York society, however, is easy in its mind just now, and the upper world of millionnaire [sic] merchants, bankers, contractors, and great traders are glad that the vulgar Republicans are suffering for their success. Not a man there but resented the influence given by universal suffrage to the mob of the city, and complained of the intolerable effects of their ascendency . . . but it did not require proof that universal suffrage in a city of which perhaps three fourths of the voters were born abroad or of foreign parents, and of whom many were the scum swept off the seethings of European populations, must work most injuriously on property and capital. I confess it is to be much wondered at that the consequences are not more evil."[45]

From New York Russell went to Washington. On the train he was annoyed by "a big man, with a broken nose, a mellow eye, and a very large display of rings, jewels, chains, and pins, [who] was in very high spirits, and informed us he was 'Going to Washington to get a foreign mission from Bill Seward!' "[46] On this trip the correspondent also met another man who said that he too was bound for Europe on a diplomatic mission.[47] This man, Henry S. Sanford by name—the same who had dined with Cassius M. Clay—was fully Russell's equal in experience and manners. At Washington, Sanford's carriage was waiting at the station and he drove the correspondent to Willard's Hotel. The two new friends dined together that evening and on the following day Sanford escorted Russell to the State Department. Seward sat behind his desk in a smoke-filled office surrounded with bookshelves and a few engravings. He received his guests affably, and said he was expecting Chevalier Bertinatti of Savoy. Lincoln was scheduled to receive him as minister from the new kingdom of Italy. Would Russell like to be introduced at the same time?

As Seward spoke, the tall, slim and handsome Italian appeared in diplomatic suit of blue with silver lace, sash, sword, and ribbon of the Cross of Savoy. His white-gloved hands held a cocked hat. Neither Seward nor Russell, as they looked at this splendid figure of a man, dreamed that he was destined to be a secret agent between Napoleon III and Abraham Lincoln. The men walked out of the State Department and across the lawn to the White House. They entered by a side door and were ushered into "a handsome spacious room, richly and rather gorgeously furnished," with "gilt chairs and ormolu ornaments."[48]

Russell wrote in his diary:

"Soon afterwards there entered, with a shambling, loose, irregular, almost unsteady gait, a tall, lank, lean man, considerably over six feet in height, with stooping shoulders, long pendulous arms, terminating in hands of extraordinary dimensions, which, however, were far exceeded in proportion by his feet. He was dressed in an ill-fitting, wrinkled suit of black, which put one in mind of an undertaker's uniform at a funeral; round his neck a rope of black silk was knotted in a large bulb, with flying ends projecting beyond the collar of his coat; his turned-down shirt-collar disclosed a sinewy muscular yellow neck, and above that, nestling in a great black mass of hair, bristling and compact like a ruff of mourning pins, rose the strange quaint face and head, covered with its thatch of wild republican hair, of President Lincoln. The impression produced by the size of his extremities, and by his flapping and wide projecting ears, may be removed by the appearance of kindness, sagacity, and the awkward bonhommie of his face; the mouth is absolutely prodigious; the lips, straggling and extending almost from one line of black beard to the other, are only kept in order by two deep furrows from the nostril to the chin; the nose itself—a prominent organ—stands out from the face, with an inquiring, anxious air, as though it were sniffing for some good thing in the wind; the eyes dark, full, and deeply set, are penetrating, but full of an expression which almost amounts to tenderness; and above them projects the shaggy brow, running into the small hard frontal space, the development of which can scarcely be estimated accurately, owing to the irregular flocks of thick hair carelessly brushed across it. One would say that, although the mouth was made to enjoy a joke, it could also utter the severest sentence which the head could dictate, but that Mr. Lincoln would be ever more willing to temper justice with mercy, and to enjoy what he considers the amenities of life, than to take a harsh view of men's nature and of the world, and to estimate things in an ascetic or puritan spirit.

A person who met Mr. Lincoln in the street would not take him to be what—according to the usages of European society—is called a 'gentleman;' and, indeed, since I came to the United States, I have heard more disparaging allusions made by Americans to him on that account than I could have expected among simple republicans, where all should be equals; but, at the same time, it would not be possible for the most indifferent observer to pass him in the street without notice.

"As he advanced through the room, he evidently controlled a desire to shake hands all round with everybody, and smiled good-humoredly till he was suddenly brought up by the staid deportment of Mr. Seward, and by the profound diplomatic bows of the Chevalier Bertinatti. Then, indeed, he suddenly jerked himself back, and stood in front of the two ministers, with his body slightly drooped forward, and his hands behind his back, his knees touching, and his feet apart. Mr. Seward formally presented the minister, whereupon the President made a prodigiously violent demonstration of his body in a bow which had almost the effect of a smack in its rapidity and abruptness, and, recovering himself, proceeded to give his utmost attention, whilst the Chevalier, with another bow, read from a paper a long address in presenting the royal letter accrediting him as 'minister resident;' and when he said that 'the king desired to give, under your enlightened administration, all possible strength and extent to those sentiments of frank sympathy which do not cease to be exhibited every moment between the two peoples, and whose origin dates back as far as the exertions which have presided over their common destiny as self-governing and free nations,' the President gave another bow still more violent, as much as to accept the allusion.

"The minister forthwith handed his letter to the President, who gave it into the custody of Mr. Seward, and then, dipping his hand into his coat-pocket, Mr. Lincoln drew out a sheet of paper, from which he read his reply, the most remarkable part of which was his doctrine 'that the United States were bound by duty not to interfere with the differences of foreign governments and countries.' After some words of compliment, the President shook hands with the minister, who soon afterwards retired. Mr. Seward then took me by the hand and said—'Mr. President, allow me to present to you Mr. Russell, of the London "Times."' On which Mr. Lincoln put out his hand in a very friendly manner, and said, 'Mr. Russell, I am very glad to make your acquaintance, and to see you in this country. The London "Times" is one of the greatest powers in the world,—in fact, I don't know anything which has much more power,—except perhaps the Mississippi. I am glad to know you as its minister.' Conversation ensued for some minutes, which the President enlivened by two or three peculiar little sallies, and I left agreeably impressed with his shrewdness, humor, and natural sagacity."[49]

In the evening Russell dined with Secretary Seward and, like a true reporter, kept his ears open for possible news. At the table was Frederick Seward, son and private secretary of the Secretary of State, Mr. Sanford and "a quaint, natural specimen of an American rustic lawyer," who was introduced as Sanford's future secretary of legation. The newspaperman noticed that the diplomat "did not appear altogether happy" over the selection.[50] Sanford loved simplicity, and had once resigned a diplomatic post because it required wearing gold lace, but when confronted with the democratic practice of accepting a subordinate who knew little about foreign conditions he did not like it. Russell enjoyed watching him squirm and prophesied unpleasant complications in Belgium.

Seward's dinners were famous in Washington but the Secretary himself, although brilliant in conversation, remained an incorrigible outlaw, rough and blunt as a British squire. Seward had traveled extensively and was full of anecdotes. Only two years before, when a member of the Foreign Relations Committee of the Senate, he had been entertained by the Emperor Napoleon at Compiègne. The two men had talked freely and Seward had been impressed with the anxiety of the great powers to maintain peace in Europe.[51] Russell noted that the Secretary of State was well versed in foreign affairs. Belch and bluster as he might in his republican way, Seward was no novice in diplomacy. Tonight he had an opportunity to say things that he could not convey to an official minister, and William H. Russell got the full broadside of Seward's belligerency toward foreign nations. After the wine began to flow in his veins, Seward's tongue wagged unrestrainedly. With overbearing jocularity he impressed upon the British government, through W. H. Russell, a few bellicose facts. "The Ministers of England or of France," he said pointedly, "had no right to make any allusion to the civil war which appeared imminent. . . . The Southern Commissioners who had been sent abroad could not be received by the Government of any foreign power, officially or otherwise, even to hand in a document or to make a representation, without incurring the risk of breaking off relations with the Government of the United States."[52]

After the dinner, when Russell returned to his hotel, he found a note awaiting him, an invitation to dine with the President on the following night. Truly the Lincoln administration considered Russell as important as any official envoy. Yet why had the Secretary of State gone out of his way to insult Great Britain? This was something about which Russell as well as the United Kingdom might ponder. Had the President now invited him to make amends or to administer another dose of Seward's medicine? Russell did not know that Charles Francis Adams believed Seward's talk nothing but bluff to intimidate the European powers in their precarious peace. Adams knew diplomacy and he also knew William H. Seward as well as any man, but in the months that followed even he demonstrated an inability always to plumb the motives and character of diplomats.

At the White House next evening, Russell found Mrs. Lincoln seated to receive her guests.

"She is of the middle age and height, of a plumpness degenerating to the *embonpoint* natural to her years; her features are plain, her nose and mouth of an ordinary type, and her manners and appearance homely, stiffened, however, by the consciousness that her position requires her to be something more than plain Mrs. Lincoln, the wife of the Illinois lawyer; she is profuse in the introduction of the word 'sir' in every sentence, which is now almost an Americanism confined to certain classes, although it was once as common in England. Her dress I shall not attempt to describe, though it was very gorgeous and highly colored. She handled a fan with much energy, displaying a round, well-proportioned arm, and was adorned with some simple jewelry. Mrs. Lincoln struck me as being desirous of making herself agreeable; and I own I was agreeably disappointed, as the Secessionist ladies at Washington had been amusing themselves by anecdotes which could scarcely have been founded on fact."[53]

Russell was surprised to note that in the whole republican assemblage there was "not a scrap of lace or a piece of ribbon, except the gorgeous epaulettes of an old naval officer who had served against us in the last war."[54]

"In the conversation which occurred before dinner, I was amused to observe the manner in which Mr. Lincoln used the anecdotes for which he is famous. Where men bred in courts, accustomed to the world, or versed in diplomacy, would use some subterfuge, or would make a polite speech, or give a shrug of the shoulders as the means of getting out of an embarrassing position, Mr. Lincoln raises a laugh by some bold west-country anecdote."[55]

If Russell had expected Lincoln to continue Seward's policy of intimidating England he was disappointed. Russell had no way of knowing that a great gap of misunderstanding existed between the President and the Secretary, that their two foreign policies in no way agreed at this time. Almost daily, members of the government and officers of the Army and Navy resigned to join the Confederacy. Every man looked on his neighbor with suspicion. Even Mrs. Lincoln was accused of listening at keyholes and rummaging wastebaskets for information to send relatives in the South. Lincoln did not tell his own cabinet the policies he had in mind. Often he asked their advice and then solved the problem in a different manner. The cabinet learned this characteristic of Lincoln's when James Gordon Bennett persisted in making trouble in New York. His *Herald* published many articles to alienate the people of Europe from the administration—innuendoes about Lincoln's weakness—"there is nothing going wrong." The President asked his cabinet to name someone suitable to talk to the editor, someone capable of winning Bennett to the Union cause. Thurlow Weed's name was suggested. Seward insisted that he was the worst man possible for the task. Weed had quarreled with Bennett in 1827 and the two men had not spoken to each other for thirty-three years. Lincoln's eyes twinkled. Instead of taking Seward's advice he called Weed to the White House and convinced the politician that he should win Bennett for the Union.

Weed agreed to try. This was precisely the kind of mission in which he believed that he excelled. Lincoln might not succeed in winning the friendship of James Gordon Bennett, but if he won Thurlow Weed the experiment would be a success.

Weed took the train for New York. His eyebrows balanced perfectly today—one benevolent, the other devilish as could be. In New York he held two conferences, one with Bennett to help the administration, the other with Henry J. Raymond, editor of the *Times*,[56] to ruin the President. Shortly thereafter people noticed that the *Herald's* policy changed. Bennett's son offered his yacht to the government and in exchange received a commission.[57] Weed claimed the credit for the miracle. Lincoln was satisfied and in the future he dealt directly with the editor.

In the meantime Weed and Raymond came back to Washington as thick as thieves. The big city editor was convinced that he would soon get the scoop of the century—a story of the abdication of Abraham Lincoln. Weed had been working on a plan for some time. He was sure that it would happen any day now.

Lincoln, as has been said, made a practice of delegating duties to individuals and then attending to them himself. He never knew how long his most trusted supporter would remain in the government. The disloyalty that honeycombed the Army and Navy had spread to the civil service. It was sure to break out next in the cabinet—the council of enemies—and Weed had brought Raymond down to see the show.

Lincoln's first hint that a plot was aimed at him personally came on the first day of April. Seward bustled into his office with two young men and a bundle of papers to be signed. Lincoln was harassed with the disorganized business of a new administration, the breakdown of government under spreading rebellion, and by the clamor of office seekers. People said that a hundred and forty thousand appointments, many of them small, devolved upon him.[58] Without looking at Seward's papers Lincoln affixed his signature.[59] The young men hurried from the room. Seward followed them. Outside Weed learned that Lincoln had signed the papers. A private note bearing Seward's signature was sent in to the President.[60] Raymond was notified. A wire was cleared for New York.

Lincoln had been worried for several days about the advisability of asserting his authority over Federal property in the South. Two forts, Sumter in South Carolina and Pickens in Florida, were garrisoned by United States soldiers who would soon have to evacuate them if supplies were not sent. The adjacent states had seceded from the Union and insisted that the forts must be given up. Lincoln's cabinet had discussed the problem and failed to agree on the best policy. It was generally conceded that Fort Pickens might be

supplied with impunity, but batteries had been constructed across
the bay from Sumter and a rebel army threatened to shell any ship
that came with provisions. Lincoln ordered an expedition to outfit
in New York. He did not tell his cabinet whether the supplies
were destined for Sumter or Pickens. That was Lincoln's business.
Seward decided that the President was flustered, incompetent,
weak. He himself must save the Union. If Sumter was reinforced, a war was inevitable. Seward consulted Justice Campbell
of the Supreme Court, a known Secessionist, and he also opened
communications with the Confederacy. Seward assured the Southerners that Sumter would not be reinforced. Next he prepared
plans in detail for sending the New York expedition to Fort Pickens. He wrote orders in the President's name for both the Army
and Navy—departments headed by his rivals. These orders were
in the papers that Seward brought to be signed on April 1. The
Seward note delivered to Lincoln on the same day has been attributed to Weed.[61] Raymond was waiting with the wires open for
Lincoln's reply. The President picked it up and read, "We are
at the end of a month's administration, and yet without a policy
either domestic or foreign." The note then requested Lincoln to
turn his office over to a stronger man, someone with a rigorous
policy. War must be declared at once against either France or
Spain. "I neither seek to evade nor assume responsibility,"[62] Seward's note concluded.

Lincoln put down the paper. This insolence had come from his
second in command, from one of the best-informed statesmen in the
United States. "I have endured a great deal of ridicule without
much malice; and have received a great deal of kindness, not quite
free from ridicule,"[63] Lincoln once said, and a similar thought must
have come to him on this night at the end of his first month in the
White House.

Late at night Secretary Welles came into Lincoln's office. He
was in high dudgeon. Why had the President countermanded his
orders for the New York expedition? Lincoln was incredulous.
Then it dawned on him that he had been tricked by Seward as well
as insulted. He mollified Welles with soft words and the Secretary
of the Navy retired.

A quick-tempered President would have dismissed the Secretary

of State at once but with him might have gone Charles Francis
Adams and Thurlow Weed—the best of his foreign ministers and
also the strongest wing of the Republican party. Had these men
and all they stood for withdrawn as a political entity, the war
could not have been waged, the will of the majority could not have
been enforced and the American experiment with democracy would
have failed.

Abraham Lincoln took up his pen to reply to William H.
Seward.

# III. *Whom Could He Trust,*
## *If Not the Secretary of State?*

LINCOLN wrote slowly, patiently. His pen scratched across the paper. Now and again he stopped to push back his coarse hair with long, bony fingers. Since the revolutions during the 1830's and 1840's the world trend had been away from democracy in England, France, Austria and the German states. The South had followed the trend. Only the North, eager, aggressive, vulgar, moved counter to it. The future of American democracy was the real issue Lincoln had at stake. He must keep the power vested in him by popular election, and he must also keep Seward. Lincoln had found out that Seward's trickery was not confined to stopping the Sumter expedition. One of the papers he had given Lincoln to sign commissioned a man who happened to hold an important post in the Confederate Navy. An order he had sent to the military overrode the Secretary of War. Whom indeed could Lincoln trust, if not the Secretary of State?

Seward had warned Lincoln that the Navy Department was full of traitors. Any order emanating from it would be known to the enemy instantly, he said. Was this an excuse to usurp that department's functions? Seward was known to be an intimate friend of Jefferson Davis. Lincoln had caught him negotiating with the rebel commissioners and the Secessionist Justice of the Supreme Court, John A. Campbell. Was Seward a traitor, or was he only a usurper who believed that the country's salvation depended on him?

Lincoln finished writing his reply. Every one of Seward's charges was skillfully denied in such a way that no offense could be taken. Seward's concluding sentence about devolving the executive authority on someone who would be "all the while active in it" was answered in Lincoln's last sentence:

"If this must be done, I must do it. When a general line of policy is adopted, I apprehend there is no danger of its being changed without good reason . . . still, upon points arising in its progress I wish, and suppose I am entitled to have, the advice of all the cabinet.

"Your obedient servant,
"A. Lincoln."[1]

Was such a reprimand too gentle, too subtle, for Secretary Seward? Would the words, "I wish, and suppose I am entitled to have, the advice of all the cabinet," sink with full significance into Seward's brain?

The next day it appeared not. Seward wrote a letter to Señor Tassara. He threatened to declare war on Spain if that country was found to have any hand in the revolution in Santo Domingo which led to the reannexation. Tassara acknowledged receipt of the dispatch and the matter dropped.[2] A Spanish bull might have swung his tail at a fly and continued grazing with similar disdain. Two days later William H. Russell called at the State Department to see Seward. The Secretary of State occupied an inner office reached by passing through a carpeted corridor and an anteroom. He had not yet removed the pictures left by his predecessor. On one wall a large map of Cuba recalled the slaveholders' aspirations to extend their territory. On a mantelshelf a large unframed photograph showed President Buchanan, the Prince of Wales and the Duke of Newcastle at Niagara.[3] Russell entered the inner office. Seward got up from behind a desk piled high with papers and open books. He welcomed the correspondent as cordially as he had previously, then threw himself back in his chair, crossed his legs, put his thumbs and forefingers together on a level with his chin, looked contemplatively at the skeins of tobacco smoke above his head and began to talk. He looked old and frail today, but every word bristled with his eagerness to fight Great Britain and if need be to "wrap the world in flames." Russell thought this was bold talk for a minister who had just been flouted by decadent Spain.[4] The Britisher was unable to make up his mind whether Seward was bluffing or really threatening to batter out his own brains in a war with England.

As the talk continued Russell became more perplexed. Seward

followed his belligerent boasting with an account of the weakness of his government. The last cabinet, Seward said, had plotted treason. Rather than let the government pass into the hands of the opposition they had encouraged the Secessionists. One cabinet member had purposely sent the Navy away to distant and widely scattered stations. Another had shipped an undue proportion of the nation's matériel into the South where it would fall into the hands of the rebels. Government funds had been diverted for "traitorous purposes." The little man in the mussed clothes could make words crackle when he talked. "In every port, in every department of the State, at home and abroad, on sea and by land," he told Russell, "men were placed who were engaged in this deep conspiracy." Such political chaos had forced Lincoln to take a temporizing policy of inaction.

Russell looked at Seward with haughty, incredulous eyes. The old terrapin did not understand how a Secretary of State who was in as bad a way as Seward intimated dared fight the world. That night the correspondent asked his diary:

"Was it consciousness of the strength of a great people, who would be united by the first apprehension of foreign interference, or was it the peculiar emptiness of a bombast which is called Buncombe?"[5]

Russell did not know that on the very day Seward delivered this doleful picture, Lincoln had ended the "temporizing policy of inaction." On March 30 he had ordered the expedition to Sumter without telling Seward, and on April 4, the same day that Seward was in conference with William H. Russell, the President sent word to the commander at Sumter: "The expedition will go forward, and, finding your flag flying, will attempt to provision you, and in case the effort is resisted, will endeavor also to reinforce you"— fighting words.[6]

That evening Russell dined with Senator Stephen A. Douglas and other rivals of the President, all of whom were ignorant of Lincoln's order to aid Fort Sumter. Among the guests were Secretary of the Treasury Salmon P. Chase and Secretary of the Interior Caleb Smith, as well as one of the Southern commissioners who were in the city to arrange a dissolution of the Union—a strange medley of rivals, rebels and administration officials. Russell looked with curiosity upon the strange creatures from the South who countenanced human slavery. Purposely he drew them out on the subject and he wrote in his diary the next evening:

"Slavery is their *summum bonum* of morality, physical excellence, and social purity. I was inclined to question the correctness of the standard which they had set up, and to inquire whether the virtue which needed this murderous use of the pistol and the dagger to defend it, was not open to some doubt; but I found there was very little sympathy with my views among the company."[7]

On the following day Russell dined with the Southern commissioners at a French restaurant on Pennsylvania Avenue. He was introduced to Colonel John Pickett, soon to loom large in Confederate foreign policy. Russell described him as "a tall good-looking man, of pleasant manners, and well-educated. But this gentleman was a professed buccaneer, a friend of Walker, the gray-eyed man of destiny—his comrade in his most dangerous razzie."[8] Russell found the commissioners determined to attempt no reconciliation.

"Mr. Lincoln they spoke of with contempt; Mr. Seward they evidently regarded as the ablest and most unscrupulous of their enemies; but the tone in which they alluded to the whole of the Northern people indicated the clear conviction that trade, commerce, the pursuit of gain, manufacture, and the base mechanical arts, had so degraded the whole race, they would never attempt to strike a blow in fair fight for what they prized so highly in theory and in words. Whether it be in consequence of some secret influence which slavery has upon the minds of men, or that the aggression of the North upon their institutions has been of a nature to excite the deepest animosity and most vindictive hate, certain it is there is a degree of something like ferocity in the Southern mind towards New England which exceeds belief. . . . They believe that we, too, have had the canker of peace upon us. One evidence of this, according to Southern men, is the abolition of duelling. This practice, according to them, is highly wholesome and meritorious."[9]

As the men dined together Russell learned further that these slaveholders considered themselves physically superior to Free State men. Russell's round head came out of his coat collar like a turtle coming out of its shell, slowly, with dignity and disapproval. The gentlemen who wielded knives and forks on both sides of him expounded strange theories of morals and physics which proved—to themselves—that Southerners were chosen people. Russell's wrinkled eyes distended with outrage as he learned that Southern congressmen boasted of insulting Northerners on the floor of Congress just for sport. The Yankee cowards would not come out and fight! Sumner's case was cited; how Preston Brooks with a gutta-percha cane had floored him in his seat. Mudsills all of them! Thus the common people would fare always before aristocrats. Northern rabbledom would never dare fight Southern chivalry.

Russell could stand no more. History was not taught that way in monarchical England. His old turtle head was extended on the extremity of his wrinkled neck. His proud eyes scanned the table. "Gentlemen," he said, "the descendants of the Puritans were not to be despised in battle." Russell's clipped British speech possessed an aristocratic drawl. "The best gentry in England," he continued, "were worsted at last by the train-bands of London, and the 'rabbledom' of Cromwell's Independents."[10]

The Confederates made no reply. Russell barged away from the dinner convinced that Southern life had produced people out of step with all mankind.

On the following day, April 6, Secretary Seward learned that his orders to divert the Sumter expedition were going awry, that conflicting orders from the Navy Department had embarrassed the commanders. Secretary Welles did not seem to realize that Seward had taken command. Seward called his son Frederick and the two set off to see Old Neptune. It was after eleven o'clock at night. They found him in his room at Willard's Hotel. The Secretary of the Navy listened to Seward's complaint. Then he replied. The President himself had agreed to all the acts, he said. Lincoln's orders, and not Seward's, must be obeyed. The cockatoo looked sharply at the rabbit-faced Secretary behind the thicket of beard but Welles did not give in. The time had come for Seward to find out whether he or Lincoln ran the government. The three men, joined by Commodore Silas H. Stringham, set out for the White House.[11]

Lincoln had been extremely busy all day. Work came to his desk faster than he could dispose of it. Occasionally he slipped away and let it pile up. In the family wing of the White House, he took off his shoes, slumped in a chair, one leg across the arm, the Bible or Shakespeare in his hands, his sock foot waving slowly to the rhythm of his reading. From time to time he looked over his glasses at the boys. Willie and Tad had extended their explorations from the White House to the entire neighborhood, the conservatory, the stable, the War, Navy and Treasury buildings— and, best of all, a near-by alley where black servants lived. They had discovered, too, that the Fourth Presbyterian Church was more to their liking than the New York Avenue Church which their parents attended. Strange, wasn't it! Lincoln put down his book. "Why do you like Mr. Smith's church better than ours, Tad?"

The little fellow replied that it was "livelier." Members there were mostly "Secesh." It was fun to hear the pew doors slam when the minister prayed for the President. Lincoln's eyes twinkled. His waving foot came to rest but Tad had not finished. "Why do the preachers always pray so long for you, Paw?" Tad spoke with a broad Western accent.

Lincoln's face became grave. A shadow of worry puckered his forehead. "I suppose it's because the preachers think I need it," he said, looking wearily out the window, "and I guess I do." Lincoln put on his boots, got up and walked slowly back to his office and the accumulating documents.[12]

At midnight Lincoln was still at his desk when Seward, Welles and their companions arrived. The case of the conflicting orders was explained. Both Lincoln and Seward were in a peculiar position, but if the two men thought about the "note" in which Seward had stated that he would not "evade" the responsibility of running the administration, neither man's eyes wavered sufficiently to be noticed by the witnesses who watched them intently. Lincoln looked at the papers on his desk. He spoke quietly as though relieved from the unpleasant problems before him. The fault, he said, was all his. He should have been more attentive. Lincoln paused for a moment, then continued, "On no account must the Sumter expedition fail or be interfered with."[13]

Seward fidgeted. His plan to divert the expedition faced ruin. He said it would be difficult to countermand the order at this hour of the night. Was not the other expedition quite as important? Lincoln insisted that it must be done.

Such modesty and tolerance combined with firmness, immediately after Seward's insulting "note," opened the eyes of the Secretary of State. Seward began to understand his chief, an understanding that grew in the months that followed into great respect and finally into something like love. "The President has a curious vein of sentiment running through his thought," Seward confided to a friend, "which is his most valuable mental attribute."[14] In June he wrote to his wife: "There is but one vote in the cabinet and that is cast by the President. . . . The President is the best of us all."[15]

Seward buckled down to the new leadership patriotically. The Sumter expedition was irretrievably on its way; war, a blockade and foreign complications were only matters of a few days and the Secretary of State was not prepared. First he must make his word good to the South. He must accept the humiliation of admitting that his assurance about reinforcing Sumter was a usurpation of authority. He must hold no more intercourse with the Southern commissioners. This was severe medicine for a man of Seward's disposition. Externally the transition to the new position was slow, face-saving. Lincoln helped Seward do it this way. When secret-service operatives intercepted a telegram warning the Confederacy about the secret decision to reinforce Sumter, Lincoln quashed the investigation. The wire had been written by a friend of Seward's, James E. Harvey. Lincoln sent him to Portugal as minister— another use for foreign posts.[16]

To get Charles Francis Adams to England in time to meet the storm which would break the minute firing started on Sumter was obviously out of the question. Seward had told Adams there was no hurry. Complacently he had granted Adams permission to remain in America until the last of April in order that he might attend the wedding of his son. The Secretary of State had been positive that he and not Lincoln was running the government and that no reinforcement of Sumter would be attempted. Now when it was too late, Seward saw, and said, that this Adams marriage was "the greatest misfortune that ever happened to the United States."[17] He liked to talk in superlatives.

Seward did not repeat this error in Mexico. On the day that Lincoln told Seward with so much gentleness what "must be done," Tom Corwin was ordered to leave for Latin America. The advantage that Lincoln had lost by Seward's negligence in letting the Southern commissioners go to England six weeks ahead of the North's envoy might be offset by sending the Ohioan to the next most important post, Mexico, ahead of the South's representative.

Corwin was well suited for the mission. Like Lincoln, he had opposed the Mexican War, the injustice that now plagued Northern diplomacy. Lincoln, as a cub politician serving his one and only term in Congress, remembered—though not present—a day when Corwin challenged a war-minded Senate, thundering:

"If I were a Mexican I would tell you: Have you not room in your own country to bury your dead men? If you come into Mexico we will greet you with bloody hands and welcome you to hospitable graves."[18]

Lincoln was sure that Mexicans would remember that day also. And if they did not he would remind them of it. Yes, Corwin was ideal for the post. Besides he was a good party man and had worked in Lincoln's campaign. True, Corwin could not speak a work of Spanish[19] but he had what was more important in a democracy—a likable personality and a brimming flow of language. What he said did not matter with the masses. Moreover, Corwin could entrance an audience with his sympathetic eyes— great brown orbs—sparkling, affectionate. "Those eyes will remind Mexican ladies of their hairless Chihuahua terriers," said congressmen and smiled to each other. Lincoln knew that those eyes were worth ten thousand words. In Ohio it was common gossip that Corwin's eyes had outtalked a preacher in his own church. The minister opposed Corwin in politics and thundered at him from the pulpit. Corwin, sitting in a pew, answered only with his eyes, eloquently, persistently. The minister gave up. He said later that he felt the eyes of the Almighty were upon him.

At another time, friends of the Ohioan related, Corwin was speaking to an apathetic audience when a bulldog sauntered down

*Reprinted from Reminiscences of Carl Schurz (McClure Co., 1907-1908)*

WILLIAM H. SEWARD AND DAUGHTER FANNY

GIDEON WELLES, SECRETARY OF THE NAVY

the aisle. Corwin stopped. He looked at the dog. People remembered that the silence was so intense they could hear the gas lamps sputter. Then Corwin raised a long finger and leveled it at the intruder. "What are you doing here?" he demanded. The dog stood transfixed, his stub tail sinking from the vertical. "By the cut of your jib, your bow legs, your pug-nose carried so haughtily in the air," Corwin boomed, "I am sure that you are a Democrat." The bull pup turned and fled. Roars of laughter followed him like a can on his tail. "A bucket of cold water could not have taken the starch out of that dog any quicker," one of the onlookers remembered. Others said that the dog gave a yelp of relief when he crossed the doorsill and was last seen running south with his tail between his legs.[20]

Lincoln was sure that Corwin could give a good account of himself in Mexico. Critics noticed this friendly attitude of the administration toward Latin America. They also noted the belligerent attitude toward Great Britain. Was there method in this madness, this bullying big Britain and cajoling weak Mexico? Or was the Mexican policy Lincoln's and the British policy Seward's? "We'll know before long," they told one another.

The critics noticed also that Jefferson Davis played his cards very differently from Abraham Lincoln. The Confederate was conciliatory with Britain instead of belligerent. He had trade advantages to offer. His countrymen hinted that the South hoped to return to British allegiance. But to Mexico he sent a fighting man—a soldier of fortune, John Pickett, filibuster and fomenter of revolutions in Santo Domingo, in Cuba, in Nicaragua with Walker. Colonel Pickett looked the part. He affected brilliant uniforms, had his picture taken wearing a cocked hat like a grand marshal in Bonaparte's Old Guard. Swashbuckling in the Caribbean was his meat. He sailed south eager to beat Tom Corwin. The Ohioan might win people's hearts. Pickett would appeal to their military instincts. In his trunk he carried twenty signed commissions for privateers. The Gulf of Mexico under his direction might become a haven from which pirates could raid all Northern commerce.

For lawless intrigue Mexico was ripe, and Lincoln had no time to study the situation. His mind was occupied with the details devolving upon a new President, plus concern for the fleet on its way to Sumter. In Mexico an Indian lawyer, Benito Juárez, had opposed the power of the army and the church. With a rabble of sandaled soldiers in enormous hats, he had deposed President Miramón and installed himself in the palace. Mexico was indebted to citizens of Britain, France and Spain. Juárez found himself no more able to pay than Miramón had been. Lincoln and Seward heard a rumor that the three powers planned sending a joint fleet to take Mexico's customhouses, collect the revenue and pay the indebtedness. The rumor was not verified. It had come to Washington at the time Spain affronted the Monroe Doctrine by reannexing Santo Domingo. Success then had undoubtedly given the powers courage for further aggression. Lincoln had been warned before he left Springfield that Europe would try to wipe out the Monroe Doctrine. The danger was upon him.

Lincoln and Seward learned, too, that Miramón had fled to France seeking the alliance many Mexicans believed necessary to save their country. In Paris he interviewed the Duc de Morny, manipulator of Napoleon's plot to declare himself Emperor after being duly elected President of France. The duke was typical of the adventurous spirits upholding the Second Empire. Mexico offered an unusual opportunity. The powers, the Catholic Church, and the Miramón party in Mexico all promised to abet De Morny's scheme to make easy money and increase the prestige of France. Few noblemen have inherited more qualities of intrigue, shady diplomacy, verve and worldly ambition than the Duc de Morny. As minister to Russia he had traveled to St. Petersburg with forty-three carriages filled with laces and feminine finery. Every servant had his own carriage and every secretary at least two. Diplomatic immunity saved the cavalcade from customs duties. A few days after arrival the goods and carriages were auctioned for a profit of 800,000 rubles. A practical realist in other ways as well, the duke promoted the sugar-beet industry in France, became an entrepreneur and president of the Railway Club. A leader in fashion, he collaborated with writers of operettas and producers of vaudeville. He was a connoisseur of liqueurs and an inveterate gambler. Victor Hugo, exiled in Guernsey by the Emperor, said of the duke:

"He was dissipated, yet well concentrated; ugly, good-humoured, ferocious, well-dressed, fearless; willing to leave under lock and key one brother in prison, but willing to risk his head for another upon the throne; conscienceless, irreproachably elegant, infamous and amiable—at need a perfect duke."[21]

The duke and his protégé, Napoleon III, had already made France one of the great powers of the world. The prospect of Abraham Lincoln's locking diplomatic horns with the duke was truly ludicrous—the peasant's son against a man whose family for five generations had kept themselves at the top of Continental society. De Morny was a son of Queen Hortense, a half brother of the Emperor, a grandson of Talleyrand and a great-great-grandson of Louis XV.[22] Lincoln's father had emigrated into the Northwest trudging beside a wagon, his worldly wealth in a few kegs of homemade whisky, so people said.

The diplomats lifted their eyebrows and coughed politely when it became known that Jeff Davis had sent Pickett, the gallant soldier of fortune, to negotiate with the Latin military men who generally ruled below the Rio Grande. Lincoln's Tom Corwin, who deprecated war, could appeal only to the mudsills down there—people with neither power, ambition nor prestige.

Lincoln was equally democratic and conciliatory with other Latin-American countries. In Peru a ready-made war had been prepared for him by President Buchanan. The Peruvian government had seized two American vessels loaded illegally with guano in November 1860. Diplomatic relations were broken off. The stage was set for the foreign war which some people hoped would unite the North and South. Now Lincoln dashed their hopes to the ground. He reversed his predecessor's policy and re-established friendly relations. Christopher Robinson—good Republican from Rhode Island, recently defeated in his race for Congress—was sent to Lima[23] with instructions to extend cordial greetings to all the countries in the Western Hemisphere which had "commercial, social and political institutions" similar to those of the United States. The Peruvian offer to arbitrate the American dispute, which President Buchanan had turned down, Lincoln accepted. For referee the King of Belgium was agreed upon. His Majesty looked over the briefs and declined to act. The United States had no case, he said. Lincoln immediately bowed to the Peruvian contention. If Seward was sincere in believing that foreign conflict would re-unite the North and South, he watched the chief brush aside a con-venient war without remonstrance.

The appointments of Corwin and Robinson indicated that Lin-coln intended to be a good neighbor to all Latin America. Next he sent Thomas Nelson to Chile—another promising Republican who had just been defeated in his canvass for Congress in Indiana. Nelson was famous for his nice manners and winning personality. Spanish temperaments were sure to warm to him as they would to Corwin.

The Washington diplomats noticed another peculiarity in Lin-coln's foreign appointments. The men he sent abroad were out-spoken abolitionists. Foreign countries abhorred slavery. Was Lincoln getting rid of troublemakers at home and at the same time making it plain abroad that the North was antislavery?[24] In the United States Lincoln maintained that the war, if it came, was for a constitutional principle. In Europe abolitionist ministers were bound to tell a different story. The Washington diplomats noticed also that Lincoln used his foreign service to placate his cab-inet. His rival Secretaries were piqued about the Sumter expedi-tion, about associating with one another. They remained in the cabinet reluctantly. Lincoln oiled their annoyances with offices for their friends. He appointed, also, some of Seward's enemies to positions in the State Department. He kept each cabinet member strong, but not too strong. His official family must be in a position to "eat each other up" and not the chief.

To The Hague Lincoln sent Seward's most resourceful maligner, James S. Pike, the Washington correspondent of Greeley's *Tribune*. Seward's rival in Albany, Bradford Wood, was sent to Denmark.[25] To please Seward he appointed Andrew Dickinson to Nicaragua, William H. Vesey to Le Havre, George P. Marsh to Italy. For Cameron, Jacob S. Haldeman of Pennsylvania was sent to Stockholm. For Bates and the Germans, Lincoln appointed Carl Schurz to Spain, the position Cassius Clay declined. A post was found in Venice for William Dean Howells, whose campaign life of Lincoln had elected the Rail Splitter—according to the author. James Q. Howard, another campaign biographer, was sent as consul to New Brunswick. Joshua Giddings, the old war horse "sweenyed" from a thirty-year pull for abolition, was appointed consul general to the British North American Provinces. Hinton Helper, whose *Impending Crisis* had seemed to slaveholders as incendiary as *Uncle Tom's Cabin,* was sent as consul to Buenos Aires. To Switzerland, the only republic of any size in the civilized world which had survived, Lincoln sent George Gilman Fogg, a New Hampshire journalist. Fogg was a Free-Soiler, a Welles man opposed to Seward. He had helped organize the Republican party and as a delegate to the Chicago convention had supported Lincoln.[26] Seward, no doubt, bit his lip but he wished Fogg Godspeed. His formal instructions read:

"We very much want a good history of the Swiss Confederacy, since its reformation, especially showing how faction develops itself there, and how the Government works in preventing or suppressing designs subversive of the federal unity of the republic. The President hopes you will furnish it, as he knows your ability for such a task."[27]

To Brazil, a slave country ruled by an emperor, Lincoln sent James Watson Webb, who came to him for a major general's commission and declined to accept a brigadier's stars. Webb was bold and adventurous—another likable man for Latin America. He had distinguished himself as a frontiersman among the Indians of the West. Later, as a newspaperman, he had introduced innovations such as a pony express for dispatches, and packet boats to meet incoming schooners. Webb set off for his post by way of France. He wanted to call on his old friend who had become Napoleon III of France.

Perhaps the most iridescent of Lincoln's appointments, next to Corwin, was Anson Burlingame, who was paid for his campaign services by appointment as minister to Austria. His mission was not strategic like Corwin's and there was no necessity for getting to the post before the fleet arrived at Sumter. Indeed Burlingame might take his time and enjoy some of the row before he sailed.

Anson Burlingame was the son of a shouting evangelist. He applied his father's technique to politics so successfully that Massachusetts sent him to Congress. In Washington he gained a renown for pugnacity[28] which he climaxed with a duel he did not fight. In 1856 Congressman Preston Brooks had attacked Senator Sumner with a gutta-percha cane. Southern fire-eaters sent dozens of canes to their champion. Burlingame denounced him from the floor and was promptly challenged to fight.

Dueling was illegal. Burlingame designated Niagara Falls for the meeting, then slipped out of town ahead of the sheriff. Brooks did not come north to fight. He intimated that Burlingame had run away. Burlingame's friends gave their man a dinner in the Astor House and admired his marksmanship in a near-by shooting gallery. Henceforth he became a secondary constellation in the Republican firmament.[29]

Seward told Burlingame, as he told so many others, that there was no need for hurrying away. Tom Corwin alone was urged to get to his post at once.

Lincoln had many more diplomatic stations to fill. His little book contained plenty of applicants' names, and men waited in the anteroom every day for interviews and jobs. Lincoln made it a point to admit everyone, but his mind was often far away. What would happen when the expedition arrived at Sumter? Lincoln's eyes drifted toward the window. It was raining. The White House lawn had become wet as a sponge. Patronage hunters tracked mud into the office; the hallway steamed with dripping hats and cloaks —wet human odors. One by one, hopeful, worried men came in with forced smiles, bragged about their ability, their past services to the party. The melancholy President behind the walnut desk under the cracked portrait of Andrew Jackson shook their hands, made promises or explanations. Raindrops pelted on the windowpanes, blurred the familiar landscape—the budding trees, the half-finished Washington Monument, the gray surface of the Potomac. Somewhere out yonder in the ocean in this storm the transports were nearing Fort Sumter.

People in the streets heard a rumor about the naval expedition. They asked each other where the ships were going, what would happen next? Office seekers in hotels, on the streets, in barber shops, in saloons, getting ready to make a good appearance for their new jobs, talked about Fort Sumter. Every train brought more transients to the city. Hacks loaded with trunks and carpetbags splashed in the rain. William H. Russell, looking for news, elbowed his way through hotel crowds and noted that the hallways and lobbies were tracked full of mud and sluiced with tobacco juice, like a barnyard. The Englishman left the republican crowds and sought cleaner comfort with more respectable residents. Southern sympathizers speculated on the Sumter expedition also. They said that Lincoln was a traitor if he had ordered the ships to go south. Russell was puzzled. "How can the United States Government be guilty of 'treachery' toward subjects of States which are preparing to assert their independence?" he mused.[30] Russell wanted to get something definite about the expedition for publication. He wrote a note to Seward for a statement. The Secretary replied by messenger. Would Russell favor him with a call at his residence at nine that evening, April 8?

Such efficiency was gratifying. Russell did not know, as Seward did, that the meeting must be held at once so the Department of State could prepare England for the news of Sumter, soon to break upon the world. This interview, also, was the first for the correspondent with Seward since his "understanding" with the President, and if the State Department's policy had changed Russell would be the first to report it to the British government—in a manner more effective than Lord Lyons'.

Seward undoubtedly knew that Russell had just dined with the Southern commissioners and that he was planning to go south and learn more about the Southern people. In fact the newsman might be able to tell Seward more than Seward cared to tell him. At least the Secretary of State could say the last word before Russell left.

As the gloomy afternoon faded into dank night and the lamps were lighted, Russell watched the time. At the appointed hour he set out for Lafayette Square. The street lights, misty with rain, illuminated a watery Washington. Continued downpour had converted the streets into swirling torrents through which cab horses splashed in water sometimes to their knees. The correspondent rang the bell at Seward's house on the east side of the square.[31] The Secretary of State, his wife and son Frederick were enjoying the comforts of an evening at home. Russell made a foursome for whist, playing partner with the Secretary while the rain beat on the windowpanes. Their score was low. Seward talked state affairs. Russell followed the conversation instead of the game. Watching his chance, Russell remarked that he had heard rumors of an expedition to reinforce Sumter. Seward struck the bait. "All the preparations of which you hear," he replied, "mean this only. The Government, finding the property of the State and Federal forts neglected and left without protection, are determined to take steps to relieve them from neglect, and to protect them. But we are determined in doing so to make no aggression. The President's inaugural clearly shadows out our policy."[32] Seward laid down his hand at cards. He had not shown interest in the game from the beginning. He wished to read the correspondent a paper he had prepared to send to England. Mrs. Seward lighted the droplight of the gas and left the room. Seward unfolded the paper. Mr. Adams, he said, was going to read it to Lord John Russell. Then Seward lighted a cigar and began to read with marked emphasis. Russell listened. He considered the tone of the paper hostile to Great Britain. An undercurrent of menace insinuated that England would split up the American republic if she could.[33] Russell was baffled. Evidently Seward's attitude had not changed.

Late at night he picked his way to the hotel along the muddy streets. Russell wondered why the Secretary of State, on the eve of conflict, sought to antagonize instead of make friends with Britain. He did not realize that Charles Francis Adams, who was to deliver the message, was still in America and that he would not be in England for at least five weeks. He did not know either, as Seward did, that the fighting at Sumter might start within a week and that complications with England over blockading the cotton ports would follow immediately. Obviously Seward was continuing his old policy of threatening war—unofficially—still confident that the political balance in Europe was sufficiently precarious to prevent England from starting hostilities.

Both Russell and Seward overlooked the greatest factor in American foreign policy at this time. Neither reckoned with Abraham Lincoln. The man without a policy might take it on himself to alter Seward's dispatch long before it reached the British government. Whether Lincoln knew what was going on at Seward's residence and was waiting to see how it worked or whether

Seward had not yet come sufficiently under the influence of his chief to follow the administration's policy is a matter for conjecture. Lincoln may have been too harassed by domestic duties to give much attention to foreign affairs at this time. On the other hand he may have been playing the double game of letting his lieutenant threaten, knowing that if such tactics did not work he could always quietly assume command and rectify things with conciliation—a policy hard to beat in world politics.

Certainly Seward, when he read the threatening dispatch to William H. Russell, knew that the correspondent would run to Lord Lyons immediately and that the British government would learn the contents of the note unofficially. True to Seward's plans Lord Lyons, on the following day, wrote to his home office, but he did not say what Seward might have expected. Long schooled in diplomatic affairs, Lyons was not so much baffled by the tenor of the note as Russell had been. Seward, he believed, was bluffing. He recommended that his Foreign Office in England try a little counterbluff. Northern arrogance, Lyons wrote Lord John, would probably increase if England showed any timidity. Better receive the Southern commissioners unofficially. This might make Seward talk louder but it would probably make him act more cautiously.[34] Thus two could play the game of bluff.

On April 13, 1861, before dawn, the Confederates knocked the chip from the North's shoulder, with cannon firing at the American flag over Sumter. Thirty-four hours later, the ruined fort surrendered. Lincoln called for 75,000 volunteers to put down the rebellion and ordered a blockade of the rebel ports. Southern trade was thus officially denied to all foreign nations, and the issue had come to a head. Henceforth the foreign policy, which Lincoln and Seward had been testing with talk, had to be pounded out on the anvil of action.

# IV. *No Lawyer and No Statesman*

FROM Wisconsin to Maine, boys on farms and in factories, shipyards and shoeshops dropped their tools to fight for democracy as they understood it. Lumberjacks from the north woods, railroad men, whalers from Nantucket, hurried to the courthouses and the public squares to enlist. Lincoln knew his America when he called for volunteers to put down the rebellion. At Galena, in northern Illinois, a storekeeper's helper, Ulysses S. Grant, packed his grip and followed the local company to Lincoln's Springfield. In New York City volunteers from upstate and from New England surged down Broadway under banners inscribed "Remember Lexington and Concord." To Theodore Tilton in Boston the tramp of marching men sounded like the throbbing toll of the great bell Roland that rang to arms the burghers of Ghent when their liberty was in danger.

> "Timid hearts grew bold
> Whenever Roland tolled,
> And every hand a sword could hold,
> And every arm could bend a bow!
> So acted men
> Like patriots then—
> Three hundred years ago!
> Toll! Roland, toll!
> Bell never yet was hung
> Between whose lips there swung
> So grand a tongue!
> If men be patriots still,
> At thy first sound,
> True hearts will bound,
> Great souls will thrill!
> Then toll, and let thy test
> Try each man's breast
> Till true and false shall stand confest!
> Toll! Roland, toll!
> Snatch pouch and powder-horn and gun,
> The heritage of sire to son
> Ere half of Freedom's work was done.
> Toll! Roland, toll!"[1]

Many men in the first Northern regiments carried copies of Tilton's poem in their knapsacks. Steamboats carried the heroic cadence to Europe—perhaps the first propaganda of the war. Long-haired Southerners heard the rumbling rhythm—relentless as marching Roundheads, the Covenanters coming! Trainbands from the towns to exterminate landlordism and the landlord way of life! With grim determination the slaveholding South resolved to defend the old order from republicans—red or black. Virginia, across the river from Washington, called a convention and voted to secede. A minority in the mountain counties promptly seceded from the seceders and came back into the Union. Equally revolutionary, Maryland went into a state of chaos. Slaveowning farmers saddled their horses, rode off to join wild boys from Baltimore and defy the Federal authority. In Washington fortifications to repel invasion were hastily erected.

Thurlow Weed, with his long nose hunting for news, discovered as he prowled around Washington that a large party of rebels was concentrating for an attack on the Federal arsenal at Harper's Ferry, up the Potomac from Washington. Weed strode away to tell Secretary Cameron. The latter, elderly and happy with the prospect of many business "deals," was incredulous that a real attack could be imminent. Going next to General Scott, Weed found the old commander thoroughly alarmed but helpless. "My effective force, all told, for the defense of the capital is twenty-one hundred," said the hero of the War of 1812. "Washington is as much in danger as Harper's Ferry."[2]

On April 19, 1861, newspapers announced that the commander at the Ferry had been compelled to demolish the arsenal, burn the armory and abandon the town.[3] This disastrous news reached Washington with a rumor that Gosport, the Navy Yard down the Potomac from Washington, was being menaced. Gosport's arms, vessels, munitions and supplies had cost the government many millions. If they fell into rebel hands the enemy would possess more war matériel than the government had in all its other depots.[4] Protecting this property was a job for the Secretary of the Navy. Weed hunted up Gideon Welles at Willard's Hotel and talked with him first at breakfast and later at dinner, but at neither time could he convince the Secretary of the danger. In desperation Weed hurried to the White House. Lincoln was gone. He had driven out to inspect the city's fortifications, Weed was told. Early next morning Weed tried again, grimly pleased at being able to expose the old "ship's figurehead." Lincoln listened to the story.

"Well, we can't afford to lose all those cannon," he said. "I'll go and see Father Welles myself." He went immediately, but relief did not reach the port in time to prevent its evacuation and destruction. The whole fabric of the nation began to disintegrate. Business in the capital came to a standstill. Stores closed. Windows were boarded. Groups of people at street corners exchanged forebodings of disaster. The wildest rumors gained credence. Rebels were reported to be marching from Baltimore to sack the city. Confederate gunboats were said to be coming up the Potomac to shell the White House. A mob with pistols and bowie knives was reported galloping north from Richmond. Another was coming down from Harper's Ferry. Secession sympathizers in the city prepared to welcome the conquerors. Government clerks vacated their desks. More officers in the Army and Navy resigned their commissions. Colonels Joseph E. Johnston and Robert E. Lee both joined the Confederates. No leader with known military initiative was left in the Federal Army.

Thurlow Weed decided that he must save the country. Ignoring Lincoln's rebuff to Seward, he interviewed people of importance, called again on General Scott, and asked about possible officer material for the Army. But Scott, with one foot in the grave and the other swollen with gout, only sighed. No officer material was available! Weed left. "The question pained him,"[5] he remembered later. Weed went next to see Colonel Joseph P. Taylor, a brother of the ex-President. The two men thumbed through the *Army Register*. The available men they noted were either on the side of the Confederacy or out of the service. The best prospects were George B. McClellan and William T. Sherman, both in civil life. Weed forwarded their names to the President for consideration and fled on the first train for Albany. Looking from the car windows he saw peaceful farmsteads, but the absence of young men working in the fields was ominous. At Baltimore an excited crowd on the station platform said that the bridges behind Weed's train had been burned. Washington was cut off from the North—an island in Secessia.

Troops in the North concentrated in Pennsylvania, but it was impossible to move them by train to the capital. That night, at the Astor House in New York, Weed received a wire from Seward: "The danger is imminent. Hasten movement of steamers with troops via Annapolis." An hour later a wire from Cameron stated: "Charter steamers and despatch troops to Annapolis."[6] Then silence. The wires were cut. The North could only speculate what might be happening in the beleaguered capital.

Lincoln was a stranger to war. As a young man he had spent one summer in an Indian campaign, but military tactics had not interested him since. He turned the emergency over to General Scott. The feeble old warrior drove down Pennsylvania Avenue in his buggy. He distributed a half-dozen companies of regulars about the city. The bridges were guarded with artillery. The Capitol was barricaded. The District Militia, some fifteen companies mustered for the inauguration, was ordered to guard public buildings. Loyal clerks were handed rifles to protect their offices. The owners of some private residences fixed loopholes in their windows and doors for defense. Senators, representatives and transients at the hotels organized into two companies for guard duty throughout the city. One of these companies, the Strangler Guard, was captained by Cassius M. Clay, Lincoln's minister to Russia, who had no intention of leaving for a foreign post while excitement ran high at home. Swaggering along the street with three pistols and an "Arkansas toothpick" clanking against his legs, Clay boasted about battles in Mexico and clattered up and down the White House steps "like an admiral vignette to 25-cents-worth of yellow-covered romance," as John Hay wrote in his diary. Clay's men were quartered elegantly in Willard's Hotel. Between details they lounged on the benches, drank coffee and scribbled in editorial notebooks. The "grizzled captain," according to Hay, "talks politics on the raised platform and dreams of border battle and the hot noons of Monterey."[7]

The suspense lasted for days. On one occasion John Hay took a message upstairs to the President and found him in a room overlooking the Potomac—up whose broad waters enemy ships were reported to be coming to attack the city. Lincoln was spraddled out in a chair with his feet on the window sill, "calmly looking out the window," Hay wrote, "looking at the smoke of two strange steamers puffing up the way, resting the end of the telescope on his toes sublime."[8]

On April 23, 1861, just five days after Washington became isolated, Lord Lyons requested safe passage for a friend to Baltimore.[9] The pass could not be granted. The administration admitted that it controlled only the lower end of the railroad. Lyons reported this hopeless weakness of the government to his home office. Surely the North could never win the war.

The state of affairs at the capital was quickly relayed into Secessia and William H. Russell, touring the South for his paper, heard in Savannah:

"the most terrible accounts . . . of the state of things in Washington. Mr. Lincoln consoles himself for his miseries by drinking. Mr. Seward follows suit. The White House and capital are full of drunken border ruffians. . . ."[10]

On the Atlantic Ocean, Mann, Yancey and Rost, confident of recognition, approached nearer and nearer to England and France. No representative of Lincoln's administration had even prepared to counteract them. Southern cotton and Southern trade were vital to Europe. Powerful leaders of industry and commerce in both England and France looked to their governments to protect their investments. The Governor of Maryland suggested to Seward that Lord Lyons arbitrate the American difficulty.[11] The Secretary of State scoffed at the suggestion. Then Lincoln with equal audacity declared a blockade on the ports of two more states that had seceded—fine talk when Washington was surrounded by the enemy. Was this some more of Seward's bluff or did Lincoln sincerely believe that he could enforce his authority?

Five days later the diplomats wagged their heads knowingly. Seward had got Lincoln's permission to pass minister Schleiden, of Bremen, through the Federal lines to effect a reconciliation in Richmond. The opposing policies of Lincoln and Seward were clear now. Seward still hoped to reunite America with a foreign war. He would scrap the Constitution to avert a war at home. Lincoln would not sacrifice as much as one punctuation mark in the Constitution to reconcile the South. The principle of majority rule under the Constitution must be tested once for all. The President instructed Schleiden to say that the Federal government had no compromise to offer, but the seceded states might suggest any proposition for readmission into the Union. The diplomats speculated on the terms Seward was sending *sub rosa.*

On April 29, 1861, Yancey and Mann arrived in London. The time had come for England to make a decision. Would the commissioners be given an audience and would that mean war with the North? Lyons had recommended calling Seward's bluff, but Lord John Russell, Secretary of Foreign Affairs, was cautious. On April 30 he requested the American minister, George M. Dallas, to come for a conference at the Foreign Office. Dallas was the Democratic holdover awaiting his successor. Lord John Russell told him that he had heard rumors that Lincoln planned a blockade. If one was attempted, Russell said frankly, it might be necessary for Great Britain to recognize the Confederacy. Dallas, without authority or knowledge, assured His Lordship that this rumor was unfounded. Returning to the legation, he told his secretary that this "seemed to give satisfaction."[12]

Yancey and Mann were immediately given an audience. They submitted a request for recognition of the Confederate States of America. His Lordship listened to their plea with aristocratic reserve. He thanked them with cool punctiliousness, said the whole matter would be submitted to the cabinet. Then he bowed them out.[13] Two days later Lord Russell learned that Lincoln had ordered a blockade. Dallas had misinformed him.[14] Another audience was held with the commissioners but this time Lord Russell was briefer than before. Perhaps Seward's bluff had had its effect. The commissioners, in their reports, attributed their failure to another cause. Slavery, they said, was as intolerable to Europeans as to New Englanders. They wrote:

"We are . . . satisfied that the public mind here is entirely opposed to the Government of the Confederate States of America on the question of slavery, and that the sincerity and universality of this feeling embarrass the Government in dealing with the question of our recognition."[15]

Russell did not see the commissioners again. Across the Channel Rost seemed to be having more success. Napoleon III, himself a political adventurer, hinted co-operation. Perhaps the American revolutionists could join with the Mexican revolutionist, Miramón. Between them they could reinstate the Catholic Church in Mexico, guarantee payment on the French debt and give Napoleon a new empire. *N'est-ce pas?*

Lincoln's ability as a political manipulator would be taxed to the utmost to counteract such tempting prizes. Long before he decided on a way to outmaneuver Napoleon, he got into trouble with England. The unpleasantness started innocently enough. Washington was full of spies and traitors. Every day somebody was arrested and led away to jail. In many cases these men were held on suspicion without being told their alleged offense. Frantic lawyers stormed into the office of Ward Hill Lamon, District Marshal, and also into the White House. Their clients must be given a trial.

Lincoln listened to the complaints, asked the lawyers to leave their briefs for him to examine. Interruptions came so often that Lincoln sometimes hid himself in the back room where John Hay copied letters endlessly. At mealtime he retreated down the main hall to the west wing where his family lived. Occasionally pursuers waylaid him. Then Lincoln smiled innocently, shook hands, told stories, and slipped away in a gale of laughter.

Under no circumstances did Lincoln intend to let the culprits out of confinement. The safety of the country demanded that they be held, trial or no trial, until the revolution was in control. This denial of the writ of habeas corpus estranged Britishers. "Egad, the North must be on the verge of collapse, to adopt such tyranny." Arbitrary arrests numbered close to 13,000 during the war. It was useless to tell Englishmen that concentration camps were justified in a so-called liberal government. Nor could sympathy be gained for Lincoln by pointing out that many of the imprisoned men were being protected from inflamed juries eager to condemn them without evidence or mercy. Englishmen prized the right of trial by jury as the most sacred provision in their constitution. If the writ of habeas corpus was suspended, all guarantees might be set aside.

The question of inalienable rights assumed international importance[16] when a man claiming to be a British subject was denied the writ. Soon Chief Justice Taney and Abraham Lincoln were arguing the constitutional points of this sacred Anglo-Saxon heritage. Lord John Russell attempted to open a diplomatic inquiry into the question. Seward cut him off, peremptorily refusing to discuss a question of American constitutionality with a foreign power.[17] The exchange of notes served as ammunition for British reactionaries to hurl at the liberals. "Just as we said," they sneered. "History always repeats itself. Democracy leads always to dictatorship."

Adding to the insult of Lincoln's arbitrary arrests, the inconsistency of his maritime policy increased irritation in England. Jeff Davis replied to Lincoln's order of blockade by offering letters of marque and reprisal to any shipowner who desired to prey on Northern commerce. Seward, under Lincoln's name, promptly announced that such privateers would be treated as pirates. If caught, they would be hanged instead of confined as prisoners of war.

This harsh order was announced during the delirious days when Washington verged on chaos. Complications grew endlessly from it. Lincoln, harassed as he was, decided that henceforth he must give the State Department closer supervision.

When Lincoln investigated the full meaning of the blockade that Seward had got him to declare,[18] he realized that the situation was worse than it appeared at first. At Seward's suggestion Lincoln had declared the blockade "in pursuance . . . of the law of nations." The law of nations in this case was the Declaration of Paris subscribed to five years before by seven of the principal nations of Europe. The Declaration defined "blockade" and abolished privateering. The United States had been asked to join but declined. At that time the provisions of the Declaration were not deemed advantageous. Now the Declaration became suddenly beneficial and when Lincoln proclaimed his blockade according to "the law of nations," Seward made haste to call in Lord Lyons and tell him that the United States wished to subscribe to the convention. Such subscription, Seward explained, would not only legalize Lincoln's blockade but at the same time it would outlaw Jefferson Davis' "inhuman" privateers.

Lord Lyons was almost as slow to think as Lincoln himself. He was also devastatingly logical. The North, he was sure, would be welcomed to the fellowship of the Declaration, but by joining it could not bind the South. Seward remonstrated. Any treaty negotiated by the United States bound all the states, North and South. Rebels did not constitute an independent country. To this Lord Lyons replied, "Very well. If they are not independent then the President's proclamation of blockade is not binding. A blockade, according to the definition of the convention, applies only to two nations at war."

Lincoln pondered in his slow, sure way over the blockade-privateer proposition. Seward had led him into a bad complication this time—one of the worst for international amity in his administration. Suppose the European nations did agree to the North's commitment to the Declaration of Paris "abolishing privateering everywhere in all cases and forever." What good would that do when it would not bind the Confederacy? Furthermore, if Lincoln by his own proclamation had recognized the South as a nation, could the North complain if Britain also recognized her? In short, Seward had accomplished the one thing he had tried to prevent, and in addition he had succeeded only in committing his own country not to use privateers. When questioned about these inconsistencies Seward's answer was always the same. "Europe must interpret the law our way or we'll declare war, commission enough privateers to prey on English commerce in every sea and wrap the world in flames." What could Lincoln do with such a renegade? Perhaps he approved of him. Was the President as incorrigible as his Secretary of State? The diplomats did not like the new government.

Lord Lyons worried. England could not remain friendly with an American Department of State in such a frame of mind, and he, as minister, was sure to be held responsible. On May 2, 1861, the House of Commons discussed American affairs. Lord John Russell pleaded, "For God's sake, let us, if possible, keep out of them!" But he said further, "A power or a community (call it which you will) which [is] at war with another, and which [covers] the sea with its cruisers, must either be acknowledged as a belligerent, or dealt with as a pirate."[19]

England could hardly be expected to treat the warships of 9,000,000 people as pirates, but Seward had got things into a situation where she must either do that or recognize them as belligerents, perhaps as a nation, yet Seward had said such recognition would be just cause for the North to declare war on England. Things looked bad.

Seward's colleagues in the cabinet accused him of getting the nation into this predicament because he was ignorant of international law. Postmaster General Blair, rat-eyed, sniffing daintily at his own words, said that in his opinion Seward knew "less of public law than any man who ever held a seat in the Cabinet." Dingy little Bates, who constantly surprised strangers with forthright terseness, pronounced Seward "no lawyer and no statesman." Welles went home and whimpered in the consoling covers of his diary about a Secretary of State "so little acquainted with the books."[20] Lincoln listened, still learning the multifarious duties that devolved on a President of the United States. His peaceful capital had become a fortified camp. Without doubt he could not trust his Secretary of State. Yet he must be kept. The only solution was for Lincoln to take an active part in international relations himself. Two months had elapsed. His ministers to France and England had not yet arrived at their stations. Just what could be done to straighten out affairs was problematical. Fortunately England was slow to act. Was public opinion dictating her tolerance? If so, the letters William H. Russell sent to Europe describing his experiences in the South deserved study. Abraham Lincoln, first and foremost a statesman, could go to no better source of suggestion for a future foreign policy.

These dispatches came to Lord Lyons in Washington by messenger. From his office they went by packet boat to London for publication.[21] Lincoln did not see them until they came back to the United States as newspaper articles at least a month after they were written. The first thing to catch Lincoln's eye in the newspaper reports must have been the apologetic attitude of the Southerners toward the *Times* correspondent. Evidently they felt remorse for their own imperialistic, filibustering foreign policy during the years they had ruled America. Russell told the English people continually that the Southern leaders were trying to ingratiate themselves with the European powers. They wanted help from abroad. One of these news notes stated:

"The people of the seceding States, aware in their consciences that they have been the most active in their hostility to Great Britain, and whilst they were in power were mainly responsible for the defiant, irritating, and insulting tone commonly used to us by American statesmen, are anxious at the present . . . to remove all unfavorable impressions."[22]

When Lincoln read this he knew whom to blame for America's unsavory reputation. Foreign policy had been directed by the Democrats, with few interruptions, for two generations. Should Lincoln, as leader of the Republicans, change this impression or should he allow Seward to continue in it? Which would be the better for the interests of America?

Russell's notes showed, too, as England expected they would, that Southern society was based on property to a much larger extent than the Northern. The English people were informed that at no place did Russell find any sentiment for reunion.[23] On the other hand the North's enthusiastic response to the firing on Sumter, Russell found, had given the South a real shock. Russell wrote:

"I am pretty well satisfied that if they [the North] had always spoken, written, and acted as they do now, the people of Charleston would not have attacked Sumter so readily. The abrupt outburst of the North and the demonstration at New York filled the South, first with astonishment, and then with something like fear, which was rapidly fanned into anger by the press and the politicians, as well as by the pride inherent in slaveholders."[24]

Russell reported a sample of Southern oratory that he heard in Charleston. His subject was the fire-eater who had tired of the Sumter negotiations and, in petulance, gave the signal to commence firing.

"How they cheer the pale, frantic man, limber and dark-haired, with uplifted arms and clenched fists, who is perorating on the balcony! . . . 'That's Roger Pryor—he says that if them Yankee trash don't listen to reason, and stand from under, we'll march to the North and dictate the terms of peace in Faneuil Hall!' "[25]

The closer Russell studied Southern society the more he became convinced that the boasted cultural supremacy did not exist except in the minds of a rather backward people. The greatest disillusionment came to him in New Orleans where he saw with horror a debtors' prison. He had seen nothing so archaic as this in the North. Seward had crushed out imprisonment for debt in New York almost a generation before. More and more Russell came to realize that the crusade against slavery was only one phase of a crusade against social backwater. From respectable people everywhere Russell heard, "We are bound to go through with this thing if we would save society."[26] But was the society that Russell saw worth saving? That troubled him. Property, Russell said again and again, was threatened by mob rule in the North, but the South, with its fixed order, was more intolerable. Only England, he believed, had struck a commendable balance between these two dilemmas. When Abraham Lincoln read that observation in the dispatches he must have seen his chance. Here was the touchstone by which England could be reached.

Time and again Russell told his readers that the Confederacy hoped to be readmitted to the British Empire. Would England give them one of her Royal Princes? "Let there be no misconception on this point," Russell wrote. "That sentiment, varied in a hundred ways, has been repeated to me over and over again."[27] Russell was amused when Southerners bragged that their place names were sentimentally English, witness: Charleston, Cooper, Ashley, Gadsden, Sumter, Pinckney, etc.—all names of true cavaliers, Southerners maintained. Russell looked at their bowie knives and pistols, their tobacco juice and long hair curling over the collars of their frock coats. He recalled names that did not sound so sentimentally British. How about Pedee, Tombigbee, Sullivan's Island, etc.?

Another idea which Lincoln might use with effect to gain the respect of Europe for the Northern cause was repudiation of debts. Russell pointed out that the South in the past had led in the policy of repudiation and that the worst offender was the Confederate President himself, Jefferson Davis.[28] Lincoln must have smiled when he saw this fact printed in the leading financial newspaper in England. The facts of the case seemed so apt that both Lincoln and Seward took a tip from the correspondent and made additional memoranda about it for their ministers abroad.

Lincoln noted that one topic impressed Russell more than the evils of democracy and the repudiation of debts. Day after day the correspondent wrote about slavery. On this subject British sentiment was most vulnerable. For page after page Russell described the horrors of this unnatural institution. No Britisher, he was sure, could make an alliance with it. In the London *Times* on May 30 he wrote that Southerners defended slavery as a civilizing influence on a jungle savage. The correspondent had traveled extensively and he could not help comparing the stark poverty of slave cabins in Mississippi with the native villages in Africa. He doubted if the Negro in servitude was as fortunate as his African progenitors[29] who had attained a culture in many villages comparable with ancient Greece. The Southerners' rationalization of the service they were rendering the Negro so preyed on Russell that he wrote a special dispatch on the horrors of a slave auction:

"I am neither sentimentalist nor Black Republican, nor negro worshipper, but I confess the sight caused a strange thrill through my heart. I tried in vain to make myself familiar with the fact that I could, for the sum of $975, become absolutely the owner of that mass of blood, bones, sinew, flesh and brains as of the horse which stood by my side. There was no sophistry which could persuade me the man was not a man—he was, indeed, by no means my brother, but assuredly he was a fellow creature."[30]

And again:

"I have seen slave markets in the East . . . and the idea of its taking place among a civilized Christian people, produced in me a feeling of inexpressible loathing and indignation."

Russell's loathing and indignation increased in New Orleans when he dined with the president of a railroad and the son-in-law of John Slidell, boss politician of the state and nephew of Mrs. August Belmont who in New York had notified the papers that she wished it known that she had not attended the reception for Mrs. Abraham Lincoln. At the dinner, Russell wrote, "one of the slave servants who waited at the table, an intelligent yellow 'boy,' was pointed out to me as a son of General Andrew Jackson."[31]

The Southerners continually told Russell how happy the Negroes were.[32] Traveling to Montgomery, the Confederate capital, he wrote once more that there was something suspicious in the constant, never-ending statement, "We are not afraid of our slaves." To Russell, a realist, the curfew, night patrol, prisons and watch-houses belied such statements.[33] Again he wrote:

"It has often been said to me that no one will ill-use a creature worth £300 or £400, but . . . many a hunting-field could show that if value be a guarantee for good usage, the slave is more fortunate than his fellow chattel, the horse."[34]

On a plantation Russell was amused to hear an overseer praise the intelligence and skill of his workmen and then later expatiate on "the utter helplessness and ignorance of the black race, their incapacity to do any good, or even take care of themselves."[35] Russell noted, too, how Southerners justified slavery on biological grounds, how they eased their consciences with subtle arguments.

"The negro skull won't hold as many ounces as that of the white man's. Can there be a more potent proof that the white man has a right to sell and to own a creature who carries a smaller charge of snipe dust in his head? He is plantigrade and curved as to tibia! Cogent demonstration that he was made expressly to work for the arch-footed, straight-tibia'd Caucasian. . . .

"Our Saviour sanctions Slavery because he does not say a word against it, and it's very likely that St. Paul was a slave-owner. . . . Besides, the negro is civilized by being carried away from Africa and set to work. . . . What hope is there of Christianizing the African races except by the agency of the apostles from New Orleans, Mobile, or Charleston. . . . If these high, physical, metaphysical, moral and religious reasonings do not satisfy you . . . I advise you not to come within reach of a mass meeting of our citizens, who may be able to find a rope and a tree in the neighborhood."[36]

The idea of enslaving the Negro for his own good, to save his soul by Christianizing him, had been prated by Englishmen two hundred years before. But the persistence of a concept from the religious wars in Europe brought home to Russell's mind the extreme narrowness which had resulted from the Southern policy of isolation. To the correspondent these people had learned nothing and forgotten nothing for two hundred years. That they were sincere he could not believe; rather it must be the rationalization of capitalists against red republicans.[37] He told his diary:

"I declare that to me the more orderly, methodical, and perfect the arrangements for economizing slave labor . . . are, the more hateful and odious does slavery become."[38]

For publication in the *Times* he wrote:

"Admitting everything that can be said, I am the more persuaded from what I see, that the real foundation of slavery in the Southern States lies in the power of obtaining labor at will at a rate which cannot be controlled by any combination of the laborers."[39]

Russell reported another aspect of slavery particularly obnoxious to all Britishers. In 1808 Great Britain and the United States had contemporaneously abolished the slave trade. Since that time cooperative agreements permitting British men-of-war to stop suspected slave ships had been made with all the maritime nations— excepting only the United States. The slave-owning South had been in power almost continually, and it was useless for Americans to claim that the United States would not tolerate the right of search because that was an issue on which they fought the War of 1812. Britishers believed that the real reason was the South's desire to permit the trade. Englishmen had smarted for half a century from their futile efforts to stop the nefarious traffic. Now Russell, traveling in the South, irritated the old sore by reaffirming that British suspicions were true. On April 30 he wrote from South Carolina:

"Although they profess (and I believe, indeed, sincerely) to hold opinions in opposition to the opening of the slave trade, it is nevertheless true that the clause in the Constitution of the Confederate States which prohibited the importation of negroes was especially and energetically resisted by them, because, as they say, it seemed to be an admission that slavery was in itself an evil and a wrong. Their whole system rests on slavery, and as such they defend it."[40]

Again, in June, England was warned to appreciate the full significance of this threat to reopen the slave trade when Russell wrote:

"The success of the South—if it can succeed—must lead to complications and results in other parts of the world for which neither it nor Europe is now prepared. Of one thing there can be no doubt—a Slave State cannot long exist without a slave-trade. The poor whites who will have won the fight will demand their share of the spoils. The land is abundant, and all that is wanted to give them fortunes is a supply of slaves."[41]

Russell's greatest disappointment in the South was his inability to find a refined civilization there. His notes to the *Times* coincided with the report which Consul Bunch had sent at the time Yancey, Mann and Rost had set out for Europe. Between the two of them Britain was getting a very definite picture of Englishmen's ideas of the South. Russell was particularly impressed by the same thing which impressed so many Northerners. Slavery had degraded the masses down South to a status below other civilized Anglo-Saxons.

Russell noted that a man with an income of £800 and a house believed the society to which he belonged "the highest development of civilized life, notwithstanding the fact that there are more outrages on the person in his State, nay, more murders perpetrated in the very capital, than were known in the worst days of mediaeval Venice or Florence."[42]

Russell dwelt in detail on people's respect for violence in Montgomery, Alabama, "the very capital." He reported the hotel where he stayed there to be "full of Confederate congressmen, politicians, colonels, and place-men" all of whom had a "bowie-knife, or a six-shooter, or Derringer about them."[43] In this Southern society Russell was told how he must act to qualify as a "gentleman" and he noted the cardinal qualifications in his diary:

"I was warned, for example, against the impolicy of trusting to small-bored pistols or to pocket six-shooters in case of a close fight, because suppose you hit your man mortally he may still run in upon you and rip you up with a bowie-knife before he falls dead; whereas if you drive a good heavy bullet into him, or make a hole in him with a 'Derringer' ball, he gets faintish and drops at once. . . .

"Altogether the impression produced on my mind was by no means agreeable, and I felt as if I was indeed in the land of Lynch-law and bowie-knives, where the passions of men have not yet been subordinated to the influence of the tribunals of justice."[44]

The picture Russell sent back to England disclosed a rude people. Always he saw the South as a society gone to seed, reactionary, closed mentally to new ideas, respecting only property and violence. "No security for life! Property is quite safe," he wrote.[45] Russell reported that local conversation consisted of stories about how one man shot another and was afterwards stabbed by a third, or how this fellow and his friend hunted down in broad daylight and murdered one obnoxious to them, etc.

Astute Abraham Lincoln read these dispatches and decided for himself the best propaganda for Great Britain. Russell had found the North vulgarly democratic, with universal suffrage threatening to confiscate all property. In the South he had found a society that prized property above human life. Always the Britisher noted how Her Majesty had avoided these two extremes by granting a moderate amount of democracy and yet preserving property. Once more Lincoln was reminded that his foreign problems might be solved by jarring British opinion from the middle position.

The two extremes of civilization, North and South, were graphically explained by Russell when he described the Presidents of the two governments. After meeting the Confederate chief executive he wrote:

"[Jeff Davis] did not impress me as favorably as I had expected, though he is certainly a very different looking man from Mr. Lincoln. He is like a gentleman—has a slight, light figure, little exceeding middle height, and holds himself erect and straight. . . . 'Yes, sir,' he remarked. . . . 'In Eu-rope' (Mr. Seward also indulges in that pronounciation) 'they laugh at us because of our fondness for military titles and displays. . . . But the fact is, we are a military people.' "[46]

Delving deeper into this military civilization which held property higher than human life, Russell reported an interview with the Confederates' Attorney General, later to be Secretary of State, Judah P. Benjamin—the man reported already to have opened

negotiations with Great Britain for a foreign prince. Of this individual lover of property he wrote:

"He is a short, stout man, with a full face, olive-colored, and
most decidedly Jewish features, with the brightest large black eyes,
one of which is somewhat diverse from the other, and a brisk,
lively, agreeable manner, combined with much vivacity of speech
and quickness of utterance."[47]

Inquiring into the background of this man who had thrown in
his destiny with the agricultural civilization, Russell reported that
until recently Benjamin had had a large law practice in Washington
amounting to some £8,000 to £10,000 "but his love of the card-
table rendered him a prey to older and cooler hands."[48]

Slave driver, militarist, filibuster, gambler—this was the type of
man that ruled the Confederacy, according to the reports sent to
Europe by William H. Russell and other Britishers. The rank
and file of the fighting men under this kind of leadership Russell
found equally peculiar. The soldiers' names and uniforms appeared
strange to him. He reported:

"In the train which preceded us there was a band of volunteers
armed with rifled pistols and enormous bowie-knives, who called
themselves 'The Toothpick Company.' They carried along with
them a coffin, with a plate inscribed, 'Abe Lincoln, died ———,'
and declared they were 'bound' to bring his body back in it, and
that they did not intend to use muskets or rifles, but just go in
with knife and six-shooter, and whip the Yankees straight away.
How astonished they will be when the first round shot flies into
them, or a cap-full of grape rattles about their bowie-knives."[49]

Russell returned to the North by way of the Mississippi Valley.
Crossing the Ohio to free soil, he saw Union soldiers everywhere.
He compared the fighting men of the Northern and Southern
civilizations as he traveled toward Washington. To his English
readers he wrote:

"Coming so recently from the South, I can see the great difference which exists between the two races, as they may be called,
exemplified in the men I have seen, and those who are in the
train going towards Washington. These volunteers have none of

the swash-buckler bravado, gallant-swaggering air of the Southern men. They are staid, quiet men, and the Pennsylvanians, who are on their way to join their regiment in Baltimore, are very inferior in size and strength to the Tennesseans and Carolinians. . . . There is certainly less vehemence and bitterness among the Northerners; but it might be erroneous to suppose there was less determination."[50]

Lincoln mulled over these dispatches. Obviously the British correspondent looked unfavorably on the South. By no stretch of understanding could Russell reconcile the institution of slavery with British tradition. A Virginia philosopher, George Fitzhugh, had got some sympathy for the South by preaching the dangers of democracy. The rule by many, he said, was "Socialism and communism . . . no private property, no church, no law, no government."[51] This had appealed to the ruling classes abroad, but when Fitzhugh went one step farther and said that slavery was necessary for all labor "black or white," even the conservatives turned away. Lincoln knew, too, that a liberal Frenchman, Count Agénor de Gasparin, had written a book about the impending American war which made a great impression on Frenchmen. His *Un Grand Peuple qui se relève—Les Etats-Unis en 1861* warned all liberals that the American war was a world civil war. The tide of reaction already high in England and France must be stopped by a Northern victory. An abridged London edition of this Frenchman's work was on sale in paper covers for a shilling. In New York, Charles Scribner was preparing a full-length American translation. In the appendix of the British printing an extract from a speech of Alexander H. Stephens, Vice-President of the Confederacy, appeared. If sincere Englishmen had any doubts in their own minds about the purpose of Southern secession they could be informed here by the next to highest authority. The extract said in part:

"The prevailing ideas entertained . . . at the time of the formation of the old Constitution, were that the enslavement of the African was in violation of the laws of nature; that it was wrong in principle, socially, morally, and politically. . . .

"Our new government is founded upon exactly the opposite idea; its foundations are laid, its corner-stone rests, upon the great truth that the negro is not equal to the white man; that slavery—

subordination to the superior race—is his natural and moral condition.

"This, our new government, is the first, in the history of the world, based upon this great physical and moral truth. . . . It is upon this, as I have stated, our social fabric is firmly planted; and I cannot permit myself to doubt the ultimate success of a full recognition of this principle throughout the civilized and enlightened world. . . .

"This stone which was rejected by the first builders 'is become the chief stone of the corner' in our new edifice."[52]

The London publisher offered a separate printing of this enlightening speech for sixpence.

Everywhere Lincoln turned he was reminded that Europe's friendship could be gained by declaring the American war a crusade against slavery. Yet he could not do that. The Constitution of the democracy under which he had been elected protected the archaic institution. Until Lincoln could work out some means by which he could make the war a war to exterminate slavery he could expect little sympathy in Europe. This was plain to any man.

# V. *Noisy Jackasses*

O N MAY 11, 1861, the war seemed far away from Washington. Thousands of children trudged through the White House to shake hands with the President. John Hay commiserated with Lincoln—but learned with surprise that the President enjoyed endless handshaking. In the afternoon the Marine Band played on the south lawn. It was May in Washington. All the trees were in leaf. Lincoln rested on the balcony, listening. Beside him Carl Schurz fidgeted nervously, his eyes sparkling under Lincoln's benign flattery. Nine years before, Schurz had escaped Europe as a dangerous revolutionist. Now, as reputed ruler of the German vote, Lincoln welcomed him to the White House. Carl Schurz possessed boundless energy. He crackled with ideas, things to do, plans. The Negroes must be freed. An army of volunteers must sweep down across the South, exterminate aristocracy, wipe out chivalry, landed gentry—*Junkers* they were called in Germany. Lincoln looked at Schurz's sharp nose and chin, his steel-trap lips—tokens of uncompromising devotion to principle. Schurz rattled on. He said young men would kindle to his oratory, flock to his standard, uphold democracy. Confident, brimming with anecdotes, names, dates, purposes, fluent with facts, unable to remain silent, expressing snap judgments, Carl Schurz looked eagerly at Lincoln through thick glasses. He wanted to be a guerrilla, he said, a cavalryman, a leader of horse, light horse—mighty light horse. Lincoln asked to be excused. Work in the office demanded his attention. He walked away slowly, thoughtfully. Carl Schurz's long hair, waving in winds of anticipated adventure, looked remarkably like the long locks of a troublesome young cavalryman, George A. Custer, already in the service.[1]

Lincoln sat down at his desk. Music from a piano came faintly to his ears, pensive, gay, bold, furious, ecstatic—a master hand. The German, restless as a caged bear, had found the instrument. He had drawn up a stool, and his nervous fingers danced and hurdled across the keys, tickling laughter from the strings, pounding out rage, then triumph—composition after composition until Lincoln came by and took him down to tea.[2] Lincoln could use such versatile men. Let Schurz raise the nation's youth, recruit the regiments. Then he might serve his country best by going away to Spain where the Secretary of Legation, Horatio Perry, with full instructions and a lifetime of experience, knew exactly what to do. Lincoln was not one to value glib knowledge above slow common sense.

As Lincoln sat with Schurz, sipping tea, chatting with other friends, William Dayton arrived in Paris to assume his official duties. Two days later, May 13, 1861, Charles Francis Adams arrived in London. He had spent almost two weeks crossing the Atlantic. The same boat carried Cassius M. Clay, bound for Russia with his wife, her companions and a contingent of frock-coated Kentucky orators.

Henry Adams attended his father as private secretary. Mrs. Adams, a younger son and a daughter eighteen years old completed the suite. As the packet's chugging engine carried the vessel out of sight of the American coast Adams told his son how his great-grandfather had sailed on a similar mission from Mount Wollaston in midwinter, 1778, on the little frigate *Boston,* taking his eleven-year-old son John Quincy with him for secretary, on a diplomatic adventure which ended in the independence of the United States. The minister also told his son how the boy John Quincy, grown to manhood in 1809, had sailed for Russia with his two-year-old son, Charles Francis, to cope with Napoleon and Czar Alexander.[3] Henry Adams, leaning on the ship's rail, looking across the waste of waters, pondered pleasantly that the third generation was following the pattern which inevitably led to the White House.

Arriving in the choking fog of Liverpool, Adams and Clay were greeted with bad news. Queen Victoria had recognized the Confederacy as belligerents. She declared England neutral in the war, warned British subjects not to enlist under either flag, and not to supply munitions or fit out privateers. Such a proclamation was considered by the Adams party as the first step toward recognizing the South as an independent nation. Deeply depressed by the news as well as by a pea-soup fog, the Americans hurried to the railway station.

Cassius M. Clay attracted attention. Britishers stared at his heroic six feet clad in a blue dress coat with gilt buttons,[4] his bone-handled bowie knife in a shoulder scabbard beneath his arm. The sharp-faced Kentucky retainers in high hats and skirted coats added a theatrical touch to his retinue. The Adams family were indistinguishable from well-dressed Londoners even to their accent. On the railway train, rattling out of the city, past the Welsh coal mines into the clearer air of the English Midlands, Clay in his compartment could dream of stubborn defenses at every thatched cottage. The green hillsides were ideal for gallant charges of Kentucky cavalry.

Twenty-three-year-old Henry Adams, locked in another "carriage" with his family, amused himself by teasing his nervous mother. He likened her little party to "a family of early Christian martyrs about to be flung into an arena of lions, under the glad eyes of Tiberius Palmerston."[5] This foreboding of evil was not altogether imaginary on the part of Henry Adams. His father, the minister, shared it. England's recognition of the belligerent rights of the Confederacy seemed an unfair advantage to take before his arrival. Later he said that the Queen's proclamation was a very fortunate circumstance, for had the British taken this action after, instead of before, his arrival he might have been blamed for the occurrence. At the time, however, he felt as though his mission had failed before it began. He was discouraged and fatigued when the train puffed and rattled into the London station that night. On the platform, waiting for the Americans, stood the Secretary of Legation, Charles Wilson of Chicago, and the Assistant Secretary, Benjamin Moran. The two secretaries escorted the party to cabs and then drove with the Adamses to "an hotel," as Moran called it. The secretaries had much to say. Moran, an old employee of the legation, knew the city intimately and hoped to be of "sarvice." The wild young Chicagoan was more of a stranger to London than the Adamses and much more unhappy. He had arrived in the British capital a few days before and with western energy he determined to get things done. Applying to the British government for guns, he had been informed coldly that the government would

Courtesy of Lincoln National Life Foundation. Inset by courtesy of F. H. Meserve

LINCOLN AND HIS CABINET DISCUSSING THE EMANCIPATION PROCLAMATION
Painting by Francis B. Carpenter. *Inset*: The Capitol photographed during Lincoln's first
inauguration.

CHARLES FRANCIS ADAMS, MINISTER TO GREAT BRITAIN

furnish no guns.[6] The rebuff chilled Charlie to the marrow. He spent the succeeding hours sitting with his feet on a table at Morley's, abusing the English.[7]

As soon as the Adamses were ensconced for the night, Moran and Wilson set out once more to see if Clay had found comfortable accommodations. They drove first to the hotel where the Kentuckians planned to lodge. The "clark" said the Americans were not there. They had been sent to another hostelry. Once more the secretaries set out through the lamp-lighted city only to find that Clay had been sent to a third hotel. Following his trail the secretaries went to a fourth and finally overtook him at the fifth hotel. As they approached, the secretaries saw four cabs piled high with baggage, standing before the door. The "Kentucky ambassador," they learned, had employed them all for the convenience of his suite. In the hotel Clay stalked up and down the magnificent hall "like a chafed lion . . . a man to be avoided."[8] Moran and Wilson heard sleepy menials refuse the Americans admittance. Big Ben was striking 12:30 A.M. over London town.

Benjamin Moran took things in charge. Accommodations were provided for the women in the party and the men traveled on to a third-rate house in Charing Cross—not luxurious but better than some lodginghouses Clay knew in the backwoods of Kentucky. At least it served as a place for him to hang his bowie knife.

On the following day Charles Francis Adams inspected his official residence. The bare rooms, scant staff and humble accommodations were not prepossessing. Probably as weakly manned as the legations of Guatemala or Portugal, his son Henry observed.[9] The force consisted of Wilson, Moran and Henry Adams, secretary, assistant secretary and private secretary. Great stacks of correspondence had accumulated. The secretaries would be obliged to spend tedious hours copying duplicates in longhand of all official correspondence. Adams determined to get a larger appropriation. He knew that he owed his appointment to William H. Seward. He did not know that his erstwhile friend, Charles Sumner, chairman of the Foreign Relations Committee, had opposed him. In the months that followed, he suspected as much when, with increasing friction with England, he encountered difficulty in getting the money he required.

On the third day after his arrival, Adams was presented to Queen Victoria. The day before, he and his wife stewed over diplomatic formalities. Mrs. Adams was exercised about the etiquette of cards. Her husband sketched elaborate designs for male court dress—a navy-blue coat with stand-up collar and profuse embroidery on sleeves and breast, white kerseymere vest and breeches, white silk stockings, black shoes with gold buckles, and a fine gilt-headed sword. If the British court expected anything Lincolnian in Adams' dress they were disappointed. The Queen was reported as saying, "I am thankful we shall have no more American funerals."[10]

Unfortunately Adams' costume was not ready for his presentation. Instead he wore a dress coat with tails.[11] Queen Victoria at this time was described by another American as:

"A very short woman with a dumpy figure, though erect, no grace of outline. Her complexion was florid, and with the least provocation grows red all over; her eyes gray and very pop. She peels her teeth to the very top of her gums when she laughs, which is not becoming at all, as her front teeth are quite too prominent to bear such exposure. Her smile is pleasant, but when she puts on a severe or cold expression she looks as though her features had been accustomed to it. I was led to suspect that her temper was capricious."[12]

The opinion of this little woman would make or mar Charles Francis Adams' diplomatic reputation. Her decisions would be the most important in Lincoln's foreign relations. England prided itself on the liberalism of its constitutional monarchy, but when Her Majesty tapped her foot nervously the Prime Minister, old bull Palmerston, jumped to her service. In England the Queen represented the interests of all her people, the humblest coster as well as the richest banker. Lord Palmerston owed his premiership to votes of certain big interests. The difference in responsibility between Queen and premier might become very significant in foreign relations if the workers and shipping interests differed on England's policy toward the American war. Suppose the workers became convinced that the American war was a war for democracy? What would they do then to their overlords?

On the morning following the presentation John Bright blustered through the legation door and stopped to chat democratically with the secretaries. Few Englishmen were better known in America than this doughty liberal and the young men looked him over with enthusiasm. Bright's face betokened strength of will, independence and capacity. Though he was perfectly at ease, his strong voice made the inkstands rattle. A practical man not given to generalizations or speculations of any kind, he beamed under praise, the boys noticed, and snapped with contempt at any remark questioning his perspicuity. No person and no institution in England was sacred to John Bright. He shouted his dislikes and criticisms with licentious British freedom of speech. He flayed the ruling powers of England as bravely as he would have done had they been present and with as loose language as he would have used before an earl or a London cabbie.[13] The *Times,* Bright blustered, was as profligate as the *New York Herald* and equally as unscrupulous. Palmerston, Russell, Gladstone, he shouted, were politicians with no principles beyond their own personal advancement.

The young Americans watched the British bull paw the ground. He's 110-percent American already, they chuckled. No missionary work was necessary here. But how about the other great liberal, Richard Cobden, the free trader, a quiet, studious man? Rumor said that Cobden had been offended by Seward's arrogance and the high tariff endorsed by the Republican party. Would his belief in democracy and the abolition of slavery outweigh these prejudices? Bright thought they would. He'd win him over. Liberals, by Gad, must stand together! Great Britain must maintain the North in this struggle.[14] The flushed and hearty fellow stamped out of the legation.

Charles Francis Adams, coldly thoughtful, knew too much of the conservative quality of the British Parliament to share Bright's optimism. He knew that Bright had annoyed British conservatives for years by pointing to America as an example of the benefits of universal suffrage and democratic government. No national debt, by Gad, no standing army, no poor laws nor workhouses. Adams knew, too, that members of Parliament had greeted the American Civil War with a sigh of relief, telling one another at teatime, "Now Mr. Bright will be forced to stop wearying us with his blessings of universal suffrage and of government by numbers."[15]

The American minister knew that Bright's friendship was valuable, but did he have the power? The Britisher's blunt vehemence annoyed the cold Adams temperament as much as it did "respectable" Englishmen. Henry, following the Adams tradition of diary writing, noted later:

"Every one called Bright 'un-English,' from Lord Palmerston to William E. Forster; but to an American he seemed more English than any of his critics. He was a liberal hater, and what he hated he reviled after the manner of Milton, but he was afraid of no one. He was almost the only man in England, or, for that matter, in Europe, who hated Palmerston and was not afraid of him, or of the press or the pulpit, the clubs or the bench, that stood behind him. He loathed the whole fabric of sham religion, sham loyalty, sham aristocracy, and sham socialism. He had the British weakness of believing only in himself and his own conventions. . . . Bright was singularly well poised; but he used singularly strong language."[16]

On the day following Bright's call at the legation, Minister Adams paid his first respects to Lord John Russell, Secretary of Foreign Affairs—a momentous meeting and the beginning of Lincoln's foreign policy with Great Britain. The two men were equally cold, formal, diplomatic, almost equally British. A diamond come to cut a diamond. Both were small, funereal men: Charles Francis Adams with a mouth straight and lipless as a gash, an aurora of whiskers encircling his stern face; Russell with pointed and protruding nose, wizened face, high, slanting, partially bald forehead, unfriendly blue eyes. The American minister might have been confronting a picture of his own father, so drolly did Russell resemble John Quincy Adams.[17] Seldom have two more conservative radicals come face to face in the same room. Charles Francis Adams was the third generation of rebels. His grandfather had been a traitor to England. His father had founded the Whig party in America to fight the alleged despotism of Andrew Jackson, and now Charles Francis represented those horrible Republicans who had been elected with Abraham Lincoln. Russell had also come to power as a rebel, a generation earlier, first gaining renown for a radical speech in the House of Commons in favor of the Reform Bill. But after the bill passed and more liberal legislation followed, Russell changed and finally won the name of "Finality Jack" on account of his opposition to further reform. As Adams studied the man before him he may have recalled the words of his erstwhile friend, Charles Sumner, who, after seeing Russell speak in 1838, had said:

"He reminded me of a pettifogging attorney. . . . He wriggled around, played with his hat, and seemed unable to dispose of his hands and feet; his voice was small and thin, but, notwithstanding all this, a house of five hundred members was hushed to catch his smallest accent."[18]

Charles Francis Adams knew that foreigners cut sorry figures before Americans schooled to the democratic habit of stump speaking. He looked at Lord John with the punctilious respect of a toreador for the bull that is destined to act as a foil for the display of his most dexterous thrusts. Specters of John Adams and John Quincy always walked with him, admonishing their offspring to exploit once more the source of their renown.[19] Family tradition demanded ultimate victory. As Charles Francis talked formalities, planning his course of action, he became aware that Lord John esteemed only two things in the world—high birth and great intellect, with two exceptions. He greatly admired John Bright and Charles Dickens, both popular figures in America, but a small bond for diplomatic negotiations. The American minister did not know that on Russell's desk a recently received dispatch from Lord Lyons in Washington suggested the course to be followed in dealing with the American situation.

"The sympathies of an Englishman are naturally inclined towards the North—but I am afraid we should find that anything like a quasi alliance with the men in office here would place us in a position which would soon become untenable. There would be no end to the exactions which they would make upon us, there would be no end to the disregard of our neutral rights, which they would show if they once felt sure of us. If I had the least hope of their being able to reconstruct the Union, or even of their being able to reduce the South to the condition of a tolerably contented or at all events obedient dependency, my feeling against Slavery might lead me to desire to co-operate with them. But I conceive all chance of this to be gone for ever."[20]

When Adams broached the question of recognizing the Southern commissioners, Russell's cold, impersonal eyes must have glanced at his dispatch files. He replied that England's traditional policy had been not to oppose rebels fighting for independence. He had received "unofficially" Polish, Hungarian and Italian revolutionists in recent years—America too had done the same with Kossuth, Garibaldi, etc.—but this did not remotely mean recognition. Russell stated further that he had already seen the Southerners "some time ago" and "once more sometime since." His fishy eyes looked calmly at the surface of the ceiling. "But," he concluded, weighing every word in order that he might not commit himself, "I have no intention of seeing them any more."[21]

With this, Adams had to be content. Returning to the legation he told Moran, "His Lordship was provokingly diplomatic."[22] Private secretary Henry Adams, as much interested in newspapers as in diplomacy, noted that *Punch* commonly drew Russell as a schoolboy telling lies.

The Adamses completed their formal introduction to the British government by attending the Saturday night levee of the Prime Minister, Lord Palmerston. Benjamin Moran warned the Adamses what to expect. Well acquainted with the British government, Moran had found Palmerston "an intellectual wonder." Over eighty ears of age, robustly healthy, the Prime Minister enjoyed chuckling over "an inexhaustible fund of anecdotes"[23]—and was the noisiest man in any assembly, boisterous as John Bright. But the responsibility of long political power had made Palmerston cautious.

Minister Adams knew Palmerston's background. Like Weed in America, Palmerston bridged the gap between the Revolution and the Civil War. His two obsessions were a hatred of slavery and distrust of France. As a Cambridge student he had drilled for Napoleon's threatened invasion. He was thirty-one when Waterloo was won. As Prime Minister one of his first acts censured President Buchanan's failure to co-operate with England for suppression of the slave trade.

Palmerston's hatred for slavery and distrust of France should have given the American minister a clue for his British policy, but the noisy Prime Minister was beyond his understanding. The two men never understood each other. Lord Palmerston's total lack of interest in the Adamses' personalities was more than son Henry could tolerate. He became furious because a footman at one of the Prime Minister's receptions did not recognize him. Adams, in white breeches and stockings, had presented himself to the lackey at the foot of the stairs, gave his name and heard it shouted above as "Mr. Handrew Hadams." In Boston this could not have occurred, and Henry corrected the error. The footman shouted again more loudly, "Mr. Hanthony Hadams!" Adams lost his temper and repeated his name again. He finally was introduced as "Mr. Halexander Hadams." Under this name he bowed to the Prime Minister, who was telling an anecdote to a henchman and let the American pass with perfunctory civility.[24]

The minister and his family were invited to many formal dinners and receptions but they felt that they were able to penetrate the English reserve of only four people. John Bright, Richard Cobden, William E. Forster and Richard Monckton Milnes, or Lord Houghton, showed no prejudice against red foreigners from radical countries. The two former were never seen in the best society. In Parliament they had only a small radical following. Forster was a Yorkshireman with no social or political experience. Of Quaker ancestry and antislavery convictions, he had a rough upcountry exterior. As a new member of Parliament he needed a cause and hoped the Americans might supply it. His friendship with them soon passed political bounds. The Adamses discovered that his apparent roughness covered an emotional, almost sentimental nature.[25]

Of the four men, Milnes alone had social position. His Lordship's breakfasts were famous—coarse, witty, rude, honest, English.[26] The Americans might be socialists or atheists for all he cared, provided they could turn a good story. Even Lord Brougham, the worst swearer in Mayfair,[27] dared not do the things Milnes did. Friendship with such people was diverting, but these men could have only minor influence on the nation's foreign policy.

Minister Adams attended to his office, watched his country's interests, was efficient and alert. In leisure hours he collected coins and studied sales lists. His son tried, in a small way, to influence unofficial English opinion. Lincoln in time noticed his success and eventually threw all his resources into Adams' form of propaganda. In America young Adams had been a correspondent for Henry J. Raymond's *Times*. Looking over the London field, Henry Adams saw that the Northern cause was safe in the columns of the *Morning Star*, a small paper owned by John Bright. Adams wrote a few articles for it. The *Morning Post* was the personal organ of Lord Palmerston[28] and Adams believed that he could write nothing to change the policy of such a sheet. The London *Times* was also practically a government publication representing conservative Britishers. Its news was being colored somewhat satisfactorily by William H. Russell's friendly reports from America. The *Daily News* had a large circulation among people not represented in Parliament—Lincoln's kind of people. Here was Adams' chance. For this organ of the underprivileged he wrote many articles. Three other papers, the *Economist,* the *Saturday Review* and the *Spectator,*[29] had all been pro-Northern at the time of Lincoln's election; but after Seward's bellicosity and Lincoln's inaugural address proclaiming that the war was not to be fought over the question of slavery, the first two had changed, returning to the traditional British policy of neutrality toward rebels fighting for independence. The *Spectator* alone remained sympathetic to the North. A paper with a conscience, Adams thought, and contributed articles for its pages also.

Henry Adams did not know, however, that the *Spectator's* conscience might have been subsidized. Windy George Francis Train claimed later that he had purchased the *Spectator* and also the *Chronicle*[30] for the French Emperor, who wished to build up America to counter England and thus help France. Train was openly known to be the mainstay of another paper, the *London American,* a propaganda sheet so scurrilous that Henry Adams ignored it completely. Other conservative Americans believed that the *American* did incalculable harm to their cause.[31] Lincoln's administration never countenanced it, although Train himself maintained that Seward secretly sent him $100 to keep the paper in circulation.

If the *London American* lacked the dignity Adams admired, it certainly played upon the strings that Lincoln saw were tuned to the ears of lower-class Englishmen. Train held numerous public meetings in England and reported them in his paper. Thus people not fortunate enough to attend might get a secondhand jag from his intoxicating words. Train's editorials shocked scholarly Henry Adams. He sniffed when he read:

"Dissolve the Union!—What! Divide the Constitution? Which half for the northerners, which the southerners? And, great God! What will they do with the Declaration of Independence? . . .

"Dissolve the Union!—Who will pay the public debt? Who is to have the National arms? How is the army to be divided? How the Navy? How are you to manage West Point? and what will you do with General Scott?"[32]

Train's rallies were attended by many people. The entertainment was fulsome. The meetings were enlivened at times with song and laughter. One of Train's specialties was singing "De Camptown Races," with improvised verses. He called on the audience for the chorus. Always Train was willing to get a laugh at the expense of himself as well as America. During a speech at the opening of the Exmouth Railway, shortly after the surrender of Fort Sumter, he said: "We invented railways and Mississippi steam boats. . . . We have invented a new kind of war, fighting without killing anybody—forty hours of bombardment and no bloodshed."[33]

The impertinent utterances that annoyed upper-class Americans certainly were not overlooked by conservative Englishmen. The language may have sounded ungenteel but the facts could not be gainsaid. The Confederate commissioners had come to Europe prepared to explain the Civil War as a Southern protest against the Northern desire for a high tariff on English goods. Time and again they claimed that the tariff and not slavery was the kernel of the dispute. This contention had been given space in English newspapers, especially the *Times*. Train struck back, at a dinner of the London and Provincial Discount Company. He reported his speech in his paper:

"You alluded to the tariff—that question you do not understand. Our entire revenue from customs is but twelve million pounds; yours is twenty-six million pounds—who, then, exercises the most free trade? Your idea of reciprocity is, take all your goods free of duty, and give you our cotton for nothing. (Hear, and laughter.)"[34]

At the Westminster Palace Hotel he told another audience: "I can only tell you, gentlemen, it is a notorious fact when the *Times* takes snuff all England sneezes."[35]

In Washington, Lincoln could study the foreign newspapers at the State Department. He learned that garrulous talk in the European press was not limited to George Francis Train. His own ministers, the smaller fry on the way to their posts, joined the chorus. Burlingame had not been acceptable to Vienna—too pink. He had entertained Austria's exiled revolutionist Kossuth in America! Burlingame returned to Paris for instructions on what to do next. He met Cassius M. Clay, who found it difficult to get past Paris on his way to Russia. The two men decided to give Europe a taste of American oratory. Clay, forever warlike, flung about words more dangerously than derringer balls. From Paris he sent the *Times* a letter equal to Seward at his worst. Let the British beware of America and her democracy. In fifty years, he warned, the population of the United States would be twice that of Great Britain. He appealed to French traditional hatred of Englishmen who might "mingle the red crosses of the Union Jack with the piratical black flag of the Confederate States of America." France, he was sure, would unite her tricolor with the Stars and Stripes, nor would she forget what power it was that had in the past checked her advance at every turn, the power that "had hedged in all the fields of her glory" and had confined "an earlier Napoleon on St. Helena."[36]

Henry Adams shook his head in dismay. How could he hope to build up friendship with England? To his brother he wrote:

"Those noisy jackasses Clay and Burlingame . . . have done more harm here than their weak heads were worth a thousand times over."[37]

In more sober vein, John Lothrop Motley, the American historian who had spent much of his life abroad, joined the argument, writing "Causes of the Civil War in America" for the London

*Times.*[38] The war of words was soon taken up by Southern sympathizers resident in Paris. Edwin De Leon, one-time consul general to Egypt whence he had shipped a proud Arabian stallion[39] to Jefferson Davis, dashed into print. Davis liked De Leon's argument as well as his studhorse. The man might be valuable as a permanent propagandist for the South. Train, still working on his own, summed up the tongue-lashing in the *London American* on June 19, 1861:

"We must hang some new pictures on the wall, such as abolitionist England sitting affectionately on the lap of negro slavery. . . . Mr. Clay's athletic Western argument was brought out the more forcibly by the weakness of Mr. De Leon's Southern reply. . . . The *Times* rejoinder could not erase the crushing logic of the author of the Dutch Republic in his strong array of facts. Everyone reads the *Times,* and everybody knows how it has ignored the great North in its admiration for the little South. . . . The *Times* declared war, and England cheered—when the *Times* lays an egg, the nation cuckles [*sic*]."[40]

This battle of words in 1861 was only a prologue to the great contest in propaganda which Lincoln and Davis began a year later. Both Presidents had yet to learn the importance of European opinion. When Lincoln read reports of this preliminary skirmish he issued some innocent orders. Burlingame he dispatched as minister to China on the opposite side of the world only to hear, in time, wondrous tales of strife with shrewd Confederate agents over there. To the post in Austria, where Burlingame was not acceptable, Lincoln sent Motley. The Austrian Emperor had a brother, Maximilian, a poor nobleman looking for a home. If by chance the powers of Europe decided that some throne, perhaps Mexico, offered a good opportunity for the promising young man, Motley might be the first to hear of it and warn Lincoln or Seward.

Quiet was further restored to Europe by the departure of Clay for Russia, but St. Petersburg proved a poor substitute for Lexington. Clay could not long tolerate the monotony of being away from Kentucky. His first official act, after taking off his knife, was to write a long letter to the State Department asking for a military command back home.[41] Clay knew that two months would elapse before he could hope for a reply. During that time he sat night after night with his quill in hand, writing letter after letter by the light of the midnight sun. The State Department must have his ideas on the technique of war, the construction of iron ships, the beauties of Kentucky. General Scott, he reported solemnly, would no doubt subdue the rebellion, "stock, lock, and gun barrel." Yes, by the Etarnal! "Hook and line, bob and sinker."[42] Clay worried, too, about receiving money for his expenses so far from home. Clerks in Washington filed the letters away.

Between letters, Clay brooded over his loneliness. Czar Alexander II was absent in Poland. When the Little Father returned to his capital Clay was asked to present his credentials. After the ceremony he wrote Lincoln officially: "The Emperor is about my size and weight, grey eyes, auburn hair." Clay also told Lincoln that he favored His Majesty with a stump speech congratulating him for emancipating the serfs. "The Emperor seemed much gratified and really moved," Clay wrote. Russia and America, the Czar replied, "were bound together by a common sympathy in the common cause of emancipation." Clay remembered also that the Czar asked if England would interfere in the American war. Clay wrote Lincoln that he told His Majesty, "We did not care what she did, that her interference would tend to unite us the more—we fought the South with reluctance."[43]

In a later letter Clay told Lincoln about Prince Alexander Mikhailovich Gorchakov, the Minister of Foreign Affairs. He was a man of medium size, about sixty years old, wearing European dress, Clay said, with short hair, a little gray—shrewd and agreeable.[44] The Prince made it a point to seat visitors with their faces toward the window in order to detect the slightest change in their expressions while he sat with his face in shadow.[45]

On such notes Lincoln constructed his Russian policy, but fortunately the Czar's attitude was well known in Washington. Lincoln and Seward were both too busy to exchange banalities with Cassius Clay, but Secretary Welles, watching always from behind his thick whiskers, noted in his diary that Lincoln seated his cabinet with their faces toward the light and sat with his own in shadow.

On the streets of St. Petersburg, Cassius Clay's nostalgic eyes looked critically at the recently liberated serfs. Only a short time ago these poor people had been virtual slaves hired out by land-owners to work in the cities or act as house servants for resident noblemen. Clay noted the stupid, bestial features, the calm, illiterate eyes of the men, women and children, their love of colorful costumes, holidays, music. Certainly they had been as happy as Negro slaves in Kentucky. Human slavery seemed to press the features of all human beings, black or white, into the same mold. The great landowners and their foremen, with free-swinging whips, did not differ widely from American slaveholders. Cassius Clay knew the breed. Perhaps the grand dukes could furnish meat for his ready knife as the Southerners had done. Lincoln's minister to all the Russias spit on his whetstone.

Clay's baggage contained bowie knives for every occasion. For formal dress he had brought an eighteen-inch blade with pearl handle and an eagle on the haft. For street wear he preferred bone-handled knives. Before long, rumors of bloody affrays came to America from Russia.[46] A pretty mess for Lincoln! The American minister was reported to have been challenged repeatedly to duels. Having the right, according to the code, to select the weapons, Clay invariably chose bowie knives in a grapple. Pugnacious Muscovite swordsmen were beside themselves. The big American must be tricked into making the challenge. Then they could select rapiers—and *voilà!* Meester Clay would be skewered upon the field of honor, so! With this in mind two noblemen swaggered through St. Petersburg seeking the Kentuckian. They found him in a café. One of the Russians slapped Clay across the face with the gauntlet of his glove, then stood back prepared to receive the American's card in a challenge for a duel. "Cash" Clay leaped to his feet and with a fist, big and red as a Kentucky ham, he struck with the full force of his two hundred pounds, square on the nose of his antagonist. The expert swordsman went down with an over-turned table and a clatter of china. Clay stood for a moment challenging anyone else who cared to take up the fight. Then he sat down again to his dinner.[47] He was beginning to like Russia as he became better acquainted. Perhaps he had been hasty in writing

Lincoln for his recall. Strangely enough the Russian grand dukes also admired the American. Lincoln's appointment was a happy one.

The legation in Madrid, which Clay had declined, remained to be filled. Carl Schurz's speaking tour of the West was over. Lincoln ordered him to come and take the post. Schurz's new political boss, Seward, was an old political rival. Gossips said that Seward still dominated Lincoln's foreign policy. Schurz's meeting with him might tell the truth of the rumor. The German, a student at heart, prepared himself for the new mission by reading the State Department dispatches to Horatio Perry, Secretary of Legation in Madrid. Schurz noted that Seward had instructed Perry to make a sharp protest against the annexation of Santo Domingo, which the United States should "expect to maintain."[48] Well primed, Schurz called on Seward and asked him to be more specific. Did the administration wish to break off diplomatic relations in case Santo Domingo was retained? The Secretary replied that Schurz's actions must be confined to "protests."[49] So, Schurz mused, Seward's belligerent days are over. All thought of forcing a war on Spain is forgotten. Lincoln's policy dominated the administration at last.

After the interview Schurz stepped across to the White House to call on his friend the President. Lincoln offered him a chair. The tall, near-sighted German sat down and shook back his long hair. Lincoln looked at the hatchet-faced man with the stooped shoulders of a scholar and an ambition to lead light horse. The President smiled, then began the conversation by apologizing for his own ignorance. He had been able to devote "so little attention to foreign affairs" and felt the necessity of "studying up."[50] Lincoln hoped that the German would watch public opinion abroad and "whenever anything occurs to you that you want to tell me personally, or that you think I ought to know, you shall write me directly." Schurz squinted his weak blue eyes through his thick glasses at the President. Certainly, he concluded, Lincoln does not trust Secretary Seward.

Aristocratic Castilians received Carl Schurz with apprehension. Red republicans were not popular with the government in power. Horatio Perry arranged an introduction to the Queen and called on the appointed day at the new minister's lodgings to conduct him to the reception. Schurz appeared in evening clothes instead of embroidered court regalia. This was his first mistake. In the carriage the two men rehearsed the formalities of presentation. Schurz discovered that he had forgotten his letter of credence—his second mistake. There was no time to return. The minor catastrophe did not disturb successful revolutionist Schurz on his way to meet a Queen. He resolved on a bold stroke. A newspaper was folded carefully into an official envelope. On it Schurz inscribed, "Doña Isabella, Queen of Spain."[51] He then instructed Horatio Perry to explain to the Foreign Secretary the true contents of the envelope. The Queen, Schurz knew from careful study, was wont to receive letters of credence with Her Own Hand, then pass them to the Foreign Secretary to open with a flourish and read to the court—a boring procedure for everyone concerned. "You must whisper to the Foreign Secretary," Schurz told Perry, "to get the letter from the Queen as soon as possible. He can acknowledge it with a grand gesture and then omit the reading."

The republican diplomats chuckled over their proposed deception of the monarch and before long the carriage stopped at the palace door. The Americans walked inside. A guard of halberdiers in gorgeous medieval costumes guarded the foyer. Two of them spied Schurz's evening clothes. With a clash of arms the stairs were barred with crossed halberds. The Americans explained and gesticulated, displayed their identification papers—the envelope containing the newspaper. Finally Perry shouted to a flunky to run for the Master of Ceremonies. The halberdiers stood grim, stolid and unmoved. In a few moments an official in knee breeches came tripping down the stairs. With voluble Spanish he parted the halberds with his own delicate hands. The envoys were escorted into the hall of state where gaily dressed courtiers awaited the Queen. Never having been received by royalty, Carl Schurz was relieved to learn that the British minister would be introduced before him and thus serve as a model. In the meantime Horatio Perry called aside Don Saturnino Calderón Collantes, Minister of Foreign Affairs, and whispered to him about the missing letter. Saturnino nodded gravely. Soon a door was flung open. A brilliantly attired official shouted through the hall. The Queen! "A portly dame with a fat and unhandsome but good-natured looking face,"[52] Schurz noted and remembered.

The British minister stepped forward to be introduced. Schurz, a blackbird among the gay courtiers, watched with bright eyes. When his turn came he stepped forward, letter in hand. Delivering a speech in English, he handed the envelope to Her Majesty. The Queen held the letter in her jeweled hand and replied formally in Spanish. To Carl Schurz the speech seemed unnaturally long. At last she looked down at the letter as though to open it, then handed the envelope to Don Saturnino who bowed profoundly. Her Majesty then chatted for a few minutes in French and retired.

Carl Schurz's Castilian mission was not remarkable. The government could not be expected to sympathize with a republic and the radicals were disappointed because Lincoln did not declare a war against slavery. On the whole, Schurz's residence in Spain was as fruitless as Cassius Clay's in Russia. Both men could smell powder burning across the Atlantic and neither liked a life of diplomacy.[53] Schurz's dispatches disclosed an active mind fretting in the idleness of Old Spain. Unlike Clay, who wanted to come home at once—until he got acquainted—Schurz decided to stay until fall. Lodging in a picturesque castle, he described the extreme poverty of the lower classes, the brutality of bullfights. Always he had time to tell Lincoln how to run the government. It was the old story. Slavery must be abolished to get the wholehearted support of Europe.

Lincoln, with a first-class civil war getting hotter by the hour, had little time to answer Schurz's observations on domestic policy or to consider Clay's "hook and line, bob and sinker." As President he had instructed all his ministers to report the popular sentiment in their respective countries. These reports were important to his future policy, and the story told by all his ministers was much the same. Liberals in the monarchical countries favored the North as an example of the possible success of democracy. Conservatives, too, unless they had some ulterior motive, could not overlook the bad example of a successful revolution even if it were reactionary, and none could stomach slavery. To the State Department reassuring messages came from all over Europe. Jacob Haldeman wrote from Scandinavia: "In Sweden the public voice, represented by a free press, is clearly and emphatically in favour of my government, and views secession as a causeless rebellion."[54] The American minister at Turin wrote that Piedmont and the House of Savoy were "entirely by sympathy on the side of the President."[55] Even in Spain, the *Iberia,* a radical sheet fined many times for its political utterances, began in July to translate and publish Lincoln's speeches.[56] Germany divided on the Civil War along lines similar to America's—the great landowners and army officers on one side, the middle class, bankers, commercial groups and lower urban classes on the other. German bankers held American bonds and with them a real stake in the Northern government. The common people had many relatives in the Northern Army. National unity had been a German aspiration for over a generation. Such aspirations in America were understood. Norman Judd in Berlin, annoyed by men seeking enlistment and transportation to America, posted on the doors of his office: "This is a Legation of the United States, and not a recruiting-office."[57]

From Austria, Motley wrote that there was more interest in the Civil War and more sympathy for the North in Vienna than in any other city in Europe.[58] Austria was a federal state. The principle of secession challenged the framework of their government. Lincoln looked over the accumulated testimony of all the ministers. Great Britain alone seemed the most loath to take sides with the North. Lincoln knew that America's experiment in government threatened England more than any other government in Europe—the bonds were closer. The British Parliamentary system was more apt to be affected. The awful truth that Northern victory meant more democracy in England shuddered up and down the spines of the "best people" in their country houses.

Lincoln decided to let things take their course, seek their own level, run down. Seward, never happy unless he was writing something, if only another letter to contradict one written the day before, sent a private note to Adams in London. Every nation in Europe, he said, except England, has expressed to the President a wish for the preservation of the Union. "Liberal Constitutional England is now the only favorer of Slavery!"[59]

# VI. *They're Having Fits in the White House Tonight*

"ONE war at a time. One war at a time!" Lincoln murmured[1] to himself as he mused on a long dispatch written on sheets of foolscap. As the President read and reread the manuscript he crossed out words, wrote others, made marginal suggestions, added phrases that took the sting from Seward's words. The dispatch, dated May 21, 1861, was important to Lincoln's domestic as well as to his foreign policy. It marked the beginning of the end of Seward's struggle to bolster his waning prestige as the leader of a "foreign war" minority. The dispatch was addressed to Charles Francis Adams, instructing him categorically to sever diplomatic relations with Great Britain if her government continued to have intercourse of any kind with the Southern commissioners.[2] Lincoln paused. Reading further he noted that Seward left nothing to the discretion of his minister. The ultimatum must be read to Lord John Russell word for word. Lincoln drew his pencil through this sentence. In the margin he wrote that Adams might consider the tenor of the note a personal memorandum of what the United States hoped to accomplish. Reduced to this form, with all its teeth drawn, the communication still remained so radical that Adams was shocked when he received it. Henry wrote his brother in America on June 11, 1861:

"A dispatch arrived yesterday from Seward, so arrogant in tone and so extraordinary and unparalleled in its demands that it leaves no doubt in my mind that our Government wishes to face a war with all Europe. . . .

"I do not think that I exaggerate the danger. I believe that our Government means to have a war with England; I believe that England knows it and is preparing for it; and I believe it will come within two months—if at all."[3]

Lord Lyons also felt sure that war was inevitable and he warned the home office. Lincoln in the meantime turned to the problem of

getting Seward out of another tangle—his proposal to join the
Paris Convention of 1856. The powers had taken Seward's offer
seriously and appeared to be going forward with a project to include
the United States. To block the North from using privateers and
allow the South to use them would be a real catastrophe. Seward's
offer must be reversed, but how could it be done without making a
fool of the Secretary of State? Before Lincoln decided on a plan the
smoldering Civil War broke into flames. For a week a rebel flag
had been flying at Alexandria. Lincoln could see it with a telescope
from the White House. Soldiers were sent across the Potomac to
surround the town. Colonel Ellsworth, Lincoln's Springfield
friend, went directly to the rebel city with his Fire Zouaves. No
Confederate soldiers were encountered. The flag was found to be
flying from the top of the Marshall House. Ellsworth tore it from
the staff with his own hands. As he came down the hotel stairs the
proprietor stepped out, raised a double-barreled shotgun and fired.
The young colonel's companions killed the man instantly but it
was too late.

Ellsworth's death was the first of consequence in the Civil War.
He lay in state in the East Room at the White House. A solemn
march was composed for him by a member of the Marine Band,
Antonio Sousa, an immigrant whose seven-year-old son John
Philip Sousa showed unmistakable signs of musical appreciation.
Ellsworth's companions presented the rebel flag to Mrs. Lincoln.
Young Ellsworth's death cut the President deeply. He was responsible for bringing him to Washington. At the funeral a great
armchair was placed before the casket for General Scott. When
the impressive service was completed, aides helped Scott to his feet.
His chair fell backward with a crash. Willie and Tad Lincoln,
the imps, had perched on the chair back to see in the coffin. Staff
members hurried them from the room.

Before Lincoln's heartache passed away, word from Europe disclosed that adherence to the Declaration of Paris had become doubly
disadvantageous. The British Parliament had unwittingly played
into the North's hands. No vestige of advantage remained now for
the Federal government in that international agreement. The Parliamentary action—or more properly failure to act—was reported by
Henry Adams and Charlie Wilson. They had learned that a resolu-

tion to recognize the Confederacy was calendared. On May 27, 1861, both of them attended the session.[4] The young men, politically wise, studied the ruddy faces of the British lawmakers. Palmerston and John Bright were both present—two bulls grumbling across a partition fence. Sitting beside Lord Palmerston on the government bench, Lord John Russell appeared as indifferent as a little white hen in the stall of a puffing ox. Near by, Gladstone sat with countenance of thunder and Zeus-like brow—a left-wing Tory in a coalition government that needed the votes he could command. Americans who knew Gladstone said that he possessed a bell's tongue, furious earnestness and a willingness to champion any principle for the advancement of himself. Richard Cobden was also present. As a liberal he might be expected to favor the Northern democracy but could he be counted on? The leading passion of his life was international free trade—a commercial policy the Confederacy favored, while Lincoln's party planned a tariff on English goods. One other man attracted the Americans—Bulwer-Lytton, the author. Henry Adams watched him the way a young writer looks at a great master.

The spokesman of the bloc, intent on passing the resolution to recognize the South, was W. H. Gregory, an Irish landlord and also a free trader. Indeed the free-trade element in English politics threatened to be dangerous for the Northern cause. Henry Adams knew that Gregory sympathized financially and socially with the planters. Their agricultural problems were his problems. Shortly before Lincoln's election Gregory had traveled through the South. He knew its actual situation as well as any man in Parliament. Impatient of the mobocracy that had come to power in America, Gregory deemed the Civil War a struggle to preserve property and the landlord's way of life. Like a true conservative, he was cautious. He did not want to offer a resolution, have it defeated, and thus expose the weakness of his following. As a "feeler" of party strength Sir John Ramsden tried a speech favoring the Confederacy. To the assembled statesmen he announced that in America "the great republican bubble had burst." Loud cheers from the Tory benches encouraged him.[5] Gregory felt confident.

Under the gallery Charlie Wilson, who had been adept in creating artificial applause for Lincoln, might have told Gregory the danger

of counting too much on noise. Palmerston, too, seemed to be
undecided on the genuineness of the cheering. He appeared to be
napping in his seat—a sure sign that he was mentally alert. Then
he nodded a signal. His party should not reply. Did Palmerston
feel so weak, was his majority so small, that he dared not make the
Southern question a party issue, or did he want Gregory to present
his motion and have it killed so dead the opposition would have to
reorganize on different lines? The Americans wondered. They
noticed also that Gregory saw the danger and hesitated. "Old
Pam" seemed almost asleep, breathing heavily, a poker player
daring the board to call the turn. Gregory decided to let the opportunity pass. The Queen's proclamation of neutrality remained.
Both Northern and Southern warships were denied the privilege of
bringing prizes into British ports.[6] France, Holland and other
countries followed Britain's lead. Thus the South had no port
where she could send prizes. The Federal government could employ
her own North Atlantic ports. This was the situation that made
adherence to the Declaration of Paris doubly disadvantageous.
Seward realized that his offer must be countermanded at once. But
how? Lincoln as yet had suggested no solution. Seward must get
out of his impossible situation alone. He had asked specifically for
permission to join the convention and the powers might send their
authorized ministers any day now.

On the morning of June 15, 1861, the Secretary of State sat at
his desk when the page announced, "The British minister is here to
see you, sir, and the French minister also."

Seward knew that the time had come. Not only might these
foreign ministers deliver the articles on the unpalatable convention but the fact that they came together intimated that the two
nations were acting in accord.

Lincoln's and Seward's whole foreign policy was based on keeping them separated, to divide and conquer. "Which came first?"
Seward asked.

"Lord Lyons, sir, but they say they both want to see you together."

Seward paused a moment, thinking fast. "Show them both into
the Assistant Secretary's room, and I will come in presently."

The two men were ushered into Frederick Seward's room and

seated on a sofa. In a few minutes the Secretary of State appeared, waving his arms in his ill-fitting clothes. His disheveled hair stood up like a cockatoo's crest on his head; his thin, wrinkling eyelids blinked over his wise macaw eyes. "No, no, no!" he screamed. "This will never do. I cannot see you in that way."

The ministers rose to meet him in confusion. "At least," said one of them, "you will allow us to state the object of our visit?"

"No!" Seward screeched. "We must start right about it, whatever it is. M. Mercier, will you do me the favour of coming to dine with me this evening? Then we can talk over your business at leisure. And if Lord Lyons will step into my room with me now, we will discuss what he has to say to me."

"If you refuse to see us together——" began the Frenchman with a shrug.

But Seward cut him off. "Certainly I do refuse to see you together, though I will see either of you separately with pleasure, here or elsewhere."[7]

Later, when he was alone with each of the ministers, Seward said that negotiations on the Convention of Paris had been transferred from Washington to the ministers in the field. He did not add that he had instructed the ministers to make agreements as ambiguous as possible, leaving loopholes for argument in case the North might need to employ privateers. Nor did he say that the involved instructions would probably consume considerable time in negotiation until the whole subject might die from old age and exhaustion.[8]

After the crisis had passed, Seward said, with a twinkle in his eyes, that the most impudent men in history were Hernando Cortez, Lord Lyons and Henri Mercier, the first when he set fire to the ships that had brought his handful of men to Mexico and then set out to capture the kingdom of the Montezumas, and the other two when they came together "to announce an agreement between the British Government and the Emperor as to the course they should jointly pursue in regard to the American question"[9]—a typical Seward superlative. The Secretary of State was undoubtedly resourceful, but he appeared to have little understanding of foreign affairs.

Lincoln realized that a scholar was needed in the State Department, someone familiar with international law and the history of Europe. Letters were constantly coming to Seward in languages that none of the clerks could read. Adam Gurowski, a Polish count, was recommended. Besides reading sixteen languages he was familiar with foreign court procedure and could advise Seward on customary usages. In Paris he had been a favorite of Lafayette, so it was said. Moving to America in 1849, he became acquainted with the New England intellectuals—Prescott, Ticknor, Longfellow, Lowell, Parker and Sumner. President Everett appointed him to teach jurisprudence at Harvard. Gurowski contributed fluently to the newspapers. His *Slavery in History,* published in 1860, was the product of ten years' research.[10] His opinion of the peculiar institution satisfied the most exacting Garrisonian. With the objective viewpoint of a European economist he could write:

"The Africo-Americans are the true producers of the Southern wealth—cotton, rice, tobacco, etc. When emancipated and transformed into small farmers, these laborious men will increase and ameliorate the culture of the land; and they will produce by far more when the white shams and drones shall be taken out of their way. In the South, bristling with Africo-American villages, will almost disappear fillibusterism, murder, and the bowie knife, and other supreme manifestations of Southern *chivalrous high-breeding.*"[11]

The count first distinguished himself in Washington by joining Cassius Clay's Strangler Guard and then refusing to accept a certificate of service signed by Lincoln, because he had done no fighting.[12] A few days later he informed the President confidentially that the French Emperor planned to follow Spain's example in Santo Domingo. The count's knowledge of foreign intrigue in America was uncanny. He warned Lincoln about a French spy in New Orleans. Then, in a strictly confidential letter, he explained, after it was too late, that closing the Confederate ports instead of blockading them would not have forced England and France to recognize the belligerency of the South.[13] Lincoln decided to employ him. Ostensibly the count was hired "to explore the Continental newspapers for matter interesting to the American government, and to furnish the Secretary of State, when called upon, with opinions upon diplomatic questions."[14]

Gurowski came to work in a broad-brimmed, bell-shaped hat and a long sky-blue veil. Blue goggles hid the fact that he had but one eye. A bright red flannel waistcoat hung from his rotund stomach like an apron. Seward found him argumentative, conceited, quick to detect a weakness in a new acquaintance and take advantage of it with sadistic pleasure. Having learned English from books, he talked with an accent hard to understand. His knowledge was amazing. The pedigree of every diplomat in Washington was on his tongue's tip. Lord Lyons, he said, was the son of a commoner. His uncle was a farmer near Chicago. Henri Mercier, the son of a French consul, was born in Baltimore. Don Tassara, a journalist, had come to the surface in a Spanish revolution. Stoeckl was no baron. He owed his position to his clever American wife. In Russia he was not recognized socially. Bertinatti had been educated for the priesthood, had tried journalism for a while. His good looks commended him as a diplomat. Baron Gerolt was an engineer who had served as director of an English mining company in Mexico. Edward, Count Piper of Sweden, with the sweet face and Cupid's-bow lips, was the only old-line aristocrat of the lot.[15] Being "promiscuous" aristocrats themselves, Gurowski said, the diplomats considered the slaveholders to be gentlefolk, thus giving themselves "an aristocratic perfume." Seward could take this for what it was worth. Surely he and Lincoln could hold their own with men like these. Before long it was whispered in Washington that Gurowski's own background was not so brilliant as it had at first appeared. His noble birth proved true. So did his intimate association with the New England intellectuals. However, the best Boston families had received him with condescension as an odd character. An exciting rumor that he was a Russian spy paled under cold Bostonian logic. What was there in the parlors of the literati to spy upon? Gurowski had been dismissed from Harvard because his accent was unintelligible to the students. His missing eye was due to a childhood accident instead of a duel as some supposed.

After Lincoln appointed him to the State Department, a Washington journalist remembered an experience with the eccentric fellow and published it unsigned. Some years before, so he said, he had called at the count's apartment in Boston. Gurowski received him stark naked, a big hideous head on a potbelly and spindly legs. Torrents of broken English rattled from his lips. The amazed reporter slowly became aware of the fact that his host was lecturing him on medieval history, establishing a point that had been questioned in a previous argument. The count talked too fast to have time to dress. He held his underwear in his hands. Unabashed, Gurowski conjured premises for his harangue and built his argument. He drove home point after point with a flourish of his drawers for emphasis. A maid knocked at the door. "Come in," shouted Gurowski, without ceasing to elaborate his contention. Unperturbed by her horrified retreat the nobleman continued to add source and quotation to prove his evidence. Another knock was heard at the door. Again the count shouted, "Come in." This time the intruder was a caller. Gurowski waved him to a seat without stopping his discourse. Finally, as dinnertime approached, the Pole retired to his dressing room but now and again he padded back partly dressed to add a new citation to his theme.[16]

A man with Gurowski's power of concentration could not be expected to understand the slow mind of Abraham Lincoln. The Count pronounced him a stupid fellow, a *bête*. The diplomats of Europe, he said, were all making fun of Seward's dispatches and looked on him as a "clever charlatan." Secretary Welles he called "Neptune-Methuselah-Van Winkle."[17] Scornfully he told friends that he himself had been employed "to read the German newspapers, and keep Seward from making a fool of himself." Browsing through the Department library, he discovered that Phillimore's work on international law did not have the pages cut.[18] No wonder the President misunderstood the implications of blockade!

Gurowski was not the only brainy man in Washington who believed that President Lincoln had displayed his ignorance of international law by the wording of his blockade proclamation. Pompous doctrinaires were slow to attribute any subtlety to a country lawyer from Illinois. As a matter of fact Lincoln had Phillimore's work in his law library in Springfield and the volume on blockade showed signs of being read. Had Lincoln studied the possibility of ordering a blockade, before he went to Washington? Could he by chance have purposely worded his proclamation in such a way that he would be obliged to modify it later and by so doing establish loopholes which might serve to defend some unforeseen exigency? The diplomats argued this question over their coffee and wine.

To meet the war emergency Lincoln called a special session of Congress to meet July 4, 1861. Perhaps the President's message to the solons would give some clue to his peculiar interpretation of a blockade. The diplomatic corps looked forward to his explanation. William H. Russell made it a point to be back from his tour of the country to report it.

Washington had turned into a military camp since Russell had left it eleven weeks ago. Bugle calls and the tramp of marching men and the sharp orders of command awoke the city at dawn each morning. Long lines of white-topped commissariat wagons trundled endlessly down the dirt streets and rattled across the cobbles on Pennsylvania Avenue. Hundreds of white tents had arisen like mushrooms in the green fields around Washington. In the heart of the city, men crowded the streets, stirred up clouds of July dust. Sweating horses were gray with it. Hot human faces, opaque as ripe peaches, flowed along the crowded sidewalks. Here and there the bright pompon on a military shako bobbed among the stovepipe hats. On street corners farm boys in uniform gaped open-mouthed at the unfinished dome of the Capitol. Cavalry columns clattered by, the horses' hoofs strangely silent on the dirt streets. Women in hoops round as cupcakes stood at intersections, waiting for a gap in the traffic. Now and again they lifted their farthingales with mitted fingers and darted like covies of startled quail before advancing columns of horsemen.

Up at the White House, Lincoln in his office on the second floor put the finishing touches on his message for the special session of Congress. From the window he could look across the still waters of the Potomac where skeins of smoke marked the camp sites of his assembled army. In the dust of the city below him red, white and blue bunting draped on the fronts of brick houses along Pennsylvania Avenue had become almost colorless with grime. The civil and military population were engrossed with personal affairs. No one except the lawmakers, the lobbyists and the diplomats showed any interest in Congress.

William H. Russell, with notebook in his pocket, climbed the hot steps to the Capitol. With relief he emerged on the hill in the clear air above the ceiling of dust. In the subdued light of the legislative chambers he noted that the galleries were only partly filled. When his eyes became accustomed to the room he saw M. Mercier watching the solons intently. The French minister sat with his intelligent and eager bearded face between both hands.[19] At the appointed time John Hay brought the President's message into the room. A clerk read it perfunctorily. The diplomats listened to the droning voice. Lincoln began by summarizing his actions since his inauguration. He corrected the inconsistency of declaring a blockade in "pursuance of the law of nations" against a domestic insurrection, stating: "A proclamation was issued for closing the ports of the insurrectionary districts by proceedings in the nature of blockade." Shrewd way to justify his international interpretation of blockade and apply it to a district in revolt!

The diplomats noted, too, that Lincoln had a debater's gift for making the most of the case before him. His study of international opinion had just begun, and an appeal to the antislavery sentiment of Europe was denied him by his constitutional oath as well as the proslavery border states. Other grounds must be found to delay European intervention. With the acumen of a lawyer preparing a brief for a jury, Lincoln played upon the point which, if properly argued, might influence hardheaded European businessmen to take an interest in a war between abstract principles of "State rights" and federalism. Lincoln was obviously hoping that the foreign ministers in the gallery would transmit to European bondholders his query:

"If one State may secede, so may another; and when all shall have seceded, none is left to pay the debts. Is this quite just to creditors? Did we notify them of this sage view of ours when we borrowed their money?"[20]

Lincoln knew that his message would reach London at a time when investors were reading that the Confederate issue of 10,-000,000 sterling in twenty-year bonds was already found insufficient for the South's needs.[21] Let bankers beware of this or future issues. With this warning to investors Lincoln turned to the idealists, the masses, the underprivileged—people he understood. The American Civil War, he said, "presents to the whole family of man the question whether a constitutional republic or democracy—a government of the people by the same people—can or cannot maintain its territorial integrity against its own domestic foes. It presents the question whether discontented individuals, too few in numbers to control administration according to organic law in any case, can always, upon the pretenses made in this case, or on any other pretenses, or arbitrarily without any pretense, break up their government, and thus practically put an end to free government upon the earth. It forces us to ask: 'Is there, in all republics, this inherent and fatal weakness?' 'Must a government, of necessity, be too strong for the liberties of its own people, or too weak to maintain its own existence?' "[22]

Reviewing for Congress the attitude of foreign powers toward the Civil War, Lincoln said that the government's "forebearance" had led some nations to expect an early destruction of the Union but now "a general sympathy with the country is manifested throughout the world."[23]

This was the first time Lincoln had referred to foreign relations in a message. Did it mark the beginning of his appreciation of the importance of foreign nations in the American Civil War? From now on could the diplomats expect Lincoln's attention to this phase of his executive duty to increase as Seward's diminished?

After the President's message had been read, Russell left the Capitol and drove from the clear air on the hill down into the hot July dust that hung like gossamer above the city. Emerging again at the State Department, he called on Seward. Russell was not shunted into the Assistant Secretary's room as Lyons and Mercier had been. Instead he was ushered to the Secretary. A great change had come over Seward. The cockatoo's plumage showed signs of molting. The slow, easy discipline of Lincoln's methods had taken the crackle from his raucous voice, but his haggard eyes showed the determination of a gamecock.

Russell sat back on the slippery horsehair upholstery. Noting the change in the man before him, he spoke of the change that had come over Washington since his last visit; of the great army surrounding the capital. A military despotism, he reflected, would destroy the democracy it was mustered to preserve. He said aloud, "But, Mr. Seward, has not this great exhibition of strength been attended by some circumstances calculated to inspire apprehension that liberty in the Free States may be impaired?"[24]

Seward could not answer this abstraction any better than he could solve the knotty problem of blockade. He did not attempt it and Russell went away without a story.

Outside in the streets and in the army camps Russell found no indication that individual liberty had been given up by the democratic army of boys from farms and factories who were eager only to fight "aristocrats and slaveholders." South of the Potomac Russell knew the Southerners were also assembling, contemptuous of Northern tradesmen.

Every day now Lincoln worked from seven in the morning until late at night, with political placemen, with insatiable office seekers, and with organization problems for his army—usual and unusual civil and military affairs. Only occasionally did he spare time to be plagued with foreign policy and his avowed "proceedings in the nature of blockade." America, he knew, had been a neutral in many European wars and in all of them had complained about Britain's so-called "paper blockades" which interfered with American commerce. Since the conference of 1856 international law had prescribed that a blockade must be really effective to be binding. Lord Stowell had defined "effective" as an arch of ships around the mouth of the prohibited port, "where, if the arch fails in any one part, the Blockade itself fails altogether."[25]

The definition pleased American shippers at that time but now a "paper blockade" was all that Lincoln could maintain. The British interpretation was beyond anything he could command, yet strangely enough Britain did not hold America to Lord Stowell's definition. Instead she accepted the "paper blockade" in spite of the fact that it was against her own immediate interests. Without doubt Britannia, old and wise, was taking the long view. She did not intend to establish a precedent that would plague her in more vital wars to come. Or perhaps, as Seward maintained, England was really afraid that a war with America would start a European conflict.

To make the blockade "dangerous," Lincoln employed almost any boat that would float while Northern yards built suitable craft. The Confederates, on their side, owned but one vessel, a 500-ton commercial steamer, the *Sumter,* commanded by Raphael Semmes, a dashing Washingtonian with a wax-tipped mustache like that of Napoleon III.[26] The *Sumter* was blockaded for over two months in the delta below New Orleans by the Federal warship *Brooklyn.* One day Semmes saw the Yankee on the horizon chasing a distant sail. He decided to make a dash for the open sea. Putting on full steam, his little vessel churned across the bar. Almost at once the *Brooklyn* spied him, turned, and the race began. Hour after hour the two ships matched each other's speed. Semmes noticed to his dismay that the *Brooklyn* was growing larger, gaining on him, slowly but surely as she came across the saucer of the sea. Then Semmes resorted to a trick of navigation that he hoped would save the day. The *Brooklyn* was using sails to help her engines. Semmes changed his course, steering so close into the wind that sails became useless. The great sheets on his pursuer flapped dismally, checking the *Brooklyn's* speed. Semmes noted that they were being hauled down. Having reduced her adversary to this rigging, the *Sumter* soon slipped away across the horizon with a grinning crew and a captain curling the waxed ends of his mustache—the first Confederate warship to get to sea. Three days later she overtook and burned her first prize.[27] Almost daily, dispatches reached Washington stating that more vessels had been destroyed.

Excited merchants pounded on Lincoln's desk: send enough warships to catch the enemy. Lincoln replied with funny stories. The frantic men accused him of being trivial. Lincoln let them talk. He had no intention of lifting the blockade. He planned to strangle the Confederacy along the sea, then give a quick knockout blow on land. The Northern 'Army had now mobilized around Washington to strike Richmond—now the Confederate capital. The Southerners could not resist long if all manufactured goods—munitions of war—were shut off from abroad.

Lincoln learned that other Confederate ships were in the offing. A New Yorker with an intimate knowledge of the sea and the technicalities of maritime and international law had arrived in London. His head was large, his hair thin with a curl plastered carefully on the center of his bald forehead. His mustache and beard were brushed away from his mouth. The first impression he made on strangers was one of gentility and correctness in dress. He called at the offices of the biggest shipbuilding firms in England. His card disclosed his name to be James Dunwody Bulloch, the retired Navy man who operated a steamship line to the South and whose sister married a Roosevelt. Bulloch held a commission from Jefferson Davis to negotiate the construction of vessels[28]—not for the Confederacy, which was prohibited by the neutrality proclamation, but for private parties. When built these ships could sail to Southern ports, run through Lincoln's blockade and be hastily converted into ships of war. Thus transformed they could turn on Lincoln's wooden blockaders and scatter them like spray. Shipbuilders did not ask embarrassing questions of such a good customer.

The first month Bulloch was in England he closed a contract for construction of the *Oreto,* ostensibly a merchant ship for a Palermo firm, in reality a war vessel later known as the *Florida.* Next Bulloch visited the Birkenhead Ironworks.[29] He was introduced to the Messrs. Laird and with them negotiated for the construction of another ship, later notorious as the *Alabama.* The South Carolina banking house, Fraser, Trenholm and Company, supplied funds through their Liverpool branch.

Rumors of the contracts came to Lincoln as he shook hands with lines of tourists, job seekers, politicians asking favors, officers hinting for promotion. At least a year would be required to build these vessels and Lincoln hoped to end the war long before that time. He had put General Irvin McDowell in active charge of the Army, under Scott's direction. On July 16, 1861, the citizen soldiers marched across the Potomac to disperse the rebels in Virginia. All day long men in uniform tramped through the streets of Washington. Democracy under arms, the hope of common people around the world marching out to crush slavery.

The spectacle thrilled sixteen-year-old Julia Taft with conflicting emotions. A friend of the Lincoln family, nicknamed "the Flibbertigibbet who flies when she walks," Julia saw everything with her bright eyes. Still a wondering schoolgirl, she remembered later that martial music ebbed and flowed through the streets with the passing regiments. The Germans, she said, stepped quickly to *"Ach, du lieber Augustin."* Scotch Highlanders from New York marched by in kilts, with bagpipes skirling. Irishmen carried green banners beside the Stars and Stripes. French emigrants in zouave uniforms, white gaiters twinkling below red culottes, made Pennsylvania Avenue ring with the stirring cadence of *"La Marseillaise"*[30]—*"Aux armes, citoyens!"*

Thirty thousand patriots thumped across the Potomac bridges. Congressmen with their ladies, lunch baskets and bottles of wine followed in carriages. All the gigs, hacks and saddle horses in Washington were hired by merrymakers eager to see the rebels routed—constitutional government upheld.

The prospect of a decisive action enlivened the foreign legations. William H. Russell prepared to join the throng and get another story. Before leaving he reported that the diplomats were unable to maintain their professional calm. M. Mercier "is moved by a vivacious interest." Stoeckl, the Russian minister, "becomes more animated as the time approaches when he sees the fulfilment of his prophecies at hand." The Spanish minister Tassara "cannot be indifferent to occurrences which bear so directly on the future of Spain in Western seas."[31] In the confusion, Russell wrote in his diary on July 18, 1861:

"On my way to dinner at the Legation I met the President crossing Pennsylvania Avenue, striding like a crane in a bulrush swamp among the great blocks of marble, dressed in an oddly cut suit of gray, with a felt hat on the back of his head, wiping his face with a red pocket-handkerchief. He was evidently in a hurry, on his way to the White House, where I believe a telegraph has been established."[32]

Only the day before, as though nothing were happening, the British government had written to the State Department proposing a joint commission to be established by Great Britain, France and the United States for the protection of the fisheries off the coast of Newfoundland and Labrador. Such international questions would have to wait until after the impending battle. On July 21 distant cannonading could be heard plainly at the White House. Lincoln hurried to the War Department. The telegraph station had been installed there, not in the White House. Seward, Cameron, Chase, Welles and Bates all came in. A map of northern

Virginia was spread on the table. Colored pins showed the order of the regiments. Old General Scott drew up his chair, ready to explain the reports as they came in.

Down at the front a young Scotsman named Andrew Carnegie, with a gift for organization, had charge of mounted couriers instructed to bring the news to the wire head at Fairfax Courthouse.[33]

The wires began to tick. Reports stated that the two armies had met. Scott arranged the pins. The next wire announced that the rebel lines had given way. The statesmen looked at each other and smiled, then listened again to the ticking instrument. The Northern troops advanced to position after position. Scott moved up the pins. A victory was assured. The cabinet members went back to their offices in high spirits. They could now discuss appointments to the fisheries commission. In the afternoon no marked advances were reported. Then the dispatches ceased. Was this a sign of victory? The long silence made Lincoln nervous. A sudden ticking on the receiver brought all the men who had remained to their feet. The telegrapher spelled out the message. "O-u-r a-r-m-y i-s r-e-t-r-e-a-t-i-n-g."[34] The sudden reverse was overpowering. The men walked out of the room silently. They wanted to be by themselves. The telegraph operators jotted down later messages alone. Lincoln came back a dozen times during the evening. The news got worse and worse. The Northern Army was reported to be in a panic, with Confederate cavalrymen cutting down retreating soldiers the way farm boys club rabbits when they jump from a woodpile. Next, word came through that the enemy's vanguard was forming for an attack on Washington. Lincoln strode from the room in despair. Where was General Scott? Lincoln found him asleep in his chair. His strength had been overtaxed by listening to the telegraph all day.[35] The President looked at the sagging features, then stepped out of the room into the night, a lonely man.

Down in the city the streets were ominously silent. Heavy clouds rose rapidly and obscured the moon. Lights blazed in all the windows along Pennsylvania Avenue. A chill of trepidation pervaded the atmosphere. Shortly before midnight W. H. Russell galloped across the Long Bridge into town. His horse's hoofs echoed in the ghastly silence. A sentry challenged him. "Stranger, have you been to the fight?" Soldiers, civilians and women crowded around the horseman for news. Russell spurred away. He had a dispatch to write for England. At the livery stable Russell returned his mount. The liveryman was in high spirits, hilariously unconcerned about pay for his horses. "Such news! such news!" said he, rubbing his hands. "Twenty thousand of them killed and wounded! Maybe they're not having fits in the White House tonight!"[36]

Russell went at once to his lodgings to write up the disaster. In a few minutes he heard a knock at the door. Lord Lyons' servant called, requesting him to come to the legation. The correspondent declined. He must get his dispatch ready for the Boston mail.

General Scott, blinking, tired out, a virtual invalid, woke up and was told the news. He ordered sentries on all the bridges to stop the retreating soldiers. Let them pile up along the south bank of the Potomac. In the morning he would reorganize them and make a last stand to defend the capital. At dawn it was raining. Lincoln could see from his office window unhappy groups of men huddled on the bank, drenched, mud-caked and miserable, drinking, looking fearfully toward the South. The magnitude of the disaster was reported by senators and other men of dignity who were passed into the city. Congressman Ely of New York was a prisoner of war. The enemy cavalry might arrive at any moment.

Fortunately for the North, the Battle of Bull Run disorganized the victors almost as much as it did the vanquished. No attack was made on Washington. In foreign lands the spectacle of military incompetence on both sides lowered American prestige. The fact that no one was killed in the bombardment of Sumter coupled with the precipitate stampede from Bull Run made Europeans question the tales of American ferocity.[37] Britishers complained that the Federals had dishonored the common heritage of England. Democracy and an intermingling of immigrant races, they said, had weakened Anglo-Saxon stamina and character.[38] Londoners looked forward to Russell's dispatches and read them with wonder. The battlefield, he wrote, was "strewed with coats, blankets, firelocks, cooking tins, caps, belts, bayonets" but no dead soldiers. Then he described the retreat:

"The scene on the road had now assumed an aspect which has not a parallel in any description I have ever read. Infantry soldiers on mules and draught horses, with the harness clinging to their heels, as much frightened as their riders; negro servants on their masters' chargers; ambulances crowded with unwounded soldiers; wagons swarming with men who threw out the contents in the road to make room, grinding through a shouting, screaming mass of men on foot, who were literally yelling with rage at every halt."

To his friend John Bigelow he wrote:

"The world will only see in it all, the failure of republican institutions in time of pressure as demonstrated by all history—that history which America vainly thought she was going to set right and re-establish on new grounds and principles."[39]

When the London papers reached America a remonstrance was raised. Seward stigmatized Russell as "a foreigner who perverts our hospitality to shelter himself in writing injurious publications against us for the foreign press." Newspaper reporters set to work to make the Englishman a scapegoat. *Harper's Weekly* discovered that "Dr. Russell" had recently been arrested in Illinois for shooting prairie chickens on Sunday.[40] Other journals announced that the Britisher could not have seen the rout he described. By his own allegations he beat the retreat back to Washington. Englishmen did not understand the American sense of humor. George Francis Train was also misunderstood when at a lecture at Hanley he reported himself as saying:

"At Bull Run the great fact was proved that I have always failed to convince Englishman [*sic*] that the Americans were not troubled with the gout. . . . In charity to our troops that moved backward faster than the laws of brave men allow, I believe that they thought that some of the rebel army had got behind them, so they rushed back to the attack. (Loud laughter and oh.) Munchausen Russell was the first to get to Washington in order to give an eyewitness picture of a battle that he not only never saw, but was not within some miles of. (Hear, hear.) Like the hound sent to clear the field of wolves, the latest report was, by the old farmer, who said they were going about forty miles an hour: but if anything the dog was a leetle ahead!"[41]

Americans laughed at Russell but the joke was expensive. It

lost forever the friendship of the turtle-headed correspondent—a loss that Lincoln could ill afford.

All the diplomatic advantages which Lincoln had established since his inauguration were wiped away by the defeat at Bull Run. Seward's threat to fight the world mocked him now. The Secretary of State had received two crushing blows in four months. First he had learned that Lincoln would not let him run the administration. Now his boast to "wrap the world in flames" turned to ashes in his loose mouth. Demoralized soldiers and citizens thronged the streets around the State Department and sat disconsolately in Lafayette Square. Seward, versatile always, pulled the chair up to his desk and wrote a dispatch to be sent to all foreign ministers for their information.

"You will receive the account of a deplorable reverse of our arms at Manassas. For a week or two that event will elate the friends of the insurgents in Europe, as it confounded and bewildered the friends of the Union here for two or three days. The shock, however, has passed away, producing no other results than a resolution stronger and deeper than ever, to maintain the Union, and a prompt and effective augmentation of the forces for that end. The heart of the country is sound. Its temper is now more favourable to the counsels of deliberation and wisdom. The lesson that war cannot be waged successfully without wisdom as well as patriotism has been received at a severe cost, but perhaps it was necessary."[42]

After finishing this circular and handing it to his clerks to copy manifold, Seward began another letter, very confidential, to Sanford in Brussels. The minister to Belgium was requested to cross France at once, take ship to the little island of Caprera out in the Mediterranean, find Garibaldi, the Italian Liberator, get him to come to America and accept high rank in the republican army. Democracy was a world concept and no stone to strengthen its structure must be left unturned.

# VII. *Dictators and Soldiers of Fortune*

THE Union Army was routed at Bull Run on July 21, 1861. On July 27 Lincoln opened negotiations[1] with the Italian revolutionist, Giuseppe Garibaldi. The soldier of fortune was well known in America, having been popularized by Orville Victor for Adams & Beedle, an enterprising firm experimenting with "dime novels." In paperback publications the Italian's picturesque life had been written with a glamour that endeared him to the hearts of adults learning to read.

Garibaldi started his career as a revolutionist in Nice where he had been born. Compelled to flee to South America, he became a noted crusader for the abstract principle of liberty. He returned to Italy for the revolution of 1848 and won renown as leader of the Red Shirts. After driving Austria from northern Italy he purchased the island of Caprera, a rock in the sea near Sardinia, and, Cincinnatus-like, retired to his vine and fig tree. Almost immediately he was sought to lead revolts in Sicily and Naples.

Italian peasants rallied to Garibaldi's standard. A striking figure on a white horse, he led his men into battle shouting, "Here we make Italy one or we die."[2] The King of Savoy, with trained soldiers, helped the revolt. His Majesty also wanted to make Italy one—a great monarchy. Startling victories were achieved over the Bourbon rulers of southern Italy. The part played by the King's forces was minimized in the popular mind. Everybody acclaimed Garibaldi's peasant army. The Red Shirts became symbols of freedom. Victor Emmanuel was crowned King of Italy in Naples and Garibaldi admonished his peasants to accept the new regime. The gesture was construed by many people as democratic modesty. American imagination was particularly captivated by the simplicity with which Garibaldi left the coronation pomp, wrapped a gray blanket around his red shirt, and with a bag of beans to be planted

133

on his Caprera farm, sailed away to become a legendary figure, the ideal of democracies everywhere.

Garibaldi's home, a one-storied house, was built in the style he had admired in Montevideo. Sea breezes drenched the island's sparkling granite cliffs and the tang of salt blended with the perfume of myrtle and thorny acacias. Most pleasing to Garibaldi were the red geraniums dancing in the wind under the brilliant Mediterranean sun—red geraniums risen from the earth like his peasant Red Shirts.

Garibaldi was happy on the days he clambered over the rocks hunting goats that grazed where the highest headlands towered toward the turquoise sky. On the face of the cliff the wind blew his great beard against his chest, and Garibaldi's eyes swept the Mediterranean to the horizon. Across the blue waters to the north he could see the islands of San Stefano and La Maddalena, dark rocks collared with surging spray. Beyond them lay Napoleon's Corsica. The goats, when disturbed, plunged down the precipitous slopes, blatting to each other, their strong hoofs dislodging rocks which hurtled hundreds of feet into the sucking, surging tempest of waters. In the Tyrol, Garibaldi had seen Austrian soldiers flee in a similar manner while Red Shirts instead of red geraniums waved exultantly.

One day a ship appeared on the horizon under a smudge of smoke in the sky, due north—the direction of Genoa.[3] The ship did not follow the trade route south along the horizon to Naples and Palermo. Instead it came straight for Caprera. Perhaps the King was sending for Garibaldi once more to lead his Red Shirts into Rome, to conquer the Papal States and thus make Italy one. The ship hove to under the bluffs, churning a wake of milky water. Ribbons of kelp rose to the surface for a moment, then sank from sight. From the headlands which furnished pasture for the goats the ship appeared like a lozenge on the purple satin of the sea, a lozenge crosshatched with ropes and spars, lines of anchor chains, a smoking funnel. The red and white stripes of an American flag on the mast lashed the wind—a thing alive, a coal glowing against the purple waters. Garibaldi had once lived in America. On Staten Island he had worked in a candle factory.

As he watched the ship he must have recalled how, a few months earlier, admirers in America had written requesting him to lead an Italian legion in the Civil War,[4] and how, after that, the American consul at Antwerp, James A. Quiggle, had written Garibaldi offering him supreme command of the American Army.[5] Garibaldi's steel-blue eyes had dreamed of unifying Italy, not the United States.[6] Perhaps the Americans' offer would serve his own purpose. Garibaldi had written Victor Emmanuel for permission to go.[7] Surely this suggestion that he might leave Italy would force the King to give him active service at home.

The King valued Garibaldi and he also feared him. Then, too, Napoleon had helped as much as Garibaldi in the overthrow of the Bourbons, and Victor Emmanuel knew that the Emperor did not want to antagonize his Catholic subjects by a conquest of the Papal States.[8] It seemed best to let the Liberator go. Garibaldi had been disappointed when his request was granted. In any event he was free and here was an American, Henry S. Sanford from Belgium, with a chartered ship to carry him away.

The conference between Sanford and the Italian revolutionist may be reconstructed with sufficient accuracy—the two men seated at a rude table on the terrace before Garibaldi's Montevidean house, a great loaf of bread and a golden cheese, tankards of sharp red wine, the salt wind playing with the red geraniums and their deep green leaves, voices mingling with the coughing of the sea. The American did not bring as good an offer as Quiggle had intimated. A commission as major general, not commander in chief, was the best that Sanford could do. Garibaldi insisted that he must have supreme command—also that the slaves must be emancipated. The war must become a crusade for liberty.

Both of these demands were more than Sanford had authority to grant. He promised to take up the matter with Lincoln. Then he steamed back over the horizon to Genoa. At the water front, in the shipping office above the arcaded shops where great two-wheeled carts loaded and unloaded freight on the quay, Sanford canceled the charter of the ship on which he had hoped to carry away the chief of the Red Shirts in triumph. The Connecticut Yankee was sick at heart. Wending his way through streets narrow as those of a city in the Levant, he dodged pack donkeys, stumbled over the open sewer, looked dolefully up at the tenements with upper stories jutting over the streets; clotheslines stretched from windows above his head, clothes of many colors hanging like banners above him. Sanford decided to go back to Turin, to the King's court, and consult Minister Marsh, the linguist whom Lincoln had sent there.[9]

The two Americans pieced together the intrigue and Sanford returned to Paris.

The Italian press expostulated loudly at Italy's indifference to her hero. International newspapers took up the theme. In London Lincoln's putative offer seemed an acknowledgment of weakness. Insult and abuse were heaped upon him. Garibaldi, on the other hand, read the Italian newspapers and decided to strike for Italy without the King's permission. He landed on the mainland and rallied his peasants for a march on Rome.

The King was torn between desire to add the Eternal City to his kingdom and the inexpediency of doing so. His Premier insisted that Garibaldi must be stopped. The King agreed and ordered the army to disperse the Red Shirts. Garibaldi resisted, was wounded and imprisoned—a dangerous captive for any king to keep. One thing was certain. Italy loved him.

Up in Vienna, Austria, Theodore Canisius, the unsuccessful Springfield newspaperman, read about the fiasco. Canisius felt sure that he would not have failed to get the Liberator. Perhaps there would be another opportunity. Canisius waited. Next time the story might be different.

The news of the offer to Garibaldi brought to Washington a flood of military adventurers seeking commissions: Hungarians, Poles, officers of the Turkish army with illegible testimonials from European wars and revolutions. General McDowell had been relieved after the defeat at Bull Run, George B. McClellan succeeding to the command. The whole Army was reorganized. Politicians struggled to get commissions for their friends. They came to the State Department with importantly bedecked foreign military men. Secretary Seward bent his shaggy eyebrows over their undecipherable credentials. "It is best to detain them with the hope of employment on the Northern side," he told a friend, "lest some legally good man should get among the rebels."[10] William H. Russell noted the influx of soldiers of fortune in Washington—swivel-eyed gentry with foreign medals and ribbons on their coats. Before long he met McDowell and said to him, "A great many Garibaldians are in Washington just now."

"Oh," the general replied in his quiet way, "it will be quite enough for a man to prove that he once saw Garibaldi to satisfy us in Washington that he is quite fit for the command of a regiment. I have recommended a man because he sailed in the ship which Garibaldi came in over here, and I'm sure it will be attended to."[11]

One young man, neatly attired in the uniform of an officer of Austrian Uhlans, appeared in the capital with authentic-looking papers, a glib tongue and thorough knowledge of aristocratic military life. Introducing himself as Count von Schweinitz, he borrowed money from two foreign ministers and was appointed to a minor post. Later it was discovered that his mother was a washerwoman and that he had served as valet for an Uhlan officer.[12]

A genuine prince, Felix Salm-Salm, came from Germany. Trained as an officer since a child, schooled in the manual of arms and of the horse and little else, the Prince had accumulated troublesome gambling debts in both Vienna and Paris. In Washington he presented a letter to Baron von Gerolt. The kindly German minister accompanied him to the State Department much as a farmer might lead a sportive thoroughbred from his stall. Seward and Lincoln, both rustics in appearance, looked at Prince Felix' elegant figure, his dark hair, light mustache, fine dark eyes, the monocle which he could toss and catch in his right eye "with all the skill of a Prussian officer of the guard."[13] Lincoln commissioned him a captain and said with artless simplicity, "That you are a prince shall be no impediment to your success with us."[14] Shortly afterward, Salm-Salm met and married a circus bareback rider, beautiful, dashing, clever. With her little dog she rode with him everywhere, the talk and toast of the camps. On long wet marches the Prince carried her scarlet ostrich plume under his cloak to keep it dry, while she, devoted to his military ambition, made it a point to offer anything in her power to advance his position, and once at least prevented his dismissal from the service.

A more important foreigner, Prince Napoleon, cousin of the Emperor, arrived as military observer in his yacht shortly after the Battle of Bull Run.[15] Nicknamed "Plon-Plon" by French soldiers because, rumor said, he feared lead—*plomb*—Jerome Bonaparte's tongue wagged unrestrainedly. His reckless remarks had made it advisable for him to come to America instead of staying at home to fight a duel. Prince Napoleon was a patron of the arts. His suite included the son of George Sand,[16] then at the height of her literary reputation. The opinion of these French observers was sure to have wide publicity abroad. Jerome, unlike the Emperor whose study of history had led him to conclude that permanent forms of government were imperial, spoke candidly of his friendship for democracy. Formally introduced to Abraham Lincoln, he was tendered a state dinner and other official ceremonies both at the French legation and at the Secretary of State's residence. Frederick Seward described the Prince in his memoirs:

"As he stood on the hearth rug, wearing a white vest with red ribbon and decorations, and with his hands behind his back, his features, hair, and attitude showed a startling resemblance to the pictures of the first Napoleon—a resemblance that he was said to cultivate, although he was a trifle taller than his uncle."[17]

Later, at the President's dinner, the master of the Marine Band stationed in the vestibule committed a diplomatic blunder. Not versed in French politics, he struck up *"La Marseillaise,"* a revolutionary lyric banned in Paris during the Second Empire. The guests smiled as they looked toward the Prince, who took it with good humor, saying, *"Mais, oui, je suis Républicain—en Amérique."*[18]

Another gesture of Napoleonic friendship during the early months of Lincoln's administration threatened more serious consequences. A French frigate steamed up the Potomac on another "visit of observation" and anchored off the Navy Yard. The commander invited Lincoln to come on board and receive a national salute. A day was selected and the President rowed out with Captain John A. Dahlgren in the Navy Yard barge. The frigate lay draped with bunting, her bow toward midstream. The barge pulled under the frowning stern, then around to the side where the presidential party was greeted by gesticulating officers on the gangway. Drums rolled. Bugles sounded. When the President stepped on deck the Stars and Stripes broke from the top of the mainmast.

Lincoln inspected the vessel, her wardroom, quarters and armament, chatting with unpretentious dignity. Returning to the side ladder, the party stepped down and took their seats in the barge, the President in the stern. "Suppose we row around her bows," he said. "I would like to look at her build and rig from that direction."

The barge moved forward and the Frenchmen prepared to fire the national salute. They did not notice that the President's boat had pulled forward instead of returning as she had come. Frederick Seward remembered the next few minutes of near tragedy:

"We had hardly reached her bow, when, on looking up, I saw the officer of the deck pacing the bridge, watch in hand and counting off the seconds, '*Un, deux, trois,*' and then immediately followed the flash and deafening roar of a cannon, apparently just over our heads. Another followed, then another and another in rapid succession. We were enveloped in smoke and literally 'under fire' from the frigate's broadside. Captain Dahlgren sprang to his feet, his face aflame with indignation, as he shouted: 'Pull like the devil, boys! Pull like hell!'

"They obeyed with a will, and a few sturdy strokes took us out of danger. After he had resumed his seat and calmed down, I said in a low voice: 'Of course those guns were not shotted, and we were below their range?'

"He answered, gritting his teeth, 'Yes, but to think of exposing the President to the danger of having his head taken off by a wad!'

"I did not know, until he explained, that the wadding blown to pieces by the explosion sometimes commences dropping fragments soon after leaving the gun. Whether Mr. Lincoln realized the danger or not, I never knew. He sat impassively through it, and made no reference to it afterwards."[19]

Three French princes also arrived in Washington unofficially. Lincoln and the cabinet showed them marked attention but M. Mercier made it a point never to see them in any company. They were members of the House of Orleans which Napoleon had succeeded. Two of them, the Count of Paris and the Duke of Chartres, were sons of the deposed King. The third, Prince de Joinville, was his brother. Before they arrived, Charles Francis Adams had warned Seward to look out. Napoleon, he said, had a deep plot to conquer Mexico and establish them as rulers there. Thus he would increase French prestige and at the same time dispose of dangerous rivals.[20]

De Joinville had unwittingly helped ruin his own house in France. To please the people, he had brought back from St. Helena the remains of the first Napoleon. Frenchmen saw with horror that the Little Corporal had been buried with holes in his boots[21]—by the English swine. Some people said politicians had supplied the boots to engender hatred of Britain. Who knows? In any event the return of Bonaparte, dead, aroused a nostalgia for his great name. Napoleon III played upon it until the French people turned against the ruling House of Orleans and placed him upon his uncle's throne. Thus De Joinville served his rival and now he and his nephews were exiled for his pains. Lincoln decided to appoint the three noblemen to McClellan's staff. So the President, like the Emperor, considered it good policy to give them employment! Did he want to keep them out of Mexico until Corwin got affairs straightened out down there?

The French princes proved popular acquisitions for the Army. De Joinville's tall slim figure was topped with a forage cap and a beard pointed like the bill of a tall heron. Being deaf, he stood aloof and talked little but made a fine appearance in any company. His nephews, popeyed and active as bullfrogs beside their slow-stepping mentor, both spoke English fluently, liked to dance and have a good time. Captain Orleans and Captain "Chatters" were the names by which they passed. John Hay reported De Joinville as having the finest mind he ever met in the Army. Hay also remembered a day when he, Seward and Lincoln encountered Orleans:

"We came to McClellan's quarters and met in the telegraph office a long and awkward youth who spoke in a high-pitched and rapid tone to Seward, 'We are just in from a ride of all day.' Seward introduced him to me as Captain Orleans. He went upstairs to call McClellan and the President said quietly, 'One doesn't like to make a messenger of the King of France, as that youth, the Count of Paris, would be if his family had kept the throne.' "[22]

Lincoln haunted McClellan's headquarters almost as persistently as he did the War Department. The Northern cause grew darker day by day. McClellan drilled his men endlessly but fought no battles. His men were not yet ready, he said. Politicians told Lincoln that the new general was no fighter. They urged the President to appoint their favorites in his place. Lincoln insisted that McClellan must be given a chance. The Little Dragoon himself became almost insolent with the President. One day when Lincoln sat at headquarters McClellan came in, climbed the stairs and went to bed without speaking to him. Seward used to treat the President in that manner. Lincoln took it from Little Mac as he had from Seward—no remonstrance. He said that he would hold McClellan's horse[23] if that would bring a victory.

In the midst of the bickering a dispatch arrived from Japan. The Shogun asked to be excused, please, from his recent treaty with the United States for the opening of certain ports to Yankee traders. Had American prestige got so low that the Japs, too, dared follow the lead of Spain and France?

Neither Lincoln nor Seward had time to study the treaty in question, nor the alleged antiforeign disturbances in Japan which made further opening of ports seem undesirable. Lincoln evaded the responsibility of a decision. The problem, he told Seward, would have to be decided by the American representative in Japan, Townsend Harris, an appointee of Buchanan's.[24]

Here was a new diplomatic policy. Statesmen sitting in on the game speculated on Lincoln's finesse. With South America Lincoln had been conciliatory, reversing his predecessor's policy. With England he had permitted Seward to be firm to the edge of quarrelsomeness. Now he left Japanese diplomacy to a Democratic appointee without instructions. Was such fickleness part of a studied foreign policy or was it opportunism? Some diplomats deemed it inconsistent carelessness. Others were not so sure.

Within a few days, more bad news reached Washington. The North had received another setback almost as disastrous as Bull Run. Out in Missouri the Federal General Nathaniel Lyons had been defeated and killed at Wilson's Creek. In both East and West the shaken armies lay panting in the hot sun of August. Lincoln must build up reserves, recruit more men, make a new army if he could. William H. Russell watched the bungling and delay. To English readers he reported Republican ineptness.

To add to the annoyance and confusion, governors of states made peremptory demands on the President for protection. Governor Morton wired from Indiana. His state was threatened by armed bands of rebels. A telegraph messenger came running to the White House. Lincoln put on an old linen duster, called one of his boys and followed the man out the door. As soon as the three of them reached the walk leading to the War Department, the President stooped over and picked up a pebble. With thumb and finger he flipped it down the path. "Who can come nearest to that?" he challenged—the customary beginning of a rural game known as "followings." The President played all the way to the War Department while Governor Morton waited.[25]

Such indifference! Russell noted too that executive authority crumbled everywhere. He reported that mobs had burned and gutted newspaper offices. Antiadministration editors were ridden on rails. But worst of all, mutinies were reported continually in the Army. An outbreak in the New York 79th[26]—the Highlanders who had marched off so valiantly to save democracy—was followed by another mutiny in the 2nd Maine regiment, both serious until stopped by a display of cannon and cavalry. "The President was greatly alarmed," Russell wrote dryly, "but McClellan acted with some vigor."[27] Dispatches from abroad were also discouraging. The London legation reported Yancey and Mann, the Southern commissioners, as "being dined and feasted widely."[28] Such cordiality might be a prelude to recognition of the South, the first step toward European admission that the Union was severed.

While the gloom of Bull Run and Wilson's Creek, together with adverse reports from Europe, cast a triple shadow across the North, the armies were reorganized for the grim business ahead. Lincoln succeeded in recruiting more soldiers. He began also to reorganize his foreign service. First he sent John Bigelow to Paris, ostensibly as consul general but really to head a publicity campaign against Confederate propaganda.[29] Seward was responsible for the appointment. John Bigelow's influence over the Secretary of State was second only to Charles Francis Adams'. A man with John Bigelow's standing in the party might be expected to use his own discretion in carrying out orders from a chief whom he had bent to his own will. Soon people were saying that Bigelow's appointment marked a change in the United States Government's policy abroad. Diplomats never could be sure whether the guiding hand belonged to Lincoln, Seward or John Bigelow.

Bigelow's fitness for his diplomatic post was almost equal to Adams'. His acquaintance in Europe was large. He had been presented to Queen Victoria, knew the British Prime Minister, Lord Palmerston, and the Secretary of Foreign Affairs, Lord John Russell. Bigelow was on friendly terms with such parliamentarians as Gladstone, Cobden and Bright. Among English literary lights Bigelow was a welcome guest. He knew the latest gossip about Dickens' love affairs[30] and Mrs. Dickens' jealousy. He had seen Thackeray in his cups,[31] and was an old friend of war correspondent Russell. Through the latter, Bigelow had met J. T. Delane, editor of the London *Times*.[32] In addition to these qualifications, Bigelow was what might be called "a gentleman"—very important to England in a war alleged to be between red republicanism and the older order of civilization. He might be expected to do officially for the snobs what eccentric George Francis Train was doing for the mobs. Already, at a reception with Lord Shaftesbury, son-in-law of Palmerston,[33] Bigelow had listened with apparent sympathy to British aristocracy's scorn for penny postage and street railways.[34] "It will be the ruination of our servants, eh what?"

On the Continent Bigelow was equally at home. He had been entertained by the embassy set in Paris, had discussed political economy with the French liberal scholar Edouard de Laboulaye, had argued with Sainte-Beuve and endeared himself to the French people by studying the intimate life of Benjamin Franklin, whose autobiography he discovered later in Paris. Moreover, Bigelow was an abolitionist. Study convinced him that the decline of the ancient democracies of Greece and Rome was due to "the demoralizing influence upon the ruling class of their conquered bondsmen." A white master, he believed, appropriated more of the savagery of the African slave than slaves appropriated of civilization.[35] In France, Bigelow had traveled to the Vosges Mountains, to the dungeon in which Toussaint L'Ouverture had died. He looked at the Negro's cell with something like reverence.

A man with these sentiments and attainments was exactly what Lincoln needed in Europe to oppose the representatives of the slaveholding South. No time must be lost while Yancey and Mann were being "dined and feasted widely." John Bigelow was at his country home in New York when he received word from Lincoln to be ready to sail in one week. He set out at once for Washington. Two days later he met Abraham Lincoln for the first time. Like Charles Francis Adams, he was disappointed in the uncouth figure democracy had brought to the highest position in the nation. With a heavy heart he embarked on the *Persia* for Liverpool on August 28, 1861—a week behind schedule. Crossing to France, he established his headquarters in Paris. The situation seemed as discouraging to Bigelow in Europe as it did to others in America. He wrote that the only loyal representatives of our government, "so far as I knew, at the Continental Courts" were W. L. Dayton, minister to the French Court, H. S. Sanford, minister to Belgium, and David Fuller, colored messenger at the Paris consulate.[36] The North's failure in battle, Lincoln's unwillingness to emancipate the slaves, and the reports of the breakdown of democracy in America, Bigelow found to be alienating sympathy for the North rapidly. In England, John Bright's lusty loyalty was too radical to have much weight, and when Bright's colleague, the more thoughtful Richard Cobden, recommended conceding independence to the Confederates[37] Bigelow realized that Southern propaganda was having its effect. Bigelow's pessimism was further increased by his impression of Napoleon III, whom he had met in 1860. He wrote:

"The Emperor also . . . disappointed me. He is short, with broad shoulders, large chest, and barrel tapering off into two legs, so short as to seem very, very small. His head, too, seemed rather large for his legs, and he looked, as the sailors say, 'all by the bows,' like a catfish."[38]

The Emperor made an equally unpleasant impression on John Hay, who at a later date was sent to Paris to fill Bigelow's position. Hay said:

"The moustache and imperial which the world knows, but ragged and bristly, concealing the mouth entirely, is moving a little nervously as the lips twitch. Eyes sleepily watchful—furtive—stealthy, rather ignoble; like servants looking out of dirty windows and saying 'nobody at home,' and lying as they say it. . . . He stands there as still and impassive as if carved in oak for a ship's figure-head."[39]

Empress Eugénie, Bigelow described as "a pretty woman; has a graceful figure; moves gracefully; has beautiful sloping shoulders, drooping eyelids; and yet there seemed to be nothing regal and sovereign in her appearance."[40] But the thing that hurt Bigelow the most, as it also hurt the Adamses in England, was the lack of personal attention he received from the Emperor and Empress. Bigelow, a recognized conversationalist, was unable to arouse interest in the sallow face of Napoleon III, who sat silent, paying no attention to the vivacious talk around him. When Eugénie called the Emperor's attention to some remark he smiled sweetly, but Bigelow noticed that the smile stopped abruptly—unmistakable evidence of preoccupation and insincerity.[41]

In France, as in England, the red republicans could expect little sympathy from the ruling classes. Only through the people might pressure be brought to bear. As Bigelow planned how best to begin his campaign to popularize the American cause his eye noted a sympathetic article in the *Journal des Débats*. On the following day another appeared. The two articles, reviewing a recent book by Count Agénor de Gasparin entitled *L'Amérique devant l'Europe,* were signed by Bigelow's old friend Edouard de Laboulaye, "de l'Institut." Gasparin declared the American Civil War part of the world struggle for liberalism. Laboulaye enlarged and popularized the theme. Bigelow was delighted. He hunted up the French reviewer, renewed his old acquaintance, and planned sound, realistic propaganda for the Northern cause. The great scholar was not popular with the Emperor, who feared his liberal principles and suspected, with reason, that Laboulaye was striking at the Empire through a screen of sympathy for the North.[42] In consequence everything he published was liable to suppression. Bigelow helped the scholar play a trick on the Emperor. Napoleon III prided himself on remodeling France to Bonaparte's design. Laboulaye and Bigelow took pains to show that the great Napoleon always favored building a strong United States as a counterbalance to England. The Corsican's statement at the time he sold Louisiana to America seemed prophetic.

"To emancipate the world from the commercial tyranny of England, it is necessary to give her for a counterpoise a maritime power that shall become her rival. Such are the United States. The English aspire to dispose of the wealth of the world. I can be useful to the universe if I can prevent their ruling America as they rule Asia. . . . In ceding Louisiana, I strengthen forever the power of the United States, and give to England a rival upon the sea, which sooner or later shall abase her pride."[43]

This sentiment, printed in a pamphlet, was sent to two hundred members of the Institute, all the diplomatic representatives, prominent journalists, barristers and statesmen in Paris. Such propaganda would undoubtedly help keep France and England from uniting against the American democracy, which Seward's untimely offer to join the Convention of Paris had encouraged. Bigelow and the Frenchmen, each for different ends, were doing exactly what Clay and Burlingame had done, but they were more skillful. Adams did not call them "noisy jackasses."

Laboulaye followed his pamphlet with a book entitled *Paris en Amérique*[44] and a year later with *Les Etats-Unis et la France,* both of which were translated into English and sold widely in the North. As his fame spread, Laboulaye's portrait was hung in the Union League Club in New York. His bust in bronze was placed in the clubrooms in Philadelphia.

In London the anti-British propaganda was received with stoicism. The vessels which J. D. Bulloch had ordered were progressing on schedule. The Charleston-Liverpool banking firm, Fraser, Trenholm and Company, outfitted an iron steamer, the *Bermuda,* with war supplies to be run through the American blockade.[45] Adams learned about the preparations and warned Earl Russell[46] on August 15, 1861.[47] The earl replied that the matter would "be looked after." But on August 20 word was received that the ship had got away. The negligence seemed inexcusable to Adams. He prepared a strong remonstrance but Earl Russell beat him to the gun. With double-edged diplomacy the Britisher sent word that he was ready to receive the American's signature to the Declaration of Paris,[48] a touchy question better not brought up. Adams discontinued the conversation with pleasure. The toreador's first encounter with the British bull was contrary to tradition. In September 1861 the *Bermuda* reached Savannah safely[49] with the first supply of war material from abroad.[50] Once more it was demonstrated that the North had established only a paper blockade which by the law of nations none was obliged to respect.

Lincoln learned about the arrival of the *Bermuda* in a series of maritime dispatches—all bad. The *Sumter,* which had slipped out to sea from New Orleans, had called at the Dutch port of Curaçao. Instead of being interned as a pirate, she was allowed to coal and depart, and called later at Trinidad and then at Paramaribo. Lincoln realized that no power in the Caribbean could be counted on to help the North. Every island, a European possession, was a potential outfitting place for Confederate raiders.[51] People noticed that Lincoln looked old and tired when he climbed into his carriage for his daily drive to McClellan's headquarters—stiff as an old man. Then good news revived his youthful spirit and his laugh. General Benjamin Franklin Butler had been ordered to sail secretly against Cape Hatteras, the eastern tip of North Carolina, while McClellan covered the movement with his diligent drilling and reviews. The expedition had succeeded. The sand batteries at the entrance of Pamlico Sound were destroyed and the great coastal sea was at the mercy of the North. Much Southern coast line remained to be patrolled, but the new base served admirably for the beginning of an anaconda movement to constrict all Southern ports and make the blockade real. The North had a victory at last and also a first hero of the war.

Lincoln knew that the Cape Hatteras victory would incite the South to retaliate. Rebel troops camped south of Washington were reported to be moving ominously. Lincoln urged McClellan to attack, not be attacked. On September 3 the President went to visit the Union Army. Some residents of Washington, Secessionists at heart, prepared furtively to receive the invaders. This time, they whispered, the capital will fall.

That night Russell slept fitfully, disturbed by the endless rumbling of heavy guns trundling through the dark streets. Sometime in the night a group of men knocked at his lodgings—three foreign ministers and a banker—and breathlessly inquired whether the city was being attacked. Russell noticed that the visitors were in "high spirits" over the prospect of seeing the red republicans "flying before Southern bayonets."[52] Respectability in Washington meant Secession. "Only one representative of a foreign power here," Russell said, was friendly to the government in power.

The threatened attack did not materialize. The ministers and the banker returned to their homes, resigned to the discomfort of a few more days of republicanism. So preposterously rude did American democracy appear to the foreign ministers that two days later Russell noted in his diary:

"The event of the day was the appearance of the President in the Avenue in a suit of black, and a parcel in his hand, walking umbrella-less in the rain."[53]

The correspondent did not know that this democratic figure was turning over in his mind a *coup d'état* worthy of Napoleon. Not being bred to American traditions, Russell did not understand how Lincoln might perpetrate a tyrannical act to save the country, then relinquish his arbitrary power and let the country return to its democratic way. The usurpation Lincoln had in mind at this time concerned the Maryland Legislature, scheduled to meet on September 17, 1861. A majority of the representatives, he believed, would vote for the state to secede. Lincoln planned to stop this by an act of such an illegal and dictatorial nature that he dared not write it in the most confidential letter. Instead he ordered a carriage and with Seward and his son Frederick called on General McClellan. Come take a drive! they invited. Rattling away apparently to inspect the troops, they proceeded to General Banks's headquarters at Rockville, Maryland. Here in a grove, free from underbrush, where none could overhear, the conspirators ordered the general to arrest all the legislators suspected of being Secessionists and to detain them until after the session.[54] The details of this outrage against democracy were perfected verbally, then the presidential party returned to Washington unnoticed in the dark. The plot succeeded, but when a report of this tyranny reached Europe, political scientists saw in it another proof that democracy leads to dictatorship. William H. Russell wrote:

"The news that twenty-two members of the Maryland Legislature have been seized by the Federal authorities has not produced the smallest effect here; so easily do men in the midst of political troubles bend to arbitrary power, and so rapidly do all guarantees disappear in a revolution."[55]

Outwardly unconscious of this tyrannical perfidy, Abraham Lincoln was seen on the following day, September 12, 1861, in his same old "gray shooting suit" with a number of dispatches in his hand, walking to the State Department "quite unnoticed by the crowd."[56]

The accounts of Lincoln's dictatorial actions were published in England at a time when friction between Great Britain and America was growing rapidly. Two incidents particularly annoyed both sides. One was the arrival of troops in Canada, in apparent anticipation of a war with America—an answer to Seward's threat. The other was the announcement in Northern newspapers of the discovery that British consuls were forwarding rebel mail to Europe with their official correspondence. Consul Bunch had even issued passports to couriers captured with rebel dispatches.[57] These two incidents, combined with a dislike of democracy on one side and of monarchy on the other, produced what almost amounted to a war hysteria between England and the North in the fall of 1861.

Moreover, the examination of the diplomatic mails disclosed that the English and French consuls had approached the Confederacy with a proposition to join the Convention of Paris,[58] obviously a first step toward recognizing the South as an independent nation. The disclosure foreboded further connivance. It was useless to explain that the reinforcements to the Great Lakes were merely the usual reliefs.[59] Seward, always quick to fly into a tempest of wrath, prepared a circular letter[60] to all the Northern border states admonishing them to prepare men and defenses to repel an invasion.

Plans for mobilization on the Canadian border went forward and Seward published what would be called a "white paper" half a century later. This publication for British consumption printed the correspondence between the State Department and Lord Lyons on the question of arbitrary arrests of British subjects carrying rebel mail. The evidence of the Britishers' guilt was too conclusive to be denied. War preparations accelerated on both sides, and Earl Russell could only reply that "Her Majesty's government have not recognized and are not prepared to recognize the so-called Confederate States"[61]—weasel words full of many meanings. William H. Russell and John Hay watched the war clouds grow. They studied the faces of the principal actors, speculated on their motives, tried to unravel the duplicity of diplomacy and prophesy the future. Hay noted in his diary that Seward stormed and fumed about "the double dealing and lying of our young English friends."[62] Next day W. H. Russell reported that Seward was dining and driving with Lord Lyons in the most friendly manner. Surely the difficulty had been settled. But on the following day Russell heard that Seward was preparing a dispatch to demolish the British government's position and vindicate the preparations of the United States.[63] Was Seward trying to provoke a war with England or to avert it without losing face? Almost five months had elapsed since Lincoln had toned him down to "one war at a time," and since Bull Run Seward had realized the seriousness of the war at home. When he fumed to Lincoln about "the double dealing and lying of our young English friends," was he sincere or was his friendly smile while driving with Lord Lyons a grin of pain? The men watching him did not know. Perhaps time would tell. Then, as so often happens in the worst crises, news arrived of a greater danger. Jeff Davis and his cabinet had sent two more commissioners to Europe, James Murray Mason and John Slidell—two men who might succeed where Yancey, Mann and Rost had failed.

On October 11, 1861, the second contingent of Southern envoys, with their secretaries, wives and daughters, had driven down to the wharf in Charleston, South Carolina. Rain sluiced from the sky with the violence peculiar to this region of the Atlantic. The women's shawls and dresses were drenched. The gentlemen's long hair dangled in Gorgon locks on the sopping shoulders of their frock coats. After farewells the group separated. Some ran back to the waiting carriages; others tripped down the slippery planks into a small steamer. The ropes were cast off. In the cabin James M. Mason and John Slidell, his wife and his two daughters, Mathilde and Rosina, shook the rain from their garments. Also in the party were Slidell's secretary, George Eustis, and Mrs. Eustis, whose father, a former head of a Washington bank, pined in prison at Fort Lafayette. Mason's secretary, J. E. McFarland, and two or three other dripping individuals completed the party. The vessel chugged doggedly away from the lighted city. When Fort Sumter, the last Confederate outpost, was approached, the ship's lights were turned out. The engine was slowed so that it could not be heard above the patter of the rain. In this manner the little craft slipped past the blockade into the open sea.

The timing of the departure of the Southern envoys was almost perfect. Friction over the arbitrary arrests of British subjects, the seizing of the mails and the mobilization of troops along the border had set both countries' teeth on edge. Lincoln was nagging McClellan to attack the rebels. Then he learned that Mason and Slidell had got through the blockade. He watched daily for a report of their arrival in some neutral country. As he waited, a dispatch came from Corwin. More bad news. The rumored expedition of France, Spain and Great Britain to collect their debts in Mexico had become a fact. Corwin was sure that the powers contemplated taking the entire country and establishing a monarchy there.[64] The United States, he said, could prevent this catastrophe by lending Juárez sufficient money to pay the interest on their foreign obligations. Napoleon was the leading aggressor. A dispatch was hurried to Dayton: interview the Emperor and find out if the expedition would be called off in case Mexico paid the interest. In quick time the reply came back. Napoleon insisted that he must have the principal,[65] even if he were forced to occupy Mexican ports and collect the customs. Let the United States submit or fight.

Lincoln went to see McClellan again. The general must strike. With England mobilizing on the Northern border and France preparing to occupy the country to the south, the United States would be smothered. Only a Union victory could save the day.

Copies of the London *Times* dated September 10, 1861, prophesied that British and French intervention in Mexico was inevitable.[66] A dispatch from Adams stated that he had called on Earl Russell for an explanation and was told that no treaty existed between France and Great Britain for such intervention "nor does

Great Britain approve of such a scheme."[67] This sounded like diplomatic evasion.

A fortnight later Earl Russell upset the American State Department with a speech at a public dinner at Newcastle upon Tyne. Russell compared Britain's foreign policy toward the Italian rebels fighting for freedom with its action toward the Confederates in America. Was he preparing British public opinion for recognition of the Southern states? Clerks scoured the British press for other keys to future policy. Seward called the pronouncement to Lincoln's attention. The Englishman was no doubt sarcastic when he said it would be a great pity if anything should happen to the "great experiment of the new continent in free institutions."[68] Evidently Earl Russell did not believe that the American war was being waged over slavery, for he said:

"We now see the two parties contending together, not upon the question of slavery, though I believe that was probably the original cause of the quarrel—not contending with respect to Free Trade and Protection, but contending, as so many states in the Old World have contended, the one side for empire and the other for independence."[69]

Surely this was an effort to prejudice British public opinion against the United States as intervention in Mexico loomed. One American voice in Europe seemed unafraid to protest the rising storm. Irrepressible George Francis Train screamed with his usual loquaciousness:

"The noble earl made one mistake in his celebrated speech—he said the South was fighting for independence, and the North for empire.—He should have reversed it to express the nation's sense— the North is fighting for independence and the South for empire."[70]

Lawyer Lincoln knew that a good argument could be developed for either side of such a proposition. Train was a comical fellow who warranted watching. If McClellan would only disperse the rebels around Washington, Lincoln could talk with Train's assurance. But McClellan did not act. He said the army was not yet in shape for battle. Politicians told Lincoln again and again that

McClellan was no soldier. Lincoln walked to the State and War Departments two and three times a day, with Tad and Willie whooping ahead of him, chasing pebbles. The boys were his only consolation. Lincoln decided to get them a goat.

Finally McClellan ordered an advance across the Potomac at Ball's Bluff, where the enemy appeared to be weak. Senator Baker accompanied the troops, acting as colonel of a California regiment. Lincoln's spirits revived. He wished Baker Godspeed and waited for the news of victory. In the afternoon black clouds covered the sky. A storm broke over the city. Late at night Lincoln learned that the sortie had been another Bull Run. Baker was dead. Lincoln paced up and down through the gloomy corridors, unconsolable.[71] Rain pelted on the White House windows. Lincoln could not adjust himself to the fact that his old friend Baker would never come to the White House again—Baker who could always be counted on for little diplomatic tasks like placating the hurt feelings of Cash Clay. Lincoln had named one of his sons Edward Baker Lincoln—the son he buried back in Springfield. First Ellsworth and now Baker, both practically members of the President's personal family, had paid the supreme price for democracy. Harried and sleepless, Lincoln went next day to see McClellan. The Little Dragoon said the officers had disobeyed his orders.[72] They had advanced too far. His men were not yet hardened for war.

Back in the White House a self-appointed committee of Senators Wade, Trumbull and Chandler called on Lincoln. They insisted that the President order a great battle and retrieve the loss. He must throw the Army ruthlessly across the Potomac.[73] Better another defeat than the uncertainty of delay.

Lincoln shook his head. McClellan needed more time. There must be no more ill-conceived attacks. The soldiers must be better trained. The officers must know their duties. Then a new mailbag from Europe arrived—diplomatic gossip from Schurz in Madrid. A Spanish prince was to be called to the throne of Mexico. A revolution similar to the one in Santo Domingo would make the call appear to come from the people.[74] Both France and Great Britain were said to be behind the movement.

What could Lincoln do? His big untrained army seemed to be no match for the rebels. Washington itself was blockaded. Cold weather had come and sufficient fuel was not available to keep people warm.[75] Then definite confirmation arrived concerning joint intervention of England, France and Spain in Mexico. The three powers had signed a convention in London on October 30, 1861, in spite of Earl Russell's assurance that Britain did not "approve of such a scheme." It was no longer a secret. The London *Times* described the opportunities for investors in the new country. Other articles explained the advantageous provisions of the Anglo-French commercial treaty.[76] Seward's plan to keep France and England separated had failed miserably. Worst news of all: Mason and Slidell had reached Cuba.[77] Henceforth they could travel under neutral flags, reach Europe and offer the powers any concession for recognition and aid.

# VIII. *The Capture of Mason and Slidell*

"WELL, boys, I am down to raisins."[1] Lincoln turned from the drawer where telegrams were filed and shuffled across the room to his upholstered chair. The cipher operators wondered what he meant but did not like to ask. The President spent many hours in the telegraph office since he had appointed McClellan commander in chief. One of Little Mac's first acts after assuming his exalted station had been to hide incoming telegrams from the President. Lincoln heard about it and he also heard that McClellan planned to take over the United States with his great army and make himself dictator. Lincoln made no comment but he asked for a rocking chair in the telegraph office. He spent many hours there. Every time Lincoln came in the office he read all the telegrams in the file until he came to those he had seen on his last visit. Then he said, "I am down to raisins." The boys determined to ask him what he meant as soon as they knew him better.

The news from abroad seemed strange indeed. The cotton famine had not materialized. Instead cotton was reported to be a glut on the British market.[2] Unemployment, then, could not reasonably be blamed upon the American blockade. Lincoln decided to tighten his strangle hold on the Confederate coast. He ordered a fleet of old vessels, sixteen of them, loaded with stone. When ready, the fleet could be sunk in Charleston Harbor. Blockading warships would thus be released to strangle ports farther south. Lincoln decided also to send some prominent Americans to Europe to counteract the influence of Mason and Slidell. He selected Thurlow Weed, General Scott, Archbishop Hughes and Bishop McIlvaine. The appointments strengthened Lincoln's hand at home as well as abroad.[3] The Archbishop was old, wise, and influential with foreign-born Catholics in America. A Whig in politics, he had been intimate with Weed and Seward for twenty years.[4] Advanc-

ing age had not dulled the twinkle in his eye nor palsied the firmness of his step.[5] Before he embarked, Lincoln called him to Washington. Busybodies who saw the Archbishop enter Lincoln's office
speculated on the conference. The prelate came out with the mien
of a man entrusted with a secret mission. He said that he was going
to Europe—France, Spain, Italy—the Catholic countries. "Neither
the North nor the South knew my mission," Hughes wrote a
friend. "I alone knew it."[6]

Hughes was a Weed man. To preserve the balance between the
Weed and Chase factions in his cabinet Lincoln appointed Charles
P. McIlvaine,[7] Episcopalian Bishop of Ohio. Next Lincoln
broached the question with Thurlow Weed.[8] The spoilsman was
coy, suspicious of being sent away from the throttle of his machine.
Chase's friends might attempt to remove Seward while Weed was
gone. Weed gave Lincoln many courteous excuses. Then he accepted the appointment. After all, it gave him an opportunity to
be absent from a looming investigation of war contracts in which
he might be implicated. Weed remembered later that he had decided to go when he became convinced that Archbishop Hughes
would not go without him. Weed said, too, that he paid for the trip
out of his own pocket in order to prevent criticism from Democratic
members of the cabinet—Chase, Welles and Blair. Members of the
State Department noted that he wrote secretly for funds.

It was a relief to Lincoln when all the good-will ambassadors
were gone. He walked over to the telegraph office and "got down
to raisins." One of the boys could stand it no longer and asked
him the meaning of that odd phrase. Lincoln sank wearily into the
rocker, crooked his leg over the arm and leaned his head against
the cushion.

"Back to home," he said, "a neighbor girl celebrated her birthday by eating too much and topping off with rice pudding. During
the night she got sick. The doctor arrived while she was busy cast-
ing up her accounts. He looked at the contents of the bowl and
said, 'All danger has passed. She's down to raisins.' "[9]

Lincoln looked out the window dreamily. Somewhere in the
Atlantic Ocean the fleets of Spain, France and England were
steaming belligerently toward the Caribbean. Mason and Slidell,
Weed, Scott and Hughes were racing for Europe. An American

ship, the *San Jacinto,* had recently returned from an African cruise. The commander, Captain Charles Wilkes, was looking for Semmes and the raider *Sumter* or any other excitement. The Atlantic was full of ships shuttling hither and yon. Northern and Southern ships scoured the sea for each other's envoys. Weed and his daughter, Scott, his wife and family, all on the *Arago* bound for Le Havre, France, made a tempting prize for some Confederate ship.

Old Winfield Scott's vivid military past and present love of good living made him desirable company on such a journey. The days on shipboard were whiled away watching the horizon for Confederate cruisers and playing whist. Weed and Scott, card partners during the entire voyage, were equally fond of telling stories drawn from the gamut of over half a century of American life. Two wars and a constant association with political leaders had developed in Scott a taste for resplendent uniforms, a studied ostentation in language, a fondness for poetic couplets and a desire to display his ability at fine writing.[10] Short of breath from his extreme weight, the old general enjoyed panting grimly about his youthful escapades with women during the War of 1812 and his victory over the British at Chippewa when the soldiers had irreverently compared him to a beanpole.[11] The general's romantic wife delighted in writing poems, conjuring her spouse to "Sail on, gallant Scott,"[12] and she was rewarded with whinnied approval by the spavined war horse.

Thurlow Weed, unlike Scott, had grown old without gaining undue weight. The two men made an odd appearance promenading the deck, scanning the horizon for a sail—the fat and the lean of American diplomacy. Both men were over six feet tall. Both men were a little lame.[13] The weight of Scott's stomach arched his spine forward, tossing his head aloft with an air of military hauteur. Weed's head habitually bowed a trifle as though listening to someone shorter than himself. Among the passengers along the rail the two men looked like two letters of the alphabet: f and O.

The two men differed in dress as widely as in stature. For Weed fine clothes had no appeal. He dressed like a farmer or, as he liked to phrase it, with the simplicity of Franklin and Jay. Eighteen years before, when he had visited Europe, Weed complained about the undemocratic court dress affected by American

ministers. On that trip he had crossed the ocean with Bishop
Hughes and Father DeSmet, the latter returning from exploring
the Rocky Mountains. Weed remembered a difficulty that had occurred with the British customs officers. Father DeSmet's trunk,
full of Indian relics, was passed without question but Bishop
Hughes had to pay eighteen shillings' duty for some snuff.

"You must do this, sir," said the officer, "in honor of the
Queen."

"For which I should like to give her Majesty a *pinch*," replied
the Bishop.[14]

When not playing whist or scanning the horizon for enemy
raiders the passengers watched the ship's log and speculated on the
number of days the journey would consume. They wondered also
whether Mason and Slidell would beat them to Europe. Weed
knew both the Confederate commissioners and could tell his companions that Slidell's brother, Ronald, had a record none too
praiseworthy. As captain of a school ship he had hanged three
midshipmen—one of them the son of the Secretary of War.[15] The
boys had not been given a fair trial, Weed said. Their court-
martial had been "fixed" by the commander. Weed liked to tell
too how all the officers implicated in the boys' trial met a tragic
end,[16] one in a shipwreck, one by suicide, while the captain himself
had died in an accident as he rode his horse in the village of Sing
Sing, New York. The captain had felt an approaching heart
attack. Drawing his feet from the stirrups to keep from being
dragged to death, he fell to the ground, hit his head, and died.[17]
The curse had followed the school ship, too. A hurricane in the
Caribbean had laid her on her side, trapping most of the crew,
drowning them like rats. Her commander in that accident had
been Raphael Semmes, who was now on the *Sumter* somewhere
out yonder over the horizon looking for Weed or Scott or any
other Americans who dared sail the Atlantic under the Stars and
Stripes.

Weed could also tell his companions stories of foreign courts and
potentates. European diplomats, he believed, were more hardened
than Americans to political trials that were "fixed" and executions
that were convenient. They were more cynical, more opportunistic
and harder pressed by the economic problems of feeding and

employing a congested population. Millions were always on the verge of starvation, yet the upper classes were always finding it difficult to invest their capital profitably. To get support for the North from such people in this crisis, hard facts, not sentiment, would be required. Weed said that when he visited Europe in the 1840's Americans were taunted with their country's repudiation of foreign debts.[18] "And let us not forget, gentlemen, that Jeff Davis was leader in that repudiation."

Lincoln had acted none too soon in getting his extra ambassadors to Europe. The anti-Union sentiment which had been constantly growing since the North's failure at Bull Run increased in tempo during November. A flood of pro-Southern pamphlets descended upon British readers. One of these, by Charles McKay, a *Times* correspondent and author of *Life and Liberty in America,* argued that the Civil War was not a struggle over slavery but over which section—North or South—should rule politically and economically. Early in November another book appeared—*The American Union* by James Spence. The author, a Liverpool businessman, had once filled an iron contract for the Illinois Central Railroad.[19] He might now profit by Confederate war orders which were making shipyards hum. The author followed the cunning subterfuge of stating in his preface that his interests and friendships were on the Northern side, "hence the opinions formed and expressed have not been adopted from choice."[20] With this introduction, designed to take the reader off guard, Spence's book was read widely. It became the manual for all Southern propagandists. With the long vision of political scientists Spence showed that throughout history federal republics had not endured; that America's material wealth was no indication of political strength. Lincoln no doubt saw the book in Washington, and if he thumbed the pages he read that America's statesmen had become decadent since the bright days of Washington, Madison, Jefferson, Webster and Clay. Lincoln may have been interested, too, in Spence's statement that slavery, although abhorred by the civilized world, was in reality an advantage to the Negro. Reviewing the relations between England and America since the outbreak of the rebellion, Spence pointed out the inconsistency of Lincoln's blockade proclamation and the futility of objecting to England's recognition of the South as a belligerent. Had not the United States in 1836 recognized the revolting Texans as belligerents but not as an independent country? Referring to the blockade, Spence turpentined Lincoln's and Seward's sore spot when he wrote:

"The Northern party, in fact, demanded that we should recognize a state of war by admitting their blockade, and at the same time deny a state of war by treating Southern vessels as pirates."[21]

Spence's best points, the ones that most affected English businessmen, concerned the potential danger of American industrial rivalry. The North Spence saw as the self-appointed antagonist of his country, the Southern portion its natural ally.[22] Politically America offered another threat. Her size if she were not divided would make her the greatest nation in the world.

"Any American will admit that the dimensions of France are ample for a great power, yet as a Unionist he plunges into the horrors of civil war, because his country with half the population of France would be reduced to twelve times the size."[23]

Rationalizing these fears, the author could not see the Civil War as a struggle for democracy with its freedom of speech, of the press and of election. In case of a Northern victory he prophesied:

"It would probably be followed by a foreign war—free institutions would cease to be practicable—a military hero would take, as a dictator, the seat that Washington filled. . . ."[24]

Letter writers answered Spence's book with long missives to the press. The whole question of the American war was rehashed. The London *Times* published[25] a three-and-a-half-column protest from Theodore S. Fay, late minister resident of the United States in Switzerland. Fay censured a recent speech of Lord John Russell's against the North as a body blow to the humane cause of abolition. This letter was followed by one from Dion Boucicault, the playwright—flagrant propaganda, Northerners said when they read it. Boucicault stated that, after long residence in the South, he had become convinced that *Uncle Tom's Cabin* was not a true picture of Southern slavery. Europeans had changed their senti-

*Courtesy of Baker & Taylor, N. Y.*

*Courtesy of Illinois State Historical Library*

THURLOW WEED

WINFIELD SCOTT

*Courtesy of Baker & Taylor, N. Y.*

*Courtesy of F. H. Meserve*

JOHN BIGELOW

WILLIAM L. DAYTON

EARL JOHN RUSSELL          LORD PALMERSTON

JOHN BRIGHT               RICHARD COBDEN

*Courtesy of F. H. Meserve*

ment against slavery, he said, as they learned more about it. His play *The Octoroon*, the tragedy of a slave girl sold to a brutal overseer, had been so badly received by the public that he was compelled to rewrite the drama and show the sunny side of Negro life.[26]

This letter called out others. Henry Adams wrote leisurely from the legation. It was plain that English sentiment was shifting on the slavery issue—at least the sentiment of the upper classes, confronted now with the danger of republicanism. Weed, Scott, Hughes and McIlvaine would have plenty to do.

Then another ship, the *Finegal*, loaded with naval guns as well as thousands of rifles, cutlasses and other munitions, evaded the British officials and got to sea in October 1861. Americans blamed the British for complicity.[27] As a matter of fact J. D. Bulloch had manipulated the escape. He knew that the government had become vigilant since the *Bermuda* had got away. Bulloch used every precaution to keep his own movements a secret. He suspected that the United States Government had created an espionage fund for the London consulate. An ex-congressman, Freeman H. Morse, had been appointed United States consul there. Born near the sea, Morse had made a hobby of carving ship's figureheads during an active political career. Bulloch was sure that this Northern man prowled around the wharves for more than artistic designs. The Southerner soon became convinced that the British yards were full of Federal spies.[28] Bulloch made it a point not to visit the vessels being built for him except on rare occasions. He stayed away from the *Finegal* while she was loading and arranged for the ship's officers to sign up a crew for the British island of Bermuda. As the time approached for the *Finegal's* departure Bulloch and his Southern companions took passage for Holyhead Island, in the Irish Sea. From here they planned to board the vessel as she came by. At the appointed time a heavy fog disrupted the schedule. The channel was blotted out for three days. Bulloch fretted in a country inn on the island. On October 14, 1861, the gale subsided. By four in the afternoon blue sky appeared through the fog. Soon the mists arose from the silvery ocean. No *Finegal* in sight! Bulloch watched and waited as dark settled across the sea. Finally he returned to the inn where a fire burned cheerily.

Early next morning a knock awoke Bulloch. His bedroom was cold, black and silent at that hour. Two men entered with a dark lantern. Bulloch rubbed his sleepy eyes. In the half-light he saw the gloomy figures of the inn porter and an officer from the *Finegal*. The seaman, muffled in a sou'wester and dripping slicker, brought bad news—a wreck. His ship had rammed a Sardinian coaler when she slipped around the breakwater in the dark.[29] The coaler, heavily loaded, sank almost immediately. Come daylight and an investigation, the *Finegal* would be detained and her identity disclosed. What must be done? Bulloch threw back the covers, slicked the curl down on his bald forehead and called his sleeping companions. All dressed hurriedly, stuffed clothes into their bags, then stumbled out into the dark street, shivering with memories of warm beds.

Day was breaking when they boarded the *Finegal*. In the dim light they could see the upper spars of the sunken brig "with the bunt of the main-top-gallant sail awash." She had sunk squarely to the bottom without capsizing. Bulloch ordered the *Finegal's* engines full speed ahead. They got to sea without meeting the port authorities.[30]

Arriving at Bermuda, the *Finegal* did not unload. Instead she put out to sea once more, bound for Nassau, so the captain said. The next day the crew was piped aft to hear passenger Bulloch explain from the quarter-deck that the ship intended to run the blockade into Savannah and gain great profits. He explained also that this profit would be lost if the ship were overhauled by one of Mr. Lincoln's makeshift blockaders, a contingency Bulloch had guarded against by stowing cannon on board which could be quickly mounted on the decks. "So long as the *Finegal* is under the British flag, we have no right to fire a shot," Bulloch shouted above the throbbing engines. "But I have a bill of sale in my pocket, and can take delivery from the captain on behalf of the Confederate Navy Department at any moment."[31]

Bulloch asked the crew to join him in this adventure, explaining that the ship would run the blockade as a British vessel unless she encountered an American her own size. Then she would become a Confederate and open fire. The crew cheered. "We knowed it all the time."

The *Finegal* steamed across the empty waters toward Savannah. No blockading vessel was sighted. One day a billow of fog rolled out of the west. Pine and cypress swamps were near. Soon the ship was enveloped. Thick as "mulligatawny soup," said Bulloch,[32] who had lived enough of his life in the South to know the idiom. The sun disappeared overhead. The helmsman steered by compass alone while sailors with lead lines made constant soundings in the shallow water. Night settled around the little ship. Running close to shore, skirting sand bars in water too shallow for a large vessel, the *Finegal* slipped along toward Savannah. All hands on deck talked in whispers, listening to the slowed throb of the engines and the lap of water on the prow. The forward watch could not see the stern. As dawn approached excitement became intense. A near panic occurred when a cock in a crate on the deck crowed lustily. To the seamen's overstrained ears the sudden clarion sounded like a siren whistle. The enemy must hear it! A sailor ran to the coop to wring the chicken's neck. A great mistake. The whole coop cackled wildly. Noise enough to straighten the curl on Bulloch's forehead!

Fortunately no blockader was near. The *Finegal* got into the Savannah River, steamed up the channel and then, at the end of the long, hazardous voyage, ran aground. The accident occurred well inshore and so close to the city that Federal blockaders dared not approach. The precious cargo of munitions was transferred to Confederate barges. The *Finegal* floated free and was towed away to be converted into a ship of war. Jeff Davis' navy had grown apace. Let Lincoln's blockaders beware.

While this bad news filtered North on Lincoln's secret grapevine and while dispatches from the English press argued the pros and cons of the American war, Mason and Slidell made arrangements for the second step of their passage from Havana to the British Isles. In the meantime copies of Seward's circular letter mobilizing the border states to repel an invasion from Canada reached Great Britain. The *Times* published a sarcastic leader.[33] George Francis Train answered the *Times* from every platform in England where he could get an audience. Week after week he served sumptuous breakfasts and luncheons in order that his guests might see him enjoy his own eloquence. He wrote long letters to the *New York*

*Times* and *New York Herald,* then published them in pamphlet form for distribution. He gave the names of British firms speculating in contraband trade and their profits. He named the British ships outfitting for the Southern run and enumerated the number and make of rifles on board. Train hinted at the only remedy—a class struggle. "I say, when you see the entire dress circle of England is secession to the back bone, it is time to declare . . . that the English pit is sound, and goes for the Union to the last."[34] Lincoln had hinted at this same approach in his message to the special session of Congress. Perhaps he should dig deeper into it.

Upper-class Englishmen were incensed at the turn of events—America's uncalled-for crusade against their institutions. Seward's order to mobilize along the Canadian border appeared like a threat. His aggressive nature was well known. The blockade and idle cotton factories hurt everybody's nerves—even if they were not cause and effect. Spence's book had painted a very bad picture of the aggressive North. Anything could be expected of those unscrupulous rascals. Then astounding news arrived.

An American man-of-war had stopped a British packet on the high seas, searched the ship and taken off four passengers—the Confederate commissioners, Mason and Slidell, with their two secretaries. "Han hinsult to the flag!"

The commissioners were typical of the characters that might be expected to come to the top in a reactionary revolution. Mason was master of Selma Plantation, a rural aristocrat, large, dull, his contemporaries said, the product of inherited opportunity, opposed to the mandate of democratic majorities which might deprive him of his way of life. Slidell was a city slicker, Northern-born, self-made, seeking a gambler's opportunity in revolution. James Murray Mason boasted of his descent from Virginia Cavaliers. His grandfather, George Mason of Gunston Hall, had been prominent in the Revolution, author of the Virginia constitution and compounder in large part of the American Bill of Rights—the first ten amendments of the United States Constitution. The grandson, James Murray Mason, sincerely believed the seat he had held in the United States Senate to be a birthright.[35] He was known as the orator of slavery, a believer in the institution as "a positive good," author of the Fugitive Slave Act. A leader in the secession movement, he saw nothing inconsistent in preserving slavery by repealing, if necessary, the Bill of Rights[36]—the source of his family's fame. Philosophical Charles Francis Adams, Jr., enjoyed the inconsistency as a biological example of the influence of environment on the minds of men, the radical of one generation becoming the reactionary of the next. William H. Russell, the correspondent, described him as "a fine old English gentleman but for tobacco" which, rumor said later, he provincially expectorated in the House of Commons.

John Slidell was in many ways the opposite of his colleague. Contemporaries called him keen and shrewd. Mason's honesty was unquestioned; not so Slidell's. Like many of the Northern adventurers who joined the Confederate cause, Slidell was more typically Southern than men to the manor born. William H. Russell, on his Southern trip in the spring of 1861, visited Slidell's plantation above New Orleans. He was introduced to Mrs. Slidell and her sister, Madam Beauregard, wife of the general. Conversation was carried on in French. He met also Slidell's daughters, "two very charming young ladies."[37] Russell did not dream of the international notoriety in store for Slidell as well as for one of the "two very charming young ladies." Of the future envoy he wrote:

"I rarely met a man whose features have a greater *finesse* and firmness of purpose than Mr. Slidell's; his keen gray eye is full of life; his thin, firmly-set lips indicate resolution and passion. . . . He is an excellent judge of mankind, adroit, persevering, and subtle, full of device, and fond of intrigue . . . what is called here a 'wire-puller.' Mr. Slidell is to the South something greater than Mr. Thurlow Weed has been to his party in the North."[38]

When Charles Francis Adams heard that Slidell had been appointed as envoy to Napoleon in France he raised his eyebrows. The Southerner, Adams mused, will find the Emperor "a man of his own sort who'll be delighted to see him."

Mason and Slidell both had the personal appearance and experience which qualified them for social life in official circles. At Havana they had been lionized by the diplomatic set, but not officially, the British government maintained. While they were enjoying this revelry the American *San Jacinto* dropped anchor at

Cienfuegos, Cuba. Captain Wilkes, a rugged, studious, irascible man, happy to be back from stifling equatorial seas, went ashore for news and learned that Mason and Slidell were across the island in Havana. Steaming around the Pearl of the Antilles, he headed straight for Morro Castle, entered the harbor and got more news.[39] The United States Navy, he learned, was watching the commissioners. Officers assumed that the Southerners would continue their voyage in the Confederate steamer *Nashville*. The bluejackets planned taking the ship, commissioners and all, before she reached England. Wilkes learned too that the Confederates intended to foil their pursuers by engaging passage to St. Thomas on the British mail steamer *Trent* and thus escaping under the protection of the British flag.

Captain Wilkes had known John Slidell as a boy in New York. In that distant day they had quarreled over a girl and the two men's paths had not crossed again. Wilkes remembered Slidell as a man-about-town who played politics, and was often one jump ahead of the sheriff and the debtors' prison; he recalled that he had left New York for New Orleans after fighting a duel with a theater manager over an actress.[40] Wilkes and Slidell had both succeeded, each in his chosen field. Wilkes, on the sea, had distinguished himself the hard way, leading an exploring expedition for four years in Antarctica—a success partly marred by a court-martial held after his return on charges preferred by his disgruntled companions. He had been acquitted on all charges except "illegal punishment of subordinates,"[41] for which he received a reprimand.

When Wilkes had returned from Antarctica the whole country was agog with the Plaquemines Parish scandals, a tale of fraud in which Slidell was charged with chartering two steamboats in New Orleans, loading them with toughs, and sailing down the river where he stopped at several landings for his hired men to vote repeatedly. Captain Wilkes also heard over and over again all the Navy gossip about the court-martial of Slidell's brother for hanging the school-ship students.

Wilkes wanted to catch his old rival. He talked the matter over with his ship's officers. To arrest Mason and Slidell on a British ship would be identical to the British practice which had aggravated the War of 1812. However, the opportunity of capturing the commissioners ahead of the entire United States Navy was more than Wilkes could resist.

Lieutenant D. M. Fairfax, second in command, ruled against the enterprise but Wilkes was no man to be easily dissuaded. The *Trent* was due to carry Confederate mail and was thus subject to capture. Captain Wilkes got the packet's itinerary and steamed away.

On November 7, 1861, the *Trent* put to sea. Shortly after noon on the next day, her captain looked across the cobalt waters of the Bahama channel and saw what was known as a "tea kettle"—a sailor's name for an ocean-going steamship. The "kettle" was lying to on the horizon, with fires banked, no smoke above her funnels and no flag flying at the masthead. As the captain of the *Trent* watched her from the bridge he noticed a gush of black smoke. Fire had been released to her boilers. The vessel moved forward to intercept him. As she came nearer the captain recognized her as the American *San Jacinto*. He noted also that her gun ports were open; cannon showed with the tampions pulled from their mouths. When she was within a few hundred yards a puff of white smoke burst from a pivot gun on the forecastle. The captain of the *Trent* watched it float into the rigging like a summer cloud and disappear. Then he heard the boom of a cannon. A geyser of spray leaped from the ocean where the ball hit. The captain ran up the British flag and chugged doggedly along. Another puff of smoke from the American! This time a shell burst ahead of the *Trent*. The captain shouted an order. His engines were shut down and the ship lay to. Two hundred yards away the *San Jacinto* came to a halt, her broadside cannon grinning at the mail packet. Marines lowered a boat from her davits. With long sweeping oars they came alongside. The packet carried an officer commissioned in the British navy, Commander Richard Williams, in charge of Her Majesty's mail. Williams watched the approaching boarders with irritation, then ran below to put on the uniform of his rank.

The marines' boat grated against the side of the *Trent*. The officer in command, Lieutenant Fairfax, climbed on board. He demanded the list of passengers. The captain hesitated, then led the way to his cabin. Fairfax thumbed through the sheets. Mason and Slidell, he said, must be surrendered. The captain remonstrated. The Confederates overheard the demand and stepped from the passengers assembled on the deck. The two men, politicians of long standing, were at home before an audience. They demanded their rights to immunity under international law as belligerents on a neutral ship. Slidell's daughter Mathilde watched with sparkling eyes. The great men thundered on the deck with the pomposity they used in the halls of Congress when denouncing the tyranny of the Northern majority. At the hatchway a noise was heard. Commander Williams, puffed out like a turkey cock in full uniform, brass buttons and gold lace, strutted into view. According to one chronicler, "He danced about the deck in an ecstasy of rage, and made the most fearful threats of the wrath of the British people."[42]

The Confederates refused to be taken without a show of force. The lieutenant must clap his hands on their shoulders to signify involuntary arrest. Let him do so if he dared. Fairfax signaled his ship. Three more boats were lowered. In short order they took positions around the *Trent*. The crew from the lieutenant's boat clambered over the rail. Fairfax mustered them smartly on the deck. He told off men to make the arrest. Each stepped forward. The two commissioners as well as their secretaries, George Eustis and J. E. McFarland, were slapped on the shoulder. All agreed to go without further resistance.

This punctiliousness, this intimation that some ruling of international law was involved in the technicality of slapping the prisoners' shoulders, caused endless argument in wardrooms. Some maintained forever after that the irate British naval officer had suggested the formality. Others believed the whole proceeding a trick formulated in the resourceful brain of John Slidell. Lieutenant Fairfax had questioned his chief's right to make the capture. He had acted under orders which he disapproved. Slidell, some Navy men said later, noticed that the lieutenant showed hesitancy. With a master politician's intuition he hoped to intimidate his captor.

Mason accepted his arrest stolidly. Gentlemanly reserve, some called it; others called it sweet stupidity. Slidell, whose close-set, foxy eyes looked down his long straight nose, was agitated. Captain Wilkes had been an ancient enemy. Perhaps an unpleasant reception awaited him on the *San Jacinto*. Mathilde shrieked with rage. She faced the marines, taunted them for cowards. The commissioners pleaded for silence, then asked permission to go to their cabins and pack their bags. Fairfax agreed. Slidell did not return and a marine was sent for him. At the door of his cabin, Mathilde, who had followed her father, barred the passage. Throwing herself on the deck she screamed that he would be taken only across her dead body or something to like effect. While this scene was being enacted at the door Slidell climbed out the port. He was immediately apprehended and taken to the other prisoners,[43] his head blushing beneath his thin white hair "like the shell of a boiled lobster." The two commissioners with their secretaries, Eustis and McFarland, climbed down onto the longboat and were rowed away to the *San Jacinto*. The *Trent* steamed off in a huff.

Petty officers watched the *Trent* go with regret. They would have enjoyed taking her in as a prize. Why had the lieutenant disobeyed the order of his chief and not done so?[44] Had the lieutenant been deterred by his own disinclination coupled with Slidell's astute insinuation that some technicality of international law depended on the forcible laying on of hands? Why did Captain Wilkes not censure the disobedient lieutenant? Did he too question the legality of the act? Perhaps he still smarted under his last court-martial and the official censure for "illegal punishment of subordinates." Sailormen never did agree.

News about the capture of Mason and Slidell arrived in Washington on November 16, 1861. It was a cold, raw day but excitement warmed all loyal spirits. McClellan's army was in the pink of condition, recruited to full strength, and drilled to exactitude. A grand review was scheduled for the twentieth. The North felt confident. The people were wild with joy. They understood that England would resent the capture of Mason and Slidell as an insult to the flag, but war or no war, the mob insisted that the men be held.

Henri Mercier heard the cheering. He wrapped himself in a cloak and left the warmth of his fire to hurry to the British legation for details of the *Trent* incident.[45] Lord Lyons knew nothing more about it than the men in the street, but he was sure that Lincoln must release the prisoners or Seward would have his foreign war.

Ministers from Italy, Prussia, Denmark—even Russia—called on Lord Lyons and all agreed that the United States was in the wrong.[46] The stock market, sensitive to the threat of a new war, went down. The price of gold went up. What of it? The North was jubilant. Bull Run, Ball's Bluff, Wilson's Creek—three rebel victories were partially atoned for by the capture. Hurrah for the Navy! 'And the Army too was now trained and eager for any foe. Only the capture of Jeff Davis himself could have been received with more enthusiasm. A dinner was given Wilkes in Boston. Congress voted him a resolution of thanks. When he visited his home on H Street in Washington a cheering crowd serenaded "the hero of the *Trent*."[47] Wilkes had done more than stop two diplomatic emissaries. He had provided the North with two valuable hostages. Now let the rebels retaliate against Lincoln's pirate proclamation by hanging Northern prisoners! Already Confederates boasted that fourteen men had been selected to pay the penalty as a reprisal in case any privateersmen were executed. When hanging began it would not end until Mason and Slidell died upon the scaffold.[48]

Lincoln listened to the joyful demonstrations, the exultation. He knew that Wilkes had violated the principle for which America had fought the War of 1812. Lincoln knew, too, that the will of the people in a democracy is hard to resist. The commissioners, he said sadly, might become "white elephants."[49] Charles Sumner in the Senate and Montgomery Blair in the cabinet both urged Lincoln to surrender the men immediately. Lincoln was reminded of a story. The great statesmen went away provoked. Damn a man who would never make a decision! The prisoners were ordered confined in Fort Warren in Boston Harbor.

On November 20, 1861, Lincoln drove out with Secretary of War Cameron to review the army. John G. Nicolay, Lincoln's private secretary, accompanied them. Fifty thousand men were drawn up in solid formation—acres of blue uniforms—artillery, cavalry, bands, commissary wagons, as far as the eye could see. Lincoln mounted a charger provided for him and galloped away. Officers clattered in his rear. Secretary Cameron dropped out before the inspection was half complete.[50]

Such an army, so well equipped, was enough to put heart into any people. Let England declare war if she had the nerve!

Meanwhile, Southerners rejoiced to know that England was preparing to fight with them against the Northerners. Mason and Slidell had served them better by being captured than they could have with arguments in Great Britain. Jeff Davis ordered J. D. Bulloch to rerun the blockade with the *Finegal,* proceed to England and take command of the *Alabama,* now nearing completion. Should England declare war he would have little trouble getting the ship released from British yards.

Lincoln's advisors knew that the President faced a great crisis. Would the village lawyer be equal to it? The cabinet did not agree on what to do. Lincoln had no plan. Another muddle! The critics who howled loudest did not know that two important letters went out from two of Lincoln's departments on the same day—one from Seward to Minister Adams and the other from Welles to Captain Wilkes. Both letters might become public property and they were worded in such a way as not to inflame the people who insisted, war or no war, on keeping the prisoners. On the other hand the letters were also worded to assuage England. Seward's letter to Adams stated that the minister might tell Earl Russell that Captain Wilkes had not acted on instructions from the government.[51] Welles's letter to Wilkes was equally guarded. He congratulated his commander, warned him that international law had been violated and cautioned: "The forebearance exercised in this instance must not be permitted to constitute a precedent."[52]

Obviously Lincoln watched every word that might be used against him by his enemies at home, who suspected that he planned to turn loose the prisoners. At the same time he left an open passage for retreat with honor if popular sentiment veered sufficiently to permit him to do so. Had he said definitely that he would hold the commissioners it would have amounted to an ultimatum to England and had he said definitely that he would return them he would have lost power at home. Only a few intimates noted Lincoln's guarded words, his hope for the cooling influence of time. Most of the people raged at what they called his indecision. Later they called it masterly intuition.

William H. Russell watched the trend of American opinion. He felt positive that war was coming. On November 19, 1861, the "stone fleet" set sail to destroy Charleston Harbor as heedlessly as though no crisis existed. Had the President no fear of Britain? A week later all hope of the Northern people's willingness to release the prisoners vanished with a statement told confidentially by Russell and soon known by everyone. The British crown lawyers had anticipated that Mason and Slidell would sail on the *Nashville* and would be transferred to a British packet before reaching England. Russell quoted the barristers as saying that in such a contingency a United States man-of-war would be justified in taking the commissioners from the British ship.[53] Americans crowed triumphantly.

Lincoln listened to the popular acclaim of Charles Wilkes and decided that it would be unwise to release the prisoners. Yet William H. Russell, Lord Lyons, all the diplomats, insisted among themselves that the men must be given up or England would fight. Russell was surprised to see the President and all the cabinet in good spirits as the danger increased. He told his diary that Lincoln "indulges in quaint speculations."

"He calculates, for instance, there are human beings now alive who may ere they die behold the United States peopled by 250 millions of souls. Talking of a high prairie, in Illinois, he remarked, 'that if all the nations of the earth were assembled there, a man standing on its top would see them all, for that the whole human race would fit on a space twelve miles square, which was about the extent of the plain.' "[54]

Russell wondered what was on Lincoln's mind. Surely it was not the *Trent* affair. Perhaps he was bluffing England with a picture of America's future might. More likely he was dreaming that in Washington he might argue the case for democracy before the world, as he and Douglas had argued before assembled farmers on the prairies in Illinois.

# IX. *Give Up the Men!*

IN ENGLAND, before the capture of Mason and Slidell was known, speculation as to their fate assumed the excitement of a Derby. The commissioners were expected on the Confederate *Nashville*. Palmerston knew that England and America tottered on the verge of war. One more misunderstanding might push both into the abyss. He ordered a warship to patrol the three-mile limit and prevent the capture in British jurisdiction.[1] On November 21, 1861, the Confederate *Nashville* steamed into Southampton,[2] her decks fore and aft of the great churning side-wheels black with marines. But no Confederate commissioners were on board. The whereabouts of Mason and Slidell were still unknown. The captain had sighted the *Arago* just before sunup. His hold was already full of prisoners; his engine knocked badly. He decided not to give chase.

Thurlow Weed and General Scott had recognized the *Nashville*. They expected a fight. General Scott forgot his gout and strutted the deck, eager for battle. Weed said Old Fuss and Feathers looked "an inch or two higher." Both were surprised when the *Nashville* kept her distance and permitted them to go on to Le Havre.

Two days later a steamer brought word of the capture of Mason and Slidell.[3] The danger that Palmerston feared—and Adams too—had struck at last. The people of England appeared stunned—dazed.[4] On November 27, 1861, the full reports from the *Trent's* purser and several of the packet's passengers arrived.[5] Excitement swept like a hurricane across the country. Popular passion, people said, had not been so inflamed at any time in their memory.[6] Mass meetings were called. Anonymous letters threatened to burn the American legation. Yancey and Mann realized that for them the sun now shone. On the day that the news arrived they wrote Earl Russell for another interview.

In due time the reply came back. The Earl presented his compliments and hoped that the gentlemen would put in writing any communication they might have.[7]

173

The envoys received this snub with humility. In a long letter they described Southern victories and the hopelessness of the Northern cause. The lengthy reply did not reach its destination until after the cabinet met to determine Britain's policy on the *Trent* affair.

The cabinet's proceedings were secret but soon leaked out. The crown lawyers had been present. They reiterated their recent decision but the cabinet was brusque. Their seats in Parliament depended on votes, not on principles of international law. Palmerston sent the minutes of the meeting to the Queen. The cabinet, not the law officers, he reported, insisted that "a gross outrage and violation of international law has been committed."[8] Russell sent a proposed ultimatum to Her Majesty. Lincoln was given seven days to relinquish the prisoners and apologize. The Queen held the papers for a day and returned them. The Americans at the legation wondered if the Queen had given her approval.

Spies reported that three dispatches were prepared and sent to Lord Lyons in America. A fourth to the Admiralty ordered the North Atlantic squadron to prepare for action.[9] Next Earl Russell replied to the long letter from the Confederate envoys.

Surely the Foreign Secretary intended to welcome the Confederates as allies. Breaking the seals on the dispatch, the Southerners read:

"Lord Russell presents his compliments to Mr. Yancey, Mr. Rost and Mr. Mann. He has had the honor to receive their letters of the 27th and 30th of November, but in the present state of affairs he must decline to enter into any official communication with them."[10]

As a studied insult this exceeded the previous letter. One thing was certain. Russell was marking time, using caution, being scrupulously neutral while the war threat gained momentum.

Both parties in Parliament were against war now the crisis had come, but popular clamor could not be ignored. Seward had talked so long and so belligerently that the average Englishman believed, without waiting for confirmation, that the American government sanctioned the capture. This belief increased with a rumor from France. Old General Scott was reported as saying that the American cabinet had planned the capture to excite a war. He, Scott, had come to enlist France on the Northern side, humiliate England, and take Canada.[11]

The American envoys—Weed, Scott, McIlvaine and Hughes—had scarcely unpacked when the hurricane burst upon them. Meeting with Dayton, Sanford and Bigelow, Weed mapped out their course. First a letter must be prepared for the British and French newspapers explaining the American position. Scott must quash the rumor of his alleged statement. To get such a letter from "the old cipher" was not as simple as might be assumed. The general knew Byron better than he did international diplomacy. He liked to write and prided himself on his ability to indite fine letters. He resented suggestions from anyone. Wire-puller Weed had an idea, a plot within a plot. Bigelow, with his long experience in international affairs, must write the letter. While he was working, Weed went out to see the general. Old Fuss and Feathers fumed with a swollen hand. Weed saw his chance. Suavely he discussed the matter of writing a letter for the press. Point by point the letter was mapped out in such a way that the general believed each idea to be his own. The foundation and the super-structure of the letter were agreed upon. Then Weed clinched the nails. Would it not be permissible, Weed inquired in his quiet way, to get someone to write down the general's ideas for him, especially since the general's malady made writing so painful? Scott, grunting with pain, agreed, and Weed retired. Bigelow soon had the letter finished and Weed took it to Scott for the old general's signature. Bigelow believed that he had written the first great bit of diplomatic propaganda for the war.[12] The letter was addressed "To a friend" and began:

*"My dear Sir:* You were right in doubting the declaration imputed to me that the Cabinet at Washington had given orders to seize Messrs. Mason and Slidell, even under a neutral flag, for I am not aware that the Government has ever had that point under consideration. At the time of my leaving New York it was not known that the *San Jacinto* had returned to the American seas; and it was generally supposed that those persons had escaped to Cuba for the purpose of reëmbarking in the *Nashville,* in pursuit of which vessel the *James Adger* and other cruisers had been dispatched."[13]

Scott then discussed the British contention that Wilkes would have been justified in taking a vessel which carried contraband, but not in taking off the men—"a very narrow basis on which to fix a serious controversy." In short, Scott continued, England contends "our offence had been less if it had been greater."[14] Then Scott discussed Britain's "right of search," the War of 1812 which had not settled the right, and the inadequate definition in international law.

Bigelow watched the press to see the effect of this letter. The London *Times* replied on December 5, 1861, that Scott obviously was trying to assuage British anger, that this was no time to argue. Let America accept or challenge the British view! The *Spectator* declared that the capture of the commissioners was not analagous to the British right of search.[15] This right, the *Spectator* maintained, had always been a right in war, but the United States denied that there was a war. Therefore Mason and Slidell could not be contraband. They could not be "enemies." They were traitors. And political refugees were always safe under a British flag. Time had come to rehash the whole tangled argument about belligerents, blockades and rights of neutrals, the meaning of laws, and what so-and-so said and what so-and-so meant; time for hustings oratory and explanations. Lincoln had sent to London and Paris two of the best American politicians, two of the best diplomats and two of the highest-ranking theologians in America. If they could not talk themselves out of a predicament of this kind American ingenuity had declined.

The propagandists agreed that Archbishop Hughes should remain in France and interview the Emperor. Weed set off for London to consult with Bishop McIlvaine. To America he wrote that the prisoners must be surrendered.[16] Reading the papers, Weed could see plenty of evidence to show that war was not inevitable. True, *Punch* published a cartoon of Britannia leaning on an Armstrong cannon, but the *Saturday Review* stated that nothing should be done until America had time to explain the seizure. Furthermore, the *Review* continued, "We none of us wish that the demand should be put in any but a conciliatory way."[17] However, the editor continued, England should not dream of surrendering political rebels to any power on earth. He hoped that Wilkes had not acted under instructions.

Weed consulted other papers. The London *Times* announced that Seward desired to annex Canada as compensation for the loss of the Southern states. If Canada wanted to retain its independence, the *Times* warned, she should prepare her own defense. Britain would help her if necessary but "our fellow subjects" were really a free people. "They would not be worth a dollar less to us were they to-morrow the tributaries of the Northern Republic or the members of an independent state."[18] Here was another angle for Weed to ponder as he traveled from Paris to London on his mission to avert the war. The American trend toward a strong federal government was counter to the British political concept of loose confederation—a serious difference when every similarity of the two governments was being published.

More encouraging to Weed was the news of an antiwar meeting at Rochdale on December 4, 1861. John Bright had spoken strongly in favor of the Northern cause, castigating Earl Russell and the *Times* eloquently. Bright had said that Southern secession was not analogous to the American Revolution. Southerners could not complain of "taxation without representation." The South had always been represented—more than represented. In Congress they were allowed to vote for themselves and for their slaves also. Nor was the tariff a valid complaint. A tariff could not be passed without Southern votes. A tariff would be hard on the agricultural West, too, yet it did not secede. The only real cause of the Civil War, Bright boomed, was slavery, slavery, slavery! The *Trent* affair, he said, was irritating, "but let us wait calmly and see if it is not disavowed."[19] At the meeting the mayor of Rochdale also read a paper prepared by Richard Cobden, urging Englishmen to respect American legal opinion in the *Trent* case, to refrain from interfering in the American war and to settle the involved question by a codification of maritime law.

Weed had not finished the account of this meeting when his train rattled into London. Next morning at the legation he found Charles Francis Adams discouraged. "America was doomed to fall like ancient Rome." Weed had been 'Adams' political rival in the same party at home. He did not care to listen to ancient history in this crisis. Could Adams tell him what kind of ultimatum had been sent to America? If not, could he get Weed an interview with Palmerston or Russell? Adams, cold and formal, agreed to arrange an audience. Fine! The tall, warmhearted man hoped that the appointment would be soon. Then he bowed himself out of the ministerial icebox and hurried away to renew acquaintances with old friends. A prominent businessman in London said he would get Weed an audience with Russell in the morning. Weed hurried back to the legation. Casually—and cruelly—he mentioned that the interview was already arranged. That night Weed dined with British friends, merchants, bankers, officers talking war and preparations for war. Shipyards clattered day and night, they said. The officers discussed the vessels assigned to carry them to Canada. They drank toasts to gallantry in action. Whatever attitude the government might have, the army and navy were keen for combat.

On the following day Weed drove to Pembroke Lodge to lunch with Earl Russell. The American felt confident. If any diplomatic secrets were to be divulged he expected to hear them. At least he would discover whether or not the government wanted war. The tall, gray, almost farmerlike Weed was ushered into the drawing room to meet the little, aged Secretary of State for Foreign Affairs. The American stooped slightly in his confidential way and began: He regretted the recent unpleasantness, pointed out the British precedent of 1812, the taking of British citizens from American ships.

Earl Russell snapped off the conversation as only a British aristocrat can. He absolutely refused to discuss such a comparison. Warm, easygoing, bent on intrigue, Weed chilled in the cold, rational atmosphere of international diplomacy. In the formal Victorian hall he sensed the climate as accurately as he had in Lincoln's little parlor back in Springfield ten months before. Tactfully he changed the subject, started again on a warmer basis. For years, he said, the Earl's political career had interested him. As a founder of the Whig party in America he always felt close to the Whigs in England. Russell listened, perfunctorily, Weed thought, too well schooled to thaw. Weed did not give up. His persuasive voice massaged the Englishman patiently, enlarging on the parallel principles of the Whigs in America and in England. When Weed thought the time opportune, he drifted back to the point at issue. Prior to 1812, he said, six thousand American seamen had been taken from under the American flag before the United States resorted to war.

"The danger of a collision—" Russell's words tinkled icily—"might be averted by the surrender of the rebel commissioners."

"English history," Weed persisted, "taught us that English noblemen had gone from the Tower to the block for offenses less grave than those which Messrs. Mason and Slidell had committed." Still playing on British history and prejudice he continued, "Our government would be strongly tempted to maintain that this seizure was sanctioned by the early practice of the English government." Weed paused for a moment. His next remark was designed to bring out the information he wanted. Without asking a direct question he said nonchalantly, "I do hope that the British demand for the release of the prisoners was made in a friendly spirit." Another pause. "If so the request will be complied with, I believe."[20]

Little Earl Russell, cold, important, made no reply. At the end of an hour luncheon was announced.

Lady Russell presided at the table. When the meal was over the Earl asked to be excused. Any man but Weed would have felt his mission a failure. Her Ladyship suggested that the American gentleman might enjoy a stroll through the grounds—obviously a polite form of dismissal. Weed glanced out the heavily draped windows. The day was dark and blustery with threatening clouds blowing in from the Thames estuary. He would be delighted, he said, to see the grounds. Lady Russell called a servant to get her hat and shawl. As Weed waited he noticed that the Earl called his wife to one side for a few moments and talked earnestly. Then Lord John bade the "quasi-ambassador" a formal good day. Lady Russell took Mr. Weed's arm and the two stepped out under the lowering clouds. The air, saturated with moisture, was cold but indescribably soft, atmosphere famous for giving English women matchless pink and white complexions. The tall man and the hoop-skirted woman strolled across the lawn, green in winter, jade velvet, spongy under foot as only English sod can be. Weed remembered that walk all his life and told, with travelers' license, how Her Ladyship pointed out the towers of Hampton Court, Kew, Kingston, the round tower of Windsor and other localities made famous by the residence of such men as Pope and Walpole. The American noticed a mound some two or three feet above the level of the lawn. He asked if that too had a history.

"Oh, yes," replied Lady Russell, as Weed, limping a little, mounted its summit. "Look through that avenue of elms. You are now standing precisely where Henry VIII stood watching for a signal from the dome of St. Paul's church, announcing the execution of Anne Boleyn."

Strolling farther they came upon the Russell children building a fort in this sacred soil of England, constructing in their imagination new wars on the nursery tales of their nation's past. Lady Russell turned toward the tall gray man who habitually stooped a little, listening. She spoke suddenly as though an idea had just come to her. "Ladies, you know, are not supposed to have any knowledge of public affairs. But we have eyes and ears, and sometimes use them. In these troubles about the taking of some men from under the protection of our flag, it may be some encouragement to you to know that the Queen is distressed at what she hears, and is deeply anxious for an amicable settlement."[21] Weed bowed courteously, and as they walked back to the lodge in silence he remembered that the Earl had called Her Ladyship to one side for a curtain lecture. Surely Lady Russell had delivered a confidential message direct from the Secretary of State for Foreign Affairs.

A few minutes later Weed completed the tedious formality of farewell prescribed by American society. Then he drove away convinced that the British government would not force a war. Back in London he continued to study the British press. He read the daily issues assiduously. His long nose plowed up and down the columns. An account of the Royal Yacht Club dinner at Plymouth fanned anew the war spirit in Britain. Commander Williams had added some lurid embellishments. The brutal marines, he said, "advanced with their bayonets pointed at the undefended breast of Slidell's daughter." Just in the nick of time, the heroic commander himself, so he said, stepped between the beautiful victim and her destroyers, crying, "Back, you damned cowardly poltroons!"[22]

George Francis Train attempted to answer the Britisher before an audience at the new assembly rooms for the benefit of the

Aldershot Institution for Mental and Social Recreation. The crowd was unfriendly and boisterous. "All I ask," Train shouted, "is not to interrupt me when I get my steam up."[23] Then the tramway promoter cited cases when the British had taken passengers off neutral ships—the Laurens case, the *Leopard* and *Chesapeake* affair, and also the incident in the Levant when a British man-of-war took Lucien Bonaparte from the American *Hercules*. "I believe," said Train, "the American had no mail agent on board, and that Bonaparte had no daughter to throw herself in the door-way, and slap the face of the British officer, which may prevent this case from being exactly analogous."[24]

Train scoffed at the sophistry which enabled Britishers to find an insult in the *Trent* affair. What nonsense to admit that Wilkes had authority to send the packet in as a prize, and that he insulted the flag because he spared the owners and let the ship go. "As General Scott has clearly put it, the greater crime would have been the lesser."[25]

Train's voice was shouting against the tempest of thirty millions. Newspapers and politicians continued to print and prate for votes and circulation. War talk helped both. The English people were plainly out of hand unless Lincoln mollified them with a soft answer. On December 10, 1861, a dispatch came from Seward to the legation.[26] The Secretary of State wanted information about the capture during the Revolution of the American envoy, Henry Laurens, on a neutral ship, by a British man-of-war. Apparently Lincoln was hunting precedents to justify keeping the prisoners.

Weed was disappointed. Three weeks to a month would be required for him to get a reply from any remonstrance he might write. Then it would be too late. From the very beginning he had written that the men must be given up, right or wrong.[27]

Weed rooted through the papers again, silent and diligent as a mole. On December 12, 1861, the *Times* called its readers' attention to the fact that recent elections in America had repudiated the President.[28] Weakened and tottering at home, the *Times* continued, Lincoln must now choose between "justice and peace or outrage and war." Next day the *Times* printed an account of a meeting at Bury. Politicians were adding to the war fever by blaming unemployment on the American war, scoffing at the reports of overproduction of cotton goods, displaying statistics to prove it.[29]

Then Weed received a letter from Paris bitter enough to make even his sweet face curdle. Bigelow wrote that Scott was packing his trunks to go home. In vain his colleagues argued that such a move might precipitate a war. Scott was perverse. America needed him. He must go. Weed published a disclaimer of Scott's hostile intentions. On the same day the *Times* announced that the "stone fleet" had left New York to be sunk in Charleston—an unfortunate coincidence. Englishmen told each other that "the fleet" was designed to release blockaders to fight Great Britain. At best the destruction of a great harbor was ruthless vandalism, an admission by the North that they could not defeat the Confederacy by legitimate warfare.

On December 14, 1861, Delane wrote scathingly about Weed the "quasi-ambassador" who was trying to smooth out the *Trent* affair and was not succeeding. The same issue announced the serious illness of Prince Albert.

Two days later, December 16, 1861, newsboys came through the streets selling papers with heavy black borders. Weed unfolded a copy curiously. He read that the Prince Consort was dead. An abstract of Lincoln's message to Congress and an announcement of the fact that Captain Wilkes had received a vote of thanks also appeared in the issue.[30] Britishers were sure to construe this vote as another insult to the flag. Would the English people blame Albert's death, too, on the Americans? If they did, neither the Queen, Russell nor Palmerston could stave off the demand for revenge by war. Everything seemed to be goading the people to great heights of hate. Lincoln's message suddenly attained a new significance. Weed read it critically. He wondered how it would impress the English. He looked carefully for some clue in Lincoln's words that would disclose his attitude in the *Trent* affair. Did the President endorse the congressional resolution of thanks? Did he intend to hold the men? Weed knew that suspicious experts would sift every word and every phrase of the message. Lincoln began:

"Fellow-citizens of the Senate and House of Representatives: In the midst of unprecedented political troubles we have cause of great gratitude to God for unusual good health and most abundant harvests.

"You will not be surprised to learn that, in the peculiar exigencies of the times, our intercourse with foreign nations has been attended with profound solicitude, chiefly turning upon our own domestic affairs."[31]

A tantalizing beginning! Next Lincoln explained that Europe would not get more cotton if the Union were destroyed. Then he recommended the fortification of the Atlantic coast as well as the Great Lakes. Was this a threat of war? If so, Lincoln followed it at once with a conciliatory proposal. Englishmen, he said, must be reimbursed for the illegal capture of the *Perthshire*. Surely he would state his position on the *Trent* next, but instead Lincoln recommended the recognition of Haiti and Liberia. Then, turning from foreign affairs, he called the attention of the Senate to the advisability of reorganizing the Army and Navy and the Supreme Court. He suggested creating a Department of Agriculture. But he had not finished matters that interested Englishmen—there was the slave trade. Five vessels, he said, had been seized and condemned. Lincoln then discussed emancipation, his own preference for compensating slaveholders and colonizing the bondmen. Turning next to his definition of a blockade, Lincoln artfully blended the distinction between closing a port in insurrection and blockading an enemy harbor. Even Seward's inconsistencies began to make sense. Next Lincoln recommended congressional sanction of the exalted rank of general in chief for McClellan. Then the President turned to the subject uppermost in all his state papers—democracy as the hope of the common man in Europe as well as in America. The insurrection, he pointed out, was essentially a counterrevolution against a republican form of government, against the right of the people "to participate in the selection of public officers. . . . Monarchy itself is sometimes hinted at as a possible refuge from the power of the people. . . . In my present position I could scarcely be justified were I to omit raising a warning voice against this approach of returning despotism."[32]

Lincoln then outlined the relation of capital and labor in America, where every laborer had the right to expect to become a capitalist—an enticing message for prospective immigrants. He concluded by referring to the figures that had amused William H. Russell—the tremendous growth of America in the seventy years of its existence and its potentialities. Men now living, he said, might see the country expand to a population of two hundred and fifty million. "The struggle of to-day is not altogether for to-day—it is for a vast future also."[33]

Weed looked further through the *Times*. How would Delane interpret Lincoln's omission of any reference to the *Trent?* A leader gave the answer. The absence of allusion to Mason and Slidell, Delane said, was so remarkable that it went some way toward neutralizing Englishmen's ill conclusions on the vote of thanks to Captain Wilkes.[34]

This seemed to be an encouraging attitude, but the next day the *Times* was more outspoken. The editor accused Lincoln of being unwilling to make up his mind. "The American nation," the paper concluded, "is step by step committing itself to a war policy with England."[35]

The situation looked very sour to Thurlow Weed. Popular resentment fermented throughout England. There seemed to be no way to allay the agitation. At Tunstall, George Francis Train was heckled viciously in a debate. "I was invited to meet an intelligent audience of ladies and gentlemen," he shouted above the din, "not to be brought into a poultry yard."[36] Train stood up under a volley of hoots and queries. In the next lull he bellowed, "Let us have the evidence that Wilkes has broken the law. . . . England might have the right of asylum, but if they went to war it would be a lunatic asylum." It was no use. The tramway patriot's jokes failed to console tonight's crowd.

Outside the Tunstall assembly hall, across the city of London, the indignant conflagration licked higher, crackling wickedly. Bright and Cobden worked diligently to calm England's outraged feelings. Both played fluent streams of eloquence onto the inflamed people, stressing the horrors of slavery and the hope of American democracy as the salvation of the world.

The impassioned oratory died in the flames. Weed watched

shipowners on the Tyne and Clyde grasp the chance to wipe out American competitors. Birmingham, Sheffield and South Staffordshire ironmongers, with profits in sight, fanned the glowing passions.[37] A meeting of six thousand at Birmingham, Bright's bailiwick, gloated over the economic advantage of manufacturing arms for an Anglo-American war. They rejected the idea of arbitration and voted confidence in Earl Russell.[38] Were the manufacturing districts, center of Bright's power, turning against him? The pitch of war was rapidly becoming fanatic.

Then a ray of hope pierced the lowering sky. The dissenters, reformers and idealists worked like ants for peace, petitioning for arbitration. Old Palmerston, with half a century's observation of British political trends, had said that England followed in the end the consciences of the nonconformists.[39] The movement grew. At Exeter Hall the Evangelical Alliance convened with four thousand praying to avert war. On December 17, 1861, a general meeting of ministers of the chief dissenting denominations adopted resolutions calling for arbitration. A joint deputation of Baptists and Independents called on Earl Russell.[40] The Peace Society and the Anti-Slavery Society memorialized the government. The Quakers—only body in Britain who could consistently preach peace without being howled out of hearing—prepared a long petition. The Society of Friends had moral weight and influence. When they spoke even the *Times* listened. Delane printed their petition and with it a leader:

"In this solemn interval—for such it undoubtedly is—between the sending of a just demand and the arrival of the momentous reply, the Society of Friends have come forward with their accustomed gravity to urge the old remedy of an arbitration. They review the crisis with a force and simplicity of language which itself will commend the document to our readers. Did any of us want to know what is meant by a war with the United States, and especially one in which the Slave States are to be our allies against the Free, they would find it told here."[41]

The tide of frenzy against America subsided unmistakably during the third week in December. The peace societies, the nonconformists, had done their work well, and the death of Prince

Albert saddened rather than enraged the people. On December 22, 1861, at the Prince Consort's funeral services in Westminster Abbey, Dean Trench stated:

"One great sorrow has already overtaken us, and there is another, perhaps, travelling up behind, the tidings of which may now be on their way to us—but by God's mercy, may that threatening evil, an unnatural and fratricidal war, a war between the children of the same mother, be averted."[42]

In speaking thus Dean Trench voiced the Prince's dying wish. In the agony of approaching death he had given his last strength to prevent this fratricidal war. Victoria in her diary noted that "he could eat no breakfast . . . and looked very wretched" but still forced himself to revise Earl Russell's words, take the insult from the ultimatum.[43] Englishmen could not ignore such a sacrifice. Americans said that Prince Albert's funeral marked the change in British opinion. The press, the people, everyone became more tolerant toward America. Queen Victoria, before sending the *Trent* memoranda to the archives, autographed them in her own hand: "This draft was the last the beloved Prince ever wrote."[44]

The first news about Great Britain's attitude toward the capture of Mason and Slidell came to Abraham Lincoln at teatime in the White House on Sunday, December 15, 1861. A few intimates were chatting together. Seward bustled into the room in a state of high excitement. Lincoln's guests set down their teacups.

Secretary Seward liked to clothe his remarks in mysterious importance. Word had been received, he said, from the British cabinet. They pronounced the arrest of Mason and Slidell "a violation of international law," and insisted that "we must apologize and restore them to the protection of the British flag."[45] Seward added with a wise nod that this was not official but Lord Lyons would confirm it. Moreover, newspapers recently received from Europe disclosed the English people to be furiously clamoring for war.

All eyes turned to the President. Lincoln looked thoughtful. The issue was already a month old. The long interval had made many Americans believe that England intended to acquiesce.[46] The ultimatum—if Seward were right—would take the scab off an old sore!

Senator Browning picked up his teacup. "I don't believe England has done so foolish a thing," he said. "But if she is determined to force a war upon us why so be it. We will fight her to the death."[47] The Senator was sure England was only bluffing. She dared not fight. Europe would jump on her from behind.[48]

Lincoln said nothing. He knew the people down on Pennsylvania Avenue were talking like Senator Browning. Yet Great Britain had the best navy in the world and the United States was unable to lift the blockade on the Potomac.[49] Lincoln remembered a vicious bulldog back in Springfield. Neighbors told one another that the dog was not dangerous. One man was not sure. He said, "I know the bulldog will not bite. You know he will not bite, but does the bulldog know he will not bite?"

On the night after the fatal news arrived, Senhor de Lisboa gave a ball. All the diplomats as well as Seward were invited. William H. Russell decided to attend also. The first news of a war with England would be the journalistic scoop of his life. For over twenty-four hours Russell had been thumping in and out of the legations. He had dined with Baron Gerolt, whose family was intimate with John Hay. He had called on Senator Sumner. But in all his visiting he heard only evasive rumors. At the ball he was sure that he could pump Seward and get the inside story of Lincoln's intentions.

The dance was gay. Bare-shouldered women, beautiful as tulips, waltzed with uniformed escorts. The French princes appeared to be happy and carefree with a dark-eyed Brazilian girl. A group of older men, including De Joinville, stood around Seward. Russell joined them. The Secretary of State was in an excellent humor, full of talk. With blinking eyes he expatiated on the terrible disaster to England of a war with America. "We will wrap the whole world in flames!" Russell heard him say. "No power so remote that she will not feel the fire of our battle and be burned by our conflagration."[50]

Russell strolled away irritated and resentful. One of the guests said to him, "That's all bugaboo talk. When Seward talks that way he means to break down. He is most dangerous and obstinate when he pretends to agree a good deal with you."

Russell went home baffled. The next day he was surprised to get an invitation to dine with the Secretary. No doubt Seward had some message for the British press which he did not care to disclose before all the diplomats. Russell looked forward to the meeting. All day long he listened to people on the street boast what the United States would do in case of a new war. England must mind her own business. What right had Europe to object to the "stone fleet"?

At last the dinner hour arrived. The newsman presented himself, eager to receive a confidence. Seward was cordial. As the wine flowed he became hilarious, but he had no message for the correspondent. Russell gave up trying to understand him. The peculiar chap had been irritable in May and June when England professed neutrality and now when war loomed he showed good humor.[51]

On December 19, 1861, Lord Lyons called at the State Department with the Queen's ultimatum. The Secretary of State was not in. A clerk said that he had gone down to the Capitol for a conference with the Foreign Relations Committee. Lyons returned to the legation. Seward had gained a day before he would have to answer.

The Foreign Relations Committee was torn with other problems equal to that of Mason and Slidell. Spain had already landed troops in Vera Cruz—her second affront to the Monroe Doctrine in nine months. The English-Mexican expedition had been diverted to Canada to attack the United States. Seward offered a solution for the Mexican problem—a treaty Tom Corwin had negotiated to lend Mexico $9,000,000, enough to buy off some of the powers and finance Juárez to fight the others. The committee doubted the wisdom of raising so much money. The war had already weakened America's credit and gold was rising in price. The senators talked, then adjourned.

Next day Lord Lyons found Seward at his desk. The Secretary of State, guessing the object of Lyons' mission before it was stated, asked him to postpone the formal presentation for a short time.

Lyons, prone to be friendly, agreed. He gave Seward a written memorandum of the Queen's request. Seward might study it and prepare his reply for the official presentation. Seward bent his shaggy eyebrows over the note, mumbling audibly. As soon as Lyons left, Seward closed the door to all visitors. All day long he scribbled and scratched, consulted books, preparing a reply.[52] Below his window on the street he could hear passers-by say that Mason and Slidell must be held at any cost. Seward knew that in the White House Lincoln was listening to the same opinions from the people. The President was so sensitive to the popular will! A Treasury official reported Lincoln as saying, "Sir! I would sooner die than give them up!"[53]

For ten days the British crisis kept Washington in suspense. People forgot McClellan's inactivity to predict fabulous victories over the British navy. Other people were sure that the nation was on the verge of collapse. One night Lincoln went to the theater— his favorite form of relaxation in trying times. The play was dull, but in one act he was amazed to see his son Tad in a uniform twice too big for him with trousers and sleeves rolled up, marching on-to the stage waving an American flag, singing at the top of his childish treble, "We are coming, Father Abraham." Lincoln knew Tad chummed around with the son of the theater manager but he had not expected this. Executive laughter pealed uncontrolled from his box.[54] No worries of impending war with England clouded his humor.

In the days that followed, the cabinet, the Foreign Relations Committee, independent senators and many incumbents of foreign legations[55] offered Lincoln advice. The Mexican loan and Mason's and Slidell's release were tied together inexorably. Dayton wrote that Baron Rothschild had called. He had money to lend the North.[56] On the other hand Corwin seemed to be getting along rather well without any help. The files were full of correspondence showing his Mexican career to have been successful as well as picturesque. He had got the Mexican espionage agents to open Swashbuckler Pickett's mail. They discovered that the freebooter urged the South to conquer their country. They read, too, that Pickett considered them "a race of degenerate monkeys . . . robbers, assassins, blackguards and lepers."[57]

Señor Don Juan Pickett of the cocked hats and resplendent Napoleonic uniforms was arrested on a charge of assault and battery and lodged in jail. After his release thirty days later, he hurried to New Orleans, delivered his correspondence to the postmaster there, to be forwarded to Jeff Davis. The postmaster sent it to Seward instead.[58] Lincoln was paying him for such services. The fiasco became known in Washington in due time. When the Foreign Relations Committee considered Corwin's treaty they knew enough of the story to be satisfied with Corwin's performance. The loan was a good thing but it might upset the national currency. The committee adjourned. Senator Browning went to the White House to tell Lincoln. The two men talked for a long time. Lincoln was worrying about the *Trent* affair, said he "feared trouble," already had an answer "reduced" to writing.[59] The President went to his desk, took out a paper, adjusted his glasses and read a plan to be submitted to Lord Lyons. Two alternatives were suggested. Either the question be submitted to arbitration or the United States give up the men in return for an acknowledgment by Great Britain that the principle so fixed be regarded as "the law for all future analogous cases."[60]

Strange phenomenon! Both Lincoln and Seward preparing replies before the official demand was made.

The next day was Sunday, just a week since the first word had been received. Lord Lyons called on Seward again.[61] The Secretary of State told him that an answer could not be given until Christmas. Lord Lyons appeared irritated when he came down the steps into the street. Lincoln had known about the demand for a week. Seward had stalled off an answer for three days. The American people were noisy for war. Lincoln must make up his mind. Next day Lyons delivered the British demand officially. It was hot—a very hot day for December. People's nerves were jangled. They looked anxiously at the sky, said it was going to storm. In the afternoon a deluge swept the city with tremendous fury. Houses shook to their foundations. Fugitives huddled in the lobbies of hotels and in saloons, looking out the windows, making way for drenched individuals who stamped in from the streets. "Did you hear about Lord Lyons? Lost his temper with Seward this morning. It's war sure."

An officer from the Navy Yard ran face to face into William H. Russell. War was as good as declared,[62] he boasted, and old General Scott was on his way home to lead the Canadian campaign.

Between cloudbursts Seward and Welles and Chase called repeatedly at the White House. Senator Sumner urged Lincoln to give up the men. Lincoln brooded, grave and thoughtful. "Natural slowness," the senator grumbled behind Lincoln's back, when he left with no assurance.[63] Down along Pennsylvania Avenue the shrill strains of "Yankee Doodle" floated out of saloon doors. Blue-coated soldiers who had seen no battles bragged with thick tongues, "We've whipped England twict. We kin do it again."

A cabinet meeting was called for the morrow. It met and could not agree. The proposed invasion of Mexico, the hope of saving Juárez with a loan, the ill success of Northern arms after a whole summer of campaigning, diverted the discussion. The meeting adjourned and the men started downstairs to go home for Christmas Eve. Seward tarried. Lincoln looked down at the little man and said, "Governor Seward, you will go on, of course, preparing your answer, which, as I understand, will state the reasons why they ought to be given up. Now I have a mind to try my hand at stating the reasons why they ought not to be given up. We will compare the points on each side."[64]

On Christmas Day the cabinet met again. The decision could not be put off longer. Lincoln closed the door to the reception room. Everyone sat down. Word had been received the night before that Prince Albert was dead. The cabinet did not know what effect this would have on the English people. Samples of British opinion on hand reflected the sentiment of a fortnight ago. How did the British people feel today?

As the men deliberated a knock was heard at the door. A letter was handed in. The French minister requested Lincoln to give up the men and avert war. More discussion behind closed doors. Then another knock. Sumner begged to present two letters he had received from Cobden and Bright. Both Britishers urged giving up the men, justice or no justice.[65] England, they both said, did not want war. If the present dispute were settled amicably Britain would not interfere further in the North's problems. After more

192

discussion the cabinet opened the doors and filed out solemnly, adjourning for Christmas dinner at their respective homes.

Seward returned to his desk to prepare the official reply. Lincoln joined his wife's guests for dinner in the White House—among them Senator Browning, anxious to learn the cabinet's decision. Other guests included the Blairs, father and sons, Attorney General Bates, Phineas D. Gurley, who was the minister of Lincoln's church, and a Springfield friend of the Lincoln's, all with their families. Three of the men present had attended the cabinet meeting. Senator Browning watched them, listened to the conventional trivialities of their talk. No word or look from anyone indicated the decision reached. When the guests arose to leave, Browning knew no more than he had when Gurley offered thanks. The senator determined to stay in the White House until he had an opportunity to speak to Lincoln alone. Surely the President would tell him the decision. Finally the last guest departed and Browning broached the subject. Had a decision been reached?

"Yes," Lincoln replied, "but the cabinet agreed not to divulge what had occurred." Lincoln paused. "But there will be no war with England."[66]

Next day Seward's answer was ready, twenty-six pages of foolscap explaining the American case.[67] Lord Lyons, glancing over the sheets, could not have been impressed by the profundity of the argument, but the document was remarkable as an essay which kept the reader in suspense. Seward opened by taking the position that America was suppressing an insurrection. Next he asked himself five questions. 1. Were the persons captured contraband? 2. Might Captain Wilkes lawfully search the *Trent* for contraband? 3. Did he make the search in a lawful manner? 4. Having found contraband did he have the right to take it? 5. Did he exercise that right in the manner recognized by the law of nations? At this place in the narrative Lyons read, "If all these inquiries shall be resolved in the affirmative the British government will have no claim for reparation."[68]

Seward answered each question in detail. He decided that America was at war and not suppressing an insurrection. If this were so Captain Wilkes had acted within the law in all but the last question. He had erred only by not sending the ship to an Amer-

## ONE HEAD BETTER THAN TWO.

Louis Napoleon. "I SAY, HADN'T WE BETTER TELL OUR FRIEND THERE TO LEAVE OFF MAKING A FOOL OF HIMSELF?"

Lord Pam. "H'M, WELL, SUPPOSE YOU TALK TO HIM YOURSELF. HE'S A GREAT ADMIRER OF YOURS, YOU KNOW."

*Cartoon from Punch, by Tenniel*

NAPOLEON URGING PALMERSTON TO INTERVENE IN THE
AMERICAN WAR
Cartoon by John Tenniel

*Courtesy of F. H. Meserve*

*Courtesy of F. H. Meserve*

JOHN SLIDELL

JAMES MURRAY MASON

*From Harper's Weekly, 1863*

RAPHAEL SEMMES

ican port as a prize. In other words he had done wrong because he had not hurt the British owners as much as the law permitted. As Scott had said, "the offence had been less if it had been greater." Seward's argument followed the outline printed in many English newspapers.[69] This alone should soothe British sensibilities. At the same time he dexterously pointed out that England was agreeing to the principles for which Americans had fought the War of 1812. In short, England was getting everything she asked and at the same time the American State Department had won a diplomatic victory. What matter if strictly legal minds punched the paper full of holes? As a parting shot Seward admitted that his decision was based on opportunism. "If the safety of this Union required the detention of the captured persons it would be the right and duty of this Government to detain them."[70] The Secretary ended in true form. After commencing his argument with the premise that Mason and Slidell were insurgents, he stated next that they were enemy aliens, then concluded that they were American citizens in rebellion.

Newsman Russell was reading a Washington paper when Seward delivered his reply to Lord Lyons. Russell noted a leader stating that Mason and Slidell would not be surrendered. He believed the paper to be Lincoln's organ and considered the announcement almost official.[71]

In the next issue of the paper Russell read Seward's reply. These Americans! There would be no war and nobody felt ashamed. The price of gold came down and the stock market went up.[72]

The famous prisoners were delivered to a British man-of-war at Provincetown on the tip of Cape Cod.[73] The commander gave the State Department a receipt for the goods. Seward reached for his pen and wrote Lord Lyons that he had given up Mason, Slidell, Eustis and McFarland, "citizens of the United States"—not alien enemies—today. George Francis Train crowed: "Seward . . . is, without exception, the cleverist Secretary of State that America has ever possessed. . . . He can talk diplomacy with Lyons, war with Palmerston, Latin with Russell, Greek with Gladstone, or Hebrew with Rothschild."[74]

# X. Stone Fleets and
## Wooden Nutmegs: January 1862

W HEN the *Trent* excitement began to subside a new war
scare arose. The blockade! Ill will between England
and America threatened to become a malignant infec-
tion. Napoleon with his industries disrupted by the American war
could ride the wave of British prejudice and alleviate French suffering. The Deputies and Parliament were both preparing to
assemble. Charles Francis Adams wrote Seward that the next six
weeks would determine the future of the American government.
The English war party, disappointed over the *Trent* affair, would
seek a rupture on the efficiency of the blockade—or the hardship
wrought on England because it was too good.[1] England disapproved Napoleon's Mexican conquest, Adams said, but dared not
object. France might be a useful ally in a war to break the American blockade.

Lincoln treated the threat of intervention with exasperating un-
concern. To France, Seward sent a dispatch calling the Emperor's
attention to the fact that Northern wheat might be more important
for his starving workers than Southern cotton. To British soldiers
arriving in icebound Canada, he sent an invitation to disembark at
Portland, Maine, and thus avoid the inconvenience of a march
across snow-covered New Brunswick.[2] Lord Lyons protested.
No soldiers need land in the United States. The offer was a
Lincoln trick to put Britain off guard. In like manner Northern
wheat was probably unimportant in face of the supplies in eastern
Europe. Trick or no trick, British soldiers could not take seriously
a war in which the enemy helped them reach their battle stations.
Industrial workers in France would not want to destroy the hand
that promised bread.

George Francis Train joined the effort for international reconciliation by advertising a debate and "for want of speakers on the
Southern side" he appointed himself to defend the Confederacy.

194

In doing so, Train made his position clear by stating, "We in Secessia have based our Constitution and reared our Temple of Despotism on one acknowledged corner-stone—NEGRO SLAVERY."[3] Train then proceeded to denounce the Lincoln administration for permitting the British soldiers to cross Canada:

"Now, I submit that we of the South have a right to complain of the manner in which Mr. Seward acted. Did he not in this prove himself England's friend, instead of America's?"[4]

The two nations were not apt to fight while they laughed at each other's horseplay. At the same time the American blockade became more effective daily—so effective that J. D. Bulloch, eager for news of the vessels he had ordered for the Confederacy, found it difficult to get back to England. The blockade's deadly certainty goaded Southern propagandists to dire prophecies. European workers would starve. The Secessionists handed M. P.'s tabulated data on the destructive blockade—urged them to preach that unemployment was the result of cotton shortage, and to vote to break the blockade.

In January 1862 the price of cotton reached a new peak. The Indian fiber offered for sale was not adequate. Agitators doubled their protests against complacency before impending famine. Speculators reaped their harvest. Other countries besides England became excited. Lincoln's ministers warned him that the cotton shortage might ruin industry on the Continent. Something must be done or several of the powers might unite to open a Southern port for the export of cotton. The "stone fleet" for Charleston Harbor was construed by some critics as a vicious blow at European prosperity. James S. Pike and William L. Dayton both urged Lincoln to capture New Orleans and send cotton, or suffer the consequences.[5] John Bright wrote a "private" letter explaining the necessity of taking the Crescent City. With a Southern port opened, he said, "the pretense of the injuriousness of the blockade" could be used by neither England nor France as excuse for intervention. No country of Europe could stand the odium of being a party to "the restoration and perpetuation of slavery."[6] Seward wrote Weed: "I am concerned deeply about the agitation apprehended in Parliament. I fear that there may be precipitancy there."[7]

On both sides of the ocean statesmen watched sentiment, followed the press, collected data on the blockade, listened to the legislators as they arrived in London and Paris. Weed reported to the State Department by every boat. Lincoln held his trump card and waited for Parliament and the Deputies to meet. Soon a new problem of neutrality arose. A Union naval commander, Tunis Craven, openly defied the port authorities at Southampton. He kept his decks cleared and his boilers fired for action against the Confederate *Nashville* that lay near by. A great howl came up to London against this insolence—an insult to the flag as great as the *Trent* affair. Weed and Adams waited on tenterhooks. Next they learned that the pesky little *Sumter* had sailed into Cadiz on January 4, 1862. She had destroyed sixteen vessels and evaded the entire Union fleet. In the French West Indies the *Sumter* had touched for supplies at Martinique. Officials had greeted the Confederate flag with respect. The native Negroes were hostile. They knew the meaning of the Stars and Bars. Marines kept them from cutting the ship's mooring cables.[8] The "tea kettle" got away before a Federal man-of-war arrived. In Cadiz she stopped next for repairs.

The American consul called for a battleship to come and capture her. In all probability there would be a fight in Spanish territorial waters. Then again the *Sumter* might get away to the coast of France or to Gibraltar. Some nation's jurisdiction was almost sure to be violated. Weed prepared himself to iron out the approaching trouble. On January 15, 1862, he received a dispatch from Dayton to come at once—not on account of the *Sumter,* but a much more threatening disaster. The French people suffering from unemployment were more volatile than the English. They might overturn the government. The Corps Législatif would soon convene. The Emperor, Dayton said, planned to recommend a strong American policy to the Deputies. Could Weed prevent it?

The danger seemed greater in France than in England—a domestic crisis, more important than a trespass on territorial waters. Thurlow Weed stuffed clothes and papers in his bags. By eight o'clock that night he was on his way. At Dover he took the boat. Weed always got pleasure from his surroundings, or pretended to. It was a matter of principle with him. In spite of the winter weather that stiffened his old joints, making him more lame, he enjoyed the exhilaration of the salt air drenching his face, curling his hair, his devilish eyebrows. He watched the flickering beacons on the English coast sink lower and lower into the horizon as the lights appeared in the harbor of Calais. At six in the morning he reached Paris.

Suave Satan Weed called on Archbishop Hughes. The cloth and cloven hoof breakfasted together. Then Weed drove to the legation where Bigelow and Dayton awaited him. The Americans' anxiety had increased in the last few hours. On good authority they had heard that Napoleon, in his address to the Deputies, would demand the opening of the blockade. Could anything be done to head him off? Weed smiled artfully, left the legation and went back to see Archbishop Hughes who, he knew, had already talked to the Emperor. Next Weed planned to use a letter of introduction given him by Seward to Prince Napoleon, now back in France—the imperialist who was *"républican—en Amérique."* 'At the Archbishop's lodgings Weed learned that Hughes had no suggestions. Weed set off to see the Prince. Perhaps the little nobleman who dressed and acted like his illustrious uncle might have a fertile idea.

While driving to the palace, Weed remembered later, he was struck by something familiar about the name of the street through which he was driving. Then it occurred to him that he had a letter from an old friend, Anthony J. Hill, a West Indies planter, to one M. Alphonse Loubat, who resided on his street. With a politician's intuition—"special intervention of an all-wise Providence," Weed preferred to call it—he decided to deliver this letter at once. He shouted to the driver, the carriage was turned around and before long stopped at the door of M. Loubat. Mr. Weed introduced himself to the concierge and was ushered into the Frenchman's parlor.[9] After the first formalities had been exchanged Weed broached the subject of politics and learned that M. Loubat knew of the aggressive policy proposed in the Emperor's message. Loubat sympathized with the Union and deplored a provocative message to the Deputies. "I hope it may prove that you have arrived in season to prevent a great calamity," he said. After some more conversation M. Loubat concluded, "An interview with the Emperor must be arranged. Leave that to me. But no, the Emperor is hostile. For you to see him might avail nothing. You must see his brother, the Duc de Morny—shall we say at ten o'clock tomorrow morning?"

That evening Weed discussed his good luck with Archbishop Hughes. The prelate was incredulous. At the legation both Bigelow and Dayton told Weed that there must be some mistake. However, later in the evening, M. Loubat called at Weed's apartment to say that De Morny—the perfect duke—would receive him in the morning. Furthermore, Loubat had learned definitely that the first paragraph of the Emperor's message was fully as hostile as had been expected; that the sinking of the "stone fleet" at Charleston would be stigmatized as "a monstrous and barbarous policy, which, from a mere sentiment of revenge upon a people struggling for freedom, would forever close and destroy harbors necessary for the commerce of mankind."[10]

Weed knew that so hostile a declaration from the Emperor might well be followed by a similar one from England. Joint action of this kind was exactly what Lincoln feared most. Already Seward had refused to treat with the nations together on any subject. His whole policy depended on keeping them apart. Weed knew, too, that the opportunity of interfering in America under the guise of alleviating the suffering in Europe was tempting adventurous politicians on both sides of the Channel.

After M. Loubat left the hotel Weed tried to sleep. He had manipulated American politicians and democratic conventions all his life, but now he worried. De Morny he knew to be the shrewdest and most artful operator in all Europe. A statesman who had made a president into an emperor was probably a match for any American. Jacksonian spoilsmen were small fry beside an ambassador who unblushingly imposed on diplomatic immunity by selling carriages and laces duty-free. Thurlow Weed arranged and rearranged his pillow, pitched and tossed in his bed, planned and replanned arguments he intended to use on the kingmaker in order to change the message planned for the Deputies. By morning he had an outline in mind that he thought would work. Going to the legation, he searched volume after volume for a certain precedent which he remembered, a precedent the duke could not bear to hear.[11] While he was hunting, the *London Post* arrived. Palmerston's own paper contained an article which virtually invited the Emperor to make his dangerous announcement.[12] Weed needed no further warning of the impending united action between England and France. He told himself that the crisis would require his most persuasive eloquence. He had found a key, he hoped, which would open Napoleon's eyes and shut his mouth on this delicate subject. As the hour approached for his conference with "the perfect duke," Weed gained self-assurance. The New York politician liked to think of himself as an American diplomat with simple, benevolent manners. People who saw him that day might have noticed that his left eyebrow curled up suspiciously.

At the appointed hour Thurlow Weed and M. Loubat set out for De Morny's palace. The account of the interview with the duke has been preserved in the American's memoirs, written in the third person, as befitted a modest follower of the author of *Poor Richard:*

A servant, taking their cards, ushered them into the luxurious *salon* reserved for visitors in waiting. It was customary for callers, while De Morny was engaged, to beguile the time by walking through his art galleries, which were the talk of Paris. Several gentlemen of distinction were thus occupied when M. Loubat and Mr. Weed entered. Returning in a few moments, the servant said that the Duke wished to see the American gentleman immediately. Mr. Weed was introduced by M. Loubat, who, remarking that a pressing business matter required his attention withdrew. "Do what you can with the Duke," he had said to Mr. Weed that morning. "If you gain him, the way is clear. If you fail, the result cannot but prove most unfortunate."

The Duke assumed at once the leading part in the conversation. He was exceedingly affable and unreserved. It gave him great pleasure, he said, to meet Mr. Weed. He extended an invitation to the opera. The season was rather dull, to be sure, but a new singer was soon to make her appearance.

Mr. Weed referred to public topics by gradual stages. He could not let the Duke know that he had been informed of the nature of the Emperor's message. He was obliged to criticise a policy which

France had not adopted, and which he was not supposed to have any information that she intended to adopt. But he was equal to the occasion.

"After some general remarks in regard to the tone of the British press," writes an ex-diplomat, "Mr. Weed finally succeeded in breaking ground.

" 'Nothing,' he said, 'could be more absurd than for England, which had never hesitated at any miscreancy requisite to uphold or extend her power,—for England, yet bloody to the armpits from the massacre of many thousand unarmed Sepoy prisoners,—belligerents as much as our southern rebels,—to pretend to affect horror at our attempted blockade of southern ports by means of sunken vessels. Certainly England had no right to become the champion of humanity or civilization, whatever claim might be put forward on the part of France to that distinction.'

"De Morny acknowledged the compliment to France with a cold bow. In this matter, however, he must think that England's complaints were justified. Harbors were places of refuge for distressed ships, as well as ports of entry for commerce. They were constructed by nature, and should not be held subject to the wrath of man. To turn from an unpleasant subject, however, if Mr. Weed and his charming daughter would do him the honor, and afford him the pleasure, etc., etc.

"The disinclination to discuss the question of the stone fleet blockade, on the Duc de Morny's part was so obvious, and yet so courteously expressed, that our American diplomatist—plain, farmer-like person that he was, in appearance—had no little difficulty in returning to the charge. To return, however, was a necessity; and, mentally deciding that his next sentence must either close the conversation or arouse De Morny's interest, he made a dash at that point of character which his experience told him is the most sensitive in every true Frenchman's organization.

"Pushing aside the social invitation with a polite and complimentary acknowledgment, he resumed: 'But, let England's course be what it will, France certainly, with her very peculiar position in history (De Morny suddenly became attentive), cannot afford to take sides with her on this question.'

" 'Ah,' said the Duke, 'you were saying'—

" 'I was saying,' continued Mr. Weed, who saw that the point of the barb was in the palate, and only needed a scientific jerk to be sent home,—'I was saying that, from the historical position of France on this question, and the noble pride of your nation, which so keenly dislikes to be placed in a self-condemnatory or in the least humiliating attitude, that we of the United States expect the cordial support of your government in our right to blockade or destroy any ports on our own seacoast.'

" 'Ah—ah—indeed!' The Minister was evidently troubled,—evidently at sea as to what could be the meaning of the farmer-like personage, with shaggy gray eyebrows and a long forefinger, from the working of which some mysterious power of electricity seemed to radiate.

"At length De Morny brightened. He had, he thought, caught the meaning, and it was not so serious as he had supposed. 'Ah, yes. You doubtless allude to Napoleon the First's blockade of the Scheldt with piles,—but that was an entirely different matter'—

" 'No, no, no,' was the slow but impressive rejoinder, made impressive by three shakes of the long forefinger,—a smile, as if in half sympathy for unfortunate France, and half at the Minister's error passed quickly over Mr. Weed's face. 'I allude—but pardon me. You are a Frenchman—almost the highest Frenchman. I do not wish to give you pain. Let me take my leave. The interest awakened by your conversation led me further than I intended. If my daughter be well enough, we shall certainly have much pleasure,' etc., etc.

"Oh! subtle angler of men, your hook was well home by this time. The leviathan of the French Cabinet could now be played as easily as a drum-fish in Port Royal harbor.

" 'Stay, stay, Mr. Weed,' said the Minister. 'If any precedents have escaped me, which could have the effect you imply, it might possibly be of importance that my attention should be drawn to them.'

"Mr. Weed shook his head. The chief and controlling precedent, to his view, could not possibly have escaped the Duc de Morny. Perhaps he had overestimated the punctilio of honor,—the sensitiveness of the French people. For his part, he could not imagine that the Duke could . . . have overlooked that painful paragraph in one of France's most important treaties which bore upon this subject. As it had been one of England's greatest and most durable triumphs—indeed her most durable, and, therefore, the most afflictive to French pride, he was not able to do more than thus remotely refer to it. Even for this distant reference he apologized sincerely; and would now beg to be allowed to take his leave.

"No more coldness in the Duc de Morny now—no more disinclination to discuss the topic of the stone fleet. He paced the room with fingers locked behind his back and twitching nervously. He was ransacking his memory vainly for the treaty in which this disastrous paragraph was encased. At length, recovering himself, he sat down, and motioned Mr. Weed, who had risen as if to take his leave, to be again seated.

" 'It is important, my good friend—that is to say (correcting himself), it is not important to my government, but it would give me personal pleasure to know the treaty to which you refer, and the character of the paragraph therein to which you but now alluded.'

" 'The treaty of Utrecht'—

" 'Ah. Well, what of that?'

" 'Its second paragraph'—

" 'Well—well.'

" 'The principal advantage therein taken by Holland and Great Britain of the temporary weakness— But pardon me! This reference, made as delicately as possible, will recall all the facts to your remembrance.'

" 'No—no; spare me nothing. Punish my memory for its default by telling me all our humiliation; for to this, I see, though you would avoid it, you must come.'

" 'Since you compel me, then, thus briefly: The second paragraph of that treaty provided for the destruction by the French of the second best harbor in their Empire; for the permanent sealing up and total destruction of Dunkirk, the Hollandaise and British averring openly that the continuance of this harbor was injurious to their maritime interests, and a constant menace against their coasts.'

" 'And France submitted?'

" 'Two years after that treaty you will find a formal complaint from the government of Holland to the Court of St. James, that France had not fully carried out the destruction of the works and harbor; that ships of light draft could still pass in and out.'

" 'And after this, what?'

" 'England represented the alleged breach of faith to the French Court, demanding, in her own name and that of Holland, that instant measures should be taken by France for the total sealing up, by stone barriers, of the harbor.'

" 'And it was done?'

" 'The harbor is sealed up to this day for all but smacks or vessels of the lightest draft. You see no large river emptied into the harbor of Dunkirk, and there was no current to cut new channels for the imprisoned waters. With us, at Charleston, Mobile, and the mouths of the Mississippi, the thing is different. Our stone fleets are a farce—a scheme of folly. One week of the river-flow will, beyond any doubt, cut deeper, because narrower, channels than those we are attempting to blockade. Our action, therefore, will have no practical ill effect upon the commerce of the world. But any discussion of it at this time could not fail to embarrass France by directing the attention of her proud and gallant people to the desolate memorial in the harbor of Dunkirk of British ascendancy at one time, and the brutal manner in which that ascendancy was exercised. The Emperor still continues on terms of friendship, does he not, with the British Court?'

" 'The best terms—the best,' said De Morny, suddenly rousing himself out of a profound reverie, which had not been a pleasant one, to judge by his countenance during its continuance. 'I confess with something of shame that the Utrecht treaty, or rather the second paragraph of it, had escaped me. You have put me under an additional obligation by recalling it. Adieu, my very good friend, I have an engagement with the Emperor, and already the interest of your conversation has detained me past my time.'

"Mr. Weed retired, bowing, to the door, well satisfied with his interview. Never in state or national convention did he feel more certain of the success of his arts. Leviathan was hooked and might struggle. But the hook was tangled round and round, backwards and forwards, in and out, through all the tissues of national pride, and the hook would hold.

"Driving home, our farmer-like diplomatist called upon the Prince Napoleon, and briefly gave an outline of the interview here roughly but faithfully sketched.

" 'You have him,' said the Prince, rubbing his hands and laughing heartily. 'You have him, my dear sir, and may now go to your hotel and enjoy yourself. Think no more of the matter. It is all settled. The speech will be silent about the stone fleet. I rejoice that you have succeeded. You know that my heart is with you in American affairs; but I am regarded as a northern partisan, and can do nothing with the Emperor.' "[13]

Thurlow Weed did not always remember things as others did. His colleagues questioned his importance in changing the Emperor's message. The old fellow was a great talker. Entertaining, yes, but his facts didn't bear investigation. Almost anybody knew that the Dunkirk clause was not in the second paragraph of the Treaty of Utrecht. Perhaps the rest of his account was out of place too. A week after Weed's visit, Bigelow printed in the *Moniteur* several other precedents in which harbors had been destroyed during military sieges. Louis XIII, Bigelow showed, had been guilty of such actions at La Rochelle in 1628. The Scheldt had been sealed in 1648. Britain threatened to "stone" Napoleon in Boulogne in 1804. Alexandria had been blocked in 1807; and Russia only a few years before had resorted to the practice in her defense of Sevastopol.[14]

Bigelow liked to believe that he, instead of Weed, had quashed the "stone fleet outrage," but he did not give himself credit for changing the Emperor's policy. John Bigelow knew the Emperor was pondering many projects—the situation in Mexico, the importance of Northern wheat to feed his people,[15] the possibility that the South would win the war. These considerations the Emperor must turn over and over in his mind, playing one against the other. The "stone fleet" at worst was only a pretext for voicing some larger decision. When the time came the Emperor would decide.

The "stone fleet" agitation had ceased to be a vital issue by the time Mason and Slidell arrived in England. The Confederates stepped unnoticed from a train in London. They had been mentioned in the papers almost daily for months. Now England had tired of them. Their escapade was reckoned to have cost the British government $20,000,000 and the Exchequer was jolly well sick of it.[16] Socially prominent people received Mr. Mason. The poor chap had had such a time, and at his age and with his weak heart, and he such a dear—"a bit slow to understand, rather, but that's so British you know, especially with the gentry on the large estates." The Anglican Church, sympathetic with Virginia since Revolutionary days, showed Mason marked attention.[17] Opposed to this, the London *Times* scorned the Southerners as "blind haters and revilers of this country." With brutal British bluntness the paper added: "We should have done just as much to rescue two of their own negroes." A convention of English workingmen pronounced the commissioners "sworn enemies . . . of the working classes of all countries."

In spite of this warning Mason approached the Foreign Secretary with confidence. Earl Russell proved provokingly diplomatic. John Mason received the same cold shoulder that had been offered Yancey, Mann and Rost. James Murray Mason could not believe it. Surely these Englishmen would thaw! To Earl Russell he sent statistics proving the blockade ineffective and therefore proper to be broken. The Earl found the figures "very interesting" but did not encourage further correspondence. When Earl Russell referred to "the so-called Confederate states" after James Mason himself had explained to him in his letter the fallacy of the term, James Mason was provoked. When Earl Russell referred to Senator Mason himself as a "pseudo-Commissioner"[18] it was more than a slaveholder should be expected to bear. The Virginian lost his temper and struck back petulantly at the Englishman he had come to ingratiate. If Great Britain had no respect for Southern culture the South indeed must secede from the world! Minister Adams noted James Mason's provincial shortcoming with pleasure and henceforth considered him the greatest Northern asset in Europe.[19]

Jeff Davis had erred once more. Yancey, Mann and Rost had proved to be useless as "paps on a boar," as Lincoln liked to say. Pickett in Mexico, with his cocked hat and fancy uniforms, had made an organ-grinder's monkey of himself. Now the fifth man to represent the South, James Murray Mason, had failed. Slidell, still untried, was the South's great hope abroad.

Lincoln had every reason to believe the Union cause safe in Parliament. Throughout January 1862, he sat at the big table with the cannel coal sputtering behind him in the marble fireplace under the ancient picture of Andrew Jackson. The press of office seekers had not abated, but war activity slowed down in midwinter. France must be hog-tied and made impotent as England seemed to be. Napoleon had been scotched in his opening address to the Deputies, but Slidell might soon undo Weed's successful propaganda. The sharp New Yorker differed from the other commissioners Davis had sent to Europe. As perpetrator of the Plaquemines Parish voting scandal Slidell had much in common with "the perfect duke." He might make plenty of trouble in the adventurous French court. The two men's practical and active minds delighted in cards. Before long it was known in Washington that they played together regularly. Slidell wrote home: "The Duc de Morny, whom I frequently see, is now and has been for some months a warm sympathizer with our cause."[20]

The only member of the Emperor's cabinet loath to favor the Confederacy was Edouard Antoine Thouvenel, who, fortunately enough for Lincoln, was Minister for Foreign Affairs. Thouvenel was younger than his colleagues and strangely less adventurous. At the time of the *coup d'état* he was serving the republic at Munich. Not being forced to declare his politics, he had remained in the service of the imperial government. His diplomatic training fitted him admirably for his position. Lincoln learned that Thouvenel did not have much power, but without doubt he would act as a brake on his impetuous chiefs who toyed with plans to divert the economic distress—open a cotton port or excite the people's martial ardor and conquer Mexico. Thouvenel did not treat Slidell with the sharp-edged coolness Earl Russell had used to chill James Mason, but he was noticeably reserved. France, he said, would not act until England took the lead.[21] Thus the issue was thrown squarely upon James Mason back in London, and he had already antagonized the British government. Months might be required now for Slidell to organize "a party" in both England and France. No wonder Lincoln was pleased.

Before long, news arrived that a shift had been made in the Confederate personnel abroad. The new "pseudo-commissioners" had automatically ended the official careers of Yancey and Rost. Mann, a favorite of Jeff Davis, was appointed as commissioner to Belgium—an important post. King Leopold, uncle of Queen Victoria and member of almost every royal house in Europe, was a recognized opponent of republicanism. The King's daughter, Carlotta, had married an Austrian grand duke out of a throne. If Mann in Belgium had the stuff in him, he might yet be useful to the Southern cause.

Thurlow Weed kept busy watching all the Confederate agents. He studied their methods, their tricks, and reported to the State Department. His sharp ears sampled opinion everywhere. He heard people in France say that the Emperor had secret information. Otherwise he would have urged the Corps to act against the blockade. Weed dashed back across the Channel. In London he heard Britishers haw-haw incredulously about Napoleon's uncertain stand. A prominent member of the House had gone to France to consult with the Emperor and had come back with assurances that the blockade would be denounced. Why had His Majesty changed? Weed attended teas, receptions, dinners. He was happy. Before long he saw and reported the beginning of the Confederate campaign to gain popular sympathy and then organize a political bloc. A Swiss writer, Henry Hotze, recently on the *Mobile Register*, appeared to be employed in London. He indoctrinated free-lance writers with Southern propaganda, paid for articles they wrote and then urged them to collect additional fees from any paper that accepted their copy. Weed suspected that Jeff Davis furnished the money—through Slidell perhaps. Next the Englishman, James Spence, who in his recent book had "reluctantly" taken the Southern side, wrote leaders for the *Times,* and organized a pro-Southern society in Lancashire. Weed saw people point to him as a British subject who worked for nothing but the lofty principle involved.

Weed watched Southern propaganda flower like Jimson weeds in the long columns of the press which Bigelow and Henry Adams had been cultivating. He saw Yancey deliver a swan song before turning over his portfolio to his successor. The Alabamian detailed all the bitterness of the South for Yankees who did not appreciate true culture. New England tradesmen, said Yancey, had tricked the planters for a generation, lending them money at prohibitive interest, imposing a high tariff to protect Northern manufacturers, adulterating goods which the South was obliged to buy, even selling them at times "wooden nutmegs." The true cause of the rebellion, Yancey maintained, was economic discrimination, the tariff which the North forced on the South.

Thurlow Weed, scanning the papers for some protest against Yancey's declamation, noted in time a long "letter" replying point by point. Its style was not that of either Bigelow or of Henry Adams. Bad puns and pungent anecdotes spiced the lines. Figures and facts fluently answered each contention. The protective tariff, the correspondent said, did not cause the war. Many Northerners believed in free trade. The South had controlled the majority in Congress. The present tariff had passed after secession. Yancey's tariff talk, according to the writer, was an attempt to "throw dust in people's eyes." If the fire-eater was sincerely interested in the tariff instead of slavery, why had he always voted for the extension of the "peculiar institution"? Why had he introduced his motion in a Southern convention to reopen the slave trade? If the tariff had been so important why had the Vice-President of the Confederacy spoken as he did at the Georgia convention when secession was being considered? Why had he challenged any member to produce one act of aggression on the part of the North which would warrant secession? "Show me one act!" he had taunted the assembly.

The cause of the war, the writer continued, was amply explained by this same Confederate Vice-President, and the tariff "cut no ice." No, the Vice-President had said, "African slavery was the immediate cause of the late rupture and the present revolution."[22] Drawing the letter to a conclusion, the writer summed up Yancey's philosophy.

"Nobody must interfere—England—civilization—the world must all stand back. He must be let alone—God or man have no right to tread on Secession soil—no freedom of speech—no freedom of press—no freedom of thought—nothing but hang—burn, and destroy. The bowie knife—the revolver—and eternal slavery of the white man as well as the black—and this is Secession!
"Yours truly,
"George Francis Train."[23]

Weed knew that Gentleman Adams and Gentleman Bigelow did not write or talk in this fashion. He knew, too, that Train's description agreed with the accounts that William H. Russell had been sending to the London *Times.* Thousands of Englishmen read these accounts and believed them. Yancey, notorious for swaggering deadly weapons in the halls of Congress, was done for. That was plain. In Europe his fiery oratory fell dead, but the new man—shrewd, skillful John Slidell—what would he accomplish? Surely the New York adventurer could outwit and shut up George Francis Train? Scheming with the Emperor and De Morny, he might also counteract anything Weed, Bigelow and Dayton could do with moderate Thouvenel.

In Washington Lincoln waited for his propagandists to collide with the Southern writers. Parliament and the Chamber of Deputies had both convened now. The fate of the blockade hung in the balance. Callers at the White House noticed lines of care deepening in the President's melancholy face. He still planned to take the field himself in the spring. Neither Parliament nor the Deputies would be apt to recognize the South if the Federal Army struck a crushing blow. Scott, McDowell, McClellan—all had failed. More-over, Cameron must be got out of the War Department. Yet Cameron's votes had nominated Lincoln. The Pennsylvania politician must not be offended. Lincoln had better go slow.

Throughout January 1862, European statesmen scowled and mumbled but made no threats. The Old World had not made up its mind about the American war. One day a tall, lathlike figure wearing thick glasses ran up the White House steps, two at a time, eager to see the President. He had just arrived from Europe with a plan to end all difficulties.

It was Carl Schurz.

Lincoln's minister to Madrid had many things to tell. The monarchies of Europe all feared the example of American republicanism. On the other hand they disliked revolution—even a revolution to set up a conservative government. Above all they could not stomach the institution of slavery.

Lincoln had heard dozens of persons, committees, fanatics, say this same thing. He listened patiently, then replied, "You may be right. . . . I cannot imagine that any European power would dare to recognize and aid the Southern Confederacy if it becomes clear that the Confederacy stands for slavery and the Union for freedom."[24]

Lincoln, however, had not been elected to emancipate the slaves. He hated slavery—had been born in a slave community with its jail and whipping post—but his first duty was to save democracy as defined in the Constitution. Carl Schurz went away without any definite commitment.

The harried President received another bit of distressing news before the long slow month of January 1862 rolled into history. The joint Mexican expedition was going forward successfully. As Adams had prophesied, England did not object. Instead, she had joined forces with France and Spain. The Monroe Doctrine was being violated flagrantly again—this time by the greatest powers in Europe. The men and ships which England had detailed to Canada were rerouted to the Caribbean. Long lines of soldiers were reported to be marching inland from Vera Cruz toward the healthful highlands. Americans blamed England more than the other countries. Fourth of July orators could always rouse childhood hatred of redcoats. Some congressmen still believed in Seward's discarded doctrine. War with Britain would solve America's civil war. A noisy representative from Illinois, Owen Lovejoy, shouted from the floor of the House that Great Britain should pay dearly as soon as the war was over. America should stir up Ireland, appeal to the Chartists, get the French in Canada to revolt.[25]

A fine way to be talking while Confederate propagandists organized a bloc to vote in Parliament for American intervention! Lincoln did not wince. Freedom of speech and of the press were American traditions. Lincoln knew Lovejoy to be a Congregational preacher crazed by the memory of how his brother had been murdered by a proslave mob for insisting, on another day, that freedom of speech and of the press was his birthright. Lovejoy was an uncompromising abolitionist, one of the group that was growing stronger daily, threatening Lincoln's power in Congress. Many of Lincoln's colleagues censured him for refusing to squelch these firebrands. They said the President lacked decision, willingness to act. But Simon Cameron and Cassius Clay both learned that Lincoln could act firmly enough. He removed the latter and put the former in his post. The transfer was made adroitly, so gently that neither man was publicly mortified.

The trip to Russia appealed to Simon Cameron. He had never crossed the ocean. In England he tarried, visited Scotland for genealogical research, gratified the ambitions of a poor boy who had become wealthy. His heart had never been in the War Department. His contracts for munitions were notorious.[26] General Butler reported that uniforms he supplied could be torn with a soldier's fingernail. Not content with appointing friends in his own department, he had annoyed Lincoln with requests for political preferment in the diplomatic service. For him the President had trespassed in Seward's department, appointing E. Joy Morris as minister to Constantinople and Jacob S. Haldeman to Sweden and Norway.[27]

Lincoln knew that Cassius Clay wanted Cameron's job more than anything else. Before the Kentuckian had time to get back to America and claim it, Lincoln got Edwin M. Stanton confirmed as Secretary of War, January 15, 1862. For Clay he arranged a major general's commission. Stanton was a Democrat who had served in Buchanan's cabinet but Lincoln thought him suited to the job. A capable lawyer, he had a reputation for being outspoken and for getting things done. Before Lincoln was elected President he had once been associated with Stanton on a legal case. At that time Stanton ignored Lincoln's counsel, jockeyed him out of participating in the oral argument, and said, "I will not associate with such a damned gawky, long-armed ape as that!"[28] Lincoln overheard him and was deeply hurt. But now if Stanton could win the war Lincoln would welcome him as willingly as he would hold McClellan's horse.

The rest of the cabinet were as antagonistic to Stanton as they had been to Cameron. Welles called him "a hypocrite, a moral coward";[29] Blair referred to him as "this black terrier,"[30] "great scoundrel" and "thief."[31] The cabinet still promised to eat one another long before they ate the President. Stanton himself, when he accepted the position, told his friends that he intended to make Abraham Lincoln President of the United States. "Oyster supper" generals like McClellan would have to move or be removed.

Lincoln knew that the reorganization of the War Department came none too soon for the critical situation in Europe. Carl Schurz had told him that nothing but abolition would save the Northern cause abroad. Seward warned that abolition would be construed as a sign of weakness, a ghastly effort to enlist the blacks in a servile insurrection. A smashing Northern victory was what was needed. Seward knew the diplomatic field better than Schurz. His advice should be the better. A great military victory must be attained.

Energetic Stanton, now in charge of the Northern armies, struck the Confederates in southeast Kentucky five days after he became Secretary of War. The skirmish, small as it was, gave the North confidence in Stanton. Lincoln pushed his preparations for the New Orleans expedition. He would open a cotton port, placate the solons sitting petulantly in Parliament and in the Corps, then deal with the violation of the Monroe Doctrine in Mexico. Lincoln heard that Napoleon was in conference with the Confederates, scheming to recognize the South. Mexico would, no doubt, be partitioned—England and Spain to get the southern half, France the north—a natural springboard for the reannexation of the old French territory of Louisiana.[32] Lincoln knew a good way to thwart them all. On January 24, 1862, he asked the Senate, for the second time in little over a month, to consider the loan Tom Corwin had negotiated for Benito Juárez.[33] With help Mexico might pay off some of her enemies and whip the rest.

The Senate squabbled and took no action. A clique was intent on getting Secretary Seward out of office. He had failed, they alleged, in all his foreign negotiations. European troubles were all his fault as surely as military failures had been Cameron's. One had been dismissed; the other must follow.

Seward reacted with characteristic rashness. He attempted to let his diplomatic actions speak for themselves in a publication of the correspondence between the Department and the legations. Seward might better have saved himself the trouble. His opponents replied with a sly political artifice. A special pamphlet entitled *A Review of Mr. Seward's Diplomacy* drew from Seward's own publication innumerable diplomatic blunders, including the tactless printing of ministers' confidential dispatches thus exposed to foreign view "without a fig leaf of protection." Seward could not reply that the letters had been expurgated. Such an admission would defeat the original purpose of the publication. He was caught, said nothing, and his enemies formed their line for attack.

On January 25, 1862, elegant Orville Browning and a group of legislators went to Representative William Sheffield's room after tea.[34] The failure of America's foreign policy was on everybody's lips. Senator Thomas Ewing of Ohio said that Seward had gone out of his way to insult every foreign power since he had been in office. Browning, who thought he knew as well as any man what was in Lincoln's mind, asked Ewing whether this bluster on Seward's part was due to want of sense and discretion, or whether he supposed the Secretary had some motive in doing so designedly. Ewing, slow to see a possible finesse in Seward's bluff, replied, "Seward was not a gentleman, but a low, vulgar, vain demagogue."[35]

Lincoln heard the storm brewing on Capitol Hill. Obviously it was a plot of the Chase forces to oust an enemy from the cabinet —to upset the President's balance of power. Soon pompous and powerful politicians called at the White House, saying, "Seward must get Cameron's medicine, by God, sir!"

Lincoln asked them to sit down. He was reminded of a story.

There was once a farmer out in Sangamon County whose hen house was disturbed nightly. The farmer determined to destroy the source of his trouble and he posted himself at an advantageous place with his shotgun. Before long a skunk appeared, followed by five little black and white kittens—Seward and the cabinet—all with their tails erect, waddling down the path toward the hen house. The farmer aimed his gun at one of the little black and white animals and fired. Next day the farmer's friends asked why he had killed only one of the marauders and the farmer replied, "When I saw the stink that was raised over getting rid of one I decided to stop."

# XI. *Cold, Fever, and then Delirium*

CASSIUS MARCELLUS CLAY, Grand Duke of White Hall, Kentucky, now United States minister plenipotentiary to the Czar of all the Russias, called for pen and ink, drew a chair up to the table, parted his coattails and sat down. He had received a package of newspapers from America. In these columns from the opposite side of the world, he learned for the first time that he was to be succeeded by Simon Cameron. Having asked repeatedly to be relieved during the unhappy days before he made fighting friends in Russia, Clay could not complain.[1] Instead he wrote a long letter for the State Department files. Clay refuted Adams' reference to him as a "noisy jackass," summed up his own accomplishments and outlined a plan for an "international judicature, which will diminish the necessity of war, if it shall not abolish it altogether." Thinking this proposition over in the days that followed, Clay became more belligerent and wrote Seward again.

"Since steam can throw, in twelve days or less, the entire navies of Europe upon our country, it is useless to deceive ourselves with the idea that we can isolate ourselves from European interventions. We become, in spite of ourselves—The Monroe Doctrine—Washington's farewell—and all that—a part of the 'balance of power': and constitute a portion of that 'universal equilibrium' of which Prince Gortcshacow [*sic*] so aptly spoke. We must then strengthen ourselves like other nations. . . . We must make and keep a navy equal to any other nation. This we can well do: without jeopardizing our liberties, and will ever be, loyal to the *Union:* and incapable of domestic tyranny. Here has been the secret of English liberty—a *small army,* and a *large navy.* Let us go, and do likewise."[2]

Lincoln decided to replace Cassius Clay's nephew, Green Clay, with Bayard Taylor,[3] the traveler-poet who after a previous visit to Russia wrote romantic prose about the land of serfs and grand dukes. Taylor was a middle-class conservative, safe enough for any court. Success had changed him physically; friends who remembered him in the early days when he tramped afoot across

Europe remarked that he now looked "as fat and burly as a well-to-do butcher . . . gross and unpoetic, having lost the litheness we usually attach to men of active mind."[4] Furthermore he had been so often complimented upon his shyness that it had become the most forward thing about him. As a literary man, Bayard Taylor did not relish subordination to a wealthy politician. But he accepted[5] the position of secretary believing that he would soon be promoted to the more responsible position of minister.[6]

While Lincoln worked out his Russian posts, an international situation similar to the *Trent* affair arose in 'Africa—this time with France instead of England. The *Sumter,* Captain Semmes commanding, had steamed into Gibraltar for more repairs. Two Confederates on board, Myers and Tunstall, decided to take a pleasure trip on a French passenger steamer across the straits to Tangier, a town of romance and adventure.

The Southern gentlemen landed in the picturesque city of low white buildings—a blend of the Old Testament and *The Arabian Nights*—shimmering on the shore beneath a dazzling African sky. Together they strolled up the main street, mingling with polyglot people—Mohammedans, Jews, Italians, Spaniards, Portuguese, Turks in red fezzes, black slaves, white-turbaned Indians, Arabs, grunting camels, proud Berbers on prancing horses. Brilliant birds whistled in wicker cages, monkeys chattered on chains, mangy dogs slept in the sun.[7] Over one of the buildings an American flag, the Stars and Stripes, waved in the blue sky. The Confederates had not expected this and made some loud, disparaging remarks. The American consul general, Judge James DeLong from Ohio, sitting in the spiced shade beneath the Star-Spangled Banner, heard amid the babel of tongues the traitorous terms drawled in his own language. The judge did not like it. He sent word to Sidi Mohammed Bargash, Minister of State, requesting a file of soldiers to arrest the Confederates and bring them to the consulate for imprisonment. The swarthy minister was relieved to know that the men would not be jailed at his expense in a dungeon of state or even beheaded. He complied willingly, and his dusky constabulary marched the proud upholders of white supremacy to the consulate. Loudly the Confederates pleaded for their rights as belligerents on neutral soil. Judge DeLong said that they were traitors and locked them up. Black men with arms stood at the door. The prisoners professed to know Negroes. They believed that African guards could be bribed. A hundred dollars and a gold watch, their combined wealth, were offered the constabulary. Judge DeLong overheard the bargain and put the prisoners in irons.

By this time word had reached Europe concerning the fiasco. Captain Semmes on the *Sumter* twirled his waxed mustache and sent a peremptory demand for the Southerners' release. He threatened to cross the straits and blow the white-walled city into the Atlantic. Sidi Mohammed Bargash called on Judge DeLong. What should he do? The Ohioan reassured the Vizier. The *Sumter,* he said, was coaling and could not make the trip at once. Besides, Northern vessels would capture her when she left the harbor. At this juncture a warship was sighted coming into port under a cloud of sail. An American flag sparkled on her staff. A few moments later she saluted with a dip of colors, then hove to. A puff of smoke hid her broadside. The thunder of the friendly salvo rolled across the water. Shore batteries returned the salute. A longboat with glistening oars came ashore. Courtesies were exchanged between the commander of the U. S. S. *Ino* and Sidi Bargash. Would the Grand Vizier permit the American to land marines and take the pirates to his ship?

Sidi Mohammed Bargash was eager to comply, but French influence was strong in the city and his arrest of the Confederates had stirred up a hornets' nest. French nationals and other foreigners in the Moroccan city insisted that political refugees were safe on neutral soil. The Confederates must not be detained, ironed and hanged like common pirates. Had not a Hungarian revolutionist, sailing on an American ship some years ago, been arrested by the Austrian consul when he landed in Smyrna, exactly as these Confederates had done? At that time the United States had insisted that the Hungarian was under the protection of their flag even while disembarked. The refugee had been returned. Now the Americans had reversed their principles as they had done when Mason and Slidell were captured less than three months ago.

A mob formed in the market place. Enraged Frenchmen marched down to the American legation, flourishing knives, threatening vengeance. The Sidi ordered the water gate closed, leaving the American marines outside.

In his palace the Viceroy, Prince Muley-el-Abbas, leisurely enjoying the perfection of Allah as he smoked, was annoyed by the noise. Taking the narghile from his lips he signified that the military must disperse the mob. By this time the rabble had entered the legation, but before they found either the prisoners or the judge the Viceroy's army swung into the street, cleared the halls, compound and doorways. Order was restored. The city gates swung open again. A squad of marines marched up to the consulate, then marched back with the Confederates bound hand and foot like felons on the way to execution.[8]

The *Ino* made sail and skimmed away. Traffic was resumed in the streets of Tangier,[9] and Judge DeLong returned to the purple shadows of the consulate. The Frenchmen pouted, and at Gibraltar Captain Semmes realized that he was blockaded. He sold the *Sumter*[10] and took his crew to England.[11] The *Ino* sailed back to America and placed the prisoners in Fort Warren. France protested formally and Lincoln released the men. Northerners acquiesced. The Mason and Slidell incident had taught a grim lesson, and no traditional prejudice urged Americans to hate the country which had produced Lafayette.

The African adventurers had returned against their will to a dreary United States—cold, wet, but bright. In the month of January 1862 it had rained or snowed almost every day. In February the weather improved. Lincoln looked through the White House windowpanes at blue sky again. North, over the tops of bare trees, he could see the bronze statue of Andrew Jackson on a horse rampant. Soldiers took heart.

The camps quivered with activity. Even the commissary mules jigged through Washington in quick step to the obbligato of rumbling covered wagons. The expedition against New Orleans set sail. Admiral Farragut left Hampton Roads on February 2 to take command. Next day Lincoln had a breathing spell. He sat down and wrote a letter to the King of Siam, declining a gift of some breeding elephants. His Majesty, eager to spread the benefits of Oriental culture to the New World, had offered the animals as a solution for the labor and transportation problem in America. Lincoln appreciated the spirit in which the gift was offered and answered:

"Our political jurisdiction, however, does not reach a latitude so low as to favor the multiplication of the elephant, and steam on land, as well as on water, has been our best and most efficient agent of transportation in internal commerce."[12]

The correspondence was published for general distribution as a "white paper." People smiled when they read it. Good times must be coming. Then three days later the telegraph announced that the Confederates' Fort Henry in Kentucky had been captured. In a week their Fort Donelson fell, too. The gateway was opened to the Deep South—Alabama and Mississippi. And this was not all. Out in Arkansas, at the Battle of Pea Ridge, the last Confederate army west of the Mississippi was defeated. Now if Farragut took New Orleans the South might soon be cut in two. Forts Donelson and Henry had been hammered down by an unknown general, U. S. Grant, who, when the enemy asked for terms, replied, "Unconditional surrender." The crisp finality of these military words thrilled Americans after ten months of minor victories and major defeats. "Unconditional Surrender" Grant took the laurels from Butler as the first hero of the war. The North was developing generals. With superior man power she might yet overcome the self-supporting agricultural enemy.

Lincoln felt strong for the first time since Bull Run, seven months ago. Now he could play antislavery cards and gain the friendship of Europe without being accused of resorting to them after all other means of victory had been exhausted. All the foreign ministers were invited to a grand levee. Mrs. Lincoln renovated the White House with new wallpaper, new carpets. Then, after the invitations were sent, the little boys, Willie and Tad, became suddenly ill.

The guests assembled in the East Room. Upstairs Lincoln stood in the sickroom watching his sons. Willie's breath rasped in his throat. Eddie had suffered like that before he died. Distant voices drifted up from the East Room. Frock-coated notables and their brilliant mates were being ushered into the White House. Lord Lyons and De Stoeckl arrived—the two cronies from rival countries. The French princes came—carefree and debonair. Henri Mercier made it a point never to see them. Morose Tassara grumbled across the threshold—a bull surveying his pasture. Count Piper with his sweet childish face—the only real nobleman—and resplendent Bertinatti were both announced. A group of young blades circled about plumed Princess Salm-Salm, the circus rider, and her monocled hussar—a striking couple in any assemblage.

Lincoln leaned wearily on the mantelpiece in the sickroom. This was to be Mrs. Lincoln's big night and his too, after the great victories in the West. The boys tossed feverishly. Washington society had snubbed the Rail Splitter's wife ever since she came to Washington—and she a Todd from Kentucky. Her gown for tonight was to be the envy of the capital. Let "smiling friends" scoff, she told her maid sarcastically. In the sickroom Lincoln knew how much the evening meant to his wife. Poor little Willie whimpered in his sleep. His breathing was very unnatural. A rustle of satin at the door made Lincoln look up. His wife stood before him. Her dress had a gorgeous white train flounced with black lace—half mourning for Prince Albert. Lincoln smiled. "Whew! our cat has a long tail to-night."[13]

Mrs. Lincoln took his arm and the two went downstairs to meet their guests. She did not tell her husband that she had overspent her allowance for renovating the White House. This was to be her big night. Gaiety must not be marred.

A few days later, February 20, 1862, little Willie died. Ellsworth, Baker, now Willie—all dead within a year! Lincoln was almost beside himself with grief. Behind closed doors servants and secretaries heard the agonized tramping back and forth of the great flat feet that could not rest. Mrs. Lincoln was stricken to the verge of insanity. Comforting her, Lincoln assuaged his own sorrow. Seward knew that hard work was grief's opiate. A new international crisis had arisen and he brought the papers for Lincoln's consideration. The sad, patient man pulled himself together and with tear-blurred eyes read a dispatch from Earl Russell. The Britisher objected to Seward's interpretation of international law in his letter of December 26 releasing Mason and

Slidell. Lincoln forced his mind to focus on the involved language. He talked the case over with his Secretary of State. Something must be done too with France, England and Spain in Mexico, and English smuggling into the Confederacy must also be stopped. Great Britain was sure to take offense when blockade-runners were captured. France and England might yet combine against the United States. That old specter of united foreign intervention constantly haunted Lincoln and Seward. They talked a long time. The antislavery cards Lincoln held in his hand would be useful now. He also held other diplomatic cards which might be led first—holding the trumps to the last. Finally the two men agreed on the best way to play the game. Seward bustled off. Back in the State Department he wrote Lord Lyons: "There is no melioration of the maritime law, or of the actual practice of maritime law, that the leading maritime states, including Great Britain, shall think desirable, which will not be cheerfully assented to by the United States."[14] Seward also offered to arbitrate all future difficulties— Lincoln's original solution for the *Trent* affair.

When Seward finished writing he looked at his manuscript. His extremely conciliatory reply was by no means a retraction. It was instead an effort to use the surrender of Mason and Slidell as a comb for currying favor with Britain. England showed signs of quitting the joint occupation of Mexico with France. Seward and Lincoln intended to aid that separation. As soon as France stood alone they had another plan for knocking her out of Mexico—the Tom Corwin treaty. Again Lincoln urged the ratification of the loan—his first play in this little hand at diplomacy. His trump cards were ready but held in reserve. Surely the Senate would take the opening trick for him.

The Senate refused on February 25, 1862. Lincoln lost the hand and the game turned against him at once. Reports at the State Department revealed that English ships were evading the blockade and carrying goods to the Confederacy by way of the Mexican port of Matamoros across the Rio Grande from Brownsville, Texas. Lincoln could not legally blockade a neutral country's port. Britain, in the Napoleonic Wars, had established what was known as the "continuous voyage" doctrine, under which goods were seized moving between neutral ports when they were ultimately bound for an enemy country. The "continuous voyage" doctrine, however, had not applied to goods moved from the last neutral port to the enemy country by internal transportation, as was obviously being done at Matamoros. England had the law on her side, yet if the trade south of the Rio Grande was not stopped, the Confederacy could not be blockaded. Lincoln worked alone with this problem in the Executive Room on the second floor of the White House. After midnight he was able to concentrate—"get in his best licks." The last guest had gone home then and the great house was quiet. Servants swept the reception room and the stairs, cleaned up the crumbs on the carpet where Edward, the doorman, had munched his lunch. The oven fires in the basement were banked and all lights were turned down except the lamp in the President's room. Lincoln disclosed his policy for dealing with the foreign powers to no one, but the acts soon spoke for themselves.

A British ship, the *Labuan,* bound for Matamoros, was sent in as a prize. Lyons objected. Seward evaded the issue, procrastinated for time. Lincoln on March 6, 1862, recommended that Congress compensate any border state that would emancipate its slaves. On March 18, slavery was abolished in the District of Columbia. In April a treaty to stop the slave trade was ratified. No one could prove that any of these domestic issues were part of a studied foreign policy but the effect on English liberals was unmistakable. Lincoln had split Britain class from class, precisely as he and Seward had separated England and France. The Northern cause had become definitely antislavery. The liberals cheered even while Lincoln stopped and confiscated their countrymen's ships.

Lincoln's long hours in the lamplight upstairs in the White House were crowded with many things besides foreign affairs. He had a long argument with McClellan. The Little Dragoon wanted to go down Chesapeake Bay with his army and strike Richmond from behind. Lincoln wanted him to strike straight across Virginia for the Confederate capital. McClellan got his way. His troops were moving when letters from Adams and Dayton warned Lincoln that Parliament had scheduled a motion to break the American blockade. Bulloch was back in England with renewed credit for Confederate ships and two iron rams designed especially for piercing wooden blockaders. One Confederate vessel, the *Oreto,* later *Florida*, had got to sea. Semmes had arrived from Gibraltar to command the next vessel finished. British neutrality appeared a travesty. Pike wrote that all Europe awaited England's action.

Lincoln knew that the shipping interests he had hurt possessed more votes than the idealists he had assuaged with his antislavery cards. Perhaps he had played too soon. The discouraging assembly of dispatches in the State Department had not got into the files before bad news came from Fortress Monroe. The Confederacy had launched an ironclad—a strange monster known as the *Merrimac*. She had sunk two wooden warships and now threatened to cut off McClellan down on the peninsula. She might steam up the Potomac and take Washington. Lincoln's cabinet were almost frantic. Seward cackled in and out of Lincoln's room with his hackles up. Terrier Stanton trotted repeatedly to the window and with both hands on the sill cocked his head down the silvery Potomac looking for the iron freak. The Federal Union was doomed.

England, France and Spain all had armies in Mexico; all had great populations of poor people to be fed and capital to be invested. Statesmen expected the United States to collapse. The three powers, like vultures, were waiting. A few liberals could not divert autocracy from this feast on democratic corruption. Lincoln's diplomacy seemed to have failed miserably.

Next day a Federal monitor arrived in Fortress Monroe to challenge the *Merrimac*. The two monsters locked horns, pounded each other's iron sides and parted—both claiming victory. At least the Confederacy was no longer undisputed master of the bay. A few days later another European dispatch bag was delivered at the State Department. The news from abroad was good. International jealousy had started the vultures pecking one another's eyes. Prussia threatened to fight Denmark. Revolution menaced Poland and Italy. Garibaldi was back on Caprera. If war broke out in Europe, Red Shirts would blossom around him like geraniums in spring. Down in Mexico, Spain and England concluded that they were pulling Napoleon's chestnuts from the fire. They had better look to their own diplomatic hearths at home. On April 9, 1862, they formally terminated the joint occupation and began to withdraw. France was being isolated in both Mexico and Europe. The

cynical old story of European turbulence had played into the hands
of America again.

Lincoln read the dispatches. The split between England and
France was good news. Divided, they would be much easier to
handle. Lincoln immediately executed one of those diplomatic
movements which his friends called deeply subtle and his enemies
pure accident. He gave Minister Mercier a pass through the
Union lines, to visit Jefferson Davis in Richmond and ostensibly
arrange a truce.[15] An innocent errand surely, but Lord Lyons suspected that the astute Frenchman had imposed on guileless Lincoln
to make a secret commercial treaty with the Confederacy ahead of
all other nations. The schism between England and France widened. With good management the two strongest nations on earth
might be kept forever more from uniting against the North.

Lincoln learned that Jeff Davis had struck at the North's new
advantage. A new propagandist had been sent to Europe in April[16]
—a man with more authority than Henry Hotze. Edwin De Leon,
formerly consul general of the United States at Alexandria, Egypt,
had distinguished himself the year before by entering the lists in
a newspaper argument in Paris against Henry Adams. De Leon
was a favorite with the Confederate President. Jeff Davis gave him
$25,000 "as a secret service fund, to be used by him in the man-
ner he may deem most judicious."[17] Thus the old planter civilization was to be represented in the foreign press by Swiss Hotze and
Jewish De Leon—Lincoln's mobocracy by the New England
scholars Henry Adams and John Bigelow.[18] Hotze had been
given £2,000 per year,[19] and he had made plenty of trouble in
foreign newspapers. If De Leon used the same judgment he could,
with his funds, swing most of the press against Lincoln. Jeff Davis
also promoted another of his Jewish friends, Judah P. Benjamin, to
the position of Secretary of State. Benjamin had a new scheme for
winning France's friendship. He sent it to Europe with De Leon:
Give Napoleon four and a half million dollars' worth of cotton,
worth twelve and a half million abroad, France to open the blockade
and receive it.[20] In addition the French ships to be sent for the
cotton might import goods duty-free. The combined profits should
net $25,000,000—enough to help finance the Mexican venture.
Moreover, the cotton would relieve unemployment in France.

Lincoln realized that the Confederate bribe might tempt the Emperor, especially since he was going ahead with the Mexican conquest alone. The threat to America throbbed like a bad tooth. Lincoln could give it only part of his consideration as he sat in the lamplight at midnight. McClellan's advance up the peninsula engrossed most of the President's time.

Before long Lincoln heard that Napoleon still refused to see John Slidell. Good! The bribe was not sufficient to induce the Emperor to recognize the Southerner until England recognized John Mason. The Emperor felt that France was being isolated in Europe too much already. He wanted to work with England, not independently, especially since the Polish and Italian problems were becoming more acute. Lincoln had the satisfaction of knowing that he and Seward had added to France's isolation. Their diplomacy was not so bad after all.

Then a strange story came to America. John Slidell, desperate to get recognition, had determined on a bold act.

A New Orleans soubrette, Mlle Sophie Bricard, had announced her debut in Paris. Slidell, with a weakness for grease paint since his New York days, patronized the performance. The Duc de Morny acted as sponsor also. The Emperor, archadventurer of them all, signified an imperial desire to see the show. William L. Dayton bought tickets also. At the end of the second act the Emperor went in person to the greenroom to congratulate the actress. (Impartial critics pronounced her acting poor.) Slidell and his secretary Eustis hurried backstage. Mlle Bricard saw them coming. She threw herself on her knees before the Emperor. "*Voilà, Sire, le représentant de mon pays souffrant!* . . . On my knees, I supplicate your Majesty. Give us the friendship of France!"[21]

The startled Emperor shook hands solemnly with the white-haired Southerner, then raised *la petite Bricard* from the floor. The curtain rose for the third act, and people whispered that the sly vixen had forced a recognition of the South behind the scenes. Dayton looked inquiringly at the Emperor's box. It was empty. Napoleon had left the theater. Surely he was mortified by the intrigue. Slidell had outwitted the Emperor but he had not helped the Confederacy.

This diplomatic *opéra bouffe,* if true, was good news for Lincoln. France would not be dangerous for some time at least now. Lincoln could tighten the screws on English shippers without fear. He had split British idealists from the shipping interests after the *Labuan* capture; now he trod on the shipmen as though sure of his ground. He ordered British ships stopped on the high seas and inspected for contraband wherever they might be found. The *Bermuda,* long suspected of being a Fraser-Trenholm bottom, was overhauled between the two British ports of Bermuda and Nassau. Her cargo, including blankets, swords, uniform buttons and postage stamps, was unmistakably for the Confederacy. The British flag was struck and the vessel was sent to New York as a prize.[22] Lincoln's plan to divide and conquer had given him the whip hand. People who watched his long figure walk daily to the War Department for the latest dispatches reported him to be confident and calm. The expedition to New Orleans that had meant so much to his foreign relations no longer seemed to worry him. Everything was too good to be true. George Francis Train had warned, three months before, to beware of the London *Times.* Upper-class opinion, he said, was slow, fickle and dangerous—"first cold, fever, then delirium"—and the cotton-topped orator had an eccentric way of saying what was so.

Lincoln got a hint of the coming fever—a clue that financial interests would outweigh idealism and reunite England and France—in a dispatch from Bigelow dated April 28, 1862. Napoleon, he wrote, could not hold out much longer without cotton. The Deputies were debating poor relief. An increase in taxes would cut deep into the property of the upper classes,[23] wipe out the middle class. Napoleon might try to save France from revolution by fighting the United States.

Later dispatches from Dayton, Pike and Sanford all insinuated that Lincoln should divide France internally as he had England and thus let class play against class—like his cabinet at home. Already the Catholics had prepared an opening for him. French bishops had announced that it would "not be objectionable" to pray for the emancipation of the American slaves.

Before Lincoln had time to fit a wedge in this opening, New Orleans fell, April 28, 1862. General B. F. Butler invested the city.

A cotton port was open at last. Trouble should be over with Europe now.

Hotze and De Leon had been sent abroad to meet just such an emergency. They rushed into print. The press in London and Paris was plastered with feature stories of "Beast" Butler's brutality, horrendous accounts of ruthless Northern conquerors determined to subjugate the South to a vassal state and impose a protective tariff. A new weekly newspaper, the *Index,* appeared on London streets. It was apparently a British publication and six or eight of the most successful leader writers in the city contributed to its columns. The writers displayed an intimate knowledge of Southern affairs. Readers did not generally know that the editor was Henry Hotze.

The Confederate publicity was answered by three booklets. In England, Professor John Elliot Cairnes published *The Slave Power.* In France, M. Picard and Edouard de Laboulaye wrote *Le Conflit américain* and *Les Etats-Unis et la France* respectively. John Bigelow undoubtedly had a hand in the last, but the other two seem to have been unprompted. All the works refuted the arguments advanced by De Leon and Hotze. The war could not be a struggle between a rural and an industrial civilization, between free traders and high-tariff industrialists, as the Southerners maintained. All the writers explained that Northern farmers took a bigger part in the war than did the people in the cities, and a tariff discriminated against these agriculturists as much as against the Southern planters. Readers put down the booklets convinced that the fundamental reason for the American war was slavery. The old, old story. If Lincoln could keep such publications before the reading public abroad, he would control the French Emperor as well as the British government. Moreover it was interesting to note that the French books recommended "hands off America." Let the North crush her own slaveholders. Cairnes, on the other hand, maintained that slavery must be stamped out in the United States even if England interfered to do it. Thus the liberals in the two countries recommended two distinct policies. Policies that would keep England and France apart—exactly what Lincoln wanted. Did Lincoln plan it that way? Who knows? Without doubt John Bigelow collaborated in Laboulaye's work. The fever Train had prophesied abated.

Lincoln had a breathing spell, but not for long. Late in May 1862, General Banks was defeated in the Shenandoah Valley southwest of town. The capital was at the mercy of the Confederates. With this bad news came a dispatch from Adams: five ships were being built for the South—Bulloch's work. The British government showed no inclination to investigate them. Evidently the shipping interests had gained the upper hand over the idealists. Secretary Seward's reply oozed conciliation. He shamed England for being dominated by capitalists who put profits above humanity. Britain, he said, would cause a servile insurrection by aiding the Confederacy. The arson and massacre would all be chargeable directly to her. He no longer threatened to wrap the world in flames. After all, the domestic enemy might challenge Union sentries on the outskirts of Washington any time now.

Days dragged by and the rebels did not come—another scare, like the one following Bull Run, that failed to materialize.

The White House lawn was lovely in June 1862—no sign of the political fever beginning to circulate again at home and abroad; no stench yet from the Potomac marshes that befouled the hot weather in Washington. Robins nested in the shade trees, and ran across the sward hunting worms. Tad, childlike, had forgotten his dead brother. Willie's place was filled adequately by the neighboring theater manager's son. The two youngsters played in the White House conservatory.[24] They caught goldfish in the greenhouse tank with bent pins on lines. Lincoln could hear them shout with glee as he walked to the War Department for the latest news from the front. Stanton reported that Banks had got his army out of the Valley. Washington was temporarily safe and McClellan wanted the men shipped south to help him. Lincoln said that they must not go. Washington must be protected. The President strolled back to the White House. He had many diplomatic posts to fill and the anteroom was always crowded. Deserving friends twitched the tails of his frock coat with hopeful hands.

On June 5, 1862, Lincoln signed a bill for the appointment of commissioners to Liberia and Haiti—the first time any Congress had recognized a Negro government. Perhaps the liberals abroad would eventually believe that the Union stood for freedom. When sufficient Europeans became convinced of this they might exert enough pressure on the conscience of their governments to squelch the vested interests and let the Northern democracy triumph.

Lincoln's next diplomatic problem came from Russia. Simon Cameron wanted a furlough ten days after he was presented to the Czar.[25] Lincoln read his letter and looked out the window, out across the treetops to the Potomac. So, the Russian post was open again! Cameron might almost beat Clay home. Would a major general's stars satisfy him too? Perhaps Lincoln could keep the two troublesome fellows on shipboard traveling from post to post throughout the war.

The next dispatches from England disclosed that the friends of Secessia had heard about Banks's defeat in the Valley. They believed that the time had come to force a new resolution through Parliament to recognize the South. Lincoln knew that the shipping interests had failed twice in such an attempt; that Lindsay had gone to France as an extraofficial envoy to make a deal with the Emperor, only to be snubbed by his government in England. Now in a short month military defeats had changed the situation. Britain's cold attitude toward the Confederacy had changed to heat, fever, and might go next to delirium—Train was right. Industrial conditions abroad still gave pro-Southerners ammunition and, worst of all, England and France showed signs of joining again to recognize the South. Banks's blunder in the Shenandoah cost Lincoln all his good management in separating the two big powers. The dispatch said further that the Count de Persigny, Napoleon's Minister of the Interior, had himself gone to London[26] this time—merely on a vacation, it was maintained. A resolution for intervention had been drawn. Parliament would vote on it June 20, 1862. McClellan on the peninsula might still save the day with a quick thrust at Richmond.

Came the twentieth with Little Mac advancing on the Confederate lines. London crowds waited for newspapers, prayed for word that Richmond had fallen or that the Northern Army was defeated—peace in either event. Parliament postponed the vote until July 11, 1862. Seward increased, if possible, his obsequiousness. He apologized for Butler in New Orleans, said that the general's acts were unjustified.[27]

Blatant propaganda appeared in England. Credulous people had read in the *Index* reports of Yankee rowdyism. Now they satiated their curiosity with Northern accounts of "the barbarities of the *'acknowledged belligerents,'* in murdering wounded soldiers, as they have done after almost every battle; in mutilating and disgracing the remains of the dead, and converting their bones into ornaments for their female friends, and, in more than one instance, their skulls into drinking-cups."[28]

As the time for the test vote approached, Earl Russell and Lord Palmerston felt their way cautiously, probing the possible soft spots in Parliament, watching their majority. Adams annoyed them with affidavits about the ships building at Liverpool. Earl Russell looked over the documents, sent them to various bureaus for examination and reported that more evidence would be necessary. Adams instructed Consul Dudley to prepare it. He wrote Lincoln describing his difficulties.

Lincoln did not wait for the outcome of Adams' efforts and the fatal vote in Parliament scheduled for July 11. He and Seward decided to quit their obsequiousness and try striking recklessly at Britain. A bill was prepared for Congress that would make Britain really feverish. The Privateering Bill, as it was called, authorized Lincoln to issue letters of marque for individual shipowners to go to sea, ostensibly in pursuit of the *Florida,* as well as this other new ship which Adams feared might soon be at large. Privateersmen, as soon as legalized, might also prey on English commerce everywhere. The bill made a mockery of Seward's request to join with other nations and abolish "inhuman" privateering. It marked the third time he had changed face since the first of the year. Senators in Congress complained about his inconsistency, his lack of principle. Others said anything was fair in war.

The Privateering Bill was introduced, then tabled.[29] With this threat poised over Great Britain, Lincoln asked the Senate to pass the old Tom Corwin treaty—lend Benito Juárez enough money to expel Napoleon from Mexico.[30] More foolhardy bravado, Lincoln's critics complained, thus to challenge the two greatest powers in

Europe and throw them together when the North's only hope trembled in McClellan's hands down on the peninsula.

As the fate of the Union teetered in the balance Napoleon decided to send his navy and twenty-five thousand reinforcements to Mexico. Minister Dayton warned Lincoln to be on his guard. If McClellan failed in Virginia, Napoleon expected the Union to collapse. The French fleet and French army would both be ready to pounce on the prostrate democracy.[31] Neither obsequiousness nor threats seemed to have any effect on Europe so long as McClellan could show no decisive performance.

Lincoln walked over to the War Department—awkward, silent. He fumbled through the telegrams—"down to raisins"— and got no encouragement from McClellan. The general was advancing, it was true, but his dispatches breathed caution and defeat. Over in the State Department a new set of letters disclosed that the European vultures saw McClellan falter. Chargé d'Affaires Perry wrote from Madrid that Spain planned another expedition to the West Indies under cover of the French navy. All Lincoln's ministers said that the great powers of Europe—Britain in Parliament, France and Spain in the field—all stood ready to jump on America as she fell. The buzzards had stopped pecking one another. They saw the United States begin to topple. Lincoln's darkest hour of foreign relations had arrived. Everything depended on McClellan, and Lincoln had no confidence in him. Something must be done to prevent one more defeat from turning the powers loose on America. Lincoln called Seward to the White House.

After the conference Seward wrote an innocent letter to Bigelow, dated June 25, 1862. An unofficial, private letter for the whole world to see. Lincoln was not officially responsible for anything in the letter, but its contents made the most hardened diplomat quail as from a ghost. Kind, awkward, fumbling, defeated Lincoln appeared to be standing over Europe, holding back an avalanche that threatened to crush civilization. The avalanche was Russia, and Seward's letter merely mentioned—unofficially—that the United States had a defensive alliance with her.[32] The diplomats could find no proof of the existence of such a treaty, but this only increased the suspense. They recalled that Baron de Stoeckl had conferred suspiciously with Seward in November at the time that passions were running high over the capture of Mason and Slidell. In London, shortly thereafter, Count Brunnow, the Russian minister to England, had called on Charles Francis Adams.

The time arrived for Parliament's fatal decision scheduled for July 11, 1862. Adams turned up again just before the vote. He had all the shipbuilding evidence that Earl Russell had demanded. In addition Adams had employed a queen's counsel to give an opinion on the brief. The Foreign Secretary was caught. He took the evidence and started it on another detour through the bureaus. The vote was called for in Parliament. Reports announced McClellan to be advancing slowly along the peninsula. The vote was postponed until July 18. Henry Hotze lost his temper. In the *Index* he stated that Earl Russell had made himself "the laughing-stock of Europe."[33] In America Gurowski shouted equally uncomplimentary things about the administration. Then someone in the State Department found the Polish count's diary and read in it that the failure of the war was due to the incompetence of Lincoln and Seward—"a helpless imbecile in the hands of a cunning and selfish and ruthless charlatan."[34] The journal was passed along to Seward, who decided that he had had enough of the eccentric chap. Discharged, Gurowski put on his bell-shaped hat and stamped down the stairs. Under his arm he carried the manuscript. He determined to publish it at once.[35]

Earl Russell could not dismiss so easily the annoying editor of the *Index*. Delirium had roared into his staid and ancient office. Misery from unemployment in the working classes had reached a major crisis.[36] The suffering was appalling. Through it all, the shipping interests tugged at the government from one side and Adams tugged from the other. In Lancashire the mills had worked half time, then two days a week. Finally they closed altogether. Manufacturers who had considered themselves in comfortable circumstances found their incomes and their credit exhausted. Plants were delivered to creditors who in their turn had no means of operation. In town after town, fifty percent of the required taxes was not returned on account of pauperism.[37] Hundreds of hunger-pinched people stood around the newspaper offices staring at bulletins—dispatch boards they were called—waiting for word that the Federals had taken Richmond. Workers deserted their families, their villages, to wander south begging food. A report from Burnley, Lancashire, stated that one street of forty homes possessed only one half-loaf of bread. A fever, attributed to malnutrition, swept across the slums in industrial areas. Once a "starvation meeting" resolved to end its misery in a canal. "Starvation meetings" were prohibited thenceforth. Hungry men looked into one another's delirious eyes and asked again and again about the American war. Lincoln heard the harassing stories. How long could this last before England interfered in America? If McClellan failed in the peninsula, Parliament would surely vote for mediation.

It was plain now that Lincoln had succeeded only partially in separating the idealists from the shipping interests with his anti-slavery promises and privateering threats, but he had won the hearts of the working classes better than he knew. During all their suffering there was no question on which side of the American struggle they stood. In Glossop, near Manchester, a cotton broker, confident that he could influence the workers against the North, got up to speak at a meeting. "The South," he prophesied, "would smash Lincoln and the North into cocked hats." He did not finish. The crazed population set on him like angry ants. For the rest of his life he bore a mark on his face that children a generation later pointed to as "the Lincoln mark." A participant recalled later:

"It was of no use for an aristocrat to attempt to argue with these hungry, desperate men. They had been too long already under the power of the lord and landlord, which is a synonym for oppression in that country. They had worked too long at poorhouse wages not to feel a thrill of pride and fellowship that they were counted worthy to suffer with you for liberty's sake."[38]

Both Russell and Palmerston had seen England on the verge of revolution before—at the time of the passage of the Reform Bill and during the Chartist movement. The existence of their government depended on their ability to cope with the situation, and the vote on intervention could hardly be put off again. July 28, 1862, dawned and with it came a rumor—unofficial—that McClellan had been defeated ignominiously. Unable to withdraw in orderly fashion, his army was annihilated and the general himself was a fugitive on a steamboat.[39]

Englishmen said that the last hope of a Union victory had vanished. The vote for Lindsay's motion for mediation was called and debated in Parliament.[40]

Palmerston tested the pulse of his House. He noted that the representatives of the industrial areas, the districts where the cotton famine had hit hardest, showed no disposition to vote for the slaveholders. The Prime Minister himself took the floor. A hush fell over the chamber. From a distance came the night noises of London, the rumbling of carriage wheels, the staccato cry of a newsboy, the rhythmic *plump-plump-plump* of a trotting cab horse. Palmerston was very grave. He said that the North was confronted with an overwhelming defeat. Lincoln would be obliged to sue for peace. The misery in England then would come to an end without the necessity of involving Great Britain. In view of this situation, the Prime Minister hoped that Parliament would leave the American question to the discretion of the government.[41]

Lord Palmerston resumed his seat. Lindsay withdrew his motion and the crisis passed once more. But Minister Adams, the archbishop of antislavery, wrote the State Department that a military victory and a definite stand on the question of slavery would be necessary to save the Northern cause in England.[42]

The British Parliament turned to other business, confident that the collapse of the North's resistance was only a matter of days. Adams begged the British government to consider his brief and stop the suspicious ship now almost finished. No time could be lost, he said. The assignment of his case to the bureaus appeared like a shipbuilder's trick to thwart the idealists and aid the Confederacy. James Mason believed that his day had come. He requested an interview with Russell—and was refused. What the government intended to do was anybody's guess.

For five days Adams urged a decision. He could get no word from the law office, and doubted Britain's sincerity. Finally a tracer discovered the papers untouched in the office of the queen's advocate. This worthy barrister had suffered a breakdown in health and was vacationing, on the verge of insanity. The papers were retrieved. On July 28, 1862, the attorney general and the solicitor general examined them. On the following day the vessel was ordered to be seized.[43]

It was too late.

The suspicious ship had slipped to sea for a trial trip and she never came back. "But she had no crew aboard," port authorities said. J. D. Bulloch had attended to this detail by inviting a goodly company of sailors and their molls to take an excursion along the Welsh coast. Out there the party boarded the ship. Bulloch plied them with food and drink, then offered the seamen enlistments on the vessel. A month's pay would be given each man in advance. The women's eyes brightened. They urged the tars to sign. At midnight Bulloch sent the women to shore in the rain, Jack's advance money jingling in their skirt pockets. With a full complement of men Bulloch steered north. He knew that the U. S. S. *Tuscarora* was waiting for him along the route south of Ireland. Rounding the Giant's Causeway, the ship, soon to be named *Alabama,* turned west. Bulloch instructed the captain to steam for the Azores where coal and arms would be sent. A near-by fishing boat was hailed. Bulloch boarded her and reached the coast of Ireland.[44]

Charles Francis Adams took the ship's escape in his stride—a business deal that had failed. At least his own record was clear. At heart he believed that Russell honestly tried to stop the vessel.[45] Most of the British liberals also believed that Russell was sincere. Cobden wrote Sumner: "Earl Russell was *bona fide* in his desire to prevent the *Alabama* from leaving, but he was tricked and was angry at the escape of the vessel."[46]

This was small comfort for a man confronted, as Lincoln was, with a momentous decision. Should he withdraw his blockading ships and send them out to hunt down the new marauder, or hold his blockade and alienate his own shipping interests by letting their vessels be swept from the sea? His other alternative was a resort to the Privateering Bill, the Russian alliance—if there were an alliance—and war with England.

# XII. *Antietam: Lincoln Faces the Crisis*

O N SUNDAY, July 13, 1862, Welles, Seward and Lincoln drove in the same carriage to the funeral of Stanton's infant child.[1] Lincoln leaned back wearily against the cushions. Only a few months ago he had buried his own little boy. The Lincolns had moved from the White House to the Soldiers' Home in the suburbs. Mrs. Lincoln could not bear the sight of the green lawn where Willie used to play. Seward had saved the President from too much brooding by pressing him with affairs of state. Today, as Lincoln rocked and jostled along with Welles and Seward, the three men could balance the war's debit and credit.

A year's fighting had upset Europe's economy. The powers stood poised to intervene. What had America done to get in such a bad way? What could the three men in the carriage do to correct affairs? A year ago, 1861, Gregory had failed to get a motion for the recognition of the Confederacy considered in Parliament— a good beginning for the North surely. All summer long Seward had worked to separate England and France, only to have them join for the Mexican venture. On top of this the *Trent* affair had almost precipitated a war. In the critical month of January 1862 politicians had pointed to disrupted foreign trade and idle mills as a cause for intervention in America, but both Parliament and the Deputies had stood firm. In February, Lincoln began playing his antislavery cards. Had they done any real good except to win sympathy from impotent idealists? The three men in the jolting carriage did not know for sure. England and Spain had separated from France in Mexico in April, but was not that due to a fear of war in Europe? Then, in May, Banks had made his spectacular retreat, and in June the resolution to intervene in America had been calendared, postponed and repostponed. Obviously the United States walked on trembling diplomatic sands. In addition Britain was known to be building more ships for the Confederacy, and

French and English statesmen were visiting suspiciously back and forth across the Channel—an apparent prelude to joint action against America. Less than three weeks ago Seward and Lincoln had changed their tactics. They had struck Europe left and right—with Russian treaty letter and Privateering Bill. The effect of these blows was still unknown. Would they be salutary or would they make the Northern position still more untenable? The mourning carriage lurched over the unpaved streets. Lincoln suggested that the administration take one more drastic step— emancipate all slaves in the Confederacy.

Before election Lincoln had stated, and restated, that he had no intention of abolishing slavery where it was legally sanctioned. He had continually denied petitions from abolitionists as well as wild-eyed politicians like Schurz and Clay. Yet Lincoln hated slavery. He said many times that he could not remember when he did not hate slavery.[2] Lincoln, Welles and Seward all knew that Stanton, riding up yonder behind the hearse, also opposed abolition as impolitic. But the constant urging of foreign ministers and Lincoln's own preference had modified all the men's convictions. The response in Europe to the antislavery cards Lincoln had been playing all summer was debatable—but it could not be ignored. Welles was very sure that the effect of emancipation on many people abroad would be electric. The religious middle class and the workers in England would be won irrevocably to the North. But would this gain be worth the loss of votes Lincoln would suffer in America? The President listened thoughtfully, then changed the subject. He had another device for gaining sympathy abroad. He would publish correspondence showing his government's solicitude for foreign missions—an appeal to the religious middle classes in England. British workers, too, were more devout than Americans.

The publication appeared in the form of a "white paper" entitled *Religious Toleration in Egypt*.[3] The correspondence covered a period of twelve months. Few Americans realized, until they read it, that Lincoln had taken time to deliver an ultimatum to Turkey the year before, while McClellan was endlessly organizing and drilling an army after the defeats of Bull Run and Ball's Bluff. Lincoln had been grieving then for his old friend, Edward Baker. He had partially assuaged his grief by helping Seward with foreign problems, by organizing the Navy to blockade Southern ports. During the disasters and defeats and heartaches, Lincoln had received a letter from his Egyptian minister, William S. Thayer, stating that a Syrian bookseller, a Christian employed by American missionaries, had been abused by a mob of Moslems on the Upper Nile. Thirteen wealthy and respected citizens of the district were culpable. Thayer said that an example must be made of them to preserve United States prestige. A year's imprisonment and fine of $5,000 from each would renew respect for the Stars and Stripes.

This had happened a year ago. Now Lincoln published this letter with an affidavit of the abused Syrian, Faris-el-Hakim, and the reply of the Cadi of the district. The depositions of the two principals agreed in all essential facts, yet the two accounts differed as radically as a positive and a negative photograph. Lincoln had seen many similar incidents in his wide experience as a lawyer. Faris, in his affidavit, stated that the Moslems of Upper Egypt disliked him because he sold Christian books cheaper than the native merchants could sell books in their faith. In addition, he stated, he had been persecuted because he acted as attorney for a woman who wished to become a Christian. 'All the learned doctors in the district had condemned him as a dangerous infidel and urged the populace to stone him. He had been cast in jail, where he fainted dead away. The Moudir of the district heard about Faris' plight, ordered his release, and sent a physician to examine the attorney's health. Next morning the Moudir called in person on the unfortunate Christian.

This sworn statement of grievances for the American State Department was followed in the "white paper" by the report of the Cadi, which materially changed the aspects of the case. The trouble, according to the Cadi's statement, started over a woman, Fatima, whose attorney, a Syrian named Faris-el-Hakim, enticed her from her husband and four-year-old child. Ordered to appear in the Cadi's court, Fatima came with her attorney, the Christian. She was confronted with her legal husband and admitted being married to him by Moslem law. Faris maintained that this did not bind her as she had become a Coptic Christian. The learned doctors jostled Faris for this sacrilege and made such a disturbance that the Cadi adjourned court and took Faris to jail. The Cadi concluded his report by requesting a ruling from the Moudir to determine what should be done with Faris "for reviling our religion which includes all courts and government and for his persistence in having the woman violate the law."

The "white paper" showed further that the Moudir had ordered an investigation. The learned doctors had been reproved and the Cadi had been censured for not confining his jurisdiction to a ruling on the marital status of the woman, for permitting the learned doctors in his court and for keeping Faris in custody. When this reprimand failed to satisfy the American government, the Egyptian authorities agreed to exact the punishment demanded.[4] Word of this compliance reached Lincoln while he was worrying over the *Trent* affair, but he had taken time to thank the Turkish Pasha. An exchange of letters ensued, with each complimenting the other on the firmness of their respective governments, and Turkey, shortly thereafter, announced that all her ports were closed to Confederate vessels.

This correspondence, originally published in America in May, was republished in London in July by the Evangelical Alliance, which had been Lincoln's main British defender. Count Gurowski, who could be counted on to do anything embarrassing to his former employers, published a sarcastic diatribe ending with, "Oh, Jemine! to be patronized by the Turks!"[5]

While Lincoln made this tentative effort to gain friendship with the English middle class, John Slidell in France proceeded to offset his rebuff from the Emperor by courting the Count de Persigny, Minister of the Interior. The two men had much in common. Both were adventurers, equally at home with exquisite courtiers or hireling plug-uglies. Like Morny, the count was a gambler, ready to play with nations as stakes. Persigny, having helped make an Emperor in France, now dreamed of making another one in Mexico. An independent Southern Confederacy might help his scheme. His newspaper, the *Constitutionnel,* championed the Southern cause.[6] His doorkeeper was instructed to admit Slidell at any time.

Shortly after McClellan's retreat from Richmond in July,[7] Persigny arranged the long-coveted audience for Slidell with Napoleon. The Emperor was at Vichy. Persigny suggested that the

Southerner try the healing waters there. Slidell hurried to the south of France. This meeting would be no embarrassing encounter behind the scenes of a theater. On the day of his arrival Slidell was informed that the Emperor awaited him. On the following day Slidell presented his card at the imperial chalet. The handsome pink and white Southerner was ushered into Napoleon's presence. Slidell was full of schemes and intrigues. First he disclosed Benjamin's offer of $12,500,000 worth of American cotton if His Imperial Majesty would break the blockade.[8] Slidell said, too, that the South would co-operate with France in conquering Mexico. He called the Emperor's attention to the certainty that Lincoln, if victorious, would never countenance French occupation. Already the Northern President was doing his utmost to check the advance of the French armies by financing Juárez.[9] Had not Lincoln submitted to the Senate a treaty for a loan which with subsidiary benefits amounted to $11,000,000?

Napoleon's mustache twitched eagerly, but his absent-minded eyes saw visions of Europe in chaos. Garibaldi was loose again in Italy. The Emperor must protect Rome.[10] France might help the Confederacy at a later date but not now. Slidell left the chalet with his thin white hair flying in the breeze. His hopes were high.

Lincoln had only odd moments to spend baffling the Emperor and cajoling the English missionaries. Foremost in his thoughts was emancipation of the slaves. Nine days after mentioning the subject at the funeral, he discussed the problem in the cabinet.[11] All agreed that an edict must not be issued so soon after McClellan's retreat from the peninsula. Europe would say that Lincoln was grasping at a straw to save himself. Seward became loquacious. People in England and France, he said, did not really approve of emancipation. The idealists' influence was buncombe. The industrialists would interfere in the American war to keep the blacks in bondage and thus insure a supply of cotton.

Seward knew Europe much better than Lincoln. His job as Secretary of State was to advise his chief on foreign policy. Could it be that both Weed's and Schurz's reports, as well as the dispatches from all the foreign ministers, had been misleading? After all, Lincoln had appointed abolitionists to foreign posts and they might not be able to report without bias. On the other hand Lincoln knew Seward. Was he sincere or was he just talking? Seward had been defeated for the presidential nomination because he was too much of an abolitionist. Ever since that time he had played into the hands of the slaveholders. Did Seward know Europe better than the foreign ministers or did he believe that the powers, like himself, would change their principles for political expediency? Lincoln decided to wait, to think it over.

Seward himself was not sure of his own opinion. Europe was not an open book. Two days after the cabinet meeting he wrote to Motley:

"Are you sure that to-day, under the seduction and pressure which could be applied to some European populations, they would not rise up and resist our attempt to bestow freedom upon the laborers whose capacity to supply cotton and open a market for European fabrics depends, or is thought to depend, upon their continuance in bondage?"[12]

Having taken this precaution to reassure himself on the slavery issue, Seward left his desk and went to the White House. His step showed more concern than usual. He strutted into Lincoln's room and found the President in conference with Senator Browning of Illinois. The senator rose to go. Lincoln motioned him back to his seat. Seward's message was brief. Things looked bad in Mexico and South America. Spain had a plot to reannex Peru. Senator Browning asked if there was any danger of intervention by England and France. Yes, Seward replied, very much danger, unless the Army recruited rapidly and volunteers demonstrated that McClellan's reverse had not discouraged the North.[13]

The next evening Senator Browning drove his wife out to the Soldiers' Home, ostensibly to bid the President good-by before they returned to Illinois. In reality the Senator wanted news. Lincoln was communicative, said he was convinced that there was no fight in McClellan. He had given Halleck command of the entire Army and sent him down into Virginia with instructions to relieve McClellan if advisable. Lincoln said, too, that England was clamoring for cotton and he was considering releasing

$50,000,000 worth[14]—enough to counteract Slidell's offer and help England too.

Senator Browning departed well satisfied with his knowledge. Early in August 1862, Lincoln received a letter from Count de Gasparin in Switzerland. The liberal nobleman deplored McClellan's retreat from Richmond—a great blow to liberalism throughout the world, he said. Would the President be able to recruit more men and carry on the fight? Lincoln put the letter on his desk. The cabinet arrived for the daily session. They discussed the military situation, McClellan, the advisability of besieging Vicksburg and opening the Mississippi. A rumor from Indian Territory said that the Cherokees had joined the Confederacy. These rich slaveholding red men had expelled the poor nonslaveholding tribes from the territory. Should an expedition be sent to teach them a lesson?[15]

Lincoln decided to relieve McClellan of his command by degrees—save face for him. Detachments of his men were ordered north by every boat and train. Lincoln brigaded them in Pope's Army of Virginia. Thus one force wasted away to nourish the other. From now on Pope was to be the recognized commander in Virginia. Muster rolls showed that great numbers of soldiers had disappeared—deserted! John Hay remembered that Lincoln said, "The Army dwindled on the march like a shovelfull of fleas pitched from one place to another."[16] When Lincoln answered Gasparin's letter on August 4, 1862, he expressed it differently. "With us," he wrote, "every soldier is a man of character, and must be treated with more consideration than is customary in Europe. Hence our great army, for slighter causes than could have prevailed there, has dwindled rapidly."[17]

On August 6, 1862, Lincoln addressed a great mass meeting in Washington. He deplored the rumors that McClellan had quarreled with the Secretary of War. McClellan, he said, was "a brave and able man." He had wanted more troops than Stanton could furnish. This was the only basis of their disagreement.[18] After the meeting Lincoln turned his attention to foreign affairs. On August 8, Seward sent all the legations and consulates in Europe a circular letter to be published in the leading newspapers. Prospective emigrants were told glowing tales of opportunities in America, of enlistment bounties larger than anything peasants had ever hoped to own.[19] Next Lincoln ordered Pope not to engage in any battle unless a victory was sure. A defeat at this time, Lincoln cautioned, might lose the war.

Then Lincoln picked up a memo on his desk. An Indian agent, accused of stealing, wanted the President to intercede in his behalf. Some gorgeously quilled moccasins were enclosed as a gift. Lincoln pulled off his boots, put them on, and grinned. John Hay chuckled to himself. That Indian agent was due for a disappointment if he thought moccasins would turn Abraham Lincoln's slow feet down the path to corruption.

One day Cassius M. Clay breezed into the capital, fresh from Russia. He stalked up and down the streets, called on old friends. The rebellion seemed to him as bad as it had been a year before. True, Grant had crossed Kentucky and got into the pine uplands of northern Alabama. Butler and Farragut had taken New Orleans. But Washington itself was still threatened by the rebels and enemy pickets stood within fifty miles of the city. Clay called at the White House to receive his major general's commission and bring the war to an end. He said that the first thing to be done was to emancipate the slaves, then strike like fury on a crusade of freedom into the South. No European autocracy would dare oppose the Union after that.[20]

Lincoln said that he was very glad to see his old friend again. Emancipation might be a fine idea—so novel. The President was kind and attentive as he had been when Schurz burst in upon him with the same original proposal. The interview concluded. Clay departed in ecstasy, and ever after declared that the only reason he had not been given an active military assignment then and there was that Secretary of War Stanton and Chief of Staff Halleck "opposed abolitionist generals."

Disappointed political generals always left Lincoln that way. When Clay had time to think over the interview, he remembered that he wanted to go back to Russia. A friend carried the word to the President and Lincoln wrote Clay on August 12 that he would be happy to send him, if Cameron resigned when he came back to Washington. The exchange of correspondence might take two months.

On August 13, 1862, Clay delivered an antislavery speech at the Odd Fellows Hall in Washington. He told the wondering audience that abolition was the only means of preventing foreign intervention. Lincoln had already written a draft of his Emancipation Proclamation, but he had not decided to pronounce it. He had talked a long time recently with Joseph Jenkins Roberts. Both Roberts and Lincoln were interested in freeing and colonizing the Negro. Roberts was an excellent conversationalist, intelligent, handsome, fine-mannered, familiar with the best people in both America and Europe. Born in Petersburg, Virginia, Roberts had gone as a young man to the American Colonization Society's settlement in Liberia. The director, a white man, had trouble with the natives, who resented invasion of their country. The colony was saved from annihilation by the remarkable vigor and initiative of Joseph Roberts. His Negro blood made him so natural a leader of the colonists that they elected him their first president under a constitution copied from that of the United States. Liberia owed its independence as a nation to Roberts' constructive imagination after the Colonization Society abandoned its early venture. With practically no outside help he created a unique agricultural civilization on the west coast of Africa. Amid the palm trees appeared white-pillared plantation houses. Former slaves, bearing the proudest names of the South, sat on the galleries sipping cool drinks and dispensing hospitality. All work was done by native "bond servants" who were housed in "slave quarters" and kept in ignorance. The servants' children were not permitted to attend their black masters' schools. On Sunday they sat in church in the back rows or in a balcony exactly as slaves did in Virginia. The black planters said that the servants must be treated as inferiors or they would be "insolent and saucy." They must be kept in their places lest they rise and kill their masters.[21]

Lincoln had heard white slaveholders talk like this all his life. His wife had been reared to believe this was propriety. Lincoln sent word for Cassius M. Clay to come back to the White House and discuss abolition. He also requested a deputation of free colored people in the city to come for an audience. The Negroes arrived dutifully and sat before Lincoln. The President looked into their black, stolid faces, their illiterate eyes. What could he say that they would understand? He began by explaining the unpleasantness, the injustices, the lack of opportunity which would be their lot in a white man's world. He told them about his conversation with Joseph Roberts and outlined the possibilities of forming colonies with government aid in Latin America. He said that the colonists must expect pioneer hardships. They must expect to work, but they would be their own masters and each man would have a farm of his own. For colonists, Lincoln said, he wanted "tolerably intelligent men, with their wives and children, and able to 'cut their own fodder.'" Would anybody volunteer? Could he get a hundred—fifty—twenty-five?

The freedmen stared at Lincoln stupidly. They made no reply. Lincoln told them to be in no hurry making up their minds, to think it over. The delegation arose and filed off without enthusiasm.[22]

When Clay strode into the White House in blue frock coat and brass buttons, Lincoln greeted him cordially. "I have been thinking of what you said to me," the President began, "but I fear if such a proclamation of emancipation was made Kentucky would go against us; and we have now as much as we can carry."

Clay stood with his arms folded, a heroic figure, tall enough to look straight into Lincoln's eyes. "Those who intend to stand by slavery have already joined the Rebel army," he said.

"The Kentucky Legislature is now in session," Lincoln replied. "Go down and see how they stand and report to me."[23]

Always happy when active, Clay set off. Lincoln watched him go—an ideal mission for a worthy political major general with brass buttons on his coattails. When the door closed, Lincoln turned to the military problems cluttering his desk. McClellan's army was safely delivered to General John Pope. Perhaps this new commander could retrieve the fortunes of democracy.

Lincoln no longer expected a quick victory. Every morning he rode from the Soldiers' Home to the White House to answer his mail. The August mornings were sultry. His horse steamed between his knees. The dust settled on the President's shoulders and on his hat. General Pope was marshaling his troops in the heat for a new thrust at Richmond. Lincoln dismounted at the

White House and walked across to the State Department. The dark green leaves on the maple trees were sticky with the heat. Inside the brick building it was cool. Lincoln talked to Seward. Could Europe be kept out of the fight? Blockade-running had increased amazingly. The two men discussed possible remedies. It was a bad time to stop British boats. Abolition, too, was a dangerous experiment—at least before Clay reported from Kentucky. Lincoln and Seward agreed that conciliation was the best policy until Pope showed the world that America was strong. In the meantime England must be indulged in her illegal traffic.

The cabinet met and Lincoln put the problem before his secretaries. None of them agreed. Each member had a different solution. All argued endlessly on what to do. Secretary Welles urged a strong policy—put the Privateering Bill in operation. Foreign intervention did not intimidate him. Seward's obsequiousness, Welles said, encouraged Britain to insult America in every port. Why be afraid to stand up for the nation's rights![24]

Neither Seward nor Lincoln replied. Were they both thinking of Pope in Virginia drilling to fight Lee? Two days later Welles was disgusted to learn that the administration had become more abject—promised to forward all mail captured on blockade-runners,[25] ordered sugar condemned by Butler in New Orleans restored to alleged British owners.[26] What did these soft words mean after the harsh threat of the Privateering Bill and the treaty with Russia? Was Lincoln showing that he had the power but preferred to be conciliatory? Was he playing the oldest of political tricks—offering something for all, appealing to one group with friendship and another with fear?

Night after night darkness settled over the White House before Lincoln mounted his horse to go home. The streets were gloomy at the edge of the city. Once, as Lincoln rode along deep in thought, a shot flashed from a clump of bushes. Lincoln's horse jumped forward. Horse and horseman raced down the midnight road. Turning in at the Home gate, Lincoln galloped up to the porch, dismounted and stamped up the steps laughing about his mad ride. He had lost an eight-dollar hat, he said. Lincoln's friends insisted that a guard must ride with him henceforth. A company of cavalry was posted at the Soldiers' Home and at the White House. Lincoln acquiesced reluctantly. It was undemocratic.

On August 17, 1862, Archbishop Hughes held Mass in St. Patrick's Cathedral on Mott Street, New York—the first after his return. As the organ music shuddered and died in the cathedral, the Archbishop stepped forward. His rich surplice enhanced the ruddy countenance which he had preserved through advancing years. The message he brought to the Irish in New York was not so rosy as his cheeks. Foreign nations, he warned Tammany Hall Democrats, would surely intervene unless all parties combined to back the administration. Napoleon had supported the Church. He had protected Rome from Garibaldi. For these acts the clergy was grateful but they did not support the Emperor's policy of intervention to uphold slavery. However, the economic situation in France was desperate. People were on the verge of starvation. Napoleon might be forced to act unless all Americans united to bring the war to a quick and successful end. The worshipers pondered the Archbishop's words as they filed out into the sultry streets.

Lincoln knew that Confederate propagandists in England were urging that country to join Napoleon in intervention. Henry Hotze had been working feverishly all through the summer of 1862. He hoped to have England ready to declare war against the North along with France in the coming winter. The United States' apparent military weakness, the summer's lack of military activity, gave him a great opportunity. Middle-class Englishmen were losing faith in the Union's survival. From the first, the North's case had been pronounced hopeless by leading Europeans. The London Confederate States 'Aid Association had been formed in August and forthwith appealed for funds "in the name of suffering Lancashire, civilization, justice, peace, liberty, humanity, Christianity, and a candid world."[27] Charles Francis Adams had warned Lincoln that nothing would save the North in Europe but emancipation, yet emancipation would cost him Kentucky. Everything depended on Clay's report. If Kentucky was safe then Lincoln might placate Europe.

Unfortunately Clay did not send Lincoln any assurances. Instead the Kentuckian found his home town, Lexington, wild with confusion. Breathless friends told Clay that Confederates were coming in great numbers, unopposed by Union soldiers. Bragg's Southern veterans streamed through Cumberland Gap, a long serpent of gray-clad men eager to set Kentucky free from the "Lincoln tyranny." West of them the roads that led from Tennessee were gray with the advancing army of Kirby Smith, and on their flank John Morgan's wild horsemen were already bivouacked on the edge of the Blue Grass. Clay remained a week, watching his old acquaintances hide their property or prepare a grand celebration for the invading heroes. Obviously Kentucky was lost to the Union.

On top of Clay's dejection the telegraph reported a new disaster in the East. Pope had been defeated before Washington in the second battle of Bull Run.[28] The capital was in imminent danger of capture once more. Government records were being packed. A swift vessel at the foot of C Street kept up steam day and night to evacuate the President. Major General Clay knew that his mission was a failure. He took the train back east.

In the face of this catastrophe, what could be expected of England and France with their starving thousands? Fortunately for Lincoln's democracy, communications with Europe were slow. Had these disasters been reported as soon as they occurred, Great Britain might have intervened. For a month the pressure on the English government had been almost unbearable. On August 6, 1862, Earl Russell wrote Palmerston that mediation must be considered when he returned to London. He was attending the Queen in Gotha[29] and the problem troubled him. On August 24 he wrote again:

"I have been reading a book on Jefferson by De Witt, which is both interesting and instructive. It shows how the Great Republic of Washington degenerated into the Democracy of Jefferson. They are now reaping the fruit."[30]

On August 29, before word had been received about the defeat of Pope, liberal Gladstone wrote to a colleague in the cabinet a letter on the hopelessness of the Northern cause,[31] and the next boat brought even worse news. Lee had followed Pope's defeat by an invasion of Maryland. Already he had marched north of

Washington and daily he might be expected to wheel and encircle the capital.

News that Washington was in danger reached London on September 14, 1862. Before England had time to act, Lincoln made one of those quick moves which confounded the diplomats. He had lashed out with the Privateering Bill and the Russian threat some ten weeks ago when McClellan faltered on the peninsula and the British government seemed ready to recognize the South and encourage construction of warships for her. Now after two months of conciliatory intercourse he waved a red flag before the British bull. Charles Wilkes was ordered to the West Indies. The irascible commander had not been cashiered, as Englishmen wished, after the *Trent* affair. Instead he had been promoted but kept in the Chesapeake away from tempting British prizes. In the West Indies he would be on the main contraband route and in easy striking distance of all blockade-runners. Count Gurowski squalled at the government's reckless order:

"These helpless grave-diggers, above all, Seward, are on the way to pick a quarrel with England, sending a flying gunboat fleet under Wilkes into the West Indian waters. At this precise moment it were better to be very cautious."[32]

Palmerston learned about Pope's defeat and the proposed encirclement of Washington before he knew about Wilkes's new assignment. Meanwhile, Lincoln followed his rash transfer of Wilkes with a desperate call to McClellan. He begged his deposed general to command what was left of the Union Army and defend the capital. Palmerston took up his pen and wrote Russell in Gotha that Washington in all probability would soon fall into rebel hands. He asked his Foreign Secretary:

"If this should happen, would it not be time for us to consider whether in such a state of things England and France might not address the contending parties and recommend an arrangement on the basis of separation?"[33]

Earl Russell had not been able to put off the decision, as he had hoped, until after his vacation. He replied that in his opinion the time had come for mediation whether or not Washington was captured, and he suggested a meeting of the cabinet to discuss immediate action on September 23 or 30, 1862.[34]

With mediation set to a hair trigger and Wilkes in the Caribbean ready to antagonize England at the first opportunity, George Francis Train bobbed up unexpectedly in America. Having talked himself out of audiences in England, he made one last bid for notoriety by addressing a secret meeting of the Irish Brotherhood of St. Patrick in London. For unbridled oratory irritating to the British people Train outdid himself. He was particularly vindictive against the aristocracy who controlled the English government and reported himself as saying:

"What have the people done to be denied air and water and light even? Think of 8,000 families living in Scotland in one room with no window! The statistics are sickening—227,000 families live in one room—with one window and 250,000 families live in two rooms with two windows! Think of seventy-two per cent. of the entire population of Scotland living in families of from four to eight persons, in only two rooms, with only two windows! And this is freedom! . . . The monarchies of Europe, like garrulous old men, are propping each other up with the hope of the downfall of America. Hear them chatter, and try to stand firmly on their weak legs—sans teeth, sans eyes, sans every thing. (Cheers.) Each saying to the other, Republics are dead."[35]

Having made these socialistic generalizations about the conditions in Scotland, Train gave equally unpleasant statistics about England, then concluded his speech by touching the sorest spot in the British Empire—Ireland. He appealed to his audience for armed rebellion.

"Ireland must find some Garibaldi to remember Wolf Tone, Emmet, and Daniel O'Connell, and cry Union in America and Liberty in Ireland!"

With tremendous cheers the assembled Irishmen escorted Mr. Train some way into the street, where a squad of policemen took him in hand and led the way to the nearest jail. In a less tolerant country Train would have been deported as an undesirable alien but the British court turned him loose. The indomitable Train decided next to perform the most notorious exploit of his career. A suspicious vessel, the *Mavrocordato,* was loading for America.

Though she was ostensibly bound for Newfoundland, Train became convinced that she was a blockade-runner. He engaged passage, hoping by this means to get inside the Confederate lines. With this accomplished he intended to go to Richmond with peace overtures which he was satisfied both sides would accept.[36]

Unluckily for Train, the vessel turned out to be a legitimate trader, and the eccentric orator was eventually landed in Canada without an opportunity to end the war. Train went first to Boston. He engaged a hall and gathered an audience. Always desiring to be classed with the otherwise-minded, he shouted from the stage that he was on his way to Richmond with the coffin of the Abolition Party.

Train heard that Cassius Clay had arrived in New York. He proceeded to Manhattan, got the belligerent Westerner to introduce him to an audience at the Academy of Music and then challenged Clay to debate on the following night at Cooper Union. Clay accepted, and Train, for the sake of the argument, proposed to defend slavery as a Divine Institution.

Train and Clay, the biting and the barking dogs, made a strange contrast on the stage. Newspapers reported that both men appeared in black frock coats. Train's was trimmed fore and aft with brass buttons. Patent-leather boots shone like new stove lids on his feet. Clay's hair was brushed smoothly over his large round head. Train's hair stood out fluffy as a cotton boll.[37] The Kentuckian spoke with furious sincerity. The audience displayed respect for his eloquence and also for his known combativeness. Train made them laugh, whistle, utter catcalls.

After the debate Train entrained for Washington.[38] Later he reported that Lincoln and the cabinet received him cordially. The city had changed mightily while he was abroad. During the last year a street railway had been laid on Pennsylvania Avenue and although an extra horse was required to pull a crowded car around the Treasury Building,[39] the innovation was admitted to be as successful in America as Train's enterprises in England. Secretary Seward, Train stated, invited him to dinner and regaled him with a story about Wendell Phillips in Charleston, South Carolina, before the war. Phillips objected to the slave labor in the hotel dining room. He told the slave waiter to leave. The New England abolitionist would wait on himself. "I cain't do dat, suh," replied the Negro. "I is 'sponsible for de silber on de table, suh!"

Seward told the story well. His dinner party was gay. Then Stanton came in, his face white above his bushy beard. A great battle had been fought, he announced, at Antietam Creek. No one knew which side had won. Perhaps the rebels had opened the way to Washington.

Rumor ran riot. People speculated on the magnitude of the disaster, and equally disheartening news came from the sea. The mystery ship *Oreto*, which had been released from Nassau, ran the blockade into Mobile with British colors flying. Commodore Preble had given chase, fired all around her, made a noise but hurt no one—afraid of offending England, Welles complained.[40] In a Confederate port the vessel was soon armed and ready to slip out to sea as the *Florida*. Coupled with his bad news came word from the other mystery ship, the *Alabama*, which had arrived according to Bulloch's plans at the island of Terceira in the Azores.[41] Bulloch met her there with two vessels, as he had agreed to do, one laden with munitions and the other with coal. The cannon were quickly mounted and on August 24, 1862, the ship steamed out to the high seas where the Confederate flag was broken out on her peak with due ceremony and she was commissioned a Confederate man-of-war, Raphael Şemmes commanding. Bulloch concluded the services by agreeing to send a relief ship with more coal and supplies to Saint-Pierre in Martinique. At midnight he climbed over the side and returned by devious ways to England. The *Alabama*, with a crew of English sailors of fortune, disappeared in the night, a phantom ship henceforth, sighted by few men who lived to tell the tale. The red light of burning merchantmen, spars and floating wreckage from the Caribbean to the Orient marked her trail until she came to port at last in France.

The successful commissioning of these two ships, together with the news of the doubtful engagement at Antietam, filled Lincoln's cup of bitterness to the brim. Later dispatches proved Antietam to be a draw. Lee's invasion had been stopped. Good! That was some relief. Now McClellan must strike the retreating enemy, annihilate his army, and win a signal victory. Then Lincoln could talk back to England, make the most of Wilkes in the Caribbean, check the building of more Confederate ships as well as Bulloch's rams. But McClellan did not strike back. The Confederate Army returned to Virginia without opposition. McClellan was too weak and too exhausted to follow. Politicians renewed their howl. He would not fight! Long lists of dead arrived in the War Department. Lincoln read them. His face was very sad.

The British cabinet met to consider mediation before the Antietam dispatches arrived in England. Blustering Palmerston, timid at heart, insisted that action be delayed. Wait, he cautioned, until full reports come in.

Napoleon rubbed his hands with glee, twirled the waxed ends of his mustache. He sent his great general, Louis Forey, to Mexico with more troops. Thouvenel made it a point to see Dayton and prepare him for intervention. "Would it not be better therefore," he said, "that good loyal citizens should begin to consider some way of arranging this matter instead of being entirely occupied in killing each other with bullets?"[42]

Palmerston still hesitated. If the Federals sustained "a great defeat," he said, then a cabinet should be called.[43] Palmerston knew what mediation meant. On September 25, 1862, he wrote Russell that it was tantamount to recognition of the Confederacy. He said further that it would be well to ask Russia to join them. "Her participation in the offer might render the North the more willing to accept it."[44] Palmerston suggested the middle of October as the proper time to take action. Last June Lincoln had countered a similar motion with the Russian treaty. In July he had advanced the Privateering Bill. Did he have another remedy short of war—and suicide?

Henry Hotze thought not. He was jubilant. The South, he said, was gaining sympathy so rapidly by his publicity and by the diplomatic developments, that Antietam, whether a victory or defeat, could not hurt the Southern cause. De Leon chimed in the cantata with facts to show that the North was disintegrating. He published in the English papers quotations from Lincoln's political enemies[45] to prove that the President had no support even in the North. The Confederate agents, however, were not prepared to meet Lincoln's next move—the great remedy. They had not reckoned with the trump card which the Rail Splitter held in his hand.

# XIII. *"I Am a Slow Walker But I Never Walk Back"*

INCOLN worried about the problem of caring for the Negroes in case he freed them. Roberts had made a successful Negro nation in Liberia, but Lincoln's own attempt to enlist recruits for a colony discouraged him. He considered setting aside the state of Florida as a Negro asylum.[1] The white population there was small, a few cowboys and fishermen, descendants of the buccaneers, and Seminole Indians who had sheltered runaway slaves for generations. Central and South America and the West Indies seemed better. Seward sent a circular to France, the Netherlands, Denmark, Great Britain—countries with colonies in the Caribbean—offering to make a treaty for colonization.[2] At the same time the American ministers were requested to sound out their respective countries and ascertain the probable reaction to emancipation. Seward still maintained that no Europeans except the radicals favored it.

Almost daily, promoters with alleged grants from the unstable Latin-American governments beleaguered the State Department with franchises for sale. Senator Pomeroy from Kansas came with a proposition in Panama.[3] The so-called Chiriqui grant seemed very attractive but Costa Rica claimed part of it. For months speculators tried to unload this block of land on the government.[4] Lincoln examined abstracts of the title. His administration had been noticeably friendly to Latin America.[5] Would the acquisition of such a questionable parcel appear like an act of the filibustering Democrats who had recently ruled America? Would Mexico, where Tom Corwin was working to establish friendly relations, be frightened and alienated?

Another proposition seemed less objectionable. The entire island of Vache was offered by a promoter, Bernard Kock, who held a franchise for it from the government of Haiti. The climate was ideal, so Kock said. The temperature rarely exceeded eighty de-

253

grees. Mahogany, oak and dyewood grew in abundance. Fertile prairies suitable for sea-island cotton were waiting for the plow.[6]

Lincoln was attracted to the plan. He studied geography and waited for the reports from his foreign ministers. Soon the dispatches trickled into the State Department. Most of the foreign nations favored a Negro colony in Latin America. The President decided on a preliminary step. He liked experiments. On September 22, 1862, he sent a State Department messenger to summon the cabinet to the White House at noon. The secretaries took their seats around the baize-covered table. Lincoln showed them a book Artemus Ward had sent to him. Lincoln read a chapter that he considered very funny. Secretary of War Stanton was impatient and bored. Lincoln finished and put down the book.

"Gentlemen," he said gravely, "I have, as you are aware, thought a great deal about the relation of this war to Slavery. . . . I have thought all along that the time for acting on it might very probably come. I think the time has come now. . . . I have got you together to hear what I have written down."[7]

Lincoln read the paper—his first Emancipation Proclamation. European laborers and idealists would be disappointed. The document did not free a single slave. Lincoln merely gave the seceded states until the first of January to come back into the Union or on that day be threatened with the extermination of their peculiar institution. Every member of the cabinet knew in his heart that emancipation was on its way—the ball had begun to roll. John Hay wrote in his diary that the proclamation freed the cabinet as well as the slaves. "They gleefully and merrily called each other and themselves abolitionists, and seemed to enjoy the novel sensation of appropriating that horrible name."[8]

The response to the proclamation in Europe was almost nil. However, three bits of news drew attention to the President's act. One was Jeff Davis' counterproclamation. Another was a resolution of the Southern Episcopal Church,[9] and the third was the confidential information that Bulloch's shipbuilding money was exhausted. When Englishmen read that President Davis retaliated against Lincoln's proclamation by threatening to execute any white officer captured commanding Negro troops and that the Southern Episcopalians' convention proclaimed slavery a positive good, they had to admit that the vaunted civilization of the South was as barbarous as "Beast" Butler himself. The exhaustion of Confederate funds, oddly enough, worked to the South's advantage. James M. Mason met the embarrassment by engaging an English financial adviser, James Spence, the writer who had alleged in his book that his sympathies were originally with the North—a politic appointment calculated to weld the South to the great shipping interests and financiers. Confederate bonds, cotton bonds and cotton certificates were offered at prices attractive to speculators.[10] If English investors could be sold sufficient securities, the pressure on the British government to maintain the South would be irresistible.

The Lincolns remained at the Soldiers' Home late in the fall of 1862. Every day when the President rode to the White House he heard that McClellan intended to set himself up as dictator and that the Confederates had entrenched themselves abroad.[11] In October a bombshell exploded. Gladstone, Secretary of the Exchequer, stated in a speech at Newcastle that the North would never win the war. It was presumed that Gladstone, as a member of the English government, knew the plans of the Prime Minister and was preparing the people for future government action. Surely he planned recognizing the Confederacy when he said, "Jefferson Davis and other leaders of the South have made an army; they are making, it appears, a navy; and they have made what is more than either, they have made a nation."[12]

Such talk spelled the word of doom for the American Union. The Emancipation Proclamation seemed to have come too late. Earl Russell callously called a cabinet to consider whether it was a "duty of Europe to ask both parties, in the most friendly and conciliatory terms, to agree to a suspension of arms."[13]

October 23, 1862, was set for the meeting. War or peace was up to the cabinet now, since Palmerston had asked Parliament to leave the question to the government, back in July when McClellan began his retreat. Would this shift in responsibility make any difference? Would the humanitarian principle of abolition and democracy weigh more with these men than the practical necessity of getting cotton and protecting investments? Lincoln's personal opinion of human cupidity was known to be low and good-natured. Seward, too, had said, over and over, that material considerations were paramount abroad.

The new crisis approached and each dispatch from Europe seemed worse than the last. Minister Adams asked for an interview to stop the catastrophe. Earl Russell assigned him October 23—the day of the meeting—too late to do any good.[14] In the meantime the Southern Association of Liverpool prepared a great memorial. The association was considered to be politically powerful.[15] Things looked very bad. Then Secretary Welles took an uncalled-for slap at England.

Welles needed ships, and the British *Bermuda,* captured in April, lay in the Philadelphia yards pending decision of the prize court. The Secretary of the Navy sent the purchase price and demanded delivery of the vessel before she was condemned.[16] Seward begged Welles to desist, retract the offer and show every consideration for Great Britain. Why injure the owners in this manner on the eve of a cabinet crisis?[17] Lincoln had lashed out at England several times in the last six months, it was true, but even the most offensive actions could be diplomatically explained and he had not resorted to any of them until all else failed. The Privateering Bill was an obvious precaution against the South. It would not hurt England unless she were guilty. The Russian note was unofficial and no threat at all, except indirectly. Wilkes's sudden transfer to the Caribbean could be diplomatically explained as a mere coincidence. But Welles's studied determination to affront British shipowners was sure to be construed as an insult. Welles sneered at Seward's weakness.

Lincoln's cabinet waited. The arrival of ocean packets was announced. Two days later the dispatch bags came to Washington. Foreign correspondence was delivered to Seward. Lincoln walked over every day, sometimes twice a day. The news was from countries other than England. Cameron in Russia wrote again, asking to be relieved.[18] Theodore Canisius, the Springfield printer and Lincoln's onetime partner, now consul in Vienna, had made a nuisance of himself. With no authority he had opened communication with Garibaldi, urging him to take a command in America.[19] Lincoln and Seward did not want to be laughed at again on that issue—especially on the eve of a foreign crisis. Canisius was

CARL SCHURZ          ADAM GUROWSKI

HENRY BERGH        ANSON BURLINGAME

BISHOP CHARLES PETTIT
McILVAINE

ARCHBISHOP JOHN JOSEPH
HUGHES

CASSIUS MARCELLUS CLAY

disciplined with dismissal from the service—then reinstated.[20]

On October 20, 1862, three days before the British cabinet was scheduled to meet, Newman Hall, LL.B., a Dissenting minister, addressed a meeting of London workingmen. The South, he said, had no more constitutional right to secede than had Yorkshire. Slavery was the only cause of the Civil War, and England with her traditions must perforce sympathize with the North. His speech was immediately published and distributed by the American Tract Society.

Almost two weeks elapsed after the cabinet had met before Lincoln heard the result. On the day the cabinet convened another bombshell had exploded. This time the hopes of the Confederates had been blasted and Gladstone had had nothing to do with it. At Hereford, Sir Cornwall Lewis, a cabinet member ranking next below the Secretary of the Exchequer, had delivered a speech denying all Gladstone's former implications. Thus two members of the cabinet talked two ways. The diplomats and the press had been at a loss to know what to expect. Minister Adams, completely fooled by the personalities of Russell and Palmerston, believed the suave Secretary to be America's friend and the bluff Prime Minister to be in favor of recognition. Years later his son learned that the reverse was true. Russell, cold and patient as he seemed, had decided that England could put up with the American war no longer. The Gladstone speech, given without authority, had been a sly move to publicize a wished-for government policy.

Palmerston was too old in politics and too wise to have his hand forced in this manner. He countered his colleagues by getting Lewis to speak at Hereford.[21] A few hours later, when the cabinet met, the government "doubted the policy of moving."[22] Another cabinet meeting was scheduled for November 11, 1862. Until then the fateful question was postponed. Gladstone alone remained vocally pro-South. On the following day, October 24, 1862, he circulated a rejoinder maintaining the moral duty of intervention. Henry Hotze, ignorant of the fact that suave Russell was working day and night to get support for Gladstone's policy, published a vitriolic attack on the Foreign Secretary and mailed a copy of the diatribe to Benjamin stating that he felt strong enough to attack the government.

On November 7, 1862, it had snowed in Washington—the first storm of the season.[23] The ground was white, but the snow did not last long. Dispatch bags delivered at the State Department from the railway depot were cold and soggy. A letter from William L. Dayton gave an optimistic report of affairs in France. Bigelow had publicized the Homestead Bill successfully—a hundred and sixty acres of land to anyone, regardless of "nationality," if he would live on it five years.[24] Slidell, said Dayton, was making no headway with Napoleon. A revolution in Greece, added to Napoleon's activities in Rome and Mexico, kept the Emperor busy and harmless. Dayton said, too, that "a gentleman" had come to the legation with spy information for sale and was surprised that no funds were available for the purpose.[25]

Lincoln furnished the money and before he heard from it he learned that affairs were not so rosy as Dayton had painted them. 'A' new Secretary of State for Foreign Affairs had been appointed to Thouvenel's post—a man less friendly to the North. Drouyn de L'Huys was a tall, athletic man, very English in appearance,[26] known as a gambler, an imperial henchman and opportunist like his chief. On the day before the British cabinet met, Slidell was invited to call on the Emperor at Saint-Cloud.[27] The interview lasted some time. Napoleon did not commit himself on intervention but he suggested that the Confederates give French shipbuilders a few contracts.[28] Immediately thereafter the Minister of Marine ignored France's proclamation of neutrality and granted franchises for the construction of foreign ships. Lincoln was in no position even to remonstrate. Soon a rumor leaked out of the State Department that a secret intrigue was on foot. The Union government had become so weakened from constant military reverses, some people believed, that foreign mediation was about to be accepted. Count Gurowski wrote in his diary, "Mr. Seward is desperate, downcast, and may believe he can serve his country by committing the cabinet to some such combination."[29]

Lincoln, too, was almost desperate. For two years he had been trying to find a general who could bring him victories—Scott, McDowell, McClellan, Pope, then McClellan again, only to have Little Mac, in his second opportunity, muff the battle of Antietam. Lincoln had conceded to the radical politicians who drummed into his ears that McClellan was no good. He had reduced McClellan, repented and put him back in command. Then the Little Dragoon had let Lee escape from Antietam. Lincoln's temper snapped. He told John Hay that McClellan had done nothing to make himself "either respected or feared."[30] The by-elections were coming. McClellan had many political supporters. After the votes were in, Lincoln must appoint a new general.

Lincoln marked time and continued to be conciliatory toward England and France. Seward, too, went out of his way to do England's bidding. The two men had learned to work in harmony. Welles continued to worry them. Complaining always that his department was invaded, he did everything he could with the Navy to invade the State Department with international complications. He refused to accept Seward's plea for immunity of captured mails. International law was on his side, he maintained. Fiddlesticks to conciliation!

The November elections came. The administration lost seats in Congress—a protest against the disastrous progress of the war and also, as Blair had feared, against the Emancipation Proclamation.[31] Lincoln appointed General Burnside to succeed McClellan and make another effort to save the Union. Burnside accepted reluctantly. He doubted if he were equal to the responsibility.

McClellan's friends were angry. They had just won at the polls and now Lincoln ignored them. People said openly that if the new general failed, even in the smallest degree, "McNapoleon" might set himself up as a dictator.[32] In the midst of this suspense Lord Lyons arrived in New York from London, where he had gone "on leave." The British minister drove to a hotel. A delegation of "Conservative leaders"—Copperheads whose party had gained strength in the last election—called to see him. Reports said that these men told Lord Lyons that foreign mediation would be welcomed.[33] Lyons forwarded an account of the meeting to England as a guide for his government's actions.

In the meantime Napoleon decided to act. His textile industry in fifteen Departments was prostrate. Three hundred thousand people were destitute. Eighty thousand people were out of work in Lyon alone. In Rouen, thirty thousand of the fifty thousand operatives were unemployed.[34] From all the manufacturing centers came appeals for help, appeals and also threats. "If the Emperor cannot get us cotton we must get some one else who can."[35]

Napoleon's new Foreign Secretary was eager to take the helm. He had seen Gladstone's circular pronouncing the "moral duty" of intervention. On October 30, 1862, he wrote, in Napoleon's name, to both England and Russia. Would they combine with France to mediate American affairs?[36]

Lincoln had just tallied the adverse election figures when the news came. The Emperor's request was upholstered with soft phrases. He proposed that the three powers suggest a six months' truce for the belligerents to "work out some scheme for peace." To keep from offending the North, Napoleon recommended that the powers agree not to interfere in any manner with the final settlement "unless upon the *joint request*" of the belligerents.[37]

Lincoln, deserted by his own people at the polls, knew that the American democratic experiment depended on the mercy of Britain and Russia. Mediation, as Napoleon proposed it, was a truce to separate the Union. Russia could be counted on, but how about England—the capitalists afraid of democracy, the shipping interests, contractors building warships for the Confederacy? The test had come for Lincoln's foreign policy—the Proclamation of Emancipation had evidently had no effect, nor had the studied campaign against Britain's special interests, the long struggle to isolate England and France, the recent coddling of English shippers that Welles had opposed.

Lincoln waited for Parliament's reply to Napoleon's request for joint mediation. A series of pamphlets—Northern propaganda—was being distributed in London and in the industrial cities. Most significant among them was *Correspondence on the Present Relations between Great Britain and the United States of America*—alleged letters between two attorneys, Charles G. Loring of America and Edwin W. Field of Great Britain. Appearing first in September 1862, this publication was expanded and republished in November. Lincoln knew its contents to be opportune for the cabinet decision. The average Englishman was sure to be impressed when he read the letter from his own countryman, Field, which said in part:

"I will tell you a story, just come over from some esteemed and most truthful lady friends at Cambridge, near your city. . . . There was a young and charming lady, at Boston, known to our friends, sent to Boston for education by her father, a New-Orleans merchant, devotedly attached to her. She received, just before your war, a letter, telling her to make all speed to New Orleans, if she would see her father alive, as he was fast sinking. She made all haste. When she got there, she found the letter had been written *after he was dead, and by the heirs!* Her mother had black blood in her veins; and the poor child was a slave, and the heirs had thus trepanned her home. They seized and sold her forthwith."[38]

Loring in his turn harped also on slavery as the fundamental issue of the war. He quoted the *Richmond Enquirer* at length, showing that this Southern paper admitted slavery and slave-holders' property rights to be the real issue at stake—not independence or free trade.

Lincoln knew that another pamphlet in this cabinet crisis was even more outspoken—*Cause and Probable Results of the Civil War,* by William Taylor, purported to have been written also to let England know that slavery was "the real cause of this war."[39] The author claimed to be a citizen of California. He said he was originally from Virginia and that his wife had emancipated her slaves. In the South, he stated, forty-five percent of the population were slaves, fifty-one percent nonholders of slaves, while four percent owned slaves and also most of the real estate.[40] In this highly autocratic society, he asserted, Cassius M. Clay had been the only man who dared speak out against the institution "and he could only do it by first presenting twelve substantial arguments in a pair of Colt's revolvers."[41] Taylor pronounced *Uncle Tom's Cabin* a true picture of slavery, so true and so devastating that a Negro preacher in the South had been sentenced for owning a copy.[42] With these two examples of the lack of freedom of speech and of the press in the South, the author told a few anecdotes about his own experiences with the institution. A friend of his in the Shenandoah Valley, he wrote, had seen a dark object hanging in a neighbor's barn. At first glance the man supposed it to be the carcass of a bear but on closer examination discovered a Negro woman triced up by her hands while her owner ate breakfast and held family prayers. Could the cabinet of a civilized country like Great Britain mediate to perpetuate such brutality?

The pamphlet also contained the damaging quotation from Vice-President Alexander Stephens proclaiming slavery the cornerstone of the Confederacy and prophesying the spread of the institution throughout the world.[43]

On November 11, 1862, the British cabinet met—the second critical consultation on American affairs within thirty days. On the same day a few friends of William Lloyd Garrison held a meeting in another part of London. Washington Wilks, journalist and lecturer, prominent temperance reformer, presented a strong set of antislavery resolutions which were passed. The leaders of the meeting decided to organize themselves into the London Emancipation Society and to circulate pro-Northern pamphlets throughout the British Isles. Subcommittees were formed in various boroughs and efforts were made to form auxiliary societies in the provinces. Henceforth the English people would receive a liberal education on the importance of the Emancipation Proclamation,[44] but it might be too late. Everything depended on the cabinet meeting in another part of town.

The cabinet adjourned without acting. On the next day it met again.[45] By a vote of fifteen to three Napoleon's request for joint mediation was declined. Only Earl Russell, Lord Westbury and William Ewart Gladstone dissented.[46] Charles Francis Adams wrote years later that the decision was made to punish Gladstone for trying to force the government's hand with his Newcastle speech. At the time, *Harper's Weekly* attributed the vote to Britain's fear of the newly invented ironclads. "Farragut might steam up the Thames with monitors as he did up the Mississippi."[47] Other observers said frankly that the decision was simple political expediency. In spite of the pressure exerted by big interests, the government believed that the majority of the English voters opposed intervention.

On the day after the decision, Earl Russell wrote the Emperor with perfect discipline and contrary to his own convictions that there was no ground to hope that the Federal government would accept the proposed suggestion. Gladstone, younger and more impetuous than Russell, clung to the belief that the issue was not dead. In his diary he wrote: "The matter [is] very open for the future" and "I hope they [the French] may not take it as a positive refusal. . . ."[48]

Lincoln's diplomacy had worked. England and France were separated. 'A' dispatch from Dayton stated that Napoleon would not be able to resist the economic pressure at home. "He will compel us to make peace or fight him."[49]

So Napoleon was thinking of intervening alone! Seward forwarded Dayton lists of the North's resources. Let Napoleon look over them and decide for himself whether or not he wanted to fight the North. Lincoln walked over to the War Department. He wanted the latest news from his new general, Ambrose Burnside. Out on the White House lawn, boys in the Signal Corps practiced a new code with flags. Officers told Lincoln that this signaling would be a great innovation in battle. It would save horseflesh.

Next day the Signal Corps boys appeared at the Soldiers' Home with flags and telescopes. They climbed up on the roof and waved toward the city. Lincoln watched them from his window. Mrs. Lincoln's mail was delivered and laid on a table in the hall. A copy of *Harper's Weekly*[50] displayed a cartoon of enraged British underwriters paying for the ships sunk by the *Alabama*. These financiers had been considered part of the pro-Southern bloc. Their protest was bound to weaken the British government's opposition— another lift to United States diplomacy.

Lincoln went out to see what the Signal Corps boys were doing. He climbed up on the roof. The boys' flags were attached to palm-leaf fans and they waved them with precision. Lincoln looked through a telescope at other boys on the Smithsonian Institution four miles away. They were waving also. A man beside Lincoln watched the signaling and called out letters. Another wrote them down in a notebook. Lincoln smiled as the letters resolved themselves into words and sentences.[51] This was better than the telegraph with its cumbersome wires.

Lincoln climbed down and rode to the White House. Correspondence there must be answered. A letter from Charles Francis Adams sounded almost arrogant. For the first time since he had gone to England, Adams said, he felt strong. Russell was afraid of him, now mediation had failed in the cabinet.[52] Lincoln had seen burlesque actors chase each other back and forth across the stage precisely as these diplomats were doing. If Burnside should win a victory the President and Seward might both drop their conciliatory masks and do the same. Lincoln left the White House, walked down the portico steps and over to the War Department. The leaves, fallen from the trees, rustled beneath his feet.

The cipher operators had no good news from Burnside in Maryland. Instead a message stated that the *Alabama* was reported off the New Jersey coast. The raider had sunk nineteen ships in less than three months—ten of them New England whalers intercepted in the Azores shortly after Bulloch commissioned her.[53] On the cruise across the Atlantic, vessels had been burned at night to attract other ships, which were sunk as soon as they arrived at the scene of the first disaster.[54] To fight the marauder Lincoln ordered out the gilt-edged, million-dollar, side-wheel luxury yacht his diplomacy had won from Commodore Vanderbilt.

The yacht came back, reporting that the *Alabama* could not be found. All shipping was struck with terror. No one could tell where the raider would strike now. The next mailbag from England brought an account of John Bright's latest speech at Rochdale. The old liberal had called all Englishmen's attention to Lincoln's policy of emancipation. "I wish the 1st of January to be here, and the freedom of the Slaves declared from Washington," he said. "This will make it impossible for England to interfere for the South, for we are not, I hope, degraded enough to undertake to restore three and one half millions of negroes to slavery."[55]

John Bright was afraid that Lincoln might not make good his opportunity. On December 6, 1862, he wrote Sumner, "Men are looking with great interest to the 1st of January, and hoping that the President may be firm." Two days later Bright spoke at Birmingham—one of the most impassioned orations of his career. He might have been a socialist speaking at the International when he closed:

"I blame men who are eager to admit into the family of nations a state which offers itself to us, based on a principle, I will undertake to say, more odious and blasphemous than was ever heretofore dreamed of in Christian or pagan, in civilized or in savage times. The leader of this revolt proposes this monstrous thing—

that over a territory forty times as large as England the blight and curse of slavery shall be forever perpetuated. I cannot believe, for my part, that such a fate will befall that fair land, stricken though it now is with the ravages of war. I cannot believe that civilization, in its journey with the sun, will sink into endless night in order to gratify the ambition of the leaders of this revolt, who seek to

'. . . wade through slaughter to a throne
And shut the gates of mercy on mankind.'

I have another and a far brighter vision before my gaze; it may be but a vision, but I will cherish it. I see one vast confederation stretching from the frozen north in unbroken line to the glowing south, and from the wild billows of the Atlantic westward to the calmer waters of the Pacific main,—and I see one people, and one language, and one law, and one faith, and over all that wide continent, the home of freedom, and a refuge for the oppressed of every race and of every clime."[56]

On December 1, 1862, Lincoln delivered his annual message to Congress. He still had a month before he need decide on emancipation. As a practical politician Lincoln noted what the preliminary proclamation had cost him in votes. As chief executive he watched his army march toward Richmond under Burnside's command. At Fredericksburg, Virginia, Confederate cavalry dashed around the advancing army's flanks. Gray infantry concentrated to defend the city. A great battle was in the offing and Lincoln's general admitted that he was outclassed.

Lincoln used guarded words in his message. He devoted much of his time to foreign relations. He submitted to Congress the correspondence between the State Department and the European powers. "The temporary reverses" and exaggerated reports of our "disloyal citizens," he said, had prevented Europe from withdrawing their recognition of the South's belligerent rights. He spoke of the French intrigue in Mexico and the Senate's refusal to approve the loan to Juárez. He assured Congress that the government had not acknowledged the Mexican revolution, but "left to every nation the exclusive conduct and management of its own affairs." Lincoln pointed out that the cotton famine in Europe seemed to be due to overproduction rather than to the embargo. He reviewed the foreign treaties made during his two years in office. Touching the pride of every Englishman, he cited the "complete success" of the new convention for the suppression of the slave trade. In addition, he said, proposals had been made to Great Britain, France, Spain and Prussia for the formation of "mutual conventions" to examine and pass upon "unintentional injuries" occasioned by the blockade and "complaints of the violation of neutral rights." This proposal, he said, had been "kindly received, but has not yet been formally adopted." The administration, Lincoln said, had also made commercial treaties with Hanover, Turkey, Liberia and Haiti. With Latin-American countries, he stated, "more friendly sentiments than have heretofore existed are believed to be entertained." The President then turned to the subject which all foreigners hoped would give some clue to his intention on emancipation. First he outlined his work for colonization of free Negroes. Next he discussed his offer to compensate all Southern states that would free their slaves voluntarily. He suggested that emancipation should be gradual and not completed until 1900. This, he believed, would permit both the whites and the blacks to adjust themselves, the former to hire their slaves, the latter to learn the responsibility of living on wages.[57]

European liberals read with delight the part of Lincoln's message that dealt with the Negro problem. In France, *Débats* gave three columns of praise to his plan, and Bigelow wrote William Hargreaves, the English editor:

"I feel more encouraged about the future since the receipt of the Message. I don't think 'Pam' can have a fight with us just now let him try never so hard. You may tell him however when you see him that if we do have a war, the terms of peace on your side will be settled by a prime Minister of Mr. Cobden's school of politics, and the Aristocracy of England will be put upon the road that the Aristocracy of America are now travelling. The Aristocracy will begin this war if there is to be one, but they will not finish it."[58]

A victory on the battlefield was all that Lincoln needed to make his message respected everywhere.

Down on Pennsylvania Avenue, Lincoln's enemies laughed hoarsely. Count Gurowski had published the diary that cost him his job at the State Department. Seward had him sued for libel.

The judge, an antiadministrationist, refused to let Gurowski's name on the title page be admitted as evidence that he wrote the volume. The Pole went free. Lincoln was in desperate need of some victory—almost any victory—to bolster his prestige.

At Fredericksburg, Burnside's men moved into battle line on December 11 and 12, 1862. "Copperheads" whispered in hotel rooms, made plans for the future as they had done before Pope's defeat, boasted what they would do in case Burnside also failed. Major General Cassius M. Clay was in town with some hard-eyed Kentuckians. The giant was still looking for a command and apt to make trouble if he did not get one. Burnside ordered forward his skirmishers. Lincoln sat in the White House waiting, discussing affairs with his old friend Senator Browning. The doorman brought in some cards. Lincoln looked at them and appeared annoyed.[59] Cassius Clay and his friends were at the door—on this of all days. Lincoln sent back word that he was busy and could not see them. Lincoln seldom turned away troublemakers, especially when they were men of influence. Clay would have to be sent back to Russia as soon as possible.

A telegram on December 15 told how Burnside had been defeated with terrible losses—ten thousand men killed in one futile effort to take a single position. The army had fallen back across the Rappahannock, broken and disheartened. Telegrams from New York, Philadelphia and the West showed the North to be wild with anguish. The cry for a dictator—a strong military man—thundered across the country. A caucus of senators determined to act.[60] Charles Sumner, chairman of the Foreign Relations Committee, recommended as a first step that the government get rid of Seward. The Secretary of State should have resigned with Cameron a year ago. Lincoln had no business keeping him and telling that undignified skunk story. Seward's meddlesome management of foreign affairs had caused the failure of the war.

Sumner proposed a congressional resolution for dismissal of the Secretary of State. The Senate was canvassed. A vote sufficient to remove Seward could not be got. Another expediency was tried. A less drastic resolution expressed a lack of confidence in the government and requested the President to remodel his cabinet without mentioning names. This resolution passed.

Everyone knew that Seward was the man at whom the framers of the resolution aimed. The Secretary of State, always impulsive, tendered his resignation and started to pack his things. Lincoln seemed very much annoyed. Adams and Bigelow had both pleaded with Seward when he tried to retire before Lincoln's inauguration. Now they were both in Europe and could not comfort him. On December 17, Senator King asked Lincoln for an audience. A senatorial committee, he said, wanted to request the President formally to accept Seward's resignation. Lincoln asked the committee to come for his answer at seven-thirty the next evening. On December 18, Senator Browning called. Lincoln asked if he had been at the caucus.

"Yes," said the senator.

"What do these men want?" asked the President.

"I hardly know, Mr. President, but they are exceedingly violent towards the administration, and what we did yesterday was the gentlest thing that could be done. We had to do that or worse."

"They wish to get rid of me," said the President, "and I am sometimes half disposed to gratify them." Lincoln had heard the roar for a dictator, a strong man who could hold together a strong government. "We are now," he said, "on the brink of destruction. It appears to me the Almighty is against us, and I can hardly see a ray of hope."[61]

Senator Browning left the President with his problem, but Lincoln had made up his mind what to do. First he sent a messenger to summon the cabinet to meet in the White House with the protest committee. Later, when the unsuspecting committee called, they were ushered into the room where the cabinet waited. Both groups were embarrassed. Lincoln opened the discussion. An evening of debate followed. Everybody had a chance to "blow" and there was no unanimity of opinion on the basic cause of the administration's failure. Then Lincoln asked for a vote from the senators on the removal of Seward. Four voted against the Secretary. Three refused to vote. One voted to keep him—not much of a showing from a protest committee.

Lincoln wished them all a good night.

The following day Lincoln called another cabinet meeting. Dutifully the men appeared in the little room with the baize-topped table. Chase and Stanton sat down side by side, facing the fireplace. Welles, on the sofa near the east window, watched them with sharp-shooter's eyes looking down his long nose that rested like a rifle on his beard. Every member of the cabinet knew that reorganiza-tion was in order, and when the tall figure of Lincoln appeared in the door Chase stated that he had brought his resignation.

Lincoln was eager. "Let me have it," he said, reaching his long arm and fingers toward the pompous figure, who hesitated, reluc-tant to part with the letter. Chase wished to say something further but Lincoln did not wait and hastily broke the seals. Reading the contents, he said with a triumphant laugh and a glance toward Welles, "This cuts the Gordian knot."

Chase turned his high bald head toward Welles. His face was perplexed. "I can dispose of this subject now without difficulty," Lincoln said, an air of satisfaction spreading over his features. The cabinet arose and departed, some of them still mystified.

As soon as the protest committee realized that Lincoln held res-ignations from both Seward and Chase and that the moment they insisted on Seward's removal their own Chase would follow, they wished the matter dropped. Lincoln said later, "If I had yielded to that storm and dismissed Seward, the thing would all have slumped over one way, and we should have been left a scanty hand-ful of supporters." The Chase resignation in his pocket gave him the whip hand. He said, "Now I can ride; I have a pumpkin in each end of my bag."[62] Lincoln had saved his coalition cabinet once more and it was better to be called a pumpkin than a skunk.

Seward unpacked his things and decided to remain. Much cor-respondence on foreign affairs had accumulated on his desk. Lin-coln had just ten days left to make good his threat of emancipation. Powerful politicians urged him to back down.[63] Powerful idealists urged him to go ahead. From foreign nations no serious compli-cations disturbed him. For once Lincoln had time to think through the problem without disturbance. From France, Dayton wrote that Drouyn de L'Huys and the Duc de Morny had completely reversed their policy. They desired to *"preserve the Union,"* and considered withdrawing the troops from Mexico.[64] It was even rumored that De L'Huys would resign in favor of Thouvenel. Surely nothing was to be gained abroad by emancipating the slaves.

As the day approached for Lincoln to make his decision, Burnside's broken army prepared winter quarters—cities of huts and cabins—in Maryland. Seward whiled away his time writing lengthy and conciliatory dispatches to Spain relative to a request for an extension of the neutral area around Cuba.[65] Up in New England little Harriet Beecher Stowe resolved to go to Washington and plead the Negro's case with Lincoln. English literati idolized her for writing *Uncle Tom's Cabin,* and honors had been lavished on her at aristocratic receptions abroad. She could not believe that the British had changed their attitude toward slavery. For her, Lord Shaftesbury had penned with his own hand an *Affectionate and Christian Address* to American women to end the sinful institution.[66] The address had been illuminated on vellum and sent to America with twenty-six folio volumes of signatures— more than half a million names of British women, including Viscountess Palmerston herself, all of whom now seemed cold to Bright's impassioned oratory and Lincoln's preliminary Emancipation Proclamation.[67] Harriet Beecher Stowe was unable to understand how her friends of a few years before could contribute money lavishly to abolish slavery, and now that war had come, turn their backs on the cause. She did not understand their fear of communism and the fanatical eagerness with which they embraced any speaker who attempted to convince them that the horrible democracy in America, which threatened their own security, was not sincere in abolishing slavery. Democracy did not threaten Mrs. Stowe's property and way of life as it did the life and property of these old friends in the British upper and middle classes. Harriet planned to publish a sarcastic reply in the *Atlantic Monthly* to the signers of the *Affectionate and Christian Address.* Before going into print she wanted to be sure that Lincoln intended to sign the Emancipation Proclamation. She took the train to Washington to learn from his own lips.

On the day set for her interview with the President, Mrs. Stowe furbished her two jewels—her little girl and her son, the latter in a Scotch costume, a feather in his jaunty plaid turban. Lincoln received the little family in one of the small reception rooms in the White House where a grate of cannel coal blazed warmly. Harriet, with fluttering heart, so the story goes, extended her hand toward the President. Lincoln took it and, bowing, said, "So this is the little woman who made this big war?" If Harriet Beecher Stowe thought that she could get more information out of Abraham Lincoln than Thurlow Weed or Senator Browning she was disappointed. The President, as usual, was cordial and interested in the children. As they talked he went to the fire and, extending his hands toward the glowing coals, rubbed them together saying, "I do love a fine fire in a room. I suppose it's because we always had one to home."[68] Harriet remembered the colloquial speech but when she was outside once more and drove away, she realized that she had got no satisfaction on the great question before the world— the Emancipation Proclamation.[69] She decided to take a chance and answer the *Christian Address* anyway.[70]

In England, as the day approached for Lincoln's decision, British opinion marked time. Would Lincoln be afraid to sign the momentous order? John Bright spoke to his constituents on December 18, 1862. He pleaded for the Northern cause but did not mention the proclamation.[71] Lincoln might fail! Two meetings of idealists decided that Lincoln would not let them down. They risked making themselves the laughingstock of all Europe by passing resolutions on December 31, 1862, congratulating Lincoln for signing the death warrant for the institution of slavery. One meeting was organized in London by the Emancipation Society. The principal speaker was Newman Hall. The other meeting, held in Manchester, was more informal—almost a spontaneous congregation of working people, with no prearranged chairman. The mayor was prevailed upon to act unofficially. A letter from John Stuart Mill was read. The press noted one M.P. Obviously few "respectable" people were present.

These two congregations led in a few days to the formation of the Union and Emancipation Society. The name "Union" was henceforth coupled with "Emancipation" in England as it was in America. Within a year the new organization became a real power in the land. Congregations of dissenting churches joined with enthusiasm. Quakers, always a liberal group in England, subscribed almost to a man. Ardor for abolition, which had been treading water for months, began to churn like a flood tide around Land's End. The workers, the liberals and the intellectuals were now combined into a group which no politician could ignore.[72]

On the day after the meetings at London and Manchester, Abraham Lincoln, three thousand miles away, made up his mind. As he himself said, "I am a slow walker but I never walk back."[73] Emancipation and colonization, Lincoln thought, should be attended to at the same time. The two things went hand in hand. He was in a receptive mood on December 31 when Bernard Kock called at the White House. Lincoln intended to sign the Emancipation Proclamation on the following day. Now Kock laid on his table a perfected plan for a freedmen's colony on Ile Vache.[74] For only $250,000 the promoter agreed to colonize five thousand Negroes. Congress had appropriated Lincoln over twice this amount for the purpose. The President signed on the dotted line. The state seal in Seward's office would be needed to make the contract official.

On the following day, New Year's, the cabinet assembled in the White House. The holiday was celebrated at a large reception, with Mrs. Lincoln and distinguished ladies sweet as rosebuds vased in voluminous hoop skirts. Among them stood Army and Navy officers. Old General Scott, a puffball in uniform, wheezed with the exertion of standing erect. Studious Chief of Staff Halleck, an owl in epaulets, blinked unhappily at the light of day. Lord Lyons, handsome and dignified in elaborate court dress, recited correct albeit dull speeches to the ladies.[75] Lincoln shook thousands of hands as the line filed past him. When it was over he went upstairs to the little room where the long document awaited his signature. His arm ached and he said, "If my hand trembles as I sign my name people will say that I was afraid."

His hand did not tremble—much—and Lincoln signed duplicate copies, one to be sold at the Great Sanitary Fair for the benefit of soldiers wounded in the war for democracy.

On the day Lincoln signed the Emancipation Proclamation a great battle was fought at Murfreesboro in eastern Tennessee. Both generals, Bragg and Rosecrans, claimed the victory. Some people maintained that this battle and not the liberation of the slaves changed the attitude of Europeans henceforth.

Days later Colonel McKay called at the White House. He knew

that the President enjoyed Negro dialect stories. Had Lincoln heard the one about the camp meeting?

The President had not. A good politician is a good listener even when he is the chief executive. McKay began:

A darky preacher attempted to explain the Emancipation Proclamation to his congregation as a military measure. Back in the hall a patriarch with white kinky head got up.

"Bredren," he shouted, "you don't know nothing what you talkin' about. Now you jest listen to me. Mas'r Linkum he everywhar. He know eberyting. He walk de earf like de Lord."

McKay looked at the President, but Abraham Lincoln did not smile. He got up from his chair and walked back and forth in the room. Then he said, "It is a momentous thing to be the instrument under Providence for the liberation of a race."[76]

# XIV. *Lincoln's Propaganda*

A FEW days after Lincoln signed the Emancipation Proclamation, Leonard Grover sat in his office on the second floor of the National Theatre building in Washington. Pigeonholes behind his desk were filled with bills, contracts, posters. On the wall actresses smiled at him through oval frames. A distant ripple of applause told Grover that the second act had finished. The house was full. President and Mrs. Lincoln sat in a proscenium box. Grover knew that Washington rowdies resented the Emancipation Proclamation. Would they make trouble for the President after the performance?

When the curtain rose for Act III a hush fell over the building. Grover listened for the sallies of laughter which punctuated the performance. Outside, the street was dark and quiet. Squares of yellow light from saloon windows lay across the brick sidewalk. Grover heard loud talking. Thick tongues cursed "the niggers" and "the ab'lish'nists."

Grover felt responsible for the President's safety. He knew Lincoln slightly and his little boy played often with Tad in the White House. When the last curtain bell rang, Grover went downstairs. The President and Mrs. Lincoln, with Congressman Schuyler Colfax, were walking out of their box. Grover showed them a side passageway to the street. Outside a crowd stood in a leering circle around the President's carriage. The driver staggered on the curb. His eyes were bleary, his face flushed. He was drunk. Lincoln helped his wife into the carriage. His long body followed her. Colfax scrambled after them and slammed the door. The coachman reached uncertainly for his seat and pulled himself up, then fell sprawling in the gutter. The bystanders laughed. Somebody threw a stone. A one-armed soldier boy on the driver's seat gathered up the lines. Grover leaped to the box, snatched the reins from the soldier and drove the carriage away.[1] At the gate to the White House grounds, he was relieved to see the Black Horse Cavalry on guard.

Lincoln got out at the portico and thanked Grover. Then he turned and walked into the White House. He had expected minor disturbances from the butternut riffraff of the city. That was part of the price he must pay for emancipation. Upstairs Lincoln stopped in his office before going to bed. Dispatches from Europe would tell the effect of his proclamation abroad any day now. Had foreign countries rallied to emancipation?

The next morning important Army officers called at the White House. Each had a different explanation for Burnside's failure. Bigwig politicians brushed past the officers to tell Lincoln what he must do. Then word arrived of the *Alabama*. The terror of the sea had been sighted off Galveston, where she sank the United States *Hatteras,* a side-wheel blockader originally built for the Delaware Bay passenger service.

News of the *Alabama* in the Caribbean excited the world, and with it came certain knowledge that the *Oreto,* now *Florida,* the other British-built ship, had run out of Mobile to join the *Alabama.* Emancipation or no emancipation, England could not be expected to sympathize actively with a country unable to win on either land or sea.

Over in the State Department a dispatch arrived from Dayton, dated January 15, 1863. Lincoln read that Napoleon was plotting a new scheme for mediation. Back in October 1862, the Emperor had urged the powers to join him and stop the American war. In November Lincoln had been warned that Napoleon intended to intervene alone—with war if necessary. Now in January the details of the latest intrigue arrived. Mercier, so Dayton said, had been instructed to induce Lincoln to appoint peace commissioners[2]—a smooth approach. If Lincoln initiated the movement 'America would escape the humiliation of being forced by a foreign power. Dayton said that De L'Huys had told him of the plan and wanted him to urge Lincoln to act. Dayton had replied that Lincoln did not hold the Emperor in high regard. The recent effort for joint intervention and the campaign in Mexico were both resented in America. De L'Huys shrugged. Napoleon, he said, wanted only peace—and cotton. He had no intention of staying permanently in Mexico. To do so would be "madness, madness, madness."[3]

Lincoln did not believe the French profession about Mexico.

The State Department had collected much evidence which showed that the Emperor planned to occupy Mexico permanently. Some mail had recently been intercepted which disclosed that forty-five thousand colonists were being prepared for the new empire. From another source word came to Washington that Napoleon considered laying a cable to Vera Cruz and building a railroad to Mexico City.[4] This did not sound like temporary occupation. Then, to cap the climax, an intercepted letter announced that as soon as the conquest was complete France would turn on "vain-boasting" America and "restrain" her.[5] Mercier would get an emphatic negative whenever he offered his proposal. That was certain. Burnside's defeat had not intimidated Seward. The Secretary of State always felt good after making a rash resolution. He chortled happily at his work.

Then Bernard Kock, the colonization promoter, walked into the State Department with his contract signed by the President. Kock unfolded the paper. He wanted the Great Seal attached so he could draw his money and recruit his labor for Ile Vache. Seward looked over the document. He had disagreed with Lincoln on the whole colonization policy.[6] He considered the contract a mistake. Seward called a clerk. In a jiffy the paper was carried away. Then Seward turned on Kock like an angry cockatoo. Suppose the experiment failed as such experiments usually do? People would laugh at the administration. They would accuse Lincoln of promoting contract labor—as repugnant as slavery itself. Besides, a rumor had become current that Captain Semmes planned to capture all the colonists as they were transported across the Caribbean. The Confederate boasted that he would return them to slavery in the South.[7]

"But it's an order from the President," Kock remonstrated stubbornly.

Seward's cockatoo crest rose belligerently. Kock stormed out of the old brick building, down the steps, and across the winter lawn to the White House. At the President's door he was stopped. Lincoln was in conference.[8]

Busybodies around the White House suspected that Lincoln did not want to see Bernard Kock. Others noticed that the President was pressed day and night by important callers. Congress demanded to know why he had not recognized the revolutionary government of Grenada.[9] Influential men in frock coats thrust their cards in the doorman's hand. They claimed to know inside reasons for the military defeats, secret details of France's proposed intervention. Lincoln's secretary brought quires of commissions to be signed, and whispered in the President's ear that officers wanted to see him about Burnside's incompetence. A long letter from England was placed before him. Lincoln picked it up and tipped back his chair. The workingmen of Manchester congratulated him for emancipating the slaves. The letter was dated before the proclamation had been signed. So these people had been sure that he would not let them down. Their faith mitigated some of the bitter news that came weekly from the high seas where the *Alabama,* British-built and manned, ravaged American commerce. A great people— the English. Lincoln decided to send a fitting reply—a letter to reassure his foreign friends and mortify his foreign detractors. The letter would need thought and care in writing. The President had only a superficial knowledge of England's background. From the Library of Congress he drew Hume's monumental history.[10] Lincoln worked on his reply to the workingmen along with a dozen other problems.

The doorman knocked. General Burnside wanted to see the President. The handsome soldier strode into the office. He had heard that his subordinates were carrying tales to the White House. He would like to retrieve his lost battle with a brilliant winter campaign.[11] The weather was clear for midwinter. The roads were hard and dry—ideal for action.

Lincoln listened as Burnside explained his plan. Then he told him to go ahead. The general strode down the White House steps. Back at headquarters he issued his orders. Army cooks prepared extra rations; wagons were packed. On the evening of January 19, 1863, the soldiers were ready to move at daybreak and Lincoln had finished his letter to the Manchester workingmen.

> "Executive Mansion,
> "Washington,
> "January 19, 1863.

*"To the Working-men of Manchester:* I have the honor to acknowledge the receipt of the address and resolutions which you sent me on

the eve of the new year. When I came, on the 4th of March, 1861, through a free and constitutional election to preside in the Government of the United States, the country was found at the verge of civil war. Whatever might have been the cause, or whosesoever the fault, one duty, paramount to all others, was before me, namely, to maintain and preserve at once the Constitution and the integrity of the Federal Republic. A conscientious purpose to perform this duty is the key to all the measures of administration which have been and to all which will hereafter be pursued. Under our frame of government and my official oath, I could not depart from this purpose if I would. It is not always in the power of governments to enlarge or restrict the scope of moral results which follow the policies that they may deem it necessary for the public safety from time to time to adopt.

"I have understood well that the duty of self-preservation rests solely with the American people; but I have at the same time been aware that favor or disfavor of foreign nations might have a material influence in enlarging or prolonging the struggle with disloyal men in which the country is engaged. A fair examination of history has served to authorize a belief that the past actions and influences of the United States were generally regarded as having been beneficial toward mankind. I have, therefore, reckoned upon the forbearance of nations. Circumstances—to some of which you kindly allude—induce me especially to expect that if justice and good faith should be practiced by the United States, they would encounter no hostile influence on the part of Great Britain. It is now a pleasant duty to acknowledge the demonstration you have given of your desire that a spirit of amity and peace toward this country may prevail in the councils of your Queen, who is respected and esteemed in your own country only more than she is by the kindred nation which has its home on this side of the Atlantic.

"I know and deeply deplore the sufferings which the working-men at Manchester, and in all Europe, are called to endure in this crisis. It has been often and studiously represented that the attempt to overthrow this government, which was built upon the foundation of human rights, and to substitute for it one which should rest exclusively on the basis of human slavery, was likely to obtain the favor of Europe. Through the action of our disloyal citizens, the working-men of Europe have been subjected to severe trials, for the purpose of forcing their sanction to that attempt. Under the circumstances, I cannot but regard your decisive utterances upon the question as an instance of sublime Christian heroism which has not been surpassed in any age or in any country. It is indeed an energetic and reinspiring assurance of the inherent power of truth, and of the ultimate and universal triumph of justice, humanity and freedom. I do not doubt that the sentiments you have expressed will be sustained by your great nation; and, on the other hand, I have no hesitation in assuring you that they will excite admiration, esteem and the most reciprocal feelings of friendship among the American people. I hail this interchange of sentiment, therefore, as an augury that whatever else may happen, whatever misfortune may befall your country or my own, the peace and friendship which now exist between the two nations will be, as it shall be my desire to make them, perpetual.

"Abraham Lincoln."[12]

Lincoln posted the letter. Before sunrise the columns of the Northern Army started. The rear guard burned the deserted winter quarters. Smoke hung like a fog over the dreary Maryland hills as the soldiers marched away. In the evening black clouds blew in from the east. At ten o'clock a blizzard, snow and sleet, swept across the country. Lincoln heard the frozen crystals beat on the windows in his office study. A fine night for soldiers to bivouac in the open!

Next morning the roads were impassable. The Army was bogged down. The comfortable quarters they had left the day before were charcoal and ashes in a waste of mud. The men cursed Burnside. They were through with a general who led them into misfortune. Lincoln knew that Europe would mark down another failure against him.

The first newspapers from abroad carried accounts of the growing importance of the Emancipation Proclamation. The bad news had not yet reached England. Everywhere, so the papers said, public meetings were being held. A good half of the journals had come out for the Northern cause. Richard Cobden noticed "the great rush of the people to all public meetings," and pronounced it an excellent example of Englishmen's sympathy for "personal freedom." John Bright said that every meeting in the kingdom would vote overwhelmingly in favor of Abraham Lincoln. Philosophical professional men addressed eager audiences. So did liberal university professors, leaders of the Manchester school, and lawyers who had no economic stake in the South. Professor Goldwin Smith, unhappy liberal from conservative Oxford,[13] wrote *Does the*

*Bible Sanction American Slavery?* The professor was carried away with the possible opportunities of democracy. He lectured on the war and planned visiting America to converse with the democratic demigod, Abraham Lincoln himself.

Another pamphlet, *English Criticism on President Lincoln's Anti-Slavery Proclamation,* written by Washington Wilks before word was received that Lincoln had signed the order, received wide circulation. Lincoln saw plainly that the masses were with him— ahead of him—on emancipation. Seward had guessed European sentiment wrongly. Wilks, in his pamphlet, tried to allay the fears of capitalists who deplored the confiscation of property—even slave property—by using the figures Lincoln had worked out in his December message, the figures which showed that the Negroes would all be paid for in the end. With this objection to emancipation answered, another bloc of Englishmen should be drawn to the Union.

Lincoln learned that many of the antislavery meetings were spontaneous. Adams wrote that he had taken pains to have no part in them. "The smallest suspicion of my agency would do more harm than good."[14] Consul Morse wrote that the meetings had cost him "much labor & some money . . . but I think both have been well spent & are producing results far better than [I] had any reason to hope."[15] Many of the meetings were arranged by the emancipation societies. Furthermore these organizations had begun to contain the names of prominent people on their rosters. Cardinal Newman's brother, Francis William Newman, author of *The Good Cause of President Lincoln,* was a member of the London Emancipation Society. In Newman's pamphlet English readers learned why the South suppressed freedom of speech and the press. The poor whites must not know that they were being degraded by slavery. Other prominent people joined the Emancipation Society rolls. John Stuart Mill[16] added his illustrious name but lamented that "the very best people" were disappointed by the vulgar tone of American politics—"and all the more so because it is the likeness of what we may be coming to ourselves."[17] An auxiliary Ladies' London Emancipation Society was also organized.[18]

Co-operating with the Emancipation Society, the Committee of Correspondence on American Affairs distributed pamphlets[19]—

thousands of them. Lincoln's reply to the Manchester workingmen was published in newspapers and leaflets to be cherished for years by working people as a recognition of their worthiness to suffer for liberty. School children were taught to memorize the best passages. Forty years later one of them could say, "I remember the Government inspector of schools asking 1,200 students, 'Whom do you regard as the greatest man outside of England?' 'A' chorus answered, 'Abraham Lincoln.' "[20]

Another favorite was the pamphlet by Washington Wilks. Two thousand were printed. Twenty-five hundred copies of Harriet Beecher Stowe's *Address to the Ladies of England* reminded thoughtful people of their moral inconsistency. Between November 1862 and the end of 1863, forty-three separate titles were issued by the emancipation societies. This downpour of propaganda drove to cover the Southern sympathizers. Then Lincoln turned on the faucet. His spies captured some mail disclosing that James Spence, the Englishman who claimed to have been converted to the Southern cause by high moral principles, was really a hired agent of the Confederacy.[21] This choice disclosure was released to the press as the wave of enthusiasm for Lincoln's Proclamation of Emancipation swept across England.

The jeers at Spence's hypocrisy were soon turned on Jefferson Davis. The Confederate President had shocked Europeans by answering Lincoln's preliminary proclamation with a threat to execute all white officers captured leading black troops. Now Englishmen gasped when they read that Jeff Davis answered Lincoln's final proclamation by naming Washington's Birthday, February 22, 1863, as the day on which all free Negroes should be enslaved, "they and their issue forever." The Negroes to be thus returned to bondage were enumerated as all those captured in Northern states and all those to be captured "so that the respective normal conditions of the white and black races may be ultimately placed on a permanent basis." Furthermore Davis' proclamation stated: "The day is not distant when the old Union will be restored with slavery nationally declared to be the proper condition of all of African descent."[22]

Lincoln realized that the situation looked brighter in spite of Burnside's second failure, but he was not one to mistake noise for political power. He could count on the parlor radicals in England, admirers of Garibaldi. Lincoln knew that he could depend, too, on all those people who enjoyed crusades for temperance, woman's rights, antivivisection and New Thought. Dissenters, Quakers and Unitarians were all with him—as were most of the upper lower classes—but what could he expect from the people who controlled the government?[23] The great majority of the English middle class, busy with tea and cricket and its own petty personal problems, was an uncertain quantity. The Tory gentry, High-churchmen, merchants and shippers, imperialists who believed England would profit by a weak and divided America, were few in number but influential in politics. Lincoln had seen vested interests in America rationalize the *status quo* as morally righteous. Without doubt their English counterparts would denounce the Emancipation Proclamation as the insincere utterance of an unspeakable rail-splitting President.[24]

Lincoln knew that English dominies, trotting in pony carts between neat hedgerows, stopped for tea in vine-covered manors to reassure the gentry that slavery was beneficent as practiced in the American South. Devoutly disciplined, they preached and prayed for the fixed order. Already word had come to America that the great universities, too, were not sympathetic toward democracy. Young bloods in Oxford hooted the name of Abraham Lincoln and applauded politely for Jeff Davis. Debaters at Cambridge decided in favor of the Confederacy. Samuel Wilberforce, Bishop of Oxford, whose father preached against the slave trade back in George Mason's day, openly urged recognition of the South.[25] Archbishop Richard Whately took it upon himself to answer Harriet Beecher Stowe's *Address* with the hackneyed observation that the American war was not waged to free the Negro who was treated badly in the North too. Then, using another well-worn argument, he stated that the South had as much right to secede as the American colonies in 1775.[26]

Lincoln had little hope of changing such men. England's Poet Laureate was less dogmatic. Alfred, Lord Tennyson, as mouthpiece of mid-Victorian society, expressed himself as being in sympathy with Southern culture and traditions, yet the "Battle Hymn of the Republic" haunted him. He was provoked to find himself humming the republican cadences. Why had the beautiful civilization of the South failed to produce one song that so shook men's souls?

Untroubled with Tennyson's poetic sensitivity, Lord Acton, liberal M.P., planned as a lifework to write a *History of Liberty*. He rationalized the Southern rebellion as part of the world trend in the struggle for political liberty.[27] Lincoln had heard that explanation before. He knew that realists might interpret it as liberty to enslave the Negro.

Bulwer-Lytton was another of the radicals of the past generation who had become conservative. A man with a mind softened with sentiment, Bulwer-Lytton called on the muse of melodrama to express his sympathy for the South. Fond of writing about things that were gone—*The Last Days of Pompeii, The Last of the Barons, The Last of the Saxon Kings*—he now stated that the last of the republics would be better off with a monarch and a few hereditary gentlemen. Looking on the Civil War as beneficial, he prophesied that America would split into at least four distinct countries, and thus cease to be a menace. Had the United States "remained under one form of Government," he wrote, "in which the executive has little or no control over a populace exceedingly adventurous and excitable, why, then America would have hung over Europe like a gathering and destructive thunder cloud."[28]

Charles Dickens, who knew America better than some Americans, thought with the experts that the South must win. Matthew Arnold, professor of poetry at Oxford, felt tears come to his eyes when he considered the brutality of Northern republicans and the bestiality of Abraham Lincoln. Carlyle was torn between love of revolution as typified in the Southern cause, and the rights of man as typified in the North. He said that he respected the Federalists' desire to maintain their union.[29] Herbert Spencer, author of the philosophy that the world was progressing toward a point of ultimate perfection, believed with Bulwer-Lytton that a separation of the United States was desirable. No doubt "ultimate perfection" was to be attained with England as the ruling power of the globe. Charles Darwin had just startled the world with his *Origin of Species*. Now he ignored his own philosophy of the survival of the fittest. A victorious North he feared would bully Great Britain into a war.[30] Huxley, who had recently completed *Man's Place in Nature*, a daringly revolutionary thesis denying the existence of any insurmountable structural barrier between monkey and man, including the Negro, very unscientifically begged the American question and indulged in self-analysis, saying that his heart was with the South, his head with the North.

As might be expected, Lincoln found his unqualified champions among radicals of the intellectual world as well as among radicals in other walks of life. The pre-Raphaelites, those artistic rebels from the commonplace concepts and academic rules, gloried in the Northern crusade. The Brownings and Swinburne, all emancipators of the literary formalism of English letters, spoke without reserve in favor of democracy. So, too, did the Rossettis, Dante Gabriel and his sister, both eccentric geniuses equal to the most unstable Northern idealist. The former had buried his unpublished poems with his wife and then disinterred them for publication. John Ruskin, full of sweetness and light, mildly deplored a war for a thoroughly unjustifiable cause.[31]

Lincoln knew that the battle was not yet won abroad, but English soil had become an admirable seedbed for any propaganda he cared to sow. Were conditions so good in France? How had Frenchmen reacted to the Emancipation Proclamation? In that imperial country the people were not so free to express their opinions as in England. Yet John Stuart Mill wrote from Avignon:

"Sympathy for the North . . . animated all *liberal-minded* Frenchmen from the start. It was in this moment of trial that in France all the friends of liberty recognized each other. They did not know more about the subject of slavery or secession than the English, but their instincts were truer and the prejudice against slavery was stronger in France than in England."[32]

The French Protestants were quicker than the British Dissenters to see the principle behind the American struggle, and immediately after the Emancipation Proclamation the Paris branch of the Evangelical Alliance announced its support of the North.[33] Abolition, too, was bound to be popular with the Socialists, a powerful minority under the leadership of popeyed, pint-sized Louis Blanc. The North was also openly favored by Guizot. Hugo, in exile, trumpeted for democracy and freedom on all occasions.[34] Even one of the Emperor's own family, Prince Napoleon, still *républicain* after his visit to America, supported Lincoln in his newspapers. Articles on the innate power of the Union were also published by the Orleans princes, now returned from America. Lincoln had good reason to be pleased with such payment for the cordiality he had shown these noblemen. In addition, Count Agénor de Gasparin, Henri Martin, Augustin Cochin and Lincoln's skillful consul general, John Bigelow, all wrote fluently on the "true cause" of the American war and the North's economic stamina. With this publicity one victory on the battlefield would teach the French all they needed to know, but the American soldiers had lost confidence in Burnside. Lincoln decided that a new man must supplant him. Two years of experience with Scott, McDowell, McClellan, Pope, McClellan again, then Burnside, had brought disappointments.

Lincoln studied the records of half a dozen men. One of them appealed to him—Joe Hooker, a tall, military figure with grand fighting head and grizzled russet hair. Perhaps this handsome, blue-eyed general would redeem the North before the world. "Fighting Joe" Hooker had unbounded confidence in himself. He once said that the Northern Army "was the finest on the planet." He would like to see it fighting with foreigners. Halleck and Stanton both opposed his appointment but Lincoln decided to give him a chance. Hooker's greatest handicaps were his drinking, his independence and his lack of loyalty to his superiors. The disaster at Fredericksburg, some complained, was partly due to Hooker's unwillingness to co-operate with Burnside. He was reported to have said that the Army as well as the United States needed a dictator. Sometimes troublesome subordinates make successful chiefs. On January 26, Lincoln formally appointed him head of the Army of the Potomac—a classic official document: "What I now ask of you is military success, and I will risk the dictatorship. . . . Now beware of rashness. Beware of rashness, but with energy and sleepless vigilance go forward and give us victories."[35]

Hooker did not know whether to be proud or ashamed, but he took command and prepared to belie his reputation. When old Count Gurowski heard about the new commander he immediately wrote Secretary Stanton telling him how to fight the war. He enclosed several pages translated from the German works of Boehn in order that the Secretary might learn "the qualities, the science, the knowledge and the duties of a good chief of staff."[36]

On February 3, 1863, Minister Mercier called on Seward with the proposition from Napoleon that Lincoln had already decided to reject. At the same time a draft of a treaty with Peru for the appointment of commissioners to settle claims of citizens of the United States was received from Christopher Robinson. Lincoln studied the treaty, submitted it to the Senate and discussed Mercier's proposition in the cabinet. On February 6, 1863, Seward wrote a long letter to Dayton for Drouyn de L'Huys. He reiterated his stand about treating with rebels. The Confederacy, he said, controlled in only three states—Georgia, Alabama and Texas. They had partial control of six other states, but the North's territorial gains were satisfactory. Indeed the rebellion might be stamped out without a signal military victory.[37]

Congress followed Seward's letter with a joint resolution deploring the hardships on European laborers caused by the American war and decrying the French Emperor for an act which might prolong the suffering. The resolution concluded:

"A new Government, such as they seek to found, with Slavery as its acknowledged corner-stone, and with no other declared object of separate existence, is so far shocking to civilization and the moral sense of mankind that it must not expect welcome or recognition in the Commonwealth of Nations."[38]

This resolution and Seward's letter were both printed in pamphlets and sent to all foreign ministers for distribution abroad. With them went the news that a British ship, the *Springbok,* sailing from one British port to another, had been sent in as a prize.[39] Unlike the *Bermuda,* the *Springbok* carried only a small cargo of contraband and did not appear to be ultimately bound for a blockaded port. Obviously the American Navy felt strong enough to interpret the "continuous voyage" doctrine liberally.

The Emancipation Proclamation's significance grew steadily month by month in England and Scotland as well. In February the meeting furor increased. The Manchester Emancipation Society organized subsidiary chapters. After six months' work it reported over 150 meetings and the circulation of 2,750,000 pages of information on the American war.[40] Conservatives did not like this enthusiasm. Although many of the meetings were directed solely against slavery, the implications to the social order in Europe were obvious. Trade-union leaders hailed Lincoln as "a benefactor of mankind." His name was linked with Karl Marx's as the hope of the world.[41]

Lincoln as yet had sponsored little propaganda. His speeches had been directed to the masses of mankind everywhere. Henry Adams, Weed, Bigelow, Hughes and McIlvaine had been writing for the middle classes. In December 1862, New York and Philadelphia businessmen had organized to send supplies to suffering laborers abroad.[42] In March two ships, the *George Griswold* and the *Achilles,* arrived with flour, bacon, pork and rice for delivery at Liverpool.[43] Sufferers in the Midlands blessed America. In far-off Wisconsin a colony of Lancashire people sent a carload of flour to the homeland with the simple label, "Thomas Hughes, Liverpool." Hughes, later known as a judge of the Supreme Court of Queen's Bench, London, and author of *Tom Brown's School Days,* was at this time a lawyer, stumping England for relief of the workers. Tom Hughes, according to his friends, was Tom Brown grown up. Robust but gentle in spirit, something of a dreamer, he had tried to found a socialistic colony in Tennessee.[44] The car of flour sent him from Wisconsin he rerouted for Manchester and when it arrived the door was broken open before the train stopped. Women carried the flour away in their aprons.[45]

Lincoln watched these personal contributions. He decided that they paid big dividends. Propaganda must be pushed forward more persistently than it had been by Weed, Hughes and company. Under Lincoln's direction Seward set to work with his customary vigor. Every important American he could find was sent to England to talk and lecture.[46] A number of escaped slaves, notably the former coachman of Jefferson Davis, were introduced at Union and Emancipation Society meetings. The Reverend Sella Martin, a Negro who eventually received a parish in London, worked indefatigably with the Dissenting churches. Elihu Burritt, New England's "learned blacksmith," champion of the common people, eloquent advocate of penny postage and cheap newspapers, was sent to Birmingham as consular agent. Internationally famous as a crusader for world peace, Burritt was already popular with audiences of working people for his ability to sweat convincingly as he pounded out conclusions on the rostrum. Then Lincoln put the finishing touch on his evangelical propaganda. America's most popular preacher, Henry Ward Beecher, was notified to arrange his schedule, be ready to go to England and preach if needed.

With the forum and the church represented, Lincoln turned his attention to the law. To help Adams prepare his evidence against the Confederate ships building in England, Lincoln sent William Whiting, solicitor of the War Department. Whiting had written a booklet, the *War Powers of the President,* which Lincoln used for his brief in drawing up the Emancipation Proclamation. He was a man of paradoxical character, dressing like a horse jockey, sentimental as a woman, mentally clear and cold as a cake of ice. Some people who knew Whiting complained of his unctuous, self-conscious virtue.[47] What of it? Lincoln knew Whiting would not meet the public in England.

The next selection Lincoln made for his European staff was a great financier, a man who might offer to purchase the Confederate ships if they could not be stopped legally. William H. Aspinwall was a merchant prince used to dealing in railroads or ship lines. J. D. Bulloch, with his experience running a coastal steamship, was a minnow beside such a leviathan. Aspinwall had inherited a whaling fortune which he had increased by establishing ship lines to England, the Mediterranean, the Pacific, and the East and West Indies. When gold was discovered in California he built the Panama Railroad, and, with connecting lines on both sides of the isthmus, he controlled a monopoly on all but overland travel to the Pacific coast. A financier of this caliber looked on the whole world as the theater for his ambition. He had no sympathy with sectionalism or the smug aristocracy of the South, which he believed looked backward instead of ahead to new developments. Besides, Aspinwall was a staunch supporter of Lincoln's administration. Never seeking office for himself, he had been one of the organizers of the Union League.

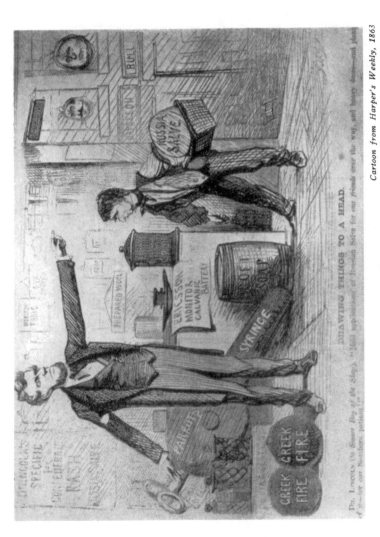

*Cartoon from Harper's Weekly, 1863*

CONTEMPORARY CARTOON OF "DR. LINCOLN" PRESCRIBING RUSSIAN SALVE
FOR NAPOLEON AND JOHN BULL

Secretary Seward (*extreme right*) and the diplomats at Trenton Falls on their grand tour in the summer of 1863. *Top row, second from the left,* Count Piper, next Bertinatti, then Schleiden and Mercier. *Lower row, second from left,* Lord Lyons, next, De Stoeckl, his usual companion.

*From Harper's Weekly, Sept. 19, 1863*

Lincoln did not let his new foreign policy stop with preachers and food bounties, with Adams' diplomacy, Whiting's counsel and Aspinwall's wealth. He decided also to send America's authority on national finance, "a most interesting old man, although small and shrivelled up."[48] Robert J. Walker had been Secretary of the Treasury under President Polk. Since that time he had studied the finances and resources of both the North and the South. His immediate job was to ruin Confederate credit abroad. Walker had been known as a die-hard Southern Democrat and his appointment seemed an anomaly. Born in western Pennsylvania of "State rights" and Whisky Rebellion stock that had looked on a strong central government as the agent of an unscrupulous majority intent on taxing the liquor of a helpless minority in the mountains, Walker had migrated to Mississippi in the boom days when cotton and Negroes were making fortunes for settlers in the Southern uplands. There he amassed wealth, lost it, and was elected to the United States Senate on the first Democratic platform to accuse New England of criminal designs against the institution of slavery. The issue thus aroused soon became popular in the South, and with it the power of Robert J. Walker increased in the party. As Polk's Secretary of the Treasury he was active in the aggressive administration which doubled the potential slave territory in the United States by conquering Mexico.

Years later, still a power in the party, Walker had been appointed Governor of Kansas by President Buchanan when that territory was engaged in a civil war of its own over the slavery issue. Walker was not successful in composing this bloody dispute. Removed from an impossible situation, he cursed the overbearing Free State men who had insisted on ruling the territory. The election of Abraham Lincoln, which followed shortly, was another blow to Walker's principles, but the little shriveled old man had changed mightily since his youthful planter days. He had seen the West, realized its possibilities, and made investments there. Like Aspinwall, his vision was no longer sectional. The surge of patriotism engendered by the firing on Fort Sumter caught him in its swell. As thousands of men and boys from farm and factory in New York and New England marched down Broadway to avenge the firing on the American flag, singing, waving banners inscribed "Remember Lexington and Concord,"[49] Robert J. Walker found himself cheering with the best of them.

A recognized authority on finance, having been rich and poor twice in his life—he had borrowed money to get to Washington when first elected senator—Walker could speak convincingly to Europeans upon the unsoundness of Confederate loans, the hopelessness of the Confederate cause and the invincibility of the Northern states. Lincoln could not send a better man to England.

After the publicity men were gone Lincoln looked out his office window at the gray Potomac. On the White House lawn the bare trees lashed to and fro in the spring wind—the third spring he had watched from that window. The Emancipation Proclamation was being displayed to advantage. The combined voices of liberal Europe had proclaimed the Civil War a fight for freedom against despotism. Every newspaper in Switzerland praised the proclamation.[50] The laborers of Barcelona passed resolutions of appreciation and sent them to Lincoln in a handsome mahogany box. The American President's act was hailed as a turning point in social history. The crisis in Europe had passed, provided the North could gain a victory and prove that it was on the way to ultimate triumph.

Could it be that the war had been won in Europe before it was in America? A great victory seemed close in the United States too. Hooker had instilled new life into the Army. Soon the roads would be dry enough for action. Democracy's day was close at hand! Good news came from everywhere. European dispatches said that the economic depression had passed.[51] The cotton famine was over. No cause remained for Europe to fight America.

Cynical statesmen sneered. The cessation of belligerency against America, they said, was temporary, a result only of the trouble brewing in Europe—the revolt in Poland. The idea of Europe's being moved by any ulterior humanitarian motive was preposterous. The influence of the Emancipation Proclamation was much overrated. Lincoln had heard politicians disagree on the basic reasons behind political changes all his life. He knew too that the European war, if it came, might reunite England and France once more. On the other hand it might make them enemies. Lincoln was confronted with a problem of many angles and no permanent solution.

Political issues seldom have! Napoleon appeared to be strong enough to continue his conquest of Mexico—still with no ulterior motives, he maintained. France was making the sacrifice for the benefit of "humanity and civilization"[52]—the old profession of dictators. French Protestant ministers at the same time had renewed their October plea to the English Evangelical churches for a joint crusade for the freedom of the American Negro.[53] In spite of the cynical commentators, the benefits derived from Lincoln's propaganda seemed unmistakable. Large popular meetings in England had assumed some of the emotionalism of the Methodist movement a century before. Lincoln, the politician, decided that he had gained all the converts he could with kindness. He would dominate the residue with fear. The old Privateering Bill had been lying on the table in Congress for six months. Lincoln called it out. In case Adams' diplomacy failed to stop the shipbuilding in British yards, or if Whiting's legal talent proved unconvincing, or Aspinwall's wealth could not purchase the ships, then Lincoln would be in a position to commission privateers and prey on England's commerce around the world. This, of course, meant war. The Privateering Bill was introduced as an administration measure. Before it was voted on, Seward wrote Adams what to tell England. The letter was obviously a threat, yet it contained no belligerent statement to which any foreign power might point. Statesmen, when they read it, pronounced Seward a genius at conveying an idea without incriminating himself in words—equal to Lincoln— almost. In part Seward's instructions said:

"I have had little hesitation in saying to Lord Lyons that if no extreme circumstances occur, there will be entire frankness on the part of the Government in communicating to him upon the subject, so far as to avoid any surprise on the part of friendly nations, whose commerce or navigation it might be feared would be incidentally and indirectly affected, if it shall be found expedient to put the Act in force against the insurgents of the United States."[54]

The bill passed the Senate and then the House with little argument.[55] Six days later, March 8, 1863, Seward sent a memorandum to Lyons, a memorandum fulsome in sweetness, which Lincoln had approved.

"If you think well of it, I should like that you should confidentially inform Earl Russell that the departure of more armed vessels under insurgent-rebel command from English ports is a thing to be deprecated above all things."[56]

Lord Lyons and Earl Russell both understood this kind of diplomatic language. Then word came to Washington that Napoleon had offered to build ships for Slidell. American privateers did not hold the threat to him that they did to England. The next bit of news set all the foreign offices agog. The Russian fleet had cleared for the open sea! The Polish and Danish problems still bubbled and in case of war Russia and the United States would undoubtedly be allies.

So quickly had the sunny diplomacy of February been clouded by the storms of March. Henry Adams, in despair between the possible failure of his father's mission and the probability of a war with England, wrote his brother, "We are in a worse mess here than we have known since the *Trent* affair."[57]

Senator Sumner became frightened. He scratched off a note to Lincoln. Privateers must not be used. If they were, the North would lose her best friends abroad.[58]

Parliament did not wait to see what Lincoln intended to do. Within a week an amendment was prepared for Britain's Foreign Enlistment Act—a provision authorizing the government to stop construction on suspicious vessels. On the night before the debate the Emancipation Society hired St. James Hall for a gigantic demonstration. The meeting became a milestone in English history. For years Professor E. S. Beesley at University College, London, had lectured on the importance of an alliance between skilled labor and the manufacturers, to oppose the landed interests. At this meeting W. R. Cremer and other trade-unionists presided.[59] John Bright represented the entrepreneurs. Henry Adams attended. The socialistic atmosphere choked the Bostonian. Well-bred Englishmen would not help the North when it was so obviously backed by labor. Bright got up to speak. With singular skill and power he told the assembled workers that the American war was a struggle between two sections, one where "labor is honored more than elsewhere in the world," and another section where it is "degraded and the laborer is made a chattel."[60] The fiery liberal thundered next against all "respectable" classes in England. Henry Adams was sure that such socialistic talk would lose the vote for the amendment on the morrow.

Next day the debate was called in Parliament. As might have been expected, the radical demonstration the night before frightened all but the extremists. Friends of the amendment who might have voted for it dared not align themselves with the socialists and trade-unionists. John Laird, M.P., a member of the great shipbuilding firm, asked for the floor and complained to the House:

"I would rather be handed down to posterity as the builder of a dozen *Alabamas* than as a man who applies himself deliberately to set class against class, and to cry up the institutions of another country which, when they come to be tested, are of no value whatever, and which reduce the very name of liberty to an utter absurdity."[61]

This outburst was greeted with great cheering in Parliament, not so much in approval of letting the *Alabama* escape but for the boldness of the attack on John Bright and his radical views. The display had an especially bad effect on Lord Palmerston. Direct attack on the negligence of his government forced the Prime Minister to take the offensive. Always quick to fight back, he was forced to oppose the motion. The Adamses thought war inevitable.

A few days later the Adamses learned that they had misjudged the situation. Palmerston might appear on the record to be on one side while in practice he was on the other, precisely as Seward appeared in Mexico. On April 5, 1863, a vessel, the *Alexandra,* being equipped to join the *Alabama,* was seized in spite of the fact that the amendment had not passed. A disgruntled Confederate ne'er-do-well, Clarence Randolph Young, clerk to Bulloch and husband of a mulatto, furnished evidence that convinced Earl Russell. The owners of the condemned vessel appealed the Foreign Secretary's decision to the courts but the people greeted the seizure with public meetings of approval. At Manchester six thousand workers applauded the act and demanded prosecution of the Lairds. On April 7, 1863, Earl Russell wrote Lord Lyons that Britain had made a change in policy—the greatest throughout the entire war.[62]

Regardless of the amendment, he told the minister in America, henceforth suspicious ships would be held in British yards if they were "apparently" intended for the Confederate service. This recognition of circumstantial evidence, this judgment of guilt until proved innocent, Earl Russell hoped would "allay the strong feelings which have been raised in Northern America by the escape from justice of the *Oreto* and *Alabama.*" Palmerston, with political subtlety not appreciated by the Adamses, had been playing the Americans' game even while he appeared to be on the other side. Then Abraham Lincoln added the finishing touch to the little love feast. He took a pen and a sheet of White House stationery and prepared the following resolution for John Bright to use at meetings of workingmen in the United Kingdom:

"Whereas, while heretofore, States, and Nations, have tolerated slavery, *recently,* for the first time in the world, an attempt had been made to construct a new Nation, upon the basis of, and with the primary, and fundamental object to maintain, enlarge, and perpetuate human slavery, therefore,

"Resolved, That no such embryo State should ever be recognized by, or admitted into, the family of Christian and civilized nations; and that all Christian and civilized men everywhere should, by all lawful means, resist to the utmost, such recognition."[63]

The Confederate sympathizers realized that their time at bat was almost over. J. D. Bulloch left for France to continue his shipbuilding in a country less vigilant. M. Drouyn de L'Huys assured Slidell that the French government would close its eyes to complaints, at least until some direct appeal was made against it.[64] Indeed only one thing prevented the shipbuilders from beginning work at once. The Confederacy had neither the money nor credit to put the French yards to work.[65] Then a French banker came forward with an idea to supply the money, an idea so fantastic and yet so workable that it taxed the imagination of Abraham Lincoln as well as Robert J. Walker and came near undoing all the advantage gained in Britain.

# XV. *A Man Whose Nights Are Sleepless*

THE great financial scheme to pay English and French ship-builders for Confederate war vessels originated in the mind of Emil Erlanger, a Frankfurt banker, resident in Paris.[1] John Slidell, the New York adventurer, soon made his acquaintance. The two men's families became intimate. Erlanger's son fell in love with the impetuous Mathilde. Erlanger was as clever a manipulator with figures as Slidell had been with votes. His proposition for raising a vast sum of money captured the imagination of the Southern commissioner. The scheme was worthy of De Morny or Napoleon. Cotton in the South was worth twelve cents per pound. In Europe it was worth fifty cents. Erlanger proposed that the Confederate government issue bonds to the amount of some $25,000,000, payable in New Orleans middling cotton at twelve cents, to be delivered at Southern wharves not later than six months after the ratification of peace—a financial transaction much better than Benjamin's 1862 bribe to Napoleon. These bonds would make all holders in both England and France eager to force a conclusion to the Civil War. Erlanger's firm offered to receive the bonds at 70, offer them at 90,[2] and in addition take a commission for sales.

As Erlanger outlined the proposition Slidell became enthusiastic. He wrote Secretary of State Benjamin for permission to make the deal. Benjamin was suspicious. The profits seemed to be too large to be fair to the Confederacy. Erlanger was sure that he could sell the idea to Benjamin in person. His agents boarded ship and ran the blockade to Richmond. These urban opportunists, Erlanger's bankers and Benjamin, sat down to play with the finances of nine million people who had rebelled in an effort to maintain a rural civilization. Benjamin looked over the figures. He limited the amount of bonds to be issued to $15,000,000, fixed the interest at seven percent and insisted that Erlanger take them at 77 instead of 70. "We would have declined it altogether," Benjamin wrote later, "but for the political considerations indicated by Mr. Slidell."

Back in Paris, Erlanger's firm prepared to put the bonds on sale. A payment of only fifteen percent purchased a bond. With promised profits of almost five hundred percent, future installments might be made from accrual of market price alone. Purchasers who got in on the opening day could thus realize over three thousand percent on their investment. With these bonds in the pockets of Europe's middle class, the problem of creating sympathy for the Confederacy would be easy. The bonds were rumored in banking and speculating circles to be the bonanza of the century. Anyone who could raise a small sum for investment would profit by a Southern victory. The sales opened auspiciously and young Erlanger led Mathilde Slidell to the altar.

The most sanguine promoter could have asked for nothing better. On the evening of the first day the bonds were oversubscribed.[3] Most of the purchasers were Englishmen. One order came from Trieste, where the Archduke Maximilian, out of a throne, watched American politics hopefully. Some British subscribers caused pro-Union men anxiety. William Ewart Gladstone enrolled for $10,-000.[4] Beresford-Hope, proprietor of the *Saturday Review,* and Mr. Rideout, editor of the *Post,* both registered orders. All three of them were in positions to make plenty of trouble. Alexander James Beresford Beresford-Hope—a Tory name for sure—was an indefatigable opponent of John Bright's humanitarian reforms and an outspoken champion of the Confederate country-gentleman ideal. A supporter of group organizations to counteract the emancipation societies, he became treasurer of a Southern aid society organized to raise a so-called Stonewall Jackson fund. Mason and Slidell both believed the bonds to be the first step in a great diplomatic victory. The latter wrote Benjamin:

"You will, before this despatch can reach you, have seen by the newspapers the brilliant success of Erlanger and his loan. The affair has been admirably managed, and cannot fail to exercise a most salutary influence on both sides of the Atlantic. It is a financial recognition of our independence, emanating from a class proverbially cautious and little given to be influenced by sentiment or sympathy."[5]

Mason, in similar vein, wrote: "I think I may congratulate you on the triumphant success of our infant credit; it shows, malgré all detraction and calumny, that cotton is King at last."[6]

Lincoln was kept posted on the progress of the loan. Dayton and Adams, and even the *Manchester Guardian*, usually pro-Southern, agreed that most of the subscribers were already creditors of the Confederacy.[7] Thus no converts to slavocracy had been gained. Other observers questioned the generalization. The bonds rose in price steadily to 95½. Erlanger's commissions and margin netted him several million. Bonds purchased on his own account swelled his profits. The Confederacy now had sufficient money for its ship payments, the rams and the cruisers—on paper at least. James Mason gloated over the rosy prospect. Slidell smiled at his daughter's successful marriage. Everybody was as merry as a wedding bell. Then Lincoln notified Robert J. Walker to kill the Confederate loan.

The President did not send minute instructions. Walker was an old hand at finance, and Lincoln's desk was piled high with problems. An odd bit of news had come from California—a quaint incident that on its face had no foreign implications. Out in San Francisco Bay, on March 14, 1863, a fast-sailing clipper, the *J. W. Chapman*, was stopped by a Federal cutter as it steamed out of the Golden Gate. Union spies had watched the vessel for several days at the wharf as she loaded lumber and boxes labeled "machinery," "reaper" and "oil mill." The crew was listed as five men, but fifteen "fighting men" were discovered hidden in the hold. The boxes were found to contain two howitzers, a case of muskets, powder, shot, pistols and uniforms. The ship's papers revealed a letter of marque from Jefferson Davis authorizing the captain to prey upon Northern commerce. A blueprint disclosed that the lumber was for the construction of a prison between decks. Most astounding of all, one of the leaders, twenty-year-old Albert Rubery, was reported to be a nephew of John Bright's.

One of the owners had got drunk before the ship set sail, and the captain had ordered the vessel away without him. Sobered by the sight of the departing ship, the owner hired a boat, overtook his craft, and climbed up the side just in time to be arrested. The entire crew was lodged on Alcatraz Island pending trial for piracy.[8] Lincoln knew that a secret Confederate organization in California plotted to take over the Far Western states.[9] Could the *Chapman* be part of the conspiracy? Lincoln was lucky to have her stopped.

Out on the Atlantic the big dangerous *Alabama* and the *Florida* were both still at large, and Captain Semmes's threat to re-enslave Kock's Negro colonists still echoed in the land. The prospective settlers assembled at Fortress Monroe. A vessel was ready to take them to Ile Vache. Newspapers announced that they boarded the ship with ecstasy and sailed away singing hallelujah. Lincoln had escaped the official responsibility of sending them as a government undertaking. But even as a private venture he felt a moral obligation for their safety on the high seas.

Then a letter arrived from Russia. Lincoln put on his small steel-rimmed spectacles and read it. Bayard Taylor, the dependable Secretary of Legation, had resigned, piqued because Lincoln had reappointed Clay minister to the Czar and he himself was not promoted.

Lincoln reached for his little book. He looked through the pages and decided to fill Taylor's place with Henry Bergh, son of a wealthy shipbuilder. Bergh ships, in the days of sail, had been recognized as models of perfection in performance around the world. Henry Bergh, scion of the family, was an odd character, but he knew Europe. Tall, slender, cadaverous, sad-eyed, he was effeminate as any woman, dressed extravagantly, was filled with horror at the sight of blood and flew into a frenzy when men were cruel to animals. Above all else he wanted to be an actor. He had quit college before graduating, wrote plays and poetry but never with success. Aged fifty-two, with purple bags beneath his melancholy eyes, thwarted Henry Bergh and wife had spent much of their time abroad, enjoying Old World culture and ill-health. Inseparable companions, their days were filled with leisurely talk about art and art galleries, private views, and the sure symptoms of a cold. Extensive travel and court life interested them. They were dazzled by the Czar's Winter Palace, marveled at the castles along the Rhine, and finally achieved the happy formality of exchanging a bow with Prince Albert at Buckingham.[10] The outbreak of the Civil War stimulated the Berghs with patriotism. Henry headed a committee to purchase arms for the North. At one of George Francis Train's *déjeuners,* Bergh mounted the platform—a real actor this time—only to learn again that he had no Thespian talent. Lincoln's appointment of Henry Bergh as Secretary of Legation in Russia filled the couple with new pride. They set off for St. Petersburg. How Cassius Clay, with his lust for blood, would get along with this precious dandy who scratched and pulled hair at the sight of it was anybody's guess.

Eccentric characters with influence at home had found their way into many diplomatic posts. Noisy jackasses were being silenced effectively. George Francis Train, Burlingame and Clay had all ceased to be problems. Only Count Gurowski remained to plague Abraham Lincoln. Official dispatches from administration eccentrics arrived at the White House from time to time but they could be ignored. A provocative communication came from China—a mysterious box exquisitely hand-painted and elaborately carved. A letter from Anson Burlingame accompanied it. The American explained that the box contained a message from Prince Kung—a greeting for the Chinese New Year. Translated with liberal Occidental brevity, Burlingame said, it meant "equality."[11]

More important dispatches attracted Lincoln's attention. Two seemed to have dangerous connotations. English conservative opinion gained strength noticeably as the emancipation meetings became socialistic[12] early in 1863. Also the British government had published a blue book revealing the semiofficial conversations of Lord Lyons with "the conservatives in New York"—Lincoln's Copperhead enemies. These two things told Lincoln how unfavorably Britain had reacted to John Bright's fight in Parliament. Obviously Palmerston was trimming his sails to navigate without the radicals. Lincoln had got too far to the left to play ball with the British government. He had better reassure the liberal wing of the conservatives. The first and best move might be to make Secretary Welles stop his wholesale arrests of British ships carrying contraband. But Welles was a hard man to force against his will.

Lincoln walked over to the Navy Department to see the Secretary. Welles was always quiet enough in a cabinet meeting but in his own den he feared nothing—not even the President. England was taking advantage of America's leniency, he said. The

Navy must not let up. It must get tough. Lincoln said he did not want another war. Welles replied that if England was given her way a war was unavoidable. The American people would insist on it. Lincoln listened intently.

"If war is to come," Welles said, "it looks to me as of a magnitude greater than the world has ever experienced—as if it would eventuate in the upheaval of nations, the overthrow of governments and dynasties. The sympathies of the mass of mankind would be with us rather than with the decaying dynasties and the old effete governments. Not unlikely the conflict thus commenced would kindle the torch of civil war throughout Christendom, and even nations beyond."

Lincoln did not reply. He appeared preoccupied. Seward used to talk like Welles but he had quit. Welles watched the President. He hoped that foreign affairs would be dealt with more firmly in the future.[13]

Next day, April 3, 1863, a ship built for the Confederates at Dumbarton, the *Japan,* alias *Virginia,* escaped down the Clyde.[14] A government order to hold her arrived twenty-four hours later. Another bungle! Welles hoped that Lincoln would strike with his Privateering Act and put a stop to foreign shipbuilding at once. Every day's delay put the rams nearer completion. Welles waited for Lincoln to get tough.

Lincoln did not do what Welles expected. He had rattled the Privateering Bill like a half-drawn saber over British shipowners' heads and he had sent John Bright resolutions for antislavery meetings—something for both sides. Now, instead of resorting to another threat of force as Welles hoped, Lincoln sent to England one more representative American, William M. Evarts, who had been practicing before the prize courts in America. All angles of maritime law were at the tip of his tongue. He must join Whiting and help prepare the briefs Minister Adams needed to stop Confederate ship construction. Many people prophesied a great future for Evarts. He was a tall, thin man who habitually wore a stovepipe hat grimly over his eyes. In court his arguments were ponderous but at banquets he could be merry. The experience he was to get in maritime law during the war would fit him admirably for the greatest service of his whole life—attorney for the United

States in the postwar *Alabama*-claims trial. Evarts would also figure prominently in the other three great trials of his generation—
the impeachment of Andrew Johnson, the election dispute between
Hayes and Tilden, and the spectacular scandal suit against Henry
Ward Beecher for illicit relations with Mrs. Theodore Tilton.

Lincoln watched Evarts depart for England with satisfaction.
In due time reports of his success would surely come back. The
shipbuilding might yet be stopped without resorting to war—a war
which the United States was in no position to wage until Hooker
showed the stuff that was in him.

After reinforcing his legal talent abroad, Lincoln decided also
to send another financier, John M. Forbes, a self-made man who
had amassed great wealth. Forbes had made his first fortune in
the China trade before he was twenty-one, and had built railroads
—the Michigan Central, the Chicago, Burlington & Quincy, and
also the Hannibal & St. Joseph, the first railroad west of the Mississippi. Like Aspinwall, Forbes was a patron of the arts, whose
hospitality at home was as manorial as any Englishman's, and
whose worldly experience was as broad. Ralph Waldo Emerson
said of him: "Wherever he moved he was the benefactor. It is of
course that he should ride well, shoot well, sail well, keep house
well, administer affairs well; but he was the best talker, also, in the
company."[15]

Forbes's and Aspinwall's commercial empires would make Mason's and Slidell's plantations look like small potatoes. If British
Tories sympathized with landed gentry, here were two for them—
two whom no possible critic could class as communists. Unlike
Aspinwall, Forbes was not a Lincoln man. Vigorous and self-
made, always impatient with Lincoln's slowness, he had favored a
relentless prosecution of the war. Lincoln knew his personal antag-
onism as well as he knew General Hooker's rashness, but he
wanted results. Perhaps these two bold and energetic men—
Forbes and Hooker—could turn the trick while Lincoln and
Seward cajoled England into complacency.

Hooker's men were ready to go. Lincoln himself had approved
the plans for the summer campaign against Richmond. A joint
naval and military expedition was also prepared to strike at
Charleston—nerve center of the Confederacy—from the sea. Lin-

coln watched the military preparation and news from abroad. The Confederate bonds were going down in price. A mysterious "bear party" was offering to take large blocks at low prices. Little old Robert J. Walker was evidently getting to work. Some subscribers lost faith. They forfeited their fifteen-percent payments. When the market closed just before the Easter holidays, the bonds had dropped below the opening price, wavering between three and three-and-a-half-percent discount.[16]

Friends of the Confederacy were in no mood to enjoy the Episcopalian services of Easter resurrection, with a new birth symbolized by eggs and Easter bunnies. The long-faced Confederate commissioners talked the matter over with the promoters. Erlanger, ever resourceful, had a scheme—rather questionable—but he was sure that it would work. Slidell was soon converted. The artful proposition was then taken to Spence and the Liverpool officers of Fraser, Trenholm and Company. All agreed that it was the only way to save the loan. The proposition was put before James Mason. A "bull party" must purchase bonds at a price above the market. None-too-bright James Mason agreed. But who had sufficient funds? The financiers, cold and precise as the figures on their ledgers, pointed out that the Confederacy had a tidy sum on deposit—the proceeds of the bonds. This must be used to "bull" the price, "but of course without disclosing the real party in the market."[17] To Mason such a proceeding was dishonest. The Confederacy could not legitimately use its own money to stimulate artificially its own bonds. He was shocked. The financiers put the question squarely to him: either use the money for this purpose or Erlanger would drop the whole transaction. The $2,000,000 on hand would then be absorbed as commissions for the promoters. Mason gave in. The city sharpers had got into the heart of his rural civilization with more deadly precision than Northern bankers had ever done. He was unhappy, and wrote Benjamin in Richmond, "All this thing is, of course, done in confidence."[18]

The price went up as Confederate funds poured into the market. The master of Selma Plantation watched the quotations and admitted that the money was well spent—a slight sacrifice now to save the loan later. James Mason did not know that Erlanger was quietly unloading his personal holdings at a handsome profit.

Robert J. Walker also watched the daily quotations, selling short whenever the Confederate "bulls" were absent.

Back in America, Lincoln followed the preparation of his land and sea forces. His naval expedition had left for Charleston—a great fleet, with wobbling ironbacked turtles churning along beside wooden ships of the line. The first week in April 1863 an assault was attempted straight into the jaws of the harbor. Batteries from all the islands opened fire. Torpedoes, mines, chains and hawsers blocked the passage. The next day Lincoln learned that the fleet had been repulsed, half of it sunk. Could enthusiasm for the Emancipation Proclamation in England survive such impotence? Surely the bonds would go up in price. Then Englishmen would have to intervene to save their investments.

Hooker replied to the naval repulse with a ringing order. "On to Richmond!" His great army began to move. Lincoln's redheaded Apollo was in the saddle. "Beware of rashness but with energy and sleepless vigilance go forward and bring us victories."

Lincoln considered joining the troops himself. Then Seward came scampering to his office with new foreign problems. Wilkes had got into trouble in the West Indies exactly as Gurowski had prophesied. Britain had not complained when he sent in prizes carrying contraband between neutral ports in the Caribbean, but he had captured a ship, the *Peterhoff,* bound for Matamoros, a mainland town, the end of a passage. The "continuous voyage" doctrine had never been applied when the last lap of the transit was overland. England had admitted that the *Springbok* capture—between two neutral ports—conformed to her own interpretation of "continuous voyage" but the *Peterhoff* capture was entirely different. It was similar to the *Labuan* case of 1862, adjudged illegal prize by the American court. Why did Welles persist in upholding Wilkes's actions? Seward's hair rose aggressively when he felt outraged. The worst of it all, Seward maintained, was Welles's attitude toward the mails found on board. He resolutely refused to give them up.[19] His excuse: they might be the only proof that the goods on board were ultimately destined for the Confederacy.

Seward appeared to be really excited. War with England would come this time surely. In the six weeks that had elapsed since the

*Peterhoff's* capture the whole affair had been aired in England. Henry Adams' gloomy augury of a second *Trent* affair was only too true.[20] The accumulation of grievances—the blockade, the suffering of the working people, fear of democracy, "Beast" Butler, Wilkes in the Caribbean, continued interference with English shipping and with the mails, the Privateering Bill not two months old —had opened the old wound and given the Confederate propagandists and special interests the opportunity they wanted. Seward banged out the door.

Welles heard about the conference. On April 18, 1863, he stalked into the President's office to tell his side of the story. He appeared very angry. Lincoln looked up over his small steel-rimmed spectacles. To hold up the mails, Lincoln said, would cause a war with England. Welles denied it. To give up the mails, he maintained stubbornly, was contrary to international law. Mail should not be surrendered in any circumstance. Lincoln said he was not sure about this point of law. He would address interrogatories on the subject to Welles, Seward and also Sumner, chairman of the Foreign Relations Committee.

Welles went down the stairs planning the reply he intended to write. On April 22, 1863, Lincoln's questionnaire arrived at his office. Then, before he or Sumner or anyone had time to reply, the newspapers announced that Lincoln had ordered the mails restored —an old trick. There would be no war with England this time.

A few days later a letter arrived from Bigelow. He wanted details of Jeff Davis' effort to repudiate the Mississippi state debt— almost $10,000,000 lost by British investors in the 1840's. Slidell had denied the charge, and no rebuttal evidence was available in Europe. Here was some good material for propaganda. Robert J. Walker could use such information to advantage in his fight against the Confederate bonds.

Bigelow stated further that Bulloch, since coming to France, was reported to have signed building contracts for four steamers. But the Emperor who had encouraged Slidell to make deals now seemed against them. Napoleon had learned that Fighting Joe Hooker had been given command. In case of a quick victory France might have to pay tremendous damages for the depredations of vessels made

illegally in her yards.[21] The Emperor, said Bigelow, had warned
Bulloch that the ships would not be permitted to leave France
unless conditions were "satisfactory."

Lincoln gathered from Bigelow's letters that Napoleon was outwardly friendly toward the North but at the same time he helped
the South whenever he could—always playing both ends against
the middle. No one could depend on him. When the *Japan,*
alias *Virginia,* had slipped unfinished from the Clyde, Adams had
wired Dayton that she was headed for St. Malo, France, for finishing. Napoleon intercepted the message, and Slidell received a
copy as soon as the American minister.[22] The Emperor obviously
wanted the Confederates to spend their money in France. Also
they might help his Mexican scheme. On the other hand, a victory
for the North would forever check the power of Great Britain.
France no longer suffered for Southern cotton. Cobden's reciprocity treaty had revived French trade. Northern wheat promised
to be indispensable in case of a Polish war. The Emperor's best
policy was to bet on the winner. He invited Slidell to his box at
the races. Bigelow was elected into the Geographical Society of
France, of which Persigny, Minister of the Interior, was president.[23]

In America Lincoln followed Hooker's progress on the map.
The gallant general had marched to Chancellorsville and established headquarters in a mansion that served as tavern for the
community. "I have Lee's army in one hand and Richmond in
the other," he exclaimed exultantly.[24]

A hundred thousand boys in blue bivouacked in the green hills
and woods around him, all eager for battle. Peace-at-any-price
Copperheads in the North protested the impending slaughter. Out
in Ohio a leading Democratic politician, Clement Vallandigham,
spoke openly against the administration. The war might have
ended, he told a meeting at Mount Vernon, if Lincoln had been willing to accept the French plan of negotiation.[25] General Burnside,
commanding the district, promptly clapped Vallandigham in jail
and denied him a writ of habeas corpus. A military court sentenced the Ohio politician to imprisonment for the duration of the
war. Lincoln commuted the sentence to banishment to the South.

Unhappy in exile, Clement Vallandigham slipped through the blockade and prepared to run for governor of Ohio while residing in Canada.

Pro-Southerners in England smiled over the demonstrations against the administration. John Bright, in his turn, continued to do everything he could to make the Civil War a class struggle. Gloating over the grimaces of the privileged people, he welded together the trade-unionists and the liberals. The Emancipation Proclamation represented a principle on which both could unite. The ruddy old bull tossed the democratic document into the most aristocratic china shops. At first the labor press had not taken the Emancipation Proclamation seriously. It had favored Lincoln only because he represented democracy. In April, George Potter's *Bee-Hive* began to applaud abolition for the first time.[26] On May 2, 1863—four months after the document had been signed—a delegation of workingmen, headed by John Bright, called on Minister Adams. They presented a letter from the trade-unions commending Lincoln's proclamation. Adams accepted the letter. It pleased him, he said, to know that English workingmen perceived secession to be an effort "to establish a Government on the destruction of the rights of labor."[27]

Without doubt the North had won labor's sympathy—an appeal started in Lincoln's July message, 1861, as a plea for democracy and the "plain people." Lincoln had never let up on the theme but he had followed it with caution. In December 1861 he added his careful definition of the rights of capital and labor. Then during 1862 he had appealed to the idealists with his antislavery program. And in January 1863 he had received the Manchester workingmen's letter congratulating him for freeing the slaves. Lincoln had fanned this responsive flame. The tempo of Northern appeals to the middle and lower classes in England increased. First Lincoln had sent his reply to the workingmen. Then food ships arrived in March. Lecturers came by almost every boat. In April Lincoln sent the resolutions for John Bright's meetings. The campaign was paying big dividends. Yes, labor and the lower middle classes were safe, but British capital remained an uncertain quantity.

In 1862 the shipping interests and manufacturers had been definitely hostile—threatening to interfere and save their markets.

Lincoln had tried to hold them down with appeals to the British people's humanitarian principles—and it had worked. Now in 1863 the capitalists were making money out of the American war. Indian cotton supplied normal needs. Linen and woolen textiles had revived under favorable competition. This in turn had helped flax growers and sheepmen at home. The manufacture of munitions and Confederate ships increased the national income.[28] The destruction of America's merchant marine eliminated Britain's greatest competitor in the world's carrying trade. Then, too, blockade-running had become an immensely profitable industry. Seward had amazing reports from his secret service, as well as the consuls in the Bahamas. Lincoln, with his army in the hands of dashing General Hooker, had time to study the blockade. Liverpool was the center of the highly speculative endeavor. Merchants had invested in long, low, side-wheelers painted gray. Special engines were designed to burn smokeless anthracite or Welsh semibituminous coal.[29] "An extraordinary instance of British energy, eh what!" On outward trips the cargoes of cotton brought the fabulous prices which made the Erlanger loan so attractive. Inbound loads of luxuries brought equally exorbitant profits—golden days —a revival of the eighteenth-century merchant adventurers who had founded the old Whig families in England. Fraser, Trenholm and Company had a practical monopoly on the cotton exported.[30] The Liverpool office became a great clandestine clearinghouse. The French branch was invited to share the business. A vessel was set aside for it, but even the offer of handsome wages did not entice Frenchmen to enlist.[31] Bulloch urged the Confederacy to purchase blockade-runners of its own. Four vessels were commissioned. The number proved inadequate.[32] English bottoms had a firm hold on the business. General C. J. McRae, Confederate business agent in England,[33] wrote on October 7, 1863, that since January 1 a hundred thousand bales of cotton had arrived in London, valued at £4,000,000—"double as much as the Erlanger loan will net (if all sold)."[34] No wonder that this business could afford an elaborate lobby in Parliament.

Lincoln put down the reports thoughtfully. England was getting rich out of the Civil War. Profiteers were not apt to intervene and kill the goose that laid the golden egg. Careful management would keep that bugaboo asleep forevermore. Lincoln and Seward had done everything in a financial way to injure Confederate credit. They had done everything in a political way to gain sympathy with English liberals and workers. They must do nothing overt in a military way to impede the blockade-runners and touch England in the quick of her maritime pride. Let Welles and Sumner whine at the government's weakness.

The next move was up to Hooker. As soon as he won a great victory Lincoln might firmly demand a stop to Confederate shipbuilding—but not blockade-running. Lincoln had slugged the contraband carriers under cover of antislavery enactments. He might be able to stop the half-finished Confederate ships by ignoring the blockade-runners—especially since the nefarious traffic hurt the Confederacy by drawing out specie to pay for imported luxuries. Of course Adams and Morse, Forbes and Aspinwall, Whiting and Evarts might stop the ships themselves. But the job would be easier if blockade-running was let alone.

In the meantime Hooker had his men set to open the ball. His army outnumbered Lee two to one—according to available reports in the North. No wonder Hooker believed that he held Lee in his hand! On April 30, 1863, Hooker began to close his fist. Lincoln haunted the telegraph office day and night, traced troop movements on the map.

Hooker maneuvered three days with sharp skirmishes but nothing decisive. On May 3, 1863, a real battle broke. All day long the telegraph ticked in the War Department. Lincoln came and went a dozen times. The fortunes of battle were hard to decipher from the dispatches. This and that regiment moved up and down the old plank road east of Chancellorsville. Lincoln read the reports, went away, came back, went away again. Late at night the operator looked up to see the tall figure of the President standing in the doorway once more. The wire began to tick. The whole story came through. Thin lines of boys in blue had advanced across green fields toward a patch of timber. New leaves on the trees hid the enemy. Battle smoke rolled out of the woods, over the boys in blue—a terrible bombardment. Trees crashed to the ground. Splintered "worm fences" blew up into the air. Hooker stood on the gallery of the tavern in Chancellorsville giving commands. A shell hit the building. A pillar toppled. The general was struck on the head and stunned. His men were not yet all in the firing line. Confused orders came from headquarters. The soldiers were baffled. They gave up, retreated.

The telegraph instrument stopped. Lincoln turned and disappeared through the dark doorway. Another glorious army clogged the roads of northern Virginia, disorganized, men "going over the hill" never to report again. Washington was exposed once more to attack. Lincoln walked back to the White House, slowly along the path across the lawn. His tired feet followed it easily in the dark. Defeats had been his main ration since the beginning of the war. A sentry noticed that the President's eyes burned unnaturally like those of a starving man—starving for victory. On the portico Lincoln greeted the doorman with absent-minded civility, then dragged his feet up the last step.

Count Gurowski felt an urge to do something important. He wrote long letters to Secretary Stanton, Senators Ben Wade and Zach Chandler. He explained the reason for Hooker's defeat, cited precedents in history from Biblical times to the Napoleonic Wars when commanders had been hit on the head and temporarily stunned without losing battles. To Secretary of War Stanton he wrote an essay on the necessity of studying certain books.[35]

In London Henry Adams heard two Britishers haw-hawing. "So the Federals have got another licking!"[36] one exclaimed as he adjusted his monocle. Then, as sympathy drifted away from the North, a sensational book appeared. Fanny Kemble, internationally known actress, published the journal of her life on a Georgia plantation. Victorian society was scandalized. Mothers forbade their daughters to read about the atrocious Southerners. The book sold well. Once more Englishmen were impressed with the horrors of slavery.[37]

Shortly after the disaster at Chancellorsville, newspapers reported that the French had captured the Mexican city of Puebla.[38] The way was now open across healthful country to the capital—a double blow to Lincoln's democracy as well as his Monroe Doctrine. Further concessions must be made to England. What could be done to stop British shipbuilding—especially the rams? Perhaps Wilkes would have to be thrown to the wolves. Letters from

Forbes, Cobden, the Duke of Argyll and Earl Russell all suggested that English relations would be benefited by his removal. Seward went to see Welles about it. The Secretary of the Navy suggested sending Wilkes to the Pacific—an "honorable but less active command."[39] Now the blockade-runners and their lobby would make hay!

Seward went next to see the President. He wanted still another concession to England—the mails on captured ships. Welles must consent to release them. Lincoln looked up at Seward. The President's face was worn with worries, political problems, Hooker's defeat, the defense of Washington, demands from party leaders with pet generals for sale, rumors of revolt in case he ordered a draft, threats of a revolution to set up a dictator.

Lincoln had argued with Welles since the *Peterhoff* capture in February about the mails, but the Secretary of the Navy was adamant. Welles's written opinion for the interrogatory lay on Lincoln's desk. Someone would have to convince the Secretary that he was wrong. Lincoln knew that Seward antagonized Welles. If the Secretary's mind could be changed, Lincoln would have to do it himself. The President took off his glasses, got up and walked across to the Navy Department alone.

Welles listened to the President. Then the lion in him rose up behind the whiskers. Always bold when with one listener, Welles gave the President a naval broadside. The mails on a prize ship, he said, were under the jurisdiction of the courts and must remain there unless Lincoln made a special treaty exempting them.

Lincoln heard him through. Then, like a lawyer back on the circuit in Illinois, he began to cross-examine his Secretary. He had read the Secretary's written opinion. It was an excellent development of legal theory but Lincoln wanted a practical example. "Have the courts ever opened the mails of a neutral government?"

"Always," Welles replied, "when the captured vessels on which the mails were found were considered good prize."

"Why, then," asked Lincoln, "do you not furnish me with the fact? It is what I want, but you furnish me with no report that any neutral has ever been searched."

Welles was caught. He answered weakly that he was not aware that the right had ever been questioned. The courts had not made reports to him, he said, whether they did or did not open the mail.[40]

Lincoln had won his point at last. Lyons was given the concession—complete submission. Then, strangely enough, the British Home Office refused to take the advantage. England was, after all, a maritime nation. Someday she might be in the Americans' position. Britain had not held the North to Lord Stowell's definition of blockade. The mails might be another bad precedent. The American interpretation of the *Peterhoff* case might also work against the United States and in favor of Britain in a later war. Sir Vernon Harcourt, in a pamphlet signed "Historicus," warned: "The danger is not that Americans will concede too little but that Great Britain may accept too much"[41]—advice that proved invaluable to Britain in World War I.

On the day after Lincoln called on Welles, John Bright wrote a letter to Sumner for the attention of Abraham Lincoln. Word had come to him concerning the retention of the privateer *J. W. Chapman* in San Francisco and the incarceration of the crew on Alcatraz. Albert Rubery, Bright's reputed nephew, though no relation, was of good family—a Birmingham boy, educated at London University. Rubery had shipped as a passenger with a trunk containing a zouave uniform and with a sword bayonet strapped on the outside. Bright expressed the hope that the "foolish young man" might be pardoned.[42] The pirates' trial had been set for October. Until they were convicted there was nothing for Lincoln to pardon. The great republic itself might collapse before that time.

Lincoln's tired eyes looked absent-mindedly out the window. Spring had burst in all the treetops. The grime and dirt of the capital was hidden from his view. But no freshness, no budding summer warmed the harried President. He had wheedled the powers through the winter of 1862-1863 with the promise of a great victory. His State Department had shifted from top of the world arrogance to the subserviency of a third-rate power. Count Gurowski wrote on June 5:

"I often meet Mr. Lincoln in the streets. Poor man! He looks exhausted, care-worn, spiritless, extinct. I pity him! Mr. Lincoln's looks are those of a man whose nights are sleepless, and whose days are comfortless. That is the price for a greatness to which he is not equal."[43]

Few curious eyes followed the President in the busy streets. The town was a-twitter with a new threat of invasion—the third in three years. Rebel cavalry was reported within ten miles of the city. Old breastworks were cleaned and reinforced at Alexandria. Rifle pits were dug to protect the capital.[44] Peace-at-any-price men urged the North to give up. Vallandigham's arrest had been protested in great mass meetings in New York, Philadelphia and Chicago. Resolutions were passed against Lincoln's tyranny, his suppression of the sacred right of free speech. In Indiana mobs resisted the draft, killed officers.[45] European governments could not be expected to put up with this much longer.

Lincoln tried one more expedient. He sent another propagandist to England—Henry Ward Beecher, brother of the author of *Uncle Tom's Cabin,* and a past master at the kind of oratory the English middle and lower classes understood. As Beecher sailed, Lee invaded Pennsylvania. This might be the long-threatened campaign to capture Washington. Perhaps Lee would first take Philadelphia, then strangle the capital. Lincoln ordered General George Meade to rally Hooker's army, to muster all available men, flank and stop Lee if possible. Another failure would be the Union's last gasp.

In Europe news of Beecher's proposed trip was broadcast by pro-Southern journalists.

"The ranting ruffian, the 'Rev.' Henry Ward Beecher, who is a sort of Spurgeon in New York . . . has been of late amusing himself by preaching perfectly devilish sermons about the war. The fellow will be received with open arms by a large party of tea and muffin-stuffing lunatics here, and will doubtless be planted on the platform of Exeter Hall. . . . Let us hope the man will be treated with indifference."[46]

The pro-Southern cause was further encouraged when an English court gave an adverse decision[47] in the case of the *Alexandra.* The Prime Minister had exceeded the authority given him in the

Foreign Enlistment Act. Palmerston appealed the case, but the decision indicated that the ministry had been more lenient toward the North than the law warranted.

Welles in the meantime urged Lincoln to take southern Texas and thus stop the Matamoros trade—an empty request when Lee was flanking Washington, taking town after town in western Maryland. Then news arrived that the French had marched into Mexico City on June 7, 1863. President Juárez fled north and established his capital in San Luis Potosí. His doughty General Diaz fled south and surrounded himself with fighting men in the town of his birth, Oaxaca. Napoleon still maintained that the French occupation was only temporary. This innocent declaration arrived in Washington along with news that France had organized a puppet government which in turn offered an imperial crown to Maximilian—brother of Franz Joseph of Austria. Lincoln was asked to accept the situation. A protest might lose him the support of the French liberals, his only friends. Seward notified Minister Corwin not to recognize the new government, to take a leave of absence and thus avoid committing himself. To his ministers in Vienna, Paris and London, Seward wrote that the American government would maintain strict neutrality. He wrote Bigelow in Paris: "[We] are too intent on putting down our own insurrection . . . to seek for occasions to dispute with any foreign power"[48] —this from Seward who wanted to fight the world in 1861.

Elated, Napoleon called Slidell to the Tuileries.[49] Could the Emperor be planning to follow his military success with a bold recognition of the Confederacy? Dayton beseeched Seward—what must be done? Seward made one more concession. On June 23 he called on Welles himself.

The Secretary of the Navy received him with suspicion. Seward began by stating that affairs had looked bad with France but "all is now right." With this prelude he told Welles that there was a large amount of tobacco in Richmond, already paid for by French merchants. Would it not be considerate to permit its shipment?[50]

The concession to France seemed so abject that Lincoln's enemies recited it as another example of his weakness—worse than his previous submission to Britain on the *Peterhoff* mails or the Spanish request to extend the maritime league around Cuba and thus make a haven for blockade-runners.[51] The North must be tottering into collapse as gray-clad men streamed up the dirt roads into the garden spot of Pennsylvania, trundling cannon past large Dutch barns on neat farmsteads. Military incompetence had rubbed out all advantage gained by the Emancipation Proclamation of six months ago. The Union and Emancipation Society, liberal lecturers, instructive leaflets, enthusiastic meetings of idealists and laborers all combined could not save a democracy that could not save itself.

The friends of Secessia in England saw another great opportunity opening before them, not for intervention—war profiteers were against that—but for recognition of the South. Anticipating the blow, Robert J. Walker assembled all the details of Jeff Davis' repudiation of the state debts back in the 1840's, and he loosed them widely, plastering the newspapers with "Davis the Repudiator." He chartered a balloon and floated across England scattering pamphlets. In order to convince Englishmen that the North's wealth was inexhaustible, he squandered his whole fortune in riotous display. With six white horses he drove about London "in an equipage more glorious than that of the Austrian ambassador."[52]

Lincoln reached into his locker for the last bolt. On the heels of Henry Ward Beecher, he sent the Reverend Dr. Moncure Daniel Conway to join the European chorus and strum with all his might on the antislavery strings. Conway was almost as eccentric as George Francis Train but he was a bigger bore. The son of a Virginia slaveholder, he had, as a Methodist circuit rider, preached that the Negro was not a human being. Personal ambition and an inquiring mind had prompted Conway to study theology at Harvard. He graduated a Unitarian. Accepting a church in Washington, he lost it with his glib antislavery sermons. In Cincinnati, the Beecher stronghold, where abolition sentiments were appreciated, Conway had taken charge of the First Congregational Church. Between Sundays he wrote magazine articles which were noticed in New England. In 1860 he became editor of the *Dial* and in 1862 of the *Commonwealth,* a Boston abolitionist sheet as outspoken but less vulgar than Garrison's *Liberator.* Conway's editorials attacked Lincoln for being unsound on the slavery question, for needlessly causing the Civil War. Several books came quickly from his facile pen.

Lincoln was desperate for men to join Evarts, Forbes and Beecher, and talk on the antislavery platform which John Bright and the emancipation societies had organized throughout England. He sent his maligner. Unfortunately Conway could not arrive in England before the new motion to recognize the Confederacy was scheduled to come up in Parliament. This time the rebel sympathizers, shipbuilders and bondholders, all with a growing interest, might have their way. Lincoln's only hope lay in postponement, delay, faith that Lee would be stopped in Pennsylvania and that the intellectual liberals in England, backed by labor, could control the nation's conscience, remind everyone that freedom and slavery were at stake. In Parliament Lincoln could count on one man, John Bright, to whom the failure of the American experiment in government spelled ruin for his dream of a democratic England. The grumbling old campaigner went down to London. He had been defeated on the amendment to stop the ships but he was not whipped. Let anyone who dared introduce a motion for the recognition of the Slave States. John Bright would be there.

# XVI. Gettysburg:
## End of British Enmity

PROPAGANDA for recognition of the South in Parliament assumed carnival proportions in June 1863. Day after day barrel organs played Southern tunes in London streets. Ragged children ran after the music, hoping to see the monkey. Scullions, on their knees scrubbing brownstone steps, stopped their work, brushed grimy locks of hair back from dirty faces and listened. "The Marster says the Yankees will get whipped, 'e do. 'E sez, sez 'e, if the Yankees win, Hengland will be Socialist. The Marster will be ruined, ruined, sez 'e. Then what's to become of such as us? Hi don't like Socialist, Hi don't."

In addition to putting barrel organs on London street corners, Hotze printed and displayed posters of the Confederate flag conjoined with the British Jack. He racked his brains to outdo the ostentation of Walker's six white horses. Carefully written leaders appeared in the *Herald* and *Standard*. First one paper, then the other, on alternate days, urged Parliament to adopt the proposed motion for recognition of the Confederacy. A large open-air meeting at Sheffield passed resolutions requesting the government to act. Confederate sympathizers chuckled over the rams and other ships being built in British yards. Pro-Southern meetings were held at Manchester, at Preston and elsewhere.[1]

The great day came. On June 30, 1863, Adams sent his son and secretary, Henry, to the House of Commons to report the result. These crises had become almost seasonal, like London fogs. Henry sat down under the gallery at the left. Out beyond the gangway he could see the profiles of the government, sharp and stolid as the profiles on his father's coins—faces ruled by expediency. Popular will in Britain seemed to have shifted completely away from the North. Military ineptness had outweighed an emancipation proclamation which could not be enforced. The law officers at Liverpool had demonstrated that they would not detain the ironclads unless forced to do so. The courts had upheld them. Financiers were becoming more deeply involved in the construction of rebel cruisers. Blockade-runners supported a powerful bloc. Munitions manufacturers gloated over prospects of new profits if the South were recognized. All holders of Erlanger's cotton loan had a real interest in the South. The case did not look good to Henry Adams.

The lecturers whom Lincoln sent to England had not had time to influence the people to any appreciable extent. Continued military reverses demonstrated that the North would never win. The Marxist meetings and John Bright's radicalism had done their share to frighten the religious middle class which did not believe in slavery but which disliked, even more, red republicanism.

Henry Adams waited restlessly in his seat under the gallery. He did not believe that politicians were ruled by altruistic principles, but he did not like to admit it. Before long, John Arthur Roebuck, an anti-Whig reactionary, introduced the dread resolution. John Bright glowered at him across the gangway. Henry Adams wondered why the Southern bloc selected so weak a man. Gregory in 1861 and Lindsay in 1862 had both been more able men. Had the Emancipation Proclamation made the Confederacy so odious that no other champion could be found? Roebuck was old and fatuous. *Punch* cartooned him as a terrier snarling at his enemies.[2] He had entered political life some thirty years before as a member for Bath. Gossips remembered that during the campaign he had been publicly slapped on the face. Big corporations used him and Lindsay as their tools.[3] In the days of the Reform Bill, when Russell and Palmerston had been considered liberals, Roebuck was a conservative, a reviler of utilitarianist Jeremy Bentham—a fig for the greatest good for the greatest number! "In all England they could have found no opponent better fitted to give away his own case," Henry Adams told himself; "a bitter tongue and a mind enfeebled even more than common by the political epidemic of egotism."[4]

At Adams' right, also under the gallery, there sat another 'American, Lucius Quintus Cincinnatus Lamar, Confederate minister on his way to Russia. Adams and Lamar would have enjoyed each other's company had they been on the same side politically. Years later they met on friendly terms and each recounted his impression of that memorable day in Parliament. Henry Adams recalled that after Roebuck had spoken, "John Bright, with astonishing force, caught and shook and tossed Roebuck, as a big mastiff shakes a wiry, ill-conditioned, toothless, bad-tempered Yorkshire terrier."[5] Lamar's account was more complete. He was a Southern gentleman of the old school, a student of law and politics—a charming raconteur, whom ill-health had caused to resign a commission in the Confederate Army. Jeff Davis ordered him to St. Petersburg as a minister—a hopeless mission—thus losing for the Confederacy the skill and charm of a personality which might have been valuable in the posts filled by dull Mason, sly Slidell and overbearing Pickett. Lamar tarried in Paris for instructions at the time Roebuck's resolution was calendared. Lindsay invited him to attend a house party at his villa on the Thames—"to meet the new champion of the South, John Arthur Roebuck." Lamar accepted. During the visit he found himself alone with the aged champion. By way of showing interest in the approaching Parliamentary session Lamar inquired if John Bright might make trouble in the impending debate. " 'No, sir!' said Roebuck sententiously: 'Bright and I have met before. It was the old story—the story of the sword-fish and the whale! No, sir! Mr. Bright will not cross swords with me again!' "[6]

Lamar remembered the incident as he sat under the balcony listening to the debate. Before long, he said later, he became aware that a bluff man with a singularly rich voice and imposing manner had taken the floor, and was giving Roebuck the most deliberate and tremendous pounding he ever witnessed. "At last," Lamar concluded, "it dawned on my mind that the sword-fish was getting the worst of it."[7]

So completely was the swordfish worsted that the friends of the motion were glad to let it drop rather than risk a vote and show their weakness. The debate, before it was finished, became extremely personal, revealing all the secret negotiations of Lindsay and company with Napoleon. The British government was accused by one side of disclosing the contents of a confidential dispatch from the Emperor to America. The other side denied that any such dispatch existed.[8] Soon the rafters of the great hall were ringing with a pertinent discussion as to whether Napoleon or

Roebuck was a liar.[9] The Emperor, when he heard of it, was not pleased. The gap between England and France widened—this time for good. Joint recognition became impossible. Henry Hotze admitted that the Southern cause was done in England. Recognition in Parliament, he said, would "never again receive serious attention, even if a man could be found bold enough to broach it."[10] Jeff Davis notified Mason to withdraw from London, his mission at an end.

The flabby collapse of the Southern diplomatic campaign was explained in various ways. Some said that the British government's attention was drawn away from America by the Polish and Schleswig-Holstein troubles. Others said that the Civil War had been won in England by the Emancipation Proclamation. The South had no chance abroad after that. Still others believed that renewed prosperity in England kept her out of the war. Whatever the true causes may have been, many people prophesied that from this time forward the big interests, the shipbuilders and bondholders would desert the Palmerston government completely and double the pressure on the Tories or any other political group that promised to enhance their investments. By strengthening the opposition they might force a change in the government, and with a new Prime Minister attack America once more.

Parliament's refusal to pass Roebuck's resolution was followed by startling news from America. The invasion of the North had been checked at Gettysburg and General Grant had captured Vicksburg—two of the greatest victories of the Civil War. The Jove-like Lee had been stopped at last, and the Confederacy was split down the Mississippi. Payday had come for democracy.

The strain at the American legation in London eased immediately. Monckton Milnes, Lord Houghton, scorned a possible overthrow of the British government. At a party he rushed through the throng "with a whoop of triumph," threw his arms around Henry Adams and kissed him on both cheeks. Minister Adams felt that the victory made him equal to any situation—Russell or Palmerston or anyone.[11] Confederate shipbuilding in general and the ironclad rams in particular would stop now or he would know the reason why.

News of Gettysburg collapsed the cotton loan to 36. The Confederate equity was gone. Only Erlanger, Slidell and Mason had profited by the grand speculation. Of the three, Erlanger's profits were the most tangible. He was said to have netted $2,700,000. Slidell had got his daughter married to the son of a rich man. Mason had got some experience. Robert J. Walker turned his attention to new forms of display and William Evarts returned to America.

Triumphant days began. Henry Ward Beecher opened his English lecture tour. He was greeted more cordially even than his sister had been. Common people flocked to his standard with a rudeness that might have shocked Harriet Beecher Stowe. England had just experienced a revival of the Methodist devotion that had swept the island a century before. Beecher fitted perfectly into the scene. Sufficiently virile to appeal to the mobs, he imparted to them some of his burning inspiration. Making democracy a religious rather than a political concept, he carried the workers with him in a revolt which would not die until they gained the franchise. At Edinburgh, Beecher's lecture at the Free Church Assembly Hall was jammed. Some of the holders of platform tickets failed to get into the building. At Exeter Hall in London the police had difficulty holding the milling crowds in hand.[12] Wise old Tories like Disraeli noted this new reform movement. Perhaps they could harness it and get back into power.

After Gettysburg, brokers realized that the war would be a long one. The price of cotton began to rise. Blockade-runners prepared to make increased profits.[13] Lincoln knew that England was traditionally laissez-faire toward big business, and that blockade-running had become a very big business, so big that it might stand a little paring down without complete destruction. Lincoln had several plans to accomplish this. Also the Confederate rams must be stopped and the French-Mexico imbroglio needed settling. Lincoln knew that all his solutions might not work out, but he hoped for a good average. Out at the Soldiers' Home the President pondered the details in the evenings. Work helped shut out from his mind the terrible losses at Gettysburg which he knew would come in soon. The battle had brought tight-lipped sorrow to the Lincoln household. On the day of victory Mrs. Lincoln had been thrown from her carriage,[14] and hurt seriously. Her mind might be affected permanently, the doctors said. Then the list of dead at Gettysburg! The longest yet in the war, it included many of the President's personal friends. Reports told, too, of a sudden flood in the Potomac with Lee trapped on the northern bank. Lincoln wrote Meade to strike before the rebels had time to reorganize for defense.

Over in the State Department the mail piled up. Weeks would elapse before Lincoln learned how Europe received the news of Gettysburg. The copy of a commercial treaty came from Sanford—new regulations for the Scheldt tariffs. Burlingame sent a far-reaching dispatch. The "noisy jackass" was making a name for himself in China. Always resourceful and energetic, he had converted the Russian minister to a new American policy—an open door in China with no territorial aspirations. The English minister, Burlingame wrote, had agreed to co-operate.[15]

Lincoln's vexed mind could not concentrate on Oriental problems. He wrote Meade again to strike at the trapped Confederates. Meade did nothing. "This is a dreadful reminiscence of McClellan," Lincoln said. The flood receded and Lee escaped. If the Confederate Army had been forced to surrender, the end of the war would have been in sight. Now Lincoln must order a new draft and prepare again for the bloody work of forcing a road to Richmond. Politicians told Lincoln that a new draft would cause trouble in the North. Gettysburg might be a victory that defeated Lincoln in the eyes of his own people. The pro-Southern bloc abroad was on the lookout for any sign of Yankee disintegration. Yet the new draft was imperative. Lee had got away and the war could not be won without more men. Lincoln was caught between the dilemma's horns. He gave the order.

Finally the echo of Gettysburg came back from England.[16] The great victory had had its effect over there. August and the draft of 1863 came and went. It was very hot in Washington. The cabinet met regularly, discussed problems and made no decisions. Bates complained as he went home, "There is, in fact, *no cabinet.*" Lincoln was still a good listener, but he acted alone. On August 6, 1863, he told his secretary, John Hay, that the danger of war with England had passed—temporarily at least.

The draft for the Army did not meet the opposition some had prophesied. A few riots had occurred. In New York City the

322

police had been powerless before a mob until "Beast" Butler marched an army into the city and declared martial law. In the West draft officers had been killed, but in all cases order had been restored—the Federal authority upheld. Dapper, smart John Hay wrote hilariously to his fellow secretary, John G. Nicolay, who was on vacation:

"The draft fell pretty heavily in our end of town. William Johnson (cullud) was taken while polishing the Executive boots and rasping the Imperial Abolition whisker. Henry Stoddard is a conscript bold. You remember that good-natured shiny-faced darkey who used to be my special favorite a year ago at Willard's. He is gone, *en haut de la spout.* And the gorgeous headwaiter, G. Washington. A clerk in the War Department named Ramsey committed suicide on hearing he was drafted. Our friend Henry A. Blood was snatched from his jealous desk. . . . Bob [Lincoln] was so shattered by the wedding of the idol of all of us . . . that he rushed madly off to sympathize with nature in her sternest aspects [in the White Mountains]. . . .

"This town is as dismal now as a defaced tombstone. Everybody has gone. I am getting apathetic & write blackguardly articles for the *Chronicle* from which West extracts the dirt & fun & publishes the dreary remains. The Tycoon is in fine whack. I have rarely seen him more serene & busy. He is managing this war, the draft, foreign relations, and planning a reconstruction of the Union, all at once. I never knew with what tyrannous authority he rules the Cabinet, till now. The most important things he decides & there is no cavil. I am growing more and more firmly convinced that the good of the country absolutely demands that he should be kept where he is till this thing is over. There is no man in the country, so wise, so gentle and so firm. I believe the hand of God placed him where he is."[17]

The foreign relations to which John Hay referred were twofold. Lincoln had decided to slice into the blockaders' profits by conquering Texas and stopping the Matamoros trade as Welles had urged. At the same time Lincoln planned to teach all the diplomats in Washington a lesson that would discourage them forevermore from considering intervention seriously. For three years the foreign representatives had lived under the guns of the enemy. Daily they were reminded of the insecurity of the capital and of the Federal government. They did not know what was happening in the rest of the United States.

Lincoln invited all the foreign ministers to take a tour of the North. Let them see with their own eyes the boundless resources of the Union, the prosperity after three years of war. Far from the fighting front, mills and factories hummed at full capacity. Bumper crops of shocked wheat dotted thousands of golden acres. No one could see this and still believe that the North would not eventually triumph.

Seward conducted the grand tour. The frock-coated gentlemen went to New York, then up the Hudson to Albany, Utica, Rome, Syracuse, Schenectady and Sharon Springs. Rambling through the woods at Trenton Falls the diplomats had their pictures taken in high hats, sitting on the rocks beside the splashing water. In the hot weather of early fall the diplomats visited the Finger Lakes. Each day's ride disclosed new wonders of wealth, rich farms, factories with whirring wheels, miles and miles of railroad trains trundling freight, rivers, lakes and canals filled with vessels. In Buffalo the harbor swarmed with commerce.[18]

Seward was at his best on a holiday. He was brilliant, sophisticated, much traveled, and it dawned on some of the ministers that the Secretary of State was not the raucous fool he had at first appeared. As they became better acquainted their eyes opened. Had Seward's apparent anger in the past been genuine, or had he been bluffing for some calculated purpose? The diplomats agreed that they did not know. They also agreed that Seward was more subtle and humorous than they imagined. When asked a direct question Seward once answered, "If I did not know I would tell you." Diplomats admired a man who could say that. They also had to admit that his erratic policy of carrying a chip on his shoulder had been eminently successful. Especially did Mercier have an opportunity to measure the caliber of the man with whom his chief, Napoleon, was getting deeply entangled down in Mexico.

As this new understanding of Seward dawned on the diplomats, some of them began to suspect that Lincoln was playing the same game. Perhaps there had been a purpose in declaring an international blockade to cure a domestic insurrection. Perhaps Seward had been a trial balloon to test the wind for the President, an erratic fellow whose actions could be modified when they did not work. General John M. Palmer, who had known Lincoln in Illinois, went one morning to the White House and found the President in the barber chair. "If I had known at Chicago," Palmer bantered, "that this great rebellion was to occur, I would not have consented to go to a one-horse town like Springfield and take a one-horse lawyer and make him President."

Lincoln pushed the barber away. "Neither would I, Palmer," he replied. "If we had had a great man for the Presidency, one who had an inflexible policy and stuck to it, this rebellion would have succeeded, and the Southern Confederacy would have been established."[19]

When Seward got back from his personally conducted tour his clerks had many dispatches to call to his attention—some that must be discussed with Lincoln. A letter from Pike dated August 19, 1863, purported to give inside information on what Napoleon intended to do next in Mexico. Copies of Henry Hotze's *Index* disclosed that the editor had given up hope of propagandizing England further, but the ram building had not stopped. Hotze had turned his attention to France. The *Index* columns praised French imperialism.[20] Dispatches from Dayton gave more details of Napoleon's intentions in Mexico. The minister to France had interviewed Drouyn de L'Huys. Dayton summarized the conversation. He said that he had been assured that France sought no territorial acquisitions in America—the old story. De L'Huys assured him that the army would not interfere with the Mexicans' right to choose any form of government they desired. The plebiscite recently taken was not considered final. Napoleon would require a more general expression from the people. De L'Huys poohpoohed the idea that England would object to French dominion over Mexico. She might grumble, but if her interests were protected she would acquiesce. The Frenchman counted also on the "good sense of the people of the United States." Dayton warned Lincoln that he suspected Napoleon of duplicity. De L'Huys's conversation reminded him of Talleyrand's observation: "Language was to disguise thought." Certainly France was flirting with the Confederacy. The *Florida* had turned up in Brest and was being repaired there. Rumor said that Napoleon had negotiated a treaty with Slidell for the cession of Texas and perhaps Louisiana also. Another rumor stated that a counteralliance had been made between the North and Russia—the old threat that no one had been able to prove or disprove.[21] The Muscovite fleet had been watched suspiciously all summer. Observers reported now "on the best authority" that it was bound for Vera Cruz.

Lincoln and Seward both received the correspondence and made no comments. They knew Napoleon. As for the rumor about the Russian fleet—let the diplomats wonder. If Seward did not know anything about it he might tell them.

A dispatch from Dayton, dated four days after his report on the conference with De L'Huys, contained some spy information.[22] Mysterious men with intelligence for sale had pestered the legation for months, but this one was different. A Frenchman "of the Gascon type,"[23] small in stature, with glittering black eyes and hair which grew far down on his forehead, had offered to furnish the correspondence between Bulloch and the French shipbuilders. Did Seward believe that 15,000 francs would be suitable compensation?[24]

Lincoln was busy planning the state election canvass when Dayton's dispatch arrived. The political prospect looked worse than last year. Party chiefs told Lincoln the war-weary people blamed his administration. Lincoln spent much time in conference. Bigelow wrote before Dayton got a reply to his last dispatch. He said that he had decided to employ the Gascon. He had guaranteed the money and in return got a pack of correspondence written by the Southern commissioners. The letters showed without question that Napoleon had agreed to let the newly constructed vessels leave French ports under a French flag if their papers showed them to be bound for the China trade. Furthermore, the companies taking the contracts contained the names of many of Napoleon's associates, and it seemed probable that the Emperor himself had invested personally in the ventures. The letters disclosed, too, that the broker who had guaranteed the preliminary payments on the contracts, for a consideration of $50,000,[25] was the notorious Emil Erlanger, agent for the cotton loan.[26] So it was proved at last that Napoleon was playing with the South. His avowed friendship for the North was all hypocrisy.

Dayton and Bigelow read the spy's letters over and over, memorizing their contents. Then they requested an interview with De L'Huys. The evidence was spread before him. The big, athletic Frenchman was "surprised and vexed."[27] The Emperor, he shrugged, did not always confide in his minister. Would the Americans give him time to consider the situation?

Napoleon was at Biarritz during the hot weather. At Villa Eugénie the windows framed gorgeous views of the Bay of Biscay and the towering Pyrenees. His court was the gayest in all Europe. John Slidell was down there also, enjoying the fashionable watering place, strengthening his ties between the Confederacy and France. His family had joined the imperial set. They reveled in banquets, games, displays and grand balls. The tall, white-headed New York adventurer and his Creole wife were favorites with the Empress. Slidell's checkered life was not unlike Napoleon's. Already he had married one daughter to Baron d'Erlanger. He married his other daughter to Comte Saint-Romain. His granddaughter by this marriage became the wife of Colonel Marchand, famous a generation later for causing an incident that came near precipitating a war between France and England at Fashoda in Africa.[28]

Back in Paris, Dayton and Bigelow realized that they were at a disadvantage. While they were debating what next to do, a dispatch arrived from London. Adams and Morse wanted a clue traced to its source in France. For months they had been working, quietly accumulating evidence against the rams being built in English yards. They had employed spies to watch the construction. Some of them worked regularly on the vessels.[29] Many suspicious facts were in the legation files, but the true ownership of the rams was still unknown. The builders maintained that the work was done for a Frenchman. Lord Palmerston accepted this story and told it to the House of Commons. Adams doubted it. Could the Paris legation verify the story?

Dayton went to see De L'Huys. The French Foreign Secretary said he believed that the rams were being built for the Pasha of Egypt—a likely enough assumption. Frenchmen building the Suez Canal worked in close conjunction with the Pasha.[30] Adams was baffled but still unconvinced.

Details of the investigation arrived in Washington. Lincoln discussed them with his cabinet. All agreed that the rams must not get away—that they alone might break the blockade. Belligerent Secretaries, flushed with the victories at Gettysburg and Vicksburg, thumped the table with their fists. The United States must take a strong stand, threaten war if necessary to keep the rams from leaving. Lincoln became sad-eyed under the bombardment— calm and absent-minded. The final lists of casualties had come in from Gettysburg and Vicksburg. They were appalling. The new draft reached into almost every Northern family. Blood, blood, blood. Better one war at a time. Seward, too, had a faraway look in his eyes. Both men seemed ready to let the rams put to sea without doing anything about it except remonstrate. Even Welles, always rigid in insistence on international rights, abstained from the discussion. The war party was at its wits' ends. Secretary Chase, with solemn mien and Websterian brow, stood up to his majestic height. The rams, he said, must be stopped at any cost. The Civil War might yet be lost by a weak foreign policy.

After the cabinet meeting Chase went to see Welles. The Secretary of the Navy, he knew, did not often agree with Seward's conciliatory policy. Warships, Chase urged, must be sent to England at once to intercept the rams when they cleared the neutral zone. Welles demurred. He was tantalizingly evasive, as he had been at the meeting. He dared not tell about a secret agreement known only to Lincoln, Seward and himself. In strictest confidence Seward had whispered that the armored vessels would not be allowed to leave England.[31] Welles was skeptical about Seward's assurance but he had to give it a trial. To Chase he replied that no warships were available. Chase went away unhappy and perplexed.

Work on the rams rushed along at top speed. In shop and forge and shipyard there was no indication that the vessels would be stopped. Had not British courts ruled against Earl Russell's order to hold the *Alexandra?* The first ram neared completion and a vessel from the Confederacy sailed into Liverpool with passengers. Spies reported to Minister Adams that British ships, at anchor along the way, dipped their colors to salute her. The passengers, seamen said, were really a crew for the new ram.

Earl Russell, too, learned about this demonstration from the seafaring population of Liverpool. These people had money and votes. Their wishes could not be ignored, yet many Englishmen, not seafarers, favored stopping the rams. Politician Russell began to count his ballots before they were cast. The Emancipation Society had prayed for the government to act.[32] Were the pro-Union Englishmen as powerful politically as the shipping interests? Would it be wise to defy the ruling of the court? John Bright could bluster about the bestiality of British courts, but he was not a member of the government. Russell's fishy eyes studied the ceiling. On September 3, 1863, he wrote his chief, "The conduct of the gentlemen who have contracted for the two ironclads at Birkenhead is so very suspicious . . . that I have thought it necessary to direct that they should be detained"—an unconstitutional act in face of the court's decision in the *Alexandra* case. Russell explained the infraction "as one of policy though not of strict law. . . . If we have to pay damages, we have satisfied the opinion which prevails here as well as in America that that kind of neutral hostility should not be allowed to go on without some attempt to stop it."[33]

Charles Francis Adams did not know about this correspondence. Two days later he wrote a famous dispatch insisting that the rams be stopped: "It would be superfluous in me to point out to your lordship that this is war!" A reply[34] to the ultimatum came from Earl Russell on September 8: "Instructions have been issued which will prevent the departure of the two ironclad vessels from Liverpool."[35] The legation boys read the cold formal words and told each other that England had been frightened into submission.

Earl Russell was not happy about the decision. In case the contractors brought suit the government might have to pay large damages. A month dragged by. The Lairds asked for permission to take the ram most nearly completed on a trial trip. October 9 was foggy—thick as the "mulligatawny soup" fog which had saved Bulloch twice before—once when he ran the blockade into Savannah and again when he got away with the *Alabama*. Perhaps the fog would help him again!

Earl Russell took no chances. The ironclad ram had a vicious reputation. Three gunboats were ordered to stations near by. Two British ships, of sixty guns each, were detailed to guard the passage down the Mersey. The *Prince Consort* was cleared for action and held in reserve. Then a file of marines marched briskly into the yards. In the ghostly fog they clambered aboard the dripping deck of the iron terror and took her in the name of the Queen.[36] The unfinished vessel was also seized.

Bulloch, the last of the Confederate agents to lose confidence in England, saw that his sun had set. Only in France could he hope to continue his shipbuilding program. The comfortable clubrooms he and his friends had maintained in Liverpool were closed.

In America the news of Russell's action was slow to arrive. Many Americans, drunk with the triumphs at Gettysburg and Vicksburg, talked belligerently about fighting England. John Hay remembered dining with Gustavus Fox, Assistant Secretary of the Navy, General Hooker and other officers. Fox was a seagoing Secretary. He had sailed with the fleet that tried to relieve Fort Sumter. At his desk in the Navy Department he was as uncompromising toward Great Britain as his chief Gideon Welles. At the dinner with John Hay everybody had something to say against England. "When the time comes," said Fox, "a publication will be made of insults and wrongs on every sea—of ports closed to us and opened to the enemy, of flags dipped to them and insultingly immovable to us, of courtesies ostentatiously shown them and brutally denied us—that will make the blood of every American boil in his brain-pan. We shall have men enough when this thing is over."

"We will be the greatest military power on earth," Hooker replied, his face flushed with ardor and strong drink, "greatest in numbers, in capability, in dash, in spirit, in intelligence of the soldiery. These fine fellows who have gotten a taste of campaigning in the last three years will not go back to plowing, and spinning and trading, and hewing wood and drawing water. They are spoiled for that and shaped for better work."

John Hay listened with interest. The United States had been an aggressive military nation since the days of the Mexican War. These fighting men who had come to the front seemed to have no limits to their ambitions. "We will make no fight on Canada," Fox continued, "that will fall of itself. But we will cast our eyes at Bermuda, at Nassau, at the islands that infest our coast."[37] Demands for war with Britain increased almost daily as autumn passed and no word came to America announcing that the rams were stopped. Even James Russell Lowell in New England wrote to Thomas Hughes, now busy lecturing as well as distributing flour to the needy in Lancashire factory towns. The United States, said Lowell, does not want war, but "if the rebel iron-clads are allowed to come out, there might be a change."[38] Lincoln, as usual, let sleeping dogs rest. Like the others, he did not know that the rams had been stopped, but he did know about Seward's secret agreement. Then word was received that Mrs. Lincoln had lost another brother, Alex, fighting for the Confederacy at Baton Rouge[39]—one brother, Sam, killed at Shiloh in 1862; another, David, invalided for life in the fight near Vicksburg; now Alex! The accumulated shocks and disasters following the carriage accident seemed to be affecting Mrs. Lincoln's mind as the doctors had predicted. Lincoln sent her to New York for a change of scene. The big stores and the resort at Long Branch, New Jersey, usually diverted her. Lincoln himself turned to the foreign problems that always waited on his desk. Rumors from Russia indicated that all was not well between Cash Clay and Henry Bergh. The latter, hurt as Bayard Taylor had been, by appointment to a subordinate post, longed for an opportunity to make a name for himself as minister. For a time he found relief performing the duties of Vice-Consul. The title was vaguely reminiscent of Bonaparte, and sounded better than Secretary of Legation, but this exalted nomenclature did not alter the fact that he was the subordinate to a Kentuckian who sometimes received guests at the legation in his shirt sleeves. Bergh, with all his zeal, felt that he had scored only one diplomatic victory. With the aid of his wife he had flung open all the legation windows and thus broken precedent and assured better health for the staff.[40] Lincoln would be lucky if the New Yorker confined himself to such inconsequential acts. The next dispatch bag from Russia might bring some unexpected story, highly entertaining if not tragic, when such a man was stationed with Cash Clay in far-off Russia.

The old problem of Negro colonization came to Lincoln's notice again as he waited. A plan for sending black bond servants to Surinam interested him.[41] A letter from Garibaldi offering his services received no consideration.[42] Daily the newspapers cheered the war spirit with grandiose threats of awful vengeance in case the rams escaped. War tension mounted. No one knew that the rams had been seized. Before they learned the news a startling thing occurred. The Russian fleet steamed into New York harbor. The wild, terrible rumor had materialized! Manhattan effervesced. Muscovite officers drove up Broadway in victorias surrounded by soldiers.[43] The merchants of the metropolis tendered a grand banquet to the visitors.[44] At a ball, the youth and beauty of the city vied with one another for dances with the resplendent foreigners. On November 21, 1863, *Harper's Weekly* reported:

"Alas! for the Russians. It is known, or should be, that these Sclavic [*sic*] heroes are not the very largest of the human race— that they are small men in fact—and what is to become of small men in such a jam? Early in the night—indeed, very soon after the dance began—we saw several of them in the embrace of grand nebulous masses of muslin and crinoline, whirled hither and thither as if in terrible torment, their eyes aglare, their hair blown out, and all their persons expressive of the most desperate energy, doubtless in the endeavor to escape."[45]

So small did one Russian officer appear beside his hoop-skirted American companion that an onlooker was reminded of "a red Indian beside his teepee." Compared to Americans the Russians might be small in stature, but New Yorkers knew that cannon equalized the size of men and the Muscovite fleet bristled with gaping guns. Bad news from the South made the Russian visit most opportune. At Chickamauga General Rosecrans had been stopped by the Confederates in a terrific battle. Reports said that he was making a masterly retreat—another masterly retreat. More long lists of casualties. The people in Washington had nothing to celebrate this time. Hurrah for the Russians!

Lincoln read the full details of Chickamauga in the War Department telegraph office. He wired Mrs. Lincoln in New York that she had lost another member of her family[46]—a brother-in-law— the third to die for the cause her husband was elected to crush.[47] Europe, Lincoln knew, would follow the defeat with new demands from the government—new humiliations. This time his reply would be different. Hurrah for the Russians! Secretary Welles, in the privacy of his room, wrote in his diary:

"In sending them to this country at this time there is something significant. What will be its effect on France and the French policy we shall learn in due time. It may moderate; it may exasperate. God bless the Russians."[48]

Some newspapers, with accounts of the disaster at Chickamauga still glaring from their pages, suggested an alliance with the Czar. Make the whole rumor good! *Harper's Weekly*[49] printed an editorial favoring such a treaty. Readers were warned that the times had changed since Washington admonished his countrymen against foreign alliances. Russia and America had much in common. Said the editor: "Certainly the least of the purposes which they [Russia and America] could achieve would be to keep the peace of the world."

In Washington, when the arrival of the Russian fleet was announced, the cabinet was summoned. The men took their places on chairs and the sofa. Lincoln did not attend. Seward called the cabinet to order. He had an important announcement, he said. A dramatic pause. Everyone was thinking about the Russians. England, said Seward, with a wise nod, had thought it best to stop the armored rams.

The meeting adjourned. The Secretaries trudged down the White House stairs, got in their carriages at the portico. Welles, slim, and silent behind his beard, scoffed to himself at the cheap dramatics of the Secretary of State—grand diplomacy, buncombe—to make Britain's order appear like fear of a secret agreement with Russia.

Members of the legations were still baffled. They remembered Seward's grand tour. Was there or was there not a secret treaty? Seward was such a sly dog and so was Lincoln.[50] Perhaps both of them had been playing with the diplomats from the beginning, judging with canny insight when to be belligerent and when to be conciliatory, always watching, always taking advantage of the fears and jealousies of European countries toward one another.

Russia's Pacific fleet had also arrived in San Francisco.

# XVII. *Lincoln Tells Europe*

INCOLN lay in bed in the White House, propped up with pillows, reading his mail. All that day of November 2, 1863, reports had come in from the state elections. They were worse than last year, and Lincoln's party had lost ground then. Lincoln laid one set of figures on the coverlet and took up another. If the trend against his administration did not change, his enemies would control Congress. For two months Lincoln had been consulting politicians from doubtful states. The Emancipation Proclamation had cost him many votes. Among the papers a letter from General Schenck caught Lincoln's eye. It must be answered at once.

Lincoln threw back the covers and swung his long bare feet onto the carpet. The mantel clock's hands pointed to midnight and it was chilly. Lincoln put on an overcoat and strode down the hall blinking sleepily. He crossed the deserted reception room, rank with the smell of stale tobacco smoke. Stepping into his office he saw a light in John Hay's room. His secretary was still working. Lincoln fumbled through the papers littering his desk, found the ones he wanted and gave them to Hay to be forwarded at once. Then the President strode back to bed.[1]

The situation in Europe appeared more favorable than in America. Ever since Chickamauga, Rosecrans' army had been shut in Chattanooga, almost surrounded by the enemy. The whole army might be lost. The thought was terrible! Meanwhile Pike wrote cheerily from The Hague that the shadow of Poland made all Europe draw back from American affairs. Wasn't it splendid! Both Napoleon and Palmerston were scurrying to diplomatic cyclone cellars. The arrival of the Russian fleet in New York disconcerted them. Pike believed Lincoln strong enough to oust Spain from Dominica. That would chill Napoleon's ardor in Mexico.[2]

Lincoln's first task was to win the election at home and relieve Rosecrans. Abroad he had stopped the rams. That was enough

333

for the present. France could be handled alone if both Britain and Russia were on the American side; but Poland might force Britain into the arms of Napoleon. Lincoln and Seward had been watching that danger for some time. They had continued to curry favor with the English—contrary to Welles's principles—since the rams had been stopped. When sure of their power they hoped to tell the Emperor to intern the *Florida,* then in French waters, and to stop the Confederate ships being built at Brest and Nantes. Then, finally, they might order him out of Mexico.

Secretary Welles stood squarely in the path of this plan precisely as he had during the *Peterhoff* trouble in April. Lincoln called him to the White House. Welles arrived at noon. Seward was reading to the President some dispatches he wanted to send by the next boat.[3] The two men showed Welles some letters for Motley, Dayton and others. Then they broached the subject on their minds. Seward said he had made a secret agreement with England last May—immediately after the *Peterhoff* affair—not to confiscate captured ships until all points of law were settled. He had just learned that the British ship *Emma,* recently sent in as a prize, had been bought by the Navy before adjudication. He hoped that she might be returned at once. Lincoln added that the Secretary of State's agreement "should be considered."

Welles sputtered. The Navy needed the ship. She was already altered beyond recognition. Why had not Seward told him of the agreement? At last Welles consented. He was learning as Seward had that "the President is the best of us all."

The next mailbag from abroad brought a new dispatch from Dayton. He reported another long "conversation" with De L'Huys. France was conciliatory now. Perhaps Napoleon saw that Lincoln had gained England's friendship past all possibility of retraction. Or perhaps diplomacy was a horse race to Napoleon— now one country ahead, now another. In any event the Emperor wanted to talk business, but it was plain from Dayton's letter that the Frenchman hoped to drive a hard bargain. The *Florida,* said De L'Huys, had come into France as a Confederate vessel. She was entitled to repairs necessary for navigation but not munitions. This was Napoleon's first point on which he could give a concession. As for the Confederate ships being built in French yards, evidence showed them to be for the China trade—armored for defense against Chinese pirates, *n'est-ce pas?* Here was a second point on which the Emperor might negotiate. As for Mexico, De L'Huys assured the American minister, the Emperor had no designs there. All Napoleon wanted was an acknowledgment that Maximilian would be recognized if the Mexican people voted to place him on Montezuma's throne. If Lincoln would agree to this, the French army would withdraw at once and let the new government take care of itself. However—and here was a threat—France would not lead or tempt the Archduke into any difficulty and then desert him.

The bribe was thinly veiled. If Lincoln would sacrifice Mexico and give up the Monroe Doctrine, which he was unable to enforce, then he could deal advantageously with Napoleon. A few days later word was received that De L'Huys had feigned anger or at least annoyance. The American warship *Kearsarge* had steamed into Brest, to lie at anchor under full steam ready to follow the *Florida* whenever she might leave French waters. This was contrary to the rule insisted on by the maritime powers. Did the Americans intend to defy France?

Then came another dispatch indicating that Napoleon was not so arrogant. Mexican successes had not stemmed the liberal tide at home. In the Corps Législatif the Left had increased its seats,[4] and some officers in the French army opposed the Mexican aggression.[5]

Perhaps France was brewing the same trouble in Mexico that Spain found in Santo Domingo. If France and England could be kept apart, the Monroe Doctrine might uphold itself.

Reports from England showed Lincoln to be holding his own there. This gave him strength to strike at France. On October 9, 1863, Henry Ward Beecher had made a great speech at Free-Trade Hall, Manchester, the heart of the country where the Civil War had borne most heavily upon British workmen, and where John Bright's following was strongest. The meeting had been preceded by a battle royal in the press between friends of the Confederacy and the Union and Emancipation Society. An audience of six thousand assembled. The people were electrified by the impending threat of war over Poland and the known disposition of the

United States to oppose France. John Bright was not present. Instead he sent a letter regretting his absence. Beecher was introduced. He stepped to the center of the platform. A thunder of applause mingled with hisses broke over his head. Beecher waited until silence was restored. Then he began to speak.

For two and a half hours the preacher spun his oratorical enchantments. First he flattered the assembly. He was happy, he said, to be able to speak in Manchester, for "where else, more than in these great central portions of England, have the doctrines of human rights been battled for, and where else have there been gained for them nobler victories than here?"[6] Britain, he said, had planted the kernel of liberal ideas in America.

"The seed corn we got in England, and if, on a larger sphere, and under circumstances of unobstruction, we have reared mightier sheaves, every sheaf contains the grain that has made old England rich for a hundred years."[7]

The war in America for civil liberty, continued Beecher, would be worth all it cost if more democracy resulted, with liberty of speech, of the press, common schools for all, division of great plantations into a plot for each.[8] The people cheered.

This was distribution of wealth—John Bright's class struggle against every Tory landlord in England.

Beecher next explained the American democratic Constitution and the peculiar growth of slavery under it, how abolition had originated in the South and become unpopular when cotton rose in value. The Civil War, he said, was the result of a section's fear of losing its political power to extend slavery. Slavery, therefore, was the mother of the rebellion.[9] The explanation was simple, impassioned and what the people wanted to hear. Beecher knew that many Dissenting ministers were in the audience. He knew the people's devotion to evangelism. With an orator's intuition he delivered a sarcastic climax. Had not Vice-President Stephens, of the Confederacy, said that the subjugation of an inferior race was the only proper way to maintain the liberty of a superior one, thus teaching Calvary a new lesson?

Henry Ward Beecher's speech was published at once in America for propaganda purposes by James Redpath, a Scotch immigrant abolitionist whose bloody pen had stabbed slavery in Kansas back in the days when Lincoln had first decided to fight the extension of the institution. A propagandist always, Redpath would live to father Memorial Day and to conduct lyceum circuits which in time grew into Chautauqua entertainments. On the back cover of his publication of Beecher's Manchester speech Redpath printed Wendell Phillips' "Toussaint L'Ouverture"—panegyric to the Negro who ranked "in the clear blue" above Washington, because the latter held slaves.

Friends of the Confederacy in England made no reply. The Emancipation Proclamation had sunk into the nation's conscience at last.

For Lincoln, the European situation was good—very good—especially with the storm rumbling over Poland. Something, however, must be done to save Rosecrans at Chattanooga. Lincoln promoted Grant to supreme command in the West. His battles at Forts Henry and Donelson, Shiloh and Vicksburg, had already made him a popular hero—"Unconditional Surrender" Grant. For the new commander, Lincoln reorganized the Army. Part of the Army of the Potomac was loaded on cars and sent with Hooker as reinforcements—a gigantic military maneuver. In the midst of it Lincoln received three messages that stood out from the routine memoranda on his desk. The United States Circuit Court in California had convicted Albert Rubery, the "foolish" young Englishman, and his two companions; the Negro colony on Ile Vache was in a bad way; and the committee in charge of dedicating the cemetery at Gettysburg requested the President to make a "few appropriate remarks."

Lincoln considered the problems before him. The case against Rubery and his accomplices was conclusive. They had been sentenced to ten years in prison and a fine of $10,000.[10] A splendid lesson for traitors in California, yet John Bright wanted the man pardoned, and England's friendship was vital.[11]

The Negro colony had not worked. Seward was right! The hallelujahs had scarcely died out as the pilgrims steamed into the Atlantic before smallpox laid low many of the passengers. On the island ill fortune persisted. The Negroes shirked their work. No crop had been raised. Reports said that the colonists were on the verge of starvation, weak and dying in miserable palm-leaf huts.

Lincoln dispatched a special agent to investigate the Negro colony. He accepted the invitation to speak at Gettysburg, and he ignored the Rubery case. Edward Everett, former president of Harvard and America's outstanding orator, was scheduled to deliver the main address at the cemetery. Without doubt it would be a masterpiece. Everyone knew that Lincoln was too busy to give more than "a few appropriate remarks." In addition to the war and shaking the hands of a constant stream of callers, Lincoln had also to prepare a message for Congress. In odd moments he jotted down ideas to be expressed at Gettysburg. William Evans, an English liberal who had come to America to view firsthand the American experiment in democracy, called at the White House on the day after Lincoln had agreed to speak. The Englishman impressed on the President the fact that the Civil War was a battle for democracy for all the world. England, he said, understood this better that it was understood in America.[12]

Lincoln remembered the democratic fervor of Henry Ward Beecher's speeches in England. John M. Forbes had also written about the hunger of all liberals for republicanism. Forbes urged Sumner to impress on Lincoln the importance of interpreting the American war as a class struggle:

". . . the Aristocrats and the Despots of the old world see that our quarrel is that of the People against an Aristocracy."[13]

Lincoln scribbled notes for his speech at Gettysburg and pocketed them. Daily he made the rounds of the State and War Departments. Leaves on the sidewalks rustled under his slow shuffling feet. The bare trees of autumn helped the Northern soldiers. Bushwhackers could no longer shoot and get away unseen. Meade's army watched Lee. Burnside's army waited for Grant to relieve the beleaguered forces in Chattanooga. When that was done, then Burnside and Grant might liberate all the loyal people in the mountains of eastern Tennessee. Banks was moving toward Brownsville to close the port of entry at Matamoros and pare down Britain's contraband profit.

On November 7, 1863, the newspapers announced that Henry Ward Beecher had delivered another smashing speech—this time at Liverpool, heart of the shipbuilding area. Newsmen had predicted a riot, but the Tories had been unable to excite the workers even in this center of war profits. Democracy had triumphed completely. Lincoln took a scrap of paper from his pocket and wrote a note, crossed out a phrase, wrote another—an idea to be expressed at Gettysburg.

Soon news came from England that the Court of Exchequer had reviewed Palmerston's appeal from the adverse decision of last June in the *Alexandra* case. The original verdict was confirmed. Palmerston and Russell were in error.[14] They had exceeded their authority when they stopped a vessel on suspicion. Luckily the rams had been purchased and the government was protected on that score, but Lincoln noticed that British courts would give him no help.

Lincoln had seen courts in America rule against popular will. He had been elected President by a party determined to reverse a decision of the Supreme Court in the case of Dred Scott. However, Englishmen were better disciplined than Americans. They might acquiesce. In fact a Confederate revival already appeared in Britain—the old specter—Napoleon still schemed to get England back on his side! A. Dudley Mann left his post in Belgium to appeal in person to the Pope at Rome to check enlistments of Catholics in the Northern Army.[15] A new society, the Southern Independence Association, had begun an "educational" campaign on the American question under the direction of James Spence and Beresford Beresford-Hope. Wealthy Britishers, some of whose fortunes had been made running the blockade, contributed to the work. These gentlemen were ambitious, confident but handicapped. The emancipation societies had almost a year's start on them. However, the Southern sympathizers organized meetings in thirty-one English and Scottish towns, mainly in the manufacturing districts.[16] From now on, meetings could be counted to fight meetings from one end of the British Isles to the other.

The first Independence Association assemblies were open to the public. Workingmen heckled the proslavery speakers without mercy. To prevent such ungenteel conduct, admission was charged to keep out rowdies. Thereafter "gentlemen" talked to partially filled benches of believers. Near by, packed houses listened to abolitionists.

Reading reports of all this, Lincoln turned with twinkling eyes to work on his Gettysburg Address. He knew which of the British meetings were preparing a seedbed for democracy.

As time approached for the dedication of the cemetery it became painfully plain that the people did not expect much from Abraham Lincoln. The only great state paper from his pen so far had been the first inaugural, and that was attributed to others. Lincoln, however, took seriously the "few appropriate remarks" he was scheduled to give. Constantly he wrote sentences, ideas, left them half-finished, had his picture taken, discussed the latest war developments—which were bad around Chattanooga.

The President was scheduled to leave for Gettysburg on November 18, 1863. That morning little Tad did not come to breakfast. He was ill. Grant was ill too—deadlocked at Chattanooga. Mrs. Lincoln became hysterical. The doctors shook their heads over Tad's malady. They had acted the same way before Willie died. Lincoln drove away from the White House, his sad face sunk on his breast. Friends waited for him at the special train. The locomotive was decorated with gay streamers. A third of the last car had been partitioned into a room for the President and his guests. Seward was there and so were Cameron and Nicolay and Hay. Welles and Stanton had declined—too busy, they said. Lincoln's pressman, John W. Forney, came with notebook and pencil. Only a few diplomats joined the party, but France was well represented. There was Admiral Renaud from the French navy, and Italian Chevalier Bertinatti and Henri Mercier, Napoleon's official and quasi-unofficial envoys, all gracious, bright-eyed, with ears alert for clues to future action against France—hopeful that Britain would swing back on their side. Army officers and other dignitaries filled the special coaches.[17]

At Gettysburg that night Lincoln dined with Edward Everett. At the table sat most of the suite who had accompanied him from Washington and in addition Governor Curtin of Pennsylvania, Lincoln's accomplice in escaping from Harrisburg over two years ago. Curtin was still the beau ideal of manhood anywhere. But two years had changed Lincoln. War and worry had cut deep scars across his forehead and around his sensitive mouth. Edward Everett, former president of Harvard, watched Lincoln critically. He had anticipated a taint of backwoods boorishness. Later he remembered that in manners and conversation Lincoln was the peer of any man at the table.[18]

Outside on the dark streets yellow lights shone from the windows of the hundred houses that made up the village of Gettysburg. Whisky circulated freely. Politicians stamped up and down stairs to one another's lodgings, sampled one another's bottles, talked loudly. Lincoln was called out for a speech. He stood in the doorway for a moment, said a few inconsequential words, and retired to his bedroom, his scraps of paper, his worries about his wife, Tad and Grant.

On the morrow the marshals organized a parade. Women in bonnets and shawls thronged the sidewalks, swept the dirt road with their long dresses, held up their children to see. A magnificent chestnut charger was led out for the President to ride. As the mettled animal pawed the ground Lincoln was handed a telegram. He read it, fixed his stovepipe hat firmly on his head, and swung into the saddle. Lincoln felt good. The wire from Stanton stated that Tad was better, that Grant had started a great battle at Chattanooga. Brownsville, opposite Matamoros, had also fallen into Federal hands.

The parade moved off down the village street between white picket fences. People noticed that Lincoln was strangely graceful on horseback, his long legs accustomed to the saddle. Beside him rode bodyguard Lamon and Secretary Seward. A few minutes later they arrived at the cemetery. Fifteen thousand people had congregated before the platform. Seward's trousers had worked up his legs, showing gray yarn socks.

Edward Everett spoke for two hours, holding the audience with the music of his voice. On the platform behind him Lincoln sat with other dignitaries, including the French admiral, Mercier and Bertinatti. Once during the address the audience noticed the President stir in his chair. He took out his steel-bowed spectacles, put them on his nose, took two pages of manuscript from his pocket, looked them over and put them back. At last the orator of the day finished. The Baltimore Glee Club rendered a selection. Then Ward Hill Lamon got up from his chair and announced, "The President of the United States."

Lincoln, tall and awkward, shambled forward with his peculiar flat-footed stride. He paused in the center of the platform and drew a manuscript from his frock coat. His high-pitched voice was tuned to prairies of upturned faces. Out West he knew one open flat capable of holding all the people in the world. To mankind everywhere his clarion voice rang out:

"Fourscore and seven years ago our fathers brought forth on this continent a new nation, conceived in liberty, and dedicated to the proposition that all men are created equal.

"Now we are engaged in a great civil war, testing whether that nation, or any nation so conceived and so dedicated, can long endure. We are met on a great battle-field of that war. We have come to dedicate a portion of that field as a final resting-place for those who here gave their lives that that nation might live. It is altogether fitting and proper that we should do this.

"But, in a larger sense, we cannot dedicate—we cannot consecrate—we cannot hallow—this ground. The brave men, living and dead, who struggled here, have consecrated it far above our poor power to add or detract. The world will little note nor long remember what we say here, but it can never forget what they did here. It is for us, the living, rather, to be dedicated here to the unfinished work which they who fought here have thus far so nobly advanced. It is rather for us to be here dedicated to the great task remaining before us—that from these honored dead we take increased devotion to that cause for which they gave the last full measure of devotion; that we here highly resolve that these dead shall not have died in vain; that this nation, under God, shall have a new birth of freedom; and that government of the people, by the people, for the people, shall not perish from the earth."[19]

The speech was telegraphed across the country. Newspapers reported it according to their political biases. The American correspondent of the London *Times,* as much out of step with the English people as *Punch* had been, wrote: "The ceremony was rendered ludicrous by some of the sallies of that poor President Lincoln. . . . Anything more dull and commonplace it would not be easy to produce."[20] Duvergier de Hauranne, ardent *républicain* who had come to the United States to see why democracy worked in America and failed in France, pronounced the Gettysburg Address the "most elevated of modern eloquence."[21]

In Massachusetts the *Springfield Republican* printed the message and admonished its readers: "Turn back and read it over, it will repay study as a model speech. Strong feelings and a large brain were its parents." *Harper's Weekly* reported: "The few words of the President were from the heart to the heart. They can not be read, even, without kindling emotion."

John W. Forney, Lincoln's pressman, set up the speech in a pamphlet for distribution, the first separate printing given it. M. Mercier could send a copy to Napoleon. It explained exactly what Lincoln had in mind. Stuffy lords in the English Parliament would shiver a little when they read it. So short, so complete. English school children could memorize every word, French liberals could translate every sentence. The echo of the Emancipation Proclamation blended perfectly with this symphony from the graves of men determined to be free. A democracy dedicated to the proposition that all men are created equal must endure.

Lincoln started back to Washington at once. His head ached and he lay down in the train drawing room. A cold towel across his forehead gave him some relief. At midnight a light still burned in the War Department but no word of importance had come from Chattanooga. In the morning Lincoln felt worse. His skin was hot, dry and feverish. Tad came running to jump on him, climb his spare frame, shout with his deformed palate, "Papa-day!" Lincoln stroked the little fellow's hair. The President felt very tired and the fever throbbed in his temples.

Across the Atlantic, in England, John Bright was writing another letter to Charles Sumner. Bright had heard about the conviction of Albert Rubery, "the foolish young man." He hoped that something could be done for him. Lincoln had a reputation for charity. Surely an English liberal's prayer would be answered.

During the days that Bright's letter traveled slowly by train and packet across England, the Atlantic and the Eastern states, Lincoln watched and waited for news from Grant. His doctor warned him that he must get more rest, refuse to see office seekers, quit handshaking. He had contracted a mild case of smallpox—

not serious but not to be trifled with. Lincoln smiled wanly. "Now I have something that I can give to everybody,"[22] he said. On November 22, 1863, Norman Judd called. Lincoln, unwilling to go to bed, insisted that his minister to Prussia be admitted. Judd came in, his face naturally as red beneath a thatch of thin silky hair[23] as Lincoln's with fever. Judd had been unhappy in Europe. A big businessman, organizer of railways, he longed for American enterprise and the hurly-burly of politics.[24] The sweetness of his reward for successfully aiding Lincoln's nomination had cloyed in his mouth. Lincoln talked with him, told a few stories. Then the stout little Illinoisan left, content to return to Berlin.

After dinner Seward came to the White House with a dispatch from another minister who had also once come home unhappy but who was now back working cheerily at his post. Cash Clay had sent a long document explaining the whole field of American politics, European diplomacy and naval improvements of the century. Seward read it out loud so Lincoln could laugh with him. "This man is certainly the most wonderful ass of the age," said John Hay when Seward had finished. Hay recalled that Clay's previous dispatch from Russia had been a diatribe against Sumner's recent address on foreign relations. Clay had concluded the dispatch in regular diplomatic style: "You will read this to Mr. Sumner and if he desires it, give him a copy."

"It is saddening to think of the effect of prosperity on such a man,"[25] said Seward.

Clay's antics relieved the war tension. The men forgot Grant and Chattanooga momentarily. The group broke up in good humor. None mentioned the tragedy that all feared in the Southern mountains. Leaving Lincoln with his worries in the White House was like leaving a sick man in a hospital after all hope was gone—everyone brave, resigned, hiding great anxiety under little pleasantries.

At last news came from Chattanooga. The Union forces had met reverses. Grant's star, bright as it had been, might yet fade in the infinity of Northern defeats. Lincoln waited for more complete reports. On November 24, 1863, Seward bustled in with a paper. Was it the latest from the battle? No, just a strong letter of remonstrance to Tassara, warning Spain not to interfere in

Santo Domingo where revolutionists threatened to oust the conquerors. Seward always talked rough when things looked the worst. Lincoln approved the letter,[26] then turned to the battle reports. Things seemed to be going better but Lincoln still worried. No decisive news came through from Chattanooga that night.

The following day the battle ended, finished by a queer quirk of war. The Northern soldiers had got out of hand. Without orders they had charged and routed the enemy from supposedly impregnable works on Missionary Ridge. A near defeat became one of the great victories of the war. In Washington on the night of November 25, 1863, the harvest moon rose at sunset out of the Potomac and frosted the White House where Lincoln waited anxiously. Looking from his window across the shimmering water, the President did not know that that same moon looked down on the bivouac fires of thousands of happy Yankees, dancing, shouting, singing in the deserted Confederate lines.

Soon the good news came dripping from the telegraph needle. Boys shouted it up and down Pennsylvania Avenue. Grant had saved the day once more. Lincoln went to bed—a bilious attack.[27] He had been under a strain for a long time and had never fully recovered from his illness. On his back Lincoln stared at the ceiling. The South was crippled badly now. It would fall. Then the United States could turn against imperial Mexico. Only one great foreign danger remained. Suppose France made an alliance with the Confederacy.

The next packet from abroad brought news that the dread alliance was consummated. Consul Morse's secret service in London had unearthed the story—undoubtedly trustworthy—although Morse said that he could not divulge the source.[28] Lincoln and Seward both read the report. Could it be true? They had received so many false reports of such an alliance!

Three days later ships from the Russian fleet steamed up the Potomac. Secretary Seward welcomed them. Secretary Welles entertained the commanders and ordered the American officers "to show them all proper courtesy."[29]

"They have vast absorbent powers," John Hay reported, "and are fiendishly ugly."[30] At night the Russians went to the theater, lolled in the proscenium boxes, "disgustingly tight and demonstrative."[31] Mercier, excessively gracious toward the administration of late, remembered Seward's grand tour. He watched the Secretary of State display himself openly with the Russian officers. The Frenchman exclaimed, *"Il est très sage!"* John Hay wrote in his diary, "The diplomatic body have all apparently stopped blackguarding and those who do not like have been forced to respect."[32] Russian guns had made the most recalcitrant diplomats understand the Gettysburg Address.

While Mercier squirmed under this pressure, Lincoln took time to consider the request of John Bright concerning the youth Rubery, lately convicted privateer in San Francisco. Here was another chance to make France uncomfortable by currying favor with England. Lincoln prepared and signed a long formal document. Rubery was pardoned on the ground that he was not of age, was a British subject, and "his pardon is desired by John Bright."[33] A copy was printed in the San Francisco papers, and recopied in the East.[34] John Bright was delighted when he read it. To Sumner he wrote, "I have not heard the subject spoken of in any society in England where it has not produced a kindly feeling towards the President and towards the Government of the United States." Bright said further that Rubery's sister had worried herself to the verge of insanity by the boy's conviction. Now the good news had restored her health.[35]

Liberated from jail, the "foolish young man" embarked on new exploits—a diamond hoax in Montana, some libel suits against English newspapers for defaming his character. Finally he sailed to Australia where fewer restrictions were put on high adventure.[36] What happened to his sister's health during these escapades may only be surmised.

Two days after Lincoln signed Rubery's pardon, John Hay reported in his diary: "Seward has just received another idiotic despatch from Cash Clay abusing the Emperor Napoleon like a pickpocket."[37] At this time too a dispatch came in from Lincoln's other "noisy jackass." Burlingame, whose originality had already started great things for America's Oriental policy, warned Lincoln that a Confederate agent had come to the Far East and was scheming with Japan. A queer situation had arisen. By recent agreements with China, Great Britain had acquired the right to regulate customs at certain treaty ports. To enforce his authority, a British inspector had ordered a flotilla of pocket gunboats to police the Yellow Sea. Before they arrived in the Orient the Chinese ousted the Britisher,[38] and no one remained with authority to pay for them. The shipowners stranded on the opposite side of the world offered their vessels to the highest bidder. Wealthy Chinese pirates rubbed their bare arms under their flaring sleeves and made handsome offers for the craft that had been constructed to suppress them. Japanese daimios, great Nipponese earls next in rank below the Shogun himself, heard about the proposed sale and made an offer. A Confederate agent added a Southern drawl to the Oriental conking. The daimios got the ships but that did not relieve Burlingame's mind,[39] for the Japs ordered them back to Europe for resale. A modern navy, they reasoned, was not necessary in the Orient if nobody had one. This gave the Confederacy a chance to buy a navy—small to be sure—but Burlingame fretted. Two days later he wrote Seward again, privately. He suspected that the Southerners might get the vessels before they reached Europe. Watch out!

Then the newspapers announced that A. Dudley Mann had been received by the Pope. The Southron had gone to Rome with buoyant confidence. Surely Pius IX would see eye to eye with him the horrors of impending mobocracy, the rise of democracy, inundation of the old ways of life. Were not Garibaldi and his Red Shirts as eager to march into Rome as Lincoln and his red republicans were to march into Richmond? Why should German and Irish emigrants to America fight for such a godless government?

The two men talked through an interpreter.[40] The Pope asked the embarrassing question about slavery that had provoked Mann in half the courts of Europe. Mann replied as he always did, with conventional platitudes about the North's unwarranted interference with the South's domestic institutions and the whole world's ignorance of the only possible relation between the races. "His Holiness," Mann remembered later, "received these remarks with an approving expression."[41] The war, Mann told the pontiff, was not waged for slavery. The South was fighting for a constitutional principle. The war was not a civil war but a war between the states. The Pope signified that he would send a letter to Jefferson Davis, and the interview terminated. Mann started back to Paris with the missive. It was addressed to the "Illustrious and Honorable Jefferson Davis, President of the Confederate States of America." This was the first time that any foreign potentate had addressed the Confederate as President and Mann was in high feather. He was not even dismayed by the letter's contents, which regretted the "Civil War" and thus showed that Mann's elaborate argument on constitutionality had been lost on the pontiff. What did it matter after all? Mann had won a near-official recognition for the Confederacy at last. A week later he burst jubilantly upon Mason and Slidell in Paris. To Benjamin he wrote:

"We are acknowledged, by as high an authority as this world contains, to be an independent power of the earth. I congratulate you. I congratulate the President, I congratulate the cabinet; in short, I congratulate all my true hearted countrymen and countrywomen upon this benign event."[42]

The Pope's letter was published for circulation during the 1863 Christmas celebrations on the Continent.[43] Instead of gaining converts to the Southern cause it produced roars of laughter. Such naïve persons these slavocrats! Imagine this beside Lincoln's Gettysburg Address.

Mann and his colleagues winced under the most exquisite of all pain, the shame of being laughed at. The Confederacy's international adventure was almost over. The quaint eggs that Jeff Davis had laid in foreign countries as representatives of his civilization were beginning to hatch.

Lincoln knew that his only real danger abroad lay in France—imperial France—that had no common people adequately represented in the government. England's plain people had helped swing their nation in line with America. There was no doubt about that now, but the common man of France had not been allowed to hear Lincoln speak at Gettysburg.

# XVIII. *It is Not Best to Swap Horses While Crossing the River*

LINCOLN held a diplomatic reception on New Year's night 1864. The plenipotentiaries drove to the White House, past the cavalry guard at each gate. At the gas-lighted portico they stopped. Edward opened the door. In the brightly lighted rooms the resplendent guests filed dutifully past the tall broadcloth figure of the President. Mercier and his American wife smiled painfully and passed on. In the line, too, was Count Gurowski. Lincoln had been told that the eccentric Pole, furious at his discharge from the State Department, might assassinate the President.[1] The count shook hands formally, then lingered where he could overhear everything that Lincoln said. Gurowski, with all his violent language, was not physically dangerous. He merely wanted diplomatic gossip to print and thus damage the administration. Before long Gurowski saw the Mexican minister approaching the President. "Stealthily," Gurowski reported, Lincoln asked for news from the war against Maximilian.

"It is good," the Mexican replied.

"Oh, I am very glad," said Lincoln. "I wish you may have the best of the invaders."[2] Count Gurowski sauntered away, happy to have caught Lincoln making an unneutral remark. He would tell Lincoln's enemies and make trouble in Congress. Upstairs a window opened. A shrill whistle pierced the night. The cavalrymen mistook the noise for their corporal's signal to change places. Each man trotted to his next station. Then the whistle blew again. The soldiers were mystified but changed once more. Again the whistle blew. Something was wrong, but the men moved dutifully. For half an hour they trotted back and forth. Then the great front door opened ever so little—a panel of yellow light. The small figure of a boy darted out. Tad, with a bowl of Roman punch purloined from the refreshment table, wanted to make amends. He had stolen a noncom's whistle and had had great sport moving the men to and fro.[3]

Lincoln could not tarry much longer before making a decision about Mexico. The country was getting deeper and deeper under French control. The Confederate ships being built in France would soon be ready for the sea. Trouble between the English-speaking neighbors seemed to be definitely past. The rams had been stopped and the blockade was admitted. The British government would surely not object to a stern policy toward France.

With a free hand to deal with Napoleon, Lincoln resorted first to diplomacy. His problem was double-edged. Could he oust France from Mexico without forcing her into an alliance with the Confederacy? If Lincoln went only halfway and aided Juárez with arms, then Napoleon was sure to retaliate halfway by letting Frenchmen build ships for the Confederates. Napoleon had called this to Lincoln's attention some months ago. At that time the President had decided not to help Juárez—openly. Thus Lincoln had kept Napoleon off his back by letting him sink deep roots in Mexico. The French now held eight of the principal cities, including the capital. But the Confederate shipbuilding had been checked —temporarily at least—and the Mexican conquest was far from complete.[4]

Lincoln decided to remain neutral in Mexico, not remonstrate with Napoleon, but work instead with the liberals in France much as he had done in England. Surely if the case were presented correctly Napoleon's own people would influence him to stop construction on the rams and withdraw his army from Mexico. In imperial France, however, this task was much more difficult than it had been in England. American lecturers could not drive home the significance of the Gettysburg Address—the value of government of the people, by the people and for the people. The French liberals themselves had not organized a counterpart for the Union and Emancipation Society to disseminate circulars and offer halls for meetings. True, liberals in the Church, in the press, in *l'Institut,* were as outspoken as censorship allowed but their combined voices had made no impression on French policy toward the Confederacy. In 1863 Charles Francis Adams had employed a queen's counsel to bore from within and stop the *Alabama.* Now John Bigelow employed a member of the Corps Législatif to do some important legal work for him—write an opinion on the legality of ship-building under Napoleon's proclamation of neutrality.[5] Bigelow did not select a liberal for the job. He already had the support of that group. Instead he retained a Legitimist—an archconservative, opposed to Napoleon as much as any liberal.

Next Seward sent Dayton a stern notice: Inform Drouyn de L'Huys that the President will hold the Emperor strictly responsible for any ships allowed to escape. Dayton sent Seward a remarkable reply. De L'Huys, he said, maintained that the suspicious ships were for Denmark. His manner, however, told plainly enough that the French minister believed that his own Emperor was trying to deceive him.[6] Obviously De L'Huys was to be the scapegoat in case Napoleon decided to let the ships go.

As the ramifications of Napoleon's foreign schemes unfolded before the diplomats, Bigelow read in the *Moniteur* that the Emperor had canceled the permit to Arman—the French Laird—for building the ships. The work on them, however, did not stop. Bigelow suspected a ruse. He noted that the *Moniteur* article had been copied from the *London Morning Star*. Strange, indeed, for official French news to come through the British press. Did the Emperor hope that the Americans would be misled without a commitment on his own part? Then on top of all the double-dealing and equivocation Napoleon permitted the *Florida,* which had been under repair for six months, to go to sea.[7] Everywhere duplicity, uncertainty—largess to both sides.

Lincoln and Seward read the record and understood what they were up against. France must be watched constantly and kept in isolation. She had been separated successfully from England but in all probabilities would seek another ally. Spain and France were both transgressors against the Monroe Doctrine. Together they might consider themselves strong enough to upset Lincoln's plans without English aid. Suddenly the new threat came to a head.

The Dominican rebels, still fighting Spain for freedom, sent a minister to Washington. Seward did not know whether he dared recognize the envoy. The year before, 1863, Lincoln had recognized a chargé d'affaires from Haiti,[8] but that country was not

352

claimed by Spain. Seward decided to put the question to the cabinet. On February 2, 1864, the chiefs met in the White House. Seward explained the dilemma. If the United States refused to help the rebels against Spain, England could say, with justification, that Lincoln was not sincere in fighting for the Negro in the South and refusing to help him in a near-by island. On the other hand, if he did help the Negro rebels, Spain would be sure to ally herself with France. Besides, the time was approaching for a national convention to nominate a President. If Lincoln did not recognize the black minister, the abolitionists were bound to make capital of it. What should be done?

The cabinet watched Abraham Lincoln. The President smiled. He was reminded of a story: Once a Negro preacher had endeavored to enlighten a lay brother on the difficulty of salvation.

"There are two roads for you, Joe," said the preacher. "Be careful which you take. One ob dem leads straight to hell, de odder go right to damnation."

Joe opened his eyes under the impressive eloquence and exclaimed, "Josh, take which road you please; I go troo de wood."

Lincoln paused. "I am not disposed to take any new trouble, just at this time, and shall neither go for Spain nor the Negro in this matter, but shall take to the woods."[9]

Lincoln's cabinet laughed politely. Privately, each member despaired at the chief's evasion—his unwillingness to make a decision. After the meeting they complained about it to their friends, the party leaders. "Just finding that out?" the politicians asked. Lincoln's evasive habits had annoyed them for three years.

The nominating convention was scheduled to meet within six months and Lincoln had not said whether he would run for re-election. Behind Lincoln's back the leaders discussed possible candidates. They whined because Lincoln's natural slowness prevented the alternates from stretching their wire. It was not fair. Lincoln's best friends, men who had known him in Springfield, were urged to take advantage of their friendship and ask the President to make a decision.

The friends agreed that they could not do so. It was unbecoming. Finally Leonard Swett, a companion of the circuit-riding days in Illinois, decided on a plan. One day, as he sat in the White

House with Lincoln and other visitors, Swett remarked artfully, "Do you know that the people begin to talk about your renomination?"

There was a pause. Lincoln turned in his chair. "Swett, do you know that same bee has been buzzing in my bonnet for several days."

That was all. The politicians left as baffled as they had come. On March 21, 1864, Judge David Davis, under whom Lincoln had tried cases back home, and who had been one of the leaders in proposing him for the first nomination, wrote Weed: "I think he ought to act, and act promptly, but his mind is constituted differently from yours and mine. We will have to wait for his decision upon the important matter."[10]

If Lincoln enjoyed watching the party leaders sweat over his indecision, his bland face did not disclose it. Before committing himself, he decided upon a great piece of propaganda. A picture fourteen and a half by nine feet must be painted of him and the cabinet discussing the Emancipation Proclamation. Such a picture had the campaign possibilities of a million words. Abolitionists, always suspicious of Lincoln's moderation, would rally to the canvas, yet a picture made no campaign promises for which Lincoln could be held accountable. In England the illiterate could understand a picture and feel a new exaltation at being considered worthy to suffer for liberty's sake. Owen Lovejoy, the radical who sometimes embarrassed Lincoln with his belligerency, suggested an artist, F. B. Carpenter by name.[11] The painting, if begun at once, should be finished before election.

Seward objected. He missed the point altogether, or appeared to. The proclamation, he said, was not the great achievement of the administration. Instead, the greatest event was the firing on Sumter or the cabinet's meeting on the Sunday following the Baltimore massacre, when the war powers of the government were put in force, when papers were issued without authority and acts were committed that might have brought all the members to the scaffold.[12]

Lincoln went ahead with plans for his picture. His silence in former times had made him President. Seward's talking had kept *him* from being President. Let Seward talk. Carpenter brought his sketch box into the White House. Lincoln showed him a chair in the cabinet room where he could study the chiefs of departments as they discussed affairs of state. Carpenter absorbed their personalities, scribbled their outlines around the long table, transfixed them on canvas. Lincoln would be remembered as the Emancipator and the people at the next election could give their verdict at the polls.

While Carpenter worked in the early spring of 1864, two exponents of the two leading ideologies—democracy and monarchy —prepared to visit England and France. Garibaldi sailed from Caprera for Southampton.[13] Maximilian left his villa on the Adriatic to visit France.[14] In England when the Italian Liberator stepped ashore in his red shirt and gray blanket the crowd went wild with enthusiasm. Greeted as "the man nations love and kings hate," Garibaldi symbolized the democracy which Henry Ward Beecher preached. His carriage was unable to proceed. A sea of faces tossed like the tide in the Strait of Bonifacio—a great ground swell of democracy.[15]

Tories did not like it. The first Socialist International was scheduled to meet in London that year. There was no telling where the thing might end. The government frowned. England must be careful, with a Continental war looming. Imperial France might be displeased. Unofficially the Liberator was "invited" to leave England. Police dispersed a meeting of protest by workingmen in London.[16] So France and England were drawing together again! Had Lincoln's three-year effort to keep them separated failed completely? Or had emancipation and Gettysburg settled that for all time? At best the threat still hung over Lincoln.

Across the Channel the representative of monarchy, Maximilian, came to France as befitted one of his station. The Archduke wished to learn from Napoleon just what French support he could depend on in Mexico. M. Mercier hurried to Paris with a last-minute report of Lincoln's attitude. The Frenchman had talked with the President immediately before departing. Lincoln, according to Mercier, had intimated that Maximilian would be recognized by the United States, if Napoleon made no negotiations with the Confederacy. The Emperor beamed with pleasure.

Slidell heard about the imperial conference between Napoleon and puppet Maximilian. The Southerner asked for an audience. It was altogether fitting and proper for the leaders of aristocratic forms of government on both hemispheres to reorganize the world.

Napoleon snubbed his onetime friend. Slidell, foiled, appealed to the Archduke for audience. Maximilian also declined the honor. Slidell wrote home to Benjamin that Lincoln had outwitted the Confederacy. By a corrupt bargain, the South had been denied its rights.[17]

Napoleon went out of his way now to show friendship for the Union cause. Drouyn de L'Huys assured Dayton that neither Napoleon nor Maximilian planned to make alliance with the Confederacy.[18] *L'Opinion* boldly warned the French government to intern the Confederate cruiser *Rappahannock,* then docked for repairs at Le Havre.[19] The Emperor twirled his waxed mustache. Maximilian returned to the Adriatic to pack his trunks. Lincoln and Seward noticed that France had become friendly at the time when Great Britain veered away. No chance of a combination there. Lincoln's persistent policy of keeping the two powers apart had borne fruit.

On April 14 the Archduke and Carlotta, his ambitious wife, with a shipload of imperial equipment, sailed away from the castled walls of Miramar. God had created him for the kingly task of bringing peace and prosperity to people somewhere on earth; of that he was certain. His parents, his teachers, his retainers had all told him so. For this duty he consented to give up forever the enchanting gardens, stately trees and terraces of his home.

Maximilian's progress to America resembled the license of a condemned man on the eve of execution. At Naples, at Rome, Gibraltar, Madeira, Martinique and Jamaica, the Archduke's suite received the pomp and ceremony due a reigning sovereign. On May 28, 1864, the flotilla arrived in Vera Cruz.[20] An imperial coach with liveried outriders and a gorgeous guard escorted the noble couple through the jungle to the healthful highlands. In Mexico City obsequious officials received them. With barbaric and shabby splendor Maximilian and Carlotta were crowned Emperor and Empress. They lived in the castle of the Montezumas on the great rock that towered above the capital. Chapultepec was its name, Aztec for grasshopper, an insect with a short and active life. Seventy-five Mexican rulers had led grasshopper lives in that castle during the forty years of Mexico's independence from Spain.

Minister Corwin was absent—temporarily—from the capital when Maximilian arrived.[21] The Confederacy had a new minister ready to greet the Austrian and negotiate an alliance with the South. William Preston had been a Buchanan Democrat. Before the Civil War he represented the United States in Madrid. Now he waited coyly at Havana for the new Emperor to call him to the capital.

Maximilian stroked his blond whiskers. Versed in statecraft, he knew Lincoln's recognition to be more valuable than Jeff Davis'. He had refused to see Slidell in Paris. Certainly he could not see Preston in Mexico. The gentleman of the South must wait.

Maximilian looked out from tall French windows across the tree-tops and the flat-roofed houses of Mexico City to the cathedral spires. Beyond lay the mountains—sleeping monsters—ridges, hips, backbones haired over with gloomy pines. Every morning Maximilian awakened to the clangor of many bells. The rare air was heady as wine with a tingle of seltzer. Below the castle, Maximilian saw skeins of wood smoke from a million braziers blanketing the city. Half an hour later the sun peeped over the mountains and struck Chapultepec with a shaft of light. The tropical rays warmed the cold stones. Crickets chirped in the crannies of the flagstone terrace. Lizards scuttled across the walls. Grasshoppers scraped their legs merrily against musical wings. They had seen other hopeful men move into those lofty rooms.

On Sundays after Mass, "Maximiliano" drove with Carlotta in the park under the cliff. Horsemen in silver and gold-embroidered costumes and enormous hats darted through the splendid cypress trees like tropical fish in a bowl. As they passed the royal couple, the cavaliers bowed gracefully from the saddle. These horsemen spent the season in the capital. Many of them had been educated in Europe. Their country estates—great self-supporting units—contained villages with churches, clergy, soldiers, overseers. Their way of life was rightly the envy of any Confederate planter. Like the Southerners, the *hacendados* were born to responsibility, the saddle and firearms. The Roman-arched dwellings on the great ranches shamed the finest pillared plantation mansions on the Po-

tomac, the York or the Mississippi. The Mexican gentry with
literary tastes read and admired Cervantes, the iconoclast, as
Americans read and admired the Declaration of Independence.
Like the Americans, they, too, failed to understand the full meaning of what they read. The better life, as these Mexicans understood it, must be supported on laboring mudsills. Maximiliano
could count on their support if he protected their property, assured
them the pleasure of responsibility, and the leisure to laugh at
Don Quixote's crusade against ideas—*muy* old-fashioned.

Carlotta set to work planning her court. The *hacendadas*—
hothouse women, trained for romance and the management of
large households—offered the Empress their services as ladies in
waiting. Wealthy duennas called at the palace. Carlotta told them
about Paris, showed them her wardrobe. She said that the man-
tilla and tortoise-shell comb were not worn by the best families.
Such gewgaws were the badges of rustics.

The ladies departed with hand-colored fashion plates under their
silk shawls. For days thereafter seamstresses, in rooms opening on
patios brilliant with bougainvilleas, stitched endlessly on new and
wondrous creations. Hairdressers' dexterous olive fingers curled
the straight Indian hair of brown-eyed damsels and fixed frizzes
in the graying locks of matrons. From Paris came boxes and bun-
dles of feminine finery. At last Carlotta was ready for a great
soiree. The guests arrived and the Empress stifled suppressed
laughter. Some of the ladies wore elegant imported bonnets
backward.[22]

In this barbarous court Maximilian felt secure. He was surrounded by Mexicans of the court party and by jaunty French
and Austrian officers. To all appearances Abraham Lincoln had
acquiesced in his rule. Tom Corwin was absent, it was true—consulting with Lincoln in Washington. When he came back the
United States would no doubt bow to the inevitable. Napoleon
had given his word to uphold the throne.

In June a genial *americano* came to Chapultepec direct from
the Emperor of France. William Gwin was a Tennessean and also
ex-senator of California. He had taken his proposition first to
Napoleon. His plan was simple. He proposed to colonize the
northern states of Mexico with Southerners and thus create a

buffer against republicanism. In recognition of his services he wanted to be made Duke of Sonora. Napoleon liked the plan as Gwin explained it. He sent him to Maximilian. The puppet Emperor listened to the details. Then he told the Tennessean that he would have to wait with his Kentucky colleague, William Preston, for a more propitious time. Maximilian walked away thoughtfully with his hands behind his back. He must not affront Lincoln. Why was Corwin staying away so long?

In the United States the time was approaching for the convention to nominate the next President. Lincoln appeared to be devoting all his time to domestic affairs. He appointed Grant a lieutenant general in charge of all the armies and in personal command of the Eastern theater—a job that had cost the military reputation of his six predecessors. The long-delayed Red River expedition was set in motion. For months Lincoln had planned to invade Texas by this route. With an army on the north bank of the Rio Grande he might tell Napoleon a thing or two, but until his soldiers got there it was best to keep Corwin on his leave of absence. Thus Lincoln had two strings to his Mexican bow. If the Red River expedition succeeded, his Army would stand as a constant threat over Napoleon's Mexico. If the expedition failed, Corwin's absence might delude the new Emperor into the belief that Lincoln intended to recognize him. In either event Napoleon might think it best to stop building Confederate ships and forego all idea of a Southern alliance.

On April 4—the day Maximilian left Miramar—the United States House of Representatives passed a resolution disapproving French occupation of Mexico.[23] That forced the President's hand. The Red River expedition was barely under way. If Lincoln agreed with Congress at this early date, Napoleon in all probability would despair of American recognition and make an alliance with the Confederacy. Certainly he would continue to make warships for her. If Lincoln opposed the congressional resolution, the American people would surely vote against him in the coming election. Lincoln was fairly caught but he saw a way out.

Seward hurried off to talk with all the diplomats. He assured them that Congress had no right to meddle in foreign affairs. He sent a dispatch to France "explaining" the resolution. He called on Sumner, his bitter enemy, and begged him to hold the Senate in check.[24] The resolution must not be concurred in by both houses.

On April 16, 1864, more bad news arrived—a lot of it. The Red River expedition had met with disaster—an end to that threat to France. Lincoln must depend now on his second bowstring— Napoleon's hope of recognition—and congressmen might cut that cord with their resolution. This was not all. Politicians reported that anti-Lincoln delegates to the nominating convention had been elected from all over the North. Lincoln listed the probable ballot on a piece of paper. He brooded over the figures, memorized them and went to bed moodily. Long after midnight, when the White House was dark except for a light in John Hay's office, Lincoln came down the hall with long bare legs striding like an ostrich under his nightshirt tail. Hay looked up, expecting to be sent on some urgent midnight errand. Instead Lincoln wanted him to stop and laugh over a paragraph in a volume of Thomas Hood's works which he held in his hand.[25]

Some days later a dispatch from Dayton warned Lincoln that the Southern commissioners were using the House resolution to stir up trouble. They were trying to convince the Emperor that Congress would overrule any agreement the President might make concerning Maximilian. They wanted Napoleon to sign an alliance with the South at once. Lincoln was too busy to reply. Then on May 17, 1864, the *New York World* and the *Journal of Commerce* published the startling announcement that Lincoln had ordered a new draft—a vicious forgery by a stock speculator who hoped to force down the market. Lincoln shuddered at the effect of this news in France. The Emperor, looking for an excuse to join with the Confederates, was bound to interpret a new draft as the precursor of defeat for the North. Lincoln denied the statement instantly and suspended the papers for the libel. But the news had already started to Europe on a New York steamer. A fast dispatch boat was sent in pursuit. Lincoln was relieved when he learned that the liner had been overtaken and the corrected report was tossed on board.[26] The guilty man was arrested.

The next day the *New York Herald* protested Lincoln's subservience to foreign powers.[27] A war against France in Mexico, the editor said, would reunite America. The press had joined Congress to ruin Lincoln politically and force his hand abroad.

Lincoln settled back into routine—his usual defense. A letter from Russia told wondrous things about Henry Bergh. The disappointed actor had found an audience at last. He had been driving one day in the legation carriage, dressed in the gilded uniform of his office. In the street he had spied a Russian peasant beating his horse unmercifully. Bergh's lifelong horror of blood blinded him. He called to his own coachman to stop, then told him to order the droshky man to desist at once. An 'American horse owner would have resented a gilded government official interfering with his personal business, telling him what he could and could not do with his own property, thus curbing his rugged individualism. In Russia the droshky driver submitted meekly, bowed deferentially, hat on breast. Bergh drove virtuously away. The next time Henry Bergh saw a droshky man beating his horse he repeated the performance. Again the recently emancipated serf complied obsequiously. Henry Bergh gloried in his new-found strength. Daily he stopped drivers on the main streets of St. Petersburg. Next he searched out the byways, alert and anxious to find cruelty to animals. The eccentric American in gold lace had become a notorious figure. He had stolen the audience from Cash Clay. The humane Czar, proud of his own record for emancipating the serfs, condoned Bergh's deeds.[28] The second of Lincoln's "noisy jackasses" to be sent to Russia was making good.

Back in America, Lincoln watched Grant fight daily and sidle, crablike, away from Lee—yet always end each battle deeper in Virginia. Lincoln watched also for the first dispatch from abroad that would tell Napoleon's reaction to the congressional resolutions. One day Seward bustled in with a great piece of news—not from abroad but almost as important. It must be kept a secret. A Cuban refugee was living in New York. He was wanted in Havana for implication in the slave trade.[29] Don Tassara had asked for his extradition. To deliver the man would be a nice gesture to Spain at a time when her friendship was needed. On the other hand, there was no extradition treaty and Congress was apt to roar about executive usurpation and further subservience of American sovereignty. Still, the man was an acknowledged slave trader. Abolitionists would not censure the administration for surrendering him to justice.

Lincoln decided to act quickly and stealthily. He did not mention the proposed action to his cabinet. Señor José Arguelles was arrested and hustled on shipboard. Some days elapsed before the incident was publicly known.[30] Lincoln, in the meantime, interviewed politicians and joked guilelessly with his secretary, John Hay.

Before long the French newspapers were delivered in Washington. Congressmen read that Lincoln had given the Emperor a satisfactory "explanation" as to the sense and bearing of the congressional resolution. Lincoln's enemies snorted.[31] What business did the President have to nullify the will of the people expressed through their representatives in Congress? Who was he to be making secret agreements and explanations with the Emperor? The fight between Lincoln and the radicals in his own party threatened to wreck the administration—and this, election year! Henry Winter Davis, chairman of the House Foreign Relations Committee, jumped to his feet and offered a new resolution. Lincoln must make a full explanation to Congress.[32]

The President summoned Seward to the White House. He felt sure that the resolution was a trick to catch him. The people would not tolerate any diplomatic understanding with Napoleon. If they suspected one, it might cost Lincoln the nomination. Congress must be answered in such a way that the people would be satisfied and at the same time Napoleon would be reassured.[33] Lincoln asked Seward to write the reply. The President himself was busy on another long letter, also for political purposes. To A. G. Hodges in Kentucky he wrote that he had never planned to abolish slavery without compensation to slaveowners. In the letter he outlined all his attempts to get them to accept pay for their bondmen. He had failed, it was true, but the effort had had a salutary effect in Europe, he said.

Then Congress learned about the surrender of Señor Arguelles. Lincoln's enemies boiled over. A resolution demanded "under what authority of law or treaty it was done."[34] This time Congress lost the support of the people. The Spaniard was a slave trader. Treaty or no treaty, he should pay the penalty. Lincoln had won his first bout with his recalcitrant colleagues. Horace Greeley devoted the columns of his newspaper to a defense of the President. Lincoln's chance of renomination looked brighter.

The echo of the squabble annoyed Europeans. Democracy always appeared so sordid, so unprincipled. International bankers became skeptical about their loans—about American inflation. When the legitimate party in a Civil War was torn to tatters by dissension, its credit could not be good.[35] Europeans read that five of Lincoln's colleagues hoped for the nomination in his stead. Seward, his prime minister, was one of them. Gossips noted that Sanford left Europe. With knowing nods, they said that he had gone to help Seward's canvass, to convince the Americans that the Secretary of State's diplomacy had prevented recognition of the Confederacy.[36]

Seward's old rival, Chase, was also working hard for the nomination. Lincoln's friends told the President that his Secretary of the Treasury was blatantly against him. Lincoln replied with a story: Back in Illinois once he saw a plow horse tormented by a fly. Neighbors asked the plowman why he did not kill the fly. "Let her buzz," the farmer said. "It keeps the horse alert and active about his work."[37]

Chase did resemble a great Clydesdale plow horse.

Behind Seward and Chase, Senator Sumner also stood ready for a call. With leonine head and prehensile tongue, he waited for the rivals to eat up each other. Stalwarts fumed! Division would kill the party. Senator Wade, grim partisan from Ohio, admitted that Chase was a good man but his theology was unsound. "He thinks there is a fourth person in the Trinity."[38]

Old Count Gurowski screamed: "If Mr. Lincoln is re-elected, then the self-government is not yet founded on reason, intellect, and on sound judgment."[39]

The Blairs, half-baked Republicans from Democratic dough, insisted that Honest Abe was the only logical candidate. William Lloyd Garrison told his abolitionist readers that the masses in Europe demanded 'Abraham Lincoln.[40]

As the time approached for the convention, the extreme radicals made a desperate move to forestall Lincoln's renomination. A week before the regular meeting they gathered in Cleveland. Calling themselves Republicans, they held a so-called convention. A "slimy intrigue," Weed called the maneuver.[41] General John Cochrane went out from Washington intent on breaking them up. On May 31, 1864, a messenger boy handed Lincoln a telegram. Frémont had been nominated for President; Cochrane for Vice-President.[42] Lincoln walked slowly across to the War Department. He was used to the double cross. Lincoln entered the telegraph office. The instruments were ticking—a message from the army in Virginia. Lee was moving his men mysteriously. Grant pushed forward around Cold Harbor. Napoleon had a military observer down there. The Emperor had heard that Grant, hero of the West, was overrated. He wanted the opinion of an expert. If the new general failed, France would be prepared to act.

On June 3, 1864, Grant ordered his men to attack Lee across an open field. The Union soldiers fell in windrows. Grant ordered forward another wave. Lincoln had found a man who would fight.

Delegates on the way to the convention stopped at the White House. These men all assured Lincoln that they were going to vote for him. How was the battle progressing? Whom would he suggest for Vice-President?

The party was no longer called Republican. That name belonged to the Frémont Secessionists. Lincoln's party hoped to enlist the war-minded Democrats. They called themselves the National Union Party. It seemed best to run a Democrat for Vice-President. Lincoln refused to name his running mate. He shook hands all around and hurried back to the War Department.

Grant had ordered another wave forward across the field. When it was cut down, he ordered out another. Reserves arrived, looked at the shambles, and wrote their names on pieces of paper. They wanted to be identified after death. In short order ten thousand men lay sprawled on the grass. Fresh troops, ordered to the front, refused to go to certain death.[43]

Lincoln walked back to the White House. Only four days until the convention! Could any president expect renomination after such a defeat? Colonel Alex K. McClure, delegate at large from Pennsylvania, called. McClure remembered later that Lincoln told him confidentially that he favored Andrew Johnson of Tennessee for Vice-President. Johnson, like the President himself, had come up from poverty. What better example could be chosen to show the opportunities in a democracy? Moreover, Johnson lived in a secession state that had been restored to Federal authority. "In no way could our friends in the European countries be so greatly strengthened," Lincoln said, "as by the election of a man to the second office of the Government from a reconstructed State in the heart of the Confederacy."[44]

During the next few days many delegations—Negroes, sutlers and carpetbaggers, claiming to represent states still in rebellion—stopped at the White House and pledged their loyalty to Lincoln. Two parties came from Florida. Each whispered that the other was bogus. Next a committee from South Carolina asked admission. "Let them in," Lincoln said.

"They are a swindle," his secretary told him.

"They won't swindle me," Lincoln replied.

The men filed in, presented a petition and retired. Both Lincoln and his secretary were sure that few of these delegations would be admitted to the convention.

At last June 7—convention day. Party representatives from all loyal states were seated—a pool of pink faces with puffs of tobacco smoke rising to the rafters. Many delegates carried newspapers in their hands. Headlines announced that Spain had invaded Peru—another violation of the Monroe Doctrine. Harrowing accounts of the tremendous losses at Cold Harbor were still coming in. Incompetence at home and weakness abroad! Senator Jim Lane, grim chieftain of Kansas, who with Cash Clay had patrolled the streets of Washington three years ago, called on the chairman for permission to speak. With spellbinding oratory and all the tricks of the pulpit and the stage, he nominated Abraham Lincoln. Andrew Johnson was selected as his running mate. Henry J. Raymond announced the party platform: war until the Union is restored, abolition of slavery and expulsion of any monarchial government "in near proximity of the United States"[45]—the ticklish Mexican problem Lincoln wanted to keep quiet.

Back in their hotel rooms disgruntled delegates packed their carpetbags, deposited empty bottles in bureau drawers, told each

other that Raymond had been offered Dayton's place in France.[46]
What would Lane get?

A delegation from the Union League brought the good news to
the White House and offered congratulations. Lincoln shook
hands and thanked them. He did not mention the embarrassing
plank that might force Napoleon into an alliance with the Confederacy. He said:

> "I do not allow myself to suppose that either the convention or
> the League have concluded to decide that I am either the greatest
> or best man in America, but rather they have concluded that it is
> not best to swap horses while crossing the river, and have further
> concluded that I am not so poor a horse that they might not make a
> botch of it in trying to swap."[47]

On June 9, 1864, just before bedtime, Lincoln went to John
Hay's room. He had received word of a gigantic plot to overthrow
the government. The Belgian consul at St. Louis was implicated.
General Rosecrans had unearthed the details in Missouri. Lincoln
asked Hay to go west at once and investigate. The private secretary set off the following afternoon. He wore a major's uniform.
Lincoln had commissioned him to this rank. Hay found the general to be a heavy man, unsteady on his feet, blond-bearded, abrupt
in speech. He invited the major to dinner. After the meal Rosecrans led the way to his hotel room, told the Negro servant to
admit no one, then offered Hay a cigar. The young man declined.

"No? Long-necked fellows like you don't need them. Men of
my temperament derive advantage from them as a sedative and a
preventive of corpulence."[48] Rosecrans puffed nervously. Then
he lowered his voice, looked over his shoulder and moved his chair
closer. The plot, he said, was large and well organized. The conspirators were bound together by a secret oath. Thirteen thousand
members were known to exist in Missouri, a hundred and forty
thousand in Illinois. Similar numbers were ready to rise in Indiana, Ohio and Kentucky. The leader of the Southern branch was
Sterling Price, a Confederate general. The Northern leader was
Clement Vallandigham up in Canada. Rosecrans' secret-service
men had suspected the Belgian consul of being a leader in the

organization. They had gained his confidence—inspected the organization's books. There was no doubt about the size and purpose of the conspiracy. The society's immediate objective was to get Vallandigham back to the United States in time to take part in the Democratic convention. If he were present, the conspirators believed all party members would unite to stop the war and throw out the Republicans. In case the government should try to arrest Vallandigham for violating his exile, the members were pledged to resist the officers at all costs. This, of course, was insurrection. John Hay agreed that the plot was serious.

The next morning Hay started back to Washington. He arrived at the capital after a week's absence. A startling event had occurred while he was gone. Newsboys shouted frantically on the streets. Vallandigham was in the United States. He had crossed the border in disguise and was now among friends in Ohio. Hay hurried to the White House.

# XIX. *A Joke Worthy of Abraham Lincoln Himself*

Young Major Hay mopped his face and felt lonely. The third week in June was stifling hot in Washington. The President was gone—down with Grant in Virginia. People talked about Vallandigham, told each other what Lincoln should do if he were any good. Major Hay had given the President a full account of the plot as soon as he returned from St. Louis. Lincoln had listened attentively, then said that the problem was more tangled than Hay imagined. Military suppression of the threatening revolt would fan a smoldering feud between General Rosecrans and Secretary of War Stanton—a major catastrophe. Then, too, Vallandigham might become a martyr if arrested. On the other hand, failure to arrest him was sure to be construed as another token of Federal temerity—like the Emancipation Proclamation, "our last shriek on the retreat."[1] Lincoln finally decided to do nothing—take to "de woods." He said he was sure that the people were sound. They would not revolt. The Democratic convention was only six weeks away. If Vallandigham was allowed to attend it, his wild talk might split his own party—as the liberals and ship-builders had split in England. So saying, Lincoln left for Virginia to see Grant.

Major Hay was sure that Lincoln had made a mistake. The people were not sound. Many of them wanted peace at any price. They would revolt to get it. Fireworks might begin any night now. On the evening of June 18, 1864, Major Hay went to see Seward. The Secretary of State greeted him with the question on everybody's mind—Vallandigham. Had Lincoln tricked the Ohioan into coming back to ruin the Democratic convention? Three years' association with his chief made Seward suspect artful statesmanship in every unexpected occurrence. Hay, a budding statesman in his own right, replied that he thought Vallandigham's uninterrupted return "too marked an exercise of good sense to be ascribed to the Administration." Instead it seemed "a visible interposition of Divine Providence." The young and the old man talked for some time about the conspiracy and the Belgian consul's part in it. Finally Seward looked down at his sleeping dog. "Midge," he said, "what do you conclude about the Major?" Looking at Hay, he continued, "Did you ever notice that the dog is the only animal that gains his impressions of the persons he meets by studying their faces?"[2] Major Hay went home turning Seward's remark over and over in his mind. He liked the old outlaw and wanted to be a great diplomat himself someday.

Down in Virginia, Lincoln learned that Grant had not quit after his defeat at Cold Harbor as his predecessors might have done. Instead he sidled around Lee's right flank and slipped deeper into Virginia. Lincoln found Grant quietly confident. He told the President that the campaign might take "a long summer's day" but he was as sure of the end as he was "of anything in the world."[3]

McClellan had never talked like this. Lincoln came back to the White House tired and sunburned but his spirit beamed. The great painting of the cabinet discussing the Emancipation Proclamation must be finished for the campaign.

Lincoln's Congress did not intend to help him in his race. Instead his party enemies prepared another punch at the administration. They were determined to thwart the President's Mexican scheme. A congressional resolution demanded all the correspondence concerning Maximilian. This included orders from the War and Treasury departments—one headed by a Democrat and the other by an abolitionist—both Lincoln's rivals, with many supporters in Congress. John Hay took the resolution to the State Department to consult Seward. Did the Secretary deem it advisable to get the information from Stanton and Chase? Seward glared at the resolutions for a moment. "Yes," he snapped, looking up from under his shelving eyebrows.

John Hay waited. He knew that the Secretary was Lincoln's exact opposite, always ready to talk and act—necessary or not.

"Send the Resolution to the Secretary of War," Seward continued, "a copy to the Secretary of the Treasury, asking reports from them, and then when the reports are in——" Seward's eyes twinkled. "Did you ever hear Webster's recipe for cooking a cod? He was a great fisherman and fond of cod. Someone once asking him the best way to prepare a cod for the table, he said, 'Denude your cod of his scales, cut him open carefully, put him in a pot of cold water, heat it until your fork can pass easily through the fish, take him out, spread good fresh butter over him liberally, sprinkle salt on the butter, pepper on the salt, and—send for George Ashmun and me.' When the reports are in let me see them." Seward got up from his chair, stumped around the room, enjoying his joke for a while, then said, "Our friends are very anxious to get into a war with France, using this Mexican business for that purpose. They don't consider that England and France would be together surely in that event. France has the whiphand of England completely. England got out of the Mexican business into which she had been deceived by France, by virtue of our having nothing to do with it. They have since been kept apart by good management, and our people are laboring to unite them again by making war on France. Worse than that, instead of doing something effective, if we must fight, they are for making mouths and shaking fists at France, warning and threatening and inducing her to prepare for our attack when it comes."[4]

Young John Hay went back to the White House. The day was hot. Girls in summer dresses—lawn and dimity—tripped across the greensward. For once Hay did not notice them. Seward's behavior lingered in the private secretary's mind. It seemed to be typical of the administration's foreign policy. Seward had blustered when blustering was advantageous. He fawned when fawning seemed the best policy. He had never been consistent in anything except an effort to keep England and France separated. Lincoln in the barber chair had said that a fixed policy would have caused sure disaster. The administration's soft words to France must have some ulterior motive. Certainly Seward had absorbed from Lincoln the idea of fighting one war at a time. Yet Seward expected to fight France in the future and boot her out of Mexico, for he had specifically mentioned "our attack when it comes."

The correspondence—hundreds of letters—was sent to the Senate. No one could find a line of it that showed any outward sign of unneutrality. Neither the Senate nor Maximilian complained.

The records disclosed repeated requests from the Juaristas for munitions that had been refused[5]—good reason for the Emperor not to recognize Confederate Minister Preston.

Lincoln followed the disclosure by transferring an officer from Brownsville who was reported to be shutting his eyes to the shipment of arms across the border.[6] Then he reached for a fresh sheet of paper and began to write a formal acceptance of the nomination for President. The Mexican plank his party had forced on him would ruin his little game with France. How could he repudiate it—walk with his party and play with Napoleon at the same time? Lincoln composed a masterpiece.

"While the resolution in regard to the supplanting of republican government upon the western continent is fully concurred in, there might be misunderstanding were I not to say that the position of the government in relation to the action of France in Mexico, as assumed through the State Department and approved and indorsed by the convention among the measures and acts of the executive, will be faithfully maintained so long as the state of facts shall leave that position pertinent and applicable."[7]

Party stalwarts could not object to this—nor could Maximilian. William Preston realized that his mission was futile. Senator Gwin, quasi Duke of Sonora, gave up and left Mexico without his fief.

Lincoln had checkmated France. Then, unexpectedly, England began to kick out of the bag. What did it mean? The British government was known to be solid with the United States. Investigation disclosed that Confederate agents had got a strong grip on the Tories as well as on the profiteers grown rich on the American war. The new agitation against the North began with letters to the British press urging the government to offer mediation. Lindsay and his shipbuilders seemed to be behind the movement. Lincoln had taken from them the profitable construction of Confederate ships, but their yards still hummed with orders for merchant ships and blockade-runners. Surely there was something queer in this demand? The shipping interests could not be sincere in wishing the American war to stop. In addition to ship construction, blockade-running had developed into a prodigious business in itself since Lincoln had studied it in 1863. In May and June 1864, forty-three ships were reported to have arrived at Wilmington and Charleston.[8] The number of ships had doubled in one year. Three large companies were now engaged in the trade: the Bee Company, Collie & Co., and Fraser, Trenholm and Company—the banking house that handled the Confederate funds for ship construction. Wilmington and Charleston were the best ports of entry. The former was protected by forts and islands which permitted blockaders to hide at the edge of open water until the coast was clear. The Confederate government manned the forts and paid for the protection they afforded, and the blockade-runners reaped the profit. A round trip was reckoned to net $300,000, of which $20,000 went to the pilot.[9] The vessels were said to average four and one-third trips before being captured. The *Kate* made forty-four passages. The *Banshee,* captured on her ninth run, netted seven hundred percent for her owners. The *Robert E. Lee* grossed $4,000,000 in twenty-one trips. Could Lindsay be sincere in wanting to stop the opportunity for such profits?

In 1863 Jeff Davis had seen that the trade might draw hard money out of the Confederacy. Now in 1864 his fears were realized. Inflation had come. A futile law prohibited the importation of English wines and beer, fur muffs, carpets, cotton lace, dolls and toys, firecrackers, Roman candles, velvets and jewelry.[10] For people in Southern cities to waste good money on such trinkets while planters sacrificed their lives and estates seemed traitorous. Yet when the Richmond government protested, states that owned blockade-runners howled about the usurpation of the central government—State rights! Secession threatened in Secessia. Jeff Davis dared not push the Richmond government's authority too far. He appointed a member of the firm of Fraser, Trenholm and Company as Secretary of the Treasury. The central government must compete with the states in the new business. Orders were sent to McRae and Bulloch in Europe for fourteen blockade-runners.[11]

Lincoln watched this menace grow as Grant lost men by the thousands in Virginia. In fact, Lincoln had helped it grow by tolerance toward British shipping and by the transfer of energetic Charles Wilkes from the Caribbean. By what form of British logic could Lindsay want to kill the bird that laid such golden eggs?

Whether the shipbuilders' reason was sound or not, their activity was unpleasant for an election year in America. Lincoln's enemies could point to the threat—shallow as it seemed—as an example of his bad diplomacy. Then suddenly the threat proved to be dangerous. Palmerston's Danish policy had weakened his government more than any other act since the beginning of the American war. The Prime Minister needed every vote he could muster to hold his portfolio. Friends of the South in Parliament held sufficient votes to upset the government at last. They saw a chance to trade—support for Palmerston's policy in exchange for a resolution to recognize the Confederacy. Thus a domestic crisis suddenly jeopardized American relations. Lindsay agreed to be spokesman for the Confederates. He asked for an interview with Palmerston. The Prime Minister cordially set May 26, 1864, for the meeting.

The two men talked alone for some time. Palmerston acquiesced in Lindsay's statement that the North's chance of ultimate victory was hopeless, but the Prime Minister preferred to put off any action until more definite news arrived from Grant's offensive—the old excuse he had made in 1862 and again in 1863. But this was different from the previous resolutions. Palmerston needed desperately the votes Lindsay controlled. If, on June 3, he said suavely, a motion were presented stating "that Her Majesty's Government will avail itself of the earliest opportunity of mediating in conjunction with the other powers of Europe to bring about a cessation of hostilities," he, the Prime Minister, "would likely be prepared *to accept it*."[12]

Palmerston had obviously left himself two means of escape. The motion did not designate a specific time for mediation and Palmerston promised only to "be prepared to accept it." Lindsay, however, felt that he had won his point. He suggested that James M. Mason be requested to return to England for an interview. To this Palmerston readily agreed. The two men parted in high spirits, one counting on more votes for his Danish policy, the other confident that a resolution for Southern mediation would be passed at long last.

On the following day a new organization, the Society for Promoting the Cessation of Hostilities in America, prepared a form letter. Members of Parliament were requested to support the proposed motion. Lindsay wrote the good news to James Mason. Four days later Lindsay called on Palmerston again. The two politicians chuckled together like thieves planning a big haul. Really intimate now, Palmerston suggested that a delay in the motion might be advantageous. Lindsay affably offered to put it off "at least 10 days or a fortnight." Later he declared that the Prime Minister "seemed much gratified" at this suggestion. Lindsay also noted with pleasure that editorials in the *Times*, on May 28 and 30, 1864, painted a dark picture of Grant's failures in Virginia. The Society for Promoting the Cessation of Hostilities in America quickly issued another circular letter inviting members of Parliament to form a committee to call on Palmerston and urge action. Lindsay wrote James Mason again. He must come at once.

Charles Francis Adams learned of the intrigue. On June 2—day of Cold Harbor—Adams warned Seward that Lindsay's motion was being held pending a "complete defeat and dispersion" of the Northern armies. On the following day forebodings of the "complete defeat" arrived. No word of Cold Harbor had reached England, but the *Times* reported Grant's losses in the Wilderness to be terrible. Sherman, too, the *Times* reported, was being drawn into the Deep South. A trap was waiting for him at Atlanta. He would be pinched off and annihilated. The North's two best generals, Grant and Sherman, were apparently on the verge of a double catastrophe. James Mason arrived in London. He conferred with Lindsay—doubted Palmerston's sincerity. The Virginian did not trust the Prime Minister. He had not forgiven the earlier rebuff at his hands. He thought it better to work with the Tories and upset the government. The horrible story of Cold Harbor was now on shipboard coming toward England. The Southern sympathizers were ready for it.

Before the news broke across Europe, stirring word thrilled the fighting youths in both England and France. The *Alabama*, after almost two years at sea, had sailed into Cherbourg for repairs.[13] Napoleon, still winking at the construction of Confederate ships in French ports, knew that Lincoln's record showed him to be meticulously neutral toward the Mexican invasion. The

Emperor would be delighted to see the North defeated, but he decided to take no chances with American friendship. Lindsay's actions promised to ruin the North without French aid. Napoleon virtuously ordered the *Alabama* to leave port—go or be interned.

In Paris Dayton wired Captain John Winslow, commander of the *Kearsarge* at Flushing, to come and sink the raider. In short order the American steamed into Cherbourg with sailors' heads at all the portholes, necks craning for a glimpse of the famous ship. Raphael Semmes, a gallant figure always, with his mustache waxed like the Emperor's, dined sumptuously on shore with officers and friends. A duel between the two vessels was arranged on waters outside the three-mile limit. Sightseers crowded an excursion train from Paris to witness the spectacle.[14] A Laird yacht, the *Deerhound,* with ladies on board, waited near by to be the first to carry news of the victory to Lindsay.

Contrary to expectations, the *Alabama* was defeated and sunk. Semmes, with a dramatic gesture on the bridge, threw his sword into the sea. Shortly thereafter he was picked up by the *Deerhound.* Sea water dripped from his imperial mustache. The Laird yacht then turned and raced for England. Raphael Semmes had been saved for the first ship Palmerston was to release after Parliament passed the pending resolution.

The seamen who did not lose their lives in the battle were captured and hospitalized in France. Of a hundred and sixty-three men, only eleven had been born in the United States. The sailors of fortune said ruefully that they had had little respect for the Americans' fighting qualities. They expected "to frighten the Yankees" by opening the fight with rapid fire.[15]

The defeat made Lindsay blink. A naval battle across the Channel cut English consciences deeper than the Cold Harbor disaster across the ocean. Then he braced up. British army and navy people tendered Semmes a great dinner. Lindsay went ahead with his plans. He was pleased to note that the Confederate captain was presented with an elaborate sword to replace the one cast into the sea. Confident aristocrats ignored the liberal press—the fun poked at Semmes's "King Arthur Excalibur incident." As gentlemen they were above noticing the *Edinburgh Mercury's* blast at the "false chivalry of the upper classes," the *London Daily*

*News's* sarcastic suggestion that the new sword be given to the Northern captain.[16] In their hearts the aristocrats realized that Americans had gained a new prestige. Yankees might run from one another on land, as Russell had reported, but they had beaten Englishmen at sea. All Europe saw, too well, that three years of war had taken "the run" out of American fighters and developed ordnance second to none in the world. The *Times* bolstered the faith of its readers with the feeble assurance that the victory was due to the chain-armored sides of the *Kearsarge*.

Lindsay knew that he must get his resolution through now or never. The Prime Minister was still in a desperate predicament. Six days after the *Alabama* had been sunk, a conference to settle the Danish question failed. Bismarck ordered his Prussians to occupy the disputed territory. Prime Minister Palmerston backed down and let him go. The House of Lords passed a vote of censure and sent it to Commons. The crisis had come. Old Pam needed every vote Lindsay could give him to save the government.

On the fatal day, the aged Prime Minister looked confidently at his fellow conspirator. Lindsay mustered his following and voted dutifully. The government was sustained and the resolution lost by a small margin. Immediately the representatives of the Southern Independence Association and the Society for Promoting the Cessation of Hostilities in America called on the Prime Minister to arrange his part of the bargain. Palmerston met them with the same cordiality he had shown Lindsay. He was full of stories and when the subject of mediating the American war was broached he became jovial. As a boy in school, he said, he had learned a little rhyme. Perhaps some of the gentlemen remembered it too:

> "They who in quarrels interpose
> Will often wipe a bloody nose."[17]

The delegation laughed piously. Palmerston treated them to a few more sallies. Then they filed out, wondering whether they had been betrayed by Palmerston or the Hon. William Schaw Lindsay. James Murray Mason returned to Paris. Slidell, the gambler, admitted bitterly that all hope of help from England had passed. Idealists pointed to Palmerston as the savior of their cause. They said he had consistently upheld the North in crisis after crisis. First in 1861 and then in 1862 cautiousness might have been his motive but since the Emancipation Proclamation in 1863 his acts had obviously been motivated by his lifelong dislike of slavery. Cynics pointed to Palmerston's dyed whiskers—symbol of insincerity. He had acted only as an opportunist, they maintained. In 1861 and 1862 he was not sure which side in America was going to win. After Murfreesboro and Gettysburg in 1863 he knew that the North would triumph in the end. Henry Hotze railed sarcastically in the *Index* at the Prime Minister's little joke.

"He proved incontestably . . . that, though he had been charged with forgetting the vigour of his prime, he can in old age remember the lessons of his childhood, by telling . . . a quotation which, in the mouth of the Prime Minister of the British Empire, and on such an occasion, must be admitted as not altogether unworthy of Abraham Lincoln himself."[18]

One more blow to the interventionists was close at hand. The shipping interests were no longer profiting by blockade-running. Hot weather in the South brought with it a plague of yellow fever to the coastal towns. People died by thousands. Blockade-runners hesitated to enter the pest ports. The traffic practically came to a stop.[19] Disease had joined Lincoln's legions and Palmerston's government to crush all opposition in Great Britain.

No sooner had Lindsay been knocked down than another danger bobbed up abroad. Pike wrote that the international bankers were frightened by the issues of greenbacks. American securities were going down.[20] Dayton and Bigelow wrote that Napoleon was acting suspiciously but they could prove nothing against him. Between dispatches friends told Lincoln that his own chance of reelection had been crushed by continued catastrophes. The *Alabama* victory made no impression on the red slaughter in Virginia. Grant was a failure—a butcher.

Lincoln mulled the problem in the quiet of his summer retreat at the Soldiers' Home. Two years had passed since Willie's death, but Mrs. Lincoln still felt happier out there than in the White House. The most suspicious thing about Napoleon was his apparent compliance with all Northern requests—sure indication that deep trickery was hatching. First he had canceled Arman's ship-building permits and ordered the half-finished hulls sold to a neutral power. Then he had dropped mediation. Perhaps he was paying Lincoln's price to keep Maximilian in Mexico. If so, things were going better for Lincoln abroad than at home. However, Napoleon could not be trusted. Grant was still fighting, slugging, reeling around Richmond—horrible losses—but he plugged on. His casualty lists would keep any President from re-election.

Soon the inside story of Napoleon's suspicious actions leaked out. The French conspirators had conspired against one another. Bulloch and Arman had planned to outwit the Emperor when His Majesty turned against them to save his Mexican empire. The plan seemed to have originated with Arman, who told Bulloch to sacrifice one of the rams he was building and thus save the other. Sell the first one to be finished to Denmark for her war, he said. The Americans would investigate and find the transfer legitimate. Then the second might be fictitiously sold to Denmark and delivered to the Confederacy. A good scheme, *oui?* Bulloch agreed and went to England to elude Lincoln's spies. Daily he expected word from Arman that the vessel was ready for delivery. At last a messenger arrived with bad news.[21] The Emperor had seen through the ruse. No ships must be sold to the Confederacy, either openly or below board. Napoleon appeared to be taking as strong a stand as England. Why?

Both Bulloch and Bigelow, in their different spheres, interpreted the act differently. Bulloch knew that Napoleon had been in on the plot from the beginning. Had he changed or was he waiting for a more opportune time? Suddenly it dawned on Bigelow that the Gascon spy might have been an agent of the Emperor. Perhaps Napoleon used him to inform the Americans of all the details and collect a few thousand francs besides. The Emperor had told the Confederates he would not go through with the deal if it became known. Now he could tell them truthfully that the North knew all about it and the ships must not be released. Lincoln's dalliance with Maximilian and Napoleon had been artful indeed. But Napoleon might reverse himself the minute Grant failed in Virginia.

Lincoln went to the War Department for the latest news. The

war, the Union, his own re-election, all depended upon Grant. The little Westerner had already moved his great army far to the south around Lee's flank. He was maneuvering toward Richmond from the rear precisely as McClellan had done. Washington was unprotected once more—the old danger. Then word came that chilled the blood in every loyal citizen in the capital. Lee had wheeled to face Grant and at the same time he had kicked out behind. Twenty thousand gray-clad veterans were coming down the Shenandoah under the command of Jubal Early, straight for Washington.

Lincoln mustered all available fighting men to guard the city. Quartermaster clerks were called from their desks and armed for the field. The President appeared to be in high spirits—happy, confident—commander in chief in his own right at last.[22] Breastworks were thrown up in the suburbs. Frantic citizens learned that the *Florida* had arrived off the entrance of Chesapeake Bay, raiding and burning ships in sight of the shore. They ran to the President but could not shake his enthusiasm.

On July 11, the rebels reached the outskirts of the city. The telegraph wires were cut.[23] Shooting could be heard out on Seventh Street. Lincoln ordered his carriage and drove to the front. The Confederates were coming across the meadows. They deployed for assault. Lincoln watched them from a parapet. Bullets hummed like angry bees past his black beard. No other President of the United States had stood thus under fire. Soldiers remembered that a young officer, Oliver Wendell Holmes, son of a Boston essayist and himself a veteran at twenty-three, lost his judicious mind in the smack and bang of battle. He shouted at the Chief Executive, "Get down, you fool!"

The gray-clad wave surged up to the defenses and then withdrew, leaving a flotsam of broken bodies in the green fields. Jubal Early, in sight of the dome of the Capitol, ordered a retreat. His army marched off up the Shenandoah, the rich valley of Virginia—corridor by which Southern armies had threatened Washington for three long years. Lincoln urged his officers to follow and harry the enemy. He was deeply depressed when they came back after one night's bivouac with nothing accomplished. This was

Meade and McClellan all over again. Only Grant knew how to strike and strike and then strike again.

News of Early's raid on Washington reached Grant in Virginia. The stubby little general shifted his cigar from one side of his mouth to the other. Reserves on the way to join him were diverted to protect the capital. That was all. Grant had no intention of withdrawing his troops as McClellan had done. Nor did Lincoln force him to do so. Grant had convinced the President that he was equal to his job. To Chief of Staff Halleck, Grant sent an order to scorch the earth of northern Virginia "so that crows flying over it for the balance of the season will have to carry their provender."[24] Two weeks later Grant sent a cavalry commander, little Phil Sheridan, to see that it was done. Sheridan stood only five feet four on the ground, but on a horse he could make men believe that he weighed a ton. Lincoln looked down skeptically at the little jockey of a man. Officers who would not follow retreating Confederates had been the bane of his presidency. He wired Grant: "I repeat to you, it will neither be done nor attempted, unless you watch it every day and hour, and force it."[25]

Sheridan trotted away across the valley of Virginia kicking the sides of his favorite black horse, Rienzi. Grant stayed where he was, down on the peninsula, killing men, champing his cigar. Eighty-four thousand Union casualties were reported in his army. Lincoln ordered another draft for five hundred thousand soldiers. Peaceful-minded citizens shuddered. Many editors demanded that the bloodshed stop. Peace-at-any-price men increased in number. The Democratic convention was due to meet in Chicago on August 29, 1864. With disaffection sweeping across the country the Democrats had an exceptional opportunity to elect the next President of the United States. Horace Greeley wrote Lincoln that the re-election could never be won unless peace was made at once. In the *Tribune* he accused Lincoln of purposely prolonging the war.[26] Did not the South have emissaries appointed to negotiate peace, yet Lincoln would not listen to them?

Lincoln challenged Greeley to produce the peace commissioners. The editor could not do so. Grant fought on. He struck and sidled. More lists of dead. Prominent party men decided that Lincoln must resign the nomination for some other man. Then Gurowski published another volume of vitriolic complaints about the progress of the war—Seward a liar, Lincoln a weakling. Soldiers who had seen the President's long figure standing on the parapet spattered by bullets did not like the tone of the publication. The author was not molested, but Gideon Welles dropped his name from the list of guests invited to a party for the cabinet and members of Congress. Gurowski's feelings were hurt.[27]

The time for the Democratic convention was close now and administration disasters piled up. Henry Ward Beecher turned against the President. Bigelow wrote that Napoleon had not stopped work on the rams. Obviously the Gascon spy was his tool and the Emperor stood ready to align himself with either the North or South on a moment's notice. Pike confirmed Bigelow's statement. He said that the Dutch Foreign Secretary had learned from De L'Huys that the Emperor did not intend to stop the rams' construction.[28] Worse news came from England. British friends of the Confederacy had raised a new hue and cry. A committee of factory workers had presented Earl Russell with a petition signed by ninety thousand laborers requesting intervention.[29] Did these people really despair of an end to the war in spite of the pamphlets and lectures by both British and American liberals?

Lincoln was deeply depressed. His administration had failed abroad as well as at home. The summer was unusually hot even for Washington. The President decided to pardon the stock speculator who had forged the call for troops. Henry Ward Beecher wanted it.[30] The cabinet was due to meet the next day, August 23, 1864. Before they assembled Lincoln wrote a strange note:

"This morning, as for some days past, it seems exceedingly probable that this administration will not be reelected. Then it will be my duty to so cooperate with the President-elect as to save the Union between the election and the inauguration; as he will have secured his election on such ground that he cannot possibly save it afterward."[31]

Lincoln folded the paper so the writing did not show. When the cabinet members filed in, he asked them to sign their names across the back. Then Lincoln put the paper in his pocket and turned to the regular order of business.

Six days later the Democrats convened in Chicago. Vallandigham presided as chairman of the Committee on Resolutions and personally nominated McClellan on a platform that pronounced "the war a failure"—incongruous for a leading general in the "failure." Peace-at-any-price men could be counted on to vote for him. War Democrats should vote for Lincoln. Independent voters, the deciding factor in this election, must be won to Lincoln's standard or he would be defeated.

Lincoln was very tired, but politics was his consuming interest. He set to work.

# XX. *Every Gambler in the Blue Grass Will Recognize You*

A TALLYHO stopped on the brink of the escarpment. The horses—Western mustangs—fretted in the harness, tossed their heads, rubbed against each other. Women on the high seats gasped with wonder at the San Joaquin Valley stretching below them like an arm of the sea. Their escorts removed their tall beaver hats and expressed awe. Then the driver tightened his reins. The tallyho lurched forward and the descent began. Wheels squealed through the brake blocks and passengers clutched the seat bars, laughing merrily. Behind them the sun peeped over the tops of the sequoias. Rays of warm light dissolved the veils on distant mountains, touched peak after peak with pale pink, until the whole Coast Range was illuminated with overwhelming splendor as far as the eye could see.

The vacationists, supporters of Abraham Lincoln and free government, had placed marble slabs bearing the names of Richard Cobden and John Bright under two giant trees in the Calaveras grove on the Wawona road to Yosemite. They had sung patriotic songs and waved flags in the cathedral gloom of the forest. An orator had spoken. The Californians had clapped their hands when he likened the big trees to the Englishmen "who, with a liberality as broad as the world, have had a kindly word for freedom, wherever a blow was struck in her behalf, or a government established in her spirit."[1]

The two Englishmen were touched by the gesture when they heard of it. Like Burke and Chatham in the American Revolution, they felt a strong kinship for America and considered the United States an experiment in English democracy. Cobden wrote Bright:

"I hope you were pleased with the compliment paid us in California. There is a poetical sublimity about the idea of associating

our name with a tree 300 feet high and 60 feet girth! Verily it is
a monument not built with men's hands. If I were twenty years
younger I would hope to look on these forest giants; great trees
and rivers have an attraction for me."[2]


Bright also hoped to see the great natural resources of the democracy that he had fought to preserve. He was past sixty, but
he planned a trip to the Far West by overland stage when the war
was over. He watched the campaign for Lincoln's re-election with
more interest than some Americans.

Lincoln appeared less careworn as the campaign progressed.
Victories accumulated on the field of battle. The old theory that a
warlike agricultural people could defeat a city civilization had run
down. Grant's order to lay waste the Shenandoah Valley had
been executed implicitly by tough little Phil Sheridan, the runt
whose feet did not touch the floor when he sat on a chair. The hoofs
of his horses tramped out the grainfields of Virginia. His men
burned barns bulging with hay, corn, oats and wheat—all needed
for Lee's army. Crows would have to carry their own provender.

In September 1864, Lincoln received two revealing dispatches—
one from Sherman in the South, the other from Henry Bergh in
Russia. Bergh sent his resignation. The climate was bad for his
and his wife's chronic colds, he said; besides, he needed a larger
audience for his new role as protector of dumb beasts. He was
eager to come back to America and organize a Society for the
Prevention of Cruelty to Animals.

Sherman's dispatch announced the capture of the great railway
center, Atlanta—accomplished without being trapped as his English critics prophesied. Lincoln's supporters who had not long
ago proposed running another man in his stead now cheered for
him heartily. News of the victories fell on Washington like manna
from Heaven. Surely the Lord wanted people to vote for Abraham
Lincoln.

The great picture of Lincoln reading the Emancipation Proclamation was boxed for a trip around the country. Lincoln felt confident about his re-election. Every afternoon he drove away from
the White House with Mrs. Lincoln. The carriage sped along the
dirt roads through sunshine and shadow. The rhythm of flying

hoofs rested the President. Cavalrymen in a cloud of dust pounded behind. Ahead, three international complications lay in wait for him during the two months that remained before Election Day. He knew that slaveholding Brazil had opposed the Emancipation Proclamation and that Canada sheltered many Confederate spies. All summer long he had heard stories of Ohio and Indiana Copperheads, Knights of the Golden Circle, followers of Vallandigham, and their plot to overthrow the government. Lincoln had given them rope to hang themselves. They had a presidential nominee of their own and surely would not revolt unless defeated at the polls. Suddenly Lincoln learned that a group of fighting Confederates had appeared on Lake Erie.

The outlaws planned to liberate Confederate prisoners on an island near Sandusky, Ohio. Knights of the Golden Circle were said to be in the plot, waiting for the signal to join and gut the unsuspecting North between the Great Lakes and the Ohio—a predicament on the eve of an election. Sherman's and Sheridan's victories would not offset such a cataclysm.

Details of the proposed raid were soon common knowledge. On September 19, 1864, the *Philo Parsons,* a steamship on the Detroit-Sandusky line, made its usual Canadian stops. Passengers trooped up the gangplank and stood innocently along the rails until the ship was well out in the lake. Then they drew pistols and took over the vessel. Another passenger ship, the *Island Queen,* was hailed, captured and scuttled. Next the pirates headed for Sandusky to release the prisoners. A suspicious vessel ahead looked like a Federal gunboat. The *Philo Parsons* was wheeled about and headed for the Canadian shore.[3] The rovers ran the ship into shallow water, grounded her and scampered away.

Canadian authorities did not learn of the raid until the men had escaped. Lincoln was told that the leader's name was John Y. Beall of Virginia.

The President might have forgotten the affair except for another border incident of a similar nature. Before this occurred, however, foreign complications shifted to South America. The *Florida,* having left France in the spring of 1864, steamed into Bahia, Brazil, in October. By chance an American war sloop, the *Wachusett,* was anchored there. Both ships were immune from attack by

*Courtesy of F. H. Meserve*

*From Century Magazine,*
*Nov. 1907*

MAXIMILIAN AND CARLOTTA

NAPOLEON III AND
EUGÉNIE

*Courtesy of Baker & Taylor, N. Y.*

*Courtesy of Baker & Taylor, N. Y.*

EDOUARD LABOULAYE

THE DUC DE PERSIGNY

*Cartoon from Punch, by Tenniel*

PALMERSTON NOT QUITE READY TO RECOGNIZE
JEFF DAVIS

Cartoon by John Tenniel

the rules of international law. The Confederate commander went ashore confidently.

On the quarter-deck of the *Wachusett,* Captain Napoleon Collins watched his enemy row to the dock. Collins had already been reprimanded for capturing a blockade-runner in the days when Seward toadied to Great Britain.[4] He might get something worse than a reprimand if he attacked the *Florida.* Then again he might not. Wilkes had profited by illegally taking Mason and Slidell at the cost of almost embroiling the United States and England in war. Napoleon Collins decided to take a chance. Late at night he rammed and disabled the Confederate, then fastened a hawser to her stem, pulled her out of the harbor and steered for the United States with the disabled Confederate in tow.

In all Latin America, slaveholding Brazil was, perhaps, the most touchy about Northern arrogance. The Brazilian minister at Washington officially demanded immediate release of the *Florida,* court-martial of the offending captain and suitable apologies.

Lincoln and Seward, each with one eye on the approaching election, closed the door for a conference. The fortunate capture of the raider might counteract the bad effect of the *Philo Parsons* affair. However, if the act must be disavowed and the *Florida* turned loose to prey on Northern commerce, the double misfortune was sure to cost votes. Could Seward, versatile as he was, think up some justification for Napoleon Collins' act? The theory that Confederate ships were pirates would hardly warrant an American to violate a foreign port. Some other pretext must be offered. The two campaigners agreed on a course of action. Seward stalled for time. Sweetly he told the Brazilian minister that a decision would have to await arrival of the ships in port. The United States would do what was right but first an investigation must be made to ascertain all facts of the case.

By that time, Seward knew, the election would be decided.

While the decision hung fire, a second outbreak occurred on the Canadian border. In the little village of St. Albans, Vermont, farmers were peacefully transacting their week-end trading, carrying armloads of groceries for near-by farms to the double row of buggies and farm wagons hitched along the rail in front of the stores. On the street corners country people gossiped, idly watching the sun, planning to be home in time for milking. Some twenty strangers, who did not appear to know one another, were in town. They had registered at different hotels. During the day some of them stepped into the banks, inquired the price of gold, looked furtively at the doors, the windows and the location of the vaults and safes. Others examined the horses along the rack. The farmers found them to be friendly fellows who knew the good and bad points of a mount. Vermonters liked "to talk horse." They were proud of their Morgan stock; "dual purpose you know, ken pull a plow all week and race of a Sunday." Boastful men pointed out the best animals. "See that 'un, short-coupled, round as a dollar, good bone and bottom, that's the idear." The strangers spit tobacco juice in the road and understood.

Suddenly, without any warning, the strangers drew pistols with the hammers racked back like snakes ready to strike. The citizens were ordered to stand still under penalty of instant death. The harness was pulled from the best of the "dual purpose" mounts. Men scrambled on their backs. Other men came out of the banks with heavy bags of money—$200,000 in specie. Now and then a shot warned the citizens that the guns meant business. In short order the strangers adjusted the heavy bags in front of the riders, jumped on spare horses and galloped away, shooting wildly in the air[5]—a bank-robbing pattern identical with that used by Jesse James and lesser bandits for the next generation. One onlooker was killed and several, including a little girl, were wounded.

Before the dust from flying hoofs had settled again on the country road, an ex-captain of volunteers in the village organized a posse. Green Mountain boys clattered off in pursuit. The trail led across the border. Some of the raiders were overtaken, but the Canadian authorities prevented the Americans from inflicting revenge. Canada was not Brazil. Thirteen men with $75,000 were lodged in jail. The leader said that his name was Bennett H. Young, lieutenant, Confederate Army of America. The raid, he said, had been ordered by Jeff Davis as retaliation for Sheridan's raids in Virginia. The defectiveness of the chemical compound he carried prevented St. Albans from being burned to the ground.

Beall's piratical adventure and the St. Albans raid led many people to suspect daily that other raids were planned. Buffalo was

pointed to as the next city to be attacked. The Northern border
jittered with panic. Farmers in Ohio and Indiana looked on their
Democratic neighbors with suspicion, whispering that they were
members of the dreaded Knights of the Golden Circle. The emotional frustration of suspense augured no good for the approaching election. The old cry for a strong man, a dictator, was heard
again. Certainly Lincoln was not such a man. His political opponent, McClellan, was a soldier. But Little Mac's military record
did not portend a policy stronger than the existing administration's—a lucky coincidence for Lincoln.

As the campaign progressed, the great picture of the cabinet discussing the Emancipation Proclamation arrived in the West, an
exhibition of art as well as political propaganda. Seward, in the
meantime, pondered the international complications on his desk.
What reply must be given Brazil concerning Napoleon Collins'
act? What could the State Department do in Canada to stop future
raids? First, Seward tried to extradite Lieutenant Young and his
accomplices as common criminals and failed. The plea was hardly
tenable in face of the leader's commission from the Confederate
government. Whether or not the Confederates were recognized as
belligerents or as rebels, the fugitives were safe in Canada. By
long tradition the British flag maintained its jurisdiction of immunity for political refugees. By no interpretation could Seward
build a case for the return of the raiders. He knew, too, that in
1837, during the Canadian rebellion, Americans had been ever
ready to give asylum to Canadian rebels. Seward's only sure
remedy was the brute force which Napoleon Collins had used in
lieu of international law.

But while Collins used military bluntness Seward continued to
be suave. He had a plan which might work—prevent future raids
and at the same time hold British friendship. On October 24,
1864, he wrote Adams to notify Earl Russell that the United States
might cancel the treaty of 1817 by which the United States and
Canada had agreed not to fortify the Canadian border. The recent
threat of mobilization during the *Trent* affair had not disturbed
this convention. Canada's inability to prevent raids seemed ample
justification for adequate defenses along the border. Yet Seward
was careful to say only that the United States "deem themselves

at liberty to increase the naval armament upon the lakes if in their judgment the condition of affairs shall then require it"—a far cry from the belligerent attitude he had taken three years before. Perhaps the Secretary had learned much from his association with the President.

Lincoln did not learn England's reaction to this notice of termination of the treaty until after the election. In the meantime, a long dispatch arrived from Burlingame in China, written three months before. On the opposite side of the world the Emperor of China had been fighting another civil war. His war, like Lincoln's, was drawing to a close. Yankee merchants in Chinese ports had taken an active part, and in return the Emperor had closed his harbors to Confederate privateers.[6] As Lincoln read the dispatches he must have noticed an interesting comparison. The rebel Chinese capital had been invested during the summer of 1864 precisely as Richmond had been besieged in America. In July, General Grant and the Chinese imperial commander both planted great mines under their respective enemies' defenses. Both succeeded in blowing up the objectives. The crater formed by Grant's mine did not permit his soldiers to enter the fortifications, but the Chinese breach proved highly successful. The Manchus swarmed into the rebel capital.

In August, Prince Kung sent a greeting to Lincoln through Burlingame.

"I am rejoiced to learn that the United States forces have recently achieved a great victory in their attack on the Southern rebels. . . . Both our countries will henceforth alike rejoice in prosperity and peace."[7]

A month later Burlingame wrote again. This time he requested leave after some three years of service. The request was granted, and like his fellow "noisy jackass," Cassius M. Clay, he returned to America only to find, like Clay, that he wanted to be back at his post. Like Clay, also, he soon did return and when he visited the United States again he did not come on a leave of absence but as an ambassador of the Celestial Empire to negotiate a treaty with his friends in Washington—Head Ambassador, Burlingame said, stroking his long youthful beard. Records disclosed later that he was really subordinate to the mandarins in the suite.

The letters from Burlingame were diverting. Lincoln might have read them with more interest at any time but on the eve of an election. All his time was engrossed with important conferences. Political advisers urged him to bid for the columns of the *Herald* by offering James Gordon Bennett a foreign post.[8] Lincoln already had got young Bennett's yacht and the foreign posts were filled. Besides the President had learned a new method as efficient as the press for broadcasting his words. At charitable functions for the benefit of wounded soldiers Lincoln explained the aims of his administration. He spoke almost daily to regiments of soldiers passing through Washington at the termination of their enlistments. These men returned to every state in the North. They circulated more widely than the *Herald* and they carried his message everywhere more convincingly than any newspaper could do. Lincoln's theme, his platform, was always an expansion of the Gettysburg Address—the importance of maintaining a democratic form of government in a world of monarchies and dictators.[9]

Foreigners took a surprising interest in the campaign. Count Gasparin, whose book on the war had already been translated twice for the English and American trade, wrote a long treatise in French for the *New York Tribune*.[10] Mary L. Booth translated the article for publication, then sent the original to Lincoln in Washington.[11] Professor Laboulaye entered the campaign with as much fervor as he could have shown had he been an American citizen. His *L'Election du président aux Etats-Unis* was translated for both the *Times* and the *New York Tribune;* his *The Great Friend of America* circulated in the North like a regular campaign document. "A victory for McClellan and reunion without abolition of slavery," Laboulaye warned, "then the North will be rightfully charged with duplicity and laughed at by Europe."[12]

In England the electioneering aroused a political contest. Friends of the South revived the hope of intervention. Old families decided to make a last fight along with the Southern planters. Gentlefolk wrote essays, shelled out their guineas,[13] provided halls for meetings. They employed speakers with position and education but not much talent. The best they could do fell flat before the voices and pens of the liberals. In Parliament a menacing letter from Seward to Earl Russell, written at the time of the *Trent* affair, was produced as a new justification for war with America. The British government—always trying to evade war—pronounced the letter spurious. No such epistle had been received at the Foreign Office.[14] Old Tories were disappointed. Nothing they could do checked the Lincoln advance. The promise of the Gettysburg Address had grown steadily, unyielding, ever since Lincoln had delivered it. The shadow of the Rail Splitter stretched across the benches in the House of Lords.

Christopher Newman Hall,[15] Goldwin Smith and William Evans all lectured for liberty and Lincoln in America, as Beecher and other Americans had done in England. Their pamphlets were published on both sides of the Atlantic. Frederick Milnes Edge decried the depredations of the *Alabama* in his *Destruction of the American Carrying Trade*. His *Whom Do the English Tories Wish Elected to the Presidency?* actually attempted to arouse American ire against the English gentry by reciting the Tory party's commissions against the Northern cause, listing the English papers that favored McClellan and peace. The battle of pamphlets was too much for the nerves of George Francis Train. He joined the lists with one of his own entitled *The Withdrawal of McClellan and the Impeachment of Lincoln.*

Then the friends of the Confederacy played their last pre-election card. Having tried to influence Earl Russell with a petition for mediation signed by ninety thousand suffering workers, a meeting was now arranged to display poor wretches, paupers, anemics, starving women with babes in arms. All this misery was blamed on the American war. Handbills summoned the audience with glaring captions: "The Crisis! The Crisis! The Crisis!" The issue was then put squarely before Palmerston in a manifesto from the Confederate commissioners in Paris demanding recognition.

Old Pam did not reply at once. He knew that skilled labor— the great unions—gave the lie to the Tory display with enthusiastic meetings. Unskilled labor—bootblacks, stevedores, almsmen, chimney sweeps, match girls—docile and downtrodden, might do anything for a sixpence. The skilled trades were not with them. Real distress in the industrial areas had been alleviated and the people knew it.[16] No self-respecting workman could forget that prominent Southerners, from the Vice-President down, had said that slavery was the solution of the age-old struggle between capital and labor—a personal insult to every man in England who worked with his hands. The dignity of mankind depended on the re-election of Abraham Lincoln. Palmerston, the politician, heard the murmur in low places. He did not intend to be caught making any commitments until the ballots were counted in America. A reply to the manifesto must wait.

In mid-November word arrived that Lincoln had won. A committee of the International Workingmen's Association marched down to the London legation to congratulate Charles Francis Adams.[17] The Civil War, they told him in a formal address, determined "whether the virgin soil of immense tracts should be wedded to the Labour of the Emigrant, or prostituted by the Tramp of the Slave Driver." When a counterrevolution was based on property in men as "the corner stone of the New Edifice . . . the Working Classes of Europe understood at once . . . that the Slaveholder's Rebellion was to sound the tocsin for a general holy Crusade of Property against Labour."[18]

Labor leaders of many European countries—including Karl Marx of Germany—signed their names to the address. W. R. Cremer, secretary of the first Socialist International, added a personal note requesting that it be sent to Lincoln.[19] Socialists as a body welcomed the Rail Splitter to their ranks. Had he not said: "The strongest bond of human sympathy, outside of family relation, should be one uniting all working people, of all nations, and tongues, and kindreds"? Yet Americans who had noted all Lincoln's speeches knew him to be no socialist. To recognize labor as a fixed status like slavery was abhorrent to him. "That some should be rich shows that others may become rich, and hence is just encouragement to industry and enterprise." Lincoln had said and resaid this all his life.[20] Lincoln replied to the International Council through Secretary Seward. His viewpoint was national, not international. The purpose of a nation, he said, was "to promote the welfare and happiness of mankind by benevolent intercourse and example." The United States "derive new encouragement to persevere from the testimony of the working men of

Europe that the national attitude is favored with their enlightened approval"[21]—a kind reply to international socialists.

The British government decided that the time had come to reply to the Southern commissioners' manifesto demanding recognition. Earl Russell wrote them formally that Her Majesty's government "deplored the commencement of this sanguinary struggle," but was determined to observe "a strict and impartial Neutrality."[22]

With the election safely past, Seward replied to Brazil. He did not attempt to justify the seizure, and replied candidly that the United States was in the wrong. Collins had erred and he would be suspended pending a court-martial.[23] As for the return of the *Florida,* Seward regretted that the vessel had suffered from a collision shortly after arriving in Chesapeake Bay. She had sunk to the bottom and her return would be impossible. Thus everybody was appeased and the rebel raider was destroyed.

While this diplomatic discussion was in progress, Goldwin Smith visited the President. A liberal professor studying the theory of democracy, he wanted to see with his own eyes how democracy appeared from the inside. Since arriving in America he had been shocked by the quality of the undisciplined persons who came to the top in such a government. Most notable among all the untrained men who attained high office was Abraham Lincoln, the uncouth rustic who joked on all occasions. With considerable curiosity Professor Smith went to the White House for his interview. The anteroom where he waited was strangely bare. He looked at a plain door, not guarded by a single sentry—the portal that separated him from the democratic chief. Goldwin Smith had read Lincoln's Gettysburg Address and had noted one or two phrases "which betray a hand untrained in fine writing." On the whole, he concluded, "it may be doubted whether any king in Europe would have expressed himself more royally than the peasant's son."[24]

When told to enter into the presence of the President, the professor found Lincoln in an ordinary office room, seated at a table littered with many sheets of paper covered with lists of figures. Lincoln was working on a message to Congress and immediately took the Britisher into his confidence—or appeared to. The figures, he said, disclosed war casualties, an appalling number. Smith agreed. Lincoln looked at his guest over the rims of his spectacles.

He had other figures for the professor to consider. The natural death rate, Lincoln pointed out, would have taken many of the men in times of peace. Then, too, deserters had been classed as casualties. Missing men were not all killed. One out of every seven men who enlisted was known to have deserted.[25] Official records of casualties, Lincoln said, reminded him of the Negro learning arithmetic. The teacher had asked, "If three pigeons set on a fence and you shot one how many would remain?" "Two," replied the black mathematician. "Dat's whar you wrong. De udder two would fly away."[26]

Goldwin Smith smiled. He noticed that Lincoln's stories always clinched a point of argument. He never told one for its own sake. The professor left the room a firm believer in Lincoln's honesty and humaneness. He remembered, too, that the most conspicuous picture in the President's apartment was a large photograph of John Bright. Goldwin Smith did not care to return to England permanently. The American experiment had won his everlasting support. He lived to help establish Cornell University.

On December 6, 1864, Lincoln delivered his annual message to Congress—a third of it devoted to foreign affairs.[27] Especially did he dwell on the friendly relations with Latin America—the recognition of Venezuela's new government, the settlement of the claims with Peru and Chile, and the amicable adjustment of the "inter-oceanic transit route." In Santo Domingo and in Mexico civil war still continued, but the United States, Lincoln said, remained scrupulously neutral. Critics might object that such neutrality was contrary to the Monroe Doctrine but Lincoln, with one war on his hands, did not bring up that question. Instead he discussed the recent depredations on the Canadian border. He said that he did not believe the Canadian authorities to be "intentionally unjust or unfriendly," but "the United States must hold themselves at liberty to increase their naval armament upon the lakes if they shall find that proceeding necessary." Lincoln turned next to the importance of his America as the haven of mankind. The abolitionist poet, John Greenleaf Whittier, referred to America as :

> The land of all who suffer—
> The dread of all who wrong.

Lincoln, too, believed that America had such a mission. Immigration had been encouraged during his administration. Unscrupulous people, he said, reaped a rich harvest organizing the foreigners into labor gangs. In some cases able-bodied immigrants had been shunted into the Army. Congress, Lincoln hoped, would amend the existing laws to stop such frauds.

"I regard our immigrants as one of the principal replenishing streams which are appointed by Providence to repair the ravages of internal war, and its wastes of national strength and health. All that is necessary is to secure the flow of that stream in its present fullness, and to that end the government must, in every way, make it manifest that it neither needs nor designs to impose involuntary military service upon those who come from other lands to cast their lot in our country."[28]

Lincoln then turned to the South, to the peace party in the North, and to any and all governments in Europe who might yet question that the North would be victorious in the war. Not only was the North prospering with wartime industries, he pointed out, but, after three and a half years of war, man power had increased mightily.

"It is not material to inquire how the increase has been produced, or to show that it would have been greater but for the war, which is probably true. The important fact remains demonstrated that we have more men now than we had when the war began; that we are not exhausted, nor in process of exhaustion; that we are gaining strength, and may, if need be, maintain the contest indefinitely."[29]

Lincoln closed by reassuring the world that slavery would be extinguished by the Civil War. The Emancipation Proclamation had been called a war measure. People had hinted that the termination of hostilities might see new laws passed to re-enslave the Negroes. Had not Congress already failed to pass a constitutional amendment abolishing the institution? Lincoln saw the danger. He wished to make it plain that he personally would not retreat from the position he had taken.

"If the people should, by whatever mode or means, make it an executive duty to reënslave such persons, another, and not I, must be their instrument to perform it."[30]

Then with Lincolnian simplicity the President concluded his message by taking full advantage of the fact that the South had begun the war by firing on Sumter.

"In stating a single condition of peace, I mean simply to say, that the war will cease on the part of the government whenever it shall have ceased on the part of those who began it."

Lincoln's message, in so far as it criticized England's policy of neutrality, was not read with equanimity abroad. Goldwin Smith pronounced the paragraphs on foreign relations to be a Sewardish complaint of England or at least "the work of a subtler genius than that of the President."[31] The London *Times* and the *Manchester Guardian,* both complacent journals dreading the social significance of a Union victory, criticized Lincoln for intimating that Great Britain had acted unwisely. Delane of the *Times* did not yet concede a final victory for the North. Sherman, who had begun his great march to the sea, appeared in Delane's columns to be making a desperate retreat to the coast. News of his annihilation was promised almost daily.

The lameduck Congress in Washington was in no mood to help the President's foreign relations. Henry Winter Davis offered a resolution in the House, announcing the constitutional right of Congress to determine foreign policy[32]—a step farther than last spring's resolution in the Arguelles case. In the Senate, Sumner spoke again and again for a termination of the reciprocity treaty with Canada.[33] In the midst of these anxious and exciting times word came to Lincoln that Dayton had died of apoplexy. The President considered offering the post to James Gordon Bennett.[34] Finally he decided to elevate John Bigelow and send his erstwhile private secretary, John Hay, to fill Bigelow's place—the beginning of a long diplomatic career which lasted intermittently into the administration of Theodore Roosevelt.

In spite of the *Times'* dire prophecies, news from down South continued to be good. General Thomas defeated General Hood near

Nashville, Tennessee, scattering his army. Sherman reached the sea almost without opposition. Reports said that he was laying siege to the city of Savannah. Delane realized what this meant to the English upper classes. He became physically ill. Tossing in bed, the newsman's pride in accurate reporting forced him to acknowledge the magnitude of Sherman's achievement.

The war was over—almost. Lord Lyons packed his plate, his boxes and portmanteaus. The Queen rewarded him with an earldom for keeping England out of the American war. His successor, whosoever he might be, would not have the trouble that confronted Lord Lyons. In spite of the finality of the news, some British papers maintained doggedly that the war would last indefinitely. Others denounced this as unwarranted news to increase circulation. Lurid accounts of bushwhackers printed in sensational sheets reminded readers that the South would not be conquered even when the last army was destroyed. The *London Telegraph,* normally neutral, sent its American war correspondent, George A. Sala, to Canada. He reported that the St. Albans raid and the *Philo Parsons* incident were only the first of a long series of similar disturbances which might be expected. Canadian liberals took this as a personal insult. To counteract the slur at the province's ability to police the border, the Reverend John Cordner delivered a lecture in Montreal. No more raids, he said, would be countenanced. Canadian taxpayers realized the tremendous expense of prosecuting lawless marauders. The St. Albans "bank robbers" and the pirates on the lakes had already cost the local government half a million dollars. "This you and I and all Canadians will have to pay."[35]

Cordner's lecture was published in Manchester, England, as *Canada and the United States.* In the pamphlet the Reverend Mr. Cordner summed up the American Civil War from the colonial and democratic point of view. He scouted the assertion that the war was fought on one side for maintenance of the union and on the other for independence. This, he said, was only a half-truth. "There would be more truth in the statement if we should say that the North fought for the Union, although Slavery should be destroyed by the war, while the South fought for Slavery though the Union should be destroyed."[36] Always this odious reference to slavery came up to curse the South. No civilized country would interpret the war on any other terms.

Cordner concluded his lecture with a flourish of oratory eulogizing Abraham Lincoln in a manner suitable for the monarchical government of Canada. He said:

"I should approach him with as much respect as if he had the blood of the Courteneys and Montmorencys and Howards all flowing in his veins. And I should certainly approach him with much more respect than if he were the owner of the largest plantation in Virginia or Louisiana, where a thousand unpaid slaves toiled perforce for his benefit, and whom, by his word or sign manual, he could send to the auction block to-morrow. All honour, then, to honest Abraham Lincoln, President of the United States, and President-elect of the *Free* United States of America."[37]

This crescendo was reported to have been greeted by the audience with prolonged applause. The speaker showed that he had been influenced by Lincoln's recent message when he concluded:

"I hope the war will be brought to a close long before the end of his second term. . . . No one desires peace more strongly than myself. But if this cannot be done, I see no immediate way to the much desired peace except the party who first took up the sword shall be the first to lay it down."[38]

Again the firing on Fort Sumter rose to plague the Confederates in foreign countries as well as in America.

The friendly tone of this lecture would have soothed the frayed nerves of an executive less sanguine than Abraham Lincoln. He knew that Seward's threats and his own messages had appeared belligerent across the border. He knew, too, that Canadian Tories, like Tories in England, scorned abolition as destruction of property—the first step toward communism. In spite of this, Canada had been the terminus of the underground railway, the asylum for escaped slaves. Canadians' natural disgust for the institution had increased as they met and talked with the fugitives. The deplorable condition of the runaway slaves, their torn clothing and bleeding feet spoke with an eloquence Canadians could not forget.[39] In Canada abolition assumed some of the political significance it had abroad. Liberals organized an Anti-Slavery Society in 1851; also a woman's auxiliary. Missions had been established to teach escaped slaves the responsibilities of freedom. One observer said of a Canadian Negro village:

"The refugees in Canada earn a living and gather property; they build churches and send their children to school; they improve in manners and morals—not because they are picked men, but because they are free men."[40]

As early as 1829, when a delegation of Negroes came to Canada hunting homes under a flag that was free, Sir John Colburne, the Governor at York, told them derisively, "Tell the republicans on your side of the line that we royalists do not know men by their colour."[41] Lincoln knew, too, that thirty-five thousand Canadians had joined the Northern Army to fight the slaveholders.[42]

As Christmas approached—the fourth since Lincoln had been in the White House—war bulletins continued to be favorable, international problems decreased. This year there was no *Trent* affair to threaten war with England; no Emancipation Proclamation to be risked. Instead the war was coming to a close. Holiday shopping reached a new peak in Washington. War wealth poured through all the stores. New buggies, phaetons, broughams, brakes, spun along the dirt streets, rattled over the cobbles. No one noticed a buggy from the country that stopped one day before a hotel near Grover's Theatre. Samuel Arnold handed the lines to a stable boy and engaged a room. He had plotted with Booth, the actor, to kidnap the President of the United States. Details would be arranged here.[43]

An unusual Christmas present came to Abraham Lincoln—the city of Savannah, Georgia, captured by William Tecumseh Sherman, the end of his march to the sea. The fall of the seaport left the Confederacy cut and cross-cut, drawn and quartered. Only European intervention could save the South now and that must come at once. Judah P. Benjamin decided to try a last expedient, so daring he hesitated to confide in President Davis. European recognition must be bought by offering to abolish slavery in the South—the only hope left for the Confederacy. A commissioner must be sent at once to negotiate the deal. Such an offer would surely win the support of all conservatives who feared democracy yet who were not sufficiently reactionary to stomach slavery. The proposition shocked Jeff Davis. Possessing the inflexible will and pious righteousness which Southerners liked to call puritanic in others, Jeff Davis' spine stiffened outrageously at the prospect of surrendering the cornerstone of his edifice. Secretary Benjamin felt no misgivings. He demanded only success. Duncan Kenner of Louisiana was selected for the job.

Kenner, a successful planter, large slaveholder and breeder of fast horses, had married into a Creole family. A younger man than Mason and Slidell, he had dabbled only in state politics, prior to the secession movement. In 1861 he was elected to the Confederate House of Representatives from Louisiana. A unique thing about Kenner was his adaptability. Many of his political contemporaries owed their eminence to an environment suitable to their peculiar talents. When the environment changed they became helpless as fish out of water. Not so Kenner, whose active mind challenged any situation and asked only for a sporting chance in it.

Duncan Kenner's greatest asset for his mission was confidence in the proposition he had to offer. His own farms, he felt sure, could be run profitably with free labor. Full of enthusiasm, he set off to board a blockade-runner. At Wilmington he learned that this form of transportation was obsolete. Precious time had been lost. Kenner returned to Richmond for permission to pass the Union lines in Kentucky and sail from New York. President Davis remonstrated. "There is not a gambler in the country who won't know you. You will certainly be captured."

"There is not a gambler who knows me who would betray me,"[44] Kenner replied. Davis decided to let him try. Kenner bought a wig, looked in a mirror and saw that it disguised him admirably. Well satisfied, he bade his friends good-by. His greatest danger, he believed, awaited him in New York. Many sporting friends were sure to be promenading the streets. When Kenner arrived at the station he hurried to a cab and drove to the American Hotel. Here the proprietor knew and sheltered him. Meals were served in his room until time for the boat to sail. A cab carried him quickly through the enemy city to the dock. On board a British steamer he was safe.

Perhaps Kenner was too late. The war was drawing to a close. Sherman had started to march north from Savannah to join Grant below Richmond. Six hundred miles of hostile country lay ahead of him. Two great Confederate Armies, one under Joseph Johnston and the other under Robert E. Lee, remained to be defeated in the East. Suppose they combined to pinch off Grant's force on the James, then turned against Sherman down there in the enemy country! With Kenner in Europe offering abolition in the South for recognition, the fortunes of war might yet be turned.

At the hotel near Grover's Theatre, actor Booth knocked at Sam Arnold's room. The two men shook hands, ordered tobacco and wine. Then Booth explained his latest plot. Next time Lincoln attended Grover's Theatre the gas would be turned off suddenly. In the dark the President would be carried away.[45]

# XXI. *A Ship Sailing to an Unknown Shore*

SHORTLY after Jeff Davis agreed to let Duncan Kenner go to Europe, old Frank Blair came to Lincoln with a proposition equally desperate. He wanted a pass to go south and see the Confederate President personally, stop the war and end the slaughter. Blair did not discuss the details of his proposition with the President. Lincoln knew that old Blair was acquainted with all the Confederate leaders, that he had served with many of them as a member of the same party. Surely he knew their characters as well as any man. On December 28, 1864, Lincoln gave him a pass to cross the Federal lines.

President Davis received Blair and the interview was friendly. Blair's plan was grandiose: Why not declare a truce between North and South, combine the armies, join Juárez in Mexico and drive out Maximilian? The joint enterprise would unite the warring factions. After the conquest a peace at home would be easy.

Blair could be eloquent at times and he thought that he understood the Confederate leader. In Mexico, Jeff Davis might become dictator, Blair hinted. "Suppose," he said, "our possessions be rounded by their extension to the isthmus." Then the name of Jeff Davis would go down in history with Washington and Jackson.[1]

The Confederate President's imagination fired with the gallant language. Always more a soldier than a statesman, his austere character mellowed with memories of his military youth. In 1847, as colonel of the Mississippi Rifles, he had fought Santa Anna in Mexico. His most cherished recollection was a vision of the American flag crackling above clouds of cannon smoke on the wide plains of Buena Vista. At Bull Run, he confided to Blair, when he saw that flag through the smoke again, he thought for a moment that it was his flag. Blair listened, sure that the rebel President would yield.

401

Blair was mistaken. The eagle in Jeff Davis was not yet dead. The North, he knew, had a million men in the field against his two hundred thousand. The South had been overrun almost everywhere except in the Carolinas. Lincoln's re-election was a clear mandate for a vigorous prosecution of the war. What matter? Johnston and Lee might yet outmaneuver Grant and Sherman. Stranger things had happened. Then, too, if Kenner succeeded in Europe, the North might have to fight the world. Frank Blair got nothing from Davis except a letter to Lincoln stating that he would gladly appoint commissioners to arrange a peace between the "two countries."

Lincoln read the letter. He would grant the Confederate States nothing but permission to return to the constitutional majority rule from which they had seceded. However, he knew that peace might be effected if the fighting men stopped to talk. Let Davis designate the time and place.

The Confederates had no intention of treating on any basis except independence, but the leaders saw in Lincoln's offer a chance to play a trick which might win the war on their own terms. They accepted, and appointed commissioners.

Seward, never innocent, went down to meet them on a steamer at Hampton Roads near Fortress Monroe. News of the proposed truce leaked out at once and with it the story that the two sections intended to combine for a foreign war.[2] Britishers heard the rumor and feared that they might be the victims. Frenchmen suspected that they were in for it. Congress, always jealous of executive authority, protested these secret agreements. The Senate called for copies of the State Department's correspondence.

Lincoln complied. He decided also to go down to Fortress Monroe himself and take part in the conference. Jeff Davis sent Vice-President Alexander H. Stephens, R. M. T. Hunter, ex-Senator from Virginia and ex-Secretary of State for the Confederacy, and J. A. Campbell, onetime Justice of the United States Supreme Court with whom Seward had dealt in the critical days before Sumter.[3] Russell of the *Times* had said of Campbell: "He seemed to me a great casuist rather than a profound lawyer, and to delight in subtle distinctions and technical abstractions."[4]

The Confederate commissioners crossed James River in a gale.

Whitecaps from Chesapeake Bay slapped their skiff, splashed them with icy foam. The Southerners shivered with cold when they reached the Federal ship. Stephens, a frail little man, five feet tall, wore an overcoat that almost dragged on the ground. Made of cotton and thick as felt, the odd pattern was a product of Confederate domestic manufacture. Lincoln, who had known Stephens for almost twenty years, thought the little man had gained weight during the war. But when the ponderous coat was removed in the warm cabin, Lincoln realized his error. The men sat down—three sly foxes come to catch big, bland, innocent, gangling Abraham Lincoln. Stephens, shrewd little hillman, began to talk. As a politician he had boxed the Southern compass. He needed watching. Years ago, Stephens had voted against the Mexican War to extend slave territory. Later he had voted against secession. Finally, as Vice-President of the Confederacy, he had proclaimed the hurtful doctrine that slavery was the cornerstone of the new edifice. Now he suggested accepting Blair's proposition to unite for a war against France in Mexico. A sure way, he said, to restore the Union. Seward discussed the subject with him at length. Lincoln draped his long legs over the arm of his chair and listened. Outside the wind hummed in the rigging. A rope slapped on the mast. Finally the men turned to Lincoln for a decision. The President's reply was gentle. The idea, he thought, might be a good one. If the South was sincere in a desire for reconciliation and joint conquest, they must first lay down their arms. As President he could not treat with rebels.

The Confederates babbled protest. They had come to catch the President, not to be caught by him. Judge Campbell, profound dispenser of technical abstractions, cited precedents in history. Charles I of England, he pointed out, negotiated with insurgent Roundheads before the cessation of hostilities.

"I do not profess to be posted in history," Lincoln said. "On all such matters I turn you over to Seward." Seward looked wise and said nothing. Four years earlier he might have discussed the legal aspects at length but he had learned what to expect when Lincoln professed ignorance. "All I distinctly recollect about the case of Charles I," Lincoln concluded, "is that he lost his head in the end."[5]

Various plans were outlined on paper for a proposed truce, but

Lincoln would not budge from his position. The Confederacy must lay down its arms. At last the commissioners rose to go. Stephens struggled into his enormous coat and the men shoved off across the tossing waters. Their intrigue had failed. They had not even succeeded in gaining a delay in the fighting while Kenner raced to Europe. Sherman's men were now swarming through the Southern swamps, choking the roads between the seaboard and the mountains, shouting "God pity South Carolina!"

Lincoln and Seward returned to the capital. At the State Department a secret-service operative handed the Secretary a note. Seward read it, then bumbled across to the White House, into Lincoln's office. The President read the memorandum in silence. The recent conference, he learned, had been a trap to entice the North to agree to interfere in Mexico so France would be justified in allying with the Confederacy.[6]

In Paris, when Duncan Kenner arrived, he found his Confederate colleagues in no mood to act on the proposition he came to offer. James Mason grumbled as sullenly as Jeff Davis had done. Abolition was too big a price to pay for recognition. Had the statesmen at home no principles?

Kenner's orders were mandatory. No time could be lost. Like it or not, Mason must act or resign. Kenner gave him the ultimatum. James Mason acquiesced, packed his luggage, and the two men set out for London. Parliament had convened on February 6, 1865. The Danish war was over, and Her Majesty's Loyal Opposition considered once more the advisability of making an issue of American intervention. Seward's threat to terminate the treaty for the Great Lakes and rumor of the Hampton Roads truce for a joint foreign war opened an opportunity. The Earl of Derby in the House of Lords put the two threats together. By Gad, England was insulted! If the government did not intend to do anything about it, the time had come to elect a new government—the Tories.

When Mason and Kenner read about this Parliamentary tirade in the *Times* they should have seen that their only hope lay with the Opposition, and when Earl Russell replied with a speech sympathetic to the North, the case was doubly clear.[7] For four years recognition of the South or mediation in the American war had progressed by regular steps in Parliament. Gregory had withdrawn his motion in 1861 rather than show his party weakness. In 1862, Lindsay had jockeyed a bill through most of the session, suffering postponement after postponement. Finally, at the news of McClellan's retreat, passage seemed almost sure, but the Prime Minister had asked Parliament, in view of the North's imminent collapse, to leave the delicate question to him. Thus Lincoln had been saved in his most critical year. In 1863, after the Emancipation Proclamation but before Gettysburg, Roebuck had tried his motion only to be flayed with John Bright's Simon Legree whip and to have his whole Tory party censured for unconstitutional negotiations with Napoleon. Old Roebuck had been glad to stop the tongue-lashing by withdrawing his motion—the last of its kind ever entered in Parliament. Next year, 1864, Lindsay had made his trade, "worthy of Abraham Lincoln himself," only to be outwitted. In case after case for four years, Palmerston, well hidden, had quashed every attempt against the North. James Mason could tell all the details but Kenner insisted on trying again.

On the day the Confederates arrived in London, bulletins announced that Sherman had occupied Charleston and that Columbia lay in ashes. Mason wanted to quit. There was no time to work with the Opposition and the government had snubbed him so many times he hesitated to ask Palmerston for another interview. Kenner was obdurate—urged him on. This time the Virginian could offer abolition and the Prime Minister would snap at the chance to check democracy. Mason hesitated. He wrote Slidell for advice. The Louisiana politician ran to the Emperor and discussed the problem.[8] Then he wrote that Napoleon was ready as ever to combine with England and interfere in America. However, Slidell added, it might be well to wait until better news came across the Atlantic.

Kenner refused to be held back any longer. He had brought instructions for Mason to act and insisted that he do so. Reluctantly the stolid Virginian requested Palmerston for an interview. The Prime Minister replied at once, setting the following day. Good! Such promptness might mean ready collaboration with the Confederates. Kenner wanted action. He was getting it.

At the meeting James Mason could not bring himself to state frankly the offer he had come to make. The words "slavery" and "abolition" stuck in his mouth. With ponderous phraseology he referred to the possibility of removing the "latent, undisclosed obstacle" which had prevented previous attempts to get recognition. Old Pam replied bluffly. All the reasons for nonrecognition, he said, had long since been stated by his government and there was no veiled consideration "underlying" them.[9] James Mason bowed himself out. He had been whipped before he called and should have stayed away.

The weary Virginian turned next to the Opposition. He would offer his wares to friends. He went to see old Earl Donoughmore, the Tory who had been cordial with him from the beginning. Two years ago he had told Mason that slavery blocked recognition of the South and Mason had replied that slavery could not be given up. Now the Virginian came to offer everything the old nobleman had wanted. Would abolition purchase recognition in England? Milord answered curtly, "The time has gone by." Two years ago, he said, such an offer would have captivated Parliament, swept all England; now only a smashing Confederate victory would arouse even the Conservatives to oppose the inevitable triumph of democracy. The grim words fell on James Mason's ears like a sentence of death after a long trial. This time he was through with England.

Unlike the Britishers, Napoleon still offered hope. The greatest gambler of his time, he had seen the fortunes of France reversed when conditions had been worse. Sherman and Grant were still separated by the armies of Lee and Johnston—the South's two greatest generals. If the Confederates got warships they might yet sweep the Union Navy from the Atlantic, cut Sherman's base and leave him helpless in a hostile country. The rams Bulloch had designed were said to be capable of crushing, like an eggshell, any wooden vessel. One such craft might be worth a fleet of wooden ships. But Napoleon had ordered that they be held from the Confederates. He owed Lincoln this consideration for acquiescing in his Mexican seizure.

Much mystery surrounded the Confederate rams. Both had been completed in the summer of 1864 and sold—one to Prussia and the other to Denmark. De L'Huys had hinted before the rams were finished that one of these proposed sales might be fictitious. Bigelow, now minister to France in Dayton's place, had not completed his investigation when the second ram appeared in January, back in France with a Danish crew. She anchored at an island off the coast. A new crew was put on board, mostly Englishmen. Then the ram disappeared. Shortly thereafter she turned up in Spain flying the Confederate flag and badly in need of repairs. Bigelow got wind of the transaction and complained to the Emperor. His Imperial Majesty was trapped at last, Bigelow believed—trapped with the information furnished the Americans by the Gascon spy. Bigelow sent Napoleon a summary of the facts, the details of Arman's negotiations with the Confederates, and the Emperor's own order not to sell the ships. Now the Emperor, if sincere in his professions of neutrality, must request the Spanish government to intern the ram as a French vessel sold contrary to his command!

Napoleon demurred. This was exactly the kind of mixup he enjoyed. He said that the ram was in no sense a French vessel. The Confederate agents had purchased her from the Danish government and christened her *Stonewall*. She had sailed into Spain as a bona fide Confederate ship. Mr. Bigelow, if he had any complaints, would have to seek redress from Denmark.

Untangling this legal skein, Bigelow knew, would consume time, and before it was accomplished the *Stonewall* might be repaired and on her way to scatter the Union fleet. He sent word at once to Horatio Perry, chargé d'affaires in Spain, to have the vessel detained if possible. He also notified Captain Thomas T. Craven on the *Niagara* at Dover of the whereabouts of the enemy.

The Spanish government was caught in an international complication. If the Confederacy won the war, Spain could be held for severe damages in case the vessel was held illegally. On the other hand, a new premier had come to power and he hoped to ingratiate himself with the United States. Already he had professed an intention to relinquish Santo Domingo, giving as an excuse the fact that Spain had reannexed the island under the belief that the inhabitants wished it. As he said this, the sly Spaniard toyed secretly with the revolution in Peru. Like Napoleon he played a double game. If the United States won the war she would be one of the best-armed powers in the world and her friendship would be valuable. But if she lost, it would be well to have some foreign possessions on the shelf. In the interim good diplomacy demanded outward neutrality.

At Ferrol, where the *Stonewall* was being repaired, the Spanish officers assured Confederate Captain Page that he would not be ordered out until his ship was seaworthy. The repairs were rushed. Before they were completed, the United States war steamer *Niagara* glided into port, then out again. Craven admitted later at his court-martial that his lofty wooden vessel was no match for the iron ram. On the open sea he waited at a safe distance to report which way the Confederate went.

The commissioners in Paris urged Captain Page to get the *Stonewall* to sea in haste. Designed specifically to break the blockade, she must strike at Port Royal, South Carolina, and destroy Sherman's base. The Northern general would thus be left at the mercy of Johnston, who had retreated before him in excellent order all the way from Atlanta and was now crouched for a spring. With Sherman destroyed, the *Stonewall* could turn south and sweep the blockade from every Confederate port. Mobile and New Orleans would be recaptured. In no time the fortunes of war would be reversed. The invincible ironclad might then steam into New York and demand ransom of the city, or better, puff up the Potomac and capture Washington while guerrillas along the Canadian border harried the Northern states.

Lincoln was preparing for his second inauguration—and Booth had organized several conspirators for his plot—when word was received that the *Stonewall* had arrived in Ferrol. Lincoln was also thinking about "a man down South"—Sherman, whose base might be cut off in case the ironclad escaped.

On March 4, 1865, Abraham Lincoln was inaugurated for the second time on the platform erected once more in front of the Capitol.[10] The diplomats took seats behind the Supreme Court justices. The day was dark, forbidding, dank as the thousands of graves that had been filled by four years of civil war. When the President got up from his chair the foreign ministers noted that he was totally different from the man who had taken the oath four years ago. Lincoln began to speak. A shaft of light pierced the low clouds and rested like a benediction on his weary shoulders.[11] The auditors forgot everything but the persuasive poetry of his thoughts.

"*Fellow-countrymen:* At this second appearing to take the oath of the presidential office, there is less occasion for an extended address than there was at the first. Then a statement, somewhat in detail, of a course to be pursued, seemed fitting and proper. Now, at the expiration of four years, during which public declarations have been constantly called forth on every point and phase of the great contest which still absorbs the attention and engrosses the energies of the nation, little that is new could be presented. The progress of our arms, upon which all else chiefly depends, is as well known to the public as to myself; and it is, I trust, reasonably satisfactory and encouraging to all. With high hope for the future, no prediction in regard to it is ventured.

"On the occasion corresponding to this four years ago, all thoughts were anxiously directed to an impending civil war. All dreaded it—all sought to avert it. While the inaugural address was being delivered from this place, devoted altogether to saving the Union without war, insurgent agents were in the city seeking to destroy it without war—seeking to dissolve the Union, and divide effects, by negotiation. Both parties deprecated war; but one of them would make war rather than let the nation survive; and the other would accept war rather than let it perish. And the war came.

"One-eighth of the whole population were colored slaves, not distributed generally over the Union, but localized in the Southern part of it. These slaves constituted a peculiar and powerful interest. All knew that this interest was, somehow, the cause of the war. To strengthen, perpetuate, and extend this interest was the object for which the insurgents would rend the Union, even by war; while the government claimed no right to do more than to restrict the territorial enlargement of it.

"Neither party expected for the war the magnitude or the duration which it has already attained. Neither anticipated that the cause of the conflict might cease with, or even before, the conflict itself should cease. Each looked for an easier triumph, and a result less fundamental and astounding. Both read the same Bible, and pray to the same God; and each invokes his aid against the other. It may seem strange that any men should dare to ask a just God's assistance in wringing their bread from the sweat of other men's faces; but let us judge not, that we be not judged. The prayers of both could not be answered—that of neither has been answered fully.

"The Almighty has his own purposes. 'Woe unto the world because of offenses! for it must needs be that offenses come; but woe to that man by whom the offense cometh.' If we shall suppose that

American slavery is one of those offenses which, in the providence of God, must needs come, but which, having continued through his appointed time, he now wills to remove, and that he gives to both North and South this terrible war, as the woe due to those by whom the offense came, shall we discern therein any departure from those divine attributes which the believers in a living God always ascribe to him? Fondly do we hope—fervently do we pray—that this mighty scourge of war may speedily pass away. Yet, if God wills that it continue until all the wealth piled by the bondsman's two hundred and fifty years of unrequited toil shall be sunk, and until every drop of blood drawn with the lash shall be paid by another drawn with the sword, as was said three thousand years ago, so still it must be said, 'The judgments of the Lord are true and righteous altogether.'

"With malice toward none; with charity for all; with firmness in the right, as God gives us to see the right, let us strive on to finish the work we are in; to bind up the nation's wounds; to care for him who shall have borne the battle, and for his widow, and his orphan—to do all which may achieve and cherish a just and lasting peace among ourselves, and with all nations."[12]

The second inaugural address caused much comment in England. With it came a dispatch from Seward revoking his order to terminate the disarmament treaty on the lakes—the last war worry on British minds. Lincoln's scriptural language took the taint from godless democracy. Middle-class hearts warmed to him. The music of the words still echoed in England when a dispatch announced Sherman's unobstructed advance across the Carolinas—another two hundred miles. The two things, combined with Seward's revocation of the order to terminate the disarmament treaty, completely nullified any proposition that Kenner had to offer. The time had passed for diplomacy to save the South. The only hope of the Confederacy lay at anchor in Ferrol, Spain, watched by a wooden war vessel which it could crush like an eggshell.

The distant menace did not dampen Washington gaiety. After the inauguration five thousand people packed the President's ball. War wealth sparkled and rustled in the crowd. The *New York Times* reported:

"Diamonds and other precious jewels were worn in great abundance, and rich laces were plentiful. Some ladies displayed the bad taste of wearing their rings over their gloves."[13]

The ballroom seethed like a caldron of colors. Ladies in silks, moires, brocades, cloth of gold and crimson velvet, with gleaming white shoulders, waltzed around and around to seductive music from the Marine Band. Along the wall hundreds of fans pulsed nervously. Over all a mist of perfume. The war had broken down conventionality—female modesty. Many women attended without hoops under their dresses. Society reporters noted in detail the costumes worn by wives of the cabinet members. Special attention was given to the plump figure of peach-cheeked Mary Lincoln, who had suffered the loss of three members of her immediate family in the Civil War and who at times had been crushed to the verge of prostration. The *New York Times* society column stated:

"Mrs. Lincoln looked extremely well, and was attired in the most elegant manner; her dress was made of white satin very ample and rich, but almost entirely covered by a tunic, or rather skirt, of the finest point appliqué. Her corsage, which was low, and the short sleeves, were ornamented richly by a pericle made of the same material, and the shawl, also of the same rich lace, was most exquisite. Passamenterie of narrow fluted satin ribbon completed the dress. Her jewels were of the rarest pearls, necklace, ear-rings, brooch, and bracelets. Her hair, which was put plainly back from her face, was ornamented with trailing jessamine and clustering violets most gracefully."[14]

Of all the thousands of women present, another caught the eye of the *Times* society reporter—the wife of a man whose voice was always the loudest in any company. This conspicuous woman was living proof of the adage that man's ambition is to be heard: woman's to be seen. According to the newspaper report:

"One of the most elaborate and rich dresses in the room was worn by Mrs. George Francis Train. It was a very finely plaited blue silk, trimmed with a flounce of thread lace, almost as deep as her skirt, and other laces to match. Her hair was powdered with gold."[15]

As soon as the festivities were over, Lincoln and his wife and little Tad boarded the President's steamer, the *River Queen,* for a trip down to Grant's army in Virginia. Lincoln had received word that Sir Frederick Bruce, late from China, was to succeed Lord

Lyons in Washington. The news did not interfere with the presidential holiday. Several weeks would elapse before the Englishman arrived. The Lincolns disembarked at army headquarters—a twenty-four-hour trip from Washington. The camp was south and east of Richmond, deep in Virginia. The supply line to the North came down Chesapeake Bay and up the James. Hundreds of wooden vessels guarded this route. Army men considered it safe. Cornwallis had been trapped on this peninsula during the Revolution. But he had lost control of the waterways.

Lincoln arrived on the historic peninsula on the same day the *Stonewall* put to sea from Spain. 'At City Point, General Grant met the President and discussed military affairs. The Confederacy, he said, was tottering to a fall. Already the railroads between Richmond and the South were threatened by blue-clad soldiers. Lee must retreat or be surrounded.

The time had come for Captain Page to act and act quickly. If the *Stonewall* could accomplish the victories over wooden ships that Bulloch had predicted, havoc could still be raised on the Atlantic coast. Both Grant and Sherman might be cut off from their bases and the President himself made a prisoner on the peninsula.

The *Stonewall* went to Lisbon, thence to Santa Cruz in the Canaries. The *Niagara,* following at a respectful distance, lost her there. Free at last, the ironclad shipped more coal and started for Bermuda—an ideal base from which to strike at the communications of either Sherman or Grant.

Lincoln enjoyed his vacation away from nagging politicians. He rode a big horse beside Grant. The two galloped through miles and miles of encampments, ordnance, cheering soldiers. The lieutenant general said victory was only a matter of days. Mrs. Lincoln returned to Washington to organize a houseboat party on the *River Queen.* She invited Charles Sumner of the Foreign Relations Committee to be one of the guests and also the Marquis de Chambrun, extraofficial visitor from France. Chambrun was not sympathetic with Napoleon although he accepted the Empire. He had come to America at the instigation of Drouyn de L'Huys, who had not forgotten that Napoleon had tried to make a goat of him in American affairs. De L'Huys was not above a little intrigue of his own. He was sure that Chambrun could gain Lincoln's friendship better than an out-and-out imperialist, and then tell De L'Huys things Napoleon did not need to know.

Along with Mrs. Lincoln's distinguished guests, a stableman led Tad's pony on board the *River Queen.* In the days that followed at inspections and reviews, Tad trotted busily after his father, his little military cape flying in the breeze. Lincoln and Grant for the first time had an opportunity to get acquainted. Lincoln talked of the peace now near at hand and the terms of surrender to be exacted from the Confederates. He talked, too, of the abortive attempt to sign a peace on his ship at Hampton Roads in February. Lincoln asked if the general saw Alexander Stephens personally when he was passed through the lines for that meeting? Grant replied that he had. "Did you see his overcoat?" Lincoln inquired next.

"Yes," Grant replied between puffs of smoke.

"Well, did you see him take it off?"

"Yes." (Puff, puff.)

"Well, didn't you think it was the biggest shuck and the littlest ear that ever you did see?"

Not a word about the South's sly game for embroiling the North in war with France and Lincoln's adroit escape. But Grant remembered Lincoln's apt description of Stephens to the end of his life.[16]

One day a messenger in boots and spurs handed Lincoln a dispatch. Jeff Davis had fled from Richmond. Lee, too, was moving south as fast as he could march his army. Perhaps he could join Johnston, still retreating in an orderly manner before Sherman. Between them Sherman might be defeated. Then they could turn about and knock out Grant. It was a soldier's last desperate chance. Grant had succeeded in such a maneuver with Pemberton before Vicksburg. Now the tables might be turned. The play would be helped immeasurably if the sharp-billed *Stonewall* appeared in Chesapeake Bay to scatter the wooden fleet like chickens. Military men considered such a forlorn hope fantastic.

On April 4, 1865—Tad's birthday—Lincoln left his guests and went with his son to Richmond to see the fallen city which had ruined the reputations of so many Northern generals. Vandals had done their work in the feverish time between the evacuation of one army and the arrival of the other. Five trunkloads of Confederate documents disappeared altogether. Some years later they turned up in the hands of ex-minister to Mexico Pickett, who sold them to the United States for some $75,000.[17] Less discriminating hoodlums set incendiary fires. Tattered Negroes, bewildered by freedom, stood in little groups along the deserted streets. As word spread that Lincoln was coming, timid ladies peered from behind curtained windows to see the barbarian. He did not enter the proud city on a prancing charger. The ladies saw, instead, a tall man in a stovepipe hat, walking hand-in-hand with a twelve-year-old boy. His only guard consisted of a scant ten sailors and four officers in blue. The tall man walked slowly, thoughtfully, but with the sure stride of a man who never walked back. Negroes sobbed when they saw him. They called him God. Tears varnished their black cheeks. One old slave, bolder than the rest, shouted, "May de good Lord bless you, President Linkum." Removing his tattered headpiece, he bowed a white kinky head before his deliverer. Lincoln turned toward him and bowing with equal gravity, removed his own hat.[18] It was a momentous thing to have struck the bonds of slavery from four million people.

Traveling back to Grant's headquarters, Lincoln learned that Seward was seriously injured. The Secretary of State's carriage horses had run away, throwing him out. Lincoln ordered the *River Queen* prepared for a return to Washington. The guests were invited to go on board. Firemen stoked the boilers. Officers and their wives tripped up and down the gangplank, waved, and wished the presidential party a safe voyage. The engineer looked anxiously at the steam gauges on his boilers. The military band played patriotic airs. Lincoln asked for the French revolutionary *"Marseillaise,"* a compliment to the Marquis de Chambrun. The band played it twice. The Frenchman beamed.

"You must, however, come over to America to hear it," Lincoln remarked.

The Marquis took this opening as an opportunity to pump the President. Since Seward lay injured—perhaps mortally—all foreign policy devolved on the tall man at his side. The urbane nobleman talked easily. He could tell Lincoln many things about diplomacy—the real attitude of the French people toward America—their reverence for Lafayette and Benjamin Franklin. It was not generally known, indeed it was very personal, but Lafayette's grandson had fallen deeply in love with Celestine Eustis, the daughter of Slidell's secretary. Family pride, Chambrun believed, kept him from proposing marriage. He could not bring himself to make an alliance with a family devoted to destroying the republic which his grandfather had helped establish.[19] French honor was always thus. International bankers were different. Erlanger did not oppose the marriage of his son into the Slidell family.

Chambrun chatted confidentially. He hoped that Lincoln would exchange confidences with him. He wondered if the victorious North would turn its great Army on France. The American people, he was sure, resented the occupation of Mexico as well as the Emperor's constant machinations for recognition of the South. The Marquis asked what Frenchmen might expect. Yes?

"There has been war enough," Lincoln replied. "I know what the American people want, but thank God, I count for something, and during my second term there will be no more fighting."[20]

At ten o'clock at night the gangplank was lifted. With churning engines the *River Queen* turned into the channel of the James. More than a hundred vessels lay at anchor on all sides. Lincoln stood for a long time watching the shore recede as his boat slugged along toward the open waters of Chesapeake Bay.

All next day the presidential party steamed north toward Washington. Lincoln did not talk about the war or the peace so close at hand. His mind was on Shakespeare and the foreign policy of a Scotch king named Macbeth. In the evening the *River Queen* docked at Washington. Lincoln dropped his wife at the White House, then drove to Seward's residence. The Secretary of State was confined in a dark room on the second floor. His jaw was broken and he could not speak.[21] Lincoln sat down on the bed and took the old man's thin hand. In a solemn monotone he told about his trip, the interview with Grant, the evacuation of Richmond. "Yes," Lincoln whispered, "I think we are near the end, at last." Seward could answer only by pressing the President's hand.[22]

Nurses waiting in the hall heard the door from the sickroom open quietly. Lincoln came out. With a silent gesture he intimated that Seward was asleep. The President returned to the White House. Soon a messenger stamped in with a telegram—Lee had surrendered. Grant said that he might be able to capture Jeff Davis also. Lincoln was silent for a long time. When he spoke he told a story about a boy back in Springfield who owned a pet coon with sore eyes and the mange. The string around the coon was frayed and the boy was crying. Lincoln asked the boy what was the matter. The boy said, "He's my coon and I got to keep him and I'm afraid he won't get away." The President, a born mimic, imitated the boy's facial expression ludicrously. Lincoln's own party contained many men who had not believed him when he said that the task remaining before them was to bind up the nation's wounds.

In the days that followed, Lincoln planned the political strategy necessary to get the seceded states back into the Union, the tricks he would play to cajole radical politicians who insisted on punishing the South. No foreign affairs pressed urgently on his attention. Seward was improving but was still dangerously ill. The new minister from Great Britain was expected daily. The English problem had long been settled, and from France came word that the liberals opposed to the Mexican venture were clamoring against the expense of wars. Already the conquest had cost more than twice the income received from Mexico—poor pay, they complained, to strengthen the financial structure of France.[23] In the Corps Législatif an angry debate brought out excited threats against "the blood-shed for a foreign prince in Mexico." Twenty-four deputies greeted the news of Lee's surrender with a vote of thanks to the United States for its "efforts on behalf of Civil Liberty."[24] Lincoln had every reason to believe that France would withdraw as Spain had from Santo Domingo. Had he not told Chambrun that there would be "no more fighting"?

On April 14 the President got up at seven o'clock—his usual hour. The day promised to be clear. Lincoln felt in "fine whack." Before breakfast he went to his office near his bedroom. Grant was in town. The city had hung out its best bunting—red, white and blue. Lincoln wrote Frederick Seward to change the cabinet meeting from nine to eleven o'clock. Grant would attend. Down in Charleston, South Carolina, Lincoln had ordered the American flag raised once more over Fort Sumter—the same old flag by the same officer who had been compelled to haul it down. On his desk a pile of correspondence marked "Assassination Letters"[25]

The State and Treasury Departments on Fifteenth Street just east of the White House on the site of the present Treasury Building

*Cartoon from Punch, by Tenniel*

BRITANNIA LAYS A WREATH ON LINCOLN'S BIER

Drawn for *Punch* by John Tenniel.

seemed strangely out of date now that peace was restored. At breakfast Lincoln told his family that he had had a dream about a vessel traveling toward an unknown shore. Lincoln enjoyed talking about his dreams and the Confederate *Stonewall* was no longer in anybody's mind. Lincoln's conversation was interrupted by a servant. Schuyler Colfax, Speaker of the House, had called. Lincoln left the table.

Colfax planned a trip to California. Lincoln became interested. "Tell the miners for me," he said, "that I shall promote their prosperity to the utmost of my ability, because their prosperity is the prosperity of the nation." The resources of the West, Lincoln hoped, would pay for the war and stabilize the currency. Hundreds of thousands of soldiers, out of employment now that the war was over, would find opportunities there.

As the two men talked, scenes of the Golden West unfolded before their eyes. Western migration, Lincoln knew, would be the cure for sectionalism—the main cause of the Civil War. Lincoln had seen bitter "State rights" men turn strong nationalists when they discovered the opportunities out West. Did not Robert J. Walker, the first man to put the slavery issue into local politics, become a Unionist after he learned in Washington that investment out West exceeded anything he had ever known in the South even in the cotton-boom days? "Immigration," Lincoln said, "which even the war has not stopped will land upon our shores hundreds of thousands more per year from overcrowded Europe. I intend to point them to the gold and silver that wait for them in the West."

All his life Lincoln had seen the steady stream of covered wagons rumbling westward. As a boy he had been part of that stream. He had seen Illinois grow from a log-cabin frontier to a railroad state. He had seen thousands of long-horned cattle from the unmeasured grasslands of the West delivered to farmers back in Illinois. He was familiar with the fortunes in furs accumulated by adventurous men in St. Louis, the great city nearest his home. Something of the lure of the West that would grip the next generation of Americans had got hold of Abraham Lincoln, a lure more compelling than being President of the United States. When his term expired, Lincoln told Colfax, he might move out West himself. The new country would be a good place for his boys to get a start. "Be sure and bring me back a special report," he said, as the Speaker departed.

Representative J. A. Creswell was the next to be ushered in. He wanted a pardon for an old schoolmate being held as a rebel prisoner. Lincoln was talkative. He kept Creswell waiting. Once at a picnic in Springfield, Lincoln remembered, the party rowed across the Sangamon and, after eating, discovered that their boat was gone. The girls were frightened. The day's fun had turned to tragedy. Then somebody suggested that all the boys roll up their trousers and each pick the girl of his choice and carry her back across the shallow water. All went well, Lincoln said, his eyes twinkling, until only one man was left. He was small and short-legged, the only woman a tall old maid. There was real trouble for that man.

"Now, do you see," said Lincoln, "you fellows will get one man after another out of this business until Jefferson Davis and I will be the only ones left on the island, and I'm afraid he'll refuse to let me carry him over, and I'm afraid there are some people who will make trouble about my doing it, if he consents."[26]

Representative Creswell left laughing, with the pardon in his hand. Two more "old friends" were ushered in. These were office seekers looking for jobs down South. Lincoln accommodated them, saying, "Make love to those people down there." Next came John P. Hale, abolitionist, recently appointed minister to Spain,[27] the "decadent country" Cassius M. Clay had refused to serve, the country that had withdrawn from Santo Domingo without being forced by the United States. Lincoln explained the foreign situation to him, outlined the minister's problems, and bade him farewell. Time was getting short before the cabinet meeting called for eleven. Several representatives and senators crowded in for last-minute favors. Lincoln talked to them as he arranged his papers. Then he walked across to the War Department for the latest news from Sherman. Since Lee had surrendered, no army but Joe Johnston's remained below Richmond. As the President entered the telegraph office, the operators looked up.

Lincoln went to the file, read a decoded dispatch which was in extremely terse and laconic phrases. Lincoln chuckled. "That reminds me of the old story of the Scotch lassie on her way to market with a basket of eggs for sale." The boys sat back in their chairs to hear the anecdote. "She had just forded a small stream with her skirts well drawn up, when a waggoner on the opposite side of the stream called out, 'Good morning, my lassie; how deep's the brook and what's the price of eggs?'

"The girl did not stop but called back, 'Knee deep and a six-pence.'" As Lincoln said the last words he gathered up the skirts of his coat and stepped through imaginary pools into Stanton's room.[28]

The Secretary of War was very busy. He did not have time to hear stories. He told Lincoln that reports from the Army were favorable. Sherman and Johnston appeared to be deploying for a battle. Sherman would win. If he did not, he could fall back on Wilmington, where the fleet would protect his base and keep him supplied.

Lincoln returned to the White House. Grant had arrived. The two men went into the cabinet room to await the assembling of the Secretaries. Lincoln sat in his usual place in the armchair by the south window where the light shone in the faces of the cabinet and left his own in shadow—the trick Cash Clay had told him was practiced in Russia. The cabinet members straggled in. Conversation was informal. Grant remarked that he was anxious about Sherman marching up from the south with Johnston ahead of him waiting for an opportunity to strike. No one mentioned the *Stonewall,* which by now had had time to reach America. Lincoln stretched at ease in his chair. Good news would come soon, he said. Last night he had had a dream which was a good omen.[29] Secretary Welles looked down over his whiskers and asked the details of this remarkable dream. Lincoln recounted his vision of the singular vessel floating toward an unknown shore. This dream, he said, had preceded many victories: Antietam, Gettysburg and Stone River. Grant puffed on his cigar. "Stone River was no victory," he said.

Stanton bustled in, a little late as usual. He did not like to waste time with small talk waiting for the members to assemble. Serious business was taken up at once.

The cabinet which Lincoln faced had only one member who

was present at the first meeting four years before. Had Seward been well, there would have been two. The ministers had eaten up each other and not the President. Secretary Welles, the ship's figurehead, had hidden behind his whiskers through many trying sessions but he still survived. The old cabinet had fought the war. The new one must reconstruct the Union. "I hope there will be no persecution, no bloody work, after the war is over," Lincoln impressed on all his men.

When the cabinet meeting was over, Frederick Seward announced that the new British minister, Sir Frederick Bruce, had arrived in Washington. When would it be convenient for the President to meet him? Lincoln thought for a moment. "Tomorrow, at two o'clock." Then with a knowing smile he added, "Don't forget to send up the speeches beforehand—I would like to look them over."

In the anteroom a press of visitors waited for interviews. Lincoln ate lunch with one of them. Time was precious. He excused himself and retired to his office, munching an apple. Card after card came to his desk announcing callers. Lincoln saw them all, and released three Confederates from jail. Late in the afternoon he ordered his carriage for a drive, then stepped into the lavatory to wash his hands. While he was gone young Charles Dana, Assistant Secretary of War, came into the office with a telegram Stanton had asked him to deliver to the President.

"Halloo, Dana!" Lincoln called. "What is it? What's up?"

Dana called back: "A wire from the provost marshal in Portland, Maine, stating that Jacob Thompson will pass through town tonight and take steamer for England. Should he arrest him?" Thompson, onetime Secretary of the Interior under Buchanan, had served more recently as secret agent of the Confederacy in Canada organizing saboteurs. Lincoln asked Dana to read the wire. When he finished, Lincoln asked, "What does Stanton say?"

"He says 'arrest him,' but that I should refer the question to you."

"Well," Lincoln replied, slowly wiping his hands, "no; I rather think not. When you have got an elephant by the hind leg, and he is trying to run away, it's best to let him run."

Dana returned and went straight to the inner sanctum where

Secretary Stanton was working in a tense atmosphere of accomplishment. "Well, what says he?" Stanton asked without looking up.

"He says that when you have got an elephant by the hind leg, and he is trying to run away, it's best to let him run."

"Oh, stuff!" Stanton exclaimed.[30]

Back in the White House Lincoln walked downstairs to take an afternoon drive with his wife. In the hallway he noticed a one-armed soldier who had come too late for an audience. Lincoln stopped a moment and spoke to the man. Then he walked down the corridor toward the door. Two women stood waiting to see him. Lincoln shook hands, asked their names, took them to the White House conservatory, showed them the lemon tree and picked a lemon for each. When he came back Mrs. Lincoln was waiting on the portico. The carriage horses stamped to be off. Lincoln helped his wife into the vehicle. The sunny April afternoon had clouded suddenly but Lincoln was in high spirits. Visions of Colfax's proposed trip danced in his mind. He told his wife he would like to take her west after his term expired. Mrs. Lincoln was more concerned with a theater party that evening. The Grants had not been able to go but other guests had accepted.

When the carriage returned, Lincoln noticed two men walking away from the portico. "Come back, boys, come back," he shouted, waving his long arms. Lincoln led the way into the White House and for an hour he talked and swapped jokes with them in the library. Taking up a volume of Petroleum V. Nasby, he read whole chapters to his friends. Time after time a servant announced dinner. Each time Lincoln said he would come in a minute, then continued reading. Finally the doorkeeper called one of the guests aside and explained that the President was going out and he had not yet dined. The visitor nudged his friends. All departed.

Immediately after dinner a newspaper correspondent called by appointment. After his visit Lincoln walked quickly over to the War Department. Surely some word had arrived from Sherman!

Lincoln came back to the White House disappointed. Speaker Colfax and George Ashmun were waiting in the library to say a last good-by. Lincoln lingered over the parting. The travelers planned to take the overland stage west of Missouri. In the Rockies they would visit Pike's Peak and the mountain parks beyond.

Lincoln liked to talk about it. Finally he tore himself away to get ready for the theater. He said he would be back in a moment. Stepping into his office, he found Senator Henderson, who had evaded the usher. Lincoln signed the senator's request. Then he noticed a blank commission for a governor of the Nebraska Territory. He signed that and left the paper on the desk. When he rejoined Colfax the usher brought him more cards. Lincoln sent word that he would be glad to see the visitors in the morning and fixed the hour. Still talking with his friends, he had started toward the front door when he was interrupted again. Two men wanted a pass to Richmond. Lincoln signed a card stating that no pass was required to go to Richmond. While he was writing, Mrs. Lincoln appeared, dressed for the theater. For four years she had contended with these endless interruptions. The party walked toward the door. On the portico Lincoln saw two more friends who had come to see him. Shaking their hands cordially, he bade them call in the morning. As he stepped into the carriage he noticed still another congressman approaching. "Excuse me now," he called. "I am going to the theater. Come and see me in the morning." Lincoln waved to Colfax and the carriage drove down the gas-lighted drive.

Late that night in Seward's hushed and darkened house the family and attendants whispered that the Secretary was asleep. The doorbell rang. A man brushed past the servant and ran upstairs. Frederick Seward, son of the sick man, met him at the landing.

"The doctor has sent me to see the Secretary," the stranger said. Frederick remonstrated. The man drew a pistol and struck him down. Rushing into the sickroom, he stabbed and slashed with a knife at the throat of the invalid, then fled.

The wounds were not fatal, but the Secretary was kept in extreme quiet. On Sunday his bed was wheeled around so he could look out the window at the April sky and the trees budding with spring. The stricken man's eyes noticed the flag on the War Department flying at half-mast. He groaned. "The President is dead."

Confused attendants, ordered to withhold all news which might excite the invalid, stammered incoherently.

"If he had been alive," Seward continued, "he would have been the first to call on me but he has not been here, nor has he sent to know how I am; and there is the flag at half-mast."[31]

# Epilogue: Silver Face in the Night

NEWS of the end of the Civil War was slow to reach Captain Page and the crew of the ram *Stonewall*. When they left the Canary Islands the ram made sail and rode before the northeast trades—a course that would take the ship south of the United States. Far out in the ocean Captain Page tacked north for Bermuda. He encountered head winds and a heavy swell. Being short of coal, he changed his course for Nassau. By the time he arrived at this British possession the war was over, but the news had not reached the Bahamas. Page steamed to Havana. Here he learned that Lee had surrendered, Lincoln had been assassinated and Jeff Davis, last of the aristocrats, had been captured attempting to escape in his wife's clothes. Page sold the vessel to pay the crew.

In Europe the commissioners were stranded. James Murray Mason was dazed—forlorn, knowing not where to go. Slidell had found congenial society for his daughters and decided to remain abroad. Turfman Kenner hurried to the American legation in Paris and asked for John Bigelow. The whole secession movement, he said, was a mistake. He wanted to take the oath of allegiance and return to the United States as an American citizen.[1] Having lost a fortune derived from slave labor, he proposed to make another with labor that was free—and did.

The diplomats in Washington were officially notified that Lincoln's funeral exercises would be held at 10:30 on the morning of April 19, 1865. They donned their formal mourning clothes and came to the White House. Carpenters had transformed the East Room into an amphitheater. Crepe curtained the large windows. Flowers filled the gloom with sweetness. In the center Lincoln's catafalque lay under draperies of black cloth fluted with white satin. The diplomats were assigned seats at the right of President Johnson and the cabinet. Tailored like bobolinks and red-winged blackbirds, the bright-eyed foreigners noted that the chairs reserved for Mrs. Lincoln and the boys were eloquently empty.[2]

424

Ward Hill Lamon, bodyguard and marshal, escorted officials to their seats.[3] The pallbearers represented the Army, Navy, Congress and the civil population. Grant and Farragut acted for the military, Ben Wade for the Senate, Colfax for the House. The latter's Western trip had been postponed. O. H. Browning, George Ashmun, Tom Corwin and Simon Cameron represented the civilians.

The diplomats had assembled for the last time around Abraham Lincoln. Most of them had heard him deliver his first inaugural address, some had heard his Gettysburg speech and second inaugural. All had read his farewell to the people of Springfield, his letter to the Manchester workingmen, and his impassioned prose to Mrs. Bixby, the mother of five sons reported lost in battle. Who but Lincoln could have written a distraught war mother:

"I pray that our Heavenly Father may assuage the anguish of your bereavement, and leave you only the cherished memory of the loved and lost, and the solemn pride that must be yours to have laid so costly a sacrifice upon the altar of freedom."

Such plain language needed no musical accompaniment, no soft lights, no incense to make the majesty of Lincoln's thought thrill common people around the world. The diplomats knew even better than many of the Americans present that Lincoln had taken with him his murderer—the old order of aristocracy. Henceforth, for better and for worse, the plain people would rule.

Few Americans appreciated the reverence felt for Abraham Lincoln by underprivileged Europeans. Eulogists gushed superlatives, but only here and there speakers, wiser than the rest, saw the real significance of the dead President. In New York City the Reverend John McClintock, who had spent many of the war years abroad, told his congregation on the Sunday following the assassination:

"Abraham Lincoln had come to be . . . the synonyme [*sic*] of hope . . . not only in every slave cabin in the South, where he is canonized already, but in many a shepherd's lodge in Switzerland—in many a woodman's cabin in the Black Forest—in many a miner's hut of the Hartz Mountains—in many a cottage in Italy, for there, as well as here, the poor had learned to look upon him as the anointed of God for the redemption of the liberties of mankind. It is but lately that Garibaldi named one of his grand-children Lincoln, little dreaming how soon that name was to be enrolled among the immortals."[4]

The Reverend Dr. McClintock knew the pulse of Europe. The triumph of Union arms was greeted with displays of enthusiasm by the liberals of all countries where free speech was permitted. George G. Fogg wrote from Switzerland that Lee's surrender caused as much rejoicing as a Swiss victory.[5] From Italy, Mazzini gloated over the benefit to be gained for Italian unity: "You have done more for us in four years than fifty years of teaching, preaching, and writing from all your European brothers have been able to do."[6] In England news of Lincoln's assassination produced a near panic. Not since Henry IV of France was slain by Ravaillac had "the whole of Europe rung with excitement of so intense a character," one paper reported.[7] Another noted:

"When the heats of party passion and international jealousy have abated, when detraction has spent its malice, and the scandalous gossip of the day goes the way of all lies, the place of Abraham Lincoln in the grateful affection of his countrymen and in the respect of mankind, will be second only, if it be second, to that of Washington himself."

The London *Times,* which made public opinion and lived on it, became confused, bewildered, remorseful. The editor reported:

"Nothing like it has been witnessed in our generation. . . . But President Lincoln was only the chief of a foreign State, and of a State with which we were not unfrequently in diplomatic or political collision. He might have been regarded as not much more to us than the head of any friendly Government, and yet his end has already stirred the feelings of the public to their uttermost depths."[8]

Press czar Delane, whose professional pride forced him to report the truth when it hurt him to illness, printed a classic editorial on the great democrat:

"Abraham Lincoln was as little of a tyrant as any man who ever lived. He could have been a tyrant had he pleased, but he never uttered so much as an ill-natured speech. . . . In all America there was, perhaps, not one man who less deserved to be the victim of this revolution than he who has just fallen."⁹

The final tribute appeared in *Punch*, comic sheet notorious for the consistency with which it lampooned Lincoln, everything American and most things English. A staff artist, John Tenniel, mural painter for the House of Lords, was illustrating a new book, *Alice in Wonderland*. He put down the pen which would make Alice, the Mad Hatter and the March Hare familiar characters to all children in America and England and drew a tragic picture of Britannia beside Lincoln's bier. The assassination had occurred at a play hit, *Our American Cousin*, written by Tom Taylor, also on *Punch's* staff. Taylor was an artist, amateur actor, and one-time professor of English literature. With mental torment he wrote:

> *You* lay a wreath on murdered Lincoln's bier,
>   *You*, who with mocking pencil wont to trace,
> Broad for the self-complacent British sneer,
>   His length of shambling limb, his furrowed face,
>
> His gaunt, gnarled hands, his unkempt, bristling hair,
>   His garb uncouth, his bearing ill at ease,
> His lack of all we prize as debonair,
>   Of power or will to shine, of art to please.
>
> *You*, whose smart pen backed up the pencil's laugh,
>   Judging each step, as though the way were plain:
> Reckless, so it could point its paragraph,
>   Of chief's perplexity, or people's pain.
>
> Yes, he had lived to shame me for my sneer,
>   To lame my pencil, and confute my pen—
> To make me own this hind of princes peer,
>   This rail-splitter a true-born king of men.
>
> My shallow judgment I had learnt to rue,
>   Noting how to occasion's height he rose,
> How his quaint wit made home-truth seem more true,
>   How, iron-like, his temper grew by blows.

How humble yet how hopeful he could be:
  How in good fortune and in ill the same:
Nor bitter in success, nor boastful he,
  Thirsty for gold, nor feverish for fame.

So he grew up, a destined work to do,
  And lived to do it: four long-suffering years'
Ill-fate, ill-feeling, ill-report, lived through,
  And then he heard the hisses change to cheers,

The taunts to tribute, the abuse to praise,
  And took both with the same unwavering mood:
Till, as he came on light, from darkling days,
  And seemed to touch the goal from where he stood,

A felon hand, between the goal and him,
  Reached from behind his back, a trigger prest,—
And those perplexed and patient eyes were dim,
  Those gaunt, long-labouring limbs were laid to rest!

The words of mercy were upon his lips,
  Forgiveness in his heart and on his pen,
When this vile murderer brought swift eclipse
  To thoughts of peace on earth, good-will to men.[10]

Twenty-four hours after reports of the assassination arrived in England, grief and indignation were publicly recorded by many constituted bodies. The Houses of Parliament, the Corporation of London, and mass meetings in the chief manufacturing cities expressed anger and consternation. The House of Lords actually noted the "absence of precedent for such a manifestation."[11] The Young Men's Christian Association, an organization of British tradesmen's clerks who met for Bible readings and prayer, planned to purchase the theater in which Lincoln was shot. They hoped to establish it as a hotel for young men visiting Washington. Lincoln's general, O. O. Howard, led the drive in America.[12] The "Christian General" he was called, not only for his efforts to expand the British Christian society in America but for his religious work with Negroes and Indians as well.

Years later an immigrant to America remembered that working people in the factory towns of Lancaster trudged to Liverpool when they learned about Lincoln's death. A ship loaded with free cotton was in port. They got a lorry, draped it with flowers and bunting, then placed a bale of cotton from the ship in the center of the platform. The British and American flags were crossed above it and under them hung "the plain picture that appeals to plain people in all the world—Abraham Lincoln." Children filled the rest of the space on the wagon. The throng dragged the lorry from the dock through Exchange Street and Lime Street to St. George Square, where twenty thousand persons congregated to hear the Bishop of Manchester preach a sermon on civil liberty. "That sermon," the immigrant declared, "and the songs of the children still echo in their hearts. . . . I have asked those men again and again, 'Would you do it again? Would you suffer again for liberty's sake?' And I asked myself, 'Would I be willing to sacrifice mother and father at an early age through suffering resultant on that starvation period for this cause?' The answer is with them, as it is with you and me, a great big 'Yes.' "[13]

In the Cotton Exchange in Manchester a miniature bale of cotton was put on exhibition under a glass globe. Behind it gilt letters announced: "Part of the first bale of free cotton. Shipped from West Virginia, U. S., to Liverpool, 1865. Free cotton is King. But what did it cost?"[14]

No one knew better than the English people in 1865 that the Civil War was their own; that a victory for republicanism in America was a victory for democracy abroad. Even the middle and upper classes could not argue effectively against a democracy which produced Abraham Lincoln. Furthermore, Grant's magnanimous terms of surrender to Lee, giving the officers their side arms and allowing every man a horse for the spring plowing, convinced all but the most obdurate that Americans displayed political generosity unknown in more autocratic governments. Both parties in Parliament realized that an immediate extension of democracy in England must come. A British liberal said exultantly:

"Our opponents told us that republicanism was on its trial. They insisted on our watching what they called its breakdown. They told us plainly that it was forever discredited in England. Well, we accepted the challenge. We staked our hopes boldly on the result. . . . Under a strain such as no monarchy, no empire could have supported, republican institutions have stood firm. It is we, now, who call upon the privileged classes to mark the result. They may rely upon it that a vast impetus has been given to republican sentiments in England, and that they will have to reckon with it before long."[15]

All the foreign countries sent mourning letters to Washington. Lincoln was eulogized for his simplicity, his liberality, his honesty, and for saving his country after four years of civil war. These were virtues any tyrant could endorse. Seward had all the letters printed handsomely on large paper. They were bound in morocco, gilt-edged. A copy was sent to every power that sent condolences. The frontispiece of this de luxe publication was an engraving of Lincoln by Francis B. Carpenter—artist of the Emancipation Proclamation picture. Surely Seward had changed his mind and believed now that abolition was the crowning event of the administration—for Europeans at least.

Queen Victoria wrote a personal letter to Mrs. Lincoln. She told her journal that Goldwin Smith suggested the courtesy. The liberal professor had acted for a short time as a tutor for the Prince of Wales, later Edward VII. The letter to Mrs. Lincoln follows:

"Osborne.
"April 29, 1865.

"Dear Madam,
"Though a stranger to you I cannot remain silent when so terrible a calamity has fallen upon you and your country, and must personally express my *deep* and *heartfelt* sympathy with you under the shocking circumstances of your present dreadful misfortune.

"*No* one can better *appreciate* than *I* can, who am myself *utterly brokenhearted* by the loss of my own beloved Husband, who was the light of my life,—my stay—*my all*,—what your sufferings must be; and I earnestly pray that you may be supported by Him to whom alone the sorely stricken can look for comfort, in this hour of heavy affliction.

"With renewed expressions of true sympathy, I remain dear Madam,

"Your sincere friend
"Victoria."[16]

On May 1, 1865, Earl Russell told the Lords that the Queen had sent this letter. The House cheered lustily. Earl Russell then eulogized the assassinated President. "There are circumstances connected with this crime which, I think, aggravate its atrocity," he said. "President Lincoln was a man who, though not conspicuous before his election, had since displayed a character of so much integrity, so much sincerity and straightforwardness, and at the same time of so much kindness, that if any one was able to alleviate the pain and animosities which prevailed during the period of civil war, I believe that Abraham Lincoln was that person."[17]

Mrs. Lincoln, still ill from the shock of her husband's murder, replied to the Queen shortly before she left the White House. The following letter was written inside mourning borders.

"Washington
"May 21st 1865.

"Madam

"I have received the letter, which Your Majesty, has had the kindness to write & am deeply grateful for its expressions of tender sympathy, coming as they do, from a heart which from its own sorrow, can appreciate the intense grief, I now endure. Accept, Madam, the assurance of my heartfelt thanks, & believe me in the deepest sorrow, Your Majesty's sincere & grateful friend

"Mary Lincoln."[18]

Victoria's next gesture made some Midwest Americans guffaw. A subscription was circulated for a great monument over the dead President's tomb. Queen Victoria contributed a tuft of down that had fallen from one of her swans—a bit of fluff that could be found under the roost of any henhouse in Lincoln's cornlands. Her intentions were no doubt sentimental and sincere.

Napoleon accepted both the Union victory and the assassination as he would a dark horse at the races. He wrote a dutiful letter of sympathy to the American government. Empress Eugénie wrote Mrs. Lincoln a formal condolence. With female intuition Her Majesty seemed to sense impending danger to her regal way of life. Over at the American legation a crowd gathered. Bigelow went to the window. He counted sixteen policemen holding back riotous young men, eager, insistent, jostling each other for an opportunity to enter and weep in the legation parlors. "I had no idea that Mr. Lincoln had such a hold upon the heart of the young gentlemen of

France," he wrote, "or that his loss would be so properly appreciated."[19] The French Academy offered a prize for the best poem on the death of the President and awarded it to Edouard Grenier.[20] Lodges of the Masonic Order, an organization beyond the control of the Emperor, sent scores of sympathetic resolutions to Mrs. Lincoln. Prosper Mérimée, venerable French senator and supporter of Napoleon, threw up his old hands in disgust. In his youthful travels he had met a certain Spanish grandee whose wife told him the story of *Carmen* and whose four-year-old daughter—*la petite Eugénie*—won his heart for life. Years later Mérimée introduced her to Parisian society and had the pleasure of seeing her marry the Emperor. The excitement over Lincoln's death, said the *ancien littérateur,* was uncalled for. The dead President at best was only *"un first second rate man."*[21]

The French author's opinion had no effect on the French people. In Lyon twenty-five thousand workmen subscribed sums as low as ten centimes each and employed their most skilled artisans to weave a flag for the United States. "The subscriptions of merchants or people belonging to the higher classes have not been solicited," read the note of presentation from the democrats of France to democratic America. As never before in history, America was looked upon as the mainstay of all that was liberal and progressive in Europe.[22] Dictators, political adventurers and gamblers who had put themselves in high places by intrigue and cabal felt the ground tremble beneath their feet. Socialists and French *républicains* started a new movement. This time they proposed a general subscription of one sou from each poor child in France for a gold medal to be presented to Mrs. Lincoln. Napoleon ordered the police to stop the collection. It was completed in secret, and goldsmiths in Switzerland cast the medal where Napoleon could not interfere. On the face was inscribed:

## "LIBERTY, EQUALITY AND FRATERNITY

"To Lincoln, twice chosen President of the United States. From the grateful Democracy of France. Lincoln the Honest abolished slavery, reestablished the Union, saved the republic, without veiling the statue of Liberty. He was assassinated the 14th April, 1865."

The medal was given to John Bigelow to be sent in his dispatch bag to the State Department, and thence to Mrs. Lincoln. A letter of transmittal accompanying the medal expressed the feelings of forty thousand *"Citoyens Français désireux de manifester leurs sympathies pour l'Union Américaine."*[23] In part they said:

"If France had the freedom enjoyed by republican America, not thousands, but millions among us would have been counted as admirers of Lincoln, and believers in the opinions for which he devoted his life, and which his death has consecrated."[24]

Conspicuous among the committeemen who signed this letter were Louis Blanc, the socialist, and Victor Hugo, the radical novelist still in exile on the island of Guernsey.

The day of reckoning came in 1867. That year Emperor Maximilian and Miramón were executed by the Mexican republicans. In England the franchise was extended to a majority of the male citizens. Oddly enough, both incidents were salted with irony. The Tories put through the franchise bill. Gladstone championed it and in the years that followed devoted some of his liberal time apologizing for the escape of the *Alabama,* promising reimbursement and making the rafters ring with his pronouncement that the American Constitution was the most perfect document ever struck off by the hand of man. Equally inconsistent, hundreds of Confederate veterans, unwilling to remain in a democracy, marched south to help Maximilian hold his tottering throne. At the Rio Grande they sold their arms to democratic Juárez and used the money for transportation to the Emperor's court. Maximilian accepted some of them in his army. Others he assigned to a tract of land—a colony, but not the duchy Gwin had suggested.

The year 1867 brought anguish, too, for Empress Eugénie. Carlotta, back in France before her husband's death, begged and wept until her mind gave way. Eugénie was powerless to help her. Seward had a million veterans eager to march into Mexico. He ordered Napoleon to withdraw his army, to quit meddling in American continental affairs. What could Napoleon do? The French army sailed away and a World's Fair opened in Paris— banners, bands, balls and barbecues. Eugénie looked ghastly in the dazzling lights. Suave courtiers at the Fair presented her with an elaborate aluminum fan—a "Lincoln fan" it was called by the donors, who were suspected of Latin subtlety.

The tide of liberalism engulfed France within three years. The Third Republic was established. In Germany Bismarck saw the tide coming. To buffet the wave he allied his militarists with the German liberals and led his country into its greatest period of cultural advancement. Censorship was abolished by the Imperial Press Act. A new municipal system allowed unprecedented democracy. German universities became the leaders of the world. The liberal wave, with Lincoln's image on the crest, passed on around the globe. Lincoln biographies formed part of the revolutionary technique in Russia, Turkey and China. Japan adopted a constitution cut to a European pattern and then printed half a dozen *Lives* of Lincoln. Writers in thirty languages told all downtrodden people about the wood chopper who became President, the plain man in carpet slippers who saved democracy "without veiling the statue of Liberty." Walt Whitman spoke for oppressed people everywhere when he hailed the dead President, "O comrade lustrous with silver face in the night."

CITATIONS, SOURCES AND
ACKNOWLEDGMENTS

# CITATIONS

## CHAPTER I

[1] Paul M. Angle, *"Here I Have Lived"; A History of Lincoln's Springfield, 1821-1865*, 252. Gideon Welles Papers, 6.

[2] William H. Herndon, *Herndon's Lincoln; the True Story of a Great Life*, III, 586.

[3] John G. Nicolay and John Hay, eds., *Complete Works of Abraham Lincoln*, VI, 110.

[4] Gideon Welles, *Lincoln and Seward*, 37-38. Compare with Welles Papers, 6.

[5] Henry Adams, *The Education of Henry Adams. An Autobiography*, 104.

[6] Charles Francis Adams, *Charles Francis Adams, 1835-1915; An Autobiography*, 65.

[7] Thomas D. Jones, *Memories of Lincoln*, 15.

[8] Salmon P. Chase, "Diary," II, 51.

[9] Allen Thorndike Rice, *Reminiscences of Abraham Lincoln*, 479.

[10] *Ibid.*, 481.

[11] *Ibid.*

[12] Paul M. Angle, ed., *New Letters and Papers of Lincoln*, 204.

[13] Henry Villard, *Lincoln on the Eve of '61*, 27.

[14] Addison G. Procter, "Abraham Lincoln," 19.

[15] Villard, *Lincoln on the Eve of '61*, 62.

[16] Edward Bates, "Diary . . . 1859-66," 167 n.

[17] *Ibid.*, 164.

[18] Nicolay and Hay, *Complete Works*, VI, 90.

[19] *Autobiography of Thurlow Weed*, 598.

[20] William Augustus Croffut, *An American Procession, 1855-1914*, pict., 205.

[21] *Harper's Weekly*, Nov. 23, 1861.

[22] *Ibid.*

[23] Oliver Dyer, *Great Senators of the United States, Forty Years Ago*, 51-57.

[24] Nicolay and Hay, *Complete Works*, X, 65.

[25] Weed, *Autobiography*, 610.

[26] *Ibid.*, 611.

[27] Forrest Wilson, *Crusader in Crinoline, the Life of Harriet Beecher Stowe*, 422.

[28] Thurlow Weed Barnes, *Memoir of Thurlow Weed, by his Grandson*, 313-314.

[29] William H. Russell, *My Diary North and South*, 62.

[30] Philip Kinsley, *The Chicago Tribune*, I, 169.

[31] George Francis Train, *Train's Union Speeches Delivered in England*, 24.

[32] *Once a Week* (Cunard), 6-7.

[33] Weed, *Autobiography*, 613-614. The verbs have been changed to conform to the text.

[34] Villard, *Lincoln on the Eve of '61*, 50.

[35] *Letters of Henry Adams*, 78.

[36] *Ibid.*, 74.

[37] Villard, *Lincoln on the Eve of '61*, 55.

[38] R. H. Osborne, *Lincoln with his People*, (2).

[39] Edna M. Colman, *Seventy-five Years of White House Gossip*, 265-266.

[40] T. D. Jones, 7.

[41] Villard, *Lincoln on the Eve of '61*, 69.

[42] Theodore C. Pease and James G. Randall, eds., *The Diary of Orville Hickman Browning, 1850-1881*, I, 432.

[43] *Letters of Henry Adams*, 72.

[44] Herndon-Weik Collection (MS), V, 6, items 713-714.

[45] Harry E. Pratt, "David Davis, 1815-1886," 98.

[46] *Directory of Chicago*, 1858, 429.

[47] Villard, *Lincoln on the Eve of '61*, 70-71.

[48] Herndon, III, 586.

[49] Nicolay and Hay, *Complete Works*, VI, 110-111.

[50] A typed copy is in Illinois State Historical Library.

[51] Wayne Whipple, *The Story of Young Abraham Lincoln*, 210, quotes Robert Lincoln as saying that this occurred in Indianapolis. Ward Hill Lamon, *Recollections of Abraham Lincoln*, 35, places the incident in Harrisburg.

[52] Carl Sandburg, *Abraham Lincoln: The War Years*, I, 52.

[53] *Ibid.*, 53.

[54] *Old Abe's Jokes*, 138.

[55] Charles Stoltz, *The Tragic Career of Mary Todd Lincoln*, 47.

[56] Sandburg, I, 60.

[57] McCirr & Co., *Lincoln's Visit to Philadelphia*, 3.

[58] Anthony Trollope, *North America*, I, 447.

[59] William Bender Wilson, *History of the Pennsylvania Railroad*, 312; Charles W. Richey, "The Pennsylvania Railroad in Philadelphia, Pa." (unpublished report). Also T. and E. Woolen letter to R. and L. Wilson, July 30, 1860 (MS).

[60] This ceremony is often erroneously fixed at 6:00 A.M. but the sun did not rise until 6:45.

[61] Charles Clothier McLean, *The Boy Who Wore Lincoln's Hat*, (4).

[62] Nicolay and Hay, *Complete Works*, VI, 159-160.

[63] Allan Pinkerton, *History and Evidence of the Passage of Abraham Lincoln from Harrisburg, Pa., to Washington, D. C.*, 17. Note also Pinkerton's MS in Herndon-Weik Collection.

[64] Alexander K. McClure, *Abraham Lincoln and Men of War-Times*, 46.

[65] W. B. Wilson, 316-317.

## CHAPTER II

[1] W. H. Russell, *Diary*, 32.

[2] Edward Bates, 205; *Harper's Weekly*, Sept. 19, 1863; Maunsell B. Field, *Memories of Many Men and of Some Women*, 319-320.

[3] Henry Adams, *Education*, 99.

[4] Milton H. Shutes, *Lincoln and California*, 54.

5 Ephraim D. Adams, *Great Britain and the American Civil War*, II, 258-259.

6 *Harper's Weekly*, Feb. 18, 1865.

7 Horace Greeley, *The American Conflict*, I, 415 n.

8 John Bigelow, *Retrospections of an Active Life*, I, 410 n. Toombs denied this allegation. See Pleasant A. Stovall, *Robert Toombs, Statesman, Speaker, Soldier, Sage*, 119.

9 Barnes, 337.

10 *Chicago Press and Tribune*, March 5, 1861, reported that Lincoln was eighth sworn in by Taney.

11 Nicolay and Hay, *Complete Works*, VI, 185.

12 W. H. Russell, *Diary*, 9.

13 George Augustus Sala, *My Diary in America in the Midst of War*, II, 152.

14 William H. Townsend, *Lincoln and His Wife's Home Town*, 305.

15 "The Diary of a Public Man," No. 274, p. 267.

16 W. H. Russell, *Diary*, 43.

17 *Ibid.*

18 Tyler Dennett, ed., *Lincoln and the Civil War in the Diaries and Letters of John Hay*, 220.

19 Charles Francis Adams, *An Address on the Life, Character and Services of William Henry Seward*, 53.

20 Gideon Welles, *Diary*, I, 137.

21 Edward Bates, 180.

22 W. H. Russell, *Diary*, 5-6.

23 Donaldson Jordan and Edwin J. Pratt, *Europe and the American Civil War*, 23.

24 Nicolay and Hay, *Complete Works*, VI, 189-190.

25 Henry Adams, *Education*, 109.

26 E. D. Adams, I, 64-65.

27 Burton J. Hendrick, *Statesmen of the Lost Cause: Jefferson Davis and his Cabinet*, 145.

28 *Journal of the Executive Proceedings of the Senate*, XI, 310.

29 E. D. Adams, I, 67.

30 C. F. Adams, *Autobiography*, 107.

31 E. D. Adams, I, 62-63.

32 *Ibid.*, I, 63.

33 Hendrick, 143 n.

34 *Ibid.*, 140.

35 E. D. Adams, I, 63.

36 W. H. Townsend, 91.

37 Rice, 294.

38 Procter, 24.

39 Rice, 300.

40 Rayford W. Logan, *The Diplomatic Relations of the United States with Haiti 1776-1891*, 293; Nicolay and Hay, *Complete Works*, VI, 237.

41 James Ford Rhodes, *History of the United States from the Compromise of 1850*, IV, 83 n.

42 W. H. Russell, *Diary*, 14.

[43] *Ibid.*, 18.

[44] *Ibid.*, 14.

[45] *Ibid.*, 21.

[46] *Ibid.*, 32.

[47] *Ibid.*, 31.

[48] *Ibid.*, 37.

[49] *Ibid.*, 37-39.

[50] *Ibid.*, 39.

[51] Frederick W. Seward, *Reminiscences of a War-Time Statesman and Diplomat 1830-1915*, 133.

[52] W. H. Russell, *Diary*, 39-40.

[53] *Ibid.*, 41-42.

[54] *Ibid.*, 42.

[55] *Ibid.*, 43.

[56] Weed, *Autobiography*, 615 ff.; James B. Swain, letter to John Hay, Feb. 21, 1881, in Nicolay and Hay Papers, III, 26.

[57] *Memoirs of Henry Villard*, I, 162.

[58] William H. Russell, *The Civil War in America*, 17.

[59] Welles, *Diary*, I, 18.

[60] F. W. Seward, 149.

[61] Swain letter to John Hay, Feb. 21, 1881, in Nicolay and Hay Papers, III, 26. Such rumors, often repeated, are almost impossible to verify.

[62] Nicolay and Hay, *Complete Works*, VI, 234-236.

[63] *Ibid.*, IX, 199.

## CHAPTER III

[1] Nicolay and Hay, *Complete Works*, VI, 237.

[2] Seward to Tassara, April 2, 1861, Nicolay and Hay Papers, V, 2.

[3] Sala, II, 127-129.

[4] W. H. Russell, *Civil War in America*, 23.

[5] W. H. Russell, *Diary*, 62.

[6] Nicolay and Hay, *Complete Works*, VI, 240.

[7] W. H. Russell, *Diary*, 64.

[8] *Ibid.*, 65.

[9] *Ibid.*, 63-64.

[10] *Ibid.*, 65.

[11] Welles, *Diary*, I, 24.

[12] Julia Taft Bayne, *Tad Lincoln's Father*, 34-35.

[13] Welles, *Diary*, I, 24.

[14] C. F. Adams, *Autobiography*, 96.

[15] Thornton K. Lothrop, *William Henry Seward*, 361.

[16] Pease and Randall, *Browning Diary*, I, 480.

[17] C. F. Adams, *Autobiography*, 112.

[18] Hendrick, 121.

[19] Addison Peale Russell, *Thomas Corwin*, 26.

[20] Another version appears *ibid.*, 29.

21 Percy F. Martin, *Maximilian in Mexico*, 51, quoting Victor Hugo, *L'Histoire d'un Crime*.

22 Hendrick, 295.

23 Harry James Carman and Reinhard H. Luthin, *Lincoln and the Patronage*, 89.

24 [William B. Reed], *A Paper Containing a Statement and Vindication of Certain Political Opinions*, 9.

25 Ward Hill Lamon Papers, 9th item, Feb. 20, 1884.

26 Letter of Fogg to Welles, Jan. 21, 1861, Welles Papers.

27 [William B. Reed], *A Review of Mr. Seward's Diplomacy by a Northern Man*, 20-21.

28 Henry B. Stanton, *Random Recollections*, 208.

29 Bigelow, *Retrospections*, 165-170. See also James E. Campbell, "Sumner—Brooks—Burlingame or the Last of the Great Challenges," 435-473.

30 W. H. Russell, *Diary*, 69.

31 Frederic Bancroft, *Life of William H. Seward*, II, 509.

32 W. H. Russell, *Diary*, 70.

33 *Ibid.*

34 E. D. Adams, I, 72.

## CHAPTER IV

1 William Abbatt, ed., *Magazine of History with Notes and Queries*, Ex. No. 89, pp. 36-39. Julia Ward Howe's "Battle Hymn of the Republic" and James Sloan Gibbons' "We are Coming Father Abraham" were both printed in 1862.

2 Barnes, 337.

3 Edward Bates, 183 n.

4 F. W. Seward, 155-156.

5 Barnes, 342.

6 *Ibid.*, 339.

7 Dennett, ed., *Lincoln and the Civil War*, 8. Other accounts appear in John Speer's life of Jim Lane; in *Transactions of the Kansas State Historical Society*, X, 419; and in *Lincoln Lore* (Fort Wayne, Ind.), No. 102, March 23, 1931.

8 Dennett, ed., *Lincoln and the Civil War*, 19.

9 *Ibid.*, 8.

10 W. H. Russell, *Diary*, 151.

11 *Ibid.*

12 Benjamin Moran, Diary, May 1, 1861.

13 Hendrick, 143.

14 Moran, Diary, May 3, 1861.

15 Jordan and Pratt, 10.

16 John Bassett Moore, *Digest of International Law*, V, 20-22.

17 Lothrop, 294.

18 Welles, *Diary*, I, 174.

19 Charles Francis Adams, *Seward and the Declaration of Paris*, 28

20 *Ibid.*, 23.

21 W. H. Russell, *Diary*, 136.

22 *Ibid.*, 337.

[23] *Ibid.*, 192.

[24] *Ibid.*, 371.

[25] *Ibid.*, 111.

[26] *Ibid.*, 325.

[27] W. H. Russell, *Civil War in America*, 42.

[28] W. H. Russell, *Diary*, 250.

[29] *Ibid.*, 157.

[30] E. D. Adams, I, 71; and W. H. Russell, *Diary*, 169.

[31] W. H. Russell, *Diary*, 232.

[32] *Ibid.*, 189.

[33] W. H. Russell, *Civil War in America*, 61.

[34] *Ibid.*, 151.

[35] W. H. Russell, *Diary*, 273.

[36] W. H. Russell, *Civil War in America*, 155.

[37] W. H. Russell, *Diary*, 271.

[38] E. D. Adams, I, 71.

[39] W. H. Russell, *Diary*, 271.

[40] W. H. Russell, *Civil War in America*, 47.

[41] *Ibid.*, 171.

[42] W. H. Russell, *Diary*, 299.

[43] *Ibid.*, 165.

[44] *Ibid.*, 301.

[45] W. H. Russell, *Civil War in America*, 174.

[46] W. H. Russell, *Diary*, 173-174.

[47] *Ibid.*, 175.

[48] *Ibid.*

[49] *Ibid.*, 303.

[50] *Ibid.*, 374-375.

[51] Arthur C. Cole, *Lincoln's "House Divided" Speech*, 26.

[52] Comte Agénor Etienne de Gasparin, *America before Europe* (London ed.), 76-78.

## CHAPTER V

[1] George B. McClellan, *McClellan's Own Story*, 364 (May 24, 1862), notes Custer as coming to prominence.

[2] Dennett, ed., *Lincoln and the Civil War*, 23.

[3] Henry Adams, *Education*, 112.

[4] Moran, Diary, May 14, 1861.

[5] Henry Adams, *Education*, 114.

[6] Moran, Diary, May 10 and 13, 1861.

[7] Welles, *Diary*, I, 301.

[8] Moran, Diary, May 14, 1861.

[9] Henry Adams, *Education*, 171.

[10] Moran, Diary, Nov. 18, 1861.

[11] *Ibid.*, May 16, 1861.

[12] Bigelow, *Retrospections*, I, 267.

[13] *Ibid.*, 255-256.

14 Moran, Diary, May 17, 1861.
15 Jordan and Pratt, 55.
16 Henry Adams, Education, 190.
17 The Reminiscences of Carl Schurz, II, 245.
18 Hendrick, 264.
19 Henry Adams, Education, 173.
20 E. D. Adams, I, 88 n.
21 Hendrick, 149-150.
22 Moran, Diary, May 20, 1861.
23 Ibid., Nov. 20, 1860.
24 Henry Adams, Education, 134.
25 Ibid., 125.
26 Ibid., 124.
27 Bigelow, Retrospections, I, 282.
28 Hendrick, 395.
29 E. D. Adams, I, 39; Don C. Seitz, The James Gordon Bennetts, Father and Son, 184, contradicts this.
30 George Francis Train, My Life in Many States and in Foreign Lands, 272-273.
31 Jordan and Pratt, 178.
32 Train, Union Speeches, 27.
33 Ibid., 34.
34 Ibid., 32.
35 Ibid., 43.
36 The Filson Club, Louisville, Ky., has text of Clay's speech at American Union Club Breakfast, May 29, 1861.
37 Letter to Charles Francis Adams in Letters of Henry Adams, 92.
38 Jordan and Pratt, 13.
39 Frank Lawrence Owsley, King Cotton Diplomacy, 176.
40 Train, Union Speeches, 41.
41 James Rood Robertson, A Kentuckian at the Court of the Tsars, 104.
42 June 21, 1861. Diplomatic correspondence.
43 Ibid.
44 Ibid.
45 Robertson, 55.
46 Clay's Russian exploits received political notoriety in the 1870's. They became popular newspaper copy in the 1880's.
47 The writer is indebted to William H. Townsend, leading authority on Cassius Clay, for this anecdote.
48 Chester V. Easum, The Americanization of Carl Schurz, 339.
49 Ibid.
50 Schurz, II, 243.
51 Ibid., 249.
52 Ibid., 250.
53 Ibid., 273.
54 Jordan and Pratt, 198.
55 Ibid., 194.
56 Ibid., 255.

[57] *Ibid.*, 197.
[58] *Ibid.*, 195.
[59] Moran, Diary, July 8, 1861.

## CHAPTER VI

[1] Henry Watterson, *Abraham Lincoln, An Oration Delivered Before the Lincoln Union*, 26.

[2] E. D. Adams, I, 105.

[3] Henry Adams, *Letters*, 93. See also C. F. Adams, *Declaration of Paris*, 21 n.

[4] Moran, Diary, May 28, 1861.

[5] *Ibid.* Also Jordan and Pratt, 57.

[6] Moran, Diary, June 3, 1861; Pike to Seward, June 12 and 16, 1861, Dip. Corres.

[7] Seward to Adams, on June 3, speaks of joint proposal on "insurrection" (Senate **Ex.** Doc.), 37 Cong., 2 Sess., No. 1, p. 97. On p. 108, Seward says Declaration of Paris was offered June 15. C. F. Adams, *Declaration of Paris*, 31 and 38, states Lyons and Mercier came with instructions to accept the adhesion of the North to the Declaration of Paris, but would not let the North bind the Confederacy.

[8] William L. Dayton to Seward, July 22 and 30, 1861, in Dip. Corres. Also Moran, Diary, Aug. 1, 1861; Dayton to C. F. Adams, July 25, 1861.

[9] F. W. Seward, 425.

[10] LeRoy Henry Fischer, *Adam Gurowski and the Civil War: A Radical's Record*, 15.

[11] Adam Gurowski, *Diary*, I, 166.

[12] Fischer, 7.

[13] Gurowski, I, 27.

[14] Robert Carter, "Gurowski," 632.

[15] Edward Bates, 205-206.

[16] Carter, 630.

[17] Gurowski, III, 183.

[18] *Ibid.*, 121.

[19] W. H. Russell, *Diary*, 388.

[20] Nicolay and Hay, *Complete Works*, VI, 317.

[21] W. H. Russell, *Diary*, 280.

[22] Nicolay and Hay, *Complete Works*, VI, 304.

[23] *Ibid.*, 311.

[24] W. H. Russell, *Diary*, 380.

[25] Robert Phillimore, *Commentaries upon International Law*, III, 294.

[26] W. Adolphe Roberts, *Semmes of the Alabama*, opp. p. 224.

[27] *Harper's Weekly*, Jan. 3, 1863.

[28] James D. Bulloch, *The Secret Service of the Confederate States in Europe*, I, 47-48.

[29] *Ibid.*, 58.

[30] Bayne, 120.

[31] W. H. Russell, *Diary*, 429.

[32] *Ibid.*, 428-429.

33 David Homer Bates, *Lincoln in the Telegraph Office,* 88.

34 *Ibid.,* 91.

35 Arthur D. Howden Smith, *Old Fuss and Feathers,* 369.

36 W. H. Russell, *Diary,* 465.

37 Jordan and Pratt, 7.

38 *Ibid.,* 18.

39 W. H. Russell, *Diary,* 453; Bigelow, *Retrospections,* I, 347.

40 *Harper's Weekly,* Oct. 19, 1861.

41 Train, *Union Speeches,* 55.

42 F. W. Seward, 181.

## CHAPTER VII

1 H. Nelson Gay, "Lincoln's Offer of a Command to Garibaldi," 67.

2 Giuseppe Garibaldi, *A Toast to Rebellion,* xiv.

3 Gay, 69.

4 Moran, Diary, Sept. 20, 1861.

5 Charles Francis Adams, "Lincoln's Offer to Garibaldi," 321.

6 Garibaldi, xiv.

7 Bigelow, *Retrospections,* I, 371-372.

8 George Macaulay Trevelyan, *Garibaldi and the Making of Italy,* 277.

9 Gay, 69.

10 W. H. Russell, *Diary,* 483.

11 *Ibid.,* 512.

12 Schurz, II, 339.

13 Princess Felix Salm-Salm, *Ten Years of My Life,* 26.

14 *Ibid.,* 29.

15 *Harper's Weekly,* Aug. 17, 1861.

16 Arnold Whitridge, "Lincoln through French Eyes," 76; Jordan and Pratt, 231.

17 F. W. Seward, 182.

18 *Ibid.,* 183.

19 *Ibid.,* 174-175.

20 Nicolay and Hay Papers, V, 2.

21 The writer is indebted to Tino Costa, French artist, for this political tradition.

22 Dennett, ed., *Lincoln and the Civil War,* 27.

23 Clarence E. Macartney, *Lincoln and his Generals,* 73.

24 Lincoln letter to Tycoon of Japan, Aug. 1, 1861, Dip. Corres.

25 D. H. Bates, *Lincoln in the Telegraph Office,* 398-399.

26 McClellan, 99. Fred A. Shannon, *The Organization and Administration of the Union Army, 1861-1865,* I, 180-181.

27 W. H. Russell, *Diary,* 489.

28 Moran, Diary, Aug. 30, 1861.

29 Bigelow, *Retrospections,* I, 365.

30 *Ibid.,* 264.

31 *Ibid.,* 263.

32 *Ibid.,* 256.

446

[33] Forrest Wilson, 376.
[34] Bigelow, *Retrospections*, I, 257.
[35] *Ibid.*, 153.
[36] John Bigelow, *Some Recollections of the Late Edouard Laboulaye*, 1.
[37] *Ibid.*, 2.
[38] Bigelow, *Retrospections*, I, 246.
[39] William Roscoe Thayer, *The Life and Letters of John Hay*, I, 236.
[40] Bigelow, *Retrospections*, I, 246.
[41] *Ibid.*, 247.
[42] Jordan and Pratt, 243.
[43] Bigelow, *Recollections of Laboulaye*, 6.
[44] *Ibid.*, 7.
[45] Bulloch, I, 71.
[46] Russell became an earl in July 1861.
[47] Moran, Diary, Aug. 15, 1861.
[48] *Ibid.*, Aug. 24, 1861.
[49] Bulloch, I, 76.
[50] *Ibid.*, 100.
[51] Letters of Pike to Seward, Sept. 4, Oct. 2, Oct. 12, 1861, in Dip. Corres.
[52] W. H. Russell, *Diary*, 523.
[53] *Ibid.*, 525.
[54] F. W. Seward, 177.
[55] W. H. Russell, *Diary*, 535.
[56] *Ibid.*, 536.
[57] Moran, Diary, Sept. 2, 1861.
[58] [Reed], *A Review of Mr. Seward's Diplomacy*, 55.
[59] W. H. Russell, *Diary*, 529.
[60] Jordan and Pratt, 27.
[61] Moran, Diary, Sept. 13, 1861. Literally "Her Majesty's Gov't."
[62] Dennett, ed., *Lincoln and the Civil War*, 29.
[63] W. H. Russell, *Diary*, 556.
[64] Moran, Diary, Aug. 31, 1861.
[65] Letter, Dayton to Seward, Sept. 27, 1861.
[66] John Musser, "The Establishment of Maximilian's Empire in Mexico," 15.
[67] Moran, Diary, Sept. 28, 1861. Literally "nor does Gt. Brit. approve," etc.
[68] Jordan and Pratt, 24.
[69] *Ibid.*
[70] Train, *Union Speeches*, 87.
[71] W. H. Russell, *Diary*, 558.
[72] McClellan, 188-190.
[73] Dennett, ed., *Lincoln and the Civil War*, 31.
[74] Letter, Dayton to Seward, Oct. 16, 1861.
[75] W. H. Russell, *Diary*, 561.
[76] London *Times*, Nov. 8, 1861.
[77] Bigelow, *Retrospections*, I, 378-379.

## CHAPTER VIII

[1] D. H. Bates, *Lincoln in the Telegraph Office*, 41.

[2] Train, *Union Speeches*, 51; London *Times*, Nov. 16, 1861.

[3] W. H. Russell, *Diary*, 566.

[4] Weed, *Autobiography*, 501.

[5] George Francis Train, *The Downfall of England*, 27.

[6] William L. Penny. *Abraham Lincoln*, 17.

[7] Barnes, 349.

[8] Croffut, 205.

[9] D. H. Bates, *Lincoln in the Telegraph Office*, 41.

[10] W. H. Russell, *Diary*, 72.

[11] Weed, *Autobiography*, 653.

[12] A. D. H. Smith, 358.

[13] Barnes, 432.

[14] Thurlow Weed, *Letters from Europe and the West Indies*, 65.

[15] Weed, *Autobiography*, 517.

[16] *St. Louis Reveille*, Sept. 30, 1848.

[17] *Ibid.*, Sept. 22, 1848.

[18] Weed, *Letters from Europe*, 210.

[19] Jordan and Pratt, 75.

[20] James Spence, *The American Union*, preface, 1st ed.

[21] *Ibid.*, 4th ed., 302.

[22] *Ibid.*, 304-305.

[23] *Ibid.*, 319-320.

[24] *Ibid.*, 313-314.

[25] London *Times*, Nov. 1, 1861.

[26] Jordan and Pratt, 131.

[27] Letter from C. F. Adams to Seward, Oct. 17, 1861, in Nicolay and Hay Papers, V, 2.

[28] Letter ("Very Confidential") from C. F. Adams to Seward, Oct. 5, 1861, *ibid.*

[29] Letter from C. F. Adams to Seward, Oct. 17, 1861, *ibid.* Bulloch, I, 115, stated that the sunken craft was an Austrian brig.

[30] Bulloch, I, 115.

[31] *Ibid.*, 121.

[32] *Ibid.*, 123.

[33] London *Times*, Nov. 5, 1861.

[34] Train, *Union Speeches*, 50.

[35] C. F. Adams, *Autobiography*, 47.

[36] Henry Adams, *Letters*, 72.

[37] W. H. Russell, *Diary*, 237.

[38] *Ibid.*

[39] *Harper's Weekly*, Nov. 30, 1861.

[40] Hendrick, 288.

[41] Jim Dan Hill, *Sea Dogs of the Sixties*, 92.

[42] Willis J. Abbot, *The Naval History of the United States*, 606.

[43] Thomas L. Harris, *The Trent Affair*, 107.

[44] *Ibid.*, 108.

[45] W. H. Russell, *Diary*, 573.

[46] *Ibid.*, 574.

[47] Margaret Leech, *Reveille in Washington, 1860-1865*, 122.
[48] Rhodes, III, 519-522.
[49] *Ibid.*, 522.
[50] MS account by John G. Nicolay in Nicolay and Hay Papers.
[51] Rhodes, III, 524.
[52] Bigelow, *Retrospections*, I, 400.
[53] W. H. Russell, *Diary*, 577.
[54] *Ibid.*, 577-578.

## CHAPTER IX

[1] J. D. Hill, 102.
[2] Moran, Diary, Nov. 21, 1861; London *Times*, Nov. 22, 1861.
[3] Weed, *Autobiography*, 639.
[4] Moran, Diary, Nov. 27, 1861.
[5] Jordan and Pratt, 28.
[6] Moran, Diary, Dec. 3, 1861.
[7] Hendrick, 151.
[8] Bigelow, *Retrospections*, I, 404.
[9] C. F. Adams, *Address on Seward*, 66.
[10] Hendrick, 151.
[11] Bigelow, *Retrospections*, I, 405.
[12] Jordan and Pratt, 36.
[13] Bigelow, *Retrospections*, I, 387-388.
[14] *Ibid.*, 388.
[15] London *Times*, Dec. 2, 1861.
[16] Barnes, 369.
[17] London *Times*, Dec. 2, 1861.
[18] *Ibid.*
[19] *Ibid.*, Dec. 5, 1861.
[20] Barnes, 352. In quoting, the writer has changed the person in the original.
[21] *Ibid.*, 353.
[22] Jordan and Pratt, 34-35.
[23] Train, *Union Speeches*, 59.
[24] *Ibid.*, 60.
[25] *Ibid.*
[26] Moran, Diary, Dec. 10, 1861.
[27] Barnes, 369.
[28] London *Times*, Dec. 12, 1861.
[29] *Ibid.*, Dec. 13, 1861.
[30] London *Times*, Dec. 16, 1861; Jordan and Pratt, 42; E. D. Adams, I, 225.
[31] Nicolay and Hay, *Complete Works*, VII, 28.
[32] *Ibid.*, 56.
[33] *Ibid.*, 60.
[34] E. D. Adams, I, 225.
[35] Dec. 17, 1861.
[36] Train, *Union Speeches*, 63. The person has been changed.

³⁷ Jordan and Pratt, 44.

³⁸ *Ibid.*, ·39-40. This was in January.

³⁹ Jordan and Pratt, 136.

⁴⁰ *Ibid.*, 39.

⁴¹ London *Times*, Dec. 9, 1861.

⁴² [Reed], *A Review of Mr. Seward's Diplomacy*, 29-30.

⁴³ Theodore Martin, *Life of the Prince Consort*, V, 421; Weed, *Autobiography*, 647. Consul Thomas H. Dudley, in "Three Critical Periods in our Diplomatic Relations with England," 43-44, states that this information was released to Dayton by Lady Cowley.

⁴⁴ Bigelow, *Retrospections*, I, 407.

⁴⁵ Pease and Randall, eds., *Browning Diary*, I, 515. Peculiar capitalization has been changed.

⁴⁶ W. H. Russell, *Diary*, 587.

⁴⁷ Pease and Randall, eds., *Browning Diary*, I, 515.

⁴⁸ *Ibid.*, 514 n.

⁴⁹ W. H. Russell, *Diary*, 585.

⁵⁰ *Ibid.*, 587.

⁵¹ *Ibid.*

⁵² F. W. Seward, 187-188.

⁵³ W. H. Russell, *Diary*, 588.

⁵⁴ Leonard Grover, "Lincoln's Interest in the Theater," 945. If the date of this incident is correct, Tad probably sang some other song.

⁵⁵ Letter of C. F. Adams to Seward, Dec. 6, 1861, Nicolay and Hay Papers.

⁵⁶ Letter of Dayton to Seward, Dec. 5, 1861, in Dip. Corres.

⁵⁷ Hendrick, 131.

⁵⁸ *Ibid.*, 137.

⁵⁹ Pease and Randall, eds., *Browning Diary*, I, 516-517.

⁶⁰ *Ibid.*, 517 n. John G. Nicolay and John Hay, *Abraham Lincoln: A History*, V, 32.

⁶¹ W. H. Russell, *Diary*, 589.

⁶² *Ibid.*

⁶³ Lothrop, 334.

⁶⁴ F. W. Seward, 189.

⁶⁵ Bigelow, *Retrospections*, I, 429; Pease and Randall, eds., *Browning Diary*, I, 518-519.

⁶⁶ Pease and Randall, eds., *Browning Diary*, I, 518. This appears in third person in the original.

⁶⁷ Seward to Lyons, Dec. 26, 1861, in Dip. Corres. The text also appears in W. H. Seward, *The Diplomatic History of the War for the Union*, V, 295-309, and in Bigelow, *Retrospections*, I, 431-436.

⁶⁸ W. H. Seward, V, 299.

⁶⁹ London *Times*, Dec. 2, 1861.

⁷⁰ Bigelow, *Retrospections*, I, 436.

⁷¹ W. H. Russell, *Diary*, 592.

⁷² F. W. Seward, 191.

⁷³ Letter of Seward to Lyons, Jan. 6, 1862, in Dip. Corres.

⁷⁴ Train, *Union Speeches*, 74.

## CHAPTER X

[1] Moran, Diary, Jan. 9, 1861; letter of C. F. Adams to Seward, Jan. 24, 1861, in Nicolay and Hay Papers, V, 2.

[2] Pease and Randall, eds., *Browning Diary*, I, 525.

[3] Train, *Union Speeches*, 78.

[4] *Ibid.*, 81.

[5] Pike to Seward, Jan. 15, 1862; Dayton to Seward, Jan. 27, 1862.

[6] Bigelow, *Retrospections*, I, 460.

[7] Barnes, 409.

[8] *Harper's Weekly*, Feb. 1, 1862.

[9] Barnes, 390-391.

[10] *Ibid.*, 391.

[11] *Ibid.*, 393.

[12] *Ibid.*, 392-393.

[13] *Ibid.*, 394-399.

[14] Bigelow, *Retrospections*, I, 458.

[15] Jordan and Pratt, 209.

[16] Hendrick, 250.

[17] *Ibid.*, 268.

[18] *Ibid.*, 267.

[19] Henry Adams, *Education*, 185.

[20] Hendrick, 296.

[21] *Ibid.*, 301.

[22] Train, *Union Speeches*, 78.

[23] *Ibid.*

[24] Schurz, II, 309-310.

[25] [Reed], *A Review of Mr. Seward's Diplomacy*, 46 n.

[26] W. H. Russell, *Diary*, 374, 411.

[27] Nicolay and Hay, *Complete Works*, VI, 191, 267.

[28] Macartney, *Lincoln and his Cabinet*, 299.

[29] Welles, *Diary*, I, 127.

[30] *Ibid.*

[31] Dennett, ed., *Lincoln and the Civil War*, 220.

[32] Moran, Diary, Jan. 23, 1862.

[33] *Journal of Exec. Proceedings of the Senate*, XII, 102.

[34] Pease and Randall, eds., *Browning Diary*, I, 527.

[35] *Ibid.*

## CHAPTER XI

[1] Clay's private letter to Lincoln, March 8, 1862, in Dip. Corres.

[2] Clay to Seward, April 13, 1862.

[3] *Journal of Exec. Proceedings of the Senate*, XII, 200.

[4] Moran, Diary, May 31, 1861.

5 Bayard Taylor to Seward, April 16, 1862.

6 James Monaghan, "Bayard Taylor, Poet and Patriot," 7.

7 F. W. Seward, 219 ff.

8 Report of acting consul general of France in Morocco to Thouvenel in *Papers Relating to Foreign Affairs* (House Ex. Doc.), 37 Cong., 3 Sess., No. 1, 413-419.

9 *Harper's Weekly*, Aug. 16, 1862.

10 *Ibid.*

11 Abbot, 591.

12 *Copy of Two Letters from His Majesty the Major King of Siam* (Senate Ex. Doc.), 37 Cong., 2 Sess., No. 23.

13 Elizabeth Keckley, *Behind the Scenes*, 101.

14 Seward to Lyons, Feb. 21, 1862, in Dip. Corres.

15 E. D. Adams, I, 280-283; Gurowski, I, 194.

16 John Bigelow, "The Confederate Diplomats," 118 n.

17 Bigelow, *Retrospections*, I, 481.

18 Bigelow's parents were from Connecticut.

19 Rhodes, IV, 356 n.

20 Bigelow, *Retrospections*, I, 479.

21 Beckles Willson, *John Slidell and the Confederates in Paris*, 74.

22 John W. Wallace, *Cases Argued and Adjudged in the Supreme Court of the United States*, III, 515.

23 Bigelow, *Retrospections*, I, 487.

24 Grover, 945.

25 Simon Cameron to Seward, June 26, 1862.

26 Dayton to Seward, June 12, 1862; *Harper's Weekly*, July 12, 1862.

27 Seward to Stuart, June 24, 1862.

28 Charles G. Loring and Edwin W. Field, *Correspondence on the Present Relations between Great Britain and the United States of America*, 48.

29 E. D. Adams, II, 123.

30 *Journal of the Exec. Proceedings of the Senate*, XII, 370.

31 Dayton to Seward, July 9, 1862.

32 Bigelow, *Retrospections*, I, 499.

33 Hendrick, 281.

34 Gurowski, II, 34.

35 Fischer, 11.

36 Owsley, 576-577, shows the amount of pauperism little higher than in previous decades.

37 Rhodes, IV, 84 n.

38 James E. Holden, "My Story of Abraham Lincoln," 719.

39 E. D. Adams, II, 21 n.

40 Rhodes, IV, 84.

41 Jordan and Pratt, 109.

42 E. D. Adams, II, 23.

43 Rhodes, IV, 89.

44 Bulloch, I, 242.

45 Henry Adams, *Education*, 149.

46 Rhodes, IV, 91.

452

CHAPTER XII

[1] Welles, *Diary*, I, 70.
[2] Nicolay and Hay, *Complete Works*, X, 65.
[3] House Ex. Docs., 37 Cong., 2 Sess., No. 117.
[4] *Religious Toleration in Egypt*, 12.
[5] Gurowski, I, 223.
[6] Hendrick, 297; *Harper's Weekly*, July 12, 1862.
[7] Bigelow, *Retrospections*, I, 531; Willson, *John Slidell and the Confederates in Paris*, 78-79.
[8] Rhodes, IV, 346.
[9] Bigelow, *Retrospections*, I, 517.
[10] Louis M. Sears, *John Slidell*, 203.
[11] Chase, 48.
[12] Schurz, II, 283.
[13] Pease and Randall, eds., *Browning Diary*, I, 562.
[14] *Ibid.*, 563-564.
[15] Chase, 51-57.
[16] Dennett, ed., *Lincoln and the Civil War*, 53.
[17] Nicolay and Hay, *Complete Works*, VII, 301.
[18] *Ibid.*, VII, 304-306.
[19] Owsley, 519.
[20] Rice, 302-303.
[21] Samuel S. Ball, *Liberia*, 11.
[22] Nicolay and Hay, *Complete Works*, VIII, 1-9.
[23] W. H. Townsend, 331.
[24] Welles, *Diary*, I, 74.
[25] *Ibid.*, 80.
[26] Seward to Stuart, Aug. 20, 1862, in Dip. Corres.
[27] Jordan and Pratt, 171.
[28] W. H. Townsend, 331-332.
[29] Rhodes, IV, 338 n.
[30] E. D. Adams, II, 285.
[31] *Ibid.*, II, 30-31.
[32] Gurowski, I, 269.
[33] Henry Adams, *Education*, 152.
[34] *Ibid.*, 153.
[35] Train, *Downfall of England*, 26.
[36] Train, *My Life in Many States*, 274.
[37] Clipping from *New York Herald*, Nov. 1 and 2, 1862, at Filson Club.
[38] Train, *My Life in Many States*, 280. Sala, II, 90, noted him at Willard's in January.
[39] Leech, 183.
[40] Welles, *Diary*, I, 140-141.
[41] Bulloch, I, 255.
[42] Dayton to Seward, Sept. 17, 1862, in Dip. Corres.
[43] Rhodes, IV, 338.

[44] Bigelow, *Retrospections*, I, 550-551.
[45] Bigelow, "The Confederate Diplomats," 119.


CHAPTER XIII


[1] Loring and Field, 136.
[2] Nicolay and Hay, *Abraham Lincoln: A History*, VI, 357.
[3] Letter of Pomeroy, Oct. 27, 1862, in Orville Hickman Browning Papers.
[4] Welles, *Diary*, I, 123, 150. Oliver R. Barrett, Kenilworth, Ill., has in his collection unpublished material on this plan.
[5] Welles, *Diary*, I, 162.
[6] Nicolay and Hay, *Abraham Lincoln: A History*, VI, 359.
[7] Chase, 87.
[8] Dennett, ed., *Lincoln and the Civil War*, 50.
[9] Note also *Address to Christians Throughout the World*.
[10] E. D. Adams, II, 156-157.
[11] Dennett, ed., *Lincoln and the Civil War*, 51.
[12] Bigelow, *Retrospections*, I, 560.
[13] Rhodes, IV, 339; Henry Adams, *Education*, 157.
[14] Henry Adams, *Education*, 157-158.
[15] Jordan and Pratt, 115.
[16] Stuart to Seward, October 10, 1862, in Dip. Corres.
[17] Welles, *Diary*, I, 170-171.
[18] Cameron to Seward, Sept. 18, 1862.
[19] *Harper's Weekly*, Oct. 25, 1862.
[20] Howard R. Marraro, "Lincoln's Offer . . . to Garibaldi: Further Light on a Disputed Point of History," 253 n., 268-269.
[21] Bigelow, *Retrospections*, I, 561.
[22] Henry Adams, *Education*, 160.
[23] Edward Bates, 266.
[24] Bigelow, *Retrospections*, I, 563-564.
[25] Dayton to Seward, Nov. 7, 1862.
[26] F. W. Seward, 421.
[27] Owsley, 356.
[28] Hendrick, 381; Willson, *John Slidell and the Confederates in Paris*, 109.
[29] Gurowski, I, 302.
[30] Dennett, ed., *Lincoln and the Civil War*, 51.
[31] Lothrop, 360.
[32] Gurowski, I, 315.
[33] *Harper's Weekly*, Apr. 11, 1863. Nathaniel B. Browne, *Address before the Union League* (1863), 13, contradicts this.
[34] Jordan and Pratt, 207-211. A clipping enclosed in diplomatic correspondence sent by Dayton, Nov. 14, 1862, stated 100,000.
[35] Dayton to Seward, Nov. 14, 1862.
[36] Bigelow, *Retrospections*, I, 572 n.
[37] Dayton to Seward, Nov. 12, 1862.
[38] Loring and Field, 139-140.

[39] William Taylor, *Cause and Probable Result of the Civil War in America. Facts for the People of Great Britain*, 30.

[40] *Ibid.*, 24.

[41] *Ibid.*, 15.

[42] *Ibid.*, 16.

[43] *Ibid.*, 32.

[44] Jordan and Pratt, 141-142.

[45] Henry Adams, *Education*, 161.

[46] Hendrick, 282.

[47] *Harper's Weekly*, Dec. 6, 1862.

[48] Henry Adams, *Education*, 161.

[49] Bigelow, *Retrospections*, I, 574.

[50] *Harper's Weekly*, Nov. 15, 1862.

[51] D. H. Bates, *Lincoln in the Telegraph Office*, 263-264.

[52] Henry Adams, *Education*, 168.

[53] *Harper's Weekly*, Nov. 15, 1862.

[54] Dayton to Seward, Nov. 13, 1862.

[55] Bigelow, *Retrospections*, I, 572.

[56] *Ibid.*, 581-582.

[57] Nicolay and Hay, *Complete Works*, VIII, 118-119.

[58] Bigelow, *Retrospections*, I, 582.

[59] Pease and Randall, eds., *Browning Diary*, I, 595.

[60] Welles, *Diary*, I, 197-198.

[61] Pease and Randall, eds., *Browning Diary*, I, 600.

[62] Nicolay and Hay Papers, VI, 12.

[63] Pease and Randall, eds., *Browning Diary*, I, 606.

[64] Dayton to Seward, Dec. 16, 1862.

[65] Tassara to Seward, Dec. 30, 1862.

[66] Forrest Wilson, 482.

[67] Stowe, "A Reply to 'The Affectionate and Christian Address,'" 121.

[68] Forrest Wilson, 484.

[69] *Ibid.*, 484-485.

[70] Stowe, 120-133.

[71] Rhodes, IV, 345.

[72] Jordan and Pratt, 145.

[73] *Lexington Observer & Reporter*, June 16, 1864, quoted in W. H. Townsend, 344.

[74] Nicolay and Hay, *Abraham Lincoln: A History*, VI, 359.

[75] Henry D. Lyman, *Abraham Lincoln A Story Hitherto Untold*, (4).

[76] McKay MS at Illinois State Historical Library.

## CHAPTER XIV

[1] Grover, 946-947.

[2] Bigelow, *Retrospections*, I, 604.

[3] Dayton to Seward, Jan. 15, 1863.

[4] Pease and Randall, eds., *Browning Diary*, I, 614.

[5] *Mexico* (House Ex. Doc.), 37 Cong., 3 Sess., No. 23, p. 18.

6 Francis B. Carpenter, *Six Months at the White House with Abraham Lincoln*, 291.

7 Charles K. Tuckerman, "President Lincoln and Colonization," 40-44.

8 Pease and Randall, eds., *Browning Diary*, I, 612.

9 Nicolay and Hay, *Complete Works*, VIII, 188.

10 Photostats in Horner Collection.

11 Burnside urged this on Lincoln in a letter dated Jan. 1, 1863, now at Illinois State Historical Library.

12 Nicolay and Hay, *Complete Works*, VIII, 194-197.

13 Jordan and Pratt, 93.

14 Rhodes, IV, 353 n.

15 Martin P. Claussen, "Peace Factors in Anglo-American Relations, 1861-1865," 521 n.

16 Jordan and Pratt, 142.

17 *Ibid.*, 67.

18 *Ibid.*, 91.

19 *Ibid.*, 142.

20 Holden, 719.

21 Jordan and Pratt, 172.

22 Jefferson Davis, proclamation, *Magazine of History with Notes and Queries*, Ex. No. 113, p. 68. A search of Dunbar Rowland's edition of Davis' works has not disclosed this proclamation. If Davis were not the author, he might have profited in Europe by a denial.

23 Jordan and Pratt, 94.

24 *Ibid.*, 158.

25 Andrew Dickson White, *A Letter to W. Howard Russell, on Passages in his "Diary North and South,"* 7.

26 Jordan and Pratt, 157.

27 *Ibid.*, 76.

28 W. Martin Jones, *Abraham Lincoln*, 24.

29 Moncure Daniel Conway, *Autobiography, Memories and Experiences*, I, 407.

30 Rhodes, IV, 359 n.

31 Conway, I, 407.

32 Jordan and Pratt, 228.

33 *Ibid.*, 140.

34 Matthew Josephson, *Victor Hugo*, 433.

35 Nicolay and Hay, *Complete Works*, VIII, 207.

36 Gurowski, II, 110.

37 W. H. Seward, V, 376.

38 Charles Sumner, *In the Senate of the United States* (Senate Misc. Doc.), 37 Cong., 3 Sess., No. 38.

39 Samuel Blatchford, *Reports of Cases in Prize . . . in the Circuit and District Courts of the United States, for the Southern District of New York*, 434.

40 Jordan and Pratt, 151-152.

41 E. D. Adams, II, 291-292 n.

42 Claussen, 521; Barnes, 423.

43 *Harper's Weekly*, March 28, 1863.

[44] Goldwin Smith, *Reminiscences,* 361.

[45] Holden, 719.

[46] Henry Adams, *Education,* 146.

[47] Gurowski, II, 280.

[48] Jordan and Pratt, 177.

[49] *New York Herald,* April 20, 1861.

[50] Jordan and Pratt, 195.

[51] Pike to Seward, Feb. 18, 1863.

[52] Frank E. Lally, "French Opposition to the Mexican Policy of the Second Empire," 42.

[53] Jordan and Pratt, 161-162.

[54] E. D. Adams, II, 125.

[55] *Ibid.,* 124.

[56] *Ibid.,* 126.

[57] Henry Adams, *Letters,* 96.

[58] Nicolay and Hay Papers, March 18, 1863.

[59] Jordan and Pratt, 161.

[60] Rhodes, IV, 353.

[61] E. D. Adams, II, 134.

[62] *Ibid.,* 136.

[63] George Macaulay Trevelyan, *Life of John Bright,* facsim., opp. 303.

[64] Bigelow, *Retrospections,* I, 633-634.

[65] E. D. Adams, II, 157.

## CHAPTER XV

[1] Dayton to Seward, March 20, 1863, in Dip. Corres.

[2] Hendrick, 223-225.

[3] *Ibid.,* 224.

[4] Bigelow, *Retrospections,* I, 620.

[5] Hendrick, 224-225.

[6] *Ibid.,* 225.

[7] Jordan and Pratt, 182.

[8] F. Lauriston Bullard, "Lincoln Pardons Conspirator on Plea of an English Statesman," [2].

[9] Shutes, *Lincoln and California,* 80.

[10] Zulma Steele, *Angel in Top Hat,* 31; Train, *Union Speeches,* 44.

[11] Anson Burlingame to Seward, Jan. 29, 1863.

[12] E. D. Adams, II, 291-292.

[13] Welles, *Diary,* I, 259.

[14] *Harper's Weekly,* May 9, 1863.

[15] Ralph Waldo Emerson, *Letters and Social Aims,* 101. See also *Dictionary of American Biography,* VI, 508.

[16] E. D. Adams, II, 161 n., attributes the price drop to the Law Officers' decision in the *Alexandra* case.

[17] Bigelow, *Retrospections,* I, 622.

[18] Hendrick, 228.

[19] Welles, *Diary,* I, 269-270.

20 *Harper's Weekly*, Apr. 25, 1863.
21 Bulloch, I, 267.
22 Bigelow, *Retrospections*, I, 636.
23 *Ibid.*, 644.
24 Greeley, *American Conflict*, II, 354.
25 J. G. Randall, *The Civil War and Reconstruction*, 395.
26 Claussen, 520.
27 *Harper's Weekly*, May 30, 1863.
28 Owsley, 572-574.
29 Rhodes, V, 397.
30 *Harper's Weekly*, Dec. 12, 1863.
31 Rhodes, V, 397-398.
32 *Ibid.*, V, 403.
33 *New York Times*, Oct. 30, 1864.
34 Rhodes, V, 404.
35 Gurowski, II, 222.
36 Henry Adams, *Education*, 130.
37 Margaret N. Armstrong, *Fanny Kemble, A Passionate Victorian*, 340.
38 *Harper's Weekly*, June 13, 1863.
39 Welles, *Diary*, I, 298.
40 *Ibid.*, 302-303.
41 *Ibid.*, 315.
42 Bullard, [2].
43 Gurowski, II, 241-242.
44 *Ibid.*, 243.
45 Barnes, 429.
46 Jordan and Pratt, 179.
47 E. D. Adams, II, 152.
48 Elizabeth Haller, "Aspects of American Opinion Regarding Maximilian's Empire in Mexico," 6.
49 Bigelow, *Retrospections*, I, 531.
50 Welles, *Diary*, I, 338-339.
51 Gurowski, II, 263-264.
52 William E. Dodd, "Lincoln's Press Agent a Marvel of Efficiency," 219.

## CHAPTER XVI

1 Jordan and Pratt, 184 ff.
2 E. D. Adams, II, 170 n.
3 Gurowski, I, 256.
4 Henry Adams, *Education*, 186.
5 *Ibid.*, 187.
6 *Ibid.*
7 *Ibid.*, 188.
8 Dayton to Seward, Aug. 5, 1863.
9 Hendrick, 319-320.
10 Jordan and Pratt, 186.
11 Henry Adams, *Education*, 171.

[12] Jordan and Pratt, 179.

[13] *Ibid.*, 187.

[14] Katherine Helm, *The True Story of Mary, Wife of Lincoln,* 211-212.

[15] Burlingame to Seward, June 20, 1863.

[16] Dennett, ed., *Lincoln and the Civil War,* 75.

[17] *Ibid.*, 75-76.

[18] F. W. Seward, 236-237.

[19] Elbridge G. Keith, "The National Republican Convention of 1860," 19.

[20] E. D. Adams, II, 180.

[21] Dayton to Seward, Sept. 7; Sept. 16, 1863.

[22] Dayton to Seward, Sept. 11, 1863.

[23] John Bigelow, *France and the Confederate Navy, 1862-1868,* 1.

[24] Dayton to Seward, Sept. 11, 1863.

[25] Hendrick, 382.

[26] Bigelow, *France and the Confederate Navy,* 7.

[27] *Ibid.*, 17.

[28] Willson, *John Slidell and the Confederates in Paris,* 57 n.

[29] Hendrick, 377.

[30] Dayton to Seward, Aug. 27, 1863.

[31] Welles, *Diary,* I, 428-429.

[32] *Harper's Weekly,* Sept. 26, 1863.

[33] Henry Adams, *Education,* 177. E. D. Adams, II, 135-136, gives slightly different text.

[34] Henry Adams, *Education,* 172.

[35] *Ibid.*, 173.

[36] *Harper's Weekly,* Nov. 7, 1863; Hendrick, 378; Bigelow, *France and the Confederate Navy,* 85.

[37] Dennett, ed., *Lincoln and the Civil War,* 87-88.

[38] Rhodes, IV, 418.

[39] Helm, 212-213.

[40] Steele, 33.

[41] Pike to Seward, Aug. 26, 1863.

[42] Gurowski, II, 311.

[43] *Harper's Weekly,* Oct. 17, 1863.

[44] Rhodes, IV, 418.

[45] *Harper's Weekly,* Nov. 21, 1863.

[46] D. H. Bates, *Lincoln in the Telegraph Office,* 163.

[47] *Harper's Weekly,* Nov. 8, 1862; Helm, 193.

[48] Welles, *Diary,* I, 443.

[49] *Harper's Weekly,* Oct. 17, 1863.

[50] Robertson, 155.

## CHAPTER XVII

[1] Dennett, ed., *Lincoln and the Civil War,* 115.

[2] Pike to Seward, Oct. 14 and 28, 1863.

[3] Welles, *Diary,* I, 445-446.

[4] Jordan and Pratt, 216.

[5] Pike to Seward, Oct. 7, 1863.
[6] Henry Ward Beecher, *England and America,* 8.
[7] *Ibid.,* 8.
[8] *Ibid.,* 15.
[9] *Ibid.,* 30.
[10] Bullard, [5].
[11] Shutes, *Lincoln and California,* 78.
[12] Sandburg, II, 459.
[13] E. D. Adams, II, 297.
[14] *Ibid.,* 136, *Alexandra* case.
[15] Owsley, 520.
[16] Jordan and Pratt, 172.
[17] Henry C. Cochrane, "With Lincoln to Gettysburg, 1863," 9-12.
[18] *Illinois State Journal,* Nov. 30, 1864.
[19] Nicolay and Hay, *Complete Works,* IX, 209-210.
[20] Sandburg, II, 474.
[21] Whitridge, 77-78. The text is the writer's translation.
[22] Sala, II, 132; Shutes, *Lincoln and the Doctors,* 85-86.
[23] Herndon-Weik Collection, V, 6, items 713-714.
[24] Dennett, ed., *Lincoln and the Civil War,* 124.
[25] *Ibid.*
[26] Nicolay and Hay Papers, V, 2.
[27] Dennett, ed., *Lincoln and the Civil War,* 128.
[28] *Ibid.,* 129.
[29] Welles, *Diary,* I, 480-481.
[30] Dennett, ed., *Lincoln and the Civil War,* 134.
[31] *Ibid.,* 136.
[32] *Ibid.,* 137.
[33] Bullard, [5]-[6].
[34] Theodore J. Irwin, *The Relations Between Abraham Lincoln . . . and John Bright,* 5.
[35] Bullard, [5].
[36] *Ibid.,* [6].
[37] Dennett, ed., *Lincoln and the Civil War,* 139.
[38] Burlingame to Seward, Nov. 23, 1863, in Dip. Corres.
[39] Burlingame to Seward, Nov. 7, 1863.
[40] Owsley, 521.
[41] Bigelow, "The Confederate Diplomats," 124.
[42] Hendrick, 406.
[43] Owsley, 524.

## CHAPTER XVIII

[1] Ward Hill Lamon, *Recollections,* 274.
[2] Gurowski, III, 81.
[3] Robert W. McBride, *Lincoln's Body Guard,* 36.
[4] P. F. Martin, 201.
[5] Bigelow, *France and the Confederate Navy,* 20-26.

[6] *Ibid.*, 35.

[7] J. D. Hill, 211.

[8] Logan, 303.

[9] Welles, *Diary*, I, 519-520. Field, in *Memories of Many Men and of Some Women*, 311, gives a different setting for this story. It was a favorite with Lincoln. Note Rice, 306.

[10] Barnes, 444-445.

[11] Fred B. Perkins, *The Picture and the Man*, 35. Welles, *Diary*, I, 527.

[12] Welles, *Diary*, I, 549.

[13] *Harper's Weekly*, Apr. 16, 1864.

[14] Hubert Howe Bancroft, *History of Mexico*, VI, 136.

[15] Trevelyan, *Garibaldi and the Making of Italy*, 289.

[16] *Harper's Weekly*, May 21, 1864.

[17] Owsley, 546.

[18] Dayton to Seward, March 11, 1864.

[19] Jordan and Pratt, 233-234.

[20] P. F. Martin, 163.

[21] *Congressional Globe*, 38 Cong., 1 Sess., p. 2475.

[22] P. F. Martin, 181.

[23] *Congressional Globe*, 38 Cong., 1 Sess., p. 1408.

[24] Gurowski, III, 169, 175.

[25] Dennett, ed., *Lincoln and the Civil War*, 179.

[26] D. H. Bates, *Lincoln in the Telegraph Office*, 231 ff.

[27] Haller, 17.

[28] Steele, 34.

[29] Edward Bates, 374; *New York Tribune*, June 3, 1864; Welles, *Diary*, II, 36, 45.

[30] Gurowski, III, 238.

[31] *Congressional Globe*, 38 Cong., 1 Sess., p. 2427. *Harper's Weekly*, May 28, 1864.

[32] *Congressional Globe*, 38 Cong., 1 Sess., p. 2427.

[33] Dennett, ed., *Lincoln and the Civil War*, 184.

[34] *Congressional Globe*, 38 Cong., 1 Sess., p. 2545.

[35] Pike to Seward, Apr. 20 and June 8, 1864.

[36] Gurowski, III, 129.

[37] Dennett, ed., *Lincoln and the Civil War*, 54. This story has been put in first person.

[38] *Ibid.*, 53.

[39] Gurowski, II, 237.

[40] *Ibid.*, III, 147.

[41] Barnes, 446.

[42] Dennett, ed., *Lincoln and the Civil War*, 184.

[43] Greeley, *American Conflict*, II, 582.

[44] Alexander McClure, *Lincoln as a Politician*, 18.

[45] Edward Stanwood, *A History of the Presidency from 1788 to 1897*, 301-303.

[46] Gurowski, III, 254.

[47] Nicolay and Hay, *Complete Works*, X, 123.

[48] Dennett, ed., 189.

## CHAPTER XIX

[1] Nicolay and Hay, *Complete Works*, XII, 51.

[2] Dennett, ed., *Lincoln and the Civil War*, 194.

[3] *Ibid.*, 195-196.

[4] *Ibid.*, 196-197. Edited slightly.

[5] *Message of the President of the United States* (Senate Ex. Doc.), 38 Cong., 1 Sess., No. 47.

[6] P. F. Martin, 139.

[7] Nicolay and Hay, *Complete Works*, X, 136-137.

[8] Rhodes, V, 400.

[9] *Harper's Weekly*, Dec. 12, 1863.

[10] Rhodes, V, 406.

[11] *Ibid.*, 408.

[12] E. D. Adams, II, 207.

[13] *Harper's Weekly*, Nov. 1, 1862, carries a picture of the *Alabama*.

[14] A. K. Brown, *Story of the Kearsarge and Alabama*, 2.

[15] Frederick Milnes Edge, *The Alabama and Kearsarge*, 27.

[16] *New York Tribune*, July 26, 1864.

[17] E. D. Adams, II, 216.

[18] *Ibid.*

[19] Rhodes, V, 400-401.

[20] Pike to Seward, June 22, 1864.

[21] Bulloch, II, 47; Bigelow, *France and the Confederate Navy*, 50-55.

[22] Dennett, ed., *Lincoln and the Civil War*, 209.

[23] Pease and Randall, eds., *Browning Diary*, I, 675.

[24] Nicolay and Hay, *Abraham Lincoln: A History*, IX, 174. Adam Badeau, *Military History of Ulysses S. Grant*, II, 446.

[25] Nicolay and Hay, *Complete Works*, X, 180.

[26] Nicolay and Hay Papers, IX, 8.

[27] Welles, *Diary*, II, 100.

[28] Pike to Seward, July 20, 1864.

[29] *Harper's Weekly*, Aug. 20, 1864.

[30] Nicolay and Hay, *Complete Works*, X, 201-202.

[31] *Ibid.*, 203-204.

## CHAPTER XX

[1] Irwin, 3-4.

[2] *Ibid.*, 4.

[3] Rhodes, V, 331; John Y. Beall, *Memoir*, 296.

[4] Gurowski, II, 277; Welles, *Diary*, I, 417-423.

[5] John Cordner, *Canada and the United States*, 22-23.

[6] Burlingame to Seward, March 17, 1864; Herbert H. Gowen, *An Outline History of China*, 265. Ward was killed in Sept., 1862. Burgevine, a North Carolinian, joined the Chinese rebels the next year. Burlingame saved him from execution by the Ever Victorious Army.

[7] Burlingame to Seward, Aug. 6, 1864.

[8] Dennett, ed., *Lincoln and the Civil War*, 215.

[9] Nicolay and Hay, *Abraham Lincoln: A History*, IX, 355.

[10] *New York Tribune*, Oct. 25, 1864.

[11] Nicolay and Hay Papers, IX, 16.

[12] The quotation varies in words but not in meaning from the translation released by the State Department.

[13] Gurowski, III, 366.

[14] *Ibid.*, 116-117.

[15] *Magazine of History with Notes and Queries*, Ex. No. 133, p. (3).

[16] E. D. Adams, II, 240.

[17] *Harper's Weekly*, Jan. 14, 1865.

[18] Department of State, *Records*, Dec. 23, 1864.

[19] *Ibid.*

[20] Nicolay and Hay, *Complete Works*, V, 361; X, 53-54.

[21] Seward to Adams, Jan. 9, 1865, photostat in Illinois State Historical Library.

[22] E. D. Adams, II, 241-242.

[23] *Harper's Weekly*, Jan. 14, 1865.

[24] Goldwin Smith, "The Death of President Lincoln," 32.

[25] Ella Lonn, *Desertion During the Civil War*, 226.

[26] Goldwin Smith, "The Death of President Lincoln," 29. The story has been edited. Goldwin Smith, true to Americans' opinion of English humor, told the story incorrectly in the original.

[27] Nicolay and Hay, *Complete Works*, X, 283-310.

[28] *Ibid.*, 291.

[29] *Ibid.*, 307.

[30] *Ibid.*, 310.

[31] Goldwin Smith, "The Death of President Lincoln," 33 n.

[32] *Congressional Globe*, 38 Cong., 2 Sess., p. 48, Dec. 15, 1864.

[33] Charles Sumner, *Reciprocity Treaty*, 8.

[34] Nicolay and Hay, *Complete Works*, XI, 38.

[35] Cordner, 25.

[36] *Ibid.*, 13.

[37] *Ibid.*, 21.

[38] *Ibid.*, 21-22.

[39] Fred Landon, "Canada's Part in Freeing the Slave," 7.

[40] *Ibid.*, 8.

[41] *Ibid.*, 4.

[42] *Ibid.*, 13.

[43] Samuel B. Arnold, *Defence and Prison Experience of a Lincoln Conspirator*, 20.

[44] Bigelow, "The Confederate Diplomats," 126.

[45] Arnold, 20.

## CHAPTER XXI

[1] Macartney, *Lincoln and His Cabinet*, 165.

[2] E. D. Adams, II, 251.

[3] Rhodes, V, 67 ff.
[4] W. H. Russell, *Diary*, 225.
[5] E. D. Adams, II, 252-253; Fitzhugh Lee, "The Failure of the Hampton Roads Conference," 477.
[6] James M. Callahan, *American Foreign Policy in Mexican Relations*, 300.
[7] Owsley, 556; *Harper's Weekly*, March 4, 1865.
[8] E. D. Adams, II, 249-250.
[9] *Ibid.*, 250.
[10] *Arrangements for the Inauguration* (1865), 5.
[11] W. H. Townsend, 367.
[12] Nicolay and Hay, *Complete Works*, XI, 44-47.
[13] Colman, 270.
[14] *Ibid.*, 269.
[15] *Ibid.*, 269-270.
[16] Ulysses Simpson Grant, *Personal Memoirs*, II, 290.
[17] Hendrick, 138.
[18] Charles C. Coffin, *The Boys of '61; or, Four Years of Fighting*, 511-512.
[19] This incident was told to Lloyd Lewis by a descendant of Chambrun.
[20] Marquis de Chambrun, *Personal Recollections of Mr. Lincoln*, (11)-(12).
[21] Elbert Hubbard, "William H. Seward," *Little Journeys*, 390.
[22] Macartney, *Lincoln and His Cabinet*, 169.
[23] P. F. Martin, 299-300.
[24] Jordan and Pratt, 243.
[25] Chambrun, (9).
[26] John W. Starr, *Lincoln's Last Day*, 13.
[27] *Ibid.*, 15.
[28] David Homer Bates, *Lincoln Stories Told by Him in the Military Office in the War Department*, 64.
[29] Starr, *Lincoln's Last Day*, 23.
[30] Charles A. Dana, *Lincoln and his Cabinet*, 67-70.
[31] Perkins, 132.

## EPILOGUE

[1] Bigelow, "The Confederate Diplomats," 125.
[2] David Brainerd Williamson, *Illustrated Life, Services, Martyrdom and Funeral of Abraham Lincoln*, 217. Noah Brooks, "The Close of Lincoln's Career," 24.
[3] John Gilmary Shea, *The Lincoln Memorial*, 116.
[4] John McClintock, *Discourse Delivered on the Day of the Funeral of President Lincoln*, 12-13.
[5] *Dictionary of American Biography*, VI, 485.
[6] Jordan and Pratt, 266.
[7] *Ibid.*, 261.
[8] E. D. Adams, II, 261.
[9] *Ibid.*
[10] *Punch*, May 6, 1865.
[11] E. D. Adams, II, 261.
[12] Oliver O. Howard, *Lincoln Memorial Temple in Washington, D. C.*

[13] Holden, 720.

[14] *Ibid.*, 719.

[15] Jordan and Pratt, 266.

[16] Helm, 261-262. Original letter at Library of Congress. See David C. Mearns, "Famous Lincoln Collections: The Library of Congress," 447.

[17] *Assassination of Abraham Lincoln,* 195.

[18] Facsim., published in *New York Herald Tribune,* Feb. 12, 1944.

[19] Whitridge, 85.

[20] Jay Monaghan, *Lincoln Bibliography,* II, 427.

[21] Whitridge, 75-76.

[22] Jordan and Pratt, 244.

[23] Mearns, 448.

[24] *French Tribute to Lincoln,* 6.

# SOURCES

Abbatt, William, ed. *Magazine of History with Notes and Queries* (1927), XXXIV, No. 1, Extra No. 133, contains a picture of the "Lincoln tower" on Newman Hall's London church.

Abbot, Willis J. *The Naval History of the United States* (New York: Peter Fenelon Collier, 1896).

Adamov, E. A. "Russia and the United States at the Time of the Civil War," *Journal of Modern History* (1930), II, 586-602.

Adams, Charles Francis. *An Address on the Life, Character and Services of William Henry Seward* (New York: D. Appleton & Co., 1873).

Adams, Charles Francis [Jr.]. "The British Proclamation of May, 1861," *Massachusetts Historical Society Proceedings* (Oct., 1914-June, 1915), XLVIII, 190-242.

──────. *Charles Francis Adams, by his Son* (Boston: Houghton Mifflin Co., 1900). American Statesmen Series.

──────. *Charles Francis Adams, 1835-1915; An Autobiography* (Boston: Houghton Mifflin Co., c1916).

──────. *The Crisis of Foreign Intervention in the War of Secession, September-November, 1862*, reprinted from *Massachusetts Historical Society Proceedings* (1914), XLVII.

──────. *A Cycle of Adams Letters, 1861-1865*, Worthington C. Ford, ed., (Boston: Houghton Mifflin Co., 1920).

──────. "Lincoln's Offer to Garibaldi," *Massachusetts Historical Society Proceedings* (1908), 3rd Series, I, 319-325. Also in *Magazine of History with Notes and Queries* (1928), XXXVII, No. 1, 33-40.

──────. "The Negotiation of 1861 Relating to the Declaration of Paris of 1856," *Massachusetts Historical Society Proceedings* (1912-1913), XLVI, 23.

──────. *Seward and the Declaration of Paris* (Boston, 1912).

──────. *Trans-Atlantic Historical Solidarity Lectures ... before the University of Oxford ... 1913* (Oxford, 1913).

──────. *The Trent Affair, an Historical Retrospect* (Boston, 1912). Also published in *Massachusetts Historical Society Proceedings* (1911-1912), XLV, 35-148.

Adams, Ephraim Douglass. *Great Britain and the American Civil War* (London: Longmans, Green & Co., 1925).

Adams, Henry. *The Education of Henry Adams. An Autobiography* (Boston: Houghton Mifflin Co., c1918).

──────. *Letters of Henry Adams (1858-1891)*, Worthington C. Ford, ed., (Boston: Houghton Mifflin Co., c1930).

Adams, John Quincy. *The Monroe Doctrine. Letter of John Quincy Adams. Balance of Power in Europe* (New York, 1863).

*Address to Christians Throughout the World by the Clergy of the Confederate States of America* (London, n.d.).

466

*Alabama Privateer. Correspondence Respecting the "Alabama," Also Respecting the Bark "Maury," at New York During the Crimean War; and the Temporary Act of Congress, passed by the United States, at the Instance of Great Britain, in 1838* (n.p., 1863?).

Allen, J. H. "American Expositions of Neutrality," *Christian Examiner* (Nov., 1864).

———. "English Expositions of Neutrality," *Christian Examiner* (Nov., 1863).

———. "Later Phases of English Feeling," *Christian Examiner* (March, 1863).

Angle, Paul McClelland. *"Here I Have Lived"; A History of Lincoln's Springfield, 1821-1865* (Springfield, Ill.: Abraham Lincoln Ass'n., 1935).

———. *Lincoln, 1854-1861; Being the Day-by-Day Activities of Abraham Lincoln* (Springfield, Ill.: Abraham Lincoln Ass'n., c1933).

———, ed. *New Letters and Papers of Lincoln* (Boston: Houghton Mifflin Co., 1930).

*Arguelles Case* (Havana, 1865).

Armstrong, Margaret N. *Fanny Kemble, A Passionate Victorian* (New York: The Macmillan Co., 1938).

Arnold, Samuel Bland. *Defence and Prison Experience of a Lincoln Conspirator* (Hattiesburg, Miss.: Book Farm, 1943).

*Arrangements for the Inauguration* (Washington, 1865).

Ashley, James Monroe. *Reminiscences of the Great Rebellion; Calhoun, Seward and Lincoln* (1890).

*Assassination of Abraham Lincoln . . . Expressions of Condolence and Sympathy Inspired by these Events* (Washington, 1867).

Atkins, John Black. *The Life of Sir William Howard Russell* (London: John Murray, 1911).

Badeau, Adam. *Military History of Ulysses S. Grant* (New York: D. Appleton & Co., 1881).

Badlam, William H. *Kearsarge and the Alabama* (Providence, R. I., 1894).

Ball, Samuel S. *Liberia* (Alton, Ill., 1848).

Balme, J. R. *Letters on the American Republic* (London, 1863).

Bancroft, Frederic. "The French in Mexico and the Monroe Doctrine," *Political Science Quarterly* (1896), XI, No. 1, 30-43.

———. *Life of William H. Seward* (New York: Harper & Bros., 1900).

Bancroft, Hubert Howe. *History of Mexico* (San Francisco: The History Co., 1890), VI.

*Bancroft and Earl Russell* (House Misc. Doc.), 39 Cong., 1 Sess., No. 110.

Barnes, Thurlow Weed. *Memoir of Thurlow Weed, by his Grandson* (Boston: Houghton Mifflin Co., 1884). Vol. I of this set is the *Autobiography of Thurlow Weed.*

Barrett, Oliver R. Lincoln Collection, Kenilworth, Ill.

B[artlett], ———. *The Present Attempt to Dissolve the American Union* (New York, 1862).

Bates, David Homer. *Lincoln in the Telegraph Office* (New York: The Century Co., 1907).

———. *Lincoln Stories Told by Him in the Military Office in the War Department during the Civil War* (New York: W. E. Rudge, Inc., 1926).

Bates, Edward. "Diary ... 1859-66," Howard K. Beale, ed., *Annual Report ...*
*American Historical Association* (1930), IV.

Baxter, James P., III. "The British Government and Neutral Rights, 1861-1865," *American Historical Review* (1928), XXXIV, No. 1, 9-29.

Bayne, Julia Taft. *Tad Lincoln's Father* (Boston: Little, Brown & Co., 1931).

Beall, John Yates. *Memoir* (Montreal, 1865).

Beecher, Henry Ward. *The American Cause in England* (New York?, 1863).

———. *England and America* (Boston, 1863).

———. *Speeches of Rev. Henry Ward Beecher on the American Rebellion delivered in Great Britain in 1863* (New York, c1887).

Bemis, George. *Hasty Recognition of Rebel Belligerency, and Our Right to Complain of It* (Boston, 1865).

———. *Precedents of American Neutrality, in Reply to the Speech of Sir Roundell Palmer in the British House of Commons* (Boston, 1864).

Bemis, Samuel Flagg, and Grace Gardner Griffin. *Guide to the Diplomatic History of the United States, 1775-1921* (Washington: Gov't Print. Off., 1935).

Beresford-Hope, Alexander James Beresford. *England, the North and the South* (London, 1862).

Bernard, Mountague. *A Historical Account of the Neutrality of Great Britain during the Civil War* (London, 1870).

Bigelow, John. "The Confederate Diplomats," *Century Magazine* (May, 1891), XLII, New Series XX, 113-126.

———. *Les Etats-Unis d'Amérique en 1863* (Paris, 1863).

———. *France and the Confederate Navy, 1862-1868* (New York, 1888).

———. *Lest We Forget: Gladstone, Morley, and the Confederate Loan of 1863* (New York, 1905).

———. *Retrospections of an Active Life* (New York: Baker & Taylor Co., 1909).

———. *Some Recollections of the Late Edouard Laboulaye* (n.p., ca. 1888).

[Black, Robert.] *A Memoir of Abraham Lincoln, President Elect of the United States of America, His Opinions on Secession, Extracts from the United States Constitution, &c. To which is appended an historical sketch on slavery, reprinted by permission from "The Times."* London: Sampson Low, Son & Co., 47 Ludgate Hill. 1861.

Blanc, Louis. *Letters on England* (London, 1866). Translated from the French by James Hutton.

Blatchford, Samuel. *Reports of Cases in Prize ... in the Circuit and District Courts of the United States, for the Southern District of New York. 1861-'65* (New York, 1866).

Blegen, Theodore C. *Abraham Lincoln and European Opinion* (Minneapolis, 1934). Reprinted from *The Friend*.

Bonham, Jeriah. *Fifty Years' Recollections* (Peoria, Ill.: J. W. Franks & Sons, 1883).

Bonham, Milledge L. "British Consuls in the Confederacy," *Columbia University Studies* (1911), XLIII, No. 3, 371-633.

Boynton, Charles B. *The History of the Navy During the Rebellion* (New York: D. Appleton & Co., 1867).

*Brig Jules et Marie* (House Ex. Doc.), 37 Cong., 3 Sess., No. 4.

Bright, John. *The Diaries of John Bright*, R. A. J. Walling, ed., (London, 1930).

———. Letters to Sumner, 1861-72, *Massachusetts Historical Society Proceedings* (1911-12; 1912-13), XLV and XLVI, 148 and 93 respectively.

———. *Speech of Mr. Bright, M. P., in the Town Hall, Birmingham. December 18, 1862* (Birmingham, 1862?).

*British Sympathies in the American Crisis. By an Irishman* (Dublin, 1863).

Brooks, Noah. "The Close of Lincoln's Career," *Century Magazine* (May, 1895), Vol. L, No. 1, 18-27.

Brown, A. K. *The Story of the Kearsarge and Alabama* (San Francisco, 1868).

Browne, Nathaniel Borodaille. *Address before the Union League* (Philadelphia, 1863).

Browning, Orville Hickman. Papers (MSS, Ill. State Historical Library).

Bullard, F. Lauriston. "Lincoln Pardons Conspirator on Plea of an English Statesman," *American Bar Association Journal* (March, 1939).

Bulloch, James Dunwody. *The Secret Service of the Confederate States in Europe* (New York: G. P. Putnam's Sons, 1884).

Cairnes, John Elliott. *The Slave Power* (2nd ed., New York, 1862). Also 2 editions, 1863, one much expanded.

Callahan, James Morton. *American Foreign Policy in Mexican Relations* (New York: The Macmillan Co., 1932).

———. *The Diplomatic History of the Southern Confederacy* (Baltimore: The Johns Hopkins Press, 1901).

———. "Diplomatic Relations of the Confederate States with England (1861-1865)," *Annual Report . . . American Historical Association* (1898), 265-283.

———. *Evolution of Seward's Mexican Policy* (Morgantown: W. Va. Univ., 1909).

———. *Russo-American Relations During the American Civil War* (Morgantown: W. Va. Univ., 1908).

Campbell, James E. "Sumner—Brooks—Burlingame or the Last of the Great Challenges," *Ohio Archaeological and Historical Quarterly* (Oct., 1925), XXXIV, No. 4, 435-473.

Carman, Harry James, and Reinhard H. Luthin. *Lincoln and the Patronage* (New York: Columbia Univ. Press, 1943).

Carpenter, Francis Bicknell. *Six Months at the White House with Abraham Lincoln* (New York: Hurd & Houghton, 1866).

Carter, Robert. "Gurowski," *Atlantic Monthly* (Nov. 1866).

Case, Lynn M. *French Opinion on the United States and Mexico, 1860-1867* (New York: Appleton-Century Co., c1936).

*The Case of the Trent Examined* (London, 1862).

Cellem, Robert. *Visit of His Royal Highness . . .* (Toronto, 1861).

Chambrun, Charles Adolphe Pineton, Marquis de. *Personal Recollections of Mr. Lincoln* (Bloomington, Ill., 1893).

Chase, Salmon Portland. "Diary . . ." *Annual Report . . . American Historical Association* (1902), II, 45-527.

*Chicago Press and Tribune.*

SOURCES 469

Choate, Joseph H. Letters to Charles Francis Adams, Jan. and Feb., 1901 (MSS, Library of Congress).

Clark, Benjamin C. *Remarks upon United States Intervention in Hayti with Comments Upon Correspondence Connected with It* (Boston, 1853).

Claussen, Martin P. "Peace Factors in Anglo-American Relations, 1861-1865," *Mississippi Valley Historical Review* (1940), XXVI, No. 4, 511-522.

Clay, Cassius Marcellus. *Memoirs, Writings, and Speeches* (Cincinnati: J. F. Brennan & Co., 1886).

———. Papers (MSS, Lincoln Memorial University, Harrogate, Tenn.).

Clay, J. Randolph. *M. Thouvenel on the Affair of the "Trent"* (London, 1862?).

Cobden, Richard. "Letters of, to Charles Sumner, 1862-65," *American Historical Review* (1897), II, No. 2, 306-319.

Cochrane, Henry Clay. "With Lincoln to Gettysburg, 1863" (Military Order of the Loyal Legion, Pa., 1907).

Coffin, Charles Carleton. *The Boys of '61; or, Four Years of Fighting* (Boston: Estes & Lauriat, 1882).

Cole, Arthur C. *Lincoln's "House Divided" Speech* (Chicago: Univ. of Chicago Press, 1923).

Coleman, J. Winston, Jr. "A Kentucky Lincolnian," *Lincoln Herald* (Feb., 1943), XLV, No. 1, 4-8.

Colman, Edna M. *Seventy-five Years of White House Gossip* (New York: Doubleday, Page & Co., 1925).

*Commodore Charles Wilkes's Court-Martial* (House Ex. Doc.), 38 Cong., 1 Sess., No. 102.

*Congressional Globe* (Washington).

Conway, Moncure Daniel. *Autobiography, Memories and Experiences* (Boston: Houghton Mifflin Co., 1904).

*Copy of Two Letters from His Majesty the Major King of Siam* (Senate Ex. Doc.), 37 Cong., 2 Sess., No. 23.

Cordner, John. *Canada and the United States: An Address on the American Conflict, Delivered at Montreal, on Thursday Evening, December 22, 1864* (Manchester, 1865).

Cornwallis-West, Mrs. George. "Reminiscences of Lady Randolph Churchill," *Century Magazine* (Nov., 1907), LXXV, No. 1, 1-23.

*Correspondence Relative to the Case of Messrs. Mason and Slidell* (Washington, 1862?).

Corti, Egon Caesar, Conte. *Maximilian and Charlotte of Mexico* (New York: Alfred A. Knopf, Inc., 1928).

Cossham, Handel. *Pitman's Popular Lecturer and Reader. Edited by Henry Pitman, Manchester. No. 3. (New Series), March 1863. 2d. America: Past, Present, and Future. By Handel Cossham, Esq. F. G. S.*

Costi, Angelo Michele. *Memoir of the Trent Affair* (Washington, 1865).

Croffut, William Augustus. *An American Procession, 1855-1914* (Boston: Atlantic Monthly Press, Little, Brown & Co., 1931).

Culthrop, S. R. "Coleridge and Kingsley on American Affairs," *Christian Examiner* (Nov., 1863).

*Daily Evening Bulletin* (San Francisco).

Dana, Charles Anderson. *Lincoln and His Cabinet* (Cleveland: De Vinne Press, 1896).

Darling, Jasper Tucker. *Address,* Memorial Day, 1912, auspices of G. A. R., Springfield, Ill.

Davis, Jefferson. "An Address to the People of the Free States," *Magazine of History with Notes and Queries* (1925), XXIX, No. 1, Extra Number 113, 67-69.

⸻. *Jefferson Davis, Constitutionalist, His Letters, Papers and Speeches,* Dunbar Rowland, ed. (Jackson, Miss.: Miss. Dept. of Archives and History, 1923).

De Cordova, Rafael J. *The Prince's Visit: A Humorous Description* (New York, 1861).

De Leon, Edwin. *Thirty Years of My Life on Three Continents* (London: Ward & Downey, 1890).

De Leon, Thomas Cooper. *Four Years in Rebel Capitals* (Mobile, Ala.: Gossip Printing Co., c1890).

Dennett, Tyler, ed. *Lincoln and the Civil War in the Diaries and Letters of John Hay* (New York: Dodd, Mead & Co., 1939).

Department of State *Records*, Washington, D. C.

"The Diary of a Public Man," *North American Review* (Sept.-Oct., 1879).

Diplomatic Correspondence, National Archives, Washington, D. C.

*Directory of Chicago* (Chicago: D. B. Cooke & Co., 1858).

[Dodd, William E.] "Lincoln's Press Agent a Marvel of Efficiency," *Magazine of History with Notes and Queries* (1928), XXXV, No. 4., Extra No. 140, 219-220. Extracts from "Little Men of Great Influence in American History."

Dudley, Thomas H. "Three Critical Periods in our Diplomatic Relations with England During the Late War. Personal Recollections of . . . Late U. S. Consul at Liverpool," *Pennsylvania Magazine of History and Biography* (1893), XVII, 34-54.

Dyer, Oliver. *Great Senators of the United States Forty Years Ago* (New York: R. Bonner's Sons, c1889).

Easum, Chester Verne. *The Americanization of Carl Schurz* (Chicago: Univ. of Chicago Press, c1929).

Edge, Frederick Milnes. *The Alabama and Kearsarge. An Account of the Naval Engagement in the British Channel . . . from . . . the Wounded and Paroled Prisoners* (London, 1864). Published in New York under title: *An Englishman's View of the Battle,* etc.

⸻. *The Destruction of the American Carrying Trade* (1863). Also 1864 and 1868 editions.

⸻. *President Lincoln's Successor* (London, 1864).

⸻. *Whom Do the English Tories Wish Elected to the Presidency?* (1864).

Einstein, Lewis D. *Napoleon III and American Diplomacy at the Outbreak of the Civil War* (London, 1905).

Ellicott, John M. *The Life of John Ancrum Winslow* (New York: G. P. Putnam's Sons, 1902).

Emerson, Ralph Waldo. *Letters and Social Aims* (Standard Library edition, Boston: Houghton Mifflin Co., c1875).

"England and America," *Frazer's Magazine* (Oct., 1863).

"England and America," *Princeton Review* (Jan., 1862).

*English Neutrality War Ships for the Southern Confederacy* (Manchester, 1863). Union League of Philadelphia pamphlet.

"English Opinion on the Inaugural," *Littell's Living Age* (April 15, 1865).

"The Evangelical Alliance and the American War," *New Englander* (April, 1863), No. LXXXIII.

Everett, Edward. "Everett's Estimate of Lincoln," *Illinois State Journal* (Nov. 30, 1864).

————. *The Monroe Doctrine.* From the *New York Ledger* (Loyal Publication Society. No. 34, 1863).

Fabens, Joseph Warren. *Facts about Santo Domingo, Applicable to the Present Crisis.* An address before the American Geographical & Statistical Society (New York, 1862).

Fairbanks, Charles. *The American Conflict as Seen from a European Point of View. A Lecture Delivered at St. Johnsbury, Vt.* (Boston, 1863).

Field, Maunsell B. *Memories of Many Men and of Some Women* (New York: Harper & Bros., 1874).

Fischer, LeRoy Henry. *Adam Gurowski and the Civil War: A Radical's Record* (abstract Ph.D. thesis, Urbana, Ill., 1943).

*La France, le Mexique et les Etats Confédérés* (New York, 1863).

*Frank Leslie's Illustrated Newspaper.*

Freidel, Frank. "Pro-Union Pamphleteering and Pamphlets in the Northern States, 1863-1865: A Survey" (M.A. thesis, University of Southern California, 1939).

*French Tribute to Lincoln* (Redlands, Calif., 1936).

Garibaldi, Giuseppe. *A Toast to Rebellion* (Indianapolis: The Bobbs-Merrill Co., c1935).

Gasparin, Agénor Etienne, Comte de. *America before Europe* (London, 1862). Also published in New York. Also in Paris as *L'Amérique devant l'Europe.*

————. *Un Grand Peuple Qui Se Relève—Les Etats-Unis en 1861.*

————. *The Uprising of a Great People,* translated by Mary L. Booth (New York, 1861; also 1862).

Gastineau, Benjamin. *Histoire de la Souscription Populaire à la Médaille Lincoln* (Paris, 1865).

Gaulot, Paul. *L'Expédition du Mexique (1861-1867), d' après les Documents et Souvenirs d'Ernest Louet* (Paris, 1906).

Gay, H. Nelson. "Lincoln's Offer of a Command to Garibaldi," *Century Magazine* (Nov., 1907), LXXV, No. 1, 63-74.

[Gilmore, James Roberts.] *Among the Pines by Edmund Kirke* (New York, 1862).

Goddard, Samuel A. *Extracts from Letters on the American Rebellion* (London, 1870). Reprinted in *Magazine of History with Notes and Queries* (1912), Extra No. 19, 483-496.

Golder, Frank A. "The American Civil War through the Eyes of a Russian Diplomat," *American Historical Review* (1921), XXVI, No. 3, 454-463.

————. "The Russian Fleet and the Civil War," *American Historical Review* (1915), XX, No. 4, 801-812.

Gowen, Herbert Henry. *An Outline History of China* (New York: D. Appleton & Co., 1926).

Grant, Ulysses Simpson. *Personal Memoirs* (New York: C. L. Webster & Co., 1885-1886).

Greeley, Horace. *The American Conflict* (Washington: National Tribune, 1899).

———. *Greeley on Lincoln*, Joel Benton, ed. (New York, 1893).

———. "Greeley's Estimate of Lincoln," *Century Magazine* (July, 1891), XLII, No. 3, 371-382.

Grenier, Edouard. *La Mort du Président Lincoln* (Paris, 1867).

Grover, Leonard. "Lincoln's Interest in the Theater," *Century Magazine* (Apr., 1909), LXXVII, No. 6, 943-950.

Gurowski, Adam. *Diary* (Boston: Lee & Shepard, 1862), I; (New York, G. W. Carleton & Co., 1864), II; (Washington: W. H. & O. H. Morrison, 1866), III.

Hale, Edward Everett. "England and America," *Christian Examiner* (Sept., 1861).

Hall, Christopher Newman. *The American War* (American Tract Society [1862]).

———. *No War with America. A Lecture on the Affair of the Trent* (London, 1861).

Haller, Elizabeth. "Aspects of American Opinion Regarding Maximilian's Empire in Mexico" (Ph.D. thesis, University of Pennsylvania, 1940).

[Harcourt, *Sir* William G.] *American Neutrality: by Historicus.* From the London *Times* of Dec. 22, 1864 (New York, 1865).

———. *Belligerent Rights of Maritime Capture by Historicus* (Liverpool, 1863).

*Harper's Weekly* (New York).

Harris, Thomas LeGrand. *The Trent Affair* (Indianapolis: The Bowen-Merrill Co., 1896).

[Haswell, John H.] *The Assassination of Abraham Lincoln* (Washington, 1867).

Haultain, T. Arnold. *Goldwin Smith, his Life and Opinions* (New York, 1914).

Haut, Marc de. *La Crise Américaine, ses Causes, ses Résultats Probables, ses Rapports avec l'Europe et la France* (Albany, 1865).

Hautefeuille, Laurent Basile. *De la Légalité des Blocus Américaines.* From the *Revue Contemporaine*, Feb. 28, 1863.

———. *Nécessité d'une Loi Maritime pour Régler les Rapports des Neutres et des Belligérants.* From the *Revue Contemporaine*, 1862.

———. *Propriétés Privées des Sujets Belligérants sur Mer* (Paris, 1860).

———. *Quelques Questions de Droit Internationel Maritime à Propos de la Guerre d'Amérique* (Leipzig, 1861).

Hay, John. Papers (MSS, Ill. State Historical Library).

Helm, Katherine. *The True Story of Mary, Wife of Lincoln* (New York: Harper & Bros., 1928).

Helper, Hinton Rowan. *The Impending Crisis of the South: How to Meet it* (New York, 1857).

Hendrick, Burton Jesse. *Statesmen of the Lost Cause: Jefferson Davis and His Cabinet* (Boston: Atlantic Monthly Press, Little, Brown & Co., 1939).

Herndon, William H. *Herndon's Lincoln; the True Story of a Great Life* (Chicago: Belford, Clarke & Co., c1889).

Herndon-Weik Collection, University of Illinois (Film, Ill. State Historical Library).

Hertz, Emanuel. "Lincoln's Diplomacy, an Unwritten Chapter," *Magazine of History with Notes and Queries* (1932), XLVI, No. 1, Extra No. 181, 3-16.

Hill, Alsager Hay. *The Oratorical Year Book for 1865: Being a Collection of the Best Contemporary Speeches Delivered in Parliament, at the Bar, and on the Platform* (London, 1866).

Hill, Jim Dan. *Sea Dogs of the Sixties* (Minneapolis: Univ. of Minnesota Press, 1935).

Holden, James E. "My Story of Abraham Lincoln," *Outlook* (Mar. 22, 1902), LXX, No. 12, 718-726.

Horner, Henry. Collection of Lincolniana, Ill. State Historical Library.

Howard, Oliver Otis. *Lincoln Memorial Temple in Washington, D. C.* (Washington, 1866).

Hubbard, Elbert. "William H. Seward," *Little Journeys* (East Aurora, N. Y.: The Roycrofters, 1898).

Hunter, John Warren. *Heel-Fly Time in Texas* (Bandera, Texas, n.d.).

Hyde, Charles Cheney. *International Law Chiefly as Interpreted and Applied by the United States* (Boston: Little, Brown & Co., 1922).

Iglesias Calderón, Fernando. *El Egoismo Norte-Americano Durante la Intervención Francesa* (Mexico, 1905).

*Illinois State Journal* (Springfield, Ill.).

"International Law vs. The Trent and San Jacinto," *Merchants Magazine* (Jan., 1862).

Irwin, Theodore J., compiler. *The Relations Between Abraham Lincoln . . . and John Bright . . .* (San Francisco, 1935).

Jones, Ernest. *The Slaveholders' War—A Lecture* (n.p., n.d.).

Jones, Thomas D. *Memories of Lincoln* (New York: Press of the Pioneers, 1934).

Jones, W. Martin. *Abraham Lincoln*, an address (Rochester, 1904).

Jordan, Donaldson, and Edwin J. Pratt. *Europe and the American Civil War* (Boston: Houghton Mifflin Co., 1931).

Josephson, Matthew. *Victor Hugo* (Garden City, N. Y.: Doubleday, Doran & Co., 1942).

*Journal of the Executive Proceedings of the Senate*, XI, XII (Washington, 1887).

Keckley, Elizabeth. *Behind the Scenes* (New York: G. W. Carleton & Co., 1868).

Keith, Elbridge G. "The National Republican Convention of 1860," *University of Illinois Bulletin* (1904), I, No. 16.

Kelley, William D. *Lincoln and Stanton* (New York: G. P. Putnam's Sons, 1885).

Kiger, John Herbert. "Federal Governmental Propaganda in Great Britain During the American Civil War," *Historical Outlook* (1928), XIX, 204-209.

Kingsley, Vine Wright. *French Intervention in America; or, A Review of La France, le Mexique, et les États Confédérés* (New York, 1863).

474

Kinsley, Philip. *The Chicago Tribune* (New York: Alfred A. Knopf, 1943), I.

Kirkland, C. P. *Liability of the Government of Great Britain for Depredations of Rebel Privateers on the Commerce of the United States Considered* (New York, 1863).

Klingberg, Frank J. "Harriet Beecher Stowe and Social Reform in England," *American Historical Review* (1938), XLIII, No. 3, 542-552.

Koerner, Gustave. *Memoirs, 1809-1896* (Cedar Rapids, Iowa: Torch Press, 1909).

Laboulaye, Edouard René Lefebvre de. *L'Election du Président aux Etats-Unis* (1864).

———. *Les Etats-Unis et La France* (Paris, 1862). Also published in Boston.

———. *Paris en Amérique* (Paris, 1863).

———. *Pourquoi le Nord ne Peut Accepter Séparation* (New York, 1863). Also translated into English.

———. *Professor Laborlaye* [sic], *The Great Friend of America, on the Presidential Election* (Washington, 1864).

———. *Upon Whom Rests the Guilt of the War? Separation. War without end* (New York, 1863). Also in Edinburgh (1863).

Lacouture, Edouard. *Mémoire à sa Majesté l'Empereur Napoléon III. La Vérité sur la Guerre d'Amérique* (Paris, 1862).

Lally, Frank Edward. "French Opposition to the Mexican Policy of the Second Empire," *Johns Hopkins University Studies* (1931), Series XLIX, No. 3.

Lambert, William H. *Abraham Lincoln, Commander-in-Chief of the Army and Navy of the United States* (Pittsburgh?, 1900).

Lamon, Ward Hill. Papers (MS photostats, Ill. State Historical Library).

———. *Recollections of Abraham Lincoln*, Dorothy Lamon Teillard, ed. (Washington, 1911).

Landon, Fred. "The Anti-Slavery Society of Canada," *Journal of Negro History* (Jan., 1919), IV, No. 1, 33-40.

———. "Canada's Part in Freeing the Slave" (n.p., n.d.). Reprinted in *Ontario Historical Society Papers and Records*, XVII.

Latané, John Holladay. *A History of American Foreign Policy* (New York: Doubleday, Page & Co., 1927).

Lawrence, William Beach. "Belligerent Rights at Sea," *London Law Magazine* (Nov., 1861). Also in *Transactions of National Association for the Promotion of Social Science* (1861).

———. "International Law," *London Law Magazine* (Nov., 1863).

———. "On Contraband of War," *Transactions of National Association for the Promotion of Social Science*.

Leary, Frederick. *Ernest Jones* (London, 1887).

Leavitt, Joshua. *The Monroe Doctrine* (New York, 1863).

Lee, Fitzhugh. "The Failure of the Hampton Roads Conference," *Century Magazine* (July, 1896), LII, No. 3, 476-478.

Leech, Margaret. *Reveille in Washington, 1860-1865* (New York: Harper & Bros., c1941).

*Legacy of Fun by Abraham Lincoln with a Short Sketch of His Life* (London, 1865).

*Lettre à Napoléon III sur l'Esclavage aux Etats du Sud. Par un Créole de la Louisiane* (Paris, 1862).

"Lincoln or Frémont," *Brownson's Quarterly Review* (New York-London, 1864).

Linder, Usher F. *Reminiscences of the Early Bench and Bar of Illinois* (Chicago: Chicago Legal News Co., 1879).

Logan, Rayford W. *The Diplomatic Relations of the United States with Haiti, 1776-1891* (Chapel Hill, N. C.: Univ. of North Carolina Press, 1941).

London *Times*.

Lonn, Ella. *Desertion During the Civil War* (New York: The Century Co., c1928).

———. *Foreigners in the Confederacy* (Chapel Hill, N. C.: Univ. of North Carolina Press, 1940).

Loring, Charles G. *Neutral Relations of England and the United States* (New York, 1863).

——— and Edwin W. Field. *Correspondence on the Present Relations between Great Britain and the United States of America* (Boston, 1862).

Lothrop, Thornton Kirkland. *William Henry Seward* (Boston: Houghton Mifflin Co., 1909).

Lowrey, Grosvenor P. *English Neutrality. Is the Alabama a British Pirate?* (1863).

Lyman, Henry D. *Abraham Lincoln: A Story Hitherto Untold* (1913). Reprinted from *Harper's Weekly*.

Macartney, Clarence Edward. *Lincoln and His Cabinet* (New York: Charles Scribner's Sons, 1931).

———. *Lincoln and His Generals* (Philadelphia: Dorrance & Co., 1925).

McBride, Robert W. *Lincoln's Body Guard* (Indianapolis: E. J. Hecker, printer, 1911).

McCirr & Co. *Lincoln's Visit to Philadelphia* (Philadelphia, 1907).

McClellan, George Brinton. *McClellan's Own Story* (New York: C. L. Webster & Co., 1887).

McClintock, John. *Discourse Delivered on the Day of the Funeral of President Lincoln* (New York, 1865).

McClure, Alexander K. *Abraham Lincoln and Men of War-Times* (Philadelphia: The Times Publishing Co., 1892).

———. *Col. McClure's Statement of Lincoln's Journey* (reprinted from *Philadelphia Press*, Jan. 19, 1908).

———. *Lincoln as a Politician* (n.p., 1916).

McCordock, Robert Stanley. *Yankee Cheese Box* (Philadelphia: Dorrance & Co., 1938).

Macdonald, Helen G. "Canadian Public Opinion on the American Civil War," *Columbia University Studies in History, Economics and Public Law* (1926), CXXIV, No. 2, Whole Number 273.

McInnis, Edgar W. *The Unguarded Frontier: A History of American-Canadian Relations* (New York: Doubleday, Doran & Co., 1942).

MacKay, Charles. *Life and Liberty in America* (New York, 1859).

McLean, Charles Clothier. *The Boy Who Wore Lincoln's Hat* (Philadelphia, n.d.).

*Magasin Méthodiste des Îles de la Manche* (Guernsey), April, 1861.

Malet, W. W. *An Errand to the South* (London, 1863).

Markins, Isaac. *President Lincoln and the Case of John Y. Beall* (New York, 1911).

Marraro, Howard R. "Lincoln's Offer of a Command to Garibaldi: Further Light on a Disputed Point of History," *Journal of the Illinois State Historical Society* (Sept., 1943), XXXVI, No. 3, 237-270.

Martin, Percy F. *Maximilian in Mexico* (New York: Charles Scribner's Sons, 1914).

Martin, Theodore. *The Life of His Royal Highness the Prince Consort* (London: Smith, Elder & Co., 1879).

Marx, Karl, and Frederick Engels. *The Civil War in the United States,* Richard Enmale, ed. (New York, 1937).

Mason, James Murray. Papers (MSS, Library of Congress).

Meade, Robert Douthat. *Judah P. Benjamin, Confederate Statesman* (New York: Oxford Univ. Press, 1943).

Mearns, David C. "Famous Lincoln Collections: The Library of Congress," *Abraham Lincoln Quarterly* (Dec., 1941), I, No. 8, 442-453.

*Memorial in Behalf of the State of New York in Respect to Adapting its Canals to the Defense of the Lakes* ... (Washington, 1862).

Mercier de Lacombe, H. *Le Mexique et les Etats-Unis* (Paris, 1863).

*Message of the President* (Senate Ex. Doc.), 38 Cong., 2 Sess., No. 33.

*Mexico* (House Ex. Doc.), 37 Cong., 3 Sess., No. 23.

Mill, John Stuart. *The Contest in America* (Boston, 1862). Reprinted from *Frazer's Magazine.*

Mills, Thomas. *Richard Cobden. A Lecture Delivered in Leigh* (London, 1865).

Milne, A. Taylor. "The Lyons-Seward Treaty of 1862," *American Historical Review* (1933), XXXVIII, 511-525.

*Mr. Russell on Bull Run* (New York, 1861).

Mitchell, James. *Letter on the Relation of the White and African Races in the United States* (Washington, 1862).

Monaghan, James. "Bayard Taylor, Poet and Patriot," *Bulletin of the Chester County Historical Society,* XXIX, I, 7.

Monaghan, Jay. *Lincoln Bibliography (Illinois Historical Collections,* XXXII, Springfield, Ill.: Ill. State Historical Library, 1945), II.

Montague, Ludwell Lee. *Haiti and the United States, 1714-1938* (Durham, N. C.: Duke Univ. Press, 1940).

Moore, John Bassett. *Digest of International Law* (Washington: Gov't Print. Off., 1906), V.

Moran, Benjamin. Diary (MS, Library of Congress).

——. "Extracts from the Diary of ... 1860-1868," *Massachusetts Historical Society Proceedings* (Oct., 1914-June, 1915), XLVIII, 431-492.

Morley, John. *The Life of William Ewart Gladstone* (New York: The Macmillan Co., 1911).

[Morse, Samuel F. B.] *The Present Attempt to Dissolve the American Union, a British Aristocratic Plot* (New York, 1862).

Musser, John. "The Establishment of Maximilian's Empire in Mexico" (Ph.D. thesis, University of Pennsylvania, 1918).

*Narrative of the Cruise of the Alabama, and a List of her Officers and Men, by One of her Crew* (London, 1864).

*New York Herald.*

*New York Times.*

*New York Tribune.*

Newell, Frederick Samuel. *Newell's Notes on Abraham Lincoln* (London [1864]).

——. *Newell's Notes on Tar and Feathers* (London [1864]).

——. *Newell's Notes on the Cruel and Licentious Treatment of the American Female Slaves* (London [1864]).

Newman, Francis William. *The Good Cause of President Lincoln* (London?, 1863).

Nicolay, John G., and John Hay. *Abraham Lincoln: A History* (New York: The Century Co., 1890).

——, eds. *Complete Works of Abraham Lincoln* (New York: Francis D. Tandy Co., c1905).

——. Papers (MSS, Ill. State Historical Library).

Noel, Baptist Wriothesley. *Freedom and Slavery in the United States of America* (London, 1863).

——. *Rebellion in America* (London, 1863).

*Old Abe's Jokes* (New York, 1864).

*Once a Week* (Cunard). *Magazine of History with Notes and Queries*, XXXIX, No. 1, Extra No. 153, 5-12. Also *ibid.*, XXXIV, No. 1, Extra No. 133, 22.

Osborne, R. H. *Lincoln with his People* (Mattoon, Ill., *ca.* 1909).

Owls-Glass. *Rebel Brag and British Bluster: A Record of Unfulfilled Prophesies* (New York).

Owsley, Frank Lawrence. *King Cotton Diplomacy* (Chicago: Univ. of Chicago Press, 1931).

*Papers Relating to Foreign Affairs* (House Ex. Doc.), 37 Cong., 3 Sess., No. 1.

Parker, Joel. *International Law. Case of the Trent* (Cambridge, 1862).

Parker, Samuel. *Legal Views of the Alabama Case and Ship-Building for the Confederates* (Manchester, 1863).

Pease, Theodore Calvin, and James G. Randall, eds. *The Diary of Orville Hickman Browning*, 1850-1881 *(Illinois Historical Collections*, XX and XXII, Springfield, Ill.: Ill. State Historical Library, c1927-c1933).

Penny, William L. *Abraham Lincoln* (Nyack, N. Y., 1886).

Perkins, Fred B. *The Picture and the Man* (New York, 1867).

Pezet, Federico. *Lincoln and Peru* (Washington, 1921).

Phillimore, Robert. *Commentaries upon International Law* (Philadelphia, 1857), III.

Picard, M. A. *Le Conflit Américain et la Solution Probable* (Paris, 1862).

Pierce, Edward L. *Memoir and Letters of Charles Sumner* (London: Sampson, Low, Marston & Co., 1893), IV.

Pinkerton, Allan. *History and Evidence of the Passage of Abraham Lincoln from Harrisburg, Pa., to Washington, D. C.* (Chicago, 1868).

——. MS account in Herndon-Weik Collection (Film, Ill. State Historical Library).

478

Pitman, Benn. *The Assassination of President Lincoln and the Trial of the Conspirators* (New York, 1865).

Pomeroy, Samuel Clarke. Letter to Orville H. Browning, Oct. 27, 1862, in Browning Papers (MSS, Ill. State Historical Library).

Porter, Horace. *Campaigning with Grant* (New York: The Century Co., 1897).

Pratt, Harry E. *Concerning Mr. Lincoln* (Springfield, Ill.: Abraham Lincoln Ass'n, 1944).

———. "David Davis, 1815-1886" (Ph.D. thesis, University of Illinois, 1930).

Pratt, J. W. "The British Blockade and American Precedents," *United States Naval Institute Proceedings* (1920), XLVI, 1789-1802.

*The Present Condition of Mexico* (House Ex. Doc.), 37 Cong., 2 Sess., No. 100.

Price, Grady Daniel. "The Secret Mission of Duncan F. Kenner, Confederate Minister Plenipotentiary to Europe in 1865" (M.A. thesis, Tulane University, 1929).

*Prize Cases in New York* (House Ex. Doc.), 38 Cong., 1 Sess., No. 74.

Procter, Addison G. "Abraham Lincoln," address at Grand Army Hall and Memorial Association of Illinois (Chicago, c1923).

*Punch.*

Randall, James Garfield. *The Civil War and Reconstruction* (Boston: D. C. Heath & Co., c1937).

———. *Constitutional Problems under Lincoln* (New York: D. Appleton & Co., 1926).

———. "Lincoln and John Bright," *Yale Review* (Winter, 1945), XXXIV, 292-304.

*Reciprocity Treaty with Great Britain* (House Report), 37 Cong., 2 Sess., No. 22.

*Record of the Testimony Taken in the Trial of Commodore T. T. Craven* (New York, 1866).

[Reed, William Bradford.] *A Paper Containing a Statement and Vindication of Certain Political Opinions* (n.p., 1862).

———. *A Review of Mr. Seward's Diplomacy by a Northern Man* (n.p., 1862).

*Religious Toleration in Egypt* (House Ex. Doc.), 37 Cong., 2 Sess., No. 117.

Rhodes, James Ford. *History of the United States from the Compromise of 1850* (New York: Harper & Bros., and The Macmillan Co., 1893-1919).

Rice, Allen Thorndike. *Reminiscences of Abraham Lincoln by Distinguished Men of His Time* (8th ed., New York: North Am. Rev., 1889).

Richey, Charles W. "The Pennsylvania Railroad in Philadelphia, Pa." (Unpublished report for company officials, 1941).

*Right of Search: Reply to an "American's Examination" of the "Right of Search;" with Observations on the Questions at Issue Between Great Britain and the United States, by an Englishman* (London, 1862).

Rimsky-Korsakoff, Nikolay Andreyevich. *My Musical Life* (3rd printing, New York: Alfred A. Knopf, Inc., 1936).

Roberts, W. Adolphe. *Semmes of the Alabama* (Indianapolis: The Bobbs-Merrill Co., 1938).

Robertson, James Rood. *A Kentuckian at the Court of the Tsars* (Berea, Ky.: Berea College Press, c1935).

Robinson, William Morrison. *Battle of Alabama-Kearsarge: A Study in Original Sources* (Salem, Mass.: Essex Inst., 1924).

———. *Confederate Privateers* (New Haven, Conn.: Yale Univ. Press, 1928).

Rogeard, M. A. *The Strictures of Labienus* (Philadelphia, 1865).

Romero, Matías. *Speech on the Situation of Mexico* (New York, 1863).

Russell, Addison Peale. *Thomas Corwin* (Cincinnati: R. Clarke & Co., 1881).

Russell, William Howard. *The Civil War in America* (Boston, 1861).

———. *My Diary North and South* (Boston, 1863).

———. *Pictures of Southern Life, Social, Political, and Military* (New York, 1861).

*Sacramento Union* (California, 1863).

*St. Louis Reveille* (1848).

Sala, George Augustus. *My Diary in America in the Midst of War* (London, 1865).

Salm-Salm, Princess Felix. *Ten Years of My Life* (Detroit: Belford Bros., 1877).

Sandburg, Carl. *Abraham Lincoln: The War Years* (New York: Harcourt, Brace & Co., c1939).

Sargent, F. W. *England, the United States, and the Southern Confederacy* (2nd ed., London, 1864).

Scharf, John Thomas. *History of the Confederate States Navy . . .* (New York: Rogers & Sherwood, 1887).

Schlüter, Herman. *Abraham Lincoln and the Working Class*, E. Haldeman-Julius, ed. (Girard, Kan. [1924]).

———. *Lincoln, Labor and Slavery; a Chapter from the Social History of America* (New York: Socialist Literature Co., 1913).

Schmidt, Louis Bernard. "The Influence of Wheat and Cotton on Anglo-American Relations During the Civil War," *Iowa Journal of History and Politics* (July, 1918), XVI, No. 3, 400-439.

Schurz, Carl. *The Reminiscences of Carl Schurz* (New York: The McClure Co., 1907-1908).

Sears, Louis Martin. *John Slidell* (Durham, N. C.: Duke Univ. Press, 1925).

Seitz, Don C. *The James Gordon Bennetts, Father and Son* (Indianapolis: The Bobbs-Merrill Co., c1928).

Semmes, Raphael. *Cruise of the Alabama and the Sumpter, from the Private Journals and other Papers of Commander R. Semmes, C. S. N.* (New York, 1864).

Seward, Frederick W. *Reminiscences of a War-Time Statesman and Diplomat, 1830-1915* (New York: G. P. Putnam's Sons, 1916).

Seward, William Henry. *The Diplomatic History of the War for the Union, Being the Fifth Volume of the Works of William H. Seward* (Boston: Houghton Mifflin Co., 1884).

Shannon, Fred Albert. *The Organization and Administration of the Union Army, 1861-1865* (Cleveland: Arthur H. Clark Co., 1928).

[Shea, John Gilmary.] *The Lincoln Memorial* (New York, 1865).

Shutes, Milton H. *Lincoln and California* (Stanford University, Calif., c1943).

———. *Lincoln and the Doctors* (New York: The Pioneer Press, 1933).

Smith, Arthur D. Howden. *Old Fuss and Feathers* (New York: Greystone Press, 1937).

480

Smith, Goldwin. "The Death of President Lincoln," *Magazine of History with Notes and Queries* (1933), XLVII, No. 1, Extra No. 185, 5-14.

———. *Does the Bible Sanction American Slavery?* (London, 1863).

———. "England and America," *Atlantic Monthly* (1864), XIV, 749-769.

———. *A Letter to a Whig Member of the Southern Independence Association* (London, 1864).

———. "Letters of Goldwin Smith to Charles Eliot Norton," Worthington Chauncey Ford, ed., *Massachusetts Historical Society Proceedings* (Oct., 1915-June, 1916), XLIX, 106-160.

———. *On the Morality of the Emancipation Proclamation* (Manchester, 1863).

———. "President Lincoln," *Magazine of History with Notes and Queries* (1933), XLVII, No. 1, Extra No. 185, 28-38.

———. *Reminiscences*, Arnold Haultain, ed. (New York, 1910).

Soley, James Russell. *The Blockade and the Cruisers*, Vol. I of *The Navy in the Civil War* (New York: Charles Scribner's Sons, 1883).

*Spanish Bark "Providencia"* (House Ex. Doc.), 37 Cong., 2 Sess., No. 38.

Spence, James. *The American Union* (London, 1861). A 4th edition, 1862, has changed text.

Stanton, Henry B. *Random Recollections* (Johnstown, N. Y., 1885).

Stanwood, Edward. *A History of the Presidency from 1788 to 1897* (Boston: Houghton Mifflin Co., c1898), I.

*Star of the West. Protest of the Master against Seizure of the Steamship "Star of the West"* (New York, 1861).

Starr, John W. *Lincoln & the Railroads* (New York: Dodd, Mead & Co., 1927).

———. *Lincoln's Last Day* (New York: Frederick A. Stokes Co., 1922).

Stebbins, G. B. *"British Free Trade," A Delusion* (Detroit?, 1865).

Steele, Zulma. *Angel in Top Hat* (New York: Harper & Bros., c1942).

Stock, John. *The Duties of British Christians, in Relation to the Struggle in America* (Manchester, 1861).

Stock, Leo Francis. "Catholic Participation in the Diplomacy of the Southern Confederacy," *The Catholic Historical Review* (April, 1930), XVI, 1-18.

Stoltz, Charles. *The Tragic Career of Mary Todd Lincoln* (South Bend, Ind., 1931).

Stovall, Pleasant A. *Robert Toombs, Statesman, Speaker, Soldier, Sage* (New York: Cassell Pub. Co., 1892).

Stowe, Harriet Beecher. "A Reply to 'The Affectionate and Christian Address of Many Thousands of Women of Great Britain and Ireland to Their Sisters the Women of the United States of America,'" *Atlantic Monthly* (Jan., 1863), 120-133.

Sumner, Charles. *The Case of the Florida Illustrated by Precedents from British History* (New York, 1864).

———. *In the Senate of the United States* (Sen. Misc. Doc.), 37 Cong., 3 Sess., No. 38.

———. "Independence of Hayti and Liberia," speech in Senate, April 23, 1862 (Washington, 1862).

———. "Letters of Marque and Reprisal," speech in Senate, Feb. 17, 1863 (Washington, 1863).

————. "Maritime Rights," speech in Senate, Jan. 9, 1862 (Washington, 1862).

————. "Our Foreign Relations," speech before citizens of New York, Sept. 10, 1863 (New York, 1863). Also published by W. V. Spencer, Boston. Translated into French and published in Paris.

————. *Reciprocity Treaty* (Washington, 1865).

Swain, James B. Letter to John Hay, Feb. 21, 1888, Nicolay and Hay Papers (MS, Ill. State Historical Library).

Taylor, William. *Cause and Probable Result of the Civil War in America. Facts for the People of Great Britain* (London, 1863). First published 1862.

Temple, Henry W. "William H. Seward" in *The American Secretaries of State,* VII, Samuel Flagg Bemis, ed. (New York: Alfred A. Knopf, 1928).

Thayer, William Roscoe. *The Life and Letters of John Hay* (2nd impression, Boston: Houghton Mifflin Co., 1915).

Thiers, Louis Adolphe. *Discours . . . sur le Mexique* (Paris, 1867).

Thomas, Benjamin Platt. "Russo-American Relations, 1815-1867," *Johns Hopkins University Studies* (1930), Series XLVIII, No. 2.

Tilley, Nannie. "England and the Confederacy, a Letter of Sir William Henry Gregory," *American Historical Review* (1938), XLIV, No. 1, 56-60.

Torrielli, Andrew J. *Italian Opinion on America as Revealed by Italian Travelers, 1850-1900* (Cambridge, Mass.: Harvard Univ. Press, 1941).

Towle, G. M. "Our Recent Foreign Relations," *Atlantic Monthly* (1864), XIV, 243-252.

Townsend, George Alfred. *Campaigns of a Non-Combatant, and His Romaunt Abroad During the War* (New York, 1866).

Townsend, William H. *Lincoln and His Wife's Home Town* (Indianapolis: The Bobbs-Merrill Co., c1929).

Tracy, Gilbert A., ed. *Uncollected Letters of Abraham Lincoln* (Boston: Houghton Mifflin Co., 1917).

Train, George Francis. *The Downfall of England* (Philadelphia, 1862).

————. *Geo. Francis Train, Unionist, on T. Colley Grattan, Secessionist* (Boston, 1862).

————. *Geo. Francis Train's Great Speech on the Withdrawal of McClellan and the Impeachment of Lincoln* (New York, 1864).

————. *My Life in Many States and in Foreign Lands* (New York: D. Appleton & Co., 1902).

————. *Train's Great Speeches in England on Slavery and Emancipation* (Philadelphia, 1862).

————. *Train's Union Speeches Delivered in England* (Philadelphia, 1862).

Trevelyan, George Macaulay. *Garibaldi and the Making of Italy* (New York: Longmans, Green & Co., 1911).

————. *The Life of John Bright* (Boston: Houghton Mifflin Co., 1914).

Trollope, Anthony. *North America* (2nd ed., London, 1862).

Tuckerman, Charles K. "President Lincoln and Colonization," *Magazine of History with Notes and Queries* (1920), Extra No. 69 [70], Rare Lincolniana, No. 15, 40-44.

Van Deusen, Glyndon. "Thurlow Weed: A Character Study," *American Historical Review* (April, 1944), XLIX, No. 3, 427-440.

[Victor, Orville J.] *The American Rebellion; Some Facts and Reflections for the Consideration of the English People* (London, 1861).

482

Villard, Henry. *Lincoln on the Eve of '61* (New York: Alfred A. Knopf, 1941).

———. *Memoirs of Henry Villard* (Boston: Houghton Mifflin Co., 1904).

Wallace, John William. *Cases Argued and Adjudged in the Supreme Court of the United States* (Washington, 1867). *Bermuda* case, III, 514; *Springbok*, V, 1; *Peterhoff*, V, 28.

*Washington Weekly Chronicle.*

Watterson, Henry. *Abraham Lincoln, An Oration Delivered Before the Lincoln Union* (Louisville, Ky., c1899).

Weed, Thurlow. *Autobiography of Thurlow Weed*, Harriet A. Weed, ed. (Boston: Houghton Mifflin Co., 1883). Vol. II of this set is *Memoir of Thurlow Weed, by his Grandson* (Thurlow Weed Barnes).

———. *Letters from Europe and the West Indies, 1843-1852* (Albany, N. Y.: Weed, Parsons & Co., 1866).

Welles, Gideon. *Diary* (New York: Houghton Mifflin Co., 1911).

———. *Lincoln and Seward* (New York: Sheldon & Co., 1874).

———. Papers (MSS, Ill. State Historical Library).

West, Richard S. *Gideon Welles: Lincoln's Navy Department* (Indianapolis: The Bobbs-Merrill Co., 1943).

West, W. Reed. "Contemporary French Opinion on the American Civil War," *Johns Hopkins University Studies* (1924), Series XLII, No. 1.

[Whipple, Edwin P.?] "The Causes of Foreign Enmity to the United States," *Atlantic Monthly* (1865), XV, 372-376.

Whipple, Wayne. *The Story of Young Abraham Lincoln* (Philadelphia: Henry Altemus Co., c1915).

White, Andrew Dickson. *A Letter to W. Howard Russell, on Passages in his "Diary North and South"* (Syracuse, N. Y., 1863). From London ed.

White, Ellsberry V. *The First Iron-Clad Naval Engagement in the World* (Portsmouth?, Va., c1906).

Whitridge, Arnold. "Lincoln through French Eyes," *Franco-American Review* (Autumn, 1937), II, No. 2, [71]-86.

Wilks, Washington. *English Criticism on President Lincoln's Anti-Slavery Proclamation and Message* (1863).

Williamson, David Brainerd. *Illustrated Life, Services, Martyrdom and Funeral of Abraham Lincoln* (Philadelphia, 1865).

Willson, Beckles. *America's Ambassadors to England (1785-1929)* (New York: Frederick A. Stokes Co., 1929).

———. *John Slidell and the Confederates in Paris (1862-65)* (New York: Minton, Balch & Co., 1932).

Wilson, Forrest. *Crusader in Crinoline, the Life of Harriet Beecher Stowe* (Philadelphia: J. B. Lippincott Co., c1941).

Wilson, William Bender. *History of the Pennsylvania Railroad* (Philadelphia, 1899).

Wish, Harvey. *George Fitzhugh: Propagandist of the Old South* (Baton Rouge, La.: State Univ. Press, 1943).

Wood, Bradford. Letter to Ward Hill Lamon, Feb. 20, 1884, Lamon Papers (photostats, Ill. State Historical Library).

Woolen, T. and E. Letter to R. and L. Wilson, July 30, 1860 (MS, Ill. State Historical Library).

# ACKNOWLEDGMENTS

To Lloyd Lewis, artist of history, who makes words give up their sound and color. He has read and reread this entire manuscript. It contains many of his suggestions together with bits of personal information gleaned from a lifelong acquaintance with the Civil War.

To Paul M. Angle, scholar unafraid, in respect for his able precision, and his courage in insisting that no evidence be suppressed to prove a thesis. His versatile and constructive imagination suggested the title of this book.

To Harry E. Pratt, for his hospitality with a vast knowledge of the details of Lincoln's life and his prodigality with precious hours spent reading this manuscript.

To Marcus Wilson Jernegan, Professor Emeritus of American History at the University of Chicago, for his New England tolerance, vision, encouragement, and for the query: "Is it dangerous to tell the truth of history?"

To James G. Randall, Professor of History at the University of Illinois and founder of a dynasty of Lincoln writers. His Lincolnian charity for some Civil War characters caused several pages of this history to be rewritten.

To Harold Clarke Goddard, Alexander Griswold Cummins Professor of English.at Swarthmore, for giving a boy on the third row by the window a view of history and literature that remains in his eyes.

To William Baringer, Executive Secretary of the Abraham Lincoln Association, for giving me the benefit of his definitive investigations, and generously taking time from his own book, *Lincoln and the House Dividing,* to read galleys on this work.

To William H. Townsend, of Lexington, Kentucky, for his charm, his humor and his suggestions regarding this narrative.

To Frederick H. Meserve of New York City and Louis A. Warren, Director, Lincoln National Life Foundation, Fort Wayne, for unearthing unique Civil War pictures and generously giving me the benefit of their labors.

To F. Ray Risdon, of Los Angeles, for lending rare pamphlets from his library; to R. Gerald McMurtry, Director of the Department of Lincolniana at Lincoln Memorial University, for sending transcriptions of Clay manuscripts; to William Wyles for the use of his collection at Santa Barbara, California, and to his secretary, Mrs. Blair Cameron, for checking notes on material discovered there; to Philip Hamer and to St. George Sioussat for access to manuscripts in the National Archives and the Library of Congress, respectively; to Martin P. Claussen, of the National Archives, for information on attitudes of the British labor press; to Matthew Josephson, Gaylordsville, Connecticut, for pertinent replies to inquiries about Lincoln and Victor Hugo; to James N. Adams of Taylorville, Illinois, for help with the manuscript and for calling attention to Rimsky-Korsakoff's account of his experience with the Russian fleet in America.

To Margaret Flint, Assistant Librarian in the Illinois State Historical Library, and Florence Nichol, Loan Desk Librarian in the Illinois State Library, for

484

skill and perseverance in searching for pertinent pictures and publications. To Anne Waller of Bolinas, California, and Betty Irwin of Springfield, Illinois, for speed, accuracy and diligence in typing the manuscript.

And to Mildred Eversole Monaghan, my wife, for patience that passeth all understanding, for reading and correcting this entire manuscript, suggesting revisions and checking footnotes; for laughing with me at the comic characters in the book and for sympathizing with the tragic ones. She has sweetened the pleasant parts of historical research and brightened the onerous tasks "that unavoidably come in due time."

# INDEX

# INDEX

*Achilles*, the, 287

Acton, Lord John, 283

Adams, Charles Francis, relations with Seward, 25, 52, 113, 114, 142; described, 26, 43, 95, 98, 100, 103; minister to England, 41-42, 44, 63, 95, 97; importance to Republican party, 56; and recognition of Confederacy, 72, 233, 256, 257; meets Russell, 100-102; Mexican intervention, 139, 151; *Bermuda*, 146-147; *Trent* affair, 165, 171, 173, 177, 205; blockade, 194, 221; Confederate shipbuilding, 227, 229, 231, 234, 328; antislavery meetings, 280; Confederate loan, 297; addressed by workingmen, 306, 391; after Gettysburg and Vicksburg, 319; intervention in 1864, 373

Adams, Mrs. Charles Francis, 43, 95, 98

Adams, Charles Francis, Jr., 165

Adams, Henry, opinions of Englishmen, 95-104, 292; opinions of Americans, 106, 114, 214; reports Parliamentary action, 115-117, 316-318; propaganda, 161, 223, 287

Adams, John, 43, 95, 101

Adams, John Quincy, 43, 95, 101

Adams & Beedle, 133

*Address to the Ladies of England*, Stowe, 281, 282

*Affectionate and Christian Address*, Shaftesbury, 270

*Alabama*, the, 127, 171, 251, 301, 432; depredations, 263, 264, 275, 298; destroyed, 373-375

Albert, Prince, 182, 185, 186, 191, 298

Alexander II, 95, 108, 360

*Alexandra*, the, 293, 312-313, 328, 339

Alexandria, Egypt, 204

Alexandria, Va., 115, 312

*Alice in Wonderland*, Carroll, 426

*American Union, The*, Spence, 159-160

*Amérique devant l'Europe*, 145

Anderson, Robert, 416

Antietam, battle of, 251, 419

Anti-Slavery Society, British and Foreign, 185

Anti-Slavery Society of Canada, 398

*Arago*, the, 157, 173

Arguelles, José, 361

Argyll, George Douglas Campbell, Duke of, 310

Arman, L., 351, 377

Arnold, Matthew, 283

Arnold, Samuel, 398, 400

Ashmun, George, 369, 421, 424

Aspinwall, William H., 288

Atlanta, Ga., 373, 383

Azores, 251

Baker, Sen. Edward D., 36, 37, 46, 153, 236

Ball's Bluff, battle of, 153

Banks, Gen. Nathaniel P., 148, 227, 228, 235, 338

*Banshee*, the, 371

Barcelona, Spain, 290

Bargash, Sidi Mohammed, 215, 216, 217

Barreda, Señor, 35

Bates, Edward, 17, 40, 45, 68, 83, 128, 192, 321

Beall, John Y., 384

Beauregard, Madam Pierre Gustave, 165

Bee Company, 371

*Bee-Hive*, 306

Beecher, Henry Ward, 288, 301, 312, 320, 354, 380; speeches at Manchester and Liverpool, 335-336, 339

Beesley, E. S., 292

Belgium, King of, *see* Leopold I

Belmont, August, 31

504

Tone, Wolf, 249
Toombs, Robert, 37
"Toothpick Company," 91
Toussaint L'Ouverture, 143, 337
Train, George Francis, biographical sketch, 22-23; promotes street railways, 48; reputed purchaser of newspapers for Napoleon III, 104; on Civil War, 105-106; appraises De Leon and Motley, 107; ridicules Russell, 131, 152; appeals to mobs, 143; comments on contraband trade, 163-164; and *Trent* affair, 180-181, 184, 193; defends Confederacy, 194; letter answering Yancey, 207-208; predicts trend of British opinion, 225, 228; speech to Irish Brotherhood in London, 249; visits U. S., 250; and election of 1864, 390
Train, Mrs. George Francis, 411
Trench, Dean Richard, 186
Trenholm, George A., 371
*Trent,* the, 166-169
*Trent* affair, British reaction to, 173, 174, 194; Scott's letter on, 175-176; Lincoln's position on, 182-184
Trenton Falls, N. Y., 323
Trumbull, Sen. Lyman, 15, 153
Tunstall, ———, 215

*Uncle Tom's Cabin,* Stowe, 21, 160, 261, 270, 312
Union and Emancipation Society, 271
Utrecht, treaty of, 202-203

Vache (island), 253-254, 298, 337-338
Vallandigham, Clement L., 305, 312, 365, 366, 367, 381
Vanderbilt, Cornelius, 23
Vanderbilt yacht, 264
Vesey, William H., 68
Vicksburg, Miss., battle of, 319, 330, 337
Victor, Orville, 133
Victor Emmanuel II, 133, 135, 136
Victoria, Queen, neutrality proclamation, 95, 96; receives Adamses, 98; described, 98; Bigelow meets, 143;

Victoria, Queen—*Cont.*
and *Trent* affair, 174, 180, 182, 186; niece of Leopold I, 206; visits Gotha, 247; makes Lord Lyons an earl, 396; correspondence with Mrs. Lincoln, 429-430
Villard, Henry, 18
Virginia, 75
*Virginia,* the, 300

*Wachusett,* the, 384-385
Wade, Sen. Benjamin F., 153, 309, 362, 424
Wales, Prince of, 58
Walker, Robert J., biographical sketch, 289-290; and Confederate loan, 297, 302-303, 304; bares Jeff Davis' repudiation of debts, 314; turns Unionist, 417
Walker, William, 60, 65
Walpole, Horace, 180
*War Powers of the President,* Whiting, 288
Ward, Artemus (Charles Farrar Browne), 254
Washington, George, 159, 160, 247, 337, 401
Washington, D. C., threatened raids on, 75-78, 147-148, 227, 247, 248; described, 122; Southern sympathy in, 148; blockaded, 153-154; Train visits, 250; Russian fleet in, 345; Early's raid, 378; threat of *Stonewall* attack, 408
*Washington Chronicle,* 322
Watson's oyster saloon (Springfield, Ill.), 13
Webb, James Watson, 69
Webster, Daniel, 159, 369
Weed, Thurlow, described, 18; conference with Lincoln, 18-24; biographical sketch, 19, 157-159; relations with Seward, 25, 40; at 1861 inauguration, 37; conciliates Bennett, 53-54; plots with Raymond, 54; reputed author of April 1, 1861, note, 55; importance to Republican party, 56; warns of unpreparedness, 75; discusses possible officers with